9

IMPRINT

PROJECT MANAGEMENT
Florian Kobler and
Inga Hallsson, Berlin

COLLABORATION
Harriet Graham, Turin

PRODUCTION
Frauke Kaiser, Cologne

DESIGN
Sense/Net Art Direction
Andy Disl and
Birgit Eichwede, Cologne
www.sense-net.de

GERMAN TRANSLATION
Kristina Brigitta Köper, Berlin

FRENCH TRANSLATION
Blandine Pélissier, Paris

PRINTED IN ITALY
ISBN 978-3-8365-3899-2

ARCHITECTURE NOW!

Philip Jodidio

TASCHEN

CONTENTS

INTRODUCTION

WE'RE AT A PLACE CALLED VERTIGO

Some of the most powerful works in this book have to do not with tall, solid buildings, but with voids, and a feeling of absence. Voids have long been a preoccupation of contemporary architecture, but those standing on the edge of Michael Arad's National September 11 Memorial (New York, New York, USA, 2006–11, page 200) will understand that it is as though the earth had swallowed up the former World Trade Center Twin Towers. Two black fountains plunge into the earth, marking the footprints of the buildings designed by Minoru Yamasaki (1912–86). This work is architectural in its reality but perhaps not in its substance, where it verges closer to art. The point is not about politics or even about how one reacts to the 2001 attacks on New York, it is about absence, and the kind of void that sucks in all that approach it. Maya Lin, then a young student at Yale, had a similar intuition when she designed the Vietnam Veterans Memorial on the Mall in Washington, D.C. (1981). Rather than a heroic sculpture, she proposed a black gash in the earth with the names of the 50 000 American dead incised in its single wall. Those who are old enough to remember the bright promise of John F. Kennedy's short presidency (1960–63) may contemplate on the relation between his assassination and the very simple design that marks the grave in Arlington Cemetery (John F. Kennedy Eternal Flame, by the architect John Carl Warnecke, 1967). A loss marked by a rising flame, and not yet the abyss; still, the time of triumph had already passed.

Granted, memorials are a genre apart, not bound to the strict rules of architecture in most cases, able to obviate many of the constraints of practicality, but Maya Lin and, again, more recently Michael Arad in New York have given voice to emptiness, to absence, to the fall. America's rise and power have had much to do with positive imagery, from the conquest of the West to such iconic works as the Iwo Jima Monument (Marine Corps War Memorial, Arlington Cemetery, Washington, D.C., 1951). In the face of adversity, Americans triumphed, or so the self-fashioned legend would have it. Maya Lin's Vietnam Memorial and Michael Arad's September 11 Memorial tell a different story, one of loss that may be more far reaching than the events commemorated.

Architecture used to be so comfortably reliable, so dense and opaque, before becoming the glazed mirror of capitalism. This is not a commentary on capitalism per se, but so many towers in a blurred international style may also leave a bitter taste, as they spread from their birthplace in Chicago or New York to the far corners of the earth. But what is left of the old order, the architecture of religion and conquest? Two works published here constitute an eloquent or perhaps humorous commentary on the passing of glory. "Reading between the Lines" (Borgloon, Belgium, 2011, page 180) by the young Belgian architects Pieterjan Gijs and Arnout Van Vaerenbergh takes on nothing else than the forms of the church, in a rural field in Limburg. But this church has an area of only 28 square meters and by any standard, it is neither functional nor a call to devotion. And yet it is solid, with a reinforced-concrete base and 30 tons of Cor-ten steel; it will surely stand longer than many contemporary buildings. The architects compare it to a drawing in space—empty, it can be seen through, quite the opposite of most churches—but symbolically speaking its void is also a commentary on the decline of religion.

1
Gijs Van Vaerenbergh, "Reading between the Lines," Borgloon, Belgium, 2011

HOW SHALL WE COMFORT OURSELVES?

Empty churches are not exactly a discovery. One hundred and thirty years ago, in a prescient text, full of horrors to come, Friedrich Nietzsche wrote:

> *God is dead. God remains dead. And we have killed him. How shall we comfort ourselves, the murderers of all murderers? What was holiest and mightiest of all that the world has yet owned has bled to death under our knives: who will wipe this blood off us? What water is there for us to clean ourselves? What festivals of atonement, what sacred games shall we have to invent? Is not the greatness of this deed too great for us? Must we ourselves not become gods simply to appear worthy of it?*
> *The Gay Science*, Section 125, 1882

And so we did try to become gods, building spires to the glory of ourselves and of money. The black fountains that empty into the abyss in New York are, in a sense, witness that the deed was too great for us. "Come, let us build ourselves a city, with a tower that reaches to the heavens, so that we may make a name for ourselves and not be scattered over the face of the whole earth" (Genesis 11:4). The tower, in its figurative and literal iterations, has fallen more than once, it is true, only to rise again and again. The Burj Khalifa in Dubai rises to a height of 829 meters (Adrian Smith, Skidmore Owings & Merrill, UAE, 2010), and an even taller expression of architectural hubris is rising in Jeddah, Saudi Arabia, the aptly named Kingdom Tower (Adrian Smith, AS+GG, ongoing) slated to break the barrier of 1000 meters in height. Both of these projects were conceived after the events of September 11, 2001. The London Bridge Tower—commonly called "the Shard"—by Renzo Piano (London, UK, 2009–12, page 370) at a height of 306 meters, relatively modest by current Middle Eastern standards, is, of course, another example of the ongoing quest for visibility and just a bit of glory. Yet the cloud of collapse and the darkness of an economy teetering on the edge will cast their shadow still. Contemporary architecture will reflect this fact more and more—for the moment, it is the province of architects who are aware of art; tomorrow, the dark reflection of a time of trouble will mark a broader swath. Or perhaps chaos will engender a new order…

THE SUN ALSO RISES

Of course there are limits to darkness as a creative impulse, and one might also characterize the time as one of reversals, imbalances, and contradictions. One of the most curious and unexpected structures to rise recently is the Orbit (Olympic Park, London, UK, 2010–12, page 252). "Unlike vertical towers that grow by being continually supported one story upon another," states Cecil Balmond, one of its inventors, "the Orbit form gathers strength from overlaps and scatter, in a new paradigm for form and its stabilities." The Orbit is in fact the creation of unexpected partners, the artist Anish Kapoor (born in Bombay, India, in 1954) and the engineer Cecil Balmond (born in Colombo, Sri Lanka, in 1943). Though England's reach across the world in a time gone by is no secret, it might be interesting to note that the most noticeable

2

2
Tatzu Nishi, "Discovering Columbus," New York, New York, USA, 2012

architecture of the 2012 London Olympics was the fruit of the collaboration of an artist and an engineer who are respectively of Indian and Sri Lankan origin, funded by a company that was founded in India. Might the "salvation" of the West come from the East and the South?

Another interesting expression of imbalance and reversal in a project that can be qualified as architectural is Tatzu Nishi's work "Discovering Columbus" (New York, New York, USA, 2012, page 332). The Japanese artist, no stranger to the exploration of contradictions, perched a 75-square-meter "living room" 23 meters above Columbus Circle in Manhattan. His work literally encircles a sculpture of Christopher Columbus, an inventor of the New World. Like Pieterjan Gijs and Arnout Van Vaerenbergh he explores not only issues of scale, but of domesticity and incongruous locations. Why would an architectural environment necessarily be confined to the solid earth when it can so easily be perched on a column in the middle of a heavily traveled square? Many others have come before Tatzu Nishi in challenging the "certainties" of architecture, and others will undoubtedly follow, but this work and others mark a kind of point of no return, beyond which architecture can never be the same. How long has solidity translated into symmetry and "durable" materials been the hallmark of architecture? Kapoor and Balmond show that balance and even elegance are not necessarily where one might think. Nishi adds a touch of humor with a very bourgeois interior sitting on a pole with a huge old sculpture in its midst. "I believe that art has the task of recapturing the familiar from a different perspective," says Tatzu Nishi. "The extraordinary experiences of this work's reversal of the public and private, and its reversal of exterior and interior, will broaden viewers' perception of the world around them, and in turn this process will lead to the expansion of humanity's imaginative powers."

HUMPTY DUMPTY SAT ON A WALL

The quest for artistic license is not new in contemporary architecture. Frank O. Gehry—who now builds huge apartment buildings in New York (Eight Spruce Street, New York, USA, 2007–11, page 174)—once praised the virtues of immediacy and invention. In his acceptance speech for the 1989 Pritzker Prize, he said: "My artist friends, like Jasper Johns, Bob Rauschenberg, Ed Kienholz, and Claes Oldenburg, were working with very inexpensive materials—broken wood and paper—and they were making beauty. These were not superficial details, they were direct, and raised the question in my mind of what beauty was. I chose to use the craft available, and to work with craftsmen and make a virtue out of their limitations. Painting had an immediacy that I craved for in architecture. I explored the process of new construction materials to try giving feeling and spirit to form. In trying to find the essence of my own expression, I fantasized that I was an artist standing before a white canvas deciding what the first move should be."1 Not long after this declaration, which indeed summarizes the freshness that he first brought to architecture in Santa Monica and Venice (California), Frank Gehry admitted that: "After years of breaking things apart, I'm trying to put Humpty Dumpty together again."[2]

Contradiction in contemporary architecture can also have to do with continuity. While Gehry seeks a wholeness that he once reputed, others like Richard Meier remain faithful to their aesthetic commitment to Modernism. Richard Meier, now in his late 70s, recently completed two structures, the OCT Shenzhen Clubhouse (Shenzhen, China, 2010–12, page 304) and the Italcementi i.lab (Bergamo, Italy, 2005–12, page 38). Both designs adhere to the fundamental whiteness and equilibrium that are the architect's "signature" qualities. The interesting thing about this coherence is that it can be compared to classicism that never really goes out of fashion. Meier has also not been insensitive to the passage of time and the new requirements of architecture. The Italcementi i.lab received the first LEED Platinum accreditation in Italy. Surely there is a virtue to longevity and to sticking to commitments. More than 30 years ago, the dandy author Tom Wolfe excoriated the Meier style in his book From Bauhaus to Our House, writing: "Every new $900 000 summer house in the north woods of Michigan or on the shore of Long Island has so many pipe railings, ramps, hob-tread metal spiral stairways, sheets of industrial plate glass, banks of tungsten-halogen lamps, and white cylindrical shapes, it looks like an insecticide refinery. I once saw the owners of such a place driven to the edge of sensory deprivation by the whiteness and lightness and leanness and cleanness and bareness and spareness of it all. They became desperate for an antidote, such as coziness and color."[3] Perhaps art and architecture fans today can find the coziness they are looking for in a living room 23 meters off the ground in Columbus Circle, but Richard Meier is sticking to his guns.

WAY DOWN UNDERGROUND

Much closer to the current spirit in contemporary architecture, the Swiss team of Herzog & de Meuron continues to explore the frontiers of design, as the Messe Basel—New Hall (Basel, Switzerland, 2010–13, page 206) and two of their recent London projects attest. The first of these London projects is the 2012 Serpentine Summer Pavilion (with Ai Weiwei; London, UK, page 212), an annual tradition inaugurated with Zaha Hadid in 2000. Working with the Chinese dissident artist Ai Weiwei, Herzog & de Meuron chose to create a pavilion that is inherently contradictory and surprising. Their structure rises barely a meter above the ground, sheltering a cork-clad environment that signals the "archeological" discoveries made on the site. Digging into the earth led the architects to the water table but also to all manner of left-over traces of the previous pavilions. These are marked by the locations of columns supporting a 10-meter steel disk that hovers over the seating areas, like a suspended reflecting pool. The 2012 Serpentine Pavilion can be said to evoke darkness, and it surely digs into the earth, characteristics that fit well with a time of troubles and doubt. The Georgian brick and limestone forms of the Serpentine Gallery are reflected in the shallow pond on the pavilion's disk, reversed, and subject to the deformations of the breeze.

A second Herzog & de Meuron project in London also has an archeological aspect, albeit in a more industrial sense. The architects made their reputation with the transformation of the old Bankside Power Station in Southwark into Tate Modern (2000). Today, they have been called on to build a new extension to the museum, due for completion in 2016. As a foretaste of their work, they have renovated nearly 6000 square meters of space originally created to store the millions of liters of oil required by the power plant. The Tanks (London, UK, 2010–12, page 39), deliberately left in a "rough and industrial" state, will be used for performances or film installations. These are "spaces where you are aware that you are underground, rich with texture and history" according to the architects. The original Tate Modern, though decidedly above grade, also explored the relations of modern art to a formerly industrial space. Here, Herzog & de Meuron go several steps further, down into a kind of netherworld of formerly unoccupied space. Here, they delve into modern archeology that is far removed from the "whiteness and lightness and leanness and cleanness and bareness and spareness" of another type of architecture that was born of a past era when it seemed that things could only get better.

WE'RE AT A PLACE CALLED VERTIGO[4]

A very definite part of the spirit of this moment is architecture and design that puts the visitor or the viewer in a situation of disequilibrium. Where are the boundaries, where is up and where is down. Clearly, artists such as Robert Irwin, James Turrell, or Dan Graham have played on notions of this kind for quite some time, but wasn't architecture supposed to be more stable, more comprehensible? Art is one thing, but isn't retail another? The young New York firm Gage Clemenceau has taken on this certainty with concept stores for the designer Nicola Formichetti (New York, New York, USA, 2011, page 154; Hong Kong, China, 2012). With a little of the hyperbole that characterizes the fashion world, they write: "Typically, fashion environments are defined by a rather restrained minimalism that focuses the attention only on the clothing—for the obvious reason of only selling clothes. In our collaboration with Nicola Formichetti, we rewrote this equation and produced a new genre of experimental space that not only showcased, but magnified, the impact of his fashion designs into a new form of immersive environment that fused the very genetics of architecture and fashion." Of their Hong Kong store for the same designer, Gage Clemenceau state: "The lighting system allows for an endless variation of effects, giving the impression that the space itself is constantly changing." It may not be that architects or designers are seeking to destabilize the built environment, but rather that the ultimate source of today's vertigo is the screen, the immersive environment where reality and fiction are easily confused. Is that young man in a uniform playing a video game, or is he piloting a drone that will kill a man half a world away? Are relationships defined by physical proximity and ancient instincts, or can we select our own disembodied avatar? Which way is up?

Although Serge Salat has degrees in architecture and engineering (amongst others), he has also chosen to express himself in the form of artistic installations that have deep historical and physiological meanings ("Beyond Infinity I," 2007, page 398; "Beyond Infinity II," 2011, page 402, both in China). In "Beyond Infinity I," he seeks to "make the spectator get out of normal space to enter a highly paradoxical space, floating, dreamlike, with deeper and deeper layers of dreams." He makes references to "personal experiences in space, experiences where you feel the encounter of time and some feeling of eternity." In the case of "Beyond Infinity II": "Visitors are levitating in the median plane of this giant structure whose replicas to infinity sink into the abyss." Purists will argue that such environments may have a relationship to the architectural background of Serge Salat, but that they are fundamentally works of art. For many years, however, it is clear that the boundaries between art and architecture have dissolved.

Efforts to evoke vertiginous space, or a space beyond immediate comprehension are also present throughout the history of architecture. Much Baroque or Mannerist architecture played on complex forms. For example, Giulio Romano's Palazzo del Te (Mantua, 1526–35)

3
Serge Salat, "Beyond Infinity II," China, 2011

brought art and architecture together in an extraordinary cacophony of forms in the famous *Sala dei Giganti* (Room of the Giants). In a true flight of the imagination, the artist-architect here associates his own structure with a fantastic scene of destruction. Scale, time, and place are swept aside in a space that seems to obviate the boundaries of the real. Giovanni Battista Piranesi (1720–78) studied as an architect in Venice, but he remains best known for his engravings, such as the celebrated *prisons* (*Carceri d'invenzione* or "Imaginary prisons"). Few architects have, in fact, had as much influence as these engravings with their brooding darkness and vertiginous plays on perspective and space. These works concerned representations of space that were somehow just beyond the edge of comprehension—deeper, darker, more sinister than reality—fiction that embodied fears. What would hell look like if not one of these prisons, more vast and incomprehensible than any earthly invention.

The doubts and complexities of Mannerism and the Baroque were at the opposite end of the pendulum swing from the ordered perspective and humanism of the High Renaissance. With all due respect to the great artists and architects of the past, might it be that Modernist certainties in the first half of the 20th century have given way to the deep ambiguities of a post-9/11 world, much as the Renaissance gave way to Mannerism? If so, there may be a long period of doubt and darkness ahead. The times when anything could be done, when Brasília could rise from the vast empty heart of Brazil, seem to belong only to the distant past. Where hope and optimism lack, money and ambition are not sufficient to breathe life into new worlds.

TEMPORARILY CONTEMPORARY

Temporary structures have become increasingly common with the economic problems posed by more permanent and costly buildings. Because they are not intended to last "forever" such ephemeral architecture can, at its best, be more inventive and free than heavy concrete and steel. Several examples in this book make the point. Humanidade 2012 (page 244) was an exhibition presented in a temporary structure designed by the architect Carla Juaçaba and the stage designer Bia Lessa. "We propose a scaffold building, translucent, exposed to all weather conditions: light, heat, rain, sounds of waves and wind, reminding man of his frailty when compared to nature," said the architects, planning further to make the building entirely recyclable. Measuring 170 meters long and 20 meters high, the building was more substantial than many temporary structures, but the idea of using scaffolding made it inherently light and airy, without recourse to expensive materials that are often more transparent on paper than they are in reality.

The New York architects SO – IL have already worked on successful temporary structures, such as their Pole Dance installation (PS1, Long Island City, New York, USA, 2010). For the New York Frieze Art Fair (page 424), they were confronted with the need for a substantial space (20 900 m²) to be created in a brief time frame, essentially using standardized tents. By inserting new pie-shaped wedges between the tent sections and extending tent fabric down to the ground at the end of the gable sections, the young designers made the plan of the fair somewhat irregular without affecting its fundamental layout. The strips of tent cloth employed made the facility seem to "dissolve into the

4

4
Shigeru Ban, Camper Pavilion, Alicante, Spain; Sanya, China; Miami, Florida, USA; Lorient, France: prefabrication June to September 2011

ground." The act of making a 457-meter-long structure original with bits of metal and cloth might be a fitting gesture for new times of austerity that challenge architects all over the world to reinvent their parameters, and to propose new solutions to clients whose main concern is cost.

The Japanese architect Shigeru Ban is, of course, well known for his temporary structures, sometimes used for disaster relief, and often made with paper tubes. His Camper Pavilion (Alicante, Spain; Sanya, China; Miami, Florida, USA; Lorient, France, prefabrication June to September 2011, page 88) was a 250-square-meter pavilion that was designed to be easily assembled and transported. Paper tubes, sized to be nested inside each other, were employed and the entire commercially oriented project was given the form of a round tent, somewhat like military tents, or perhaps the less martial, more circus type. Shigeru Ban's priorities are often related to technical issues and his desire to break new ground in architecture. Thus, he has made houses "without walls" or with paper tubes, contradicting the usual wisdom about solidity and, ultimately, about the very nature of architecture.

Another Japanese firm, Atelier Bow-Wow, was established in 1992 by Yoshiharu Tsukamoto and Momoyo Kaijima. Recently they have been working on an intriguing temporary project called the BMW Guggenheim Lab (New York, New York, USA, 2011; Berlin, Germany, 2012; Mumbai, India 2012–13, page 80). In New York, the facility, including an exhibit, workshop, lecture area, café, and storage, received 56 000 visitors in its 10 weeks of existence. Using carbon-fiber reinforced plastic instead of steel, a polyester roof membrane and double-layer polyester mesh for some cladding, the BMW Guggenheim Lab calls on fairly high technology to achieve the lightness required for easy transport. Such temporary structures can also make use of minimal sites that are between uses, or disused, a decided advantage in cities where non-space is a real problem.

HALLOWED BE THY NAME

The examples of Richard Meier and Frank Gehry in the United States do demonstrate that architecture, in the forms toward which it evolved in the 1970s and 1980s, is still very much present. There may be fewer new buildings because of the economy, but some clients naturally find it reassuring to have a Pritzker Prize winner as their architect. It would, of course, be a complete exaggeration to say that voids and non-spaces are all that is left in contemporary architecture. There are many instances where traditional values and uses are very much the order of the day. Churches, often in the form of small chapels, continue to be designed around the world by talented architects. An example published here is the All Saints Chapel (Gurita Farm, Martinho Campos, Minas Gerais, Brazil, 2011, page 366) by Gustavo Penna, an architect from Belo Horizonte. The 160-square-meter chapel actually assumes the form of a stylized cross, and was built with concrete, glass, travertine marble, and rare *peroba do campo* wood. A simple rectangular plan is underlined by a narrow basin, aligned on the center of the chapel and its sculptural evocation of Christ on the cross. This project is elegant and simple, even if the use of a cross form for the architecture itself (as seen in elevation) may be too "figurative" for the taste of some.

5
I. M. Pei and io Architects, Miho Institute of Aesthetics, Shigaraki, Shiga, Japan, 2010–12

5

Another more significant new chapel was designed by I. M. Pei in Japan (Miho Institute of Aesthetics, Shigaraki, Shiga, in collaboration with io Architects, 2010–12, page 356). Set in the midst of a school which is located in a dense Cyprus forest about one and a half hour's drive from Kyoto, the 1800-square-meter chapel assumes the exterior form of an asymmetrical cone, clad in stainless-steel panels as long as 18 meters (a technical feat). The interior of the chapel is finished in Japanese red cedar plank walls with a floor of French limestone and white oak. I. M. Pei (born in 1917) has told many acquaintances that this chapel in Shigaraki will be his last work. He has found it fitting that one of his first works was also a religious structure—the Luce Chapel (Taichung, Taiwan 1954–63). It may be of interest to recall that the small Luce Memorial Chapel is a simple hyperbolic parabolic structure roughly in the form of a 19-meter-high tent. Pei's elegance and the simplicity of his light-flooded design recall to those who have known his work, from Washington, D.C., to the Louvre in Paris, that he has been one of the most significant of modern architects. His was not the time of making do with strips of tent material, his buildings are often as close to "permanent" as one can imagine, and it can well be imagined that the chapel at the Miho Institute of Aesthetics will be standing long after today's generation of young architects has ceased to design and build.

BUILDING ON THE FRINGE

The nature of the *Architecture Now!* series of books is to be as free as possible from any formal constraints in terms of "style," location, or building types. This means that a small, inexpensive project may neighbor a huge complex, given that the books are organized by alphabetical order according to the name of the architect. It also means that projects of interest, to the extent that they can be identified, can be in any part of the globe, even if wealthy countries do tend to concentrate the highest numbers of innovative new buildings. It may again be a sign of the times that *Architecture Now! 9* contains work in countries that have hitherto been underrepresented. These include Georgia, Burkina Faso, South Africa, and Equatorial Guinea. Though the architects concerned, or sometimes their clients, may be from Europe in most instances, the work that they have been able to do in these countries is indicative of a rising level of sophistication and of a simple desire to build well that more readily available technology and information makes feasible.

The German architect Jürgen Mayer H. has made a considerable reputation with such recent projects as his Metropol Parasol (Seville, Spain, 2005–11), a 12 670-square-meter redevelopment of the Plaza de la Encarnación that involved a series of polyurethane-coated timber parasols that house or cover bars, restaurants, and public space. Even more unexpectedly, the architect has begun to realize a series of unusual buildings in Georgia. The Sarpi Border Checkpoint (Sarpi, Georgia, 2010–11, page 294), Mestia Police Station (Mestia, Georgia, 2011–12, page 26), and a series of Rest Stops (Gori, Georgia, 2011–12, page 298) on the highway linking Azerbaijan to Turkey are essentially concrete and glass structures, but their curious forms seem to explore relatively new territory in terms of design. "The building welcomes visitors to Georgia, representing the progressive upsurge of the country," says Jürgen Mayer H. about the Sarpi Border Checkpoint. Georgia is, of course, not the only country to have recently turned to talented architects in search of an image. The case of Astana, the capital of Kazakhstan, also comes to mind, where such emblematic firms as Foster + Partners have recently created public buildings (Palace of

Peace and Reconciliation, 2006; Khan Shatyr Entertainment Center, 2006). The Italian architect Manfredi Nicoletti was responsible for the surprising Kazakhstan Central Concert Hall, inaugurated in 2009. It remains to be seen if such architectural monuments can affirm a national character, or even improve a reputation, but it is true that new clients, from Qatar and other countries, have helped the profession to weather a particularly difficult economic time.

The architect Francis Kéré is already quite well known for his work in Mali—the National Park (Bamako, 2009–10) and the Museum for Earth Architecture (Mopti, 2010)—and in his native Burkina Faso. His first project, a primary school in his native village (Gando, 2001), won a 2004 Aga Khan Award for Architecture. Kéré is currently working on a more unexpected project, the Opera Village (Laongo, Burkina Faso, 2010–, page 258). A German patron, Christoph Schlingensief, suggested building an opera house in Africa. "When I was first confronted with the question of an opera house for Africa," says Kéré, "I initially thought it was a joke. Such a fantasy could only come from somebody who either doesn't know Africa, or who is so saturated that all he can think up is nonsense. That was my first, spontaneous reaction." And yet the first phase of this ambitious project, located an hour and a half by car from the capital Ouagadougou, the 14-hectare development site, which is still ongoing, has a number of housing units complete. Kéré is, of course, familiar with local building techniques and materials, which have been employed for the project. It is, in fact, in this aspect, perhaps more than in the unbuilt Festival Hall that the project shows interest and promise. There is no reason that good contemporary architecture cannot be created with an eye to local conditions—or, indeed, a style that has its roots in its country of origin. Costs are forcibly kept to a minimum and more natural, gentle methods of construction actually reply better to global concerns about the climate than do the most sophisticated Western creations that rely on technology more than common sense.

Jo Noero, a South African architect, has worked for his entire career in Cape Town, completing over 200 buildings. His most recent projects for the Red Location (New Brighton, Port Elizabeth, South Africa, 2009–11, page 336) include an art gallery and a library funded by the local Nelson Mandela Bay Municipality. The Red Location Museum (Noero Wolff Architects) that documents the struggle against apartheid, won the RIBA Lubetkin Prize in 2006. Named for typical rusted corrugated-iron barrack buildings, the Red Location was where Nelson Mandela cofounded "Umkhonto we Sizwe" (Spear of the Nation), the armed section of the African National Congress. The art gallery is devoted to "struggle art," while the digitally oriented library will provide access to the city archives and a collection of struggle literature as well as a computer school. Grouped close together the earlier museum and the newer Phase 2 buildings share such features as sawtoothed roofs to provide indirect natural light. Working on a larger scale and in a larger country than Francis Kéré, Jo Noero nonetheless has contributed in the Red Location not only to the durable commemoration of the struggle against apartheid, but has also shown that modern architecture, adapted to its specific location and function, as seen in the corrugated-iron "memory boxes" in the museum, has its own place in the developing world.

6
Jo Noero, Red Location, New Brighton, Port Elizabeth, South Africa, 2009–11

6

WELCOME TO TOMORROWLAND

As grand new airports in Doha (Qatar) or Shenzhen (China) reach completion, there is in fact no shortage of ambitious architectural projects underway. The reason that this has become less "obvious" is that the places concerned are no longer so much in the angle of view of the Western media. Internet sites chronicle new buildings at a bewildering pace and usually all use the same rudimentary texts and images. As much as this type of electronic information might seem promising for those who like to keep abreast of the latest events in the world of architecture, most searches are relatively fruitless. For this reason, books and professional magazines are still the best way to obtain information. Often, projects that are announced are not completed, or stand in a state of limbo far longer than architects would like to have most people believe. The curious case of the city of Ordos, Inner Mongolia, comes to mind. Since approximately 2005, many of the famous architects in the world, led by the artist Ai Weiwei and Herzog & de Meuron, participated in a project called "Ordos 100" which was due to create 100 exemplary houses. The lure of new architecture in China was great at the time, but even the booming economy of the world's new powerhouse clearly has its limits. *The New York Times* explains: "Ordos proper has 1.5 million residents. But the tomorrowland version of Ordos—built from scratch on a huge plot of empty land 15 miles south of the old city—is all but deserted. Broad boulevards are unimpeded by traffic in the new district, called Kangbashi New Area. Office buildings stand vacant. Pedestrians are in short supply. And weeds are beginning to sprout up in luxury villa developments that are devoid of residents… City leaders, cheered on by aggressive developers, had hoped to turn Ordos into a Chinese version of Dubai—transforming vast plots of the arid, Mongolian steppe into a thriving metropolis. They even invested over $1 billion in their visionary project. But four years after the city government was transplanted to Kangbashi, and with tens of thousands of houses and dozens of office buildings now completed, the 12-square-mile area has been derided in the state-run newspaper *China Daily* as a 'ghost town' monument to excess and misplaced optimism."[5]

Where all the Western architects came almost to a screeching halt in their Ordos adventure, one Chinese firm, MAD Architects, has succeeded in completing the 41 000-square-meter Ordos Museum (Ordos, Inner Mongolia, China, 2005–11, page 278). Founded in 2004 by Ma Yansong, MAD first gained attention in 2006 when they won an international competition to design the Absolute Towers near Toronto, completed in 2012 (published here). Inspired by the domes of Buckminster Fuller, the architects created a very unexpected structure that might be described as a metallic sand dune, a fitting symbol for the city, which is located on the edge of the Gobi Desert. The architects write: "Familiar yet distinct, the Ordos Museum appears to have either landed in the desert from another world or to always have existed." Although this building may remain to be considered as a monument to governmental excess, it does also testify to the particular ability of MAD Architects to get things done where others have not been able to succeed. Their equally surprising Absolute Towers (Mississauga, Canada, 2006–12, page 288) were completed in December 2012. Respectively 56 stories (170 meters) and 50 stories (150 meters) high, these towers almost seem to undulate since their floor plates are rotated between one and eight degrees at each story. Stunning new forms like these were quite common in the heyday of Dubai's feverish construction plans, but, again, few architects involved ever managed to see their projects inaugurated. Both because of its still strong economy and because of a rising new generation of Chinese architects like MAD's leader

7

7
Arata Isozaki, Himalayas Center, Shanghai, China, 2007–

Ma Yansong, it would seem safe to bet that Chinese influence will continue to rise in contemporary architecture for the foreseeable future. It can be said as well that the Chinese have an open attitude to new architecture, which is a kind of symbol of their success. This openness contrasts with the usually more staid reactions of European countries, or even the United States. Rising economic power is obviously a key to understanding where and how contemporary architecture will make its most stunning advances, even if, today, it is tempting to also look to countries that were hitherto ignored by cutting-edge design.

CANTILEVERS AND FLYING WEDGES

Another example of the scale and ambition of current architectural projects in China is the 155 000-square-meter Himalayas Center (Shanghai, 2007–, page 234) by Arata Isozaki. Set in the very visible Pudong district of Shanghai opposite the Bund and now populated with huge towers, the center contains a 5-star hotel, artists' studios, an art center, and the inevitable shopping malls. Isozaki also completed the ambitious National Convention Center in Doha, Qatar, a 175 000-square-meter complex finished in 2011. Both the Shanghai building and the Doha convention center have quasi-organic elements in their designs. In the case of Doha, the 250-meter-long façade evokes Sidra trees that are the symbol of the Qatar Foundation, the client for the project. Born in 1931, Isozaki is perhaps no longer at the apex of his creativity and influence, yet these projects show that his reputation and inventiveness have continued to carry his career to new heights in the countries that are today's significant builders.

What of the kind of new architectural forms that came forth with the rise of computer-assisted design and manufacturing? Are these going by the wayside with decreased funding for new buildings? There are, of course, still numerous examples of this kind of work, and every sign that such methods will continue to have an impact on design and construction in the years to come. The Herta and Paul Amir Building at the Tel Aviv Museum of Art (Tel Aviv, Israel, 2007–11, page 112) actually took almost 10 years to realize after the 2003 competition that selected the architect Preston Scott Cohen for the design. The angled, futuristic appearance of this 18 500-square-meter building is in good part the result of the architect's reaction to the site. Cohen states: "The design for the Amir Building arises directly from the challenge of providing several floors of large neutral rectangular galleries within a tight, idiosyncratic triangular site. The solution is to 'square the triangle' by constructing the levels on different axes, which deviate significantly from floor to floor. In essence, the building's levels—three above grade and two below—are structurally independent plans stacked one on top of the other." Author of other surprising structures such as the Taiyuan Museum of Art (China, 2007–12), Cohen makes intelligent use of the new liberty afforded to architects by digitally assisted methods.

The Vienna firm Coop Himmelb(l)au headed by Wolf D. Prix is, of course, one of the pioneers of the so-called Deconstructivist style in architecture. Their work continues to bear the fractured appearance that they invented in the 1980s, and continues also to engage in large-scale developments. This is certainly the case of the Busan Cinema Center / Busan International Film Festival (Busan, South Korea, 2005–11, page 128). At 51 000 square meters and with a €100 million budget, this is, indeed, a big project, and includes such features as the roof certified by the Guinness Book of Records as the "longest cantilevered roof" or a "virtual sky" covered with programmable LED systems. As is their custom, the architects name parts of the complex, like "Cinema Mountain" or "BIFF Hill." Although South Korea is not in the same category of emerging country as some others already cited in this text, it is indeed fortunate for European or American architects that the Far East still has an appetite for such large new projects, and the courage to engage in challenging forms. It is precisely the relatively long time frame that exists between the emergence of architectural styles or trends and their realization that sometimes gives the impression that the profession is in a kind of time warp where the 1980s are still quite the thing. Fortunately Coop Himmelb(l)au has found many ways to make their work evolve without losing the undoubted excitement found in something like the world's longest cantilever.

Another Vienna firm, Delugan Meissl, has also made a reputation with stunning buildings that also, frequently, include cantilevered volumes. Authors of the Porsche Museum (Stuttgart, Germany, 2006–08), they more recently completed the EYE Film Institute (Amsterdam, the Netherlands, 2009–11, page 144), which is located on the banks of the IJ river, just opposite Centraal Station. In this instance, the large wedge-shaped building juts out in the direction of the railway station, making it very difficult to miss. Perhaps less "ideological" in their design than Coop Himmelb(l)au has been over the years, Delugan Meissl nevertheless makes a very powerful architectural statement with the EYE Film Institute, and also underlines the ongoing commitment of the Netherlands to forms of artistic expression such as film and sound recordings. It may not be an accident that film is the subject of attention of both the Coop Himmelb(l)au project in Korea and the Amsterdam work of Delugan Meissl. Art museums have been the object of the attention of talented architects all over the world for so long, now areas like film are having their turn.

STILL STANDING AFTER ALL THESE YEARS

Another participant in the 1988 show at the Museum of Modern Art (New York) called "Deconstructivist Architecture" was Zaha Hadid, who has, in recent years, become one of the most active international architects. Her CMA CGM Tower (Marseille, France, 2008–11, page 188) is a 94 000-square-meter project in a city that is certainly not known for its high-rise buildings. Elegant and still imbued with Hadid's signature style, the building appears to be constituted of two rising curves that meet in the middle, echoing the forms of motorways that run around its site. Designed for 2700 employees, the project demonstrates Hadid's ability to take on large-scale corporate work as she has already done for such clients as BMW. Zaha Hadid's discourse has always emphasized the need to reform architecture, making it appear to emerge from the landscape as an almost organic entity, where walls, floors, and ceilings somehow merge into a coherent whole. The CMA CGM Tower, again, retains this sense of movement, but also ventures into the territory of the more predictable alignment of offices and parking spaces that, after all, makes up the real substance of corporate architecture.

UNStudio, led by Ben van Berkel and Caroline Bos, has long been a leader in the area of the extensive use of computer-assisted design, with such buildings as their striking Mercedes-Benz Museum (Stuttgart, Germany, 2001–06). Their Center for Virtual Engineering (ZVE), Fraunhofer Institute (Stuttgart, Germany, 2006–12, with Asplan Architekten, page 440), measures a relatively modest 3200 square meters in floor area, but involved careful 3D modeling and efforts to optimize the building's aluminum envelope, amongst other energy and material-saving gestures that allowed it to earn Gold certification from the DGNB (German Sustainable Building Council). This project actually demonstrates that formerly "exotic" digital design techniques have become much more common, and also that architects and clients have taken into account the lesson that new buildings need to be designed with a mind to their potential for energy savings.

STUFF HAPPENS

So are things as black as they might have seemed? There are certainly significant political, demographic, and economic changes underway. As China, other countries in the Far East, and powers such as Brazil "emerge" they will more and more become the driving forces in contemporary architecture. It is not that Europeans or Americans are "tired" per se, but their countries, having reached higher levels of density in modern buildings, may have fewer requirements for entirely new designs. A time of economic hardship is also one where every client counts the costs and conceivably shies away from innovation if it does not immediately make sense in terms of expense. The bold, flashy buildings that say "Here I am!" are now more for countries with the hunger and the brash need to assert themselves. Even America looks "old" by comparison. The Twin Towers of the World Trade Center were monuments to ambition and financial power. Their destruction certainly puts a damper on the hubris of some, even though, as has been pointed out, towers continue to rise, even in downtown New York. The 9/11 Memorial does, indeed, situate the psychological shock that the events of 2001 continue to represent for America. There was John F. Kennedy's assassination, the Vietnam War, and now this, all signs that the "New Frontier" of JFK may have long since been reached. The problem is that the view from here on out is not quite so bright.

The directions of architecture, like those of the economy, are hard to predict. "Stuff happens" as the former American Secretary of Defense Donald Rumsfeld famously declared. And not all of the stuff that happens is good. There are, of course, significant underlying factors in economic development, such as the huge, hard-working population of China, now eager for the material bounties of capitalism, but the economy, like architecture, is also about pessimism or optimism. An optimistic time leads to more appetite for risk on Wall Street or on the architect's computer screen. Perhaps the dust from the crash of 2008 will settle soon, just as the billowing clouds that swept over Manhattan in 2001 will dissipate. Two points can be emphasized concerning projects published here. One is that the ongoing relationship between art and architecture has continued to develop, leading to considerable creativity at the border between one discipline and another. A second point is that contemporary architecture of quality can be found in many countries, in particular because there is a new understanding that many traditional building methods were fundamentally more sound than modern techniques that have covered the earth in concrete and steel. Initiatives such as the Aga Khan Award for Architecture are at least partially responsible for this new awareness.

8
UNStudio, Center for Virtual Engineering (ZVE), Fraunhofer Institute, Stuttgart, Germany, 2006–12

If yesterday's Modernism can be likened, in all due modesty, to the bright certainties of the Renaissance, then we have certainly crossed the threshold into a new time, surely more dark and brooding than the post–World War II period. We tried to become gods, but we just weren't up to the task. The signs of this sea change are numerous, but two gaping holes in downtown New York, now filled with black stone and water, may be the most telling monument to a new era of doubt. One day, the mood will again be optimistic and creativity will bring forth new architecture that will be inventive and environmentally responsible. Buildings and projects will build the groundwork for this pro-cess even as decline and deep change are the rule for many. In between times, the world will have changed.

1 "Acceptance Speech: Frank Gehry," The Pritzker Architecture Prize, accessed September 30, 2012, http://www.pritzkerprize.com/1989/ceremony_speech1.
2 "Gehry's Crown for Bunker Hill Is a Fitting Tribute for Disney," *Los Angeles Times*, September 15, 1991, accessed September 30, 2012, http://articles.latimes.com/1991-09-15/realestate/re-3191_1_disney-hall-s-exterior/3.
3 Tom Wolfe, *From Bauhaus to Our House*, Farrar Straus Giroux, New York, 1981.
4 Lyrics of the song "Vertigo," opening track of U2's 2004 album How to Dismantle an Atomic Bomb: "Hello, hello (Hola!) / I'm at a place called Vertigo (Dónde está!) / It's everything I wish I didn't know."
5 "Chinese City Has Many Buildings, but Few People," *New York Times*, October 19, 2010, accessed October 1, 2012, http://www.nytimes.com/2010/10/20/business/global/20ghost.html?pagewanted=all&_r=0.

EINLEITUNG

DER BLICK IN DEN ABGRUND

Manche der kraftvollsten Bauten in diesem Band beeindrucken nicht durch ihre Höhe oder Massivität, sondern thematisieren vielmehr den Leerraum, die Abwesenheit. Leerräume sind seit längerer Zeit ein prominentes Motiv in der zeitgenössischen Architektur, doch erst durch den Blick in den Abgrund an der Nationalen Gedenkstätte für den 11. September, einem Entwurf von Michael Arad (New York, 2006–11, Seite 198), wird der Eindruck greifbar, dass sich der Boden tatsächlich aufgetan und die Zwillingstürme des World Trade Centers verschlungen hat. Zwei dunkle Brunnen tauchen in den Boden und zeichnen die Konturen der ehemaligen Bauten von Minoru Yamasaki (1912–86) nach. Konkret ist Arads Entwurf zweifellos Architektur, ideell jedoch stärker mit der Kunst verwandt. Im Kern geht es hier nicht um Politik, nicht einmal darum, wie auf die Anschläge in New York 2001 zu reagieren wäre, sondern um Abwesenheit, um eine Leere, die alles, was sich ihr nähert, aufsaugt. Als Maya Lin, damals noch Studentin in Yale, das Vietnam Veterans' Memorial (1981) auf der Mall in Washington D. C. entwarf, folgte sie einem ähnlichen Instinkt. Statt eines heroischen Denkmals zog sie einen dunklen Schnitt durch das Gelände und ließ in die umlaufende Wandfläche die Namen von 50 000 gefallenen amerikanischen Soldaten gravieren. Wer sich daran erinnert, welche strahlende, hoffnungsvolle Zukunft die kurze Präsidentschaft John F. Kennedys (1960–63) zu versprechen schien, erkennt den inneren Zusammenhang zwischen dem Trauma seiner Ermordung und seiner schlichten Grabstätte auf dem Friedhof von Arlington (John F. Kennedy Eternal Flame von John Carl Warnecke, 1967). Hier symbolisiert noch kein Abgrund den Verlust, sondern eine Flamme – und doch sind die Zeiten des Triumphes längst vorbei.

Mahnmale sind ohne Frage ein eigenes Genre – in der Regel nicht an strenge architektonische Vorgaben gebunden und frei vom Diktat pragmatischer Funktionalität – doch Maya Lin und kürzlich Michael Arad in New York haben es verstanden, der Leere, der Abwesenheit, dem Fall Ausdruck zu verleihen. Aufstieg und Macht Amerikas knüpfen sich an Leitmotive und Symbole der Dominanz, vom Vorrücken der Siedler in den Westen bis hin zu eindrucksvollen Gedenkstätten wie dem Iwo Jima Monument (Marine Corps War Memorial, Arlington Cemetery, Washington D. C., 1951). Amerika geht als triumphaler Sieger aus schwierigen Zeiten hervor – so die selbst propagierte Legende. Doch Maya Lins Vietnam Memorial und Michael Arads Gedenkstätte für den 11. September sprechen eine andere Sprache, eine Sprache des Verlusts, der möglicherweise schwerer wiegt als die Ereignisse, denen sie ein Denkmal setzen.

Architektur war stets eine angenehm verlässliche, kompakte, undurchsichtige Größe, bevor sie zum gläsernen Spiegel des Kapitalismus wurde. Das soll kein Kommentar zum Kapitalismus per se sein, aber viele der Hochhäuser im Internationalen Stil – von ihren Geburtstätten in Chicago und New York bis in die entlegensten Winkel der Welt – hinterlassen einen bitteren Nachgeschmack. Aber was blieb von der „alten Ordnung", der Kirchen- und Kolonialarchitektur? Zwei der hier vorgestellten Entwürfe lassen sich als eloquenter, ja humorvoller Kommentar zu vergangenen, glanzvollen Zeiten lesen. „Reading between the Lines" (Borgloon, Belgien, 2011, Seite 178), ein Projekt des jungen belgischen Architektenduos Pieterjan Gijs und Arnout Van Vaerenbergh, setzt sich auf einem Feld in Limburg formal mit dem Sakralbau auseinander. Aber diese „Kirche" hat eine Grundfläche von nur 28 m² und ist weder funktional noch für andachtsvolle Einkehr geeignet. Dennoch

9
Renzo Piano, London Bridge Tower, London, UK, 2009–12

9

ist der Bau aus 30 t Cor-Ten-Stahl und mit einem Fundament aus Stahlbeton denkbar stabil und damit auf deutlich längere Lebensdauer angelegt als viele zeitgenössische Bauten. Die Architekten verstehen ihren Entwurf als Zeichnung im Raum – leer und transparent – im Gegensatz zu den meisten Kirchenbauten. Es ist eine Leere, die sich auch als Kommentar zur schwindenden Bedeutung von Religion verstehen lässt.

WIE SOLLEN WIR UNS TRÖSTEN?

Leere Kirchen sind nichts Neues. Bereits vor 130 Jahren schrieb Friedrich Nietzsche in einem hellsichtigen Text, der spätere Schrecken der Geschichte ahnen lässt:

Gott ist tot! Gott bleibt tot! Und wir haben ihn getötet! Wie trösten wir uns, die Mörder aller Mörder? Das Heiligste und Mächtigste, was die Welt bisher besaß, es ist unter unsern Messern verblutet – wer wischt dies Blut von uns ab? Mit welchem Wasser könnten wir uns reinigen? Welche Sühnefeiern, welche heiligen Spiele werden wir erfinden müssen? Ist nicht die Größe dieser Tat zu groß für uns? Müssen wir nicht selber zu Göttern werden, um nur ihrer würdig zu erscheinen?
Die fröhliche Wissenschaft, Drittes Buch, 125, 1882

Und das taten wir: Wir erhoben uns selbst zu Göttern, bauten Türme zur Glorifizierung unserer selbst und unseres Geldes. In gewisser Weise sind die dunklen Brunnen, der Abgrund in New York, ein Symbol für unser Scheitern an diesem zu hoch gesteckten Ziel. „Dann sagten sie: Auf, bauen wir uns eine Stadt und einen Turm mit einer Spitze bis zum Himmel und machen wir uns damit einen Namen, dann werden wir uns nicht über die ganze Erde zerstreuen" (Gen 11,4). Der Turm ist mehr als einmal, buchstäblich wie metaphorisch, zusammengestürzt, nur um immer wieder neu in den Himmel zu wachsen. Der Burj Khalifa in Dubai hat eine Höhe von 829 m (Adrian Smith, Skidmore Owings & Merrill, VAE, 2010), während in Dschidda, Saudi-Arabien, ein noch ambitionierteres Symbol architektonischer Hybris in den Himmel wächst: der treffend benannte Kingdom Tower (Adrian Smith, AS+GG, im Bau), der die 1000-m-Grenze durchbrechen soll. Beide Entwürfe entstanden nach den Anschlägen vom 11. September 2001. Der London Bridge Tower von Renzo Piano (London, 2009–12, Seite 368) – gemeinhin „Splitter" oder „Scherbe" genannt – mutet mit seiner Höhe von 306 m, gemessen an den Maßstäben des Nahen Ostens, eher bescheiden an. Zweifellos ist jedoch auch er ein Beispiel für das ungebrochene Streben nach einem markanten Profil und ein bisschen Ruhm. Zugleich werfen die dunklen Wolken eines drohenden ökonomischen Zusammenbruchs, einer Wirtschaft am Abgrund, ihre Schatten. Die zeitgenössische Architektur wird diesem Umstand mehr und mehr Rechnung tragen müssen – doch für den Augenblick dominieren Architekten, die bewusst die Nähe zur Kunst suchen. Schon morgen könnte die dunkle Wolkendecke aufreißen. Vielleicht erwächst aus Chaos eine neue Ordnung …

UND IMMER WIEDER GEHT DIE SONNE AUF

Dunkelheit ist nur mit Einschränkungen ein kreativer Impulsgeber, und manche würden unsere Zeit als Zeit der Umbrüche, Missverhältnisse und Widersprüche beschreiben. Zu den ungewöhnlichsten baulichen Projekten der jüngsten Zeit zählt der Orbit (Olympiapark, London,

10

10
Frank O. Gehry, Eight Spruce Street, New York, New York, USA, 2007–11

2010–12, Seite 250). „Anders als vertikale Türme, die in die Höhe wachsen, indem ein Stockwerk auf dem nächsten ruht“, so Cecil Balmond, einer der Planer, „zieht der Orbit seine Kraft aus Schnittstellen und Streuung und definiert ein neues Paradigma für Form und Stabilität.“ Der Orbit ist das Resultat einer ungewöhnlichen Zusammenarbeit zwischen dem Künstler Anish Kapoor (geboren 1954 im indischen Mumbai) und dem Bauingenieur Cecil Balmond (geboren 1943 in Colombo, Sri Lanka). Englands ehemals weltumspannender Einfluss ist kein Geheimnis, und doch ist interessant, dass die provokanteste Architektur der Olympischen Spiele in London 2012 die Zusammenarbeit eines Künstlers aus Indien und eines Ingenieurs aus Sri Lanka ist, finanziert von einem in Indien gegründeten Unternehmen. Kann es sein, dass die „Rettung“ des Westens aus Osten und aus Süden kommt?

Auch das Projekt „Discovering Columbus“ (New York, 2012, Seite 330), eine Arbeit des japanischen Künstlers Tatzu Nishi, lässt sich als ein Auf-den-Kopf-Stellen gewohnter Verhältnisse verstehen – mithilfe von Architektur. Nishi setzt sich nicht zum ersten Mal mit Widersprüchen auseinander und realisierte mit diesem Projekt ein 75 m² großes „Wohnzimmer“ als temporäre Installation in Manhattan, luftige 23 m über dem Columbus Circle. Die Installation umbaut eine Kolumbusstatue, einen der „Erfinder“ der „Neuen Welt“. Wie bei Pieterjan Gijs und Arnout Van Vaerenbergh geht es auch bei Nishi nicht nur um ein Spiel mit den Maßstäben, sondern auch um Häuslichkeit und unvereinbare Standorte. Warum sollte Architektur auf dem Boden der Tatsachen bleiben, wenn sie doch so leicht auf eine Säule, mitten auf einen verkehrsreichen Platz zu verlegen ist? Vor Tatzu Nishi haben schon viele andere die unverrückbaren „Gesetzmäßigkeiten“ der Architektur infrage gestellt; auch nach ihm werden dies sicher viele tun. Dennoch stehen dieses und ähnliche Projekte für einen *point of no return*, nach dem die Architektur nie wieder sein wird, was sie einmal gewesen ist. Wie lange war es üblich in der Architektur, Beständigkeit mit Symmetrie und „langlebigen“ Baustoffen gleichzusetzen? Kapoor und Balmond stellen unter Beweis, dass Balance und Eleganz nicht immer das sind, was man vermuten würde. Bei Nishi kommt Humor ins Spiel – mit einem bürgerlichen Interieur, das er auf eine Säule setzt, mit einer großen Skulptur im Zentrum. „Ich glaube, dass Kunst das Vertraute aus einer ungewohnten Perspektive zeigen sollte“, so Nishi. „Der Überraschungseffekt, der sich aus der Verkehrung von Öffentlichem und Privatem, von Innen- und Außenraum ergibt, öffnet den Blick der Besucher auf ihre Umgebung. Diese Erfahrung gibt der Vorstellungskraft neuen Schub.“

HUMPTY DUMPTY SASS AUF DER MAUER

Künstlerische Freiheit als Idealbild ist kein neues Thema in der zeitgenössischen Architektur. Frank O. Gehry – der inzwischen große Apartmenthäuser in New York baut (Eight Spruce Street, New York, 2007–11, Seite 172) – war zunächst ein Verfechter von spontanen und eigenwilligen Lösungen. Als er 1989 den Pritzker-Preis erhielt, erklärte er: „Freunde von mir wie die Künstler Jasper Johns, Bob Rauschenberg, Ed Kienholz oder Claes Oldenburg haben mit denkbar billigsten Materialien gearbeitet – Holzresten und Papier – und Werke von großer Schönheit geschaffen. Es ging dabei nicht um oberflächliche Details, diese Arbeiten waren spontan und brachten mich zum Nachdenken darüber, was Schönheit eigentlich ist. Ich beschloss, mein eigenes Handwerk zu nutzen, mit Handwerkern zusammenzuarbeiten und aus den Grenzen, die sich daraus ergaben, eine Tugend zu machen. Die Malerei hat eine Spontaneität, die ich auch in der Architektur gesucht habe. Ich habe mit neuen Baustoffen experimentiert, um Gefühlen und Stimmungen Form zu geben. Auf der Suche nach einer persönlichen Ausdrucksform war ich wie ein Künstler, der vor einer weißen Leinwand steht und überlegt, wo er seinen ersten Strich setzen soll."[1] Nicht lange nach diesem Bekenntnis, das in der Tat auf den Punkt bringt, welch frischen Wind Frank Gehry in die Architekturlandschaft von Santa Monica und Venice gebracht hat, räumte er allerdings ein: „Nach vielen Jahren der Dekonstruktion geht es mir heute darum, Humpty Dumpty wieder zusammenzusetzen."[2]

Widersprüche in der zeitgenössischen Architektur können sich auch aus der Kontinuität ergeben. Anders als Gehry, der heute nach einer Geschlossenheit sucht, die er früher abgelehnt hätte, sind andere, wie Richard Meier, ihrer ästhetischen Verpflichtung gegenüber der Moderne stets treu geblieben. Meier, inzwischen Ende 70, realisierte erst kürzlich zwei Bauten, das hier vorgestellte OCT Shenzhen Clubhouse (Shenzhen, China, 2010–12, Seite 302) sowie das Italcementi i.lab (Bergamo, 2005–12, Seite 38). Beide Entwürfe zeichnen sich durch konsequentes Weiß und eine Ausgewogenheit aus, die längst zur Handschrift des Architekten geworden sind. Interessant an dieser Kontinuität ist, dass sie Parallelen zum Klassizismus aufweist, der sich ebenfalls nie wirklich überlebt hat. Dabei ignoriert Meier nicht, dass sich die Zeiten geändert haben und Architektur heute veränderten Ansprüchen gerecht werden muss. Das Italcementi i.lab wurde als erster Bau Italiens mit einem LEED-Zertifikat in Platin ausgezeichnet. Konsequenz und die Treue zu persönlichen Prinzipien können sicherlich als Tugend gelten. Vor über 30 Jahren polemisierte der Schriftsteller Tom Wolfe in seinem Buch *Mit dem Bauhaus leben: Die Diktatur des Rechtecks* heftig gegen den Meier'schen Stil: „Jedes 900 000-Dollar-Sommerhaus in den nördlichen Waldgebieten von Michigan oder an den Stränden von Long Island hat so viele Stahlrohrgeländer, Rampen, Wendeltreppen aus Metall, fabrikähnliche Fensterfronten, Neonröhren und weiße Rohre wie ein Werk für Schädlingsbekämpfungsmittel. Ich habe erlebt, wie die Bewohner eines solchen Hauses durch das Übermaß an Weiß und Helligkeit und Verschlankung und Sauberkeit und Sterilität und Reduziertheit an den Rand der Gefühllosigkeit getrieben wurden. Sie haben verzweifelt nach einem Gegengift gesucht, nach Wohnlichkeit und Farbe."[3] Wer mag, kann Wohnlichkeit heute in einem „Wohnzimmer" 23 m über dem Columbus Circle finden – doch Richard Meier bleibt sich treu.

TIEF UNTEN

Herzog & de Meuron hingegen sind eher Vertreter innovativer Tendenzen in der zeitgenössischen Architektur. Wie ihr Entwurf für die Neue Messe Basel (Schweiz, 2010–13, Seite 204) und ihre beiden jüngsten Londoner Projekte zeigen, lotet das Schweizer Architektenduo immer wieder die Grenzen architektonischer Gestaltung aus. Der Serpentine Summer Pavilion 2012 (mit Ai Weiwei; London, Seite 212) setzt eine im Jahr 2000 mit Zaha Hadid begonnene Tradition fort. In Zusammenarbeit mit dem chinesischen Künstler und Dissidenten Ai Weiwei entschieden sich Herzog & de Meuron für ein Pavillonkonzept, das auf überraschenden Gegensätzen beruht. Kaum mehr als 1 m über Geländeniveau erhebt sich die Konstruktion, die neben einer Sitzlandschaft aus Kork auch quasi archäologische Funde überdacht. Denn bei den Erdarbeiten stießen die Architekten nicht nur auf Grundwasser, sondern auch auf die Spuren früherer Pavillons. Markiert werden die Funde durch den Standort der Säulen, auf denen eine Stahlscheibe mit 10 m Durchmesser ruht, die wie ein aufgehängter Wasserspiegel über dem Sitzbereich schwebt. Der Serpentine Summer Pavilion 2012 erinnert an Dunkelheit und dringt dafür tief ins Erdreich vor – Motive, die in eine Zeit des Umbruchs und der Unsicherheit passen. In dem flachen Wasser auf der Stahlscheibe des Pavillons spiegelt sich das georgianische Backsteindomizil der Serpentine Gallery, auf den Kopf gestellt und verzerrt vom Wind.

Auch ein weiteres Londoner Projekt von Herzog & de Meuron hat archäologische Anflüge, wenn auch industriegeschichtlicher Art. Ihren Ruf verdanken die Architekten ihrem Umbau des alten Kraftwerks Bankside in Southwark zur Tate Modern (2000). Aktuell arbeiten sie an einer zusätzlichen Erweiterung für das Museum, die 2016 abgeschlossen sein soll. Einen ersten Einblick bieten die bereits sanierten 6000 m² Nutzfläche, die sog. Tanks, in denen ursprünglich Millionen Liter Öl lagerten, die das Kraftwerk benötigte. Die Tanks (London, GB, 2010–12, Seite 39) wurden bewusst „unbelassen und industriell" erhalten und sollen für Performancekunst und Filminstallationen genutzt werden. Es sind „Räume voller Charakter und Geschichte, in denen zu spüren ist, dass man unter der Erde ist", so die Architekten. Auch der bereits realisierte Bau der Tate Modern thematisiert – in diesem Fall deutlich über Bodenniveau – das Verhältnis von moderner Kunst zu einem alten Industriegebäude. Mit den Tanks gehen Herzog & de Meuron einige Schritte weiter in eine Art Zwischenreich eines ehemals unbewohnten Ortes und lassen sich auf eine moderne Form der Archäologie ein, die Welten entfernt ist von „Weiß und Helligkeit und Verschlankung und Sauberkeit und Sterilität und Reduziertheit", von der Architektur einer vergangenen Zeit, als es schien, dass alles nur besser werden könnte.

„WE'RE AT A PLACE CALLED VERTIGO"[4]

Typisch für zeitgenössische Strömungen in Architektur und Design sind Situationen, die Besucher und Betrachter aus dem Gleichgewicht bringen. Wo sind die Grenzen, wo ist oben, wo ist unten? Künstler wie Robert Irwin, James Turrell oder Dan Graham spielen schon lange mit solchen Konzepten – doch konnte man sich nicht bisher darauf verlassen, dass Architektur stabiler, berechenbarer ist? Kunst ist eine Sache, doch sollte die Architektur von Gewerbeflächen nicht etwas anderes sein? Das junge New Yorker Büro Gage Clemenceau stellt solche Gesetzmäßigkeiten infrage, z. B. mit dem Entwurf für die Konzeptstores des Designers Nicola Formichetti (New York, 2011, Seite 152; Hong Kong, China, 2012). Mit einem für die Modewelt typischen Hang zur Dramatik schreiben sie: „Räume für Mode sind minimalistisch, lenken die Aufmerksamkeit auf die Mode – wollen die Kleidung verkaufen. Bei unserer Zusammenarbeit mit Nicola Formichetti stellten wir dieses Prinzip infrage und definierten einen völlig neuartigen, experimentellen Raumtypus, der die Mode nicht nur in den Vordergrund stellt, sondern ihre Effekte und den Eindruck eines sich ständig verändernden Raums." Doch vielleicht geht es Architekten und Designern gar nicht darum, den baulichen Kontext aus dem Gleichgewicht zu bringen, vielleicht ist unsere räumliche Verunsicherung vielmehr so etwas wie ein Monitor, eine immersive Umgebung, in der Realität und Fiktion ineinander übergehen. Es bleibt offen, ob der junge Mann in Uniform nur ein Videospiel spielt oder tatsächlich eine Drohne steuert, die am anderen Ende der Welt jemanden tötet. Werden Beziehungen durch physische Nähe und Urinstinkte bestimmt oder können wir beliebig zwischen körperlosen Avataren wählen? Wo ist oben, wo ist unten?

11
Carla Juaçaba and Bia Lessa, Humanidade 2012 Pavilion, Copacabana, Rio de Janeiro, Brazil, 2012

11

Obwohl Serge Salat (u. a.) Abschlüsse in Architektur und Bauingenieurwesen hat, drückt er sich auch in künstlerischen Installationen mit komplexen historischen und psychologischen Bedeutungen aus („Beyond Infinity I", 2007, Seite 396; „Beyond Infinity II", 2011, Seite 402, beide in China). „Beyond Infinity I", lädt die Betrachter ein, „aus ihrem vertrauten Umfeld in einen faszinierend paradoxen, fließenden, traumartigen Raum mit immer tieferen Schichten von Träumen einzutreten". Salat setzt auf „persönliche Raumerlebnisse, Erlebnisse, die eine Begegnung mit der Zeit zulassen, eine Ahnung von Ewigkeit geben". „Beyond Infinity II" wiederum lässt „die Besucher scheinbar in einer Zwischenebene der raumgreifenden Konstruktion schweben, deren ins Unendliche gespiegelte Repliken in einen Abgrund stürzen". Vielleicht lassen sich solche Rauminstallationen aus Salats architektonischem Hintergrund erklären, doch in erster Linie sind sie Kunst. Dabei ist seit Jahren zu beobachten, wie sich die Grenzen zwischen Kunst und Architektur auflösen.

Auch der Versuch, Abgründe zu simulieren, Räume, die sich nicht unmittelbar erfassen lassen, zieht sich durch die gesamte Architekturgeschichte. Insbesondere die Architektur des Barock und des Manierismus spielte mit hochkomplexen Formen. Die Sala dei Giganti (Saal der Giganten) in Giulio Romanos Palazzo del Te (Mantua, 1526–35) ist ein Beispiel für ein solches Zusammenspiel von Kunst und Architektur in überbordender Formensprache. In Romanos Saal, einem fantastischen Geniestreich, verbindet der Künstler-Architekt seine Baukunst mit einer fantastischen Szene der Zerstörung. In diesem Raum, in dem die Gesetzmäßigkeiten der Realität außer Kraft gesetzt scheinen, spielen Maßstab, Zeit und Ort keine Rolle. Giovanni Battista Piranesi (1720–78) studierte Architektur in Venedig, wurde jedoch besonders für seine Kupferstiche berühmt, darunter seine „Carceri d'invenzione" (Erfundene Kerker). Im Grunde hatten nur wenige Architekten ähnlichen Einfluss wie diese düsteren Kupferstiche mit ihrem schwindelerregenden Raum- und Perspektivenspiel. Ihre Motive entziehen sich gewissermaßen einer Entschlüsselung – sind abgründiger, düsterer, finsterer als die Wirklichkeit – und stehen für eine fantastische Welt der Angst. Wie sieht die Hölle aus, wenn nicht wie einer dieser Kerker, gewaltiger und unbegreiflicher nur, als jede irdische Fantasie sie zeichnen könnte?

Zweifel und Wirrungen des Manierismus und Barock markieren den entgegengesetzten Pendelausschlag nach der geordneten Perspektive und dem Humanismus der Hochrenaissance. Ohne den großen Künstlern und Architekten der Geschichte etwas absprechen zu wollen, sollten wir uns vielleicht fragen, ob die Gewissheiten der Moderne, die bis Mitte des 20. Jahrhunderts galten, nicht längst von einer tiefen Zwiespältigkeit einer Weltordnung nach dem 11. September abgelöst wurden – ebenso wie der Manierismus auf die Renaissance folgte. Falls dem so ist, liegt vor uns möglicherweise eine lange Phase des Zweifels und der Schatten. Die Zeiten, in denen alles möglich schien, als Brasília aus dem weiten, unbesiedelten Herzen Brasiliens wachsen konnte, liegen in weiter Ferne. Wo Hoffnung und Optimismus fehlen, sind Geld und Ambition nicht genug, um neue Welten zu beflügeln.

12

12
J. Mayer H. Architects, Mestia Police Station, Mestia, Georgia, 2011–12

TEMPORÄR UND ZEITGENÖSSISCH

Angesichts wirtschaftlicher Engpässe bei langfristigen, kostenintensiven Bauvorhaben sind temporäre Bauten immer häufiger anzutreffen. Gerade weil nicht für die Ewigkeit geplant, kann solch ephemere Architektur im besten Fall innovativer und freier sein als massive Bauten aus Beton und Stahl. Etliche Projekte in diesem Band sind der beste Beweis. Die Ausstellung Humanidade 2012 (Seite 242) wurde in einem temporären Bau gezeigt, der von der Architektin Carla Juaçaba mit der Bühnenbildnerin Bia Lessa entworfen worden war. „Unser Entwurf besteht aus Gerüsten, ist lichtdurchlässig, der Witterung ausgesetzt: dem Licht, der Hitze, dem Rauschen des Meers und des Windes. Er erinnert daran, wie zerbrechlich der Mensch im Vergleich zur Natur ist", so die Planerinnen, die den gesamten Bau recyclingfähig konzipierten. Die 170 m lange und 20 m hohe Konstruktion war massiver als viele temporäre Bauten, doch das Gerüstkonzept sorgte dafür, dass der Entwurf hell und luftig war – ohne auf teure Baumaterialien zurückgreifen zu müssen, die auf Papier oft transparenter sind als in der Realität.

Das New Yorker Architekturbüro SO – IL hat bereits erfolgreich mehrere temporäre Projekte realisiert, darunter die Installation „Pole Dance" für das MoMA PS1 (Long Island City, New York, 2010). Für den New Yorker Ableger der Frieze Art Fair (Seite 424) stand das Team vor der Herausforderung, innerhalb kürzester Zeit mithilfe eines standardisierten Zeltbausystems erhebliche Nutzfläche zu schaffen (20 900 m²). Indem sie keilförmige Elemente in den Grundriss einschoben und die Zeltbahnen an den Stirnseiten bis auf den Boden herunterzogen, gelang es den jungen Planern, die Messefläche zu variieren, ohne das Grundkonzept wesentlich zu verändern. Dank der verwendeten Zeltbahnstreifen scheint sich die Konstruktion „fließend in den Boden fortzusetzen". Der Kunstgriff, einer 457 m langen Konstruktion mit lediglich etwas Metall und Textil Originalität zu verschaffen, ist eine überzeugende Geste in Zeiten der Sparprogramme, in denen Architekten vor der Herausforderung stehen, ihre Parameter neu zu überdenken und ihren Klienten, für die vor allem Kosten zählen, neue Lösungen vorzuschlagen.

Der japanische Architekt Shigeru Ban wurde für seine temporären Bauten berühmt, die punktuell auch in der Katastrophenhilfe zum Einsatz kommen und oft mit Pappröhren realisiert werden. Sein Pavillon für Camper (Alicante, Spanien; Sanya, China; Miami, Florida; Lorient, Frankreich, Vorfertigung Juni–September 2011, Seite 86) war ein 250 m² großer Pavillon, der so konzipiert wurde, dass er leicht aufzubauen und zu transportieren war. Hierbei kamen Pappröhren zum Einsatz, die ineinander gesteckt transportiert werden konnten. Der als Verkaufsraum genutzte Bau wurde als Rundzelt entworfen und erinnert an Armee- oder Zirkuszelte. Shigeru Bans Prioritäten orientieren sich an technischen Herausforderungen und dem Ehrgeiz, architektonisches Neuland zu erschließen. So realisierte er Häuser „ohne Wände" oder Häuser aus Pappröhren – und hinterfragte so überkommene Vorstellungen von Massivität und letztendlich von Architektur schlechthin.

Atelier Bow-Wow, ein weiteres japanisches Büro, wurde 1992 von Yoshiharu Tsukamoto und Momoyo Kaijima gegründet. Kürzlich arbeitete das Team an einem ungewöhnlichen temporären Projekt, dem BMW Guggenheim Lab (New York, 2011; Berlin, 2012; Mumbai, Indien 2012–13, Seite 78). In New York hatte das Projekt, das Bereiche für Ausstellungen, Workshops und Vorträge sowie ein Café und Lagerflächen umfasste, während seiner zehnwöchigen Laufzeit 56 000 Besucher. Mit kohlenstofffaserverstärktem Kunststoff statt Stahl, einem Dach aus

Polyestermembran und einer z. T. aus doppellagigem Polyesternetz realisierten Hülle setzte das BMW Guggenheim Lab auf recht anspruchsvolle Technologie und erzielte damit eine besondere Leichtigkeit, eine Voraussetzung für den problemlosen Transport. Temporäre Bauten wie diese lassen sich zudem auf kleinsten Brachgrundstücken oder Zwischennutzungsflächen realisieren – ein großer Vorteil in Städten, in denen fehlender Raum ein echtes Problem ist.

GEHEILIGT WERDE DEIN NAME

Die Beispiele von Richard Meier und Frank Gehry in den USA belegen, dass die Formensprache der 1970er- und 1980er-Jahre nach wie vor höchst präsent ist. Zwar mag es heute aus wirtschaftlichen Gründen insgesamt weniger Neubauten geben, doch so manche Auftraggeber sehen nach wie vor gern einen Pritzker-Preisträger als Architekten. Es wäre eine Übertreibung zu behaupten, Leerräume und Nichtraum seien alles, was die zeitgenössische Architektur zu bieten hat. Traditionelle Werte und Bauformen sind in manchen Bereichen nach wie vor die Norm. Fähige Architekten entwerfen auch heute noch Kirchenräume in aller Welt – häufig kleinere Kapellen. Eines der hier vorgestellten Beispiele ist die Capela de Todos os Santos (Allerheiligenkapelle, Gurita Farm, Martinho Campos, Minas Gerais, Brasilien, 2011, Seite 364) von Gustavo Penna, einem Architekten aus Belo Horizonte. Die 160 m² große Kapelle hat die Form eines stilisierten Kreuzes, gebaut wurde sie aus Beton, Glas, Travertin und seltenem Peroba-do-campo-Holz. Der schlichte rechteckige Grundriss wird durch ein schmales Wasserbecken betont, ausgerichtet an der Mittelachse der Kapelle, und der skulpturalen Beschwörung eines Kruzifix. Das Projekt ist schlicht und elegant, auch wenn das baulich interpretierte Kreuzmotiv, im Aufriss klar zu sehen, für manche zu figurativ sein mag.

Ein bedeutenderer Kapellenbau von I. M. Pei steht in Japan (Miho Institute of Aesthetics, Shigaraki, Shiga, mit io Architects, 2010–12, Seite 354). Die 1800 m² große Kapelle liegt auf dem Campus einer Hochschule inmitten von Zypressen, rund eineinhalb Autostunden von Kioto entfernt. Der asymmetrische Kegelbau ist mit Edelstahlbändern von bis zu 18 m Länge (eine ingenieurtechnische Meisterleistung) verschalt. Der Innenraum der Kapelle wurde mit japanischer Riesenthuja ausgekleidet, auf dem Boden französischer Kalkstein und Weiße Eiche verlegt. I. M. Pei (geboren 1917) äußerte vor zahlreichen Bekannten, die Kapelle in Shigaraki sei sein letzter Bau. Ein sinnfälliges Zusammentreffen, dass einer seiner ersten Entwürfe ebenfalls ein Sakralbau war – die Luce Memorial Chapel (Taichung, Taiwan, 1954–63), interessanterweise ein schlichtes hyperbolisches Paraboloid, das als 19 m hohe Zeltkonstruktion realisiert wurde. Die Eleganz und Einfachheit des lichtdurchfluteten Entwurfs machen deutlich, dass Pei nicht nur der Planer von Bauten in aller Welt ist – von Washington D. C. bis hin zum Louvre in Paris –, sondern einer der bedeutendsten modernen Architekten überhaupt. Seine Generation improvisiert nicht mit temporären Zeltbahnen, seine Bauten sind so langlebig wie sich nur denken lässt. Die Kapelle am Miho Institute of Aesthetics wird sicher noch lange stehen, wenn die heutige Generation junger Architekten längst aufgehört hat zu entwerfen und zu bauen.

13

13
Diébédo Francis Kéré, Opera Village, Laongo, Burkina Faso, 2010–

BAUEN IN DER PERIPHERIE

Die Reihe *Architecture Now!* hat den Anspruch, so offen wie möglich zu sein, sei es in stilistischer, geografischer oder typologischer Hinsicht. Und so kann es sein, dass sich – bedingt durch die alphabetische Gliederung der Bände – ein kostengünstiges Kleinprojekt direkt neben einem Großkomplex findet. Ebenso können interessante Projekte, soweit sie auffindbar sind, überall auf diesem Globus liegen, auch wenn sich die höchste Dichte innovativer Neubauten nach wie vor in finanzstärkeren Ländern findet. Vielleicht ist es ein Zeichen der Zeit, dass in *Architecture Now! 9* Projekte aus Ländern vertreten sind, die bisher eher unterrepräsentiert waren. Hierzu zählen auch Georgien, Burkina Faso, Südafrika oder Äquatorialguinea. Auch wenn die planenden Architekten (und manchmal ihre Auftraggeber) in den meisten Fällen aus Europa stammen, zeugen die Projekte in diesen Ländern von wachsendem technischem Anspruch und dem Wunsch, gut zu bauen, was durch besser verfügbare Technologien und Informationen möglich wird.

Der deutsche Architekt Jürgen Mayer H. hat mit jüngeren Projekten wie seinem Metropol Parasol (Sevilla, 2005–11) einen beachtlichen Ruf erworben. Die Umgestaltung der 12 670 m² großen Plaza de la Encarnación realisierte er mit einer polyurethanbeschichteten Holzschirmkonstruktion, in und unter der Bars, Restaurants und öffentliche Freiflächen Platz finden. Doch überraschender noch sind weitere ungewöhnliche Bauprojekte des Architekten in Georgien: Der Grenzübergang in Sarpi (2010–11, Seite 292), eine Polizeiwache in Mestia (2011–12) und Raststätten (Gori, 2011–12, Seite 298) an der Autobahnstrecke von Aserbaidschan in die Türkei sind zwar prinzipiell Bauten aus Beton und Glas, doch ihre ungewöhnliche Formensprache betritt gestalterisches Neuland. Über den Grenzübergang Sarpi schreibt Jürgen Mayer H., der Bau „steht am Eingang zu Georgien und ist ein Zeichen für den Aufschwung des Landes". Georgien ist nicht das einzige Land, das sich im Bemühen um ein neues Image in jüngster Zeit an fähige Architekten gewandt hat. Da ist etwa die kasachische Hauptstadt Astana, in der so profilierte Büros wie Foster + Partners öffentliche Bauten realisierten (Pyramide des Friedens und der Eintracht, 2006; Entertainmentcenter Khan Shatyr, 2006). Der italienische Architekt Manfredi Nicoletti plante die außergewöhnliche Zentrale Konzerthalle von Kasachstan, die 2009 eingeweiht wurde. Es bleibt abzuwarten, ob architektonische Landmarken ein nationales Profil transportieren oder ein Image aufpolieren können. Doch unbestritten tragen neue Auftraggeber – darunter Katar und viele andere – dazu bei, dass die Branche wirtschaftlich mehr als schwierige Zeiten übersteht.

Der Architekt Francis Kéré ist bekannt für Projekte in Mali – den Nationalpark von Mali (Bamako, 2009–10) oder das Zentrum für Lehmbau (Mopti, 2010) – sowie in seiner Heimat Burkina Faso. Sein erstes Projekt, eine Grundschule in seinem Heimatdorf Gando (2001), wurde 2004 mit dem Aga-Khan-Preis für Architektur ausgezeichnet. Aktuell arbeitet Kéré an einem ungewöhnlicheren Projekt, dem Operndorf in Laongo (Burkina Faso, seit 2010, Seite 256). Initiator des Opernprojekts für Afrika war der deutsche Theatermacher Christoph Schlingensief. „Als ich zum ersten Mal die Anfrage für eine Oper in Afrika erhielt", so Kéré, „dachte ich, das sei ein Scherz. So etwas kann sich nur jemand ausdenken, der Afrika entweder nicht kennt, oder so gesättigt ist, dass er nur noch dumme Ideen hat. Das war meine erste, spontane Reaktion." Dennoch konnte die erste Bauphase des ambitionierten Projekts, rund eineinhalb Autostunden von der Hauptstadt Ouagadougou entfernt, inzwischen abgeschlossen werden; auf dem 14 ha großen Gelände, auf dem weiterhin gebaut wird, wurden mehrere Wohneinheiten realisiert. Kéré ist vertraut mit ortstypischen Baumethoden und -materialien, die hier eingesetzt werden. Und vielleicht liegt es gerade daran – und weniger am bisher nicht realisierten Festspielhaus – dass dieses Projekt fasziniert und Erfolg verspricht. Es gibt keinen Grund, warum gelungene zeitgenössische Architektur nicht unter Berücksichtigung lokaler Gegebenheiten geplant werden kann oder in einem Baustil, der im kulturellen Kontext wurzelt. Kosten müssen zwangsläufig auf ein Minimum reduziert werden; natürlichere, sanftere Baumethoden sind eine bessere Antwort auf globale Klimafragen als westliche Ansätze, die eher auf Technologie setzen als auf gesunden Menschenverstand.

Der südafrikanische Architekt Jo Noero praktiziert seit Beginn seiner Laufbahn in Kapstadt und realisierte bisher über 200 Projekte. Seine jüngsten Bauten in Red Location (New Brighton, Port Elizabeth, Südafrika, 2009–11, Seite 334) sind eine Galerie und eine Bibliothek, die von der Kommunalverwaltung Nelson Mandela Bay finanziert wurden. Das Red Location Museum (Noero Wolff Architects) dokumentiert den Kampf gegen die Apartheid und wurde 2006 mit dem RIBA-Lubetkin-Preis ausgezeichnet. Red Location, benannt nach den typischen rostigen Wellblechhütten, war der Ort, an dem Nelson Mandela Umkhonto we Sizwe (Speer der Nation) gründete, den bewaffneten Arm des African National Congress. Die Galerie zeigt „Kunst des Widerstands", die Bibliothek mit digitalem Schwerpunkt soll das städtische Archiv und eine Sammlung von Widerstandsliteratur zugänglich machen; hier soll es auch eine Computerschule geben. Das Museum und die Neubauten des zweiten Planungsabschnitts bilden ein dichtes Ensemble; gemeinsame Merkmale sind Sheddächer, durch die Tageslicht einfällt. Jo Noero arbeitet in größerem Maßstab und einem größeren Land als Francis Kéré, doch sein eigentliches Verdienst in Red Location ist es, nicht nur den Widerstand gegen die Apartheid zu würdigen, sondern bewiesen zu haben, dass moderne Architektur mit Gespür für Standort und Funktion – wie die „Memory Boxes" aus Wellblech im Museum zeigen – einen eigenen Platz in sich entwickelnden Ländern hat.

WILLKOMMEN IN DER ZUKUNFT

Neue Großflughafenprojekte wie in Doha (Katar) oder Shenzhen (China) nähern sich ihrer Fertigstellung – es herrscht also keineswegs Mangel an ambitionierten Bauvorhaben. Dass diese Tatsache wenig Aufmerksamkeit erhält, liegt auch daran, dass die genannten Standorte zurzeit nicht im Blickfeld der westlichen Medien liegen. Webseiten dokumentieren neue Projekte in atemberaubendem Tempo – mit mehr oder weniger demselben rudimentären Text- und Bildmaterial. So vielversprechend diese Flut elektronischer Information zunächst erscheinen mag, will man hinsichtlich der neuesten Entwicklungen der Architektur auf dem Laufenden bleiben, erweisen sich viele Netzsuchen letztendlich als vergeblich. Ein Grund mehr, warum Bücher und Fachzeitschriften nach wie vor der beste Weg sind, um sich zu informieren. Wie oft werden Projekte angekündigt und nie fertiggestellt oder bleiben wesentlich länger ohne feste Zusagen, als uns Architekten glauben machen wollen. Da ist z. B. der denkwürdige Fall der Stadt Ordos in der Inneren Mongolei. Seit etwa 2005 arbeiten zahlreiche hochkarätige Büros, allen voran Herzog & de Meuron mit dem Künstler Ai Weiwei, am Projekt „Ordos 100", das 100 beispielhafte Wohnbauten erstellen sollte. Neue Architektur in China zu realisieren, schien damals verlockend, doch offensichtlich hat selbst die boomende Vorzeigewirtschaft China ihre Grenzen. Die *New York Times* schrieb: „Ordos selbst hat 1,5 Millionen Einwohner. Doch die Zukunftsvision von Ordos – auf dem Reißbrett auf einem

14

14
Preston Scott Cohen, Herta and Paul Amir Building, Tel Aviv Museum of Art, Tel Aviv, Israel, 2007–11

riesigen Gelände rund 25 km südlich der Altstadt geplant – ist wie leergefegt. Auf den breiten Straßen im neuen Stadtteil Kangbashi herrscht so gut wie kein Verkehr. Bürogebäude stehen leer. Passanten sind Mangelware. Und das Unkraut sprießt in den Luxusvillengegenden ohne Bewohner ... Unter dem Druck aggressiver Bauunternehmer ließen sich die Stadtverantwortlichen überzeugen, Ordos habe das Zeug zum chinesischen Dubai – eine Verwandlung ganzer Landstriche in der dürren mongolischen Steppe zur blühenden Metropole. Über 1 Milliarde US-Dollar wurden in das visionäre Projekt gepumpt. Doch vier Jahre nach dem Umzug der städtischen Regierung nach Kangbashi und der Fertigstellung Tausender Häuser und Dutzender Bürogebäude nannte die Staatszeitung *China Daily* das rund 30 km² große Viertel eine ‚Geisterstadt', den Inbegriff für Exzess und fehlgeleiteten Optimismus."[5]

Während westliche Architekten mit ihrem Abenteuer in Ordos geradezu dramatisch scheitern, konnte MAD Architects, ein chinesisches Büro, das 41 000 m² große Ordos Museum (Ordos, Innere Mongolei, 2005–11, Seite 276) fertigstellen. 2004 von Ma Yansong gegründet, erhielt MAD erstmals 2006 internationale Aufmerksamkeit, als das Büro einen internationalen Wettbewerb für die Absolute Towers bei Toronto gewann (2006–12, Seite 288). Inspiriert von Buckminster Fullers Kuppeln entwarfen die Architekten mit ihrem Museum in Ordos einen außergewöhnlichen Bau, der wie eine metallische Düne wirkt – ein treffendes Symbol für die Stadt am Rand der Wüste Gobi. Die Architekten schreiben: „Vertraut und doch ungewöhnlich wirkt das Museum wie aus einer anderen Welt, mitten in der Wüste gelandet, oder als sei es schon immer da gewesen." Obwohl man auch diesen Bau als Monument für exzessive Regierungsausgaben verstehen könnte, ist er zugleich der beste Beweis für die besondere Stärke von MAD Architects, Projekte umzusetzen, wo andere scheitern. Die ebenso ungewöhnlichen Absolute Towers (Mississauga, Kanada, 2006–12, Seite 288) wurden im Dezember 2012 fertiggestellt. Die beiden Türme, 56 Stockwerke (170 m) bzw. 50 Stockwerke (150 m) hoch, wirken – durch eine Drehung der Geschossplatten um ein bis acht Grad pro Etage – wellenförmig bewegt. Beeindruckende Formen wie diese waren in Dubai zu Zeiten des Planungsbooms keine Seltenheit, doch auch dort erlebten nur wenige Architekten die tatsächliche Realisierung ihrer Entwürfe. Dank der robusten Wirtschaft Chinas und einer jungen Generation von Architekten wie Ma Yansong, Chefplaner bei MAD, ist damit zu rechnen, dass der chinesische Einfluss auf die zeitgenössische Architektur in absehbarer Zeit weiter wachsen wird. Zweifellos ist man in China besonders offen für neue Architektur: In gewisser Weise ist sie ein Symbol der Erfolgsgeschichte des Landes. Diese Offenheit kontrastiert mit einer oft konservativen Haltung in Europa und den USA. Wirtschaftlicher Erfolg ist zweifellos ein Schlüsselfaktor, wenn es um Quantensprünge in der zeitgenössischen Architektur geht, auch wenn es heute ebenso reizvoll ist, den Blick auf Länder zu richten, in denen Avantgarde-Architektur bisher keine nennenswerte Rolle spielte.

KRAGDÄCHER UND FLIEGENDE KEILE

Ein weiteres Beispiel für die Dimensionen und Ambitionen aktueller Architekturprojekte in China ist das 155 000 m² große Himalayas Center (Shanghai, seit 2007, Seite 232) von Arata Isozaki. Das Center, gelegen im heute mit riesigen Wolkenkratzern bebauten Pudong-Viertel von Shanghai, gegenüber der Bund-Uferpromenade, bietet Platz für ein Fünf-Sterne-Hotel, Künstlerateliers, ein Kunstcenter sowie die unvermeidlichen Shoppingcenter. Darüber hinaus konnte Isozaki 2011 das ehrgeizige National Convention Center in Doha, Katar, fertigstellen,

15
Delugan Meissl, EYE Film Institute, Amsterdam, The Netherlands, 2009–11

15

einen 175 000 m² großen Komplex. Beide Projekte zeichnen sich durch quasi organische Elemente aus. In Doha greift die 250 m lange Fassade das Motiv der Sidra-Bäume auf, das Wahrzeichen der Qatar Foundation, des Auftraggebers des Projekts. Isozaki, Jahrgang 1931, mag den Höhepunkt seiner Schaffenskraft und seines Einflusses überschritten haben, dennoch zeigen diese Projekte, dass ihm sein Ruf und seine Innovationskraft in Ländern, die heute zu den großen Bauherren zählen, neuen Aufwind beschert haben.

Doch was ist mit jenen neuen Architekturformen, die dank digitaler Planungs- und Fertigungsmethoden geboren wurden? Geraten sie nun, angesichts knapperer Budgets, ins Abseits? Natürlich gibt es nach wie vor zahlreiche Beispiele für diese Bauformen, und alles deutet darauf hin, dass diese Methoden auch in den kommenden Jahren eine einflussreiche Rolle beim Entwerfen und Bauen spielen werden. Die Realisierung des Herta and Paul Amir Building am Tel Aviv Museum of Art (Israel, 2007–11, Seite 110) nahm fast zehn Jahre in Anspruch, nachdem bei einem Wettbewerb 2003 die Wahl auf den Entwurf von Preston Scott Cohen gefallen war. Die winkligen futuristischen Formen des 18 500 m² großen Gebäudes sind im Wesentlichen eine Antwort des Architekten auf das Grundstück. Cohen erklärt: „Der Entwurf des Amir Building war eine unmittelbare Reaktion auf die Herausforderung, mehrere Stockwerke mit großen neutralen, rechtwinkligen Ausstellungsräumen zu realisieren, und das auf einem knappen, eigenwilligen, dreieckigen Baugrundstück. Die Lösung lag in einer ‚Quadratur des Dreiecks' – die Stockwerke wurden entlang verschiedener Achsen ausgerichtet, die von Etage zu Etage erheblich variieren. Im Prinzip sind die Ebenen des Gebäudes – drei Ober- und zwei Untergeschosse – strukturell unabhängige Grundrisse, die übereinander gestapelt wurden." Cohen ist außerdem Urheber so ungewöhnlicher Bauten wie des Taiyuan Museum of Art (China, 2007–12) und weiß die neu gewonnenen Freiheiten digitaler Planung intelligent zu nutzen.

Das Wiener Büro Coop Himmelb(l)au unter Leitung von Wolf D. Prix zählt zu den Pionieren des Dekonstruktivismus in der Architektur. Ihre Entwürfe zeigen noch heute, u. a. bei verschiedenen Großprojekten, die visuelle Fragmentierung, die das Büro in den 1980er-Jahren entwickelt hatte. Dies gilt zweifellos für das Kino für das Busan International Film Festival (BIFF) (Busan, Südkorea, 2005–11, Seite 128): mit 51 000 m² und einem Budget von 100 Millionen Euro tatsächlich ein Großprojekt. Das Dach des Baus ist laut Guinness-Buch der Rekorde „das längste Kragdach" der Welt, ein „virtueller Himmel" mit programmierbarem LED-System. Wie üblich benannten die Architekten Teile des Komplexes, in diesem Fall „Cinema Mountain" oder „BIFF Hill". Südkorea mag nicht in derselben Liga spielen wie andere hier genannte aufstrebende Länder, doch für europäische und amerikanische Architekten ist es zweifellos ein Glücksfall, dass der Ferne Osten nach solchen Großprojekten verlangt und Mut zu provokativer Formensprache beweist. Da zwischen dem Aufkommen eines Architekturstils oder -trends und dessen Realisierung oft erhebliche Zeit verstreicht, entsteht vielleicht manchmal der Eindruck, die Branche sei in einer Zeitschleife steckengeblieben, in der die 1980er-Jahre noch immer schwer angesagt sind. Glücklicherweise gelingt es dem Büro Coop Himmelb(l)au in vielfacher Hinsicht, seine Sprache weiterzuentwickeln – ohne die Begeisterung für Experimente wie das längste Kragdach der Welt zu verlieren.

Auch ein weiteres Wiener Büro, Delugan Meissl, verdankt seinen Ruf aufsehenerregenden Bauten; auch bei ihm spielen auskragende Baukörper oft eine Rolle. Nach dem Entwurf für das Porsche Museum (Stuttgart, 2006–08) konnte es in jüngster Zeit das EYE Film Institute (Amsterdam, 2009–11, Seite 142) fertigstellen. Es liegt am Ufer des IJ unmittelbar gegenüber dem Hauptbahnhof. Hier kragt ein großer keilförmiger Baukörper in Richtung Bahnhof aus und verschafft dem Komplex eine kaum zu übersehende Präsenz. Vielleicht weniger „ideologisch" in ihren Entwürfen als Coop Himmelb(l)au, wagen Delugan Meissl mit ihrem EYE Film Institute dennoch ein kraftvolles architektonisches Statement. Zugleich bestätigt das Projekt, wie stark künstlerische Ausdrucksformen im Film- und Audiobereich in den Niederlanden gefördert werden. Vielleicht ist es kein Zufall, dass Film das Thema beider Projekte ist – bei Coop Himmelb(l)au in Korea, bei Delugan Meissl in Amsterdam. Kunstmuseen haben längst die Aufmerksamkeit großer Architekturbüros in aller Welt – vielleicht ist nun der Film an der Reihe.

NACH ALL DEN JAHREN NOCH IMMER IM SPIEL

Nicht nur Coop Himmelb(l)au war 1988 in der Ausstellung „Deconstructivist Architecture" am Museum of Modern Art (New York) vertreten – auch Zaha Hadid, deren Büro in den vergangenen Jahren international zu den aktivsten überhaupt wurde, stellte dort aus. Ihr CMA CGM Tower (Marseille, 2008–11, Seite 186) ist ein 94 000 m² großer Wolkenkratzer in einer Stadt, die nicht gerade für Hochhäuser bekannt ist. Der elegante Bau zeigt deutlich Hadids Handschrift und besteht aus zwei aufstrebenden, in der Mitte zusammenlaufenden Kurven – ein Motiv, das der Gabelung der Schnellstraße entspricht, die das Grundstück einfasst. Das Projekt bietet 2700 Mitarbeitern Platz und belegt Hadids Fähigkeit, für große Unternehmen zu planen, in der Vergangenheit etwa für BMW. Hadid thematisiert von jeher die Notwendigkeit, Architektur neu zu denken, sie aus der Landschaft wie eine organische Größe wachsen zu lassen, Wände, Böden und Decken zu einem schlüssigen Ganzen zu verschmelzen. Der CMA CGM Tower vermittelt diese Dynamik und wird dennoch den Ansprüchen konventionellerer Planung von Büroflächen und Parkplätzen gerecht, die letzten Endes den Kern der Unternehmensarchitektur ausmacht.

Das Büro UNStudio, unter Leitung von Ben van Berkel und Caroline Bos, ist seit Langem führend in der Anwendung digitaler Entwurfstechniken, etwa mit außergewöhnlichen Projekten wie dem Mercedes-Benz Museum (Stuttgart, 2001–06). Ihr Zentrum für Virtuelles Engineering (ZVE) des Fraunhofer-Instituts in Stuttgart (2006–12, mit Asplan Architekten, Seite 438), verfügt mit 3200 m² über eine vergleichsweise bescheidene Nutzfläche. Dank aufwendiger 3D-Planung, Optimierung der Bauhülle aus Aluminium und weiteren energie- und materialsparenden Maßnahmen erhielt der Bau eine Goldzertifizierung der Deutschen Gesellschaft für Nachhaltiges Bauen (DGNB). Dieses Projekt belegt, dass die anfangs noch „exotischen" digitalen Entwurfstechniken inzwischen deutlich verbreiteter sind; dass Architekten und Auftraggeber verinnerlicht haben, dass Neubauten stets mit Blick auf ihr Energiesparpotenzial geplant werden müssen.

DINGE PASSIEREN

Sieht es also so düster aus wie vermutet? Ohne Frage erleben wir eine Zeit entscheidender politischer, demografischer und wirtschaftlicher Veränderungen. Während China und andere fernöstliche Länder oder Brasilien nach vorn drängen, werden sie zunehmend zum Motor

16
Zaha Hadid, "Arum," Corderie dell'Arsenale, Venice, Italy, 2012

16

der zeitgenössischen Architektur. Dies liegt weniger daran, dass Europa oder Amerika „müde" geworden wären, sondern schlicht eine höhere Dichte an modernen Bauten erreicht und möglicherweise geringeren Bedarf an neuen Bauerschließungen haben. Wirtschaftlich schwierige Zeiten führen dazu, dass jeder Bauträger auf die Kosten schaut und vor Innovation zurückschreckt, wenn die Kosten-Nutzen-Rechnung nicht unmittelbar aufzugehen scheint. Heute sind laute Renommierprojekte eher in Ländern zu suchen, die unter Zugzwang stehen, sich zu behaupten. Im Vergleich dazu sieht selbst Amerika „alt" aus. Die Zwillingstürme des World Trade Center waren ein Symbol für Ambition und wirtschaftliche Macht. Ihre Zerstörung war ein Dämpfer für die Hybris mancher und doch werden, wie man gesehen hat, weiterhin Wolkenkratzer gebaut, auch im Finanzdistrikt von Manhattan. Das Mahnmal für den 11. September markiert den Schauplatz des großen Traumas, das die Ereignisse von 2001 für die Vereinigten Staaten bedeuten. Nach dem Attentat auf John F. Kennedy der Vietnamkrieg und nun dies: alles Zeichen, dass wir Kennedys „New Frontier" – die Grenze zum unbekannten Neuland – längst überschritten haben. Heute jedoch ist der Ausblick nicht mehr so verheißungsvoll wie früher.

In welche Richtung sich die Architektur entwickeln wird, ist ebenso schwer vorauszusagen wie die wirtschaftliche Zukunft. „Dinge passieren", so der berühmt-berüchtigte Ausspruch des ehemaligen amerikanischen Verteidungsministers Donald Rumsfeld. Dinge, die nicht unbedingt gut sind. Natürlich gibt es substanzielle Faktoren, die wirtschaftliches Wachstum fördern, etwa die schiere Größe der Arbeitsbevölkerung Chinas, die nun auch einen Anteil an den materiellen Reizen des Kapitalismus beansprucht. Doch in der Wirtschaft geht es ebenso wie in der Architektur letztendlich um Pessimismus und Optimismus. Optimismus sorgt für größere Risikobereitschaft – an der Wall Street ebenso wie auf dem Bildschirm des Architekten. Vielleicht wird sich der Staub des Wirtschaftscrashs von 2008 bald legen; auch die schwarzen Wolken, die 2001 über Manhatten zogen, werden irgendwann verflogen sein. Im Hinblick auf die hier vorgestellten Großprojekte lassen sich zwei Dinge sagen: Zum einen hat das Zusammenspiel von Kunst und Architektur zugenommen und die Kreativität auf beiden Seiten beflügelt. Zum anderen lässt sich gelungene zeitgenössische Architektur in vielen Ländern finden, nicht zuletzt deshalb, weil man inzwischen begreift, dass traditionelle Bauweisen oft wesentlich besser sind als moderne Baumethoden, die den Globus mit Beton und Stahl pflastern. Dieses neue Verständnis verdankt sich zumindest teilweise Initiativen wie dem Aga-Khan-Preis für Architektur.

Wenn man die Moderne, in aller Bescheidenheit, mit den strahlenden Gewissheiten der Renaissance vergleichen will, dann haben wir sicherlich die Grenze in ein neues Zeitalter überschritten, das dunkler, das düsterer scheint als die Nachkriegszeit. Wir wollten Götter sein und sind gescheitert. Die Zeichen für eine solche Zeitenwende sind vielfältig, doch zwei gähnende Leerstellen an der Südspitze Manhattans, heute mit schwarzem Stein und Wasser gefüllt, sind das vielleicht eindringlichste Symbol einer neuen Ära des Zweifels. Eines Tages wird wieder Optimismus herrschen, kreative Energie wird neue Architektur hervorbringen, die innovativ und umweltverträglich ist. Gebäude und Projekte werden das Fundament für diesen Prozess legen, auch wenn Rückschläge und schmerzliche Umbrüche heute noch für viele an der Tagesordnung sind. In der Zwischenzeit wird sich die Welt geändert haben.

[1] http://www.pritzkerprize.com/1989/ceremony_speech1, Zugriff am 30. September 2012.

[2] „Gehry's Crown for Bunker Hill Is a Fitting Tribute for Disney", *Los Angeles Times*, 15. September 1991, http://articles.latimes.com/1991-09-15/realestate/re-3191_1_disney-hall-s-exterior/3, Zugriff am 30. September 2012.

[3] Tom Wolfe, *Mit dem Bauhaus leben. Die Diktatur des Rechtecks*, Königstein/Taunus, Athenäum: 1982.

[4] Aus „Vertigo", dem ersten Song auf dem U2-Album *How to Dismantle an Atomic Bomb* (2004): „Hello, hello (Hola!), I'm at a place called Vertigo, (Dónde está!) It's everything I wish I didn't know".

[5] http://www.nytimes.com/2010/10/20/business/global/20ghost.html?Seitewanted=all&_r=0, Zugriff am 1. Oktober 2012.

INTRODUCTION

NOUS SOMMES EN UN LIEU NOMMÉ VERTIGO

Parmi les réalisations présentées dans cet ouvrage, certaines des plus impressionnantes se caractérisent non par la taille ou le volume du bâtiment, mais par le vide et le sentiment d'absence. L'architecture contemporaine s'intéresse depuis longtemps à la problématique du vide, mais au bord du mémorial du 11-Septembre de Michael Arad (September 11 Memorial, New York, 2006–11, page 200), on prend conscience que les tours jumelles du World Trade Center disparu semblent avoir été englouties par le sol. Deux fontaines noires s'enfonçant dans la terre marquent la trace des bâtiments conçus par Minoru Yamasaki (1912–1986). Il s'agit bien d'architecture, même si, par essence, cette création est plus proche de l'art. Il n'y est pas question de politique, ni même d'une réaction aux attaques subies par New York en 2001, mais de l'absence et du vide qui aspire tout ce qui s'en approche. Maya Lin avait eu une intuition semblable lorsque, encore étudiante à Yale, elle avait conçu le mémorial des Vétérans du Viêtnam situé sur le Mall à Washington (1981). Plutôt qu'une sculpture dans la tradition héroïque, elle avait proposé un unique mur, comme une fissure noire dans le sol, portant les noms gravés des 50 000 morts américains. Les lecteurs assez âgés pour se rappeler la perspective lumineuse qu'avait ouverte la présidence écourtée de John F. Kennedy (1960–1963) peuvent méditer sur la relation entre son assassinat et la grande simplicité de conception qui marque sa tombe au cimetière d'Arlington, la flamme éternelle de John F. Kennedy (John F. Kennedy Eternal Flame de l'architecte John Carl Warnecke, 1967). Une perte exprimée par une flamme montante, pas encore l'abîme, mais déjà la fin d'une ère triomphale.

Certes, les monuments commémoratifs sont un genre à part, généralement non soumis aux stricts canons architecturaux et aux contraintes de faisabilité, mais Maya Lin, et, plus récemment, Michael Arad ont donné voix au vide, à l'absence, à la chute. L'essor et la puissance de l'Amérique étaient pour beaucoup dans son imagerie positive, de la conquête de l'Ouest à des créations aussi emblématiques que le mémorial d'Iwo Jima (Marine Corps War Memorial, cimetière d'Arlington, Washington, DC, 1951). Face à l'adversité, les Américains triomphaient, ou du moins la légende qu'ils s'étaient fabriquée le voulait ainsi. Le mémorial des Vétérans du Viêtnam (Vietnam Memorial) de Maya Lin et celui du 11-Septembre de Michael Arad racontent une autre histoire, celle d'une perte de plus grande envergure que celle des événements commémorés.

L'architecture était très aisément fiable, dense et opaque, avant de devenir le miroir glacé du capitalisme. Ceci n'est pas un commentaire sur le capitalisme en soi, mais la dissémination de toutes ces tours d'un vague style international depuis leur lieu d'origine, Chicago ou New York, jusqu'aux confins de la terre laisse un goût amer. Et que reste-t-il de l'ordre ancien, de l'architecture de religion et de conquête ? Deux réalisations présentées ici constituent un commentaire éloquent, voire humoristique, sur la disparition de la gloire. *Reading between the Lines* (Looz, Belgique, 2011, page 180), des deux jeunes architectes belges Pieterjan Gijs et Arnout Van Vaerenbergh, ne prend rien d'autre que la forme d'une église, dans un paysage rural du Limbourg. Mais, à tout point de vue, cette église d'une superficie de 28 mètres carrés n'a rien de fonctionnel, ni n'appelle à la dévotion. Elle est pourtant solide, faite de 30 tonnes d'acier Corten sur un sol en béton armé ; elle durera sans doute plus longtemps que nombre de constructions contemporaines. Les architectes la comparent à un dessin dans l'espace – vide, on peut voir au travers, contrairement à la plupart des églises – mais, sur le plan symbolique, ce vide est aussi un commentaire sur le déclin de la religion.

COMMENT NOUS CONSOLER ?

Les églises vides ne sont pas vraiment une nouveauté. Dans un texte prémonitoire des horreurs futures, Friedrich Nietzsche écrivait déjà il y a cent trente ans :

Dieu est mort ! Dieu reste mort ! Et c'est nous qui l'avons tué ! Comment nous consoler, nous, les meurtriers des meurtriers ? Ce que le monde a possédé jusqu'à présent de plus sacré et de plus puissant a perdu son sang sous notre couteau ; qui nous lavera de ce sang ? Avec quelle eau pourrions-nous nous purifier ? Quelles expiations, quels jeux sacrés serons-nous forcés d'inventer ? La grandeur de cet acte n'est-elle pas trop grande pour nous ? Ne sommes-nous pas forcés de devenir nous-mêmes des dieux simplement, ne fût-ce que pour paraître dignes d'elle ?
Le Gai Savoir, livre troisième, aphorisme 125, 1882.

Nous avons donc tenté de devenir des dieux en construisant des flèches à notre gloire et à celle de l'argent. Les fontaines noires de New York se déversant dans l'abîme témoignent à leur manière de la démesure de l'entreprise. « Allons ! bâtissons-nous une ville et une tour dont le sommet touche au ciel, et faisons-nous un nom, afin que nous ne soyons pas dispersés sur la face de toute la terre. » (*La Genèse*, 11, 4.) La tour, au sens propre comme au figuré, s'est certes effondrée plus d'une fois, mais pour chaque fois s'élever à nouveau. La tour Burj Khalifa de Dubaï (Adrian Smith, Skidmore Owings & Merrill, EAU, 2010) culmine à 829 mètres, et une nouvelle manifestation démesurée de l'orgueil architectural, la bien-nommée tour du Royaume (Kingdom Tower, Adrian Smith, AS+GG, en cours), destinée à dépasser la barre des 1000 mètres de haut, est actuellement en construction à Jeddah, en Arabie saoudite. Ces deux projets ont été conçus après les événements du 11 septembre 2001. Avec ses 306 mètres de haut, la London Bridge Tower de Renzo Piano (Londres, 2009–12, page 370), communément appelée le *Shard* (l'éclat), bien que relativement modeste comparée aux critères actuels du Moyen-Orient, constitue un autre exemple de la quête permanente d'une visibilité et d'un peu de gloire. Pourtant, les sombres nuages de l'effondrement et les ténèbres d'une économie vacillante continueront de jeter leur ombre partout. C'est ce que va refléter de plus en plus l'architecture contemporaine. C'est, pour l'instant le domaine des architectes sensibles à l'art ; demain, le sombre reflet de temps troublés fera plus de ravages. À moins que du chaos ne naisse un nouvel ordre…

LE SOLEIL SE LÈVE AUSSI

Comme impulsion créatrice, la noirceur a évidemment ses limites, et l'époque se caractérise aussi par des renversements, des déséquilibres et des contradictions. L'un des bâtiments les plus inattendus et les plus curieux construits récemment est l'Orbit (parc Olympique,

17
Anish Kapoor and Cecil Balmond, Orbit, Olympic Park, London, UK, 2010–12

Londres, 2010–12, page 252). Selon Cecil Balmond, l'un de ses inventeurs: «Contrairement aux tours verticales qui grandissent en s'appuyant sur les étages inférieurs, la forme de l'Orbit tire sa solidité des chevauchements et de l'éparpillement et offre ainsi un nouveau paradigme pour une forme et sa stabilité.» L'Orbit est la création de deux partenaires inattendus, l'artiste Anish Kapoor (né à Bombay, en 1954) et l'ingénieur Cecil Balmond (né à Colombo, Sri Lanka, en 1943). Si nul n'ignore le rayonnement passé de l'Angleterre, il est intéressant de noter que la réalisation architecturale la plus marquante des Jeux olympiques de Londres, en 2012, est le fruit d'une collaboration entre un artiste et un ingénieur d'origine respectivement indienne et sri-lankaise, financée par une société fondée en Inde. L'Occident verra-t-il son «salut» venir de l'Est et du Sud?

On trouve une autre expression architecturale intéressante du déséquilibre et du renversement dans une œuvre de Tatzu Nishi, *Discovering Columbus* (New York, 2012, page 332). L'artiste japonais, familier de l'exploration des contradictions, a perché une salle de séjour de 75 mètres carrés à 23 mètres au-dessus de Columbus Circle, à Manhattan. Son œuvre encercle littéralement une statue de Christophe Colomb, un des découvreurs du Nouveau Monde. Tout comme Pieterjan Gijs et Arnout Van Vaerenbergh, l'artiste explore non seulement les problématiques de l'échelle, mais aussi celles de la vie domestique et des emplacements incongrus. Pourquoi un environnement architectural devrait-il forcément être limité à la terre ferme, quand il est si facile de le percher sur une colonne située au centre d'une place très passante? Nombreux sont ceux qui, avant Tatzu Nishi, ont défié les «certitudes» architecturales et d'autres suivront sans aucun doute, mais cette œuvre marque, avec d'autres, une sorte de point de non-retour au-delà duquel l'architecture ne sera plus jamais comme avant. Pendant combien d'années la solidité, traduite par symétrie et matériaux «durables», a-t-elle été la marque de fabrique de l'architecture? Kapoor et Balmond font la démonstration que l'équilibre, voire l'élégance, ne se trouvent pas forcément où l'on pense. Avec sa vieille statue imposante plantée au milieu d'un intérieur très bourgeois situé au sommet d'une colonne, Nishi y ajoute une pointe d'humour. «L'art a pour rôle de saisir le familier sous un angle différent, déclare Tatzu Nishi. L'expérience extraordinaire de l'inversion opérée dans cette œuvre, inversion du public et du privé, de l'extérieur et de l'intérieur, élargira chez le spectateur la perception du monde qui l'entoure et en retour, le processus élargira les pouvoirs imaginatifs de l'humanité.»

HUMPTY DUMPTY ASSIS SUR UN MUR

La recherche de licence artistique n'est pas une nouveauté en architecture. Frank O. Gehry, qui construit à présent d'énormes immeubles d'habitation à New York (Eight Spruce Street, New York, 2007–11, page 174), vantait naguère les mérites de l'immédiateté et de l'invention. Dans son discours de réception du prix Pritzker, en 1989, il déclarait: «Mes amis artistes, comme Jasper Johns, Bob Rauschenberg, Ed Kienholz ou Claes Oldenburg, travaillaient avec des matériaux très bon marché, des morceaux de bois et du papier, et créaient de la beauté. Ce n'était pas des détails sans importance. Ils étaient radicaux et m'ont fait me questionner sur ce qu'est le beau. J'ai choisi d'utiliser les savoir-faire disponibles et de travailler avec des artisans en faisant une vertu de leurs limites. La peinture avait cette immédiateté que je rêvais d'obtenir en architecture. J'explorais les procédés de nouveaux matériaux de construction en cherchant à donner du sentiment et de

18

18
Richard Meier, Italcementi i.lab, Bergamo, Italy, 2005–12

l'esprit à la forme. En recherchant l'essence de mon expression, je me voyais comme un artiste devant sa toile blanche, en train de décider ce que sera son geste initial [1]. » Peu après cette déclaration qui résume bien cette fraîcheur nouvelle qu'il avait apportée à l'architecture à Santa Monica et Venice (Californie), Frank Gehry admettait: « Après des années passées à tout mettre en pièces, j'essaye de reconstituer Humpty Dumpty [2]. »

La contradiction dans l'architecture contemporaine s'exprime aussi par la continuité. Alors que Gehry recherche une totalité qu'il avait jadis rejetée, d'autres, comme Richard Meier, restent fidèles à leur engagement esthétique envers le modernisme. Richard Meier, à présent presqu'octogénaire, vient d'achever deux bâtiments, l'OCT Shenzhen Clubhouse, (Shenzhen, Chine, 2010–12, page 304) et le Centre de recherche et d'innovation d'Italcementi (Italcementi i.lab, Bergame, Italie, 2005–12, ci-dessus). Ces projets respectent les principes de blancheur et d'équilibre qui constituent la « signature » de l'architecte. Cette cohérence est intéressante en ce qu'elle a de comparable avec le classicisme qui ne se démode vraiment jamais. Mais Meier n'est pas insensible aux changements des temps et aux besoins nouveaux de l'architecture. L'Italcementi i.lab est le premier bâtiment d'Italie à avoir reçu la certification de haute qualité environnementale LEED Platinum. La longévité et la fidélité à ses engagements sont indéniablement des vertus. Il y a plus de trente ans, le romancier dandy Tom Wolfe fustigeait le style de Meier dans son essai *Il court il court le Bauhaus*: « Avec toutes leurs balustrades en tuyaux, leurs rampes, leurs escaliers hélicoïdaux en tôle larmée, leurs vitrages industriels, leurs batteries de lampes halogènes et leurs formes cylindriques blanches, toutes ces résidences secondaires à 900 000 dollars, construites dans les bois du nord du Michigan ou sur le littoral de Long Island, ont l'air de raffineries d'insecticide. Il m'est arrivé de voir des propriétaires que toute cette blancheur, cette lumière, ce dénuement, cette propreté, ce dépouillement, cette austérité, avaient amenés à la limite de la privation sensorielle. Ils étaient en recherche désespérée d'un antidote, comme le confort ou la couleur [3]. » Si les amateurs d'art et d'architecture trouvent peut-être aujourd'hui le confort qu'ils recherchent dans une salle de séjour suspendue à 23 mètres au-dessus de Columbus Circle, Richard Meier, quant à lui, campe sur ses positions.

BIEN LOIN SOUS TERRE

Plus proche de l'esprit actuel de l'architecture contemporaine, l'agence suisse Herzog & de Meuron continue d'explorer les limites du design, comme l'attestent la nouvelle halle de la foire de Bâle (Neubau Messe Basel, Bâle, 2010–13, page 206) et deux récents projets londoniens. Le premier de ces projets est le pavillon d'été 2012 de la Serpentine Gallery (avec Ai Weiwei; Londres, page 212), une tradition annuelle inaugurée par Zaha Hadid en 2000. Herzog & de Meuron se sont associés avec l'artiste chinois dissident Ai Weiwei pour créer un pavillon intrinsèquement contradictoire et surprenant. Leur bâtiment, qui ne s'élève guère à plus d'un mètre du sol, est une structure recouverte de liège qui signale les découvertes « archéologiques » faites sur le site. En creusant le sol, les architectes sont tombés sur la nappe phréatique, mais aussi sur toutes sortes de traces laissées par les pavillons précédents. Celles-ci sont marquées par des colonnes supportant un disque en acier de 10 mètres de diamètre flottant au-dessus des endroits où s'asseoir, tel un miroir d'eau suspendu. Le pavillon 2012 de la Serpentine évoque les ténèbres et il s'enfonce assurément dans la terre, éléments qui s'accordent avec ces temps de troubles et de

19
Herzog & de Meuron, The Tanks, London, UK, 2010–12

19

doutes. Les formes de style georgien de la Serpentine Gallery, en briques et pierre, se reflètent, renversées et déformées par la brise, dans le bassin peu profond qui recouvre le disque du pavillon.

On retrouve cet aspect archéologique, mais sur un mode plus industriel, dans un deuxième projet londonien d'Herzog & de Meuron. Les architectes doivent leur réputation à leur transformation d'une centrale électrique désaffectée des bords de la Tamise à Southwark en un musée contemporain, la Tate Modern (2000). On leur demande aujourd'hui de réaliser une nouvelle extension du musée dont la construction s'achèvera en 2016. En prélude à ce projet, ils ont rénové un espace de près de 6000 mètres carrés construit à l'origine pour stocker les millions de litres de fioul nécessaires au fonctionnement de la centrale. Les Tanks (Londres, 2010–12, ci-dessus), délibérément laissés dans un état « brut et industriel », accueilleront des performances ou des installations cinématographiques. Selon les architectes, ces espaces « où l'on est conscient d'être sous terre, possèdent une texture et une histoire riche ». Située au-dessus du niveau du sol, la Tate Modern originale explorait également les relations de l'art moderne à un espace industriel désaffecté. Ici, Herzog & de Meuron s'enfoncent beaucoup plus loin, dans une sorte de monde des ténèbres fait de lieux jadis inoccupés. Ils fouillent une archéologie moderne très éloignée de cette « blancheur, cette lumière, ce dénuement, cette propreté, ce dépouillement, cette austérité », caractéristiques d'un type d'architecture né en un temps où les choses semblaient ne pouvoir aller qu'en s'améliorant.

NOUS SOMMES EN UN LIEU NOMMÉ VERTIGO [4]

L'esprit du moment, ce sont surtout l'architecture et le design qui mettent le visiteur ou le spectateur dans une situation de déséquilibre. Où sont les limites ? Où est le haut ? Où est le bas ? Des artistes comme Robert Irwin, James Turrell ou Dan Graham jouent, certes, sur ces notions depuis un bon moment, mais l'architecture ne se doit-elle pas d'être plus stable, plus compréhensible ? L'art est une chose, le commerce en est une autre. C'est ce que s'est dit la jeune agence new-yorkaise Gage Clemenceau en réalisant des concept-stores pour le designer Nicola Formichetti (New York, 2011, page 154 ; Hong Kong, 2012). Empruntant au style un peu excessif du milieu de la mode, ils déclarent : « Normalement, les environnements de la mode se définissent par un minimalisme assez sobre censé concentrer l'attention sur les seuls vêtements, pour la raison évidente que l'on y vend uniquement des vêtements. En collaborant avec Nicola Formichetti, nous avons reformulé cette équation et produit un nouveau genre d'espace expérimental qui, non content de mettre en valeur, amplifie l'impact de ses designs de mode au cœur d'une forme nouvelle d'environnement immersif qui fusionne les codes génétiques de l'architecture et de la mode. » À propos de leur magasin de Hong Kong pour le même designer, Gage Clemenceau déclare : « Le système d'éclairage permet une variation illimitée des effets, créant ainsi l'impression d'un changement constant de l'espace même. » Ce n'est pas que les architectes ou les designers cherchent à déstabiliser l'environnement bâti, mais peut-être plutôt que l'écran, cet environnement où peuvent se confondre réalité et fiction, est devenu la source suprême du vertige. Ce jeune en uniforme est-il en train de jouer à un jeu vidéo ou de piloter un drone qui va tuer un être humain à l'autre bout du monde ? Les relations sont-elles définies par la proximité physique et les instincts ancestraux, ou peuvent-elles passer par l'avatar désincarné de notre choix ? Où est le haut ?

20

20
Gustavo Penna, All Saints Chapel, Gurita Farm, Martinho Campos, Minas Gerais, Brazil, 2011

Bien que Serge Salat soit, entre autres, architecte et ingénieur, il a choisi de s'exprimer par des installations artistiques historiquement et physiologiquement riches de sens. *(Beyond Infinity I*, 2007, page 398 ; *Beyond Infinity II*, 2011, page 402, toutes deux en Chine). *Beyond Infinity I* cherche « à faire sortir le spectateur de l'espace normal pour qu'il entre dans un espace hautement paradoxal, flottant, onirique, fait de couches de rêves de plus en plus profondes ». Il parle d'« expériences personnelles dans l'espace, expériences où l'on rencontre le temps et un certain sentiment d'éternité ». Dans le cas de *Beyond Infinity II*, « les visiteurs sont en lévitation dans le plan médian de cette structure gigantesque dont les répliques à l'infini sombrent dans l'abîme ». Les puristes diront que ces environnements, bien qu'ayant à voir avec les antécédents architecturaux de Serge Salat, sont fondamentalement des œuvres d'art. Il est néanmoins évident depuis des années que les frontières entre l'art et l'architecture ont disparu.

Les tentatives d'évocation d'un espace vertigineux, ou d'un espace au-delà de la compréhension immédiate, ont toujours existé dans l'histoire de l'architecture. L'architecture baroque ou maniériste jouait sur des formes très complexes. Dans la célèbre salle des Géants du Palais du Té (Sala dei Giganti, Mantoue, 1526-35), Giulio Romano a réuni l'art et l'architecture dans une extraordinaire cacophonie de formes. Dans une véritable envolée de l'imagination, l'artiste-architecte combine ici sa structure avec une fantastique scène de destruction. Échelle, temps et lieu sont balayés dans un espace qui semble éviter les limites du réel. Giovanni Battista Piranesi (1720–78) a étudié l'architecture à Venise, mais il doit sa renommée à ses gravures, notamment ses célèbres Prisons (*Carceri d'invenzione*, ou « Prisons imaginaires »). Peu d'architectes ont, en fait, exercé autant d'influence que ces gravures, avec leur obscurité et leurs jeux vertigineux sur les perspectives et l'espace. Les représentations de l'espace dans ces œuvres étaient juste au-delà de la compréhension, plus profondes, plus sombres, plus sinistres que la réalité, une fiction incarnant les peurs. À quoi pourrait bien ressembler l'enfer, sinon à une de ces Prisons, plus vastes et plus obscures qu'aucune invention terrestre ?

Les doutes et les complexités du maniérisme et du baroque étaient aux antipodes de la perspective ordonnée et de l'humanisme de la Haute Renaissance. Avec tout le respect que l'on doit aux grands artistes et architectes du passé, l'on peut se demander si les certitudes modernistes de la première moitié du XXe siècle n'ont pas cédé devant les profondes ambigüités du monde de l'après 11-Septembre, tout comme la Renaissance avait cédé la place au maniérisme. Si tel est le cas, nous entrons peut-être dans une longue période de doute et d'obscurité. L'époque où tout était possible, où Brasilia pouvait naître de rien en plein cœur du Brésil, semble appartenir à un passé révolu. Lorsque l'espoir et l'optimisme font défaut, l'argent et l'ambition ne suffisent pas à insuffler la vie à de nouveaux mondes.

CONTEMPORAIN TEMPORAIRE

Avec les problèmes économiques posés par la construction coûteuse de bâtiments plus pérennes, l'on voit se généraliser les constructions temporaires. N'étant pas censée durer « éternellement », l'architecture éphémère permet, au mieux, plus de liberté et d'inventivité que le béton et l'acier, ce que démontrent plusieurs projets présentés ici. L'exposition « Humanidade 2012 » (page 244) était présentée dans un bâtiment temporaire conçu par l'architecte Carla Juaçaba et la scénographe Bia Lessa. Elles ont proposé « un bâtiment en échafaudages, translucide et exposé aux éléments : lumière, chaleur, pluie, bruit des vagues et du vent, rappelant à l'homme sa fragilité face à la nature » et, de surcroît, entièrement recyclable. Le bâtiment de 170 mètres de long pour 20 mètres de haut était plus imposant que de nombreuses structures temporaires, mais l'utilisation des échafaudages l'a rendu extrêmement léger et aérien, sans recourir à des matériaux coûteux bien souvent plus transparents sur le papier qu'en réalité.

Les architectes new-yorkais SO – IL ont déjà réalisé quelques beaux bâtiments éphémères comme leur installation *Pole Dance* (PS1, Long Island, New York, 2010). Pour la foire d'art Frieze de New-York (Frieze Art Fair, New York, page 424), ils ont été confrontés à la nécessité de construire, en un court laps de temps, un grand espace (20 900 mètres carrés) principalement à partir de tentes standard. En intercalant des triangles entre les portions de tentes et en prolongeant la toile jusqu'au sol à l'extrémité des pignons, les jeunes designers ont apporté un peu d'irrégularité dans le plan du salon sans en affecter fondamentalement la disposition. Les bandes de toile de tente donnent l'impression que la structure « se fond dans le sol ». La création d'une structure de 457 mètres de long avec des bouts de métal et de tissu semble pertinente en ces temps nouveaux d'austérité qui obligent les architectes du monde entier à repenser leurs critères et à proposer des solutions nouvelles à des clients dont la première préoccupation est le coût.

L'architecte japonais Shigeru Ban est très connu pour ses bâtiments temporaires parfois utilisés dans des situations d'urgence humanitaire et souvent faits de tubes de carton. Son pavillon Camper (Alicante, Espagne ; Sanya, Chine ; Miami, Floride ; Lorient, préfabrication de juin à septembre 2011, page 88) était un pavillon de 250 mètres carrés conçu de manière à être facilement assemblé et transporté. L'on a utilisé des tubes de carton dimensionnés pour s'insérer l'un dans l'autre, et l'ensemble, destiné à un usage commercial, est une structure rappelant un peu la forme d'une tente militaire ou, référence moins martiale, d'un chapiteau de cirque. Les priorités de Shigeru Ban sont souvent liées à des questions d'ordre technique et à son désir d'innovation architecturale. Il a ainsi construit des maisons « sans murs » ou en tubes de carton, contredisant les conceptions habituelles de la solidité et, en définitive, de la nature même de l'architecture.

Une autre agence japonaise, Atelier Bow-Wow, fondée en 1992 par Yoshiharu Tsukamoto et Momoyo Kaijima, a récemment travaillé sur un intéressant projet temporaire baptisé BMW Guggenheim Lab (New York, 2011 ; Berlin, 2012 ; Bombay, 2012–13, page 80). À New York, le bâtiment qui comprenait un espace d'exposition, un atelier, un espace de lecture, un café et un entrepôt a reçu 56 000 visiteurs au cours de ses dix semaines d'existence. Utilisant du plastique renforcé de fibre de carbone au lieu d'acier, une membrane de toit en polyester et un treillis en polyester double couche pour certains habillages, le BMW Guggenheim Lab recourt à une technologie de haut niveau pour obtenir la légèreté permettant un transport aisé. Les structures temporaires de ce type peuvent, en outre, tirer parti de sites de petite taille, temporairement inutilisés ou désaffectés, un avantage décisif dans les villes où le manque d'espace est un réel problème.

QUE TON NOM SOIT SANCTIFIÉ

Les exemples américains de Richard Meier et Franck Gehry montrent que les formes développées par l'architecture des années 1970 et 1980 sont toujours très présentes. Si les constructions nouvelles sont moins nombreuses en raison de l'état de l'économie, certains clients trouvent rassurant de faire appel à un architecte récipiendaire du prix Pritzker. Il serait, bien sûr, totalement excessif de dire que les vides et le non-espace sont tout ce qui reste à l'architecture d'aujourd'hui. Dans beaucoup de cas, les valeurs et usages traditionnels sont toujours à l'ordre du jour. Des églises, souvent sous forme de petites chapelles, continuent d'être construites par des architectes très talentueux à travers le monde. La chapelle de Tous-les-Saints (Capela de Todos os Santos, Gurita Farm, Martinho Campos, Minas Gerais, Brésil, 2011, page 366) par Gustavo Penna, un architecte de Belo Horizonte, en est un exemple. La chapelle de 160 mètres carrés, en béton, verre, travertin et *peroba do campo*, un bois rare, adopte la forme d'une croix stylisée. Le simple plan rectangulaire est souligné par un étroit bassin aligné sur le centre de la chapelle et son évocation sculpturale du Christ sur la Croix. C'est un projet élégant et simple, même si l'utilisation de la forme de la croix inscrite directement dans l'architecture (comme on la voit en élévation) peut sembler trop « figurative » au goût de certains.

Au Japon, I. M. Pei a dessiné une autre chapelle plus marquante (École d'esthétique Miho, Shigaraki, Shiga, en collaboration avec io Architects, 2010–12, page 356). Au beau milieu d'une école située dans une forêt dense de cyprès, à environ une heure et demie de route de Kyoto, cette chapelle de 1800 mètres carrés adopte la forme extérieure d'un cône asymétrique revêtu de panneaux d'acier inoxydable allant jusqu'à 18 mètres (une prouesse technique). Les murs intérieurs de la chapelle sont revêtus de panneaux de cèdre rouge et le sol est en pierre de Bourgogne et chêne blanc. I. M. Pei (né en 1917) a révélé à de nombreuses connaissances que cette chapelle de Shigaraki serait sa dernière œuvre. Il a trouvé pertinent que l'une de ses premières œuvres, la chapelle Luce (Taichung, Taïwan 1954–63), soit aussi un bâtiment religieux. Il est intéressant de rappeler que la petite chapelle du mémorial Luce est une simple structure hyperbolique-parabolique qui a, en gros, la forme d'une tente de 19 mètres de haut. L'élégance de Pei et la simplicité de son projet faisant appel à la lumière rappellent à ceux qui connaissent son œuvre, de Washington au musée du Louvre, qu'il a été l'un des architectes modernes les plus marquants. Son époque n'était pas celle des moyens du bord avec bandes de toile de tente, ses constructions sont souvent aussi proches de la « pérennité » que l'on puisse rêver, et l'on peut parfaitement imaginer que la chapelle de l'École d'esthétique Miho sera toujours debout bien après que la génération actuelle des jeunes architectes aura cessé de dessiner et de bâtir.

BÂTIR À LA MARGE

La série d'ouvrages *Architecture Now!* a pour parti pris d'être aussi libérée que possible des contraintes formelles en matière de « styles », lieux ou constructions. Cela signifie que, les livres étant organisés par ordre alphabétique suivant le nom de l'architecte, un petit projet bon marché pourra côtoyer un énorme complexe. Cela signifie aussi que les projets intéressants, pour autant qu'ils puissent être identifiés, pourront se situer aux quatre coins de la planète, même si c'est souvent dans les pays riches que l'on retrouve le plus grand nombre de bâtiments innovants. Et c'est peut-être un signe des temps qu'*Architecture Now! 9* présente des ouvrages de pays jusqu'alors

21
Atelier Bow-Wow, BMW Guggenheim Lab, New York, New York, USA, 2011

sous-représentés, comme la Géorgie, le Burkina Faso, l'Afrique du Sud ou encore la Guinée équatoriale. Même si les architectes concernés, ou leurs clients, sont la plupart du temps européens, le travail qu'ils ont pu faire dans ces pays est un indicateur d'une hausse du niveau de raffinement et d'un simple désir de bien construire, ce qu'une technologie et une information plus facilement accessibles rendent possible.

L'architecte allemand Jürgen Mayer H. s'est récemment taillé une réputation considérable avec des projets récents comme Metropol Parasol (Séville, 2005–11), la réhabilitation de la place de l'Incarnation (Plaza de la Encarnación), une place de 12 670 mètres carrés, qui consiste en une série de parasols de bois recouvert de vernis polyuréthane, abritant ou couvrant des bars, des restaurants et un espace public. Contre toute attente, l'architecte s'est aussi mis en devoir de réaliser une série de bâtiments insolites en Géorgie. Le poste-frontière de Sarpi (Sarpi, Géorgie, 2010–11, page 294), le poste de police de Mestia (Mestia, Géorgie, 2011–12) et une série d'aires de repos (Gori, Géorgie, 2011–12, page 298) sur l'autoroute qui relie l'Azerbaïdjan à la Turquie ne sont, au fond, que des structures de béton et de verre, mais leurs formes curieuses semblent explorer des territoires relativement nouveaux en termes de design. Selon Jürgen Mayer H. : « Le poste-frontière de Sarpi qui accueille les visiteurs en Géorgie représente le renouveau progressiste du pays. » La Géorgie n'est évidement pas le seul pays en quête d'image à s'être tourné récemment vers des architectes de talent. On pense également à Astana, capitale du Kazakhstan, où des cabinets aussi emblématiques que Foster + Partners ont récemment créé des bâtiments publics comme le Palais de la paix et de la réconciliation ou le complexe de loisirs de Khan Shatyr en 2006. Et c'est à l'architecte italien Manfredi Nicoletti que l'on doit l'étonnante salle de concert du Kazakhstan, inaugurée en 2009. Reste à voir si de tels monuments architecturaux peuvent affirmer un caractère national ou même améliorer une réputation, mais il est vrai que de nouveaux clients, du Qatar et d'autres pays, ont aidé la profession à résister à des temps particulièrement difficiles sur le plan économique.

L'architecte Francis Kéré a déjà acquis une certaine réputation au Mali pour son parc National (Bamako, 2009–10) et son Centre de l'architecture en terre (Mopti, 2010), ainsi que dans son Burkina Faso natal. Son premier projet, une école primaire dans son village d'origine (Gondo, 2001), a gagné, en 2004, le prix Aga Khan d'architecture. Kéré travaille en ce moment sur un projet plus inattendu, le Village-Opéra (Laongo, Burkina Faso, 2010–, page 258). C'est un artiste allemand, Christoph Schlingensief, qui a eu l'idée de construire un Opéra en Afrique. « Quand j'ai entendu parler pour la première fois d'un Opéra en Afrique, raconte F. Kéré, j'ai cru qu'il s'agissait d'une blague. Un tel fantasme ne pouvait venir que de quelqu'un qui ne connaissait pas l'Afrique ou qui était si blasé qu'il ne pouvait inventer que des idioties. Telle a été ma première réaction. » Et pourtant, nombre de bâtiments de la première phase de cet ambitieux projet, situé sur 14 hectares à une heure et demie de route de la capitale Ouagadougou, sont déjà achevés. Kéré est, bien sûr, familier des techniques et matériaux de construction locaux utilisés sur le projet. C'est peut-être cet aspect du projet, plus que le Palais des festivals encore en construction, qui est intéressant et prometteur. L'architecture contemporaine de qualité peut tout à fait prendre en compte les particularités locales, voire plonger dans les racines du pays d'origine pour y trouver son style. Les coûts sont résolument maintenus bas, et des méthodes de construction plus

22

22
MAD Architects, Ordos Museum, Ordos, Inner Mongolia, China, 2005–11

douces et plus naturelles répondent mieux, en fait, aux questions environnementales que des créations occidentales très sophistiquées qui s'appuient davantage sur la technologie que sur le bon sens.

L'architecte sud-africain Jo Noero a fait toute sa carrière au Cap où il a réalisé plus de 200 bâtiments. Parmi ses projets les plus récents pour Red Location (New Brighton, Port Elizabeth, Afrique du Sud, 2009–11, page 336), on trouve une galerie d'art et une bibliothèque financés par la municipalité de Nelson Mandela Bay. Le musée Red Location (Noero Wolff Architects), dédié à la lutte contre l'apartheid, a gagné le prix du RIBA Lubetkin en 2006. Tirant son nom du ton rouille des baraquements en tôle ondulée qui le constituaient, Red Location est le quartier où Nelson Mandela a été le cofondateur de «Umkhonto we Sizwe» (Fer de lance de la Nation), la section armée de l'ANC (le Congrès national africain). La galerie d'art est dédiée au *struggle art* (art de la lutte) alors que la bibliothèque, essentiellement numérique, offrira un accès aux archives de la ville et à des ouvrages traitant de la lutte ainsi qu'à une école d'informatique. Proches l'un de l'autre, le musée et les bâtiments de la phase 2, qui sont plus récents, partagent des caractéristiques communes, comme des toitures en dents de scie laissant passer une lumière naturelle indirecte. Travaillant à plus large échelle que Francis Kéré et dans un pays plus grand, Jo Noero a néanmoins contribué, à Red Location, à une commémoration durable de la lutte contre l'apartheid, mais aussi, comme en témoignent les «boîtes souvenir» de tôle rouillée du musée, à la démonstration que l'architecture moderne, adaptée à un lieu et une fonction, a une place spécifique dans le monde en développement.

BIENVENUE DANS LE MONDE DE DEMAIN

Alors que s'achève la construction des grands aéroports de Doha (Qatar) et de Shenzhen (Chine), il n'y a guère pénurie de nouveaux projets architecturaux ambitieux. S'ils sont moins «manifestes», c'est qu'ils concernent des lieux qui sont moins sous les projecteurs des médias occidentaux. Les sites internet font, en effet, la chronique des nouveaux bâtiments à une vitesse déroutante, en utilisant souvent les mêmes textes et iconographie de base. Si ce type d'informations électroniques peut sembler prometteur à ceux qui aiment se tenir au courant des derniers événements du monde de l'architecture, la plupart des recherches se révèlent peu fructueuses. C'est pour cette raison que les ouvrages et les magazines professionnels sont encore la meilleure façon d'obtenir des informations. Il arrive souvent que les projets annoncés ne soient pas terminés ou restent dans les limbes bien plus longtemps que ne voudraient le laisser croire les architectes. L'on pense, par exemple, au curieux cas de la ville d'Ordos, en Mongolie-Intérieure. Depuis 2005 environ, bon nombre des plus grands architectes du monde, sous la tutelle de l'artiste Ai Weiwei et de l'agence Herzog & de Meuron, ont participé à un projet appelé «Ordos 100» qui devait donner le jour à 100 maisons exemplaires. Même si l'attrait pour l'architecture nouvelle était grand en Chine à l'époque, le plein essor de la nouvelle grande puissance économique a clairement ses limites. Comme l'explique le *New York Times*: «Ordos proprement dit a 1,5 million d'habitants, mais sa version de demain, bâtie de zéro sur un immense terrain vide, à 25 kilomètres au sud de la vieille ville, est quasiment déserte. Dans le nouveau quartier de Kangbashi, la circulation est très fluide sur les larges boulevards. Des immeubles de bureaux restent vides. Les piétons sont rares. Et les mauvaises herbes commencent à pousser dans les luxueux quartiers résidentiels de villas sans habitants… Les dirigeants de la ville, encouragés par des promoteurs offensifs, espéraient faire d'Ordos la version chinoise de Dubaï, en transfor-

23
MAD Architects, Absolute Towers, Mississauga, Canada, 2006–12

mant de vastes étendues d'une aride steppe mongolienne en métropole florissante. Ils ont même investi plus d'un milliard de dollars dans leur projet visionnaire. Mais, quatre ans après l'installation de l'exécutif de la ville à Kangbashi, avec ses dizaines de milliers de maisons et ses dizaines d'immeubles de bureaux terminés, la zone d'environ 30 kilomètres carrés a été tournée en ridicule par le journal d'État *China Daily* qui la décrit comme une "ville fantôme", un monument de démesure et d'optimisme insolent[5]. »

Alors que tous les architectes occidentaux ont presque arrêté net l'aventure d'Ordos, MAD Architects, une agence chinoise, a réussi à achever le musée d'Ordos qui fait 41 000 mètres carrés (Ordos, Mongolie-Intérieure, Chine, 2005–11, page 278). Fondée en 2004 par Ma Yansong, MAD s'était fait remarquer pour la première fois en 2006, en gagnant un concours international pour les Absolute Towers, près de Toronto, projet achevé en 2012 (présenté ici). S'inspirant des dômes géodésiques de Buckminster Fuller, les architectes ont imaginé une structure très inattendue que l'on pourrait décrire comme une dune de sable métallique, un symbole qui convient parfaitement à la ville située en bordure du désert de Gobi. Selon les architectes : « Tout à la fois familier et singulier, le musée d'Ordos semble avoir atterri dans le désert en provenance d'un autre monde ou avoir toujours été là. » Même en gardant l'étiquette de monument de démesure gouvernementale, ce bâtiment témoigne aussi de la capacité particulière de MAD Architects à réussir à faire les choses là où les autres ont échoué. Leurs Absolute Towers tout aussi surprenantes (Mississauga, Canada, 2006–12, page 288) ont été achevées en décembre 2012. Avec respectivement 56 niveaux (170 mètres) et 50 niveaux (150 mètres), ces tours semblent presque onduler en raison de la rotation d'un à huit degrés appliquée au plancher de chaque étage. L'on a pu voir un grand nombre de nouvelles formes stupéfiantes à la grande époque des projets de construction effrénés de Dubaï, mais, encore une fois, peu d'architectes ont eu la chance de voir leurs projets inaugurés. En raison à la fois d'une économie encore puissante et d'une nouvelle génération montante d'architectes comme Ma Yansong, le fondateur de MAD, l'on peut certainement parier que l'influence de la Chine dans l'architecture contemporaine va continuer de grandir. Il faut ajouter que les Chinois sont très ouverts aux nouvelles architectures, sorte de symbole de leur succès. Cette ouverture contraste avec une attitude souvent plus frileuse des pays européens, voire des États-Unis. Une puissance économique en plein essor est clairement une clef pour comprendre où et comment l'architecture contemporaine fera ses avancées les plus marquantes, même si, aujourd'hui, il est également tentant de regarder vers les pays que le design d'avant-garde a ignoré jusqu'ici.

PORTE-À-FAUX ET FORMATIONS EN TRIANGLE

L'on trouve un autre exemple de l'échelle et de l'ambition des projets architecturaux actuels en Chine dans le Centre Himalayas (Himalayas Center, Shanghai, 2007–, page 234) d'Arata Isozaki, qui s'étend sur 155 000 mètres carrés. Situé dans le Pudong, le district bien connu de Shanghai face au Bund et maintenant pourvu de tours immenses, il abrite un hôtel 5 étoiles, des ateliers d'artistes, un centre d'art et les inévitables centres commerciaux. Isozaki a également achevé, en 2011, un complexe de 175 000 mètres carrés, l'ambitieux Centre national des congrès de Doha, au Qatar. L'édifice de Shanghai et le Centre des congrès partagent un design comprenant des éléments quasi-organiques. Dans le cas de Doha, la façade de 250 mètres de long évoque le sidra, cet arbre emblème de la Fondation du Qatar, cliente du projet. Si Isozaki, né en 1931, n'est peut-être plus au sommet de sa créativité et de son influence, ces projets prouvent que sa réputation et son inventivité ont continué à faire progresser sa carrière dans les principaux pays bâtisseurs d'aujourd'hui.

Qu'en est-il des nouvelles formes architecturales nées de l'essor de la conception et fabrication assistées par ordinateur ? Sont-elles en perte de vitesse du fait de financements en baisse pour les nouvelles constructions ? Il existe encore, bien sûr, de nombreux exemples de ce type de travail et tous les signes que ces méthodes continueront à avoir un impact sur le design et la construction dans les années à venir. Il a fallu presque dix ans pour réaliser la nouvelle aile Herta et Paul Amir du Musée d'art de Tel Aviv (Tel Aviv, Israël, 2007–11, page 112), après que l'architecte Preston Scott Cohen a gagné le concours du projet en 2003. L'apparence futuriste et toute en angles de l'édifice de 18 500 mètres carrés est en grande partie le résultat de la réaction de l'architecte au site. Selon Cohen : « Le design de l'édifice est directement issu du défi de donner le jour à plusieurs étages de grandes galeries rectangulaires et neutres, dans un site singulier, étroit et triangulaire. La solution est de "carrer le triangle" en construisant les niveaux sur différents axes qui se déportent fortement d'étage en étage. Fondamentalement, les étages de l'édifice, trois au-dessus du niveau du sol et deux en-dessous, sont structurellement indépendants et empilés les uns sur les autres. » Auteur d'autres structures étonnantes, telles que le Musée d'art de Taiyuan (Chine, 2007–12), Cohen fait un usage intelligent de la nouvelle liberté qu'offrent les méthodes assistées par ordinateur aux architectes.

L'agence viennoise Coop Himmelb(l)au, dirigée par Wolf D. Prix, est, on le sait, l'une des pionnières de l'architecture dite déconstructiviste. Leurs ouvrages affichent toujours l'apparence disloquée qu'ils ont inventée dans les années 1980, et ils continuent de s'investir dans des projets à grande échelle, comme par exemple le Centre du cinéma de Busan, hôte du Festival international du film de Busan (Busan, Corée-du-Sud, 2005–11, page 128). Ce programme de 51 000 mètres carrés et d'un budget total de 100 millions d'euros entre effectivement dans la catégorie des grands projets. Il offre des particularités telles qu'un toit entré dans le *Livre Guinness des records* comme le « toit en porte-à-faux le plus long du monde » ou encore un « ciel virtuel » couvert d'ampoules LED programmables. Comme ils en ont l'habitude, les architectes ont donné des noms à certaines parties du complexe, par exemple « Cinema Mountain » ou « BIFF Hill ». Bien que la Corée-du-Sud ne se situe pas dans la même catégorie de pays émergents que d'autres déjà cités dans ce texte, les architectes européens ou américains ont la chance que l'Extrême-Orient soit toujours enclin à se lancer courageusement dans d'aussi gros projets aux formes provocatrices. Un calendrier relativement étiré dans le temps, entre l'émergence de nouveaux styles architecturaux et leur réalisation, peut donner l'impression que la profession est dans une sorte de distorsion spatiotemporelle où les années 1980 sont toujours à l'honneur. Mais Coop Himmelb(l)au a heureusement trouvé le moyen de faire évoluer son travail tout en préservant l'indéniable sentiment d'ivresse que peut procurer un projet comme le toit en porte-à-faux le plus long du monde.

Delugan Meissl, une autre agence viennoise, s'est fait remarquer par des constructions étonnantes comportant souvent aussi des volumes en porte-à-faux. Auteurs du musée Porsche (Stuttgart, 2006–08), ils ont achevé récemment le EYE Film Institute (Amsterdam, Pays-

24
Coop Himmelb(l)au,
Busan Cinema Center, Busan International Film Festival, Busan, South Korea, 2005–11

24

Bas, 2009–11, page 144) situé sur les berges de la rivière IJ, juste en face de la gare centrale d'Amsterdam. Le grand édifice en forme de coin, difficile à manquer, fait saillie en direction de la gare. Peut-être moins « idéologique » dans son design que ne l'a été Coop Himmelb(l)au au fil des ans, avec le EYE Film Institute, Delugan Meissl n'en propose pas moins une formulation architecturale très puissante et souligne l'engagement actuel des Pays-Bas dans des formes d'expression artistique comme l'image ou le son. Ce n'est sans doute pas un hasard si le cinéma fait l'objet des attentions de Coop Himmelb(l)au et de Delugan Meissl dans leurs projets respectifs en Corée et à Amsterdam. Si les architectes de talent du monde entier se sont très souvent intéressés aux musées d'art, ils se tournent à présent vers des domaines comme celui de l'image.

TOUJOURS DEBOUT APRÈS TOUTES CES ANNÉES

Zaha Hadid, l'une des participantes de l'exposition « Deconstructivist Architecture » de 1988 au Museum of Modern Art (New York), est devenue, ces dernières années, une architecte internationale des plus actives. Sa tour CMA CGM (Marseille, 2008–11, page 188) est un projet de 94 000 mètres carrés, dans une ville qui n'est pas réputée pour le nombre de ses tours. Élégant et imprégné du style de Hadid, l'édifice semble constitué de deux courbes montantes se rejoignant en leur milieu, faisant écho aux formes des autoroutes qui l'entourent. Conçue pour 2700 employés, la tour prouve la faculté de Hadid de s'attaquer à des projets d'entreprise de grande envergure, comme elle l'a déjà fait pour des clients comme BMW. Le discours de Zaha Hadid a toujours souligné la nécessité de réformer l'architecture, de la faire émerger du paysage comme une entité presque organique dans laquelle les murs, les sols et les plafonds se fondent dans un tout cohérent. La tour CMA CGM, tout en gardant ce sens du mouvement, s'aventure dans le territoire plus prévisible des alignements de bureaux et de parkings qui est, il faut en convenir, le fondement de l'architecture dédiée à l'entreprise.

UNStudio, dirigé par Ben van Berkel et Caroline Bos, est depuis longtemps leader dans le domaine de l'utilisation intensive de la conception assistée par ordinateur avec des bâtiments comme, par exemple, le saisissant musée Mercedes-Benz (Stuttgart, 2001–06). Son Centre de l'ingénierie virtuelle du Fraunhofer IAO (Zentrum für Virtuelles Engineering, Stuttgart, 2006–12, avec Asplan Architekten, page 440) est un projet relativement modeste en taille – 3200 mètres carrés de surface au sol –, mais il a gagné la certification Gold du DGNB (Conseil allemand pour la construction durable) grâce, entre autres gestes pour économiser l'énergie et les matériaux, à une modélisation 3D minutieuse et des efforts d'optimisation du revêtement en aluminium du bâtiment. Ce projet prouve que les techniques de conception numérique autrefois considérées comme « exotiques » sont de plus en plus usitées et que les architectes et leurs clients ont retenu la leçon que les nouveaux édifices doivent être conçus en ayant à l'esprit leur potentiel en économies d'énergie.

STUFF HAPPENS (CE SONT DES CHOSES QUI ARRIVENT)

Les choses sont-elles donc aussi noires qu'elles ont pu le paraître ? Il existe certainement à l'heure actuelle des changements significatifs sur les plans politique, démographique et économique. Ces puissances « émergentes », comme la Chine, certains pays d'Extrême-Orient ou le Brésil, vont devenir moteurs dans l'architecture contemporaine. Ce n'est pas que les Européens ou les Américains soient « fatigués »

25
Zaha Hadid, CMA CGM Tower, Marseille, France, 2008–11

25

à proprement parler, mais leurs pays, ayant atteint des niveaux plus élevés de densité dans les constructions modernes, ont peut-être moins besoin de projets entièrement nouveaux. Les périodes de difficultés économiques sont aussi celles où les clients calculent les coûts et répugnent à l'innovation si elle ne rime à rien en termes de dépense. Ce sont aujourd'hui les pays ayant un fort besoin de s'affirmer qui s'offrent ces édifices audacieux et tape-à-l'œil qui crient « Regardez-moi ! ». Même les États-Unis ont l'air « vieux » en comparaison. Les Twin Towers du World Trade Center étaient des monuments à la gloire de l'ambition et de la puissance financière. Même si leur destruction a fait l'effet d'une douche froide sur l'orgueil de certains, les tours continuent de s'élever, même au centre de New York. Le mémorial du 11-Septembre pose bien le choc psychologique que continuent de représenter les événements du 11 septembre 2001 pour les États-Unis. Entre l'assassinat de John F. Kennedy, la guerre du Viêtnam et ceci, il semblerait que la « Nouvelle Frontière » de John F. Kennedy ait été atteinte depuis longtemps. Le problème, c'est que, vu d'ici, l'avenir ne semble guère brillant.

Les orientations de l'architecture, comme celles de l'économie, sont difficiles à prévoir. *Stuff Happens* (« Ce sont des choses qui arrivent »), comme l'a déclaré Donald Rumsfeld, l'ancien secrétaire d'État américain à la Défense. Mais toutes les « choses qui arrivent » ne sont pas forcément bonnes. Il y a, bien sûr, des éléments de fond significatifs du développement économique, comme, par exemple, l'énorme population travailleuse de la Chine, maintenant impatiente de profiter des libéralités matérielles du capitalisme, mais l'économie, comme l'architecture, est aussi une question de pessimisme ou d'optimisme. Des temps optimistes conduisent à un goût accru du risque, à Wall Street comme sur les écrans d'ordinateur des architectes. Le bruit du crash de 2008 va peut-être bientôt s'évanouir, tout comme les épaisses volutes qui ont balayé Manhattan en 2001. On peut souligner deux points en ce qui concerne les projets présentés ici. Premier point, les liens entre art et architecture ont continué de se développer, induisant une créativité considérable à la frontière entre les deux disciplines. Deuxième point, l'on peut trouver une architecture contemporaine de qualité dans nombre de pays, en particulier du fait d'avoir compris que de nombreuses méthodes traditionnelles de construction sont plus judicieuses que les techniques modernes qui ont recouvert la terre de béton et d'acier. Des initiatives telles que le prix Aga Khan d'architecture ont pour mérite d'avoir contribué à cette nouvelle prise de conscience.

Si le modernisme d'hier peut être comparé, en toute modestie, aux brillantes certitudes de la Renaissance, nous avons certainement franchi le seuil d'une nouvelle époque, plus sombre et inquiétante que la période d'après-guerre. Nous avons tenté d'être des dieux, mais sans être à la hauteur. Les signes de ce profond changement sont nombreux, mais ce sont peut-être deux trous béants dans le centre de New York, maintenant emplis de pierre noire et d'eau, qui racontent le mieux cette nouvelle ère de doute. Un jour, l'optimisme sera de retour, et la créativité enfantera une nouvelle architecture inventive et écoresponsable. Édifices et projets bâtiront les plans de ce processus, alors même que déclin et profonds changements sont la règle pour beaucoup. Entre-temps, le monde aura changé.

[1] Citation originale : The Pritzker Architecture Prize, « Ceremony Acceptance Speech Frank Gehry », http://www.pritzkerprize.com/1989/ceremony_speech1, site consulté le 30 septembre 2012.

[2] Citation originale : « Gehry's Crown for Bunker Hill Is a Fitting Tribute for Disney », *Los Angeles Times*, 15 septembre 1991, http://articles.latimes.com/1991-09-15/realestate/re-3191_1_disney-hall-s-exterior/3, site consulté le 30 septembre 2012.

[3] Tom Wolfe, *Il court il court le Bauhaus*, Les Belles Lettres, 2012.

[4] Paroles de la chanson *Vertigo*, titre d'ouverture de l'album de U2 de 2004 « How to Dismantle an Atomic Bomb » : « Hello, hello (Hola !), I'm at a place called Vertigo, (Dónde está ?) It's everything I wish I didn't know. »

[5] Citation originale : « Chinese City Has Many Buildings, but Few People », *New York Times*, 19 octobre 2012, http://www.nytimes.com/2010/10/20/business/global/20ghost.html?pagewanted=all&_r=0, site consulté le 1er octobre 2012.

ADJAYE ASSOCIATES

Adjaye Associates
223–231 Old Marylebone Road
London NW1 5QT / UK

Tel: +44 20 72 58 61 40
Fax: +44 20 72 58 61 48
E-mail: info@adjaye.com
Web: www.adjaye.com

DAVID ADJAYE was born in 1966 in Dar es Salaam, Tanzania. He studied at the Royal College of Art in London (M.Arch, 1993), and worked in the offices of David Chipperfield and Eduardo Souto de Moura, before creating his own firm in London in 2000. He has been recognized as one of the leading architects of his generation in the United Kingdom, in part because of the talks he has given in various locations such as the Architectural Association, the Royal College of Art, and Cambridge University, as well as Harvard, Cornell, and the Universidade Lusíada in Lisbon. Some of his key works are a house extension (St. John's Wood, 1998); studio/home for Chris Ofili (1999); the SHADA Pavilion (2000, with artist Henna Nadeem); Siefert Penthouse (2001); Elektra House (2001); and a studio/gallery/home for Tim Noble and Sue Webster (2002), all in London. More recent work includes the Nobel Peace Center (Oslo, Norway, 2002–05); Bernie Grant Performing Arts Center (London, 2001–06); Stephen Lawrence Center (London, 2004–06); a visual arts building for the London-based organizations inIVA/Autograph at Rivington Place (London, 2003–07); the Museum of Contemporary Art Denver (Denver, Colorado, USA, 2004–07); and the Francis A. Gregory Library (Washington, D.C., USA, 2010–12, published here), all in the UK unless stated otherwise. Current work includes participation in the ongoing Msheireb project (Doha, Qatar, 2015) and the National Museum of African American History and Culture (Smithsonian Institution, Washington, D.C., USA, 2015).

DAVID ADJAYE wurde 1966 in Daressalam, Tansania, geboren. Er studierte am Royal College of Art in London (M. Arch., 1993) und arbeitete für David Chipperfield und Eduardo Souto de Moura, bevor er 2000 in London sein eigenes Büro gründete. Er gilt weithin als einer der führenden Architekten seiner Generation in Großbritannien, auch wegen seiner Vorträge an Institutionen wie der Architectural Association, dem Royal College of Art, der Universität Cambridge, der Harvard und der Cornell University sowie der Universidade Lusíada in Lissabon. Zu seinen wichtigsten Projekten zählen eine Hauserweiterung (St. John's Wood, 1998), ein Atelier und Haus für Chris Ofili (1999), der SHADA Pavilion (2000, mit der Künstlerin Henna Nadeem), das Siefert Penthouse (2001), das Elektra House (2001) sowie ein Atelier mit Galerie und Haus für Tim Noble und Sue Webster (2002), alle in London. Jüngere Arbeiten sind u. a. das Friedensnobelpreiszentrum (Oslo, 2002–05), das Bernie Grant Performing Arts Center (London, 2001–06), das Stephen Lawrence Center (London, 2004–06), ein Haus für bildende Künste für die Londoner Organisation inIVA/Autograph am Rivington Place (London, 2003–07), das Museum of Contemporary Art Denver (Denver, Colorado, 2004–07) sowie die Francis A. Gregory Library (Washington, D. C., 2010–12, hier vorgestellt). Zu seinen aktuellen Projekten zählen sein Beitrag zum Msheireb-Projekt (Doha, Katar, 2015) und das National Museum of African American History and Culture (Smithsonian Institution, Washington D. C., 2015).

DAVID ADJAYE est né en 1966 à Dar es-Salaam, en Tanzanie. Il étudie au Royal College of Art, à Londres (M.Arch, 1993), puis travaille dans les agences de David Chipperfield et d'Eduardo Souto de Moura, avant de créer sa propre agence à Londres, en 2000. Il est considéré comme l'un des plus importants architectes de sa génération au Royaume-Uni, en partie grâce à ses conférences en divers lieux, comme l'Architectural Association, le Royal College of Art et l'université de Cambridge, ainsi qu'à Harvard, Cornell, et à l'université Lusíada de Lisbonne. Parmi ses principales réalisations, on compte une extension d'habitation (St. John's Wood, 1998) ; un atelier/maison pour Chris Ofili (1999) ; le pavillon SHADA (2000, avec l'artiste Henna Nadeem) ; l'appartement de grand standing Siefert (2001) ; la maison Elektra (2001) et un atelier/galerie/maison pour Tim Noble et Sue Webster (2002), tous situés à Londres. Ses projets récemment réalisés sont le Centre Nobel de la paix (Oslo, 2002–05) ; le Bernie Grant Performing Arts Centre (Londres, 2001–06) ; le Stephen Lawrence Centre (Londres, 2004–06) ; un immeuble dédié aux arts visuels pour les organisations inIVA/Autograph, à Rivington Place (Londres, 2003–07) ; le Museum of Contemporary Art de Denver (États-Unis, 2004–07) et la bibliothèque Francis A. Gregory (Washington, 2010–12, présentée ici), tous situés au Royaume-Uni, sauf mention contraire. Ses projets en cours comprennent sa participation au projet Msheireb (Doha, Qatar, 2015) et le National Museum of African American History and Culture (Smithsonian Institution, Washington, 2015).

EXIT
Staff Picks

FRANCIS A. GREGORY LIBRARY

Washington, D.C., USA, 2010–12

3360 Alabama Avenue, SE, Washington, D.C., USA, +1 202 698 6373, www.dclibrary.org/francis
Area: 2137 m². Client: District of Columbia Public Library
Cost: $13 million. Collaboration: Austin Harris, Russell Crader

Adjaye Associates won a competition to design two new neighborhood libraries for the District of Columbia. These are the William O. Lockridge / Bellevue Library and the **FRANCIS A. GREGORY LIBRARY** (published here). The architect states: "Our mission, with the Francis Gregory Library, has been to offer a new way to experience books, reading, and storytelling. Rather than a traditional closed building, this library is porous and open, with the canopy providing a welcoming entrance that invites people inside. Conceived as an extension to the park, it is not only a place to gather, but also a place of contemplation and learning." The structure is set in Fort Davis Park and was imagined as a "woodland folly." Designed to LEED Silver standards, the two-story structure has a reflective geometric façade with a "network" of four-sided openings that were placed to frame views of the park. Wood is the basic interior cladding material, framing the diamond-shaped window openings. The building itself is rectangular and is marked on the exterior by a generous canopy that continues the pattern of the windows.

Adjaye Associates gewannen einen Wettbewerb für zwei Stadtteilbibliotheken im District of Columbia: die William O. Lockridge/Bellevue Library und die **FRANCIS A. GREGORY LIBRARY**. Der Architekt: „Mit der Francis Gregory Library wollten wir einen Raum schaffen, in dem man Bücher, Lesen und Geschichtenerzählen neu erleben kann. Die Bibliothek ist, anders als traditionell geschlossene Bauten, durchlässig und offen, das einladende auskragende Vordach zieht Besucher in den Bau hinein. Als Erweiterung des Parks konzipiert, ist dies nicht nur ein Ort der Begegnung, sondern auch ein Ort zum Nachdenken und Lernen." Der im Fort Davis Park gelegene Bau wurde als exzentrischer Pavillon im Wald geplant. Das zweigeschossige Gebäude entspricht dem LEED-Silberstandard; seine spiegelnde geometrische Fassade besteht aus einem Netz viereckiger Öffnungen, die Ausblicke in den Park rahmen. Im Innenausbau dominiert Holz, es fasst auch die rautenförmigen Fenster ein. Markantes Merkmal des rechtwinkligen Gebäudes ist der großzügige Dachüberstand, in dem sich das Rautenmuster der Fenster fortsetzt.

Adjaye Associates a gagné le concours pour la création de deux bibliothèques de quartier dans le district de Columbia, la librairie William O. Lockridge/Bellevue et la **LIBRAIRIE FRANCIS A. GREGORY** (présentée ici). Selon l'architecte, « notre mission, avec la bibliothèque Francis Gregory, était d'offrir une nouvelle façon d'aborder les livres, la lecture et le conte. Contrairement au traditionnel bâtiment fermé, cette bibliothèque est perméable et ouverte, et l'auvent offre une entrée accueillante au public. Conçue comme une extension du parc, elle n'est pas uniquement lieu de promenade, mais aussi de contemplation et d'apprentissage ». Le bâtiment, situé dans le parc de Fort Davis, a été imaginé comme une « folie des bois ». La structure de deux niveaux, certifiée aux normes LEED Silver, a une façade géométrique réfléchissante et un « réseau » d'ouvertures sur les quatre côtés, disposées pour cadrer des vues du parc. Le revêtement intérieur en simple bois encadre les fenêtres en forme de losange. Le bâtiment, lui-même rectangulaire, se signale à l'extérieur par un grand auvent prolongeant le motif des fenêtres.

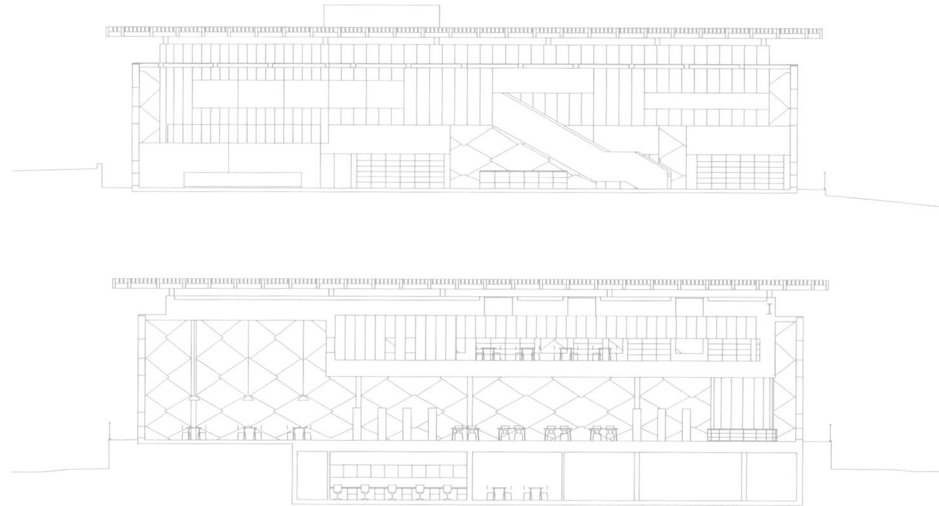

Section drawings reveal the relatively simple and essentially rectilinear composition of the structure. The honeycomb or diamond patterns seen in the canopy or the windows make the building open to light and its environment.

Querschnitte veranschaulichen die vergleichsweise schlichte, geradlinige Komposition des Baus. Das Waben- bzw. Rautenmuster des Dachüberstands und der Fenster öffnet den Bau für Tageslicht und Umfeld.

Les coupes montrent la composition relativement simple et essentiellement rectiligne de la structure. Les motifs en nid-d'abeilles ou en losange de l'auvent et des fenêtres laissent entrer la lumière dans le bâtiment ouvert sur son environnement.

Interior library spaces like the one above are relatively straightforward, though an opening overhead brings natural light into the room. Right, where the diamond-shaped openings, glass, and neon lights come together, the spatial effects are more pronounced.

Die Besucherräume des Bibliothek, wie oben im Bild, sind schlicht gehalten; Oberlichter lassen Tageslicht einfallen. Die Raumwirkung ist markanter, wo rautenförmige Fassadenöffnungen, Glas und Neonlicht zusammenwirken (rechts).

Les espaces intérieurs de la bibliothèque, comme celui ci-dessus, sont relativement simples, mais des ouvertures au plafond laissent entrer la lumière naturelle dans la pièce. À droite, les ouvertures en losange, le verre et les néons créent des effets spatiaux plus marqués.

In this double-height space, the use of wood and the glazed openings make the interior both convivial and architecturally interesting. Below, plans with the diagonal staircase visible at the bottom.

Im doppelgeschossigen Bereich wirkt das Interieur durch Holz und Verglasung einladend und architektonisch reizvoll. Unten Grundrisse mit der diagonal angeordneten Treppe unten im Plan.

Dans cet espace de double hauteur, l'emploi du bois et les ouvertures vitrées rendent l'intérieur convivial et intéressant du point de vue architectural. Ci-dessous, les plans où est visible l'escalier oblique, en bas.

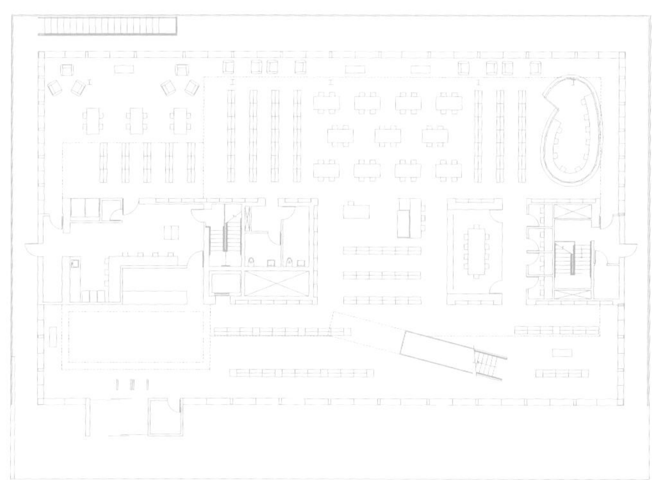

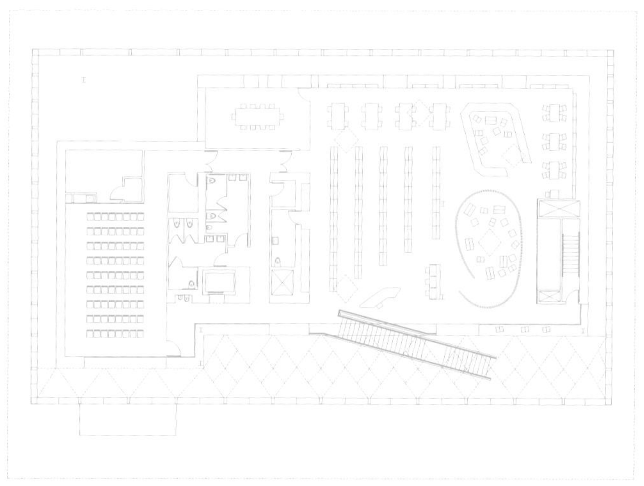

ALA ARCHITECTS

ALA Architects Ltd.
Tehtaankatu 40 B 17
00150 Helsinki
Finland

Tel: +358 9 42 59 73 30
Fax: +358 9 42 59 73 31
E-mail: info@ala.fi
Web: www.ala.fi

ALA was founded in 2004 by four Partners: Juho Grönholm, Antti Nousjoki, Janne Teräsvirta, and Samuli Woolston. ALA is a Helsinki-based firm that currently employs over 20 people in Finland. **SAMULI WOOLSTON** was born in 1975 in Helsinki. He studied at the Helsinki Upper Secondary School of Visual Arts and obtained his architecture degree from the Helsinki University of Technology (2003). **JUHO GRÖNHOLM** was also born in 1975 in Helsinki. He was the project manager for the Kilden Performing Arts Center, published here. He received his architecture degree from the Helsinki University of Technology in 2001. **JANNE TERÄSVIRTA**, too, was born in 1975 in Helsinki. He studied at the University of Arts and Design (Helsinki, 1997–98), the Technical University of Delft (2000–01), and received his degree from the Aalto University (2010). **ANTTI NOUSJOKI** was born in 1974 in Helsinki and also studied in Delft (1999–2000) and at the Oulu University, Department of Architecture (2001). As well as the Kilden Performing Arts Center (Kristiansand, Norway, 2008–11, published here), their work includes Kuopio Theater (Kuopio, Finland, 2010–14); the Keilaniemi and Otaniemi Subway Stations (Espoo, Finland, 2009–15); and Lappeenranta Theater (Lappeenranta, Finland, 2011–15).

ALA wurde 2004 von Juho Grönholm, Antti Nousjoki, Janne Teräsvirta und Samuli Woolston gegründet. Das in Helsinki ansässige Büro beschäftigt in Finnland derzeit über 20 Mitarbeiter. **SAMULI WOOLSTON**, geboren 1975 in Helsinki, studierte an der Oberschule für visuelle Künste in Helsinki und schloss sein Architekturstudium 2003 an der dortigen Technischen Universität ab. **JUHO GRÖNHOLM**, ebenfalls 1975 in Helsinki geboren, war Projektleiter für das Kilden Konzert- und Theaterzentrum und machte seinen Abschluss 2001 an der TU Helsinki. **JANNE TERÄSVIRTA**, geboren 1975 in Helsinki, studierte an der Universität für Kunst und Design in Helsinki (1997–98) und an der Technischen Universität Delft (2000–01). Seinen Abschluss erhielt er von der Aalto Universität (2010). **ANTTI NOUSJOKI**, geboren 1974 in Helsinki, absolvierte sein Architekturstudium zunächst in Delft (1999–2000) und war anschließend ein Jahr an der Universität von Oulu. Zu den Projekten von ALA gehören das Kilden Konzert- und Theaterzentrum (Kristiansand, Norwegen, 2008–11, hier vorgestellt), das Kuopio Theater (Kuopio, Finnland, 2010–14), die U-Bahnstationen Keilaniemi und Otaniemi (Espoo, Finnland, 2009–15) und das Lappeenranta Theater (Lappeenranta, Finnland, 2011–15).

ALA a été créé en 2004 par quatre associés : Juho Grönholm, Antti Nousjoki, Janne Teräsvirta et Samuli Woolston. Basée à Helsinki, l'agence ALA emploie actuellement plus de 20 personnes en Finlande. **SAMULI WOOLSTON** est né en 1975 à Helsinki. Il étudie à l'École secondaire supérieure des arts visuels d'Helsinki et obtient son diplôme d'architecture à l'Université technologique d'Helsinki en 2003. **JUHO GRÖNHOLM** est également né en 1975 à Helsinki. Il a été chef de projet pour le Centre des arts du spectacle Kilden présenté ici. Il obtient son diplôme d'architecture à l'Université technologique d'Helsinki en 2001. **JANNE TERÄSVIRTA** est également né en 1975 à Helsinki. Il étudie à l'Université d'art et de design d'Helsinki (1997–98), à l'Université de technologie de Delft (2000–01) et obtient son diplôme à l'université Aalto en 2010. Né en 1974 à Helsinki, **ANTTI NOUSJOKI** a également étudié à Delft (1999–2000) puis en section architecture à l'université d'Oulu (2001). Outre le Centre des arts du spectacle Kilden (Kristiansand, Norvège, 2008–11, présenté ici), ils ont aussi réalisé le théâtre de Kuopio (Kuopio, Finlande, 2010–14) ; les stations de métro de Keilaniemi et Otaniemi (Espoo, Finlande, 2009–15) et le théâtre de Lappeenranta (Lappeenranta, Finlande, 2011–15).

KILDEN PERFORMING ARTS CENTER

Kristiansand, Norway, 2008–11

Sjølystveien 2, 4610 Kristiansand, Norway, +47 986 47 18 39, www.kilden.com
Area: 24 600 m². Client: Kilden Teater- og Konserthus IKS
Cost: €226 million

The **KILDEN PERFORMING ARTS CENTER** includes a 1200-seat concert hall for the Kristiansand Symphony Orchestra, and a 750-seat space for the Agder Theater that can be transformed for performances of the Opera South ensemble. The city of Kristiansand is in southeastern Norway and has a population of approximately 85 000 people. A multipurpose hall and an experimental theater stage are also part of the project, as well as parking spaces for 400 cars, and office, workshop, and rehearsal spaces. The Kilden Center was built on the island of Odderøya in the port area of Kristiansand. A central feature of the project is a monumental tilted wall made of wedged CNC-milled local oak planks. The undulating forms of this wall rake forward over the entrance façade and penetrate the building, giving it an unusual form that connects the building to nature, and provides views of the neighboring dock area with its grain and cement silos and warehouses. The overall form of the structure is rectangular with the two main theaters sitting directly next to each other and oriented in the same direction.

Das **KILDEN KONZERT- UND THEATERZENTRUM** umfasst einen Konzertsaal mit 1200 Plätzen für das Sinfonieorchester von Kristiansand, einer Stadt im Südosten Norwegens mit rund 85 000 Einwohnern. Ein weiterer Saal mit 750 Plätzen für das Agder-Theater kann für Produktionen der Opera Sør genutzt werden, hinzu kommen eine Mehrzweckhalle und eine kleinere Bühne für experimentelles Theater sowie Büros, Werkstätten, Probenräume und Parkraum für 400 Autos. Kilden liegt im Hafenviertel von Kristiansand auf der Insel Odderøya. Auffälligstes Merkmal des Baus ist seine geschwungene Dachverkleidung aus CNC-gefrästen Eichenholzpaneelen aus der Region. Die Verkleidung kragt weit über die Eingangsfassade aus, durchdringt das Gebäude und verleiht dem Bau, der sich in unmittelbarer Nachbarschaft zu Getreide- und Zementsilos sowie Lagerhäusern befindet, eine naturwüchsige Anmutung. Abgesehen von der Fassade ist die Formensprache des Gebäudes geradlinig. Die beiden parallel ausgerichteten Hauptsäle liegen direkt nebeneinander.

Le **CENTRE DES ARTS DU SPECTACLE KILDEN** comprend une salle de concert de 1200 places pour l'orchestre symphonique de Kristiansand et une salle de 750 places pour le théâtre Agder, modulable pour les concerts de l'ensemble Opera Sør. Kristiansand est une ville de 85 000 habitants située au sud-est de la Norvège. Une salle polyvalente et une scène de théâtre expérimental font également partie du projet, ainsi qu'un parking de 400 places, des bureaux, des ateliers et des espaces de répétition. Le centre Kilden est situé sur l'île d'Odderøya, dans le quartier portuaire de Kristiansand. Un trait marquant du projet est un mur incliné en planches de chêne local, usinées par fraisage numérique. Les formes ondulantes de ce mur s'inclinent au-dessus de l'entrée et pénètrent dans le bâtiment, ce qui lui donne un aspect inhabituel, évoquant la nature, et permet de voir le quartier des docks, ses silos à grain et à ciment et ses entrepôts. La forme générale du bâtiment est rectangulaire, avec les deux salles principales juxtaposées et orientées dans la même direction.

The raking wood-clad façade of the building makes use of computer-controlled milling that allows for an irregular, wavelike surface.

Die ausgreifende, holzverschalte Fassade entstand mithilfe von CNC-Fräsmaschinen, wodurch die unregelmäßige wellenförmige Oberfläche realisiert werden konnte.

Pour la façade inclinée du bâtiment revêtue de bois, on a eu recours au fraisage numérique permettant d'obtenir une surface ondulée irrégulière.

Interior views emphasize a varied use of color and forms, such as the lighting (above), that are consistent with the surprising exterior of the building.

Der facettenreiche Einsatz von Farben und Formen im Innern des Baus, etwa bei der Lichtgestaltung (oben), passt zu dem ungewöhnlichen Außenbau.

Des vues intérieures mettent l'accent sur l'usage varié de la couleur et des formes, comme dans l'éclairage (ci-dessus), en cohérence avec l'extérieur surprenant du bâtiment.

Right, a section drawing shows how the theater area is inserted into the volume. Above, a curving wooden roof inside echoes the dramatic wooden exterior slope.

Ein Querschnitt (rechts) zeigt die Integration der Bühnen in den Baukörper. Die geschwungene Holzdecke (oben) setzt die dramatischen Schrägen der Holzfassade fort.

À droite, une coupe montre comment le théâtre s'insère dans le volume. Ci-dessus, une voûte intérieure en bois fait écho à l'impressionnant dénivelé en bois de l'extérieur.

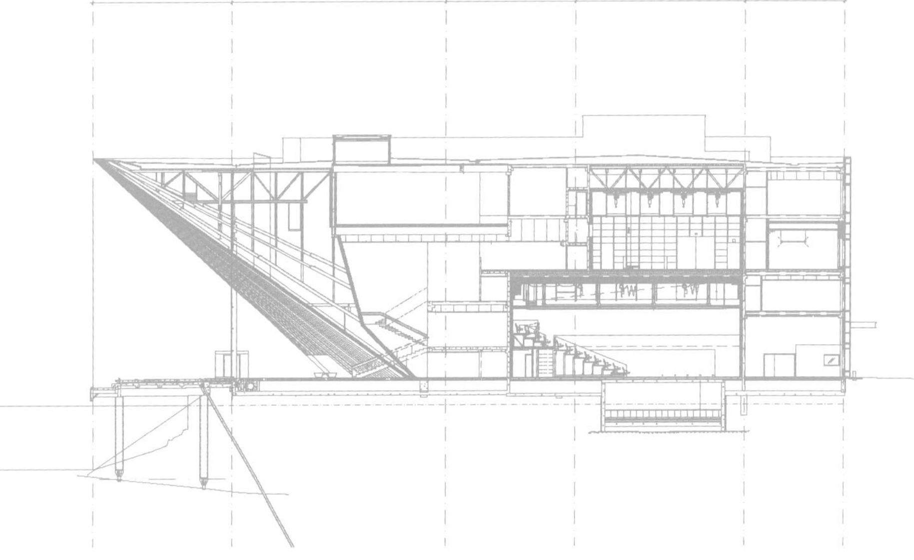

Yurihonjo City Cultural Center

CHIAKI ARAI

Chiaki Arai Urban and Architecture Design
2–14–19–2F, Yutenji
Meguro-ku
Tokyo 153–0052
Japan

Tel. +81 3 3760 5411
Fax. +81 3 3760 5415
E-mail: aoffice@nifty.com
Web: www.chiaki-arai.com

CHIAKI ARAI was born in 1948 in Shimane, Japan. He received his B.Arch from Tokyo City University (1971) and his M.Arch degree from the University of Pennsylvania (1972). He worked in 1974 in the office of Louis Kahn, and created his own firm in Tokyo in 1980. He is a Professor at Tokyo City University and has lectured at the University of Pennsylvania (1998). Recent work of his firm includes the Tonami Village Museum Information Center (Toyama, 2006); Ofunato Civic Culture Center and Library (Ofunato, Iwate, 2009); Karakida Community Center (Tokyo, 2010); Yurihonjo City Cultural Center, Kadare (Yurihonjo, Akita, 2008–11, published here); Konan-ku Culture Center (Konan-ku, Niigata, 2012); Mihama Culture Center (Mihama-cho, Fukui, 2012); Hachijo-jima Govenment Office Building and Civic Hall (Tokyo, 2013); and the Niitsu Culture Hall (Akiha-ku, Niigata, 2013), all in Japan.

CHIAKI ARAI, geboren 1948 in Shimane, Japan, machte seinen Bachelor in Architektur an der Tokyo City University (1971) und seinen Master an der University of Pennsylvania (1972). 1974 arbeitete er im Büro von Louis Kahn. Sein eigenes Büro gründete er 1980 in Tokio. Chiaki Arai ist Professor an der Tokyo City University und unterrichtete an der University of Pennsylvania (1998). Neuere Projekte sind das Informationszentrum des Dorfmuseums in Tonami (Präfektur Toyama, 2006), das städtische Kulturzentrum mit Bibliothek in Ofunato (Ofunato, Iwate, 2009), das Bürgerzentrum Karakida (Tama, Präfektur Tokio, 2010), das hier vorgestellte Kulturzentrum von Yurihonjo im Stadtteil Kadare (Yurihonjo, Präfektur Akita, 2008–11), das Kulturzentrum Konan-ku (Konan-ku, Präfektur Niigata, 2012), das Kulturzentrum Mihama (Mihama-cho, Präfektur Fukui, 2012), das Rathaus und Verwaltungsgebäude von Hachijo-jima (Präfektur Tokio, 2013) und das Kulturzentrum Niitsu (Akiha-ku, Präfektur Niigata, 2013), alle in Japan.

CHIAKI ARAI est né en 1948 à Shimane, au Japon. Diplômé de l'université de Tokyo en 1971, il obtient son M.Arch à l'université de Pennsylvanie en 1972. Il travaille en 1974 pour Louis Kahn avant de créer sa propre agence à Tokyo en 1980. Il est professeur à l'université de Tokyo et a enseigné à l'université de Pennsylvanie (1998). Les projets récents de son agence comprennent le Centre d'information du musée du village de Tonami (Toyama, 2006) ; la bibliothèque municipale/Centre culturel d'Ofunato (Ofunato, Iwate, 2009) ; le foyer municipal de Karakida (Tokyo, 2010) ; le Centre culturel Kadare à Yurihonjo (Yurihonjo, Akita, 2008–11, présenté ici) ; le Centre culturel de Konan-ku (Konan-ku, Niigata, 2012) ; le Centre culturel de Mihama (Mihama-cho, Fukui, 2012) ; les bureaux administratifs et la salle municipale de Hachijo-jima (Tokyo, 2013) et le Centre culturel de Niitsu (Akiha-ku, Niigata, 2013), tous situés au Japon.

YURIHONJO CITY CULTURAL CENTER

Kadare, Yurihonjo, Akita, Japan, 2008–11

15 Higashi-cho, Kadare, Yurihonjo, Akita, Japan
Area: 11 750 m². Client: Yurihonjo City. Cost: not disclosed
Collaboration: Ryoichi Yoshizaki, Masanori Asai

This three-story structure occupies a 13 335-square-meter lot. The complex includes a multipurpose transforming theater, library, and community center. The architect explains: "Originally, this project had two sites sandwiching a road. We combined sites by placing an indoor 'Gathering Street' that gives access to each function. Its fissure-like form lets sunlight into the deep center of the building." Workshops with local residents helped to determine some characteristics of the building, notable for its human scale and insistence on "cultural sustainability." The theater can be configured in several different ways, including a simple, flat floor, or with a centered stage. A "super box" theater, citizens' activity room, gallery, and north and south "pocket parks" can be connected to make a 135-meter-long "dynamic and spacious tunnel." The planetarium "floats above the library like a moon" on just four bent columns. The large open space of the library, designed with minimal structural elements, has space for 220 000 volumes and can seat 188 users.

Das dreigeschossige Kulturzentrum steht auf einem 13 335 m² großen Grundstück. Außer einer Mehrzweckhalle umfasst es eine Bibliothek und ein Bürgerzentrum. Der Architekt erklärt: „Ursprünglich waren für dieses Projekt zwei durch eine Straße getrennte Standorte vorgesehen. Wir haben diese Standorte zusammengelegt und im Gebäude eine ‚Straße der Begegung' konzipiert, die alle Einrichtungen verbindet. Sie wirkt wie eine Schlucht und lässt Tageslicht bis tief in das Gebäude hinein." Einige Merkmale des Entwurfs, der durch seine Nutzerorientiertheit und das Beharren auf „kultureller Nachhaltigkeit" besticht, wurden in Bürgerworkshops erarbeitet. Die Mehrzweckhalle kann u. a. als Saal ohne Bestuhlung oder mit zentraler Bühne genutzt werden. „Super-Box"-Theater, Bürgertreffpunkt, Galerie und sog. Pocket-Parks im Norden und Süden können zu einem „dynamischen und geräumigen Tunnel" von 135 m Länge verbunden werden. Über der Bibliothek schwebt an vier schiefwinkligen Säulen das Planetarium „wie ein Mond". Der große offene Raum der Bibliothek mit nur wenigen strukturellen Elementen bietet Platz für 188 Leser und 220 000 Bücher.

Ce bâtiment de trois niveaux occupe une parcelle de 13 335 m². Le complexe comprend une salle de théâtre modulable, une bibliothèque et un foyer municipal. L'architecte explique : « À l'origine, ce projet occupait deux sites séparés par une route. Nous avons lié les deux par une "rue de rencontre" couverte qui donne accès à chaque lieu. Sa forme de faille laisse pénétrer la lumière au cœur du bâtiment. » Des ateliers avec les habitants du voisinage ont aidé à déterminer certaines caractéristiques du bâtiment qui se distingue par son échelle humaine et l'importance accordée à la « durabilité culturelle ». Le théâtre permet plusieurs configurations, y compris un simple sol plat ou une disposition quadri-frontale. Un théâtre « super boîte », une salle d'activité, une galerie et deux « parcs de poche » au nord et au sud peuvent être reliés pour former un « spacieux tunnel dynamique » long de 135 m. Le planétarium « flotte comme une lune au-dessus de la bibliothèque », soutenu par quatre piliers penchés. Le large espace ouvert de la bibliothèque, conçu avec peu d'éléments structurels, peut contenir 220 000 volumes et offre 188 places assises.

Elevation drawings of the complex show the tilted roof that is also visible, in particular, in the image to the left—echoing the mountains in the distance.

Des élévations du complexe montrent le toit incliné, qui est également visible, notamment dans la photo de gauche – faisant écho aux montagnes au loin.

Aufrisse des Komplexes veranschaulichen die Neigung des Dachs, besonders deutlich auch links im Bild zu sehen – ein Echo des Gebirgszugs in der Ferne.

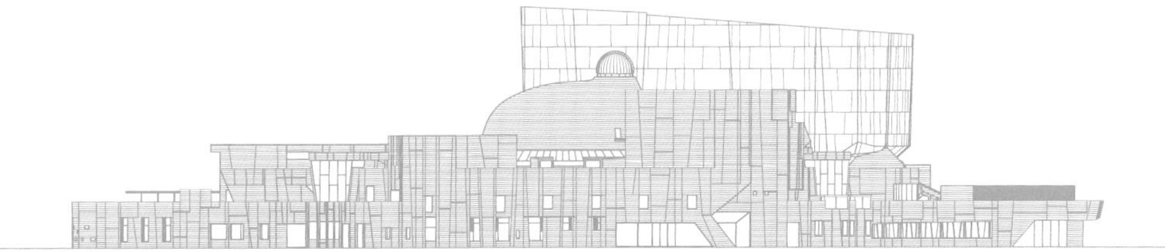

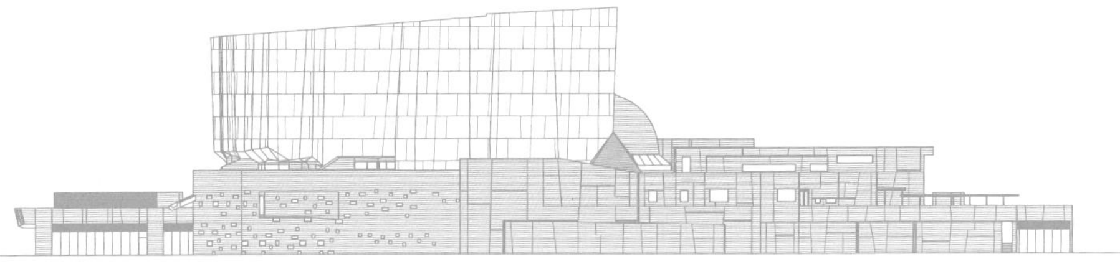

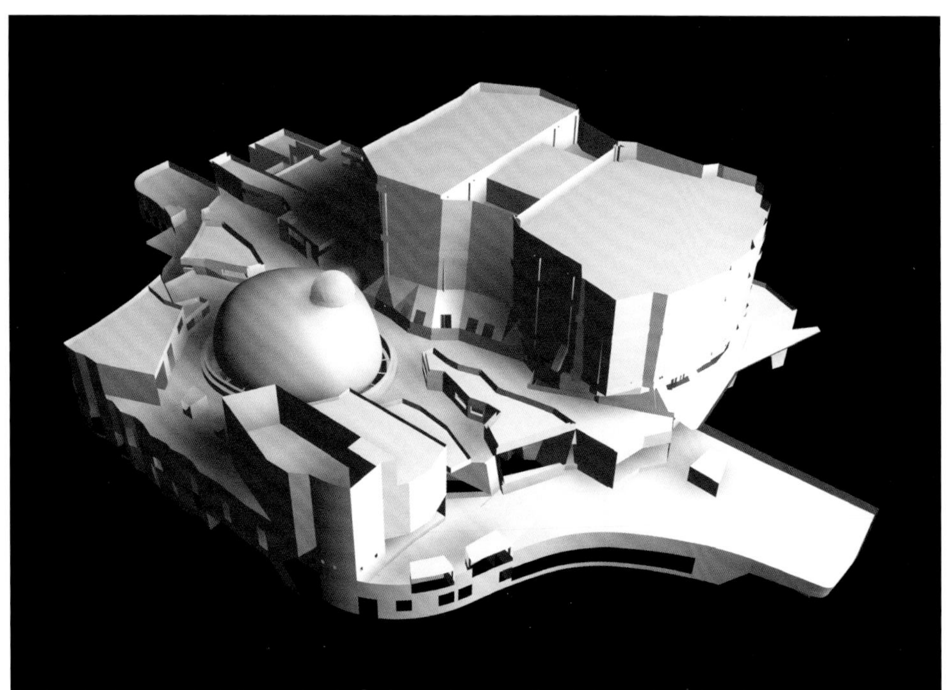

To the left, a model of the entire complex, with the main volume at the top, also visible in the image below.

Links ein Modell des Gesamtkomplexes mit dem zentralen Baukörper oben im Bild sowie auf einer Aufnahme unten.

À gauche, une maquette de l'ensemble du complexe avec, en haut, le volume principal, également visible sur la photo ci-dessous.

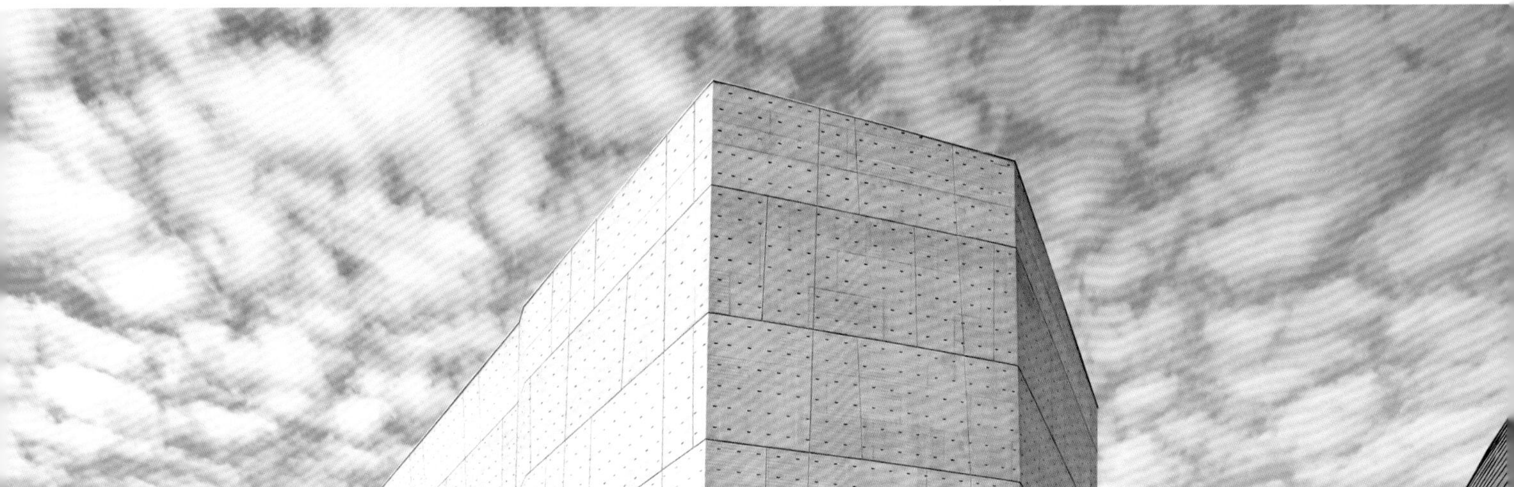

The building presents very large, essentially blank, concrete façades above ground level. Below, elevation drawings show the volume emerging from its environment.

Die oberirdischen Geschosse des Baus präsentieren sich mit monumentalen, zumeist fensterlosen Fassaden. Aufrisse unten illustrieren, wie sich der Baukörper aus seinem baulichen Kontext erhebt.

Au-dessus du niveau du sol, le bâtiment présente de très grandes façades en béton, aveugles pour la plupart. Ci-dessous, des élévations montrent le volume émergeant de son environnement.

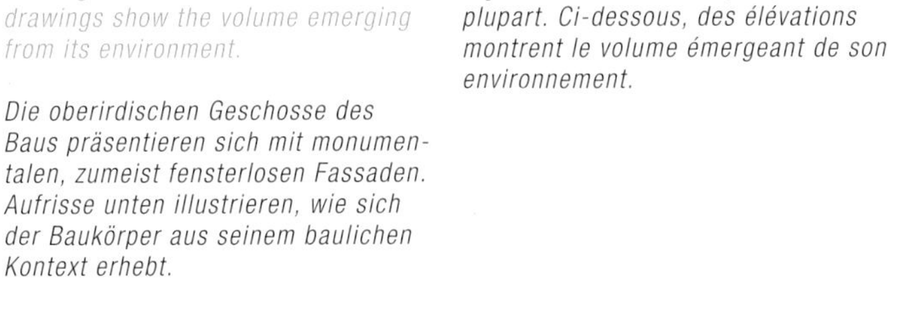

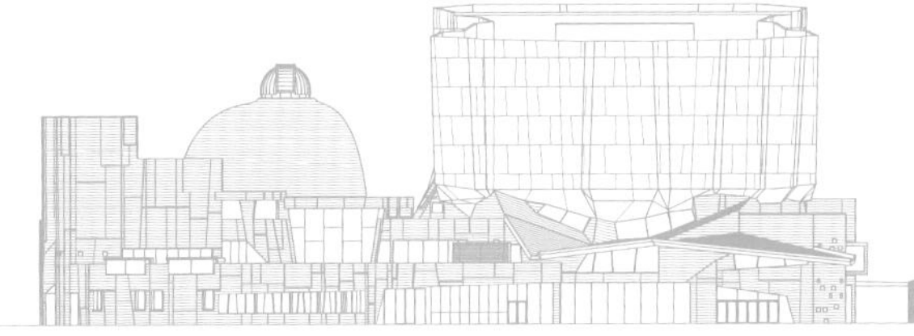

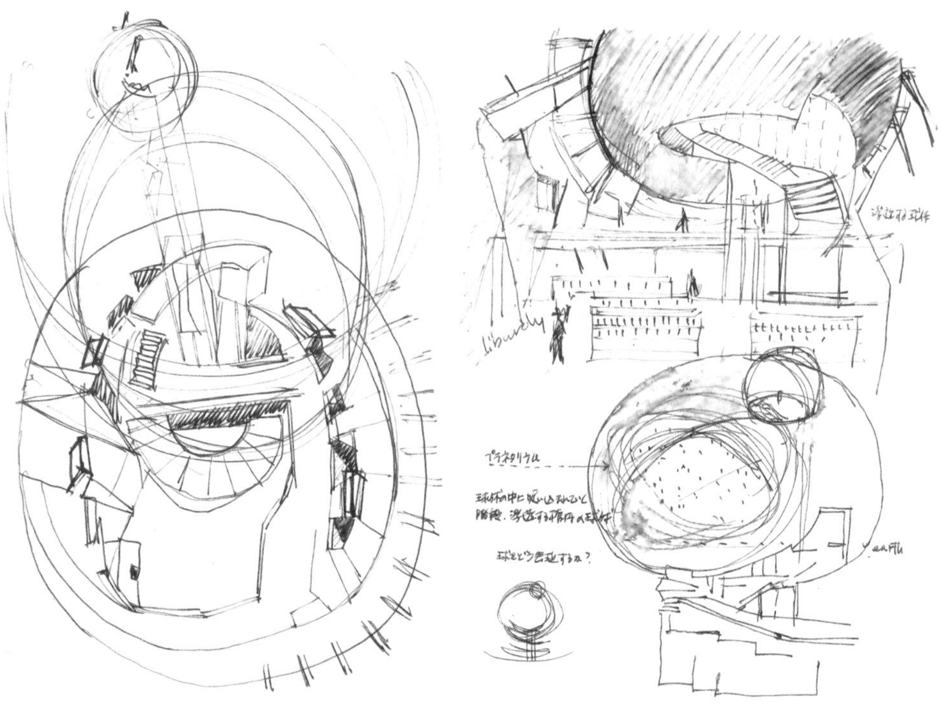

Sketches by the architect show the intricacy of the heart of the complex—also visible in the photo on the right page. Below, the main concert hall.

Skizzen des Architekten verdeutlichen die Komplexität des baulichen Kerns – auch auf der rechten Seite zu sehen. Unten der große Konzertsaal.

Des croquis de l'architecte montrent la complexité du cœur du complexe – également visible sur la photo de la page de droite. Ci-dessous, la grande salle de concert.

The library space appears as a spiraling concrete zone where wood and concrete are layered with the rows of books. Below, a lobby area and an acoustic room for music.

Der Bibliotheksbereich präsentiert sich als spiralförmige Zone aus Beton, kombiniert mit Holz und den Bücherreihen. Unten ein Foyer und ein Raum für Musik.

L'espace de la bibliothèque montre une zone de béton en spirale où le béton et le bois se mêlent aux rangées des livres. Ci-dessous, un foyer et une chambre acoustique pour la musique.

The complexity of the architectural design appears in images such as that to the left and also below, where planetarium space seems to open out onto the real sky.

Die Komplexität des architektonischen Entwurfs zeigt sich in Aufnahmen wie links und unten. Dort scheint sich ein Raum des Planetariums tatsächlich zum Himmel zu öffnen.

La complexité du concept architectural apparaît dans les photos ci-contre et ci-dessous, où l'espace du pla nétarium semble s'ouvrir sur le ciel réel.

Below, a section drawing of the whole building, with its regular elements contrasting markedly with domes and curves. To the right, the textured and angled concrete walls in an interior passage.

Unten ein Querschnitt durch den gesamten Bau, bei dem geradlinige Elemente auffällig mit Kuppeln und geschwungenen Linien kontrastieren. Rechts die ungewöhnlichen Texturen und schiefwinkligen Betonwände eines Korridors.

Ci-dessous, une coupe de l'ensemble du bâtiment, avec ses éléments rectilignes contrastant nettement avec les dômes et les courbes. Sur la page de droite, les murs en béton, texturés et obliques, d'un corridor.

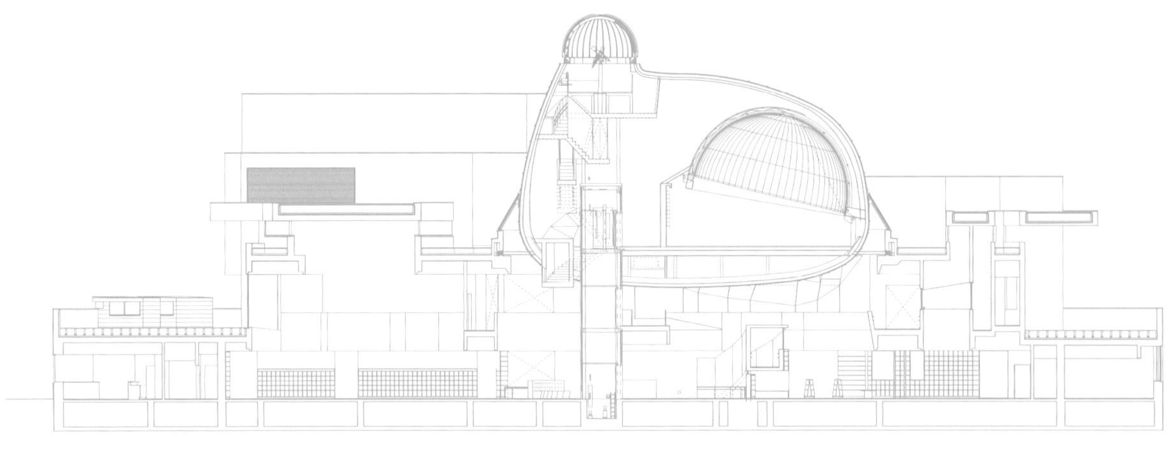

ALEJANDRO ARAVENA & ELEMENTAL

ELEMENTAL
Av. Los Conquistadores 1700, 25th Floor
Providencia / Santiago, RM 7520282 / Chile
Tel: +56 2753 3000 / Fax: +56 2753 3016
E-mail: info@elementalchile.cl
Web: www.elementalchile.cl

ALEJANDRO ARAVENA graduated as an architect from the Universidad Católica de Chile (UC) in 1992. Born in 1967, he studied history and theory at the Istituto Universitario di Architettura di Venezia (Italy, 1992–93). Aravena was a Visiting Professor at Harvard University (2000–05). He created Alejandro Aravena Arquitectos in 1994. In 2009 he became a member of the Pritzker Prize Jury and in 2010 was named International Fellow of RIBA. Since 2006 he has been Executive Director of Elemental, described as a "Do Tank affiliated to Universidad Católica and the Chilean Oil Company COPEC, its focus is the design and implementation of urban projects of social interest and public impact." Elemental is a group of architects that today includes Alejandro Aravena, **GONZALO ARTEAGA** (born in 1977), **DIEGO TORRES** (born in 1979), **JUAN IGNACIO CERDA** (born in 1980), and **VÍCTOR ODDÓ** (born in 1975). Aravena's architectural work includes the Mathematics (1998–99), Medical (2002–04), and Architecture (2004) Schools at UC (Santiago); Pirehueico Lake House (2003–04); Quinta Monroy Social Housing (Iquique, 2003–04); and the Siamese Towers at UC (Santiago, 2003–06), all in Chile. He also designed new facilities at St. Edward's University in Austin (Texas, USA, 2007–08). More recent and current work includes the Metropolitan Promenade and Children's Park for the Chilean Bicentennial (Santiago, Chile, 2010–12 / ongoing, published here); the Angelini Innovation Center at UC (Santiago, Chile, 2012–13); a building for Novartis in Shanghai (China, 2010–14); the reconstruction of the city of Constitución (Chile, 2010–15); the Tehran Stock Exchange (Iran, 2012–15); and the masterplan for the copper mining town of Calama (Chile, 2012–25).

ALEJANDRO ARAVENA, geboren 1967, machte 1992 seinen Abschluss in Architektur an der Universidad Católica de Chile (UC), studierte von 1992 bis 1993 Architekturgeschichte und -theorie am Instituto Universitario di Architettura di Venezia und war Gastprofessor an der Harvard University (2000–05). Sein Büro Alejandro Aravena Arquitectos gründete er 1994. Aravena ist seit 2009 Mitglied der Jury des Pritzker-Preises, wurde 2010 zum International Fellow des Royal Institute of British Architects ernannt und ist seit 2006 geschäftsführender Direktor von Elemental, einem „Do-Tank, der bei der Konzeption und Realisation städtebaulicher Projekte von sozialer und gesellschaftlicher Tragweite eng mit der Universidad Católica und dem chilenischen Erdölunternehmen COPEC zusammenarbeitet". Zu Elemental gehören außerdem **GONZALO ARTEAGA**, geboren 1977, **DIEGO TORRES**, geboren 1979, **JUAN IGNACIO CERDA**, geboren 1980, und **VICTOR ODDÓ**, geboren 1975. Projekte von Aravena sind u. a. die Institute für Mathematik (1998–99), Medizin (2002–04) und Architektur (2004) sowie die Torres Siamesas an der UC in Santiago, das Haus am Lago Pirehueico (2003–04) und das soziale Wohnungsbauprojekt Quinta Monroy (Iquique, 2003–04), alle in Chile. Aravana hat außerdem neue Einrichtungen für die St. Edward's University in Austin (Texas, 2007–08) entworfen. Aktuelle Projekte sind die hier publizierte Stadtpromenade samt Kinderpark, die zur 200-Jahrfeier der Unabhängigkeit Chiles entstand (Santiago, 2010–12), des Weiteren das Angelini-Innovationszentrum an der UC (Santiago, 2012–13), ein Neubau für Novartis in Shanghai (China, 2010–14), ein Stadtsanierungsprojekt in Constitución (Chile, 2010–15), die Teheraner Börse (Iran, 2012–15) und der Masterplan für die Kupferbergbaustadt Calama (Chile, 2012–25).

ALEJANDRO ARAVENA obtient un diplôme en architecture de l'Université catholique du Chili (UC) en 1992. Né en 1967, il étudie l'histoire et la théorie de l'architecture à l'université IUAV de Venise (1992–93). Aravena a été professeur invité à l'université Harvard (2000–05). Il crée Alejandro Aravena Arquitectos en 1994. En 2009, il devient membre du jury du prix Pritzker et, en 2010, il est nommé membre international du RIBA. Depuis 2006, il est directeur exécutif d'Elemental, « un groupe d'action affilié à l'Université catholique du Chili et la compagnie pétrolière chilienne COPEC qui a pour objectif de concevoir et d'implémenter des projets d'urbanisme d'intérêt social ayant un impact sur le public ». Elemental est un groupe d'architectes qui, outre Alejandro Aravena, réunit actuellement **GONZALO ARTEAGA** (né en 1977), **DIEGO TORRES** (né en 1979), **JUAN IGNACIO CERDA** (né en 1980) et **VÍCTOR ODDÓ** (né en 1975). L'œuvre architecturale d'Aravena comprend les facultés de mathématiques (1998–99), de médecine (2002–04) et d'architecture (2004) de l'UC (Santiago) ; la maison du lac Pirehueico (2003–04) ; les logements sociaux Quinta Monroy (Iquique, 2003–04) et les tours jumelles de l'UC (Santiago, 2003–06), tous au Chili. Il a également conçu les nouvelles installations de l'université St. Edward à Austin (Texas, 2007–08). Ses réalisations plus récentes ou en cours comprennent la Metropolitan Promenade et le parc des Enfants pour le bicentenaire du Chili (Santiago, 2010–12/en cours, présenté ici) ; le Centre d'innovation Anacleto Angelini à l'UC (Santiago, 2012–13) ; un bâtiment pour Novartis à Shanghai (2010–14) ; la reconstruction de la ville de Constitución (Chili, 2010–15) ; la Bourse de Téhéran (2012–15) et le plan directeur de la ville minière de Calama (Chili, 2012–25).

METROPOLITAN PROMENADE AND BICENTENNIAL CHILDREN'S PARK

Santiago, Chile, 2010–12 (ongoing)

Address: Av. Perú 1001, Recoleta, Santiago, Chile
Area: 3.8 hectares (Children's Park); 14 km (Promenade / ongoing)
Client: Parque Metropolitano - Junji. Cost: $3.8 million
Collaboration: Fernando García-Hudobro, Ricardo Torrejón, Víctor Oddó

The Santiago Metropolitan Park is located on San Cristobal Hill. In 1999, the architect Ricardo Torrejón proposed a project to transform an old agricultural water-way, the Canal del Carmen, which descends the same hill, into a 10-kilometer pedestrian promenade. This promenade was conceived to ease pedestrian access to the park, which was deemed to have too few visitors given its hilly location. In 2008, Junji, which is the National Daycare Center Service, was looking for a place to create a children's park. The architects made the steeply sloped site for the children's park into the first part of the Metropolitan Promenade, which, given its length, is the ongoing part of this project. Alejandro Aravena and Elemental, here, as in many of their other projects, have made use of circumstances to address a significant problem—the "historical debt of public space that Santiago has with its inhabitants."

Santiagos Stadtpark liegt auf dem San-Cristobal-Hügel. Der Architekt Ricardo Torrejón schlug 1999 vor, einen trockengelegten Bewässerungskanal, den Canal del Carmen, der den Hügel früher hinabfloss, in eine 10 km lange Fußgängerpromenade umzuwandeln. Auf diese Weise sollte der Park, dessen geringe Besucherzahlen man auf seine Hügellage zurückführte, für Fußgänger leichter zugänglich werden. Als der staatliche Verband der Kindertagesstätten (Junji) 2008 nach einem Standort für einen Park für Kinder suchte, entwarfen die Architekten den Hangspielplatz als Ausgangspunkt der Promenade. Aufgrund ihrer beträchtlichen Länge ist die Promenade noch nicht vollständig fertiggestellt. Alejandro Aravena und Elemental sprechen mit diesem wie auch mit anderen Projekten ein grundlegendes Problem der Stadtplanung an: die Tatsache, dass Santiago, so die Architekten, „seinen Einwohnern schon lange öffentlichen Raum schuldig ist".

Le parc métropolitain de Santiago est situé sur la colline de San Cristobal. En 1999, l'architecte Ricardo Torrejón propose un projet de transformation d'un ancien canal d'irrigation agricole, le canal del Carmen qui descend cette colline, en une promenade piétonne de 10 km. Cette promenade est conçue pour faciliter l'accès piéton-nier à un parc jugé trop peu fréquenté en raison de son terrain accidenté. En 2008, le département national des garderies d'enfants (Junji) cherche un endroit pour créer un terrain de jeux. Les architectes commencent par aménager le site en pente raide du terrain de jeux, première phase d'une promenade toujours en cours de réalisation, vu sa longueur. Ici, comme dans beaucoup de leurs projets, Alejandro Aravena et Elemental se servent de la situation pour répondre à un problème significatif – la « dette historique de Santiago à l'égard de ses habitants, en termes d'espace public ».

Alejandro Aravena has worked on significant university buildings, but here he is in a more playful mode with landscaping and areas designed for the general public and, above, for children in particular.

Alejandro Aravena hat bedeutende Bibliothekskomplexe entworfen, gibt sich hier jedoch spielerischer mit einer Landschaftsplanung und Gestaltung öffentlicher Räume, besonders für Kinder (oben).

Alejandro Aravena a travaillé sur d'importants bâtiments universitaires, mais il intervient ici sur un mode plus ludique, avec des aménagements paysagers et des espaces destinés au public et, ci-dessus, particulièrement aux enfants.

Although an obvious sense of design is at work in this park, the structures or fountains, like the one seen above and to the right, are clearly attractive to children.

Der Park wurde mit klarer Handschrift gestaltet, dabei sind Bauten und Brunnen, wie oben und rechts im Bild, bewusst auf Kinder zugeschnitten.

Bien qu'un sens évident du design soit à l'œuvre dans ce parc, les structures et les fontaines, comme celle montrée ci-dessus et ci-contre, attirent clairement les enfants.

A play area is circled by a wooden barrier, making access easier to control for parents, without creating a sense of being closed in.

Der Spielplatz ist mit einem Holzzaun eingefasst, was Eltern den Überblick über den Zugang erleichtert, ohne einengend zu wirken.

Une aire de jeu est entourée d'une barrière de bois qui permet aux parents de contrôler l'accès sans créer de sentiment d'enfermement.

ATELIER BOW-WOW

Atelier Bow-Wow
8–79 Suga-Cho
Shinjuku-ku
160–0018 Tokyo
Japan

Tel/Fax: +81 3 3226 5336
Web: www.bow-wow.jp

Atelier Bow-Wow was established in 1992 by Yoshiharu Tsukamoto and Momoyo Kaijima. **YOSHIHARU TSUKAMOTO** was born in 1965 in Tokyo and studied amongst others at the École d'architecture de Paris-Belleville (1987–88), before graduating from the Tokyo Institute of Technology (Doctorate in Engineering, 1994). He was a Visiting Associate Professor at UCLA (2007–08). **MOMOYO KAIJIMA** was born in 1969 in Tokyo, and graduated from Japan Women's University (1991), the Graduate School of the Tokyo Institute of Technology (1994), and studied at the ETH (Zurich, 1996–97). Their work includes the Hanamidori Cultural Center (Tokyo, Japan, 2005); the House and Atelier Bow-Wow (Tokyo, Japan, 2005); Mado Building (Tokyo, Japan, 2006); Pony Garden (Kanagawa, Japan, 2008); Machiya Guesthouse (Kanazawa, Japan, 2008); Mountain House (Nevada, USA, 2008); Four Boxes Gallery (Skive, Denmark; 2009); Machiya Tower (Tokyo, Japan, 2010); the BMW Guggenheim Lab (New York, New York, USA, 2010; Berlin, Germany, 2012, published here; Mumbai, India, 2012–13); and housing on Rue Rebière (Paris, France, 2012).

1992 gründeten Yoshiharu Tsukamoto und Momoyo Kaijima ihr Büro Atelier Bow-Wow. **YOSHIHARU TSUKAMOTO**, 1965 in Tokio geboren, studierte u. a. an der École d'Architecture (Paris, Belleville, UP8, 1987–88) und promovierte 1994 am Tokyo Institute of Technology in Bauingenieurwesen. 2007/08 war er Gastprofessor an der UCLA. **MOMOYO KAIJIMA** wurde 1969 in Tokio geboren und absolvierte ihr Studium an der Japan Women's University (1991), der Graduiertenfakultät des Tokyo Institute of Technology (1994) sowie der ETH Zürich (1996–97). Zu ihren Projekten zählen das Kulturzentrum Hanamidori (Tokio, 2005), Haus und Atelier Bow-Wow (Tokio, 2005), das Mado-Gebäude (Tokio, 2006), der Pony Garden (Kanagawa, Japan, 2008), das Gästehaus Machiya (Kanazawa, Japan, 2008), das Mountain House (Nevada, USA, 2008), die Four Boxes Gallery (Skive, Dänemark, 2009), der Machiya Tower (Tokio, 2010), das BMW Guggenheim Lab (New York, 2010; Berlin, 2012, hier vorgestellt; Mumbai, 2012–13) und ein Wohnbauprojekt an der Rue Rebière (Paris, 2012).

Atelier Bow-Wow a été créé en 1992 par Yoshiharu Tsukamoto et Momoyo Kaijima. Yoshiharu. Né en 1965 à Tokyo, **YOSHIHARU TSUKAMOTO** est diplômé de l'Institut de technologie de Tokyo (doctorat en ingénierie, 1994). Il a également étudié à l'École d'architecture de Paris-Belleville (Paris, 1987–88). Il a été professeur associé à UCLA (2007–08). Née en 1969 à Tokyo et diplômée de l'Université pour les femmes du Japon (1991) et de la faculté d'études supérieure de l'Institut de technologie de Tokyo (1994), **MOMOYO KAIJIMA** a étudié à l'ETH (Zurich, 1996–97). Leurs réalisations comprennent le Centre culturel Hanamidori (Tokyo, 2005) ; la maison et atelier Bow-Wow (Tokyo, 2005) ; l'immeuble Mado (Tokyo, 2006) ; le Pony Garden (Kanagawa, Japon, 2008) ; la pension Machiya (Kanazawa, Japon, 2008) ; la Mountain House (Nevada, 2008) ; la galerie Four Boxes (Skive, Danemark, 2009) ; la tour Machiya (Tokyo, 2010) ; le BMW Guggenheim Lab (New York, 2010 ; Berlin, 2012, présenté ici; Bombay, 2012–13) et des logements rue Rebière (Paris, 2012).

18 2ND AVE

BMW GUGGENHEIM LAB

New York, New York, USA, 2011; Berlin, Germany, 2012; Mumbai, India, 2012–13

Address: not applicable. Area: 184 m². Client: The Solomon R. Guggenheim Foundation. Cost: not disclosed. Collaboration: Mirai Morita, Masatoshi Hirai, Fiedler Marciano Architecture (New York), Magma Architecture (Berlin)

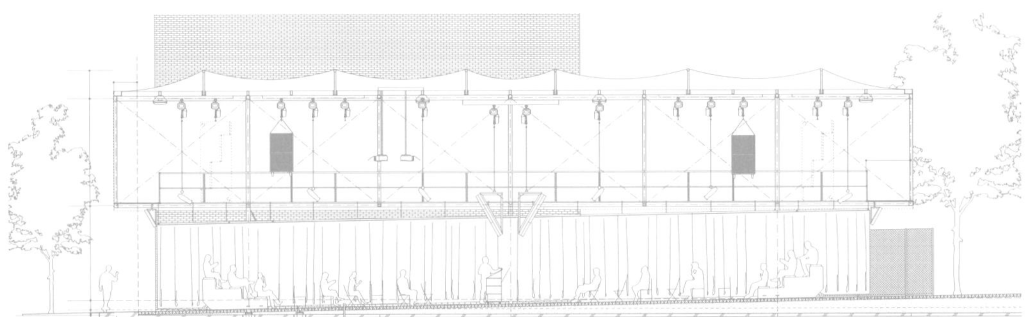

This project is the result of collaboration between the automobile manufacturer BMW and the Guggenheim Museum in New York. Part urban think tank, part community center and public gathering space, the **BMW GUGGENHEIM LAB** is a global initiative aimed at raising awareness of urban challenges. It is intended to travel to different cities, at a rate of nine locations in six years, taking into account local concerns and events. The first three-city cycle began in New York, Berlin, and Mumbai. The curators of the museum were looking for a "non-iconic" design that can be readily disassembled for transport. Air-conditioning was eliminated through plans to mount the project in "moderate" seasons. The site in New York, intended to include an exhibit, workshop, and lecture area, as well as a café and storage, was only one third of the area originally envisaged. Set between the Lower East Side and the East Village, the Lab hosted 56 000 visitors over its 10-week existence. The architects explain: "We envisioned a super-light structure that hovers above ground in between buildings. The super-light structural frame was created with carbon-fiber reinforced plastic, which has the same strength as steel with one sixth of the weight. Steel was used in combination for columns to overcome safety and fire regulations. The space under the structure is lit uniformly with light filtering through polyester roof membrane. Sides of the top half of the structure are clad with double-layer polyester mesh creating a moiré effect. At ground level, there are just six columns and curtains, resulting in architecture without a floor or walls." From June 15 to July 29, 2012, the structure was recreated in Prenzlauer Berg, Berlin, and between December 2012 and January 2013 in Mumbai, India.

Das Projekt entstand als Kooperation zwischen BMW und dem Guggenheim Museum, New York. Das **BMW GUGGENHEIM LAB** ist urbaner Thinktank, Kommunikationszentrum sowie Versammlungsort und versteht sich als eine globale Initiative, die ein Bewusstsein für drängende urbane Fragen schaffen will. Das Projekt wird in sechs Jahren an neun Standorte wandern und jeweils lokal relevante Themen und Programme aufgreifen. Die Kuratoren wollten einen Entwurf, der nicht als „Highlight" auftritt und zu Transportzwecken leicht demontierbar ist. Eine Klimatisierung des Baus ist nicht nötig, da das Projekt bei „moderater" Witterung realisiert wird. Der Standort in New York bot Raum für Ausstellungen, Workshops, Vorträge, ein Café sowie Lagermöglichkeiten und kam mit rund einem Drittel der ursprünglich vorgesehenen Fläche aus. Realisiert zwischen Lower East Side und East Village hatte das Lab in nur zehn Wochen rund 56 000 Besucher. Die Architekten erklären: „Unser Konzept ist eine ultraleichte Konstruktion, die zwischen Gebäuden über dem Boden zu schweben scheint. Das ultraleichte Tragwerk wurde mit kohlenstofffaserverstärktem Kunststoff realisiert und ist so belastbar wie Stahl bei nur einem Sechstel des Gewichts. Aufgrund von Sicherheits- und Brandschutzvorschriften kommt auch Stahl zum Einsatz, etwa bei den Stützen. Der Innenraum wird durch ein Dach aus Polyestermembran gleichmäßig belichtet. Seitlich ist der Aufbau mit einem doppellagigen Polyesternetz umhüllt, wodurch Moiréeeffekte entstehen. Die untere Zone der Konstruktion besteht lediglich aus sechs Stützen und Vorhängen – eine Architektur ohne Boden und Wände." Vom 15. Juni bis 29. Juli 2012 stand der Bau im Berliner Stadtteil Prenzlauer Berg; von Dezember 2012 bis Januar 2013 war er in Mumbai, Indien, zu sehen.

Ce projet est le fruit d'une collaboration entre le constructeur BMW et le musée Guggenheim de New York. Cellule de réflexion sur l'urbanisme et lieu de réunions publiques, le **BMW GUGGENHEIM LAB** est une initiative mondiale de sensibilisation aux défis urbains. Il voyagera dans différentes villes, au rythme de neuf lieux sur six ans, et prendra en compte les préoccupations et les évènements locaux. Le premier cycle a démarré avec New York, Berlin et Bombay. Les curateurs voulaient une structure « non emblématique » et facilement démontable. Pour éliminer la climatisation, le projet sera monté en saison « tempérée ». Le site de New York, prévu pour accueillir une exposition, un atelier, un espace de lecture, un café et des réserves, n'a occupé qu'un tiers de la surface initialement prévue. Entre Lower East Side et East Village, le Lab a reçu 56 000 visiteurs en dix semaines. Les architectes ont imaginé « un bâtiment ultra-léger, flottant au-dessus du sol entre les immeubles. La structure ultralégère est en plastique renforcé de fibre de carbone, d'une résistance équivalente à l'acier pour un sixième de son poids. L'acier a été utilisé dans les colonnes pour répondre aux normes de sécurité et anti-incendie. L'espace sous la structure est éclairé par la lumière filtrée par la membrane en polyester du toit. Les façades latérales de la moitié supérieure du bâtiment sont habillées d'un treillis en polyester double-couche, créant un effet moiré. Au sol, six piliers isolés et des rideaux créent une architecture sans plancher ni murs ». Le bâtiment a été remonté du 15 juin au 29 juillet 2012 à Berlin, et entre décembre 2012 et janvier 2013 à Bombay.

The simple, essentially industrial vocabulary employed by the architects is evident in the image to the right, where openness is also obvious. Above, section drawings show materials used and a careful attention to individual objects and spaces.

Die schlichte, eher industrielle Formensprache der Architekten zeigt sich rechts im Bild; hier wird auch die Offenheit des Entwurfs deutlich. Ein Aufriss oben illustriert Materialien und durchdachte Planung der einzelnen Objekte und Bereiche.

Le vocabulaire simple et essentiellement industriel utilisé par les architectes, et l'ouverture de l'espace, sont évidents dans la photo ci-contre. Ci-dessus, des coupes montrent les matériaux utilisés et l'attention portée aux objets et espaces individuels.

Left, an interior view of the New York installation of the Lab. Below, an overall site plan of the structure and its surrounding space.

Links eine Innenansicht des Labs am New Yorker Standort. Der Überblicksplan unten zeigt den Bau in seinem Umfeld.

Ci-contre, une vue intérieure de l'installation du Lab à New York. Ci-dessous, un plan de situation du bâtiment dans son espace environnant.

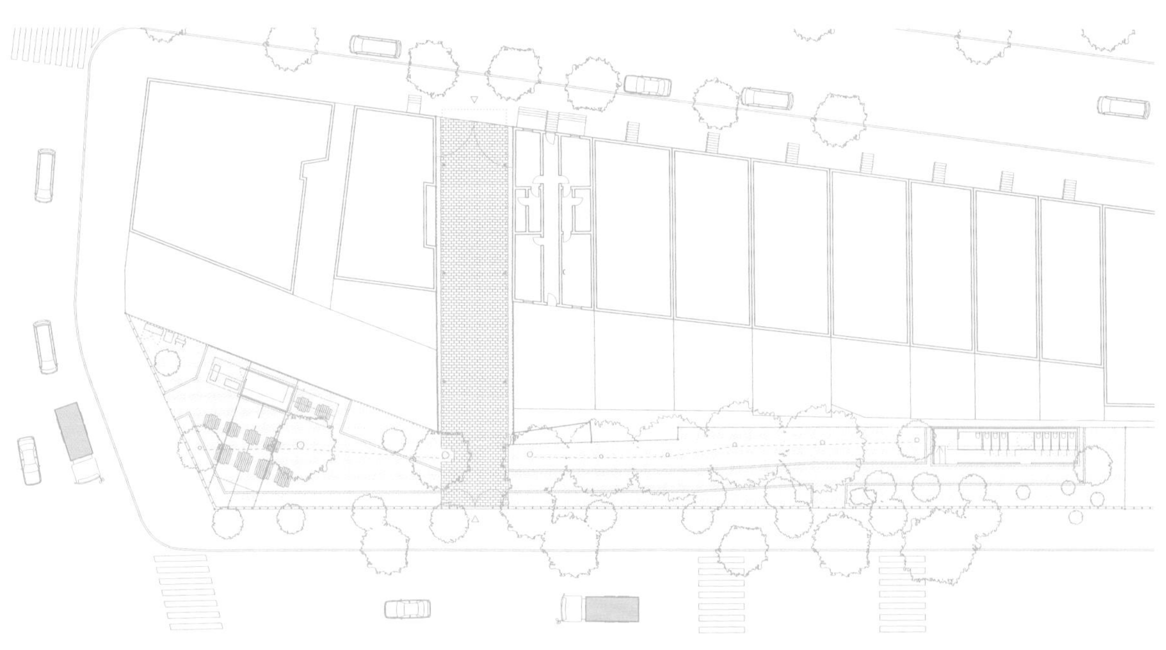

The Lab, as seen from Houston Street, offers outdoor space that is partially beneath the building.

Das Lab von der Houston Street aus gesehen; Freiflächen liegen teilweise unterhalb der Konstruktion.

Le Lab, vu depuis Houston Street, offre un espace en extérieur situé en partie sous le bâtiment.

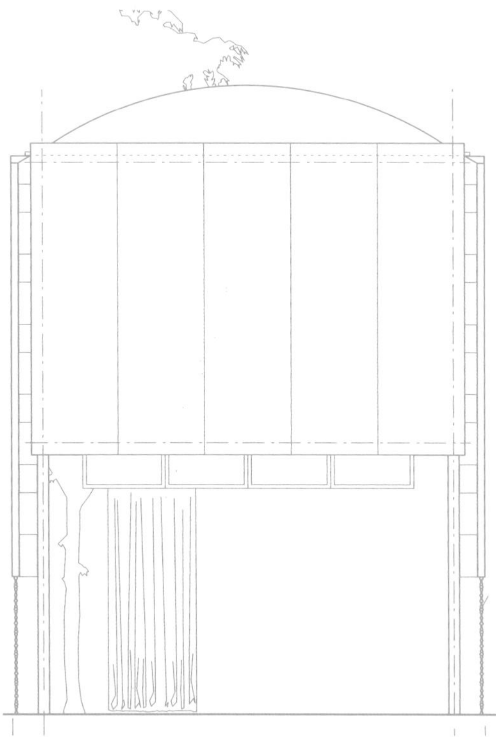

In the Berlin location, an elevation drawing showing the PVC materials employed. Also on this page, two interior views showing the open space beneath the main volume.

Ein Aufriss des Baus am Berliner Standort illustriert den Einsatz verschiedener PVC-Stoffe. Ebenfalls auf dieser Seite: zwei Ansichten der offenen Zone unterhalb der Konstruktion.

Sur le site de Berlin, une élévation montrant les matériaux PVC employés. Sur cette même page, deux vues intérieures montrant l'espace ouvert sous le volume principal.

An exterior view of the Berlin location shows how the polyester curtains allow for space to be closed off while still remaining open to the exterior.

Eine Ansicht am Berliner Standort zeigt die Möglichkeit, den Raum mit Polyestervorhängen abzuschirmen und dennoch durchlässig zum Außenraum zu halten.

Une vue extérieure du site de Berlin montre comment les rideaux en polyester permettent de fermer l'espace tout en le maintenant ouvert sur l'extérieur.

SHIGERU BAN

Shigeru Ban Architects
5–2–4 Matsubara
Setagaya-ku / Tokyo 156–0043 / Japan
Tel: +81 3 3324 6760 / Fax: +81 3 3324 6789
E-mail: tokyo@shigerubanarchitects.com
Web: www.shigerubanarchitects.com

Born in 1957 in Tokyo, **SHIGERU BAN** studied at SCI-Arc from 1977 to 1980. He then attended the Cooper Union School of Architecture, where he studied under John Hejduk (1980–82). He worked in the office of Arata Isozaki (1982–83), before founding his own firm in Tokyo in 1985. He has designed ephemeral structures such as his Paper Refugee Shelter made with plastic sheets and paper tubes for the United Nations High Commissioner for Refugees (UNHCR). He designed the Japanese Pavilion at Expo 2000 in Hanover. His work includes the Hanegi Forest Annex (Setagaya, Tokyo, Japan, 2004); Mul(ti)houses (Mulhouse, France, 2001–05); the Takatori Church (Kobe, Hyogo, Japan, 2005); the disaster relief Post-Tsunami Rehabilitation Houses (Kirinda, Hambantota, Sri Lanka, 2005); the Papertainer Museum (Seoul Olympic Park, Songpa-Gu, South Korea, 2006); the Nicolas G. Hayek Center (Tokyo, 2007); the Paper Teahouse (London, 2008); Haesley Nine Bridges Golf Clubhouse (Yeoju, South Korea, 2009); the Paper Tube Tower (London, UK, 2009); and the Metal Shutter Houses on West 19th Street in New York (New York, USA, 2010). He installed his Paper Temporary Studio on top of the Centre Pompidou in Paris to work on the new Centre Pompidou-Metz (Metz, France, 2010). Recent work includes the Camper Pavilion (Alicante, Spain; Sanya, China; Miami, Florida, USA; Lorient, France, prefabrication June to September 2011, published here); Kobe Kushinoya (Osaka, Japan, 2011); L'Aquila Temporary Concert Hall (L'Aquila, Italy, 2011); Container Temporary Housing, disaster relief project for the east Japan earthquake and tsunami (Miyagi, Japan, 2011); the Camper NY SoHo store (New York, USA, 2012); Tamedia (Zurich, Switzerland, 2011–13); and the Swatch Group Headquarters and Production Facility (Bienne, Switzerland, 2012–14).

SHIGERU BAN, 1957 in Tokio geboren, studierte von 1977 bis 1980 am Southern California Institute of Architecture (SCI-Arc). Anschließend besuchte er die Cooper Union School of Architecture, wo er bei John Hejduk studierte (1980–82). Bevor er 1985 sein eigenes Büro in Tokio gründete, arbeitete er bei Arata Isozaki (1982–83). Ban entwarf temporäre Bauten, etwa Flüchtlingsquartiere aus Papier, die er aus Plastikplanen und Papprröhren für das UN-Flüchtlingskommissariat (UNHCR) realisierte. Er plante den Japanischen Pavillon für die Expo 2000 in Hannover. Zu seinen Entwürfen zählen eine Erweiterung der Wohnanlage Hanegi Forest (Setagaya, Tokio, 2004), Mul(ti)houses (Mulhouse, Frankreich, 2001–05), die Takatori-Kirche (Kobe, Hyogo, Japan, 2005), Häuser für die Katastrophenhilfe nach dem großen Tsunami (Kirinda, Hambantota, Sri Lanka, 2005), das Papertainer Museum (Olympiapark Seoul, Songpa-Gu, Südkorea, 2006), das Nicolas G. Hayek Center (Tokio, 2007), das Paper Teahouse (London, 2008), das Clubhaus für den Haesley Nine Bridges Golfclub (Yeoju, Südkorea, 2009), der Paper Tube Tower (London, 2009) und die Metal Shutter Houses an der West 19th Street in New York (2010). Auf dem Dach des Centre Georges Pompidou in Paris hatte Ban sich ein temporäres Atelier aus Papprröhren eingerichtet, um dort am neuen Centre Pompidou Metz (2010) arbeiten zu können. Jüngere Projekte sind der Camper-Pavillon (Alicante, Spanien; Sanya, China; Miami, Florida; Lorient, Frankreich, Vorfertigung Juni–September 2011, hier vorgestellt), Kobe Kushinoya (Osaka, Japan, 2011), ein temporärer Konzertsaal in L'Aquila (Italien, 2011), temporäre Container-Notunterkünfte für das Erdbeben- und Tsunamigebiet in Ostjapan (Miyagi, 2011), der Camper Store in SoHo (New York, 2012), Tamedia (Zürich, 2011–13) sowie die Firmenzentrale und neue Fertigungsgebäude für die Swatch-Gruppe (Biel, Schweiz, 2012–14).

Né à Tokyo en 1957, **SHIGERU BAN** étudie au SCI-Arc (1977–80) puis suit l'enseignement de John Hejduk à la Cooper Union School of Architecture (1980–82). Il travaille ensuite dans l'agence d'Arata Isozaki (1982–83) avant de créer sa propre agence à Tokyo, en 1985. Il réalise des structures éphémères, comme son Paper Refugee Shelter en feuilles de plastique et tubes de carton pour le Haut Commissariat des Nations Unies pour les réfugiés (UNHCR) et conçoit le pavillon japonais pour Expo 2000, à Hanovre. Ses réalisations comprennent l'annexe Hanegi Forest (Setagaya, Tokyo, 2004) ; l'ensemble de logements sociaux Mul(ti)houses (Mulhouse, 2001–05) ; l'église de Takatori (Kobé, 2005) ; les Post-Tsunami Rehabilitation Houses pour les sinistrés du tsunami (Kirinda, Hambantota, Sri Lanka, 2005) ; le Papertainer Museum (parc Olympique de Séoul, Songpa-Gu, Corée-du-Sud, 2006) ; le Centre Nicolas G. Hayek (Tokyo, 2007) ; le Paper Teahouse (Londres, 2008) ; le Haesley Nine Bridges Golf Clubhouse (Yeoju, Corée-du-Sud, 2009) ; la tour Paper Tube (Londres, 2009) et l'ensemble Metal Shutter Houses sur la 19e Rue Ouest, à New York (2010). Il installe un atelier provisoire, le Paper Temporary Studio, au sommet du Centre Pompidou-Paris, pour travailler au projet du nouveau Centre Pompidou-Metz (Metz, 2010). Ses réalisations récentes comprennent le pavillon Camper (Alicante ; Sanya, Chine ; Miami ; Lorient, préfabrication de juin à septembre 2011, présenté ici) ; le restaurant Kobe Kushinoya (Osaka, 2011) ; la salle de concert provisoire de L'Aquila (L'Aquila, Italie, 2011) ; Container Temporary Housing, logements d'urgence pour les sinistrés du séisme et du tsunami de 2011 (Miyagi, Japon, 2011) ; la boutique Camper NY SoHo (New York, 2012) ; le siège de Tamedia (Zurich, 2011–13) et le siège et Centre de production du groupe Swatch (Bienne, Suisse, 2012–14).

CAMPER
CAMPER
VOYAGE

CAMPER PAVILION

Alicante, Spain; Sanya, China; Miami, Florida, USA; Lorient, France: prefabrication June to September 2011

Address: not applicable
Area: 250 m². Client: Camper. Cost: not disclosed
Collaboration: Jean de Gastines, Marc Ferrand

This is a paper tube structure, like others that Shigeru Ban has created in the past. It is designed to be assembled and dismantled easily in order to travel to marinas around the world where the yacht ports are located. There are four different diameters of paper tubes, which can be nested inside each other to minimize the bulk of the materials when they are shipped. The pavilion has a round floor plan and a membrane roof, assuring protection from the elements. With its Camper flag and basic form, the structure might recall military tents of another era although, clearly, the architect's intent and design are very much of this time. The ephemeral nature of the structure imposes certain constraints but also liberates the architecture from the requirements of more permanent designs.

Der Bau ist eine Konstruktion aus Pappröhren, wie Shigeru Ban sie bereits in der Vergangenheit realisierte. Der Entwurf ist leicht auf- und abbaubar, um in Jachthäfen in aller Welt errichtet werden zu können. Die Pappröhren mit vier unterschiedlichen Durchmessern lassen sich zur Minimierung des Transportvolumens ineinander schieben. Der Pavillon mit rundem Grundriss hat ein Membrandach, das vor den Elementen schützt. Mit der Camper-Flagge und seiner schlichten Grundform erinnert der Pavillon an historische Militärzelte, obwohl Motivation und Entwurf des Architekten deutlich zeitgenössisch sind. Die temporäre Natur des Baus bringt gewisse Einschränkungen mit sich, befreit die Architektur jedoch auch von vielen Anforderungen, denen dauerhaftere Bauprojekte unterliegen.

Il s'agit d'une structure en tubes de carton, similaire à d'autres déjà créées par Shigeru Ban et conçue de façon à être facilement montée et démontée, pour son transport dans des ports de plaisance à travers le monde. Les tubes emboîtables, de quatre diamètres différents, permettent de réduire le volume à transporter. Le pavillon, d'un plan circulaire, est protégé contre les éléments par un toit en membrane. Avec son drapeau Camper et sa forme simple, la structure peut rappeler les tentes militaires d'une autre époque, mais le propos et le design sont clairement actuels. La nature éphémère de la structure impose des contraintes, mais libère aussi les architectes des impératifs dictés par des projets plus pérennes.

The structure is open on all sides, which certainly encourages visitors to enter. Irregular spacing of the columns indicates the preferred entry points.

Der Bau ist zu allen Seiten offen, was Besucher zum Eintreten einlädt. Der unregelmäßige Säulenabstand deutet Haupteingangszonen an.

La structure est ouverte sur tous les côtés, encourageant assurément les visiteurs à entrer. L'espacement irrégulier des colonnes indique les points d'entrée privilégiés.

The gently sloping membrane roof of the pavilion and its paper tube columns provide shelter for the Camper installation in its Alicante setting.

Das sanft geneigte Membrandach des Baus und Säulen aus Pappröhren definieren einen schützenden Raum für den Camper-Pavillon an seinem Standort in Alicante.

La toiture en membrane légèrement en pente du pavillon et ses colonnes de carton fournissent un abri pour l'installation de Camper sur son site d'Alicante.

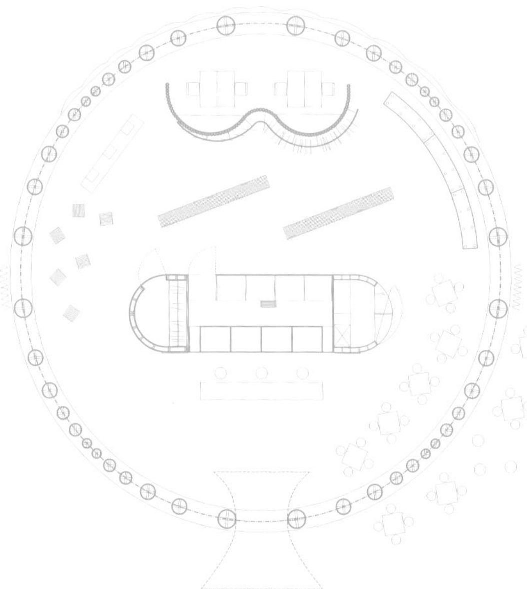

To the left, a plan of the circular structure. Below, retail space is partially defined by an undulating paper tube wall. To the right, the café area looking out on the sea.

Links ein Grundriss des Rundbaus. Der Verkaufsraum (unten) wird teilweise von einer geschwungenen Wand aus Pappröhren definiert. Rechts das Café mit Blick aufs Meer.

Ci-contre, un plan de la structure circulaire. Ci-dessous, l'espace commercial est en partie délimité par un mur ondulant en tubes de carton. Page de droite, l'espace du café face à la mer.

BENTHEM CROUWEL ARCHITECTS

Benthem Crouwel Architects
Generaal Vetterstraat 61
1059 BT Amsterdam
The Netherlands

Tel: +31 206 42 01 05
Fax: +31 206 46 53 54
E-mail: bca@benthemcrouwel.nl
Web: www.benthemcrouwel.nl

Born in Amsterdam in 1953, Mels Crouwel received his M.Arch degree from the Delft University of Technology in 1978. The following year he founded **BENTHEM CROUWEL ARCHITECTS** in Amsterdam, with Jan Benthem. Together with their Partners—Marcel Blom, Joost Vos, Marten Wassmann, and Markus Sporer—Benthem and Crouwel have offices in Amsterdam and in Aachen, Germany. In 1986 Benthem Crouwel were named master architects for Amsterdam's Schiphol Airport, in collaboration with NACO (Netherlands Airport Consultants). Their work includes the restoration and expansion of the Anne Frank House (Amsterdam, 1999); the adaptive reuse of the former Thomas de Beer textile mill in Tilburg as the De Pont Museum of Contemporary Art (1992/2003); Las Palmas Cultural and Commercial Center (Rotterdam, 2008); Deutsches Bergbau Museum (Bochum, 2009); the Stedelijk Museum (Amsterdam, 2007–12, published here); the Ziggo Dome (Amsterdam, 2012), a 17 000-seat concert venue in Amsterdam's ArenA Boulevard; and the Kulturbau and Forum Mittelrhein in Koblenz (Germany, 2013), a project that redevelops the city's central square, all in the Netherlands unless stated otherwise.

Mels Crouwel, geboren 1952 in Amsterdam, absolvierte seinen M. Arch. an der Technischen Universität von Delft (1978). Im Jahr darauf gründete er mit Jan Benthem das Büro **BENTHEM CROUWEL ARCHITECTS**. Mit ihren Partnern Marcel Blom, Joost Vos, Marten Wassmann und Markus Sperer betreiben Benthem und Crouwel Büros in Amsterdam und Aachen. Seit dem Entwurf für den Flughafen Schiphol (1986) in Zusammenarbeit mit NACO (Netherlands Airport Consultants) gelten Benthem Crouwel als Meister ihres Fachs. Projekte des Büros sind u. a. das Anne-Frank-Haus (Amsterdam, 1999), die Umgestaltung der ehemaligen Textilfabrik Thomas de Beer in Tilburg zum De Pont Museum für zeitgenössische Kunst (1992/2003), das Kultur- und Geschäftszentrum Las Palmas (Rotterdam, 2008), das Deutsche Bergbau-Museum (Bochum, 2009), das hier publizierte Stedelijk Museum (Amsterdam, 2007–12), die Ziggo-Dome-Mehrzweckarena im Amsterdamer ArenA Boulevard mit 17 000 Plätzen (2012) sowie das Forum Mittelrhein und der Kulturbau (2013), zwei Projekte zur Umstrukturierung des Koblenzer Zentralplatzes.

Né à Amsterdam en 1953, Mels Crouwel obtient son M.Arch de l'Université de technologie de Delft en 1978 et fonde **BENTHEM CROUWEL ARCHITECTS** l'année suivante à Amsterdam, avec Jan Benthem. Avec leurs partenaires – Marcel Blom, Joost Vos, Marten Wassmann et Markus Sporer – Benthem et Crouwel ont des bureaux à Amsterdam et à Aix-la-Chapelle. En 1986, Benthem Crouwel sont choisis comme maîtres d'œuvre de l'aéroport d'Amsterdam-Schiphol, en collaboration avec NACO (Netherlands Airport Consultants). Leurs réalisations comprennent la restauration et l'extension de la maison Anne Frank (Amsterdam, 1999) ; la reconversion de l'ancienne usine textile Thomas de Beer, à Tilburg, en musée d'art contemporain, le musée De Pont (1992/2003) ; le Centre culturel et commercial Las Palmas (Rotterdam, 2008) ; le Musée allemand de la mine (Bochum, 2009) ; le musée Stedelijk (Amsterdam, 2007–12, présenté ici) ; le stade Ziggo Dome (Amsterdam, 2012) ; une nouvelle salle de concert de 17 000 places, sur ArenA Boulevard à Amsterdam et le Forum Mittelrhein-Kulturbau, un réaménagement de la place centrale de la ville de Coblence (Allemagne, 2013), tous au Pays-Bas, sauf mention contraire.

schacht

STEDELIJK MUSEUM

Amsterdam, The Netherlands, 2007–12

Address: Museumplein 10, Amsterdam, The Netherlands, +31 20 573 29 11, www.stedelijk.nl
Area: 9500 m² (10 000 m², 1895 building). Client: City of Amsterdam
Cost: not disclosed. Collaboration: Joost Vos

Completed in 1895, the original **STEDELIJK MUSEUM** building was designed by A. W. Weissman. Benthem Crouwel added a six-story new building including temporary exhibition galleries, visitor services, public amenities, a library, and offices. The main entrance of the museum was moved to the former rear of the old museum, on the lawn of the Museumplein, not far from the Van Gogh Museum and the Rijksmuseum. The smooth white shape of the added structure, with its fully glazed ground-floor level, has earned it the nickname of "the Bathtub." The white façade is made with a composite material called Twaron fiber, which is five times as strong as steel and does not melt in fire. The architect Mels Crouwel states: "The Stedelijk Museum of Willem Sandberg, the Director who put the museum on the international map, was our starting point. He stripped the interior of decoration and had it painted white, creating a neutral background for art. Our plan for the exterior is based on retaining the 19th-century architecture, adding 21st-century technology and painting everything in Sandberg white." Rising to the cornice line of the existing building, the roof of the new structure creates a sheltered outdoor plaza at ground level.

A. W. Weissmanns **STEDELIJK MUSEUM** wurde 1895 fertiggestellt. Benthem Crouwel erweiterten das historische Gebäude um einen sechsgeschossigen Anbau, in dem u. a. ein Restaurant mit Terrasse, eine Bibliothek, Ausstellungsräume und der Besucherservice untergebracht sind. Der Haupteingang wurde auf die Rückseite und damit an den Museumplein verlegt, unweit des Van Gogh Museums und des Rijksmuseums. Die weiße, glatte Oberfläche hat dem Anbau mit dem verglasten Erdgeschoss den Spitznamen „Badewanne" eingebracht. Die Fassade besteht aus dem Verbundwerkstoff Twaron, der fünfmal stabiler ist als Stahl und im Falle eines Brandes nicht schmilzt. Mels Crouwel zum Projekt: „Ausgangspunkt war für uns das Stedelijk unter der Leitung von Willem Sandberg, der dem Museum zu seinem internationalen Ruf verhalf. Er entfernte dekorative Elemente aus den Innenräumen, ließ sie weiß streichen und schuf einen neutralen Präsentationsrahmen für die Kunst. Mit unserem Entwurf erhalten wir die historische Bausubstanz aus dem 19. Jahrhundert, erweitern sie um Technologien des 21. Jahrhunderts und geben dem Ganzen einen weißen Sandberg'schen Anstrich." Das weit auskragende Dach des Anbaus reicht bis zum Dachgesims des alten Gebäudes und lässt einen geschützten Museumsvorplatz entstehen.

Conçu par A. W. Weissman, le bâtiment du **MUSÉE STEDELIJK** a été achevé en 1895. Benthem Crouwel y a ajouté un nouveau bâtiment de six niveaux avec des salles d'expositions temporaires, des services d'accueil et des équipements pour le public, une bibliothèque et des bureaux. L'entrée principale du musée a été déplacée vers l'arrière de l'ancien musée, sur la pelouse de la place Museumplein, pas très loin du musée Van Gogh et du Rijksmuseum. La forme lisse et blanche du bâtiment, avec son rez-de-chaussée entièrement vitré, lui a valu le surnom de « baignoire ». La façade blanche est en Twaron, une fibre composite infusible et cinq fois plus solide que l'acier. L'architecte Mels Crouwel explique : « Nous sommes partis du musée Stedelijk de Willem Sandberg, le directeur qui lui a donné une envergure internationale. Il a débarrassé l'intérieur de sa décoration et l'a repeint en blanc, donnant ainsi un contexte neutre aux œuvres d'art. Notre projet pour l'extérieur consiste à conserver l'architecture du XIXe siècle, y ajouter la technologie du XXIe siècle et tout peindre avec le blanc de Sandberg. » Le toit du nouveau bâtiment, situé au niveau de la corniche de l'ancien, crée une place abritée au niveau du sol.

Critics have likened the new building to a bathtub in its overall form. The new wing affirms the modernity of the contents of the Stedelijk Museum, which is located next to the Van Gogh Museum and not far from the Rijksmuseum.

Kritiker verglichen den Neubau wegen seiner Form mit einer Badwanne. Der neue Flügel unterstreicht den modernen Charakter der Sammlungen des Stedelijk Museum, das neben dem Van Gogh Museum und unweit des Rijksmuseums liegt.

Les critiques ont comparé la forme générale du nouveau bâtiment à une baignoire. La nouvelle aile exprime la modernité du contenu du musée Stedelijk, situé à côté du musée Van Gogh et non loin du Rijksmuseum.

Indoor spaces are calibrated to make a clear transition from the older building (below) to the newer one (seen above with part of the former exterior façade) without damaging the older structure.

Die Gestaltung der Innenräume wurde darauf abgestimmt, den Übergang vom Altbau (unten) zum Neubau (oben mit einem Teil der ehemaligen Außenfassade) zu markieren, ohne den Altbau zu beeinträchtigen.

Les espaces intérieurs sont calculés pour faire clairement la transition entre l'ancien bâtiment (ci-dessous) et le nouveau (ci-dessus, avec une partie de l'ancienne façade extérieure) sans nuire à l'ancienne structure.

Inside the new building, with views of the older brick façade of the original structure. A generous use of glazing and light-colored surfaces emphasizes the modernity of the architecture, and, by extension, of the works displayed in the museum.

Blick aus dem Neubau auf die Backsteinfassade des älteren Gebäudes. Großzügige Verglasung und helle Oberflächen unterstreichen den modernen Charakter der Architektur und der ausgestellten Werke.

L'intérieur du nouveau bâtiment, avec des vues de la façade de briques plus ancienne du bâtiment d'origine. Un large vitrage et des surfaces aux couleurs claires accentuent la modernité de l'architecture et, par extension, des œuvres exposées dans le musée.

CADAVAL & SOLÀ-MORALES

Cadaval & Solà-Morales
C. Avenir # 1 ppal 1a
Barcelona 08006
Spain

Tel: +34 934 14 37 14
Fax: +34 934 14 62 29
E-mail: studio@ca-so.com
Web: www.ca-so.com

Cadaval & Solà-Morales was founded in New York City in 2003 and moved to both Barcelona and Mexico City in 2005. **EDUARDO CADAVAL** was born in Mexico City in 1975. He holds a B.A. from the National University of Mexico (2000), and an M.Arch in Urban Design from Harvard University (2003). Before founding Cadaval & Solà-Morales, he worked for Abalos & Herreros in Madrid, and for Field Operations in New York. He is currently a Visiting Professor at the University of Pennsylvania's School of Design. **CLARA SOLÀ-MORALES** was born in Barcelona in 1975. She obtained her architecture degree at the ETSA Barcelona (2000), and obtained an M.Arch II from Harvard University (2003). Prior to establishing Cadaval & Solà-Morales she worked at TEN Arquitectos NY, and at the Harvard University Center for Urban Development Studies. Their work includes Casa X (Barcelona, Spain, 2010–12, published here); Tepoztlán Lounge (Tepoztlán, Morelos, Mexico, 2011–12, also published here); LMB Bungalows (Tepoztlán, Morelos, Mexico, 2013); Oport 1 House (Port de la Selva, Spain, 2013); Cordoba Housing Building (Mexico City, Mexico, 2013); and the San Sebastian House (Buenos Aires, Argentina, 2014).

Cadaval & Solà-Morales, gegründet 2003 in New York, zog 2005 nach Barcelona und Mexiko-Stadt um. **EDUARDO CADAVAL**, 1975 in Mexiko-Stadt geboren, absolvierte seinen B. A. an der Universidad Nacional Autónoma de México (2000) und einen M. Arch. in Stadtplanung an der Harvard University (2003). Bevor er Cadaval & Solà-Morales gründete, war er für Abalos & Herreros in Madrid sowie für Field Operations in New York tätig. Zurzeit ist Cadaval Gastprofessor an der School of Design der University of Pennsylvania. **CLARA SOLÀ-MORALES**, geboren 1975 in Barcelona, studierte Architektur an der ETSA Barcelona (2000) und absolvierte ihren M. Arch. am Center for Urban Development Studies der Harvard University. Vor der Gründung des Büros mit Cadaval arbeitete sie bei TEN Arquitectos NY und am Harvard University Center for Urban Development Studies. Projekte von Cadaval & Solà-Morales sind u. a. die Casa X (Tepoztlán, Morelos, Mexiko, 2013) und die Tepoztlán Lounge (Tepoztlán, 2011–12; beide hier publiziert), die LMB Bungalows (Tepoztlán, 2013), die Casa Oport 1 (Port de la Selva, Spanien, 2013), das Wohngebäude Cordoba (Mexiko-Stadt, 2013) und die Casa San Sebastian (Buenos Aires, 2014).

Créé à New York en 2003, Cadaval & Solà-Morales déménage à Barcelone et Mexico en 2005. Né à Mexico en 1975, **EDUARDO CADAVAL** possède un B.A. de l'Université nationale du Mexique (2000) et un M.Arch en design urbain de Harvard (2003). Avant de fonder Cadaval & Solà-Morales, il travaille pour Abalos & Herreros à Madrid et pour Field Operations à New York. Il est actuellement professeur invité de la faculté de design de l'université de Pennsylvanie. **CLARA SOLÀ-MORALES** est née à Barcelone en 1975. Elle est diplômée en architecture de l'ETSA de Barcelone (2000) et a obtenu un M.Arch II à Harvard (2003). Avant la fondation de Cadaval & Solà-Morales, elle travaille chez TEN Arquitectos NY et au centre d'étude du développement urbain de Harvard. Leurs réalisations comprennent la maison Casa X (Barcelone, 2010–12, présentée ici) ; le Tepoztlán Lounge (Tepoztlán, Morelos, Mexique, 2011–12, également présenté ici) ; les Bungalows LMB (Tepoztlán, Morelos, Mexique, 2013) ; la maison Oport 1 (Port de la Selva, Espagne, 2013) ; l'immeuble d'habitation Cordoba (Mexico, 2013) et la maison San Sebastian (Buenos Aires, 2014).

CASA X

Barcelona, Spain, 2010–12

Address: not disclosed. Area: 300 m²
Client: Davor Gligo. Cost: €1 million

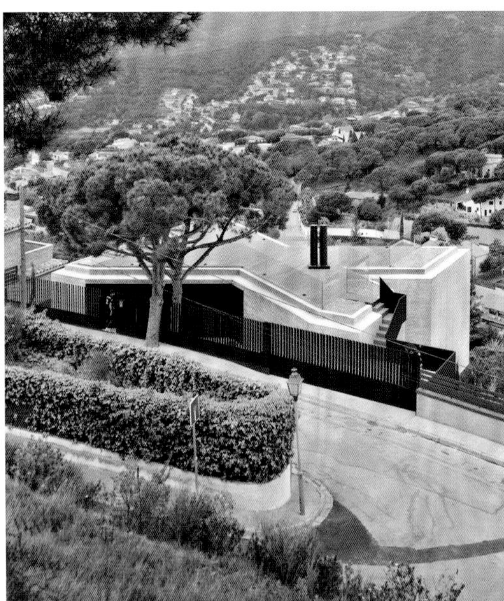

As its name implies, **CASA X** has a plan in the shape of an X. The complexities of the steeply sloped site were accentuated by the presence of a large pine tree that remained near the entrance. It was important to provide a good deal of privacy vis-à-vis neighboring houses, but also to allow views of the sea and mountains. Techniques similar to those used in bridge and tunnel construction were employed. Projected concrete was used with single-sided formwork on continuous walls that are six meters high. The precise location of the house was selected in order to minimize excavation. Its entrance is two meters lower than the upper access street. The top floor includes parking and the entrance area, together with the owners' private suite, which includes a bedroom, dressing area, bathroom, and studio. The lower floor is completely open on the front and has a double-height space near the kitchen and dining area. An eight-meter-long marble dining table marks this area as well. The architects state: "Learning from Dan Graham's reflections, the image of the sea is always present when observing the mountain, and the mountain appears as a reflection when looking at the sea: a perceptive quality that enriches the experience of the house."

Der Grundriss der **CASA X**, der Name legt es nahe, ist X-förmig. Wegen seiner Hanglage und einer großen Pinie, die neben dem geplanten Hauseingang erhalten werden sollte, erwies sich das Grundstück als erhebliche Herausforderung. Trotz unmittelbarer Nachbarbauten sollte die Privatsphäre gewahrt, die Sicht auf Meer und Berge jedoch nicht verbaut werden. Zum Einsatz kamen Verfahren aus dem Brücken- und Tunnelbau. So wurde Spritzbeton mit einhäuptiger Schalung auf die 6 m hohen Wände aufgetragen. Die Lage des Hauses ist so gewählt, dass ein Minimum an Erdarbeiten nötig war. Der Eingang liegt 2 m unterhalb der Zugangsstraße. Im oberen Stockwerk sind Garage und Privatbereich der Eigentümer mit Bad, Ankleidezimmer und Studio untergebracht. Das Untergeschoss ist über die gesamte Front verglast. Neben einer Küche liegt ein Bereich mit doppelter Raumhöhe und einem 8 m langen Marmortisch. Die Architekten: „Inspiriert von den Spiegeleffekten [der Kunstwerke] Dan Grahams, ist das Meer auch dann präsent, wenn man die Berge betrachtet, und die Berge erscheinen als eine Reflexion, betrachtet man das Meer. Dieses Spiel mit der Wahrnehmung sorgt für eine vielschichtige Raumerfahrung."

Comme son nom l'indique, **CASA X** a un plan en forme de X. Les difficultés dues à un site escarpé ont été encore accentuées du fait d'un grand pin qui a été conservé près de l'entrée. Il fallait assurer une certaine intimité face aux maisons voisines, sans condamner la vue sur la mer et les montagnes. Les techniques employées sont celles habituellement appliquées pour les ponts et tunnels. On a utilisé du béton projeté avec des coffrages à simple face sur des murs de six mètres de haut. L'emplacement précis de la maison a été choisi pour réduire au minimum les travaux d'excavation. L'entrée est à deux mètres en contrebas de la route d'accès. Le dernier étage comprend le parking et l'entrée, ainsi que l'appartement privé des propriétaires, avec une chambre à coucher, un dressing, une salle de bain et un atelier. L'étage inférieur, complètement ouvert côté façade, a une double hauteur sous plafond côté espace cuisine et salle à manger, matérialisée par une table en marbre de huit mètres. Selon les architectes, « tirant les leçons des réflexions de Dan Graham, l'image de la mer est toujours présente quand on observe la montagne, et la montagne apparaît par réflexion lorsqu'on regarde la mer : une qualité perceptive qui enrichit l'usage de la maison ».

The X-shaped plan of the house is visible in the images seen above. On the valley side, a V-shaped, fully glazed façade takes in a generous view of the valley.

Die Aufnahmen oben zeigen deutlich den X-förmigen Grundriss des Hauses. Zum Tal hin erlaubt eine V-förmige, verglaste Fassade einen Panoramablick über die Landschaft.

Le plan en X de la maison est visible dans les photos ci-dessus. Côté vallée, une façade en V entièrement vitrée intègre une large vue sur la vallée.

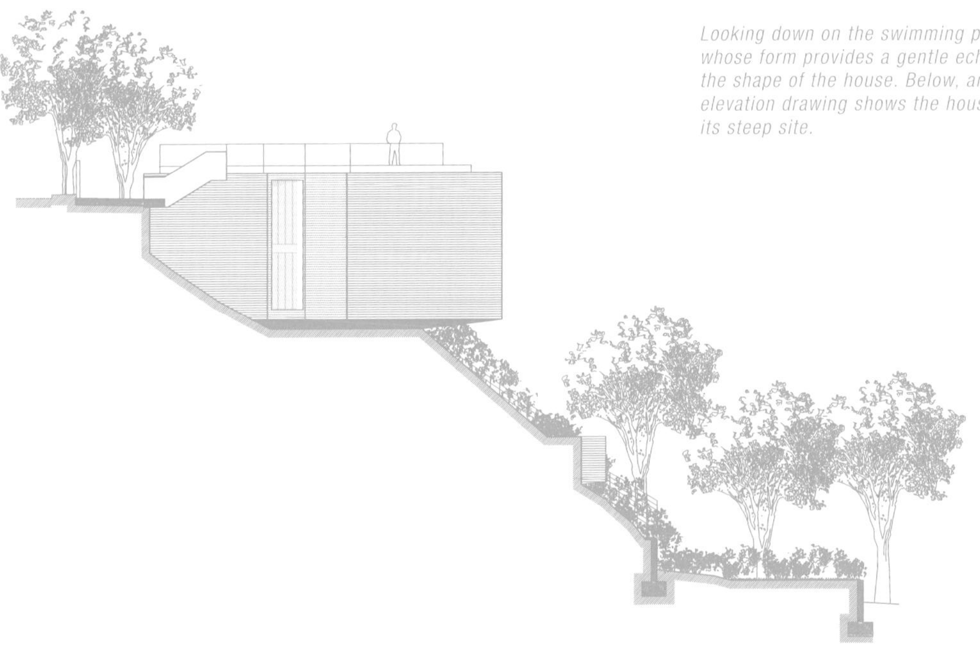

Looking down on the swimming pool, whose form provides a gentle echo of the shape of the house. Below, an elevation drawing shows the house in its steep site.

Ein Blick nach unten auf den Pool, dessen Form die Konturen des Hauses anklingen lässt. Unten ein Aufriss des Hauses, eingebettet in das steile Hanggrundstück.

Vue plongeante sur la piscine dont la forme fait délicatement écho à celle de la maison. Ci-dessous, une élévation montre la maison sur son site escarpé.

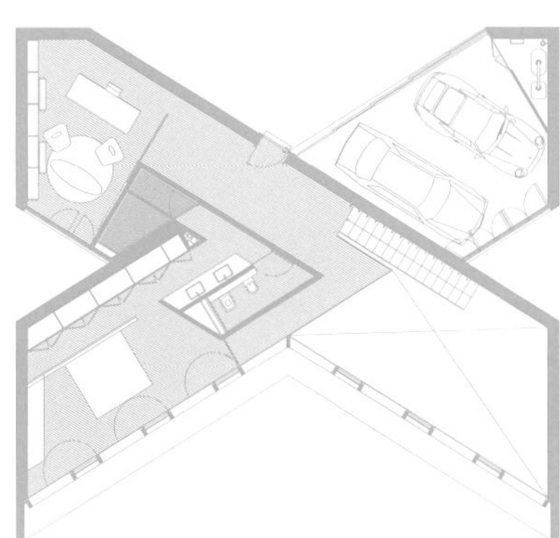

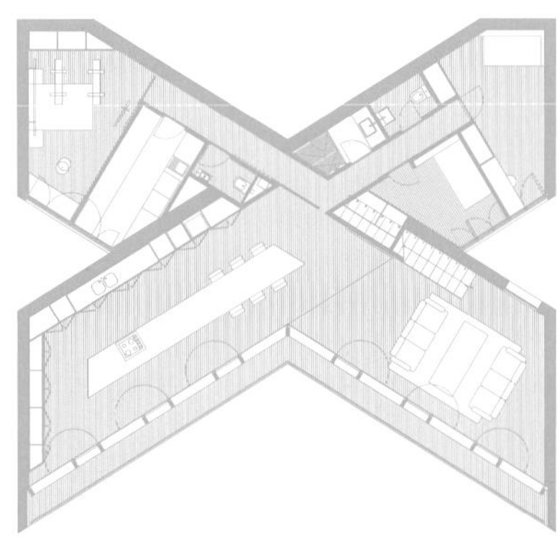

Above, plans reveal the X-shaped design. Inside, white walls and ceiling, wooden floors, and an ample use of glass emphasize both the light coming in and views of the exterior.

Oben Grundrisse des X-förmigen Entwurfs. Im Innern des Baus betonen weiße Wände und Decken, Holzböden und die großzügige Verglasung das einfallende Tageslicht ebenso wie den Ausblick.

Ci-dessus, les plans révèlent le dessin en X. À l'intérieur, les murs et plafonds blancs, les planchers en bois et l'usage intensif du verre mettent en valeur la lumière naturelle et les vues extérieures.

TEPOZTLÁN LOUNGE

Tepoztlán, Mexico, 2011–12

Address: not disclosed. Area: 250 m²
Client: Lourdes Medellín. Cost: $250 000

Tepoztlán is located 50 kilometers south of Mexico City. The **TEPOZTLÁN LOUNGE** was the first completed project in a rental community including bungalows of different sizes and designs. Shaped like a Y with a curved top, the concrete structure allows two existing mature trees to pass right through its forms. It is intended as a central communal space for leisure in the natural setting, which opens onto a neatly tended lawn. The architects describe it as an "inhabitable threshold" between interior and exterior. An open bar and small kitchen is grouped with restrooms and dressing rooms. A second area is intended either for children or as a reading area in the evening, while the third zone of the project has an enclosed area for television watching or conversation. All three areas are designed to be contiguous and continuous. The architects write: "The building is located as a plinth valuing the views of the mountains. The building wants to be respectful of the existing context, and understands that the vegetation and life in the open air are the real protagonists."

Tepoztlán liegt 50 km südlich von Mexiko-Stadt. Die **TEPOZTLÁN LOUNGE** entstand als erstes realisiertes Projekt einer Bungalowsiedlung mit Bauten in verschiedenen Größen und Ausführungen. Zwei Bäume des Bestands wachsen durch Öffnungen im kurvenförmigen Dach des Baus, der als offener Gemeinschaftsraum im Grünen konzipiert wurde. Vor der Lounge öffnet sich eine weite, makellose Rasenfläche, von den Architekten als „unbewohnbare Schwellenzone" zwischen Innen- und Außenraum bezeichnet. Neben einer offenen Bar und einer kleinen Küche liegen WCs und Umkleiden, ein zweiter Bereich dient als Spielzone oder Lesezimmer, ein dritter, umbauter Bereich zum Fernsehen oder für gemeinsame Gespräche. Alle drei Bereiche bilden ein Arrangement aus offenen, fließend ineinander übergehenden Räumen. Die Architekten: „Die Lounge liegt wie ein erhöhter Sockel auf dem Grundstück und bietet einen Ausblick auf die Berge. Unser Entwurf respektiert das vorgefundene Umfeld und erkennt an, dass die eigentlichen Protagonisten hier die Natur und die Aktivitäten im Freien sind."

Tepoztlán est situé à 50 km au sud de Mexico. Le **TEPOZTLÁN LOUNGE** est le premier projet achevé d'une résidence locative de bungalows de tailles et de styles différents. En forme de Y au sommet arrondi, le bâtiment en béton est transpercé par deux arbres adultes préexistants. Il est conçu comme un espace collectif de loisirs dans le site naturel et donne sur une pelouse bien entretenue. Les architectes le décrivent comme un « seuil habitable » entre intérieur et extérieur. Un bar et une petite cuisine ouverts sont regroupés avec des toilettes et dressing-rooms. Une deuxième zone est dédiée aux enfants ou à la lecture en soirée, tandis que la troisième zone est un espace clos dédié à la conversation ou à la télévision. Les trois zones sont contigües et continues. Selon les architectes, « le bâtiment est disposé comme un socle mettant en valeur la vue sur les montagnes. Le bâtiment se veut respectueux du contexte et part du principe que la végétation et la vie en plein air sont les vrais protagonistes ».

The Y-shape of the house (plan to the right) embraces the irregular oval pool. Existing trees poke through the roof of the house and confirm its connection to the site.

Das Y-förmige Haus (Grundriss rechts) schmiegt sich an den ovalen Pool. Bäume des Grundstücks wachsen durch das Dach des Baus und unterstreichen dessen Einbindung in sein Umfeld.

La forme en Y de la maison (plan ci-contre) épouse l'ovale irrégulier de la piscine. Les arbres existants traversent le toit de la maison et affirment sa relation au site.

With its open living space defined in part by the two trees that penetrate the volume, the house is characterized by an almost complete symbiosis between outside and inside.

Das Haus mit seinem offenen Wohnbereich, teilweise dominiert von zwei Bäumen, die den Baukörper durchdringen, zeichnet sich durch eine fast vollständige Symbiose von Innen- und Außenraum aus.

Avec son espace de vie ouvert, en partie défini par les deux arbres pénétrant le volume, la maison se caractérise par une symbiose presque parfaite entre extérieur et intérieur.

Left, the architects willfully contrast rectilinear volumes with completely open walls, and trees that rise up from the otherwise smooth floors.

Die Architekten setzen bewusst auf Kontraste zwischen rechtwinkligen Raumbereichen, vollständig geöffneten Wänden und Bäumen, die aus dem ansonsten geschlossenen Boden aufwachsen.

Ci-contre, les architectes font délibérément contraster des volumes rectilignes avec des murs entièrement ouverts et des arbres qui s'élèvent de sols d'ordinaire lisses.

In both plan and elevation (right), the house is carefully inserted into the existing site with trees playing a major role in the design. Above, open living spaces are sparsely furnished, offering ample "lounge" space.

Grund- und Aufriss (rechts) belegen, wie sorgfältig das Haus in das bestehende Umfeld integriert wurde, wobei der Baumbestand eine entscheidende Rolle spielt. Die Aufenthaltsbereiche (oben) sind nur sparsam möbliert und bieten großzügig Raum zum Entspannen.

Le plan comme l'élévation (page de droite) illustrent la soigneuse intégration de la maison au site existant et le rôle prépondérant des arbres dans le projet. Au-dessus, les espaces de vie ouverts sont sobrement meublés et offrent un large espace « salon ».

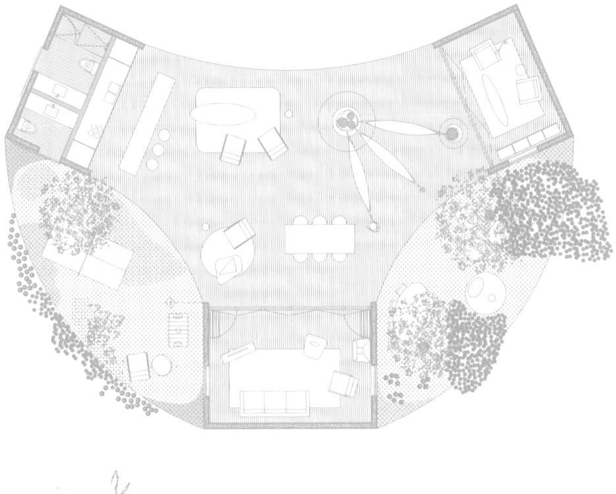

PRESTON SCOTT COHEN

Preston Scott Cohen, Inc.
77 Pleasant Street
Cambridge, MA 02139
USA

Tel: +1 617 441 2110
Fax: +1 617 441 2113
E-mail: info@pscohen.com
Web: www.pscohen.com

Born in 1961, **PRESTON SCOTT COHEN** received his B.Arch degree from the Rhode Island School of Design (1983) and his M.Arch degree from the Harvard GSD (1985). Cohen is the Chair and Gerald M. McCue Professor of Architecture at Harvard GSD. Recent projects completed or under construction include the Goodman House (Pine Plains, New York, USA, 2003–04); the Goldman Sachs Arcade Canopy (New York, New York, USA, 2005–08); the Inman House (Cambridge, Massachusetts, USA, 2008); the Nanjing Performing Arts Center (China, 2007–09); the Tel Aviv Museum of Art Amir Building (Israel, 2007–11, published here); the Taiyuan Museum of Art (China, 2007–13); Datong City Library (China, 2008–13); and the Fahmy Residence (Los Gatos, California, USA, 2007, 2011–14). The Tel Aviv Museum building was the winner of the Time and Leisure Best Museum of thc Year and the Design Review Award.

PRESTON SCOTT COHEN, geboren 1961, absolvierte seinen B. Arch. an der Rhode Island School of Design (1983) und seinen M. Arch. an der Harvard GSD (1985). Cohen ist Dekan und Gerald-M.-McCue-Professor für Architektur an der Harvard GSD. Jüngere realisierte Entwürfe und Projekte im Bau sind das Goodman House (Pine Plains, New York, 2003–04), ein Vordach für die Goldman Sachs Arcade (New York, 2005–08), das Inman House (Cambridge, Massachusetts, 2008), das Performing Arts Center der Universität von Nanjing (China, 2007–09), das Amir Building des Tel Aviv Museum of Art (Israel, 2007–11, hier vorgestellt), das Kunstmuseum Taiyuan (China, 2007–13), die Stadtbibliothek in Datong (China, 2008–13) und die Fahmy Residence (Los Gatos, Kalifornien, 2007, 2011–14). Das Amir Building des Tel Aviv Museum of Art gewann zwei Preise: den Time and Leisure Best Museum Award und den Design Review Award.

Né en 1961, **PRESTON SCOTT COHEN** obtient son B.Arch à l'École de design de Rhode Island (1983) et son M.Arch à la Harvard GSD (1985). Cohen est directeur et professeur d'architecture de la fondation Gerald M. McCue de la Harvard GSD. Ses projets récents, achevés ou en cours, comprennent la Goldman House (Pine Plains, New York, 2003–04) ; la Goldman Sachs Arcade Canopy (New York, 2005–08) ; la maison Inman (Cambridge, Massachusetts, 2008) ; le Centre des arts du spectacle de Nankin (Chine, 2007–09) ; l'aile Amir du Musée d'art de Tel Aviv (Israël, 2007–11, présenté ici) ; le Musée d'art de Taiyuan (Chine, 2007–13) ; la bibliothèque de Datong (Chine, 2008–13) et la résidence Fahmy (Los Gatos, Californie, 2007, 2011–14). La nouvelle aile du musée de Tel Aviv a été sacrée meilleur musée de l'année par le magazine Time & Leisure et a obtenu le Design Review Award.

HERTA AND PAUL AMIR BUILDING

Tel Aviv Museum of Art, Tel Aviv, Israel, 2007–11

Address: 27 Shaul Hamelech Blvd, POB 33288, The Golda Meir Cultural and Art Center, 61332 Tel Aviv, Israel, +972 3607 7020, www.tamuseum.com
Area: 18 500 m². Client: Tel Aviv Museum of Art. Cost: $55 million
Collaboration: Amit Nemlich (Project Architect), Tobias Nolte, Bohsung Kong (Project Assistants)

This project was the winner of a 2003 international competition. The building includes galleries for Israeli art, architecture and design, drawings and prints, temporary exhibitions, a photography study center and archives, a new auditorium, seminar and conference rooms, an art library, restaurant, administrative offices, and storage facilities. The museum is located in the middle of Tel Aviv's cultural area on a triangular site between the existing museum, a library and the Center for the Performing Arts. The architect states: "The design for the Amir Building arises directly from the challenge of providing several floors of large neutral rectangular galleries within a tight, idiosyncratic triangular site. The solution is to 'square the triangle' by constructing the levels on different axes, which deviate significantly from floor to floor. In essence, the building's levels—three above grade and two below—are structurally independent plans stacked one on top of the other."

Der Entwurf gewann 2003 einen internationalen Wettbewerb. Im Museum werden Kunst, Architektur, Design, Zeichnungen und Druckgrafik aus Israel sowie Sonderausstellungen präsentiert. Zum Projekt gehören auch ein Studienzentrum für Fotografie samt Archiven, ein Auditorium, Seminar- und Konferenzräume, eine Kunstbibliothek, ein Restaurant, Büros und Lager. Das Museum liegt in einem kulturell geprägten Stadtteil auf einem dreieckigen Grundstück zwischen einem bereits existierenden Museumsbau, einer Bibliothek und einem Zentrum für darstellende Künste. Die Architekten: „Der Entwurf des Amir Building war eine unmittelbare Reaktion auf die Herausforderung, mehrere Stockwerke mit großen neutralen, rechtwinkligen Ausstellungsräumen zu realisieren, und das auf einem knappen, eigenwilligen, dreieckigen Baugrundstück. Die Lösung lag in einer ‚Quadratur des Dreiecks' – die Stockwerke wurden entlang verschiedener Achsen ausgerichtet, die von Etage zu Etage erheblich variieren. Im Prinzip sind die Ebenen des Gebäudes – drei Ober- und zwei Untergeschosse – strukturell unabhängige Grundrisse, die übereinander gestapelt wurden."

Ce projet a gagné un concours international en 2003. L'édifice comprend des galeries dédiées à l'art d'Israël, à l'architecture, au design, au dessin et à l'estampe, et à des expositions temporaires, un centre de recherche sur la photographie et des archives, un nouvel auditorium, des salles de séminaires, une bibliothèque d'art, un restaurant, des bureaux et des réserves. Le musée est situé au centre du quartier culturel de Tel Aviv, sur un terrain triangulaire entre le musée existant, une bibliothèque et le Centre des arts du spectacle. Comme l'explique l'architecte, « le design de l'édifice est directement issu du défi de donner le jour à plusieurs étages de grandes galeries rectangulaires et neutres, dans un site singulier, étroit et triangulaire. La solution est de "carrer le triangle" en construisant les niveaux sur différents axes qui se déportent fortement d'étage en étage. Fondamentalement, les niveaux de l'édifice, trois au-dessus du sol et deux en dessous, sont structurellement indépendants et empilés les uns sur les autres ».

Characterized by sloping surfaces and a folded plane design, the new building looks as though it might have recently landed, fully fashioned on this site, but there are also spaces below grade not visible here.

Der Neubau zeichnet sich durch schiefe Ebenen und Faltungen aus und wirkt, als sei er als fertiges Konstrukt soeben auf dem Grundstück gelandet. Die unterirdischen Bereiche sind hier nicht sichtbar

Avec ses surfaces inclinées et son design d'avion en papier, on dirait que le nouveau bâtiment vient d'atterrir, préajusté pour ce site, mais il dispose aussi d'espaces en sous-sol qui ne sont pas visibles ici.

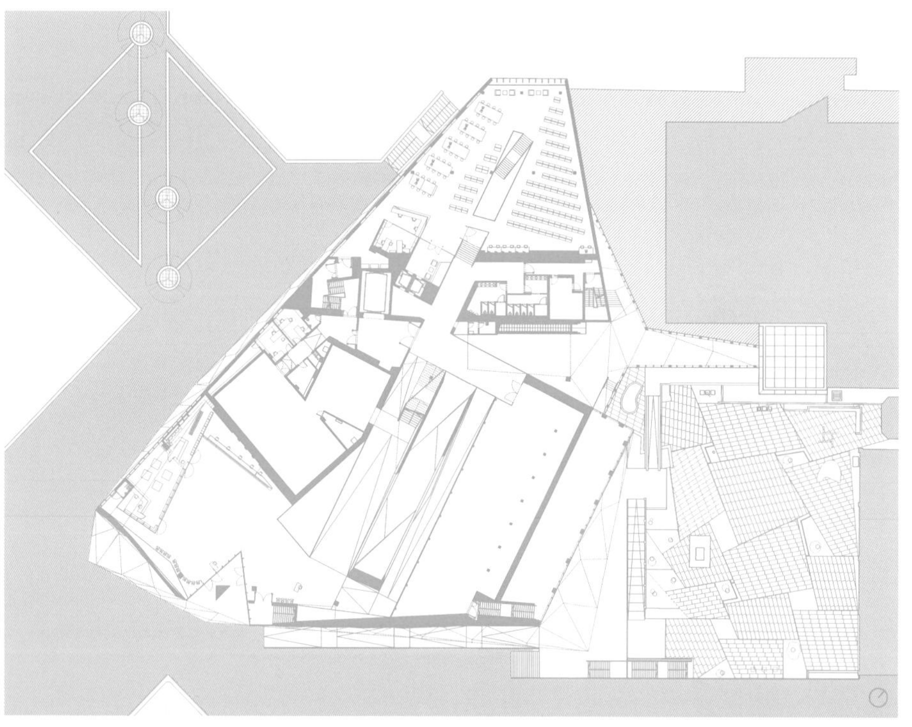

Left, a plan of the new building with its older neighbor in dark blue. Although the lines of the design are rectilinear, the continual shifting of axes and volumes gives a flowing dynamism to the interior spaces.

Links ein Grundriss des Neubaus; der angrenzende Altbau in Dunkelblau. Trotz der Geradlinigkeit des Entwurfs gewinnen die Innenräume durch zahlreiche Verschiebungen der Sichtachsen und Volumina eine fließende Dynamik.

Ci-contre, un plan du nouveau bâtiment avec son voisin plus ancien en bleu foncé. Bien que les lignes du projet soient rectilignes, le décalage répété des axes et des volumes donne un dynamisme continu aux espaces intérieurs.

Inside the museum, even spaces below grade have ample natural light and, above all, soaring ceiling heights that make visitors comfortable.

Auch die Untergeschosse des Museums sind großzügig mit Tageslicht durchflutet und verfügen über eine erstaunliche Deckenhöhe, was für die Besucher angenehm ist.

À l'intérieur du musée, même les espaces en sous-sol bénéficient d'un éclairage naturel généreux et surtout d'une belle hauteur de plafond pour le confort des visiteurs.

The architecture is all about interpenetrating planes and angled openings that offer views to other levels while also admitting natural light.

Bei dieser Architektur geht es vor allem um die Durchdringung verschiedener Ebenen und um verwinkelte Durchblicke in die übrigen Stockwerke, was zugleich Tageslichteinfall in den Bau ermöglicht.

L'architecture consiste à imbriquer des plans et des ouvertures inclinées offrant des vues sur les autres niveaux tout en permettant un éclairage naturel.

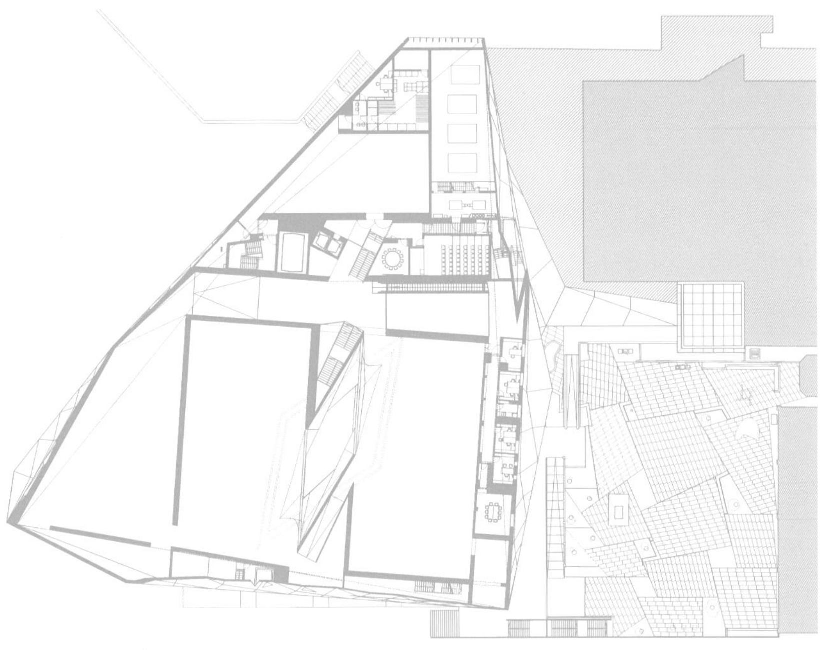

Because of the shifted volumes at each level, it is not obvious to see exactly how many levels there are in the building. Light penetrates, especially where visitors move through common space, while galleries are given less natural illumination for reasons of conservation.

Die Verschiebung der einzelnen Ebenen sorgt dafür, dass die Zahl der Stockwerke nicht auf einen Blick zu erfassen ist. Insbesondere die Verkehrsflächen werden von Tageslicht erhellt; die Ausstellungsräume sind weniger belichtet, um Exponate zu schützen.

À cause des volumes décalés à chaque niveau du bâtiment, il est difficile d'en discerner le nombre exact. La lumière naturelle pénètre en particulier dans les lieux de passage empruntés par les visiteurs, alors que les galeries en sont moins dotées pour des questions de conservation.

COOP HIMMELB(L)AU

Coop Himmelb(l)au
Wolf D. Prix & Partner ZT GmbH
Spengergasse 37 / 1050 Vienna / Austria

Tel: +43 1 54 66 00 / Fax: +43 1 54 66 06 00
E-mail: office@coop-himmelblau.at / Web: www.coop-himmelblau.at

Coop Himmelb(l)au was founded by Wolf D. Prix, Helmut Swiczinsky, and Michael Holzer in Vienna, Austria, in 1968. In 1988, a second studio was opened in Los Angeles, USA. Today the studio is directed by Wolf D. Prix, Harald Krieger, Karolin Schmidbaur, Louise Kiesling, and project partners. It currently employs 150 team members from 19 nations. **WOLF D. PRIX** was born in 1942 in Vienna, and educated at the Technical University in Vienna, at SCI-Arc, and at the Architectural Association (AA) in London. From 1993 to 2011 he was Professor of Architecture at the University of Applied Arts in Vienna, where he also served as Vice-Rector from 2003 to 2012, and he has headed Studio Prix since 2003. Completed projects of the group include the East Pavilion of the Groninger Museum (Groningen, the Netherlands, 1990–94); remodeling of the Austrian Pavilion in the Giardini (Venice, Italy, 1995); the UFA Cinema Center (Dresden, Germany, 1993–98); the SEG Apartment Tower (Vienna, Austria, 1994–98); and Expo '02, Forum Arteplage (Biel, Switzerland, 1999–2002). Recent and current work includes the Academy of Fine Arts (Munich, Germany, 1992/2002–05); the Akron Art Museum (Akron, Ohio, USA, 2001–07); BMW Welt (Munich, Germany, 2001–07); the Central Los Angeles Area High School #9 for the Visual and Performing Arts (Los Angeles, California, USA, 2002–08); the Busan Cinema Center (Busan, South Korea, 2005–11, published here); the Martin Luther Church (Hainburg, Austria, 2008–11, also published here); the Dalian International Conference Center (Dalian, China, 2008–12); the Musée des Confluences (Lyon, France, 2001–14); and the European Central Bank (Frankfurt, Germany, 2003–14).

Wolf D. Prix, Helmut Swiczinsky und Michael Holzer gründeten Coop Himmelb(l)au 1968 in Wien. 1988 eröffneten sie ein zweites Büro in Los Angeles. Heute leiten Wolf D. Prix, Harald Krieger, Karolin Schmidbaur und Louise Kiesling das Büro gemeinsam mit ihren Projektpartnern und beschäftigen 150 Mitarbeiter aus 19 Ländern. **WOLF D. PRIX** wurde 1942 in Wien geboren und studierte an der Technischen Universität Wien, am SCI-Arc und der Architectural Association (AA) London. Von 1993 bis 2011 war er Professor für Architektur an der Universität für Angewandte Kunst Wien sowie von 1993 bis 2012 Vizerektor der Universität. Seit 2003 ist er Leiter des Studio Prix. Realisierte Projekte der Gruppe sind u. a. der Ostpavillon des Museums Groningen (Niederlande, 1990–94), der Umbau des Österreichischen Biennale-Pavillons in den Giardini (Venedig, 1995), das UFA-Kinocenter (Dresden, 1993–98), das SEG-Apartmenthochhaus (Wien, 1994–98) sowie das Forum Arteplage, EXPO.02 (Biel, Schweiz, 1999–2002). Jüngere und aktuelle Arbeiten sind u. a. die Akademie der bildenden Künste (München, 1992/2002–05), das Akron Art Museum (Akron, Ohio, 2001–07), die BMW-Welt (München, 2001–07) und die Central Los Angeles Area High School #9 für bildende und darstellende Künste (Los Angeles, Kalifornien, 2002–08), das Busan Cinema Center (Busan, Südkorea, 2005 bis 2011, hier vorgestellt), die Martin-Luther-Kirche (Hainburg, Österreich, 2008–11, ebenfalls hier vorgestellt), das International Conference Center in Dalian (China, 2008–12), das Musée des Confluences (Lyon, 2001–14) und die Europäische Zentralbank (Frankfurt am Main, 2003–14).

Coop Himmelb(l)au a été fondé par D. Prix, Helmut Swiczinsky et Michael Holzer à Vienne, en Autriche, en 1968. Ils ont ouvert une seconde agence à Los Angeles, en 1988. L'agence est actuellement dirigée par Wolf D. Prix, Harald Krieger, Karolin Schmidbaur, Louise Kiesling et des partenaires de projets. Elle emploie 150 collaborateurs de 19 pays. Né à Vienne en 1942, **WOLF D. PRIX** étudie à l'Université de technologie de Vienne, au SCI-Arc, et à l'Architectural Association (AA), à Londres. De 1993 à 2011, il est professeur d'architecture à l'Université des arts appliqués de Vienne ainsi que directeur adjoint de l'université de 2003 à 2012. Depuis 2003, il dirige l'agence Studio Prix. Les projets réalisés du groupe comprennent le pavillon est du musée de Groningue (Groningue, 1990–94) ; la restructuration du pavillon de l'Autriche dans les Giardini de la Biennale (Venise, 1995) ; le complexe multisalles de cinéma UFA (Dresde, 1993–98) ; la tour SEG (Vienne, 1994–98) et le « Forum Arteplage » d'Expo.02 (Bienne, Suisse, 1999–2002). Leurs projets récents comprennent l'Académie des beaux-arts de Munich (Munich, 1992/2002–05) ; le Musée d'art d'Akron (Akron, Ohio, 2001–07) ; le BMW Welt (Munich, 2001–07) ; le Central Los Angeles Area High School #9 pour les arts visuels et les arts du spectacle (Los Angeles, 2002–08) ; le Centre du cinéma de Busan (Busan, Corée-du-Sud, 2005–11, présenté ici) ; l'église Martin Luther (Hainbourg, Autriche, 2008–11, également présenté ici); le Centre international de conférences de Dalian (Dalian, Chine, 2008–12) ; le musée des Confluences (Lyon, 2001–14) et le siège de la Banque centrale européenne (Francfort, 2003–14).

MARTIN LUTHER CHURCH

Hainburg, Austria, 2008–11

Address: Alte Post Str. 28, 2410 Hainburg, Austria, www.evang-hainburg-bruck.at
Area: 289 m². Client: Protestant Church Lower Austria
Cost: €1.1 million

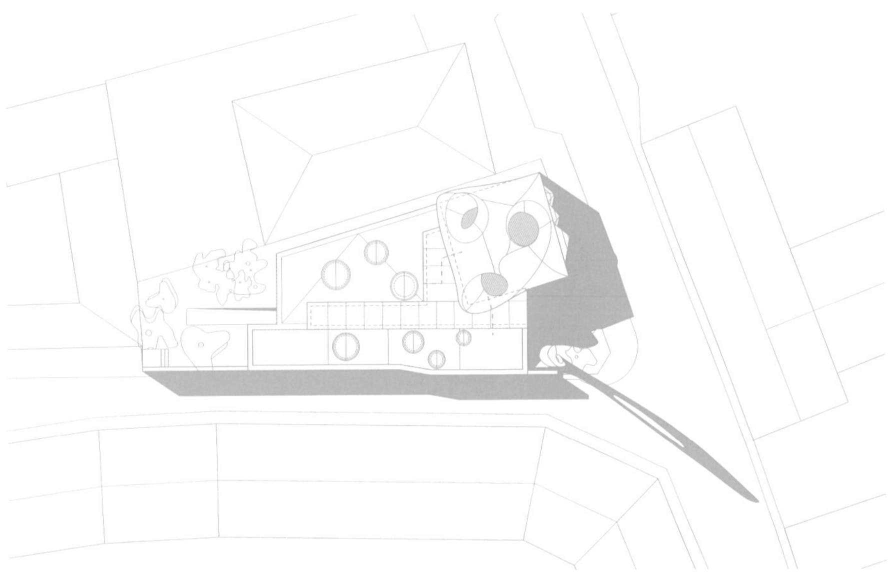

Despite the highly unusual, complex curvature of the upper volume (below), the plan of the church shows that it is made up largely of a triangular form together with rectangles.

Anders als die ungewöhnlich komplexe Kurvatur der „Kuppel" vermuten lässt (unten), setzt sich der Grundriss des Kirchenbaus aus einem Dreieck und rechteckigen Elementen zusammen.

En dépit de la complexité très inhabituelle de la courbure du volume supérieur (ci-dessous), le plan de l'église montre qu'elle est principalement constituée d'une forme triangulaire et de rectangles.

Seen from the outside, the Martin Luther Church is highly sculptural, a quality also seen in the elongated bell tower (above). Skylights bring natural light into the interior, symbolizing the Holy Trinity.

Von außen gibt sich die Martin-Luther-Kirche betont skulptural; der schlanke Glockenturm unterstreicht dies (oben). Oberlichter lassen Tageslicht in den Bau hinein, Symbole der Heiligen Dreifaltigkeit.

Vue de l'extérieur, l'église Martin Luther est très sculpturale, une qualité qu'on retrouve dans le clocher étiré (ci-dessus). Des lucarnes symbolisant la Sainte Trinité apportent une lumière naturelle à l'intérieur.

This Protestant church, which includes a sanctuary and supplementary spaces, was built in less than a year on the site of a church that had not existed since the 17th century. The architects explain: "The shape of the building is derived from that of a huge 'table,' with its entire roof construction resting on the legs of the 'table'—four steel columns. Another key element is the ceiling of the prayer room: its design language has been developed from the shape of the curved roof of a neighboring Romanesque ossuary—the geometry of this … building is translated into a form in line with the times, via today's digital instruments." Three openings in the roof, related by the architects to the Holy Trinity, bring natural light into the church. A glass-covered children's corner accommodates the baptistery. A slab structure facing a side alley houses the pastor's office, a small kitchen, and other ancillary rooms. The architects used shipbuilding techniques for the 8-millimeter-thick three-dimensionally curved steel plates on the exterior, and refer to Le Corbusier, in particular the Monastery at La Tourette. The freely formed bell tower of the church is a 20-meter-tall self-supporting steel structure.

Diese evangelische Kirche mit Altarraum und Nebengebäude wurde am Standort eines seit dem 17. Jahrhundert nicht mehr existierenden Vorgängerbaus errichtet. Die Architekten: „Die Gesamtform des Baus erinnert an einen riesigen Tisch, wobei die Dachkonstruktion auf vier Stahlstützen, den Beinen des ‚Tisches', ruht. Ein weiteres Schlüsselelement ist das Dach des Andachtsraums: Seine Formensprache ist angelehnt an die geschwungene Dachform eines benachbarten romanischen Karners – die Geometrie des Baus wurde mit heutigen digitalen Hilfsmitteln in eine zeitgemäße Form gebracht." Drei große Öffnungen im Dach stehen den Architekten zufolge für die Heilige Dreifaltigkeit und lassen Licht ins Innere. In einer glasüberdachten Kinderecke befindet sich das Taufbecken. Ein langgestrecktes Gebäude an einer kleinen Nebenstraße beherbergt Sakristei und Büro des Pfarrers, eine kleine Küche und andere Nebenräume. Die Architekten ließen die 8 mm starken, geschwungenen Dachelemente in einer Werft fertigen und nehmen mit ihrem Entwurf Bezug auf Le Corbusier, insbesondere das Kloster von La Tourette. Der Glockenturm ist eine ungewöhnlich geformte, selbsttragende Stahlkonstruktion.

Cette église protestante, comprenant le sanctuaire et des espaces annexes, a été construite en moins d'un an sur l'ancien site d'une église disparue au XVIIe siècle. Pour les architectes, « la forme du bâtiment est celle d'une énorme "table", tout le toit reposant sur les pieds de la "table" – quatre colonnes en acier. Le plafond de la salle de prière est un autre trait marquant : son langage stylistique s'inspire de la forme du toit arrondi d'un ossuaire roman situé à proximité – la géométrie de ce… bâtiment se traduit par une forme en accord avec son temps, au moyen des outils numériques actuels ». Trois ouvertures dans le toit, évoquant selon les architectes la Sainte Trinité, apportent un éclairage naturel dans l'église. Un coin des enfants, vitré, héberge le baptistère. Un bloc placé face à une allée latérale abrite le bureau du pasteur, une petite cuisine et d'autres locaux de service. Les architectes ont eu recours à des techniques de construction navale pour les plaques d'acier de 8 mm d'épaisseur courbées en trois dimensions de l'extérieur, et se réfèrent à Le Corbusier, notamment pour son couvent de La Tourette. Le clocher de l'église, de forme libre, est une structure autoportante de 20 m en acier.

The 20-meter-tall steel bell tower dominates the church in terms of height, but remains a light, airy presence next to the main structure.

Mit 20 m dominiert der stählerne Glockenturm das Ensemble in der Höhe, bleibt jedoch eine leichte Geste neben dem Hauptkirchenbau.

Le clocher en acier qui domine l'église du haut de ses 20 m conserve cependant une présence légère et aérienne à côté de la structure principale.

Left, the architects have succeeded in combining a highly contemporary design with references to a neighboring Romanesque ossuary.

Links: Den Architekten gelingt es, in den deutlich zeitgenössischen Entwurf Bezüge zu einem benachbarten romanischen Karner einzubinden.

Page de gauche, les architectes ont réussi à combiner une forme très contemporaine avec des références à un ossuaire roman situé à proximité.

The interior of the church lives up to the expectations created by the exterior forms. Simple wooden chairs face a modern altar and a wooden screen with a stylized cruciform opening that is backed by a clear glass wall.

Der Kirchenraum erfüllt, was der Außenbau verspricht. Schlichte Holzstühle orientieren sich zu einem modernen Altar und einem Wandschirm aus Holz mit einem stilisierten Kreuz, dahinter eine Glaswand.

L'intérieur de l'église répond aux attentes suscitées par les formes extérieures. De simples chaises en bois font face à un autel moderne et à un claustra en bois percé d'une ouverture en croix stylisée et donnant sur un mur en verre transparent.

Seen from below, the interior of the church is covered by a glazed ceiling that touches on the upper part of the curved exterior. Above, a section drawing shows the relatively modest volume of the structure.

Die Untersicht zeigt das Glasdach des Kirchenraums, das unten an die „Kuppel" anschließt. Der Querschnitt (darüber) lässt das vergleichsweise geringe Volumen des Baukörpers deutlich werden.

Vu de dessous, l'intérieur de l'église est couvert d'un toit en verre qui effleure la partie supérieure de l'extérieur incurvé. En haut, une coupe montre le volume relativement modeste du bâtiment.

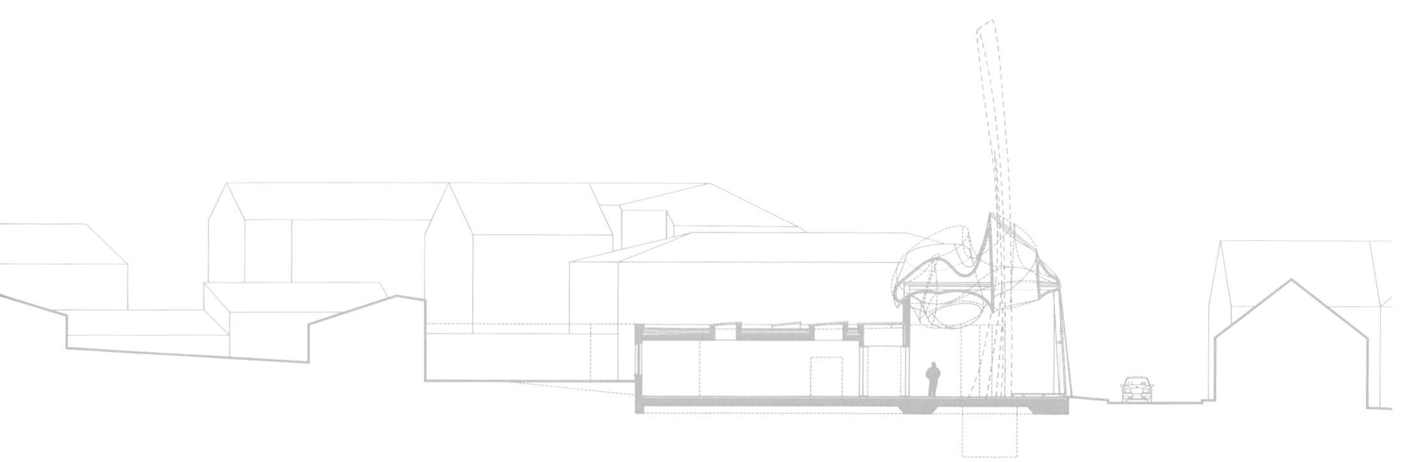

BUSAN CINEMA CENTER

Busan International Film Festival, Busan, South Korea, 2005–11

Address: 1467 Woo-Dong, Haeundae-Gu, Busan 612-020, South Korea, +82 1688 3010, www.biff.kr
Area: 51 067 m². Client: Municipality of Busan. Cost: €100 million

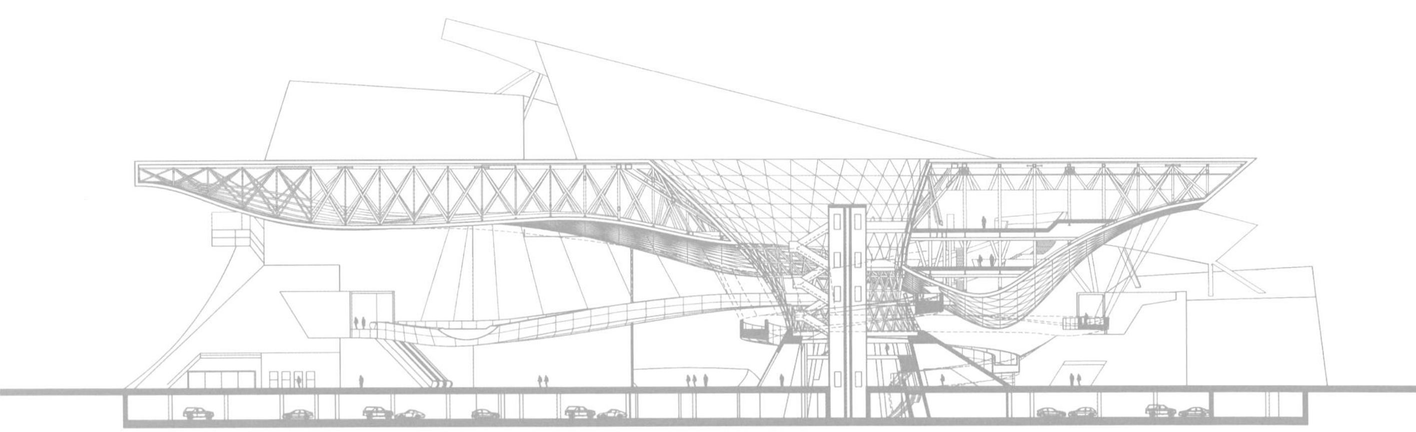

The Busan Cinema Center provides a willful contrast with its high-rise urban environment. Horizontal lines and curving volumes set the building apart and provide shelter for the entrance areas.

Das Kinocenter bildet einen bewussten Kontrast zur urbanen Hochhausbebauung. Horizontale Linien und geschwungene Baukörper machen den Komplex markant und erheben sich schützend über dem Eingangsbereich.

Le Centre du cinéma de Busan contraste délibérément avec les tours de son environnement urbain. Les lignes horizontales et les volumes courbes différencient le bâtiment et offrent un abri aux zones d'accès.

This project entered the 2011 Guinness Book of World Records for the "longest cantilevered roof" reaching 85 meters over the reception area. The architects explain: "The basic concept of this project was the discourse about the overlapping of open and closed spaces and of public and private areas." Movie theaters are located in a mountain-like building, while the center's public space is shared between an outdoor cinema and a public space that is called the Red Carpet Area. LED covered outdoor roof elements act as a "virtual sky" connecting plazas and "building-objects." The LED system can be programmed to serve as a communication platform. The "building-objects" contain a 1000-seat theater, three indoor and outdoor cinemas, convention halls, office spaces, creative studios, and dining areas in "a mixture of sheltered and linked indoor and outdoor public spaces." A "Double Cone" serves as a "symbolic landmark entrance" to the **BUSAN CINEMA CENTER**, connecting "Cinema Mountain" and "BIFF Hill." "BIFF Hill" is a "ground surface formation" with seating for the outdoor cinema. A planned riverside park dubbed "BIFF Canal Park" will eventually extend the complex toward the park across a boulevard to the south.

Dieses Projekt schaffte es 2011 mit einer Spannweite von 85 m als größtes Kragdach der Welt ins Guinness-Buch der Rekorde. Die Architekten: „Konzeptuelle Prämisse für dieses Projekt war der Diskurs um die Überschneidung offener und geschlossener bzw. öffentlicher und privater Räume." Die Kinosäle sind in einem Komplex untergebracht, der wie ein Berg anmutet; ein Open-Air-Kino und die sog. Red Carpet Area liegen öffentlich vor dem Bau. Das Kragdach wurde mit LEDs ausgestattet und dient als „virtueller Himmel", als Bindeglied zwischen Vorplatz und „baulichen Objekten". Das LED-System ist programmierbar und kann auch zur Textanzeige genutzt werden. Der Komplex umfasst einen Kinosaal mit 1000 Sitzplätzen, drei Innenraum- und ein Freiluftkino, Kongresssäle, Büroräume, Ateliers und Restaurants: „eine Mischung aus geschützten und verbundenen öffentlichen Innen- und Außenbereichen". Ein „Doppelkegel" markiert als „symbolträchtige Landmarke" den Eingang zum **BUSAN CINEMA CENTER** und verbindet die Bereiche von „Cinema Mountain" und „BIFF Hill". „BIFF Hill" ist eine „Geländeformation" mit Sitzplätzen für das Freiluftkino. Ein geplanter Park am Flussufer, der BIFF Canal Park, soll den Komplex über eine große Straße nach Süden hin ausdehnen.

Ce projet est entré dans le Livre Guinness des records en 2011, pour son « toit en porte-à-faux le plus long du monde » d'une portée de 85 mètres au-dessus de l'accueil. Selon les architectes, « le concept de base de ce projet partait du discours sur le chevauchement des espaces ouverts et fermés et des espaces publics et privés ». Les cinémas sont situés dans un bâtiment évoquant une montagne, tandis que l'espace public se partage entre un cinéma en plein air et l'espace Red Carpet. Les éléments extérieurs du toit, couverts de LED, servent de « ciel virtuel » reliant les places et les « objets-bâtiments ». Le système de LED programmables peut servir de support de communication. Les « objets-bâtiments » comportent un théâtre de 1000 places, trois cinémas en salle et en plein air, des salles de congrès, des espaces de bureaux, des ateliers de création et des zones de restauration, en un « mélange d'espaces publics intérieurs et extérieurs, couverts et reliés »; Un « double cône » marque par un « signal symbolique » l'entrée du **CENTRE DU CINÉMA DE BUSAN**, reliant « Cinema Mountain » et « BIFF Hill ». « BIFF Hill » est une « formation de surface » avec des sièges pour les projections en plein air. Un parc au bord de l'eau, surnommé « BIFF Canal Park » permettra d'étendre le complexe au sud vers le parc, en traversant un boulevard.

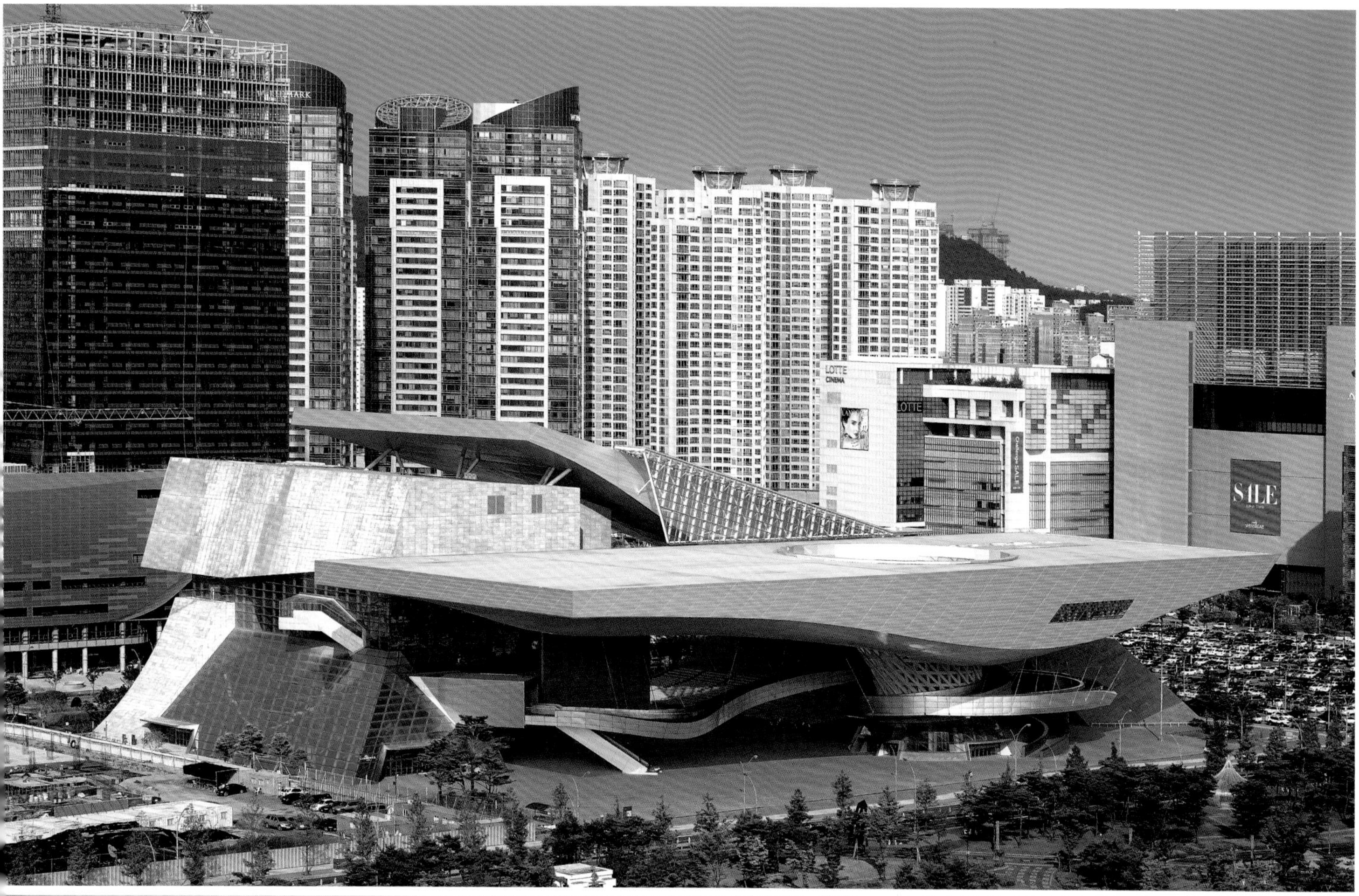
LOTTE CINEMA
SALE

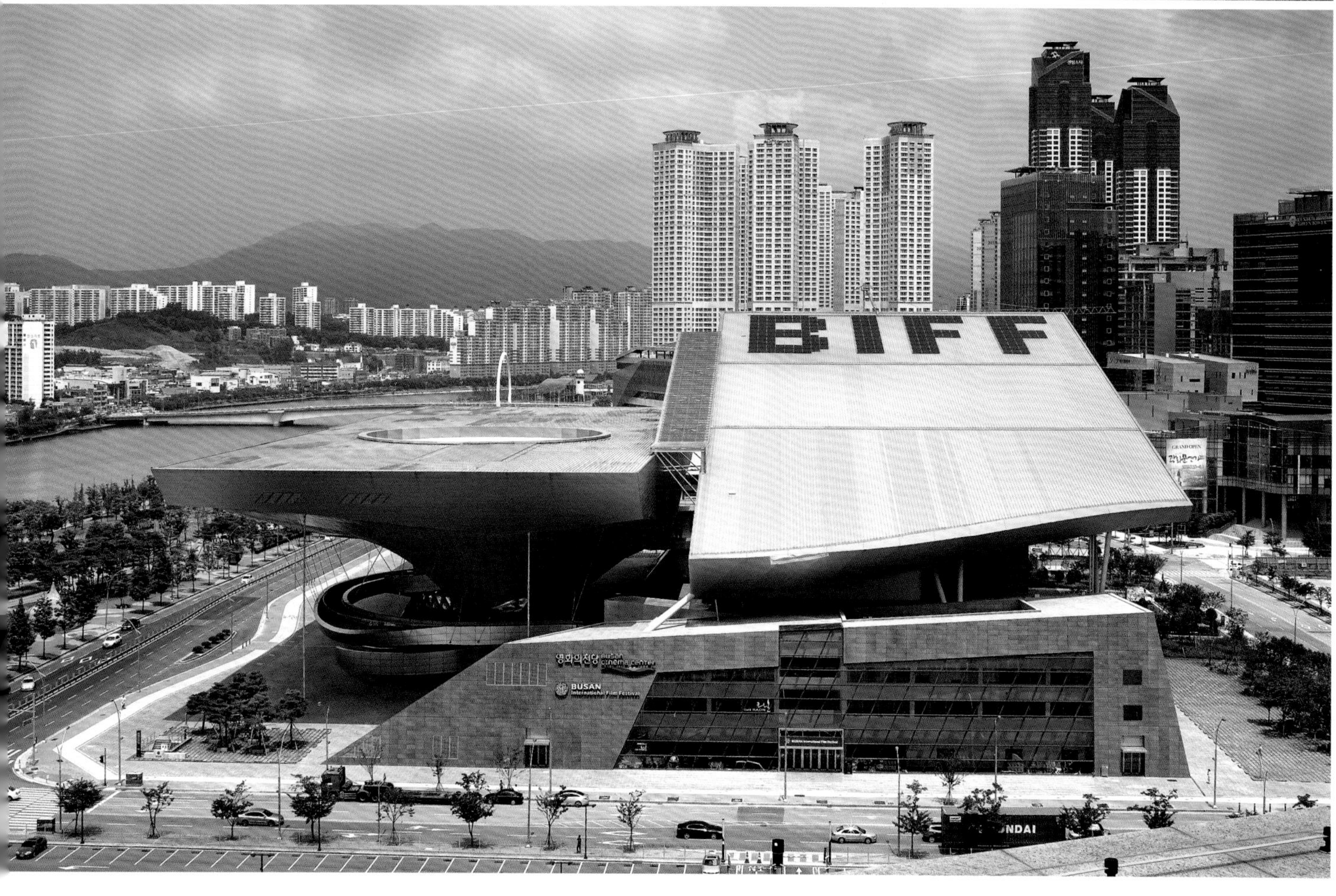
BIFF
BUSAN
HYUNDAI

The architects write that the "column-free roof covering a space comes closest to the idea of a 'flying' roof, which is further differentiated by its three-dimensionally articulated ceiling and [is] therefore not only a horizontal projection screen."

Den Architekten zufolge kommt „ein stützenfreies Dach, das schützend über bestimmten Zonen schwebt, am ehesten einem ‚fliegenden' Dach nahe. Seine Dreidimensionalität wird besonders betont; es ist mehr als eine horizontale Projektionsfläche."

Selon les architectes, « le toit sans colonnes recouvrant un espace est le plus proche de l'idée de toit "volant", qui se distingue en outre par son plafond articulé en trois dimensions et [n'est] donc pas un simple écran de projection horizontal ».

Lighting and color effects on the lower face of the "flying roof" animate the space, especially after nightfall. Below, a section drawing shows how lightly the large roof sits on the buildings.

Durch Licht- und Farbeffekte auf der Unterseite des „fliegenden Dachs" gewinnt der Bau besonders nach Einbruch der Dunkelheit an Dynamik. Ein Querschnitt (unten) illustriert, wie scheinbar leicht das große Dach auf den Baukörpern liegt.

Les effets de lumière colorée sur la face inférieure du « toit volant » animent l'espace, en particulier la nuit. Ci-dessous, une coupe montre avec quelle légèreté le vaste toit est posé sur le bâtiment.

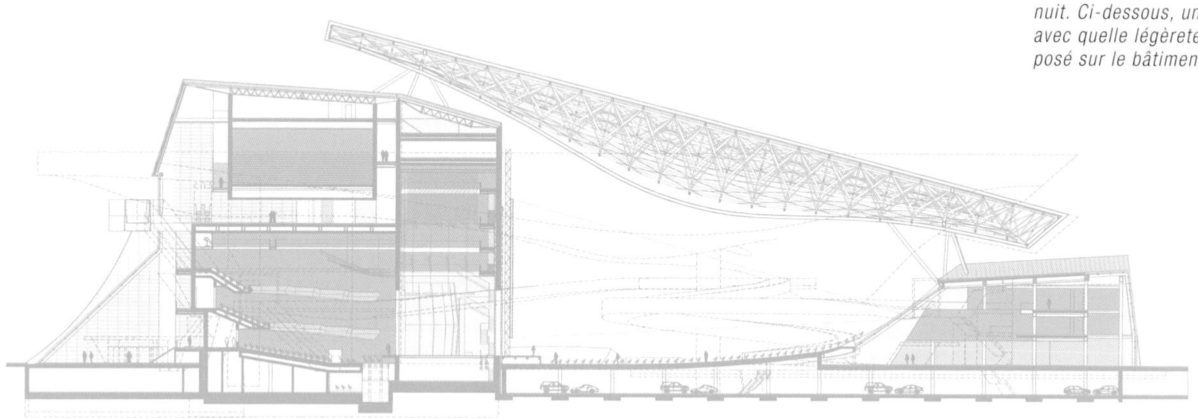

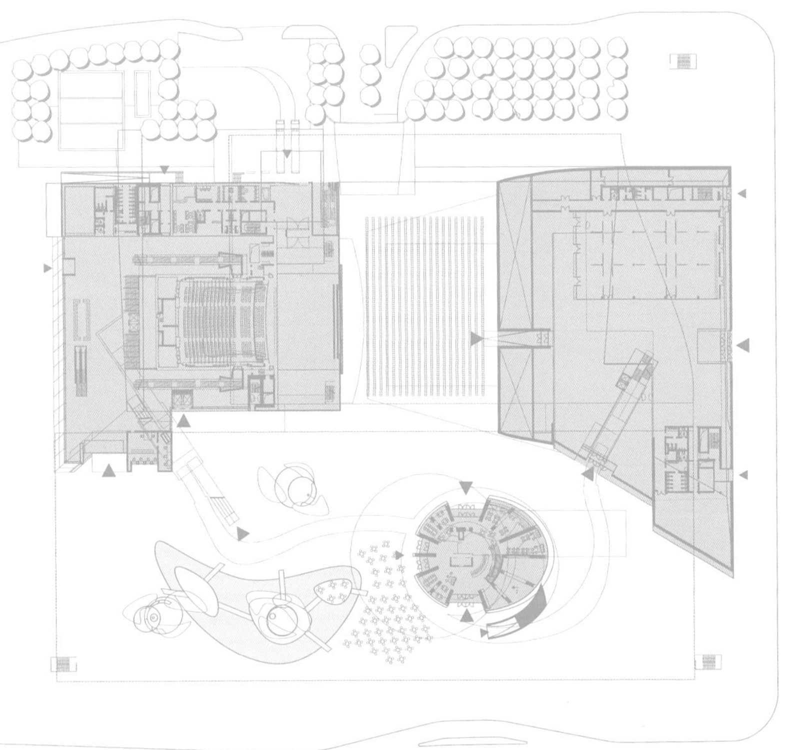

Although when it is seen from the exterior, the complex appears to be quite complicated, the plan to the left shows that it is, in fact, very rational, with spectacular spaces, such as the large projection area seen below.

Obwohl das Center nach außen komplex wirkt, erweist sich der Grundriss (links) als ausgesprochen rational, bietet aber dennoch spektakuläre Räume wie das große Filmtheater unten.

Bien que, de l'extérieur, le complexe ait l'air assez alambiqué, le plan ci-contre montre qu'il est en fait très rationnel, avec des espaces spectaculaires, tels que le vaste espace de projection ci-dessous.

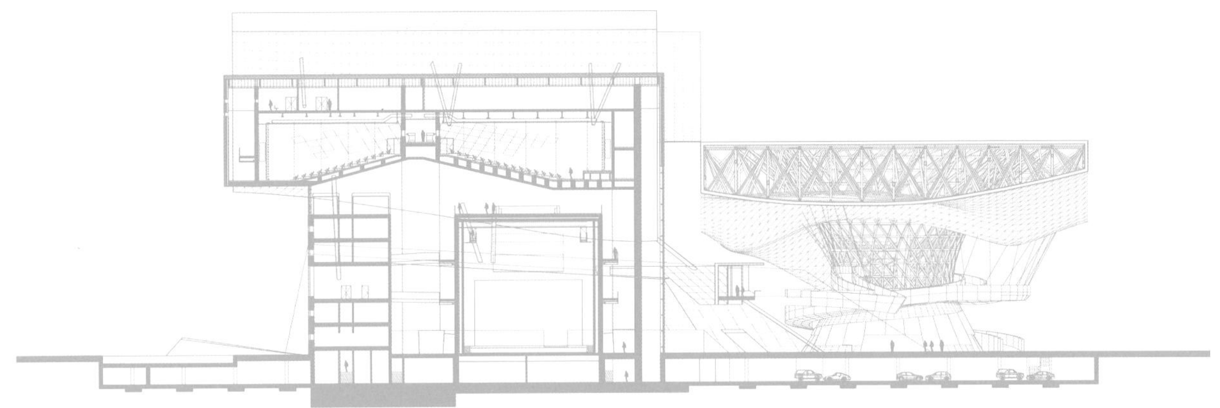

Within the complex at ground level, escalators and platforms link the different volumes and offer varied views of the architecture.

Eine Ansicht des Komplexes zu ebener Erde: Rolltreppen und Zwischenebenen verbinden die unterschiedlichen Baukörper und sorgen für abwechslungsreiche Sichtachsen.

Dans le complexe, au rez-de-chaussée, des escaliers mécaniques et des passerelles relient les différents volumes et offrent des vues variées de l'architecture.

ODILE DECQ

Studio Odile Decq
11 Rue des Arquebusiers
75003 Paris
France

Tel: +33 1 42 71 27 41
Fax: +33 1 42 71 27 42
E-mail: office@odiledecq.com
Web: www.odiledecq.com

ODILE DECQ was born in 1955 in Laval, France, and obtained her degree in Architecture (DPLG) at UP6 in Paris in 1978. She studied Urbanism at the Institut d'Etudes Politiques in Paris (1979) and founded her office in 1980. Her former Partner Benoît Cornette died in 1998. She has designed a number of apartment buildings in Paris; the French Pavilion at the 1996 Architecture Biennale in Venice (Italy); three buildings for Nantes University (France, 1993–99); a refurbishment of the Conference Hall of UNESCO in Paris (France, 2001); renovation of the Cureghem Veterinary School in Brussels (Belgium, 2001); and the Liaunig Museum (Neuhaus, Austria, 2004). Decq has been very much in the news with her recent MACRO Museum of Contemporary Art in Rome (Italy, 2004–10); the Opéra Restaurant (Paris, France, 2008–11); and the FRAC Contemporary Art Center in Rennes (France, 2009–12, published here). Winner of the Golden Lion at the Venice Architecture Biennale (1996) and the 1999 Benedictus Award for the Faculty of Economics and the Law Library at the University of Nantes, she is currently building the Great Site of Homo Erectus Fossils Museum (Nanjing, China, 2012–14).

ODILE DECQ wurde 1955 in Laval, Frankreich, geboren und erhielt ihr Architekturdiplom (DPLG) 1978 von der UP6 in Paris. Sie studierte Städtebau am Institut d'Études Politiques in Paris (1979) und gründete 1980 ihr Büro. Ihr Partner Benoît Cornette verstarb 1998. Sie entwarf eine Reihe von Apartmenthäusern in Paris, den Französischen Pavillon der Architekturbiennale 1996 in Venedig, drei Gebäude für die Universität Nantes (1993–99), realisierte die Sanierung des Kongresszentrums der UNESCO in Paris (2001), die Sanierung der Fakultät für Veterinärmedizin Cureghem in Brüssel (2001) und das Museum Liaunig (Neuhaus, Österreich, 2004). Große Aufmerksamkeit erfuhren Decqs Entwürfe für das MACRO Museum für zeitgenössische Kunst in Rom (2004–10), das Restaurant Opéra (Paris, 2008–11) und das Zentrum für zeitgenössische Kunst in Rennes, FRAC (2009–12, hier vorgestellt). Decq erhielt den Goldenen Löwen der Architekturbiennale Venedig (1996) und den Benedictus Award für die rechtswissenschaftliche Bibliothek an der Universität von Nantes. Derzeit arbeitet sie am Great Site of Homo Erectus Fossils Museum (Nanjing, China, 2012–14).

Née en 1955 à Laval, **ODILE DECQ** obtient son diplôme en architecture (DPLG) à l'UP6, à Paris, en 1978. Elle étudie l'urbanisme à l'Institut d'études politiques de Paris (1979) et crée son agence en 1980. Son associé, Benoît Cornette décède en 1998. Elle réalise plusieurs immeubles d'appartements à Paris ; le pavillon de la France à la Biennale d'architecture 1996 de Venise ; trois bâtiments pour l'université de Nantes (1993–99) ; le réaménagement du hall de conférences de l'Unesco, à Paris (2001) ; la rénovation de l'École vétérinaire Cureghem de Bruxelles (2001) et le musée Liaunig (Neuhaus, Autriche, 2004). Odile Decq a récemment défrayé la chronique avec le Musée d'art contemporain MACRO (Rome, 2004–10) ; l'Opéra Restaurant (Paris, 2008–11) et le FRAC Bretagne (Rennes, 2009–12, présenté ici). Lauréate du Lion d'or de la Biennale d'architecture de Venise (1996) et du prix Benedictus 1999 pour la faculté des sciences économiques et la bibliothèque de droit de l'université de Nantes, elle construit actuellement le Musée de géologie, d'archéologie et d'anthropologie de Nankin (Nankin, Chine, 2012–14).

FRAC BRETAGNE

Rennes, France, 2009–12

Address: 19 Avenue André Mussat, CS 81123, 35011 Rennes CEDEX, France, +33 299 37 37 93, www.fracbretagne.fr
Area: 5000 m². Client: Région Bretagne. Cost: not disclosed

The basic plan of the FRAC Contemporary Art Center is a strict rectangle, but, within this envelope, the architect experiments with angles and varying heights. She states that the project "reinterprets the apparent contradictory and dual idea" of a necessary inscription of the building in the urban landscape "simultaneously with that of immaterial escape, from nature to artificiality, from heavy to light, from shade to brightness." She places a particular emphasis on the section of the design which "reveals itself in the transfer from horizontal to vertical, from outside to inside and outside again, from the foyer toward the artworks." An atrium and ramps are the conduits for a "vertical promenade," or an exploration of exhibition areas and spaces and other activities. "The space," she says, "is never static but always dynamic and carries the visitor along in a constant exploration." Within what might appear to be a strict volume, the architect explores the ambiguity of materials, shapes, and structure. In 2004, Odile Decq wrote of "a massive block. Black material. Densities of black. From absorbing matte to reflecting lustrous black, becoming transparent matte. The inversion of weight and lightness. Gravity in suspension. Brute and sophisticated."

Der Grundriss des Zentrums für zeitgenössische Kunst, FRAC, ist ein strenges Rechteck, doch im Innenraum experimentiert die Architektin mit Winkeln und variierenden Höhen. Für sie wurzelt das Projekt in einer „widersprüchlichen und dualen Idee", die das Gebäude in die urbane Landschaft einschreiben will und „gleichzeitig ins Immaterielle drängt, aus der Natur in die künstliche Form, aus der Schwere in die Leichtigkeit, aus dem Schatten ins Licht". Odile Decq legt besonderen Wert auf „Übergänge von Horizontalität zu Vertikalität, von außen nach innen und wieder nach außen, vom Foyer zu den Kunstwerken". Über Lichthof und Rampe erschließt sich die „vertikale Promenade", ein Rundgang durch Ausstellungsräume und weitere Gebäudebereiche. „Der Raum", so die Architektin, „ist niemals statisch, immer in Bewegung und nimmt den Besucher mit auf eine unendliche Entdeckungsreise." Im Kontext des streng anmutenden Gebäudes erkundet die Architektin die Vielseitigkeit von Materialien, Formen und Strukturen. 2004 schrieb Decq über ihre Arbeit: „Ein massiver Block. Schwarzes Material. Gedrängte Schattierungen von Schwarz, von schluckend-matt über schimmernd-reflektierend bis hin zu transparent-matt. Die Verkehrung von Schwere und Leichtigkeit. Schwebende Schwerkraft. Roh und elegant."

Le plan de base du FRAC Bretagne est strictement rectangulaire, mais dans cette enveloppe, l'architecte joue avec les angles et les différences de hauteur. Elle précise que le projet « réinterprète l'idée duelle et apparemment contradictoire de la nécessaire inscription urbaine et de l'échappée immatérielle, du naturel et de l'artificiel, du lourd et du léger, de l'ombre et de la lumière ». Elle insiste sur la coupe du projet qui « est exposée dans la translation de l'horizontal au vertical, du dehors au dedans puis vers le dehors encore, du foyer vers les œuvres ». Un atrium et des rampes sont les chemins d'une « déambulation verticale » ou d'une exploration des espaces d'exposition et des espaces d'autres activités. « L'espace est non statique mais dynamique et attire le visiteur dans une constante découverte. » Dans un volume apparemment strict, l'architecte explore les ambiguïtés des matériaux, des formes et des structures. En 2004, Odile Decq décrivait son œuvre comme « un bloc. Des matières de noir. Des densités de noir. Du mat absorbant au noir mordoré, réfléchissant, devenant transparent. L'inversion du lourd et du léger. Gravité en suspension. Brut et sophistiqué ».

Above, section drawings show the relation between spaces below grade and the ground floor. Right, two pictures taken at nightfall give an idea of the originality and power of the building.

Querschnitte (oben) illustrieren das Zusammenspiel von unter- und oberirdischen Bereichen. Zwei Aufnahmen des Baus bei Einbruch der Dunkelheit vermitteln seine Originalität und Ausdrucksstärke.

Ci-dessus, des coupes montrent la relation entre les espaces en sous-sol et le rez-de-chaussée. Page de droite, deux vues à la nuit tombante donnent une idée de l'originalité et de la puissance du bâtiment.

Slanting or angled surfaces and a contrast between red and black alternate with high glazing on the ground floor.

Im Erdgeschoss zeigt sich ein Wechsel aus geneigten und schiefwinkligen Flächen, ein Kontrast von Rot und Schwarz mit hohen Fensterflächen.

Au rez-de-chaussée, les surfaces obliques ou inclinées et le contraste entre le noir et le rouge alternent avec les hauts vitrages.

A slightly industrial vocabulary of materials is employed, as seen in the images above. Right, a floor plan demonstrates the use of angled surfaces to create spaces that communicate with each other.

Die Formensprache erinnert an Industriebauten, wie die Aufnahmen oben belegen. Ein Etagengrundriss (rechts) zeigt den Einsatz schräger Linien, die einen Dialog zwischen den Räumen entstehen lassen.

Le vocabulaire des matériaux est plutôt industriel, comme on peut le voir ci-dessus. Ci-dessous, un plan au sol montre l'usage des surfaces inclinées pour créer des espaces communiquant entre eux.

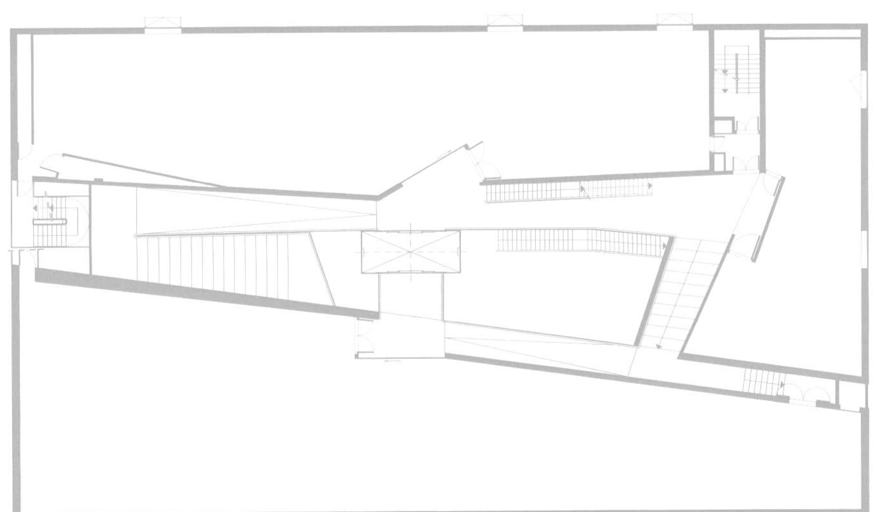

In recent years, Odile Decq has emerged as one of the most significant contemporary French architects. These sculptural volumes are carefully thought out to fulfill the functionality of the center—better understood with the plan to the right.

In den vergangenen Jahren konnte sich Odile Decq als eine der bedeutendsten französischen Architektinnen unserer Zeit etablieren. Die skulpturalen Baukörper sind höchst durchdacht auf unterschiedliche Funktionen abgestimmt, ablesbar am Grundriss (rechts).

Odile Decq est devenue, ces dernières années, l'une des plus importantes architectes françaises. Ces volumes sculpturaux sont soigneusement conçus pour remplir les fonctionnalités du centre – ce qui apparaît clairement sur le plan ci-contre.

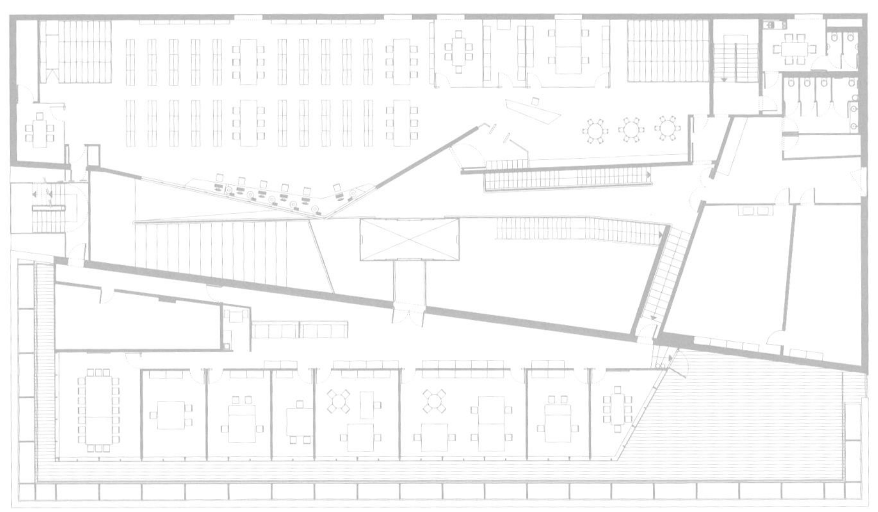

DELUGAN MEISSL

Delugan Meissl Associated Architects
Mittersteig 13/4
1040 Vienna
Austria

Tel: +43 1 585 36 90
Fax: +43 1 585 36 90 11
E-mail: office@dmaa.at
Web: www.dmaa.at

Delugan-Meissl ZT GmbH was jointly founded by Elke Delugan-Meissl and Roman Delugan in 1993. In 2004, the firm expanded into a partnership and its name changed to Delugan Meissl Associated Architects. **ELKE DELUGAN-MEISSL** was born in Linz, Austria, and studied at the University of Technology in Innsbruck. She worked in several offices in Innsbruck and Vienna, before creating Delugan Meissl. **ROMAN DELUGAN** was born in Merano, Italy, and studied at the University of Applied Arts in Vienna. **DIETMAR FEISTEL** was born in Bregenz, Austria, and studied at the Vienna University of Technology. He became a Partner at Delugan Meissl in 2004. **MARTIN JOSST** was born in Hamburg, Germany, and studied at the Muthesius Academy of Art and Design in Kiel, Germany, before working in the office of Morphosis in Los Angeles and becoming a Partner at Delugan Meissl in 2004. They were the ex-aequo First Prize winners for the Darat King Abdullah II Cultural Center (Amman, Jordan, 2008); and have completed the Porsche Museum (Stuttgart, Germany, 2006–08); the EYE Film Institute (Amsterdam, the Netherlands, 2009–11, published here); and a number of residential projects in Vienna.

Die Delugan-Meissl ZT GmbH wurde 1993 von Elke Delugan-Meissl und Roman Delugan gegründet. 2004 vergrößerte sich das Büro zur Partnerschaft und firmiert seither unter Delugan Meissl Associated Architects. **ELKE DELUGAN-MEISSL**, geboren im österreichischen Linz, studierte an der Technischen Universität Innsbruck und arbeitete vor der Gründung von Delugan Meissl in verschiedenen Büros in Innsbruck und Wien. **ROMAN DELUGAN**, geboren im italienischen Meran, studierte an der Universität für angewandte Kunst in Wien. **DIETMAR FEISTEL**, geboren in Bregenz, Österreich, machte seinen Abschluss an der Technischen Universität Wien und wurde 2004 Partner bei Delugan Meissl. Der in Hamburg geborene **MARTIN JOSST** studierte an der Muthesius-Kunsthochschule für Kunst, Design und Raumstrategien in Kiel, bevor er bei Morphosis in Los Angeles arbeitete und 2004 Partner bei Delugan Meissl wurde. Das Büro erhielt ex aequo den ersten Preis für den Entwurf des Darat King Abdullah II Cultural Center (Amman, Jordanien, 2008). Abgeschlossene Projekte sind u. a. das Porsche Museum (Stuttgart, 2006–08), das hier publizierte EYE Filmmuseum (Amsterdam, 2009–11) und eine Reihe von Wohnungsbauprojekten in Wien.

Delugan-Meissl ZT GmbH est fondée par Elke Delugan-Meissl et Roman Delugan en 1993. L'agence s'agrandit en 2004 et devient une société en partenariat sous le nom Delugan Meissl Associated Architects. Née à Linz, en Autriche, **ELKE DELUGAN-MEISSL** étudie à l'Université de technologie d'Innsbruck. Elle travaille dans plusieurs agences à Innsbruck et Vienne, avant de créer Delugan Meissl. Né à Merano, en Italie, **ROMAN DELUGAN** étudie à l'Université des arts appliqués de Vienne. Né à Bregenz, en Autriche, **DIETMAR FEISTEL** étudie à l'Université de technologie de Vienne. Il devient associé de Delugan Meissl en 2004. Né à Hambourg, **MARTIN JOSST** étudie à l'École d'art et de design Muthesius de Kiel, en Allemagne, puis travaille chez Morphosis à Los Angeles avant de devenir associé de Delugan Meissl en 2004. L'agence est premier prix ex aequo pour le Centre culturel Darat King Abdullah II (Amman, Jordanie, 2008) et réalise le musée Porsche (Stuttgart, 2006–08) ; l'EYE Film Institute (Amsterdam, 2009–11, présenté ici) et plusieurs projets de logements à Vienne.

EYE FILM INSTITUTE

Amsterdam, The Netherlands, 2009–11

Address: IJ Promenade 1, 1031 KT, Amsterdam, The Netherlands, +31 205 89 14 00, www.eyefilm.nl
Area: 6300 m². Client: ING Real Estate. Cost: €3 million
Collaboration: Bureau Bouwkunde Rotterdam, Abt-Adviseurs in Bouwtechniek, Delft; Bouwbedrijf M.J. de Nijs en Zonen BV

The architects state that this project is meant to be a new visual landmark in the developing Amsterdam Noord area, the former Shell Terrain on the opposite side of the IJ river from Centraal Station. The surprising exterior of the building, clad in white aluminum tiles, cantilevers out, and particularly at night offers an obvious destination for people visiting the area. EYE is the Dutch center for film culture and heritage. A promenade along the river leads to the entrance of the building. Broad steps allow for exterior seating, while inside, generous exhibition areas are characterized by full-height glazing that looks out on the outdoor terrace. The wedge-shaped plan points outward toward the water and Amsterdam's main railway station. Dubbed "the Oyster" by local residents, the building includes four movie theaters ranging in size from 67 to over 300 seats. The EYE Institute is located near the Netherlands Institute for Sound and Vision (Neutelings Riedijk).

Mit ihrem Projekt wollten die Architekten einen markanten Neubau für das Stadtentwicklungsgebiet Amsterdam Noord – auf dem ehemaligen Shell-Firmengelände am Nordufer des IJ, gegenüber dem Hauptbahnhof – schaffen. Das Filminstitut EYE (Niederländisches Zentrum für Filmkultur und -erbe) überrascht mit ungewöhnlich dynamischer Form und wirkt mit seiner Hülle aus Weißaluminium vor allem bei Dunkelheit sehr präsent. Über die Uferpromenade gelangen Besucher zum Eingang des Museums, vor dem sich ein großzügiger Vorplatz erstreckt, dessen Stufen zugleich eine Sitzgelegenheit bieten. Die weitläufigen Ausstellungsflächen zeichnen sich durch raumhohe Verglasung aus, durch die man auf die Terrasse blickt. Der keilförmige Grundriss des von den Anwohnern „die Auster" getauften Gebäudes verläuft spitz auf den Fluss und den Hauptbahnhof zu. Im Inneren sind vier Kinosäle mit 67 bis 300 Sitzplätzen untergebracht. In unmittelbarer Nähe liegt das Niederländische Institut für Bild und Ton von Neutelings Riedijk.

Les architectes ont voulu faire de ce projet un nouvel emblème visuel pour le quartier en expansion d'Amsterdam Noord, l'ancien site de Shell, sur les berges de l'IJ, juste en face de la gare centrale. L'extérieur surprenant du bâtiment, en porte-à-faux et revêtu d'un carrelage blanc d'aluminium, offre une attraction évidente pour les visiteurs, surtout la nuit. EYE est le centre hollandais de la culture et du patrimoine cinématographique. Une promenade longeant la rivière mène à l'entrée du bâtiment. De larges marches permettent de s'asseoir à l'extérieur, tandis qu'à l'intérieur, des espaces d'exposition généreux, caractérisés par un vitrage sur toute la hauteur, offrent une vue sur la terrasse extérieure. Le plan en forme de coin pointe à l'extérieur, vers l'eau et la gare principale d'Amsterdam. Surnommé « l'Huître » par les habitants, le bâtiment comprend quatre salles de cinéma, de 67 à plus de 300 places. L'EYE Institute est situé près de l'Institut néerlandais de l'image et du son (Neutelings Riedijk).

Located in a newly developed area of Amsterdam, near the railway station, the Eye Film Institute seems to be more isolated in these images than it is in reality. The angled, cantilevered forms give the building a dramatic presence.

Das Filminstitut EYE liegt in einem neuen Erschließungsgebiet von Amsterdam unweit des Bahnhofs und wirkt auf diesen Ansichten isolierter als es tatsächlich ist. Die schrägen auskragenden Formen verleihen dem Bau eine dramatische Präsenz.

Situé dans un nouveau quartier en expansion, près de la gare d'Amsterdam, le Eye Film Institute semble sur ces photos plus isolé qu'il ne l'est en réalité. Les formes inclinées en porte-à-faux donnent au bâtiment une présence spectaculaire.

Seen from above, the institute stands out in its dynamic white form on the water's edge. Above, a cantilevered platform overhangs other public space near the structure.

Aus der Vogelperspektive sticht das Institut mit seinem dynamischen weißen Baukörper am Wasser auffällig hervor. Oben überspannt eine auskragende Terrasse öffentliche Bereiche neben dem Gebäude.

Vue du dessus, la forme blanche et dynamique de l'Institut ressort au bord de l'eau. Ci-dessus, une terrasse en porte-à-faux surplombe un autre espace public près du bâtiment.

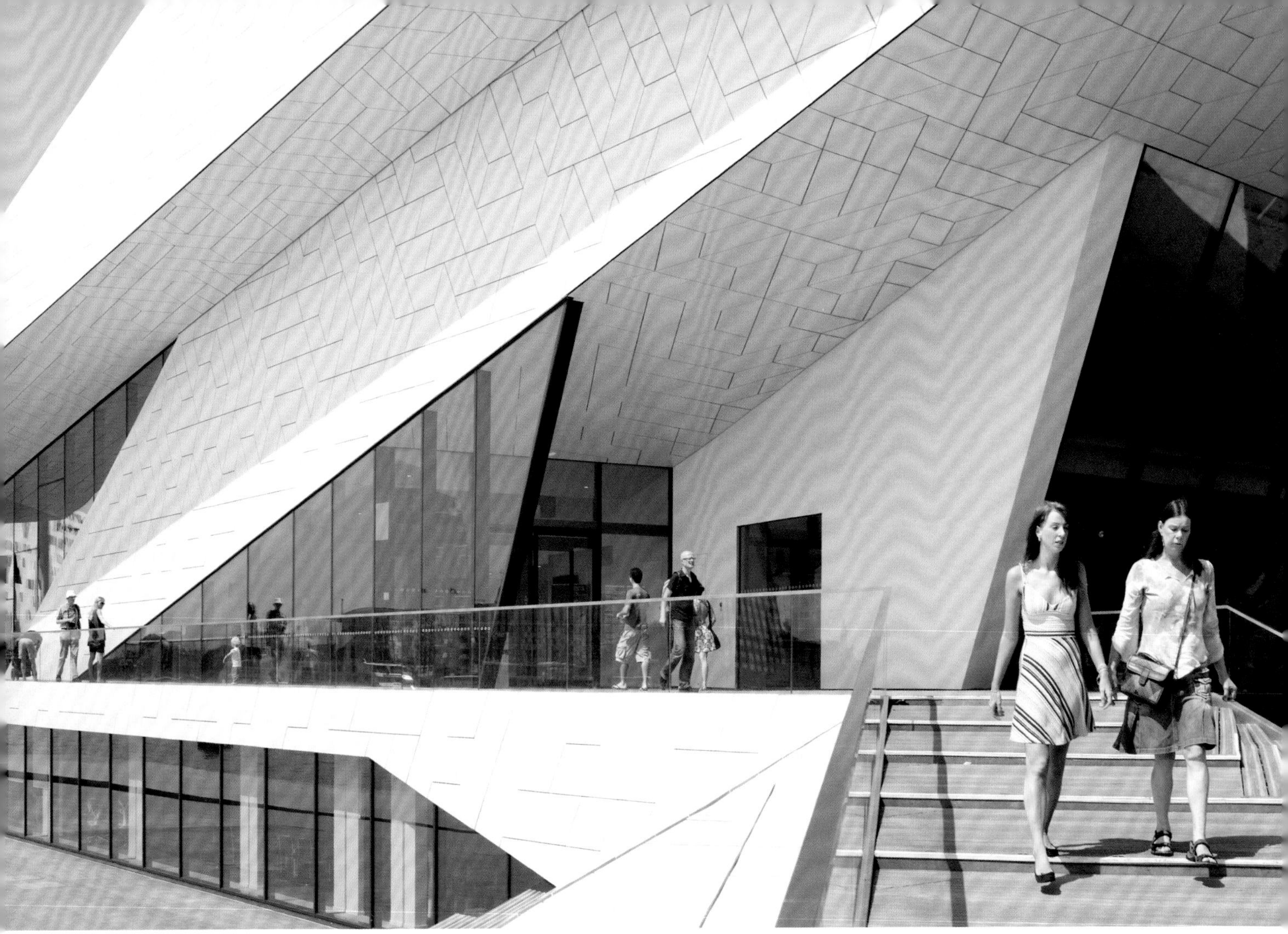

External walkways and ample glazing make the building permeable to pedestrians. Below, drawings highlight the major interior spaces of the complex.

Außenrampen und großzügige Verglasung machen den Bau durchlässig für Passanten. Zeichnungen (unten) veranschaulichen die zentralen Bereiche im Inneren des Komplexes.

Des passerelles extérieures et un important vitrage rendent le bâtiment perméable aux piétons. Ci-dessous, les dessins soulignent les principaux espaces intérieurs du complexe.

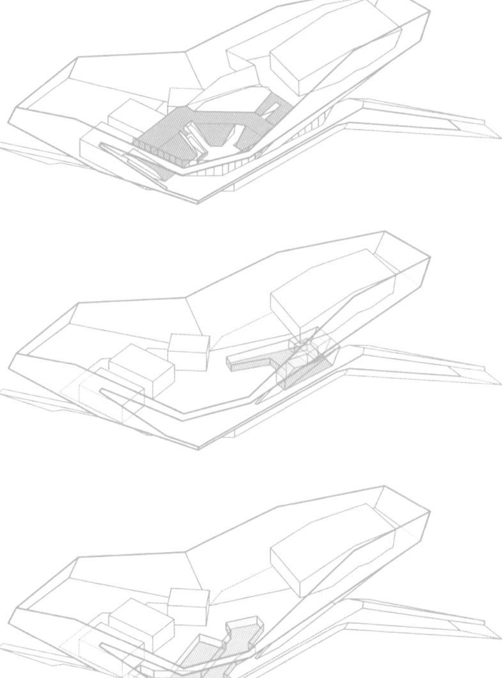

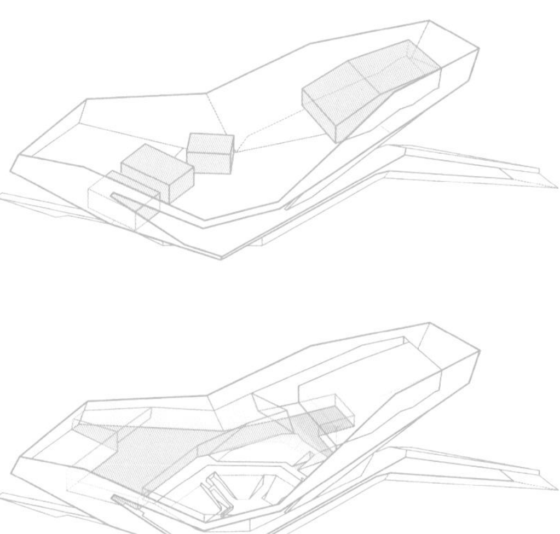

Despite its apparent opacity when seen under certain angles, the building is broadly opened to natural light in public spaces, such as the one on the left.

Obwohl der Bau aus bestimmten Blickwinkeln eher geschlossen wirkt, öffnet er sich in öffentlichen Zonen, wie links im Bild, großzügig zum Licht.

Malgré son opacité apparente suivant les angles de vue, le bâtiment est largement ouvert à la lumière naturelle dans les espaces publics tels que celui ci-contre.

The dramatic angles that characterize the exterior of the building are clearly present inside as well. Below, plans showing the theater spaces.

Die dramatische Linienführung des Außenbaus finden sich eindeutig auch im Innern des Gebäudes wieder. Unten Grundrisse mit den Kinosälen.

Les angles spectaculaires qui caractérisent l'extérieur du bâtiment sont clairement présents à l'intérieur aussi. Ci-dessous, des plans montrant les salles de spectacle.

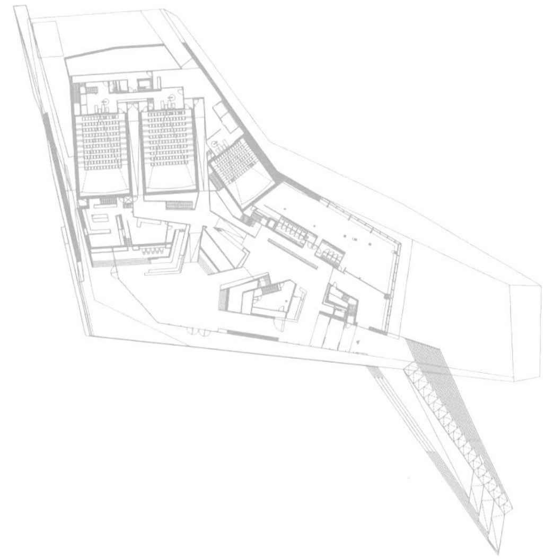

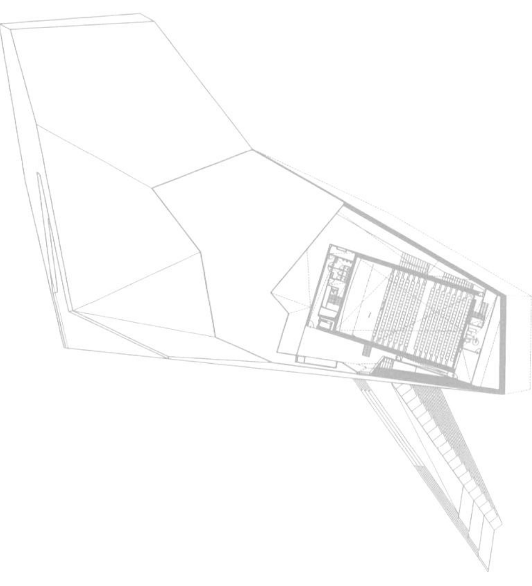

1

GAGE CLEMENCEAU

Gage / Clemenceau Architects
131 Norfolk Street Storefront
New York, NY 10002
USA

Tel: +1 212 437 2200
Fax: +1 212 437 0010
E-mail: info@gageclemenceau.com
Web: www.gageclemenceau.com

GAGE CLEMENCEAU was founded in 2002 by Mark Foster Gage and Marc Clemenceau Bailly. Mark Gage received his B.Arch degree from the University of Notre Dame (Notre Dame, Indiana, 1992–97) and his M.Arch degree from Yale (2000–01). He worked in the office of Robert A. M. Stern (2001–02), before becoming a Principal of his own firm. He is Chair of Admissions and Assistant Dean of the Yale School of Architecture. Marc Bailly is an architect, and directs the firm's design and management. Their work includes the Miller Residence (Garden City, New York, 2010); collaboration with Nicola Formichetti on a dress for Lady Gaga (New York, New York, 2011); Eich Residence (New York, New York, 2011); OMG Jeans (New York, New York, 2011); Starworks New York (New York, New York, 2011); and a large number of exhibition and design projects, all in the USA. Gage Clemenceau completed concept stores for Nicola Formichetti in Beijing, Hong Kong, and New York (2011, published here) as part of ongoing work with the designer that includes a store in Tokyo (in design, 2012). The firm was selected as one of the architecture firms to represent the United States in the 2010 Beijing International Biennale.

GAGE CLEMENCEAU wurde 2002 von Mark Foster Gage und Marc Clemenceau Bailly gegründet. Mark Gage schloss seinen B. Arch. an der University of Notre Dame (Notre Dame, Indiana, 1992–97) und seinen M. Arch. an der Yale University (2000–01) ab. Vor Gründung seines eigenen Büros arbeitete er bei Robert A. M. Stern (2001–02). An der Architekturfakultät in Yale leitet er die Zulassungskommission und ist Vizedekan. Gemeinsam mit Gage leitet der Architekt Marc Clemenceau Bailly die Firmenprojekte. Zu Gage Clemenceaus Arbeiten in den USA zählen die Miller Residence (Garden City, New York, 2010), die Realisierung eines Kostüms für Lady Gaga in Kooperation mit Nicola Formichetti (New York, 2011), die Eich Residence (New York, 2011), OMG Jeans (New York, 2011), Starworks New York (New York, 2011) sowie eine Vielzahl an Ausstellungs- und Designprojekten, alle in den USA. Gage Clemenceau realisierte Konzeptstores für Nicola Formichetti in Peking, Hongkong (2012) und New York (2011, hier vorgestellt). Die Konzeptstores entstanden als laufende Zusammenarbeit mit dem Designer. Ein Store in Tokio ist seit 2012 in Planung. Gage Clemenceau vertrat die USA neben anderen Büros auf der Internationalen Biennale in Peking 2010.

GAGE CLEMENCEAU est créée en 2002 par Mark Foster Gage et Marc Clemenceau Bailly. Mark Gage obtient son B.Arch à l'université Notre-Dame (Notre Dame, Indiana, 1992–97) et son M.Arch à Yale (2000–01). Il travaille chez Robert A. M. Stern (2001–02) avant de devenir l'un des dirigeants de sa propre agence. Il est directeur des admissions et vice-doyen de l'École d'architecture de Yale. Marc Bailly est architecte et responsable du design et de la gestion de l'agence. Parmi ses réalisations, on compte Miller Residence (Garden City, New York, 2010) ; sa collaboration avec Nicola Formichetti sur une robe pour Lady Gaga (New York, 2011) ; Eich Residence (New York, 2011) ; OMG Jeans (New York, 2011) ; Starworks New York (New York, 2011) et de nombreux projets d'exposition et de design, tous aux États-Unis. Gage Clemenceau réalise, pour le designer Nicola Formichetti, des concept-stores à Pékin, Hong Kong et New York (présenté ici, 2011). Il s'agit d'une série en cours comprenant aussi un magasin à Tokyo (en cours de conception, 2012). L'agence a fait partie des architectes sélectionnés pour représenter les États-Unis à la Biennale internationale 2010 de Pékin.

NICOLA FORMICHETTI CONCEPT STORE

New York, New York, USA, 2011

Address: 80 Walker Street, New York, NY 10013, USA, www.nicolaformichetti.co
Area: 122 m². Client: Nicola Formichetti / BOFFO. Cost: not disclosed
Collaboration: Architectural Systems Inc. (Materials), Scott Thurm (Lighting Consultant)

In marked contrast to some of the "minimalist" boutique designs seen in recent years, the Nicola Formichetti store explores the use of dense, complicated, or even chaotic backgrounds to present clothing. Light and reflections are also part of the idea.

Der Store für Nicola Formichetti ist ein auffälliger Kontrast zu den üblichen „minimalistischen" Ladenräumen vergangener Jahre und setzt auf dichte, komplexe, fast chaotische Kulissen für Mode. Auch Licht- und Spiegeleffekte sind Teil des Konzepts.

Contrastant nettement avec certains designs « minimalistes » de ces dernières années, la boutique de Nicola Formichetti explore l'utilisation d'un décor complexe, voire chaotique, pour présenter les vêtements. Lumière et reflets font également partie du concept.

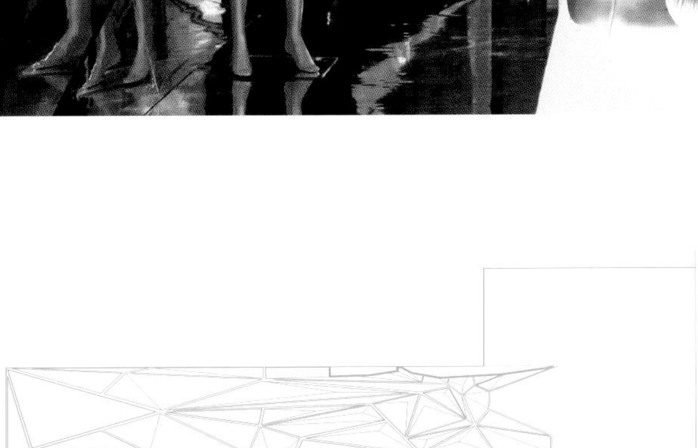

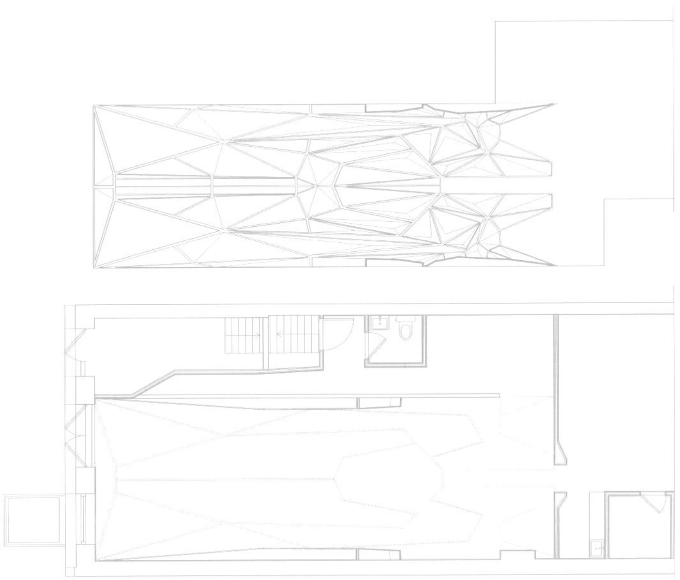

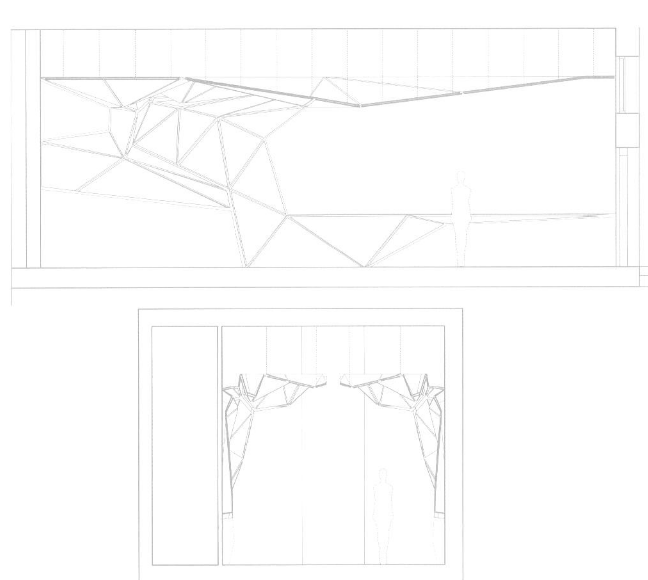

The appearance of the Nicola Formichetti stores designed by Gage Clemenceau seems to challenge the prevailing fashion aesthetic, creating an almost bewildering environment of reflections. The architects state: "Typically, fashion environments are defined by a rather restrained minimalism that focuses the attention only on the clothing—for the obvious reason of only selling clothes. In our collaboration with Nicola Formichetti, we rewrote this equation and produced a new genre of experimental space that not only showcased, but magnified, the impact of his fashion designs into a new form of immersive environment that fused the very genetics of architecture and fashion." Using robotically cut two-millimeter-thick mirrored acrylic sheets and fiberboard, the architects hung the "individual reflective facets" from the ceilings and walls. Each facet was attached to its neighbors using a system of precisely bent aluminum clips. Large sheets of mirrored abrasion-resistant plastic covered the floor.

Der von Gage Clemenceau entworfene Store von Nicola Formichetti stellt den in der Modewelt dominierenden Minimalismus infrage und setzt stattdessen auf geradezu schwindelerregendes, schillernd-reflektierendes Interiordesign. Die Architekten: „Räume für Mode sind minimalistisch, lenken die Aufmerksamkeit auf die Mode – wollen die Kleidung verkaufen. Bei unserer Zusammenarbeit mit Nicola Formichetti stellten wir dieses Prinzip infrage und definierten einen völlig neuartigen experimentellen Raumtypus, der die Mode nicht nur in den Vordergrund stellt, sondern ihre Wirkung verstärkt. Es entstand ein innovativer immersiver Raum, in dem die genetischen Codes von Architektur und Mode miteinander verschmelzen." Die robotisch gestanzten, 2 mm starken Faserplatten mit Acrylverspiegelung wurden Decken und Wänden vorgehängt und sind mit speziell gefertigten Aluminiumclips verbunden. Der Boden besteht aus verspiegeltem abriebbeständigem Kunststoff.

L'aspect donné aux boutiques de Nicola Formichetti par Gage Clemenceau semble défier l'esthétique dominant dans la mode par un environnement de reflets assez déconcertant. Les architectes expliquent que « normalement, les espaces dédiés à la mode se définissent par un minimalisme assez sobre censé concentrer l'attention sur les seuls vêtements, pour la raison évidente que l'on y vend uniquement des vêtements. En collaborant avec Nicola Formichetti, nous avons reformulé cette équation et produit un nouveau genre d'espace expérimental qui, non content de mettre en valeur, amplifie l'impact de ses designs de mode au cœur d'une forme nouvelle d'environnement immersif qui fusionne les codes génétiques de l'architecture et de la mode ». Les architectes ont utilisé des « facettes réfléchissantes individuelles » constituées de feuilles de miroir acrylique et de panneaux de fibres de 2 mm découpés au robot puis accrochés aux plafonds et aux murs. Chaque facette est rattachée à ses voisines par des agrafes en aluminium rigoureusement pliées. De larges feuilles de miroirs en plastique résistant à l'abrasion recouvrent le sol.

The interior view (above) might bring to mind some contemporary version of the Fritz Lang film Metropolis, *where art meets futuristic forms.*

Das Interieur oben wirkt wie eine zeitgenössische Interpretation von Fritz Langs Metropolis, *dem filmischen Meisterwerk, in dem Kunst auf futuristische Formen trifft.*

La vue intérieure (ci-dessus) peut faire penser à quelque version contemporaine du film de Fritz Lang, Metropolis, *où l'art prend des formes futuristes.*

The idea of complex reflections is inscribed in the design. Whether they bring to mind shattered glass or computer-generated environments, the store spaces are surprising.

Komplexe Spiegeleffekte sind integraler Bestandteil des Entwurfs. Ob man diese Effekte nun mit zersplittertem Glas oder computergenerierten Räumen assoziiert, überraschend sind sie allemal.

L'idée de reflets complexes est inscrite dans la conception. Qu'ils évoquent du verre brisé ou des environnements générés par ordinateur, les espaces de la boutique sont surprenants.

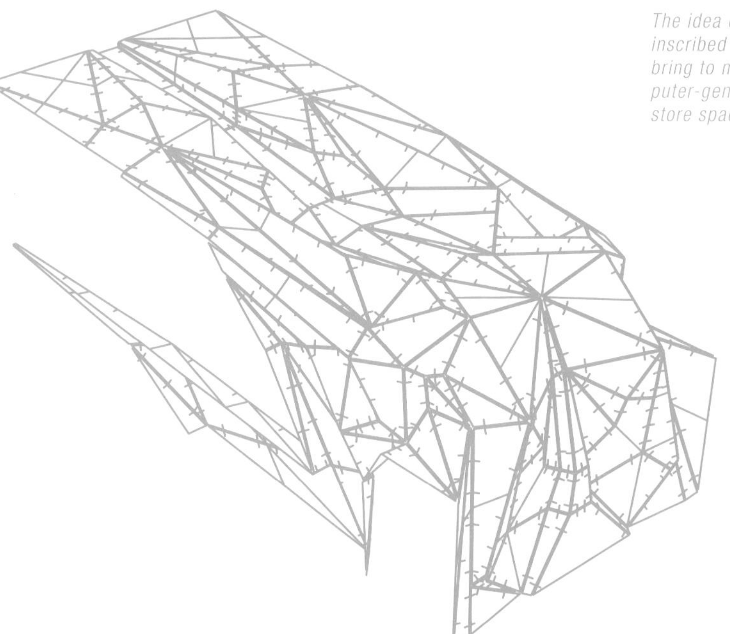

ANTÓN GARCÍA-ABRIL & ENSAMBLE STUDIO

Ensamble Studio
Calle Cabo Candelaria 9B
23290 Las Rozas
Madrid
Spain

Tel: +34 91 17 30 166
E-mail: ensamblestudio1@gmail.com
Web: www.ensamble.info

ANTÓN GARCÍA-ABRIL RUIZ was born in Madrid, Spain, in 1969. He graduated from the ETSA of Madrid in Architecture and Urbanism in 1995 and went on to receive a doctorate from the same institution in 2000. Rafael Moneo was a family friend, and García-Abril worked in the office of Santiago Calatrava (1992) and in that of Alberto Campo Baeza (1990–94). He created his first firm in 1995, and his present one, **ENSAMBLE STUDIO**, in 2000. The name of his firm is derived from "assemble," a term used in architecture, and the musical term "ensemble." His completed projects include the Musical Studies Center (Santiago de Compostela, 2002); a concert hall and music school (Medina del Campo, 2003); Martemar House (Málaga, 2003–05); Valdés Studio (Madrid, 2004); La Casa del Lector Library (Madrid, 2006); SGAE Central Office (Santiago de Compostela, 2005–07); Berklee Tower of Music (Valencia, 2007); and Paraiso Theater (Shanghai, China, 2007). More recent projects include Hemeroscopium House (Madrid, 2006–08); Lyric Theater (Mexico City, Mexico, 2008); the Fleta Theater (Zaragoza, 2008); the Cervantes Theater (Mexico City, Mexico, 2012, published here); and the Reader's House (Madrid, 2012, also published here), all in Spain unless otherwise indicated.

ANTÓN GARCÍA-ABRIL RUIZ wurde 1969 in Madrid geboren. Sein Studium der Architektur und Stadtplanung schloss er 1995 an der ETSA in Madrid ab, wo er 2000 promovierte. Rafael Moneo zählte zum Freundeskreis seiner Familie. García-Abril arbeitete sowohl für Santiago Calatrava (1992) als auch für Alberto Campo Baeza (1990–94). Sein erstes eigenes Büro gründete er 1995, sein heutiges Büro, **ENSAMBLE STUDIO**, folgte 2000. Der Name des Büros leitet sich von den architektonischen bzw. musikalischen Begriffen *assemble* (montieren) und *ensemble* ab. Zu seinen realisierten Projekten zählen das Zentrum für musikalische Studien (Santiago de Compostela, 2002), eine Konzerthalle und Musikschule (Medina del Campo, 2003), die Casa Martemar (Málaga, 2003–05), das Studio Valdés (Madrid, 2004), die Bibliothek La Casa del Lector (Madrid, 2006), die SGAE-Zentrale (Santiago de Compostela, 2005–07), die Torre de la Música (Valencia, 2007) und das Paraiso-Theater (Shanghai, China, 2007). Jüngere Projekte sind das Haus Hemeroscopium (Las Rozas, Madrid, 2007–08), das Teatro Lírico (Mexiko-Stadt, 2008), das Fleta-Theater (Saragossa, 2008), das Cervantes-Theater (Mexiko-Stadt, hier vorgestellt) sowie die Casa del Lector (Madrid, 2012, ebenfalls hier vorgestellt).

ANTÓN GARCÍA-ABRIL RUIZ est né à Madrid, en 1969. Il obtient son diplôme en architecture et urbanisme en 1995, puis son doctorat en 2000 à l'ETSA de Madrid. Rafael Moneo est un ami de la famille et García-Abril travaille chez Santiago Calatrava (1992) et chez Alberto Campo Baeza (1990–94). Il crée sa première agence en 1995 et, en 2000, **ENSAMBLE STUDIO**, son agence actuelle, qui tire son nom de la fusion du terme d'architecture « assembler » et du terme musical « ensemble ». Ses projets réalisés comprennent le Centre de hautes études musicales (Saint-Jacques de Compostelle, 2002) ; une salle de concert et une école de musique (Medina del Campo, 2003) ; la maison Martemar (Málaga, 2003–05) ; le Valdés Studio (Madrid, 2004) ; la bibliothèque La Casa del Lector (Madrid, 2006) ; les bureaux du SGAE (Saint-Jacques de Compostelle, 2005–07) ; la Torre de la Música (Valence, 2007) et le théâtre Paraiso (Shanghai, 2007). Leurs récents projets comprennent la maison Hemeroscopium (Madrid, 2006–08) ; le Teatro Lírico (Mexico, Mexique, 2008), le théâtre Fleta (Saragosse, 2008) ; le théâtre Cervantes (Mexico, Mexique, présenté ici), la Casa del Lector (Madrid, 2012, également présentée ici), tous en Espagne, sauf mention contraire.

Saks Fifth Aven
BAYSA

CERVANTES THEATER

Mexico City, Mexico, 2012

Address: C/Motolinía 20 06000 México D.F., Mexico
Area: 11 500 m². Client: SGAE - Grupo Carso
Cost: not disclosed

Seen from below (left) the theater appears to take on the form of a space frame, with large openings. Right, the structure stands next to the imposing Soumaya Museum by Fernando Romero.

In der Untersicht (links) wirkt der Überbau des Theaters wie ein Raumfachwerk mit übergroßen Öffnungen. Der Bau liegt unmittelbar neben dem monumentalen Soumaya Museum von Fernando Romero (rechts).

Vu du dessous (à gauche), le théâtre semble prendre la forme d'un châssis aux larges ouvertures. À droite, la structure s'élève à côté de l'imposant musée Soumaya de Fernando Romero.

The building, seen here when still partially under construction, is basically below grade, as the axonometric drawings to the right show.

Der Komplex, hier noch teilweise im Bau, erstreckt sich weitgehend unterirdisch, wie die Axonometrien rechts belegen.

Le bâtiment, ici partiellement en cours de construction, est essentiellement en sous-sol, comme le montre l'axonométrie, en page de droite.

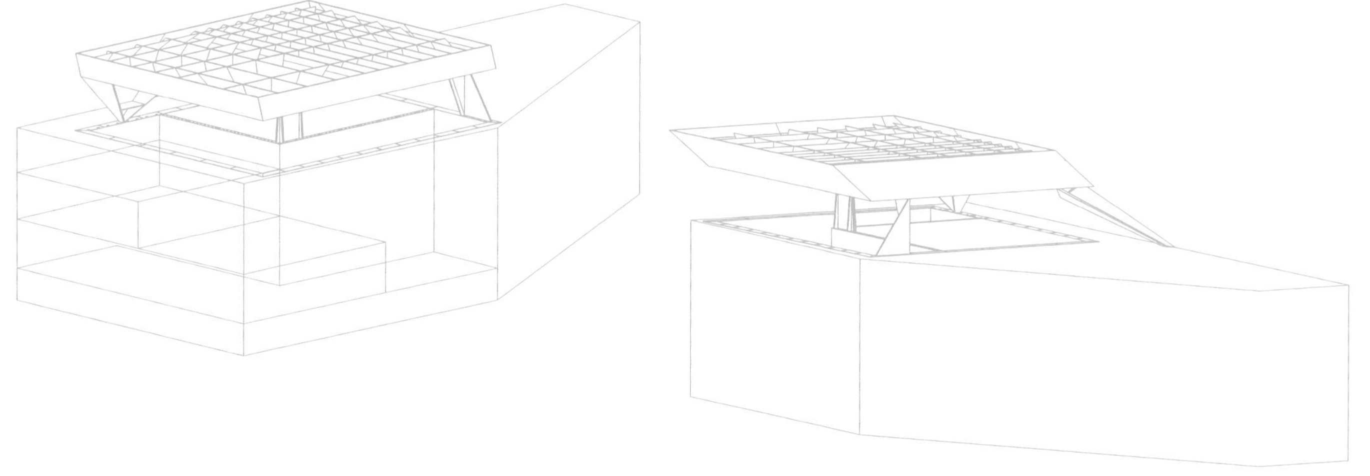

The architect compares this design to a *dovela* (keystone), or a stone that hangs in the air. In fact, it is the metallic structure that shelters this underground theater that he dubs the keystone. "The *dovela* tries to collect all the resonances of the world emerging above it, to give them order," says the architect. The actual theater is, in a sense, excavated, and the public is protected by a "symbolic" metal structure. The architect also speaks of a "negative space," and of its vertical character. "It is," he says, "a mathematical object which transposes its strict order to the space but does not impose it, allowing the natural elements (water, light, and air) to affect its last configuration." The poetic inclinations of the architect aside, this covered, yet open-air theater explores issues of interest in terms of both architecture and the stage. "By immersing ourselves in the negative space of the open excavated lobbies," he says, "we can have access to a new and final happening. Once inside the earth, the theater appears as the end of this sequence of spaces. Here the synthesis of the building culminates with the function of a halted time, recreated, a place to contemplate."

Der Architekt vergleicht seinen Entwurf mit einer *dovela*, einem Schlussstein, der frei in der Luft schwebt. Der Schlussstein aus Metall erhebt sich als schützende Konstruktion über dem unterirdischen Theater. „Die *dovela* empfängt die Schwingungen ihrer Umgebung und ordnet sie", so der Architekt. Der eigentliche Theaterbereich wurde gewissermaßen aus dem Boden herausgearbeitet, die Besucher finden unter der „symbolischen" Metallkonstruktion Schutz. Der Architekt verweist auf die Vertikalität des „negativen Raums". „Hier geht es um eine mathematische Form, die ihre strenge Logik in den Raum trägt, sie ihm aber nicht aufzwingt und sich in ihrer schlussendlichen Konfiguration von den natürlichen Elementen (Wasser, Licht, Luft) prägen lässt." Dies mag poetisch klingen, konkret geht es bei diesem Theaterbau jedoch um architektonische ebenso wie um dramaturgische Fragen. „Lässt man sich auf den negativen Raum der im Boden versenkten offenen Foyers ein", so der Planer, „erschließt sich ein neuer, zugleich der finale Aufzug des Stücks. Die Architektur ist eine Synthese; hier bleibt die Zeit stehen; es ist ein Ort der Kontemplation."

L'architecte compare son projet à une *dovela* (clé de voûte), ou à une pierre suspendue dans les airs. En fait, ce qu'il surnomme « clé de voûte » est la structure métallique qui abrite ce théâtre souterrain. « La *dovela* cherche à rassembler toutes les résonances du monde qui en émergent, à les ordonner », dit l'architecte. Le théâtre proprement dit est comme creusé dans le sol, et le public est protégé par une structure « symbolique » en métal. L'architecte parle aussi d'« espace négatif » et de son caractère vertical. « C'est, dit-il, un objet mathématique qui transpose son ordre strict à l'espace sans l'imposer, laissant les éléments naturels (eau, air et lumière) affecter sa configuration finale. » Mises à part les inclinations poétiques de l'architecte, ce théâtre de plein air explore des questions intéressantes, tant en termes d'architecture que de théâtre. « En s'immergeant dans l'espace négatif des foyers excavés, dit-il, on accède à un nouvel et ultime évènement. Une fois que l'on est sous terre, le théâtre apparaît comme la fin de cette séquence d'espaces. La synthèse du bâtiment culmine ici dans la fonction d'un temps arrêté, recréé, un lieu pour la contemplation. »

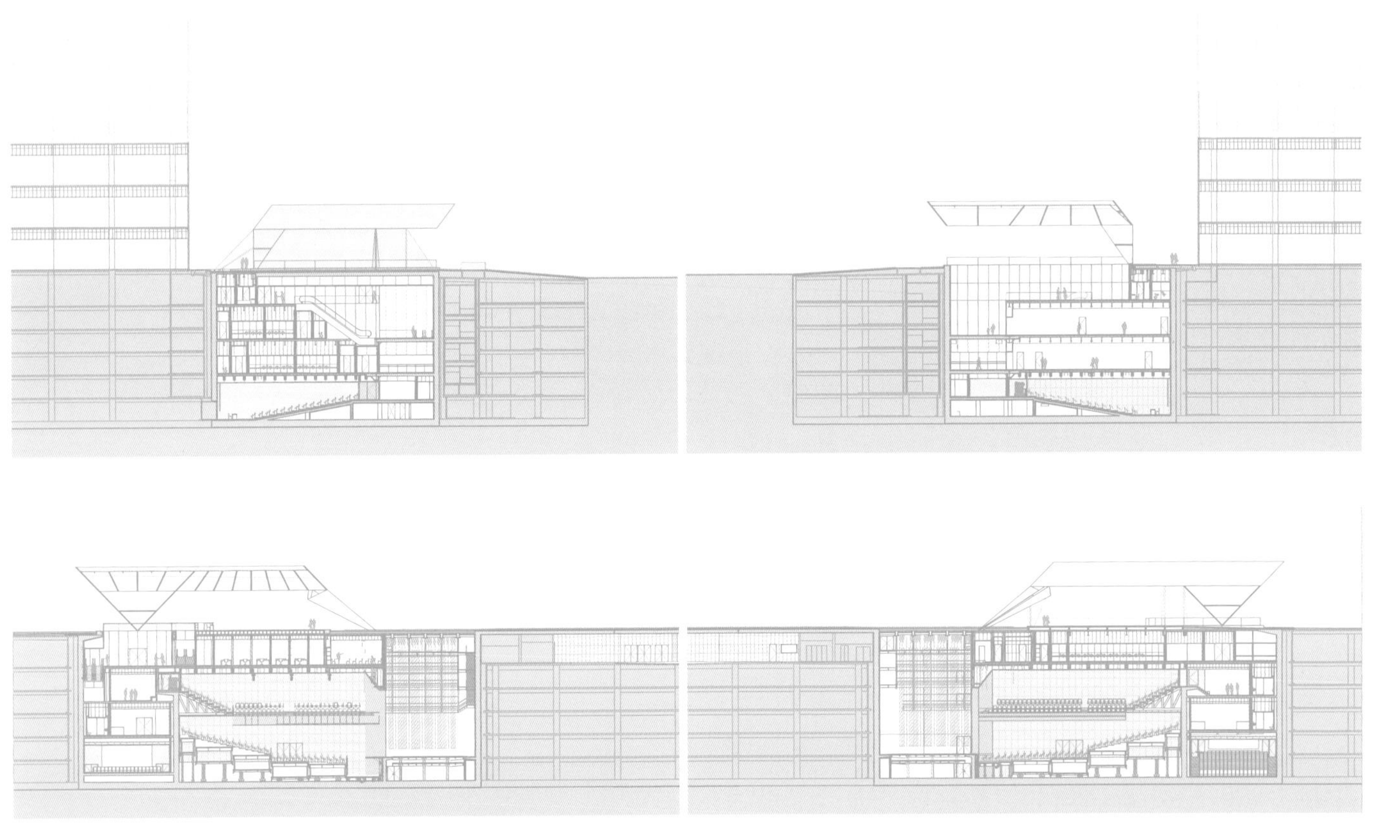

Full section drawings show the volume of the actual theater space below grade, with the relatively unobtrusive platform canopy above.

Querschnitte von allen Seiten veranschaulichen die unterirdische Ausdehnung des Theaters mit seiner vergleichsweise zurückhaltenden überirdischen Dachkonstruktion.

Des coupes d'ensemble montrent le volume du théâtre proprement dit en sous-sol et, par-dessus, la plateforme relativement discrète de l'auvent.

Only the canopy emerges from the earth, its cantilevered volume seeming fairly substantial under certain angles but hovering above the actual theater location.

Über Bodenniveau erhebt sich nur die Dachkonstruktion, deren ausgreifende Masse aus bestimmten Blickwinkeln eindrucksvoll wirkt. Sie schwebt über den eigentlichen Theaterräumlichkeiten.

Seul l'auvent émerge du sol, son volume en porte-à-faux semblant assez important selon certains angles de vue, mais flottant au-dessus de l'emplacement du théâtre.

READER'S HOUSE

Madrid, Spain, 2012

Address: Casa del Lector, Matadero Madrid, Paseo del la Chopera 14, Arganzuela, Madrid 28045, Spain
+34 91 700 06 76, www.casalector.fundaciongsr.com / www.mataderomadrid.org
Area: 7000 m². Client: Fundación Germán Sánchez Ruipérez
Cost: not disclosed. Collaboration: Débora Mesa Molina (Associate Architect)

A former slaughterhouse in Madrid is converted into a center for contemporary art. Architectural competitions were organized to gather proposals to use its vast 148 300 square meters to house artistic training and participatory dialogue between the arts. Ensamble Studio won a 2006 competition to restore warehouses 13, 14, 17b, and 17c of the old slaughterhouse to house a new educational program. The architects sought to enhance and maintain the original character of the complex. An upper level for research and study was created using 40-ton precast concrete beams. "These beams are bridges," says Antón García-Abril, "aerial streets, vectors of activity. In opposition to the basilica-like structure of the warehouses, longitudinal, light and metallic; the new structures are inserted through the windows and join the space transversally, giving unity to the complex formed by warehouses 13 and 14, which were previously independent buildings." The lower level is reserved for use by activities related to educational and cultural "diffusion." Offices are housed in former warehouse 17c, while 17b is a "multipurpose room or auditorium." An arc formed by aluminum slats "encloses, dresses, and lights the space." Granite, steel, and precast concrete are the main materials used by the architect.

Der ehemalige Schlachthof von Madrid wurde zum modernen Kulturzentrum umgebaut: Der Entwurf für den 148 300 m² großen Komplex war das Ergebnis mehrerer Architekturwettbewerbe zur Umnutzung des Standorts für künstlerische Ausbildung und partizipative Dialoge zwischen den Künsten. 2006 gewann Ensamble Studio den Wettbewerb zur Sanierung der Häuser 13, 14, 17b und 17c des alten Schlachthofs, die für neue Bildungsangebote genutzt werden sollen. Die Architekten unterstrichen bewusst den ursprünglichen Charakter des Komplexes. Mit vorgefertigten, 40 t schweren Betonträgern wurde eine obere Ebene eingezogen, die Raum für Forschung und Studium bietet. „Diese Träger sind Brücken", so Antón García-Abril, „Luftstraßen, Aktivitätsvektoren. Ein Kontrast zur Basilikastruktur der Lagerhäuser, gestreckt, leicht, metallisch; die neuen Strukturelemente wurden durch die Fenster eingeführt und halten den Raum in Querrichtung wie Nähstiche zusammen, fügen den Komplex aus Haus 13 und 14, ursprünglich separaten Gebäuden, zu einem Ganzen." Die untere Ebene ist Bildungsangeboten und kultureller „Streuung" vorbehalten. In Haus 17c sind Büros untergebracht, während 17b als „Mehrzweckraum bzw. Auditorium" genutzt wird. Ein Gewölbe aus Aluminiumpaneelen „überfängt und schmückt den Raum und filtert Licht". Die bevorzugten Materialien des Architekten sind Granit, Stahl und Betonmodule.

Les anciens abattoirs de Madrid doivent être reconvertis en centre de création contemporaine. Des concours ont été organisés pour recueillir des propositions d'utilisation de leur vaste superficie de 148 300 m² devant héberger des programmes de formations artistiques et des échanges multidisciplinaires. Ensamble Studio a gagné un concours en 2006 pour la restauration des halles 13, 14, 17b et 17c de l'ancien abattoir, pour y accueillir un nouveau programme éducatif. Les architectes ont cherché à valoriser le complexe tout en conservant son caractère original. Un étage destiné à la recherche et l'étude a été créé avec des poutres de 40 tonnes en béton préfabriqué. « Ces poutres sont des ponts, dit Antón García-Abril, des rues aériennes, des vecteurs d'activité. Par opposition à la structure en cathédrale des halles, en longueur, légères et métalliques, les nouvelles structures sont insérées par les fenêtres et relient l'espace transversalement, unissant les halles 13 et 14 qui étaient des bâtiments distincts. » Le niveau inférieur est réservé aux activités de « diffusion » éducative et culturelle. L'ancienne halle 17c abrite les bureaux et la 17b « une salle polyvalente ou un auditorium ». Un arc de lamelles d'aluminium « enveloppe, habille et illumine l'espace ». Le granit, l'acier et le béton préfabriqué sont les principaux matériaux employés par l'architecte.

The former stone slaughterhouse buildings have been renovated and connected, as seen in the image to the left, and in the section drawings (below).

Die Hallen des ehemaligen Schlachthofs wurden saniert und verbunden, wie die Aufnahme links und Querschnitte (unten) zeigen.

Les bâtiments de l'ancien abattoir en pierre ont été rénovés et reliés, comme on le voit page de gauche et sur les coupes ci-dessous.

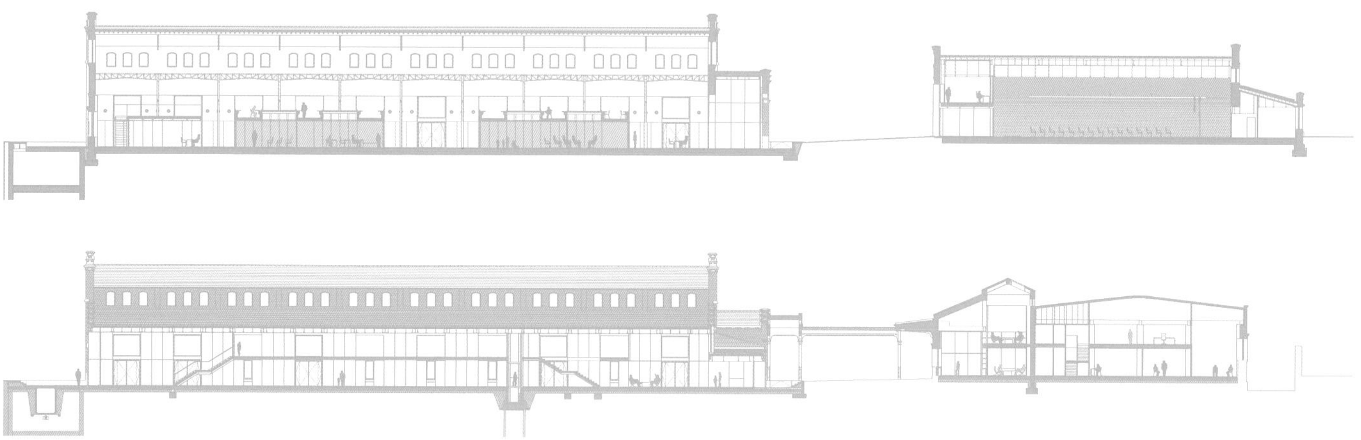

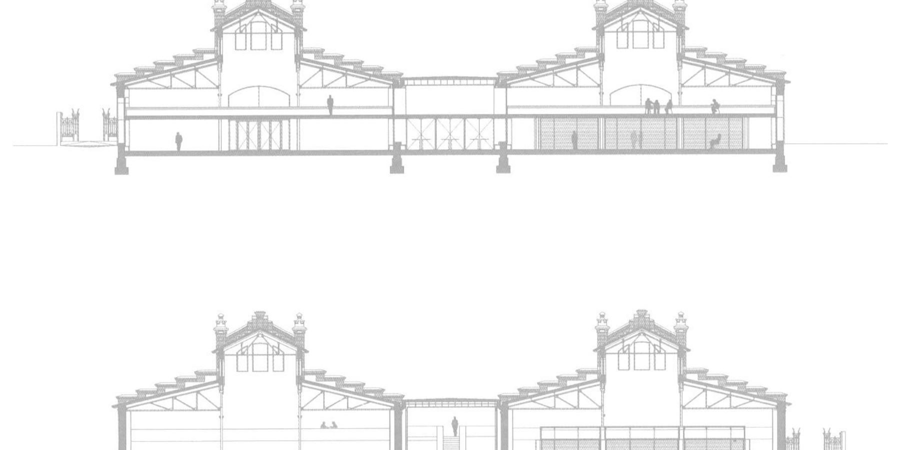

Although the basic volumes of the old buildings remain, completely redone and painted white, they take on a thoroughly modern appearance. Left, sections of the entrance and rear façades.

Obwohl die alten Baukörper erhalten wurden, wirken sie nun – saniert und weiß gestrichen – uneingeschränkt modern. Links Querschnitte von Eingangsfassade und Rückseite des Baus.

Les volumes de base des vieux bâtiments sont conservés mais, entièrement refaits et peints en blanc, ils prennent une apparence très moderne. Ci-contre, des coupes des façades d'entrée et arrière.

Elements such as the bright red stairway, round suspended ceiling fixture, and the lighting combine to make the entire project seem resolutely modern.

Elemente wie die leuchtend rote Treppe, die runde Hängeleuchte und weitere Lichtelemente geben dem Projekt ein markant-modernes Gesicht.

Des éléments tels que l'escalier rouge vif, le plafonnier rond et l'éclairage, contribuent à donner à l'ensemble du projet un aspect résolument moderne.

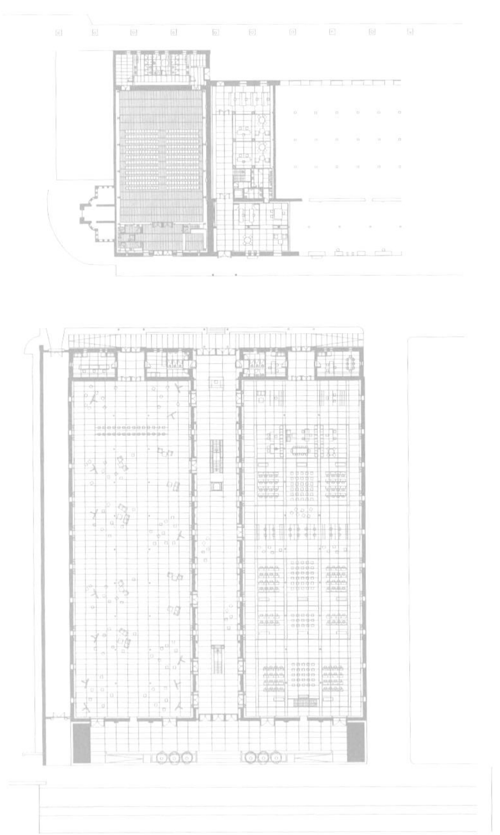

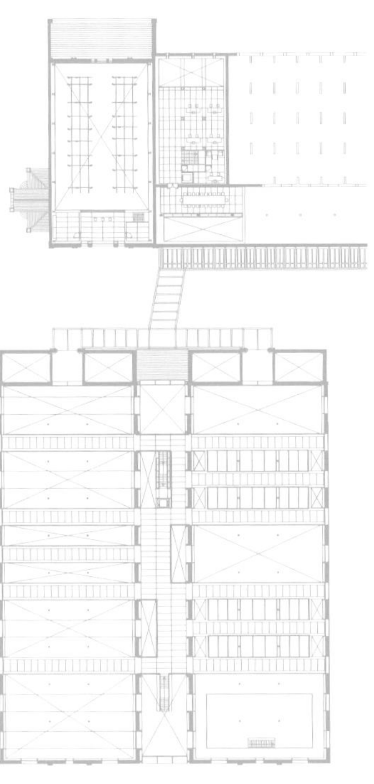

Plans show the strict rectilinearity of the building blocks. Below, and right, although the original, industrial nature of the building remains evident in its volumes and support structure, the presence of readers today does not seem contradictory.

Grundrisse illustrieren die strenge Rechteckform der Baukörper. Zwar ist der ursprüngliche Industriecharakter der Bauten nach wie vor deutlich erkennbar, etwa in Raumgröße und Tragwerkskonstruktion, dennoch ist die heutige Nutzung als Bibliothek kein Widerspruch.

Les plans montrent l'aspect strictement rectiligne des bâtiments. Ci-dessous et à droite, bien que le caractère industriel d'origine du bâtiment reste évident dans ses volumes et sa structure porteuse, la présence aujourd'hui de lecteurs ne semble pas paradoxale.

FRANK O. GEHRY

Gehry Partners, LLP
12541 Beatrice Street
Los Angeles, CA 90066
USA

Tel: +1 310 482 3000 / Fax: +1 310 482 3006
E-mail: info@foga.com / Web: www.foga.com

Born in Toronto, Canada, in 1929, **FRANK GEHRY** studied at the University of Southern California, Los Angeles (1949–51), and at Harvard (1956–57). Principal of Frank O. Gehry and Associates, Inc., Los Angeles, since 1962, he received the Pritzker Prize in 1989. His early work in California included the redesign of his own house, and the construction of a number of houses such as the Norton Residence (Venice, 1984); and the Schnabel Residence (Brentwood, 1989). His first foreign projects included Festival Disney (Marne-la-Vallée, France, 1989–92), and the Guggenheim Bilbao (Spain, 1991–97), which is felt by some to be one of the most significant buildings of the late 20th century. Other work includes the DG Bank Headquarters (Berlin, Germany, 2001); the Fisher Center for the Performing Arts at Bard College (Annandale-on-Hudson, New York, USA, 2003); and the Walt Disney Concert Hall (Los Angeles, USA, 2003). More recent work includes a Maggie's Centre (Dundee, Scotland, 1999–2003); the Jay Pritzker Pavilion in Millennium Park (Chicago, USA, 2004); the Hotel at the Marques de Riscal winery (Elciego, Spain, 2003–07); his first New York building, the InterActiveCorp Headquarters (New York, USA, 2003–07); an extension of the Art Gallery of Ontario (Toronto, Canada, 2005–08); and, again in New York, the Eight Spruce Street Tower (New York, USA, 2007–11, published here). He is currently working on the Louis Vuitton Foundation for Creation in the Bois de Boulogne in Paris (France), the Dwight D. Eisenhower Memorial in Washington, D.C. (USA), and the Guggenheim Abu Dhabi (UAE).

FRANK GEHRY wurde 1929 in Toronto, Kanada, geboren und studierte an der University of Southern California, Los Angeles (1949–51), sowie in Harvard (1956–57). Seit 1962 leitet er sein Büro Frank O. Gehry and Associates, Inc., Los Angeles. 1989 erhielt er den Pritzker-Preis. Zu seinem Frühwerk in Kalifornien zählen der Umbau seines eigenen Wohnhauses und der Bau mehrerer Wohnanlagen, darunter die Norton Residence (Venice, 1984) und die Schnabel Residence (Brentwood, 1989). Zu seinen ersten Projekten im Ausland gehören sein Bau für Festival Disney (Marne-la-Vallée, Frankreich, 1989–92) und das Guggenheim-Museum in Bilbao (1991–97), vielfach eines der bedeutendsten Bauwerke des späten 20. Jahrhunderts genannt. Andere Arbeiten sind u. a. die DG-Bank-Zentrale (Berlin, 2000), das Fisher Center for the Performing Arts am Bard College (Annandale-on-Hudson, New York, 2003) und die Walt Disney Concert Hall (Los Angeles, 2003). Zu seinen jüngeren Arbeiten zählen Maggie's Center (Dundee, Schottland, 1999–2003), der Jay-Pritzker-Pavillon im Millenium-Park (Chicago, 2004), das Hotel am Weingut Marques de Riscal (Elciego, Spanien, 2003–07), Gehrys erster Bau in New York, die Zentrale von InterActiveCorp (2003–07), die Erweiterung der Art Gallery of Ontario (Toronto, 2005–08) und der Eight Spruce Street Tower (New York, 2007–11, hier vorgestellt). Aktuell arbeitet Gehry an der Fondation Louis Vuitton pour la Création im Bois de Boulogne in Paris, am Dwight D. Eisenhower Memorial in Washington, D. C., und am Guggenheim Abu Dhabi (VAE).

Né à Toronto, en 1929, **FRANK GEHRY** étudie à l'université de Californie du Sud, à Los Angeles (1949–51) et à Harvard (1956–57). Directeur de Frank O. Gehry and Associates, Inc., Los Angeles, depuis 1962, il reçoit le prix Pritzker en 1989. Parmi ses premiers projets, l'on compte le réaménagement de sa maison et la construction de plusieurs autres, dont la résidence Norton (Venice, Californie, 1984) et la résidence Schnabel (Brentwood, Californie, 1989). Ses premiers projets à l'étranger comprennent Festival Disney (Marne-la-Vallée, 1989–92) et le musée Guggenheim de Bilbao (Bilbao,1991–97) vu par certains comme une des œuvres majeures de la fin du XXe siècle. On peut également citer le siège de la DG Bank (Berlin, 2001) ; le Centre Fisher pour les arts du spectacle à Bard College (Annandale-on-Hudson, New York, 2003) et le Walt Disney Concert Hall (Los Angeles, 2003). Ses projets récents comprennent un dispensaire Maggie's Center (Dundee, Écosse, 1999–2003) ; le pavillon Jay Pritzker de Millenium Park (Chicago, 2004) ; l'hôtel du domaine viticole Marques de Riscal (Elciego, Espagne, 2003–07) ; son premier bâtiment à New York, le siège InterActiveCorp (New York, 2003–07) ; l'extension de l'Art Gallery de l'Ontario (Toronto, 2005–08) et, de nouveau à New York, la tour de la Eight Spruce Street (New York, 2007–11, présentée ici). Il travaille actuellement sur la Fondation Louis Vuitton pour la création située dans le Bois de Boulogne, à Paris, le mémorial Dwight D. Eisenhower à Washington et le musée Guggenheim Abou Dhabi (UAE).

EIGHT SPRUCE STREET

New York, New York, USA, 2007–11

Address: 8 Spruce Street, New York, NY 10038, USA, +1 212 877 2220, www.newyorkbygehry.com
Area: 102 200 m². Client: Forest City Ratner Companies
Cost: not disclosed

This 76-story, 262-meter-high mixed-use building occupies a 4000-square-meter site between Spruce Street and Beekman Street in Lower Manhattan. The structure includes 900 apartments as well as a public school and office space for the New York Downtown Hospital. Using New York City zoning regulations, the architect developed the massing of the building, and then added bay windows for the apartments, as requested by the client. These windows are not strictly aligned, which led to the "draping effect" seen in the final design. Gehry's firm writes: "Seven sides of the tower have this configuration, while the south side of the tower is sheared into a flat plane that contrasts the curvature of the other façades and strengthens the sculptural composition. The flat side is essential to the power of the building. The tower is clad in flat and undulating stainless-steel panels. At the base of the tower is a simple five-story brick podium, which was designed to be in the spirit of the neighboring buildings." The undulation of the building leads to different apartment configurations; with units ranging from 42-square-meter studios to 158-square-meter three-bedroom apartments at the top of the building.

Das 76-stöckige Hochhaus ist 262 m hoch und liegt auf einem 4000 m² großen Grundstück zwischen Spruce Street und Beekman Street in Lower Manhattan. Außer einer öffentlichen Schule und Büroräumen für das New York Downtown Hospital sind hier insgesamt 900 Apartments untergebracht. Der Architekt entwarf den Baukörper dem New Yorker Bebauungsplan entsprechend mit Staffelgeschossen und fügte, wie vom Kunden gewünscht, erkerähnliche Fassadenausbuchtungen hinzu. Die Fenster folgen keiner geraden Vertikalachse, sodass die Fassade wie eine „textile Membran" wirkt. Gehrys Büro hierzu: „Sieben Fassadenseiten des Turms verfügen über diese Struktur, während die flache Südseite des Baus einen Kontrast zur Kurvatur der übrigen Aufrisse bildet und die skulpturale Komposition stärkt. Sie ist von zentraler Bedeutung für die Wirkung des Gebäudes. Der Turm wurde mit geschwungenen Edelstahlpaneelen verschalt. Ein schlichter, fünfgeschossiger Backsteinsockel orientiert sich an der nachbarschaftlichen Bebauung." Durch die Wellenform der Fassade entstehen unterschiedliche Apartment-Konfigurationen – von 42 m² kleinen Studios bis hin zu 158 m² großen Dreizimmerapartments in den obersten Etagen.

Ce bâtiment mixte de 262 m de haut et 76 étages occupe un site de 4000 m² entre Spruce Street et Beekman Street dans Lower Manhattan. Le bâtiment contient 900 appartements, une école et des espaces de bureaux pour le New York Downtown Hospital. L'architecte a développé les volumes du bâtiment selon les normes new-yorkaises d'urbanisme et a rajouté des bow-windows aux appartements selon le vœu du client. Ces fenêtres ne sont pas strictement alignées, ce qui crée un « effet drapé » visible dans le projet final. L'agence de Gehry explique : « Sept faces de la tour ont cette configuration, tandis que le côté sud est coupé selon un plan plat qui contraste avec les courbes des autres façades et renforce la composition sculpturale. Le côté plat est essentiel à la puissance du bâtiment. La tour est revêtue de panneaux d'acier inoxydable plats ou ondulés. À la base de la tour se trouve un soubassement de cinq étages en brique, conçu dans le même esprit que les immeubles voisins ». Les ondulations du bâtiment permettent des configurations différentes des appartements qui vont du studio de 42 m² au quatre-pièces de 158 m² au sommet du bâtiment.

Part of a recent trend in Manhattan toward taller buildings, Eight Spruce Street stands out behind the Brooklyn Bridge (above), and towers over its immediate neighborhood (right).

Bedingt durch einen Trend der letzten Zeit, höhere Bauten in Manhattan zu realisieren, überragt Eight Spruce Street die Brooklyn Bridge (oben) und die Hochhäuser seiner unmittelbaren Umgebung (rechts).

S'inscrivant dans une vogue récente de bâtir des immeubles plus hauts à Manhattan, Eight Spruce Street se détache derrière le Brooklyn Bridge (ci-dessus) et domine son environnement immédiat (page de droite).

PACE UNIVERSITY
PACE UNIVERSITY
Brooklyn Br
ONLY
TO
Broadway
11'-0" CLEARANCE
Levitan Robbins
Levitan Robbins
Local 3 IBEW
www.cooper-electric.com

The 76-story building is clad in torqued stainless-steel panels. Its exceptional height was made possible by the purchase of air rights of the neighboring Downtown Hospital.

Das 76-stöckige Gebäude ist mit teilweise gedrehten Edelstahlpaneelen verschalt. Die ungewöhnliche Höhe des Baus wurde durch den Erwerb der sog. „air rights" des angrenzenden Downtown Hospitals möglich.

L'immeuble de 76 étages est recouvert de panneaux en acier inoxydable tordus. L'acquisition des droits aériens du Downtown Hospital voisin a rendu possible sa hauteur exceptionnelle.

The building has 200 unique apartment layouts offering spectacular outlooks on the city and its rivers, as can be seen below. The undulation of the façades permits curving windows that take in the sweeping views.

Im Gebäude sind 200 unterschiedliche Apartmenttypen untergebracht, mit spektakulärem Blick über die Stadt und ihre Flüsse, wie unten zu sehen. Durch die Wölbung der Fassade entstanden erkerähnliche Fensterflächen mit Panoramablick.

Le bâtiment propose 200 plans d'appartements différents avec des vues spectaculaires sur la ville et ses fleuves, comme ci-dessous. L'ondulation des façades permet des vitrages incurvés offrant des vues panoramiques.

GIJS VAN VAERENBERGH

Gijs Van Vaerenbergh
Priester Daensstraat 26/6
Leuven 3010
Belgium

Tel: +32 485 83 78 31
E-mail: info@gijsvanvaerenbergh.com
Web: www.gijsvanvaerenbergh.com

PIETERJAN GIJS was born in Leuven, Belgium, in 1983. He studied civil engineering and architecture at KU Leuven (2001–06) and obtained a Master's degree in Urbanism and Territorial Development from the Université Catholique de Louvain (2006–07). In 2008, he cofounded Gijs Van Vaerenbergh. **ARNOUT VAN VAERENBERGH** was also born in 1983 in Leuven, and studied civil engineering and architecture at KU Leuven (2001–06). He has worked as an architect at New + Partners (2006–09) and at noA Architecten (2009–10), cofounding Gijs Van Vaerenbergh in 2008. The work of Gijs Van Vaerenbergh "consists of site-specific interventions, installations, and constructions that generate a mutual relation with their environment." Their work includes "Greenhouse Intersect" (Leuven, 2010); "SpinOff" (Brussels, 2010); "The Upside Dome" (Leuven, 2010); "Reading between the Lines" (Borgloon, 2011, published here); "Skylight" (Leuven, 2012); "Framework" (Leuven, 2012); and "Ghent 1913. A Retroactive Monument" (exhibition in DeSingel, Antwerp, 2013), all in Belgium unless otherwise indicated.

PIETERJAN GIJS wurde 1983 in Leuven, Belgien, geboren. Er studierte Ingenieurwesen und Architektur an der KU Leuven (2001–06) und absolvierte einen Master in Urbanistik und Raumplanung an der Université Catholique de Louvain (2006–07). Das Büro Gijs Van Vaerenbergh gründete er 2008 mit **ARNOUT VAN VAERENBERGH**, der ebenfalls 1983 in Leuven geboren wurde und Ingenieurwesen und Architektur an der KU Leuven studierte (2001–06). Vor Gründung des Büros arbeitete Vaerenbergh für New + Partners (2006–09) sowie noA Architecten (2009–10). Gijs Van Vaerenberghs Projekte sind oft „standortspezifische Interventionen, Installationen und Konstruktionen, die den Dialog mit ihrem Umfeld suchen". Zu ihren Projekten zählen „Greenhouse Intersect" (Leuven, 2010), „SpinOff" (Brüssel, 2010), „The Upside Dome" (Leuven, 2010), „Reading between the Lines" (Borgloon, 2011, hier vorgestellt), „Skylight" (Leuven, 2012), „Framework" (Leuven, 2012) und die Ausstellung „Ghent 1913. A Retroactive Monument" am Internationalen Kunstcampus DeSingel (Antwerpen, 2013).

Né à Louvain, en Belgique, en 1983, **PIETERJAN GIJS** étudie l'ingénierie civile et l'architecture à la KU Leuven (2001–06) et obtient un master en urbanisme et développement du territoire à l'Université catholique de Louvain (2006–07). En 2008, il est cofondateur de l'agence Gijs Van Vaerenbergh. Né également en 1983 à Louvain, **ARNOUT VAN VAERENBERGH** étudie aussi l'ingénierie civile et l'architecture à la KU Leuven (2001–06). Il travaille comme architecte chez New + Partners (2006–09) et chez noA Architecten (2009–10), et participe à la fondation de Gijs Van Vaerenbergh en 2008. Le travail de Gijs Van Vaerenbergh « consiste en interventions, installations et constructions spécifiques à un site et qui génèrent une relation avec leur environnement ». Leurs réalisations comprennent *Greenhouse Intersect* (Louvain, 2010) ; *SpinOff* (Bruxelles, 2010) ; *The Upside Dome* (Louvain, 2010) ; *Reading between the Lines* (Looz, 2011, présenté ici) ; *Skylight* (Louvain, 2012) ; *Framework* (Louvain, 2012) et « Ghent 1913. A Retroactive Monument » (exposition au centre d'art DeSingel, Anvers, 2013), tous en Belgique, sauf indication contraire.

"READING BETWEEN THE LINES"

Borgloon, Belgium, 2011

Address: pedestrian route between St. Truidersteenweg and Roman Kassel, Borgloon, Limburg 3840, Belgium
Area: 28 m². Client: IVA Beeldenproject. Cost: not disclosed

Built in a rural setting outside of the Limburg town of Borgloon, this structure, based on the design of the local church, was inaugurated on September 24, 2011. It has a reinforced-concrete foundation and was made with 30 tons of Cor-ten steel and 2000 columns. It is not a piece of architecture in the usual sense, but rather a "transparent object of art." Gijs Van Vaerenbergh explain that their work can be seen as a reflection on architectural themes, such as scale or the plan, but also as a commentary on the fact that many churches no longer fulfill their past functions since they are quite empty, in the region of Limburg and elsewhere. The work can also be seen as a kind of line drawing in space. Despite the use of such "solid" materials as reinforced concrete and steel, "Reading between the Lines" retains a fundamental fragility, which is what makes it interesting.

Das Projekt, außerhalb der limburgischen Stadt Borgloon auf dem Land gelegen und der örtlichen Kirche nachempfunden, wurde am 24. September 2011 eingeweiht. Auf einem Fundament aus Stahlbeton ruht eine Konstruktion aus 30 t Cor-Ten-Stahl und 2000 Querträgern. Dies ist keine Architektur im herkömmlichen Sinn, sondern vielmehr ein „transparentes Kunstobjekt". Gijs Van Vaerenbergh verstehen ihren Entwurf sowohl als Auseinandersetzung mit architektonischen Konzepten wie Maßstab und Grundriss, als auch als Kommentar zu der Entwicklung, dass viele Kirchen in Limburg und andernorts zunehmend leer sind und ihre ursprüngliche Bestimmung nicht mehr erfüllen. Das Projekt lässt sich auch als „räumliche Zeichnung" lesen. Trotz massiver Materialien wie Stahl und Beton ist „Reading between the Lines" von einer Fragilität, die dem Projekt einen besonderen Reiz verleiht.

Construit dans un environnement rural près de Looz, dans le Limbourg, ce bâtiment dont la forme s'inspire de l'église locale a été inauguré le 24 septembre 2011. Trente tonnes d'acier Corten et 2000 piliers ont été utilisés pour sa construction sur des fondations en béton armé. Il ne s'agit pas d'un objet architectural dans le sens habituel, mais plutôt d'un « objet d'art transparent ». Selon Gijs Van Vaerenbergh, leur création peut être vue comme une réflexion sur des thèmes architecturaux comme l'échelle ou le plan, mais aussi comme un commentaire sur le fait que de nombreuses églises ne remplissent plus leurs fonctions passées puisqu'elles sont quasiment vides, dans le Limbourg comme ailleurs. Le projet peut aussi être vu comme un dessin dans l'espace. En dépit de l'emploi de matériaux solides comme l'acier et le béton armé, *Reading Between the Lines* conserve une fragilité fondamentale qui en fait l'intérêt.

The schematic outline of a church stands out on its country hillside, a commentary on architecture, but also on religion.

Die stilisierte Kontur einer Kirche erhebt sich über der hügeligen Landschaft: ein Kommentar zur Architektur, aber auch zur Religion.

La silhouette schématique d'une église se détache sur la campagne vallonnée, un commentaire sur l'architecture comme sur la religion.

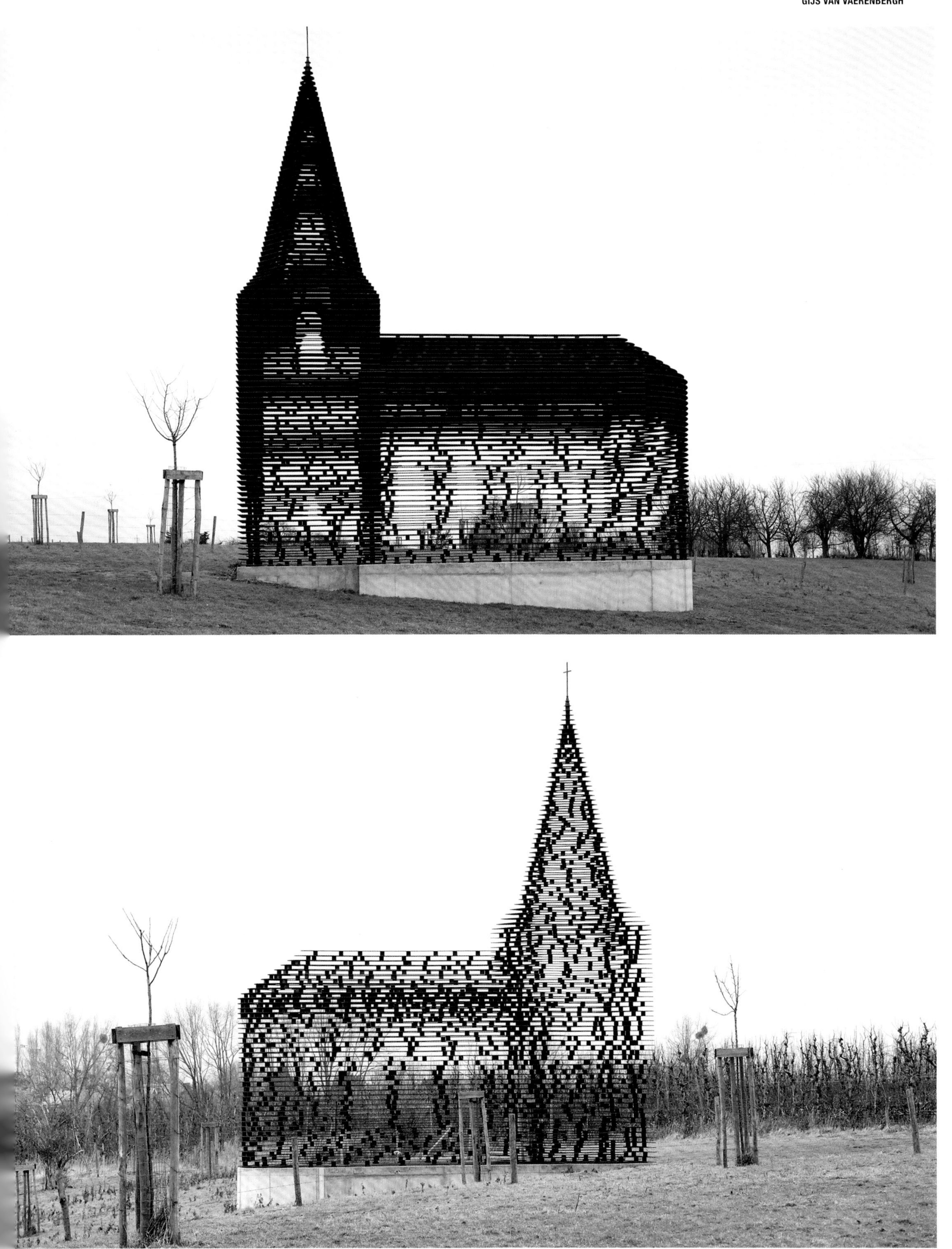

Although the exact size of this "church" is not readily grasped from a distance, when seen closer up, it becomes apparent that it is quite small.

Die tatsächliche Größe der „Kirche" ist aus der Ferne nicht eindeutig auszumachen. Erst aus relativer Nähe erschließt sich, dass der Bau recht klein ist.

La taille exacte de cette « église », qui n'est pas immédiatement perceptible à distance, se révèle bien petite quand on s'en approche.

The stacked nature of the structure is visible only from a short distance. Aside from the entrance door, the other openings are all horizontal, with variations in the density of the stacking used to create the illusion of windows.

Auch das Schichtprinzip des Baus wird erst aus größerer Nähe deutlich. Abgesehen vom Eingang sind alle weiteren Öffnungen horizontal; Variation ergibt sich durch die Dichte der Schichtelemente, die auch Fenster andeutet.

L'empilement caractéristique de sa structure n'est visible que de près. Hormis la porte d'entrée, toutes les ouvertures sont horizontales, avec des variations de densité de l'empilement qui créent l'illusion de fenêtres.

Though the idea of "Reading between the Lines" seems quite simple, the designers have used the concept to create a poetic structure that is sculptural in its essence even if it does evoke architecture.

Die Idee von „Reading between the Lines" scheint zunächst simpel, doch den Planern gelingt es, mit ihrem Konzept eine poetische Konstruktion zu schaffen, die vor allem skulptural ist, auch wenn sie an architektonische Formen anknüpft.

Bien que l'idée de Reading Between the Lines *semble assez simple, les designers se sont servis du concept pour créer une structure poétique d'essence sculpturale, même si elle évoque l'architecture.*

ZAHA HADID

Zaha Hadid Architects
Studio 9
10 Bowling Green Lane
London EC1R 0BQ, UK

Tel: +44 20 72 53 51 47 / Fax: +44 20 72 51 83 22
E-mail: press@zaha-hadid.com
Web: www.zaha-hadid.com

ZAHA HADID studied architecture at the Architectural Association (AA) in London, beginning in 1972, and was awarded the Diploma Prize in 1977. She then became a Partner of Rem Koolhaas in OMA and taught at the AA. She has also taught at Harvard, the University of Chicago, in Hamburg, and at Columbia University in New York. In 2004, Zaha Hadid became the first woman to win the coveted Pritzker Prize. She completed the Vitra Fire Station (Weil am Rhein, Germany, 1990–94); and exhibition designs such as that for "The Great Utopia" (Solomon R. Guggenheim Museum, New York, USA, 1992). More recently, Zaha Hadid has entered a phase of active construction with such projects as the Lois & Richard Rosenthal Center for Contemporary Art (Cincinnati, Ohio, USA, 1999–2003); Phaeno Science Center (Wolfsburg, Germany, 2001–05); Ordrupgaard Museum Extension (Copenhagen, Denmark, 2001–05); the Central Building of the new BMW Assembly Plant in Leipzig (Germany, 2005); the Mobile Art, Chanel Contemporary Art Container (various locations, 2007–); and the MAXXI, the National Museum of 21st Century Arts (Rome, Italy, 1998–2009). Recent projects include the Sheik Zayed Bridge (Abu Dhabi, UAE, 2003–10); the Guangzhou Opera House (Guangzhou, China, 2005–10); the Aquatics Center for the London 2012 Olympic Games (London, UK, 2005–11); the CMA CGM Tower (Marseille, France, 2008–11, published here); and "Arum" at the Corderie dell'Arsenale (Venice, Italy, 2012, also published here).

ZAHA HADID studierte ab 1972 an der Architectural Association (AA) in London und erhielt 1977 den Diploma Prize. Anschließend wurde sie Partnerin von Rem Koolhaas bei OMA und unterrichtete an der AA. Darüber hinaus lehrte sie in Harvard, an der Universität von Chicago, in Hamburg sowie an der Columbia University in New York. 2004 wurde Zaha Hadid als erste Frau mit dem begehrten Pritzker-Preis ausgezeichnet. Sie realisierte u. a. eine Feuerwache für Vitra (Weil am Rhein, Deutschland, 1990–94) und Ausstellungsarchitekturen wie „The Great Utopia" (Solomon R. Guggenheim Museum, New York, 1992). In jüngerer Zeit begann für Hadid eine Phase des aktiven Bauens, etwa mit dem Lois & Richard Rosenthal Center for Contemporary Art (Cincinnati, Ohio, 1999–2003), dem Phaeno Wissenschaftszentrum (Wolfsburg, 2001–05), dem Anbau für das Museum Ordrupgaard (Kopenhagen, 2001–05), dem Zentralgebäude des neuen BMW-Werks in Leipzig (2005), dem Mobile Art, Chanel Contemporary Art Container (verschiedene Standorte, ab 2007) sowie dem MAXXI Nationalmuseum für Kunst des 21. Jahrhunderts (Rom, 1999–2009). Ihre jüngsten Projekte sind u. a. die Scheich-Zajed-Brücke (Abu Dhabi, VAE, 2003–10), das Opernhaus in Guangzhou (China, 2005–10), das Aquatics Center für die Olympischen Spiele 2012 in London (2005–11), der CMA CGM Tower (Marseille, 2008–11, hier vorgestellt) sowie „Arum" in der Corderie dell'Arsenale (Venedig, 2012, ebenfalls hier vorgestellt).

ZAHA HADID commence à étudier l'architecture à l'Architectural Association (AA) à Londres en 1972 et en reçoit le prix Diploma en 1977. Elle devient ensuite associée de Rem Koolhaas dans l'agence OMA et enseigne à l'AA. Elle enseigne également à Harvard, à l'université de Chicago, à Hambourg et à l'université Columbia, à New York. En 2004, Zaha Hadid devient la première femme à recevoir le très convoité prix Pritzker. Elle a réalisé la caserne de pompiers de l'usine Vitra (Weil-am-Rhein, Allemagne, 1990–94) et des scénographies d'expositions comme « The Great Utopia » (musée Guggenheim, New York, 1992). Plus récemment, Zaha Hadid est entrée dans une phase active de construction, avec des projets comme le Centre d'art contemporain Lois & Richard Rosenthal (Cincinnati, Ohio,1999–2003) ; le Centre des sciences Phaeno (Wolfsburg, Allemagne, 2001–05) ; l'extension du musée Ordrupgaard (Copenhague, 2001–05) ; le bâtiment central de la nouvelle usine BMW à Leipzig (2005) ; le Musée d'art contemporain itinérant Mobile Art (lieux divers, 2007–) et le Musée national des arts du XXIe siècle MAXXI (Rome, 1998–2009). Parmi ses projets récents, on trouve le pont Sheik Zayed (Abou Dhabi, 2003–10) ; l'Opéra de Canton (Canton, 2005–10) ; l'Aquatics Center pour les Jeux olympiques de Londres 2012 (Londres, 2005–11) ; la tour CMA CGM (Marseille, 2008–11, présentée ici) et *Arum* à la Corderie dell'Arsenale (Venise, 2012, également présenté ici).

CMA CGM TOWER

Marseille, France, 2008–11

Address: 4 Quai d'Arenc, 13235 Marseille CEDEX 02, France, +33 488 91 90 00
www.cma-cgm.com / www.tourcmacgm.com
Area: 94 000 m². Client: CMA CGM. Cost: not disclosed

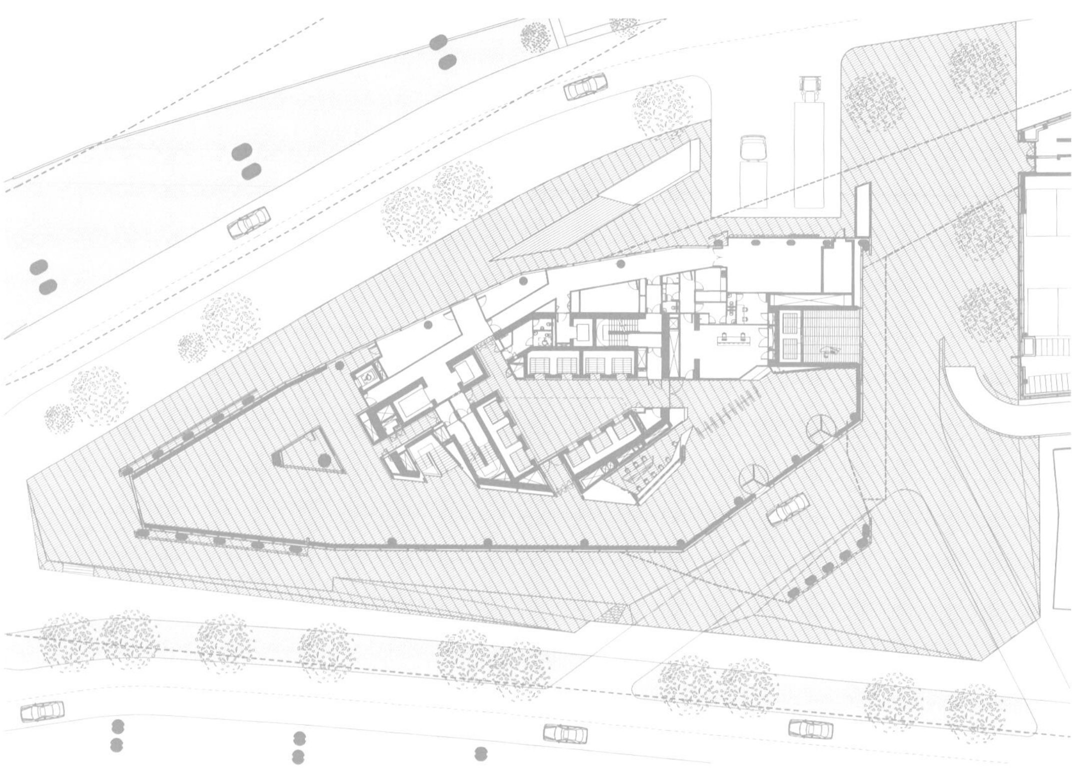

This tower is located approximately one kilometer north of the historic center of Marseille in the Euroméditerranée development zone near the city's commercial port. It is located 100 meters from the edge of the water near an elevated motorway. The project is divided into two parts, with the tower itself offering 56 600 square meters of space, and an annex that measures 36 600 square meters. Designed for 2700 employees, with parking for 700 cars and 200 motorcycles, the complex includes a corporate restaurant that seats 800 people. A gym and auditorium are also part of the facility. The architects explain: "The design strategy to deal with an awkward, elongated site was to break down the volume of the façade into vertical segments and differentiate them using light and dark glazing. These are then offset to one another with the clear glazing set forward as a separate skin which is articulated architecturally by incorporating the peripheral structural columns." The apparently diverging elements of the tower echo the split in the motorway that runs on either side of the site. In a city with few tall buildings, the **CMA CGM TOWER** offers hope of regeneration that goes beyond the immediate district.

Das Hochhaus liegt rund 1 km nördlich der historischen Altstadt von Marseille, im Bauerschließungsgebiet Euroméditerranée, nicht weit vom Frachthafen der Stadt. Der Bau befindet sich 100 m vom Wasser entfernt an einer Hochstraße. Die Anlage gliedert sich in zwei Teile: dem Turm mit 56 600 m² Nutzfläche und einem Nebengebäude mit 36 600 m² Fläche. Der für 2700 Mitarbeiter geplante Komplex umfasst Stellplätze für 700 Pkws und 200 Motorräder sowie ein Firmenrestaurant mit 800 Plätzen. Hinzu kommen ein Fitnessbereich und ein Auditorium. Die Architekten erklären: „Als Planungsstrategie für das problematische, gestreckte Baugrundstück entschieden wir uns, die Fassade in vertikale Segmente aufzulösen und durch dunkle und hellere Verglasung zu differenzieren. Diese sind voneinander abgesetzt durch das Vorhängen der Klarverglasung als separate Gebäudehaut, die architektonisch durch Einbindung tragender Stützen artikuliert wird." Die deutlich divergierenden Elemente des Turms spiegeln motivisch die Schnellstraße, die das Grundstück beidseitig einfasst. In einer Stadt mit nur wenigen Hochhausbauten ist der **CMA CGM TOWER** ein Hoffnungsschimmer, dass die Stadterneuerungsbemühungen über den unmittelbaren Stadtkern hinausgehen.

Cette tour est située à un kilomètre au nord environ du centre historique de Marseille, dans la zone de rénovation urbaine Euroméditerranée, près du port. Elle est placée à 100 mètres du bord de l'eau, près d'une autoroute surélevée. Le projet se divise en deux parties, la tour d'une superficie de 56 600 m² et un bâtiment annexe de 36 600 m². Conçu pour 2700 employés, avec un parking pour 700 voitures et 200 motos, le complexe comprend un restaurant d'entreprise pour 800 personnes ainsi qu'une salle de sport et un auditorium. Selon l'architecte, « pour s'adapter à un site ingrat et en longueur, la stratégie du projet a consisté à éclater le volume de la façade en tronçons verticaux, différenciés par des vitrages clairs et foncés. Ils sont alors décalés, verre transparent en avant comme une peau séparée qui s'articule architecturalement en intégrant les colonnes structurelles périphériques ». Les éléments de la tour apparemment divergents font écho à la scission de l'autoroute qui passe de chaque côté du site. Dans une ville qui compte très peu de bâtiments de haute taille, la **TOUR CMA CGM** offre un espoir de régénération au-delà du quartier immédiat.

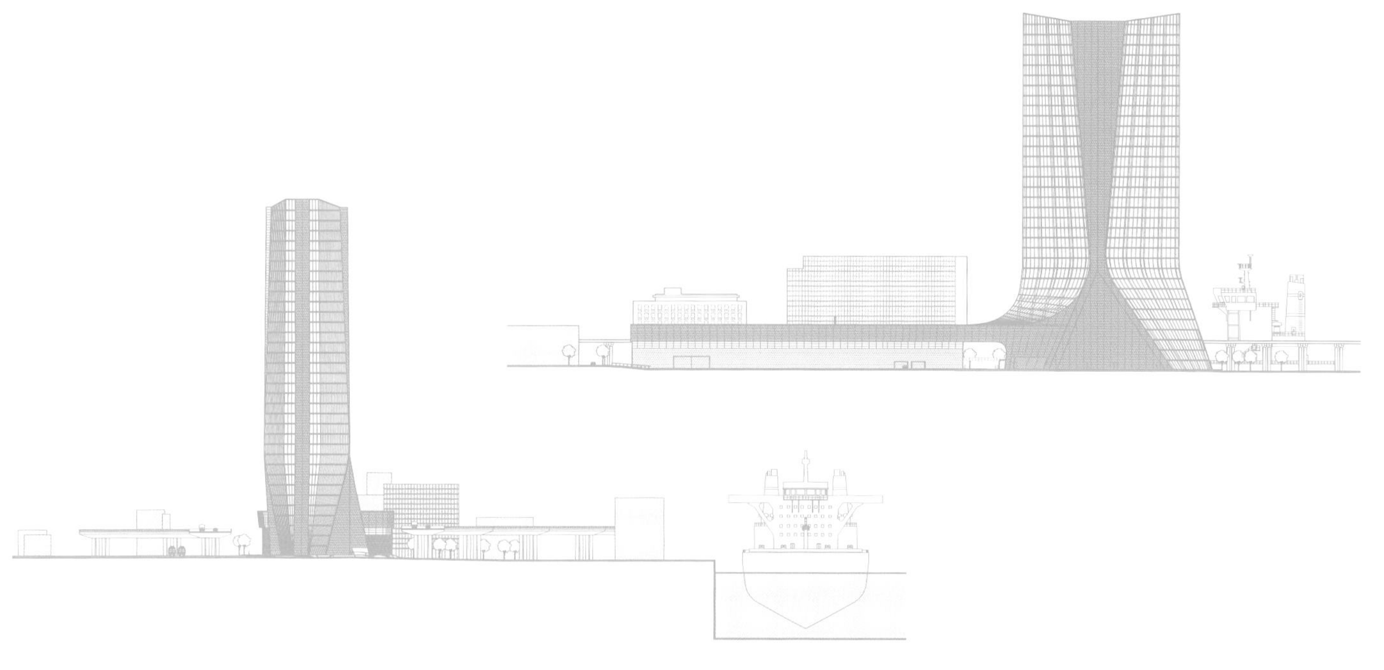

The sweeping curves of the building give it an inspiring upward movement, visible in the image to the left.

Die ausgreifenden Kurven des Baus geben ihm inspirierenden Auftrieb, zu sehen links im Bild.

Les larges courbes du bâtiment lui donnent un impressionnant mouvement ascendant, visible en page de gauche.

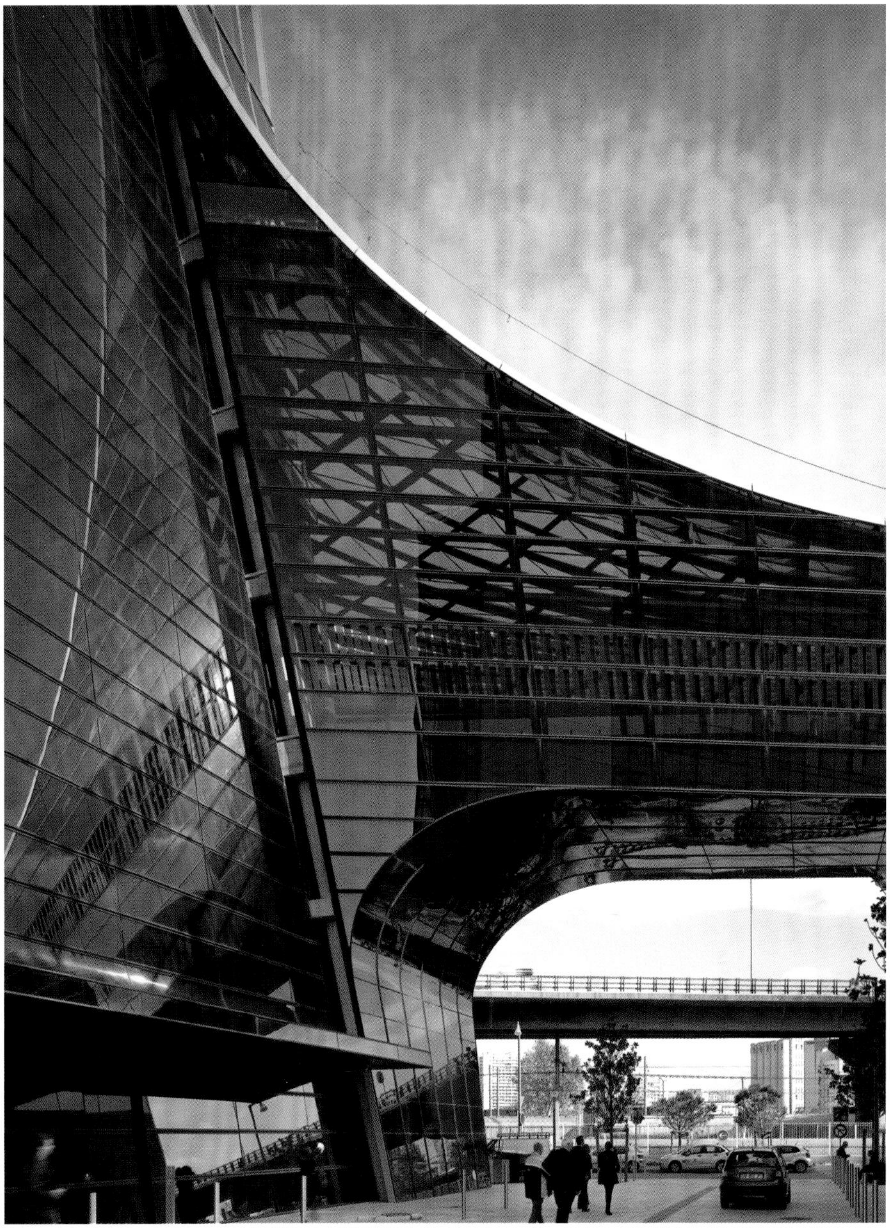

Even when seen from ground level, the building arches and curves, with an elevated passageway connecting it to other structures.

Auch zu ebener Erde sind die Wölbungen und Schwünge des Baus deutlich zu erkennen. Eine Brücke schafft die Anbindung an die Nebengebäude.

Même vu du sol, le bâtiment se cambre et se courbe, avec une passerelle aérienne qui le relie à d'autres bâtiments.

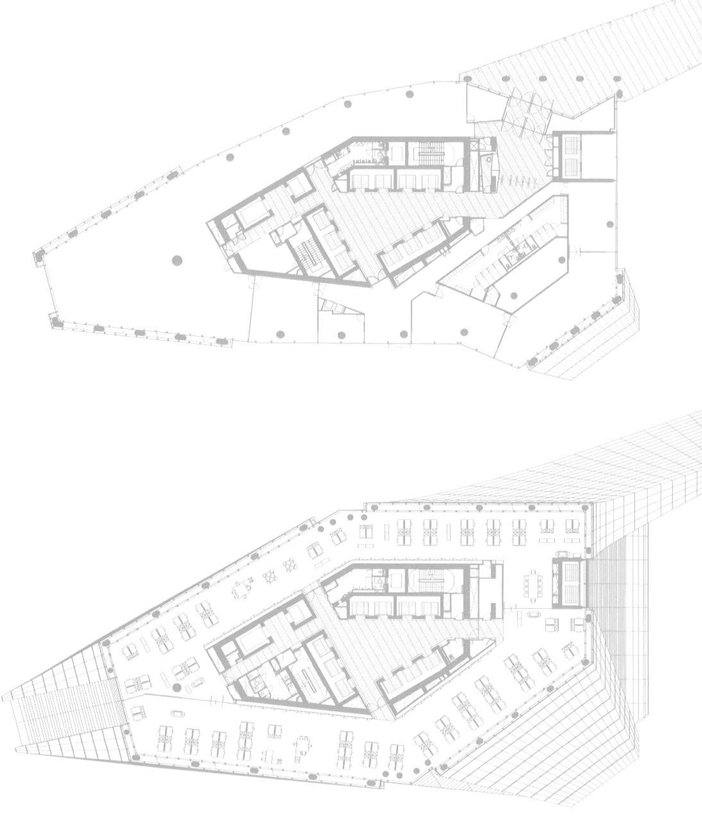

Despite its broad curves, the building offers regular floor plates and decidedly engaging public spaces (this page).

Trotz seiner ausgreifenden Schwünge bietet der Bau konventionelle Geschossebenen und attraktive öffentliche Bereiche (diese Seite).

Même avec ses larges courbes, le bâtiment offre des plateaux d'étages réguliers et des espaces communs vraiment agréables (sur cette page).

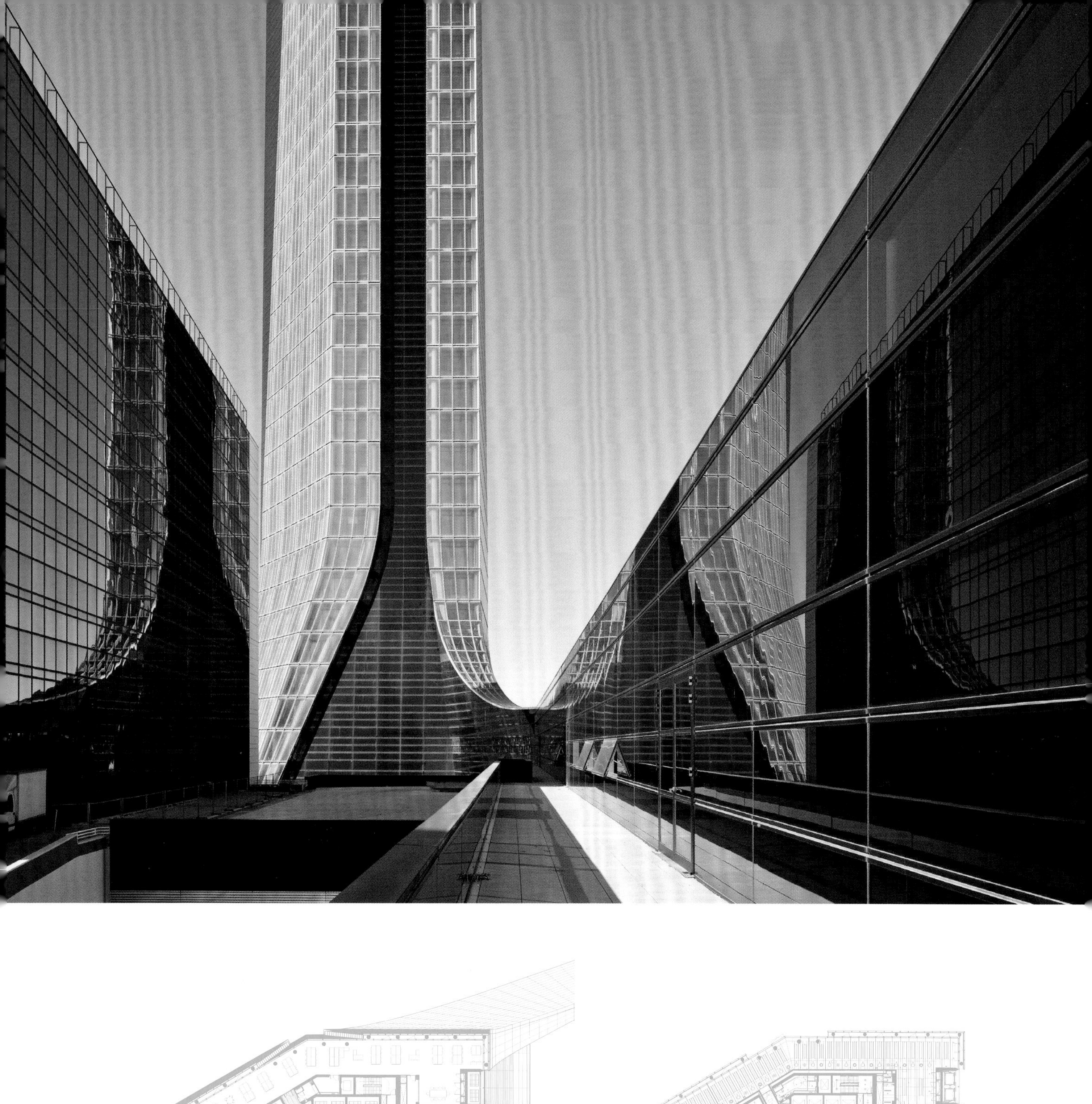

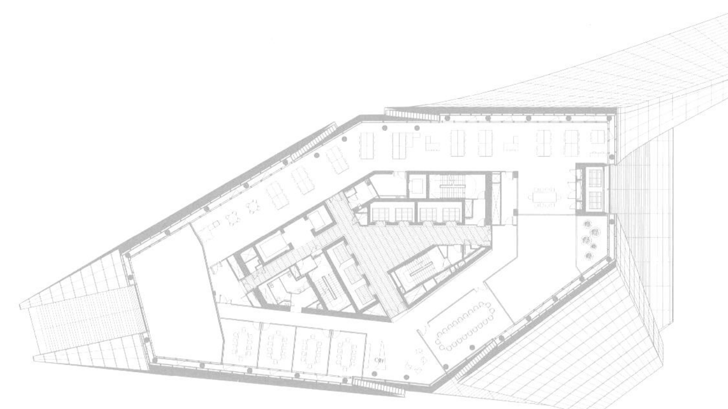

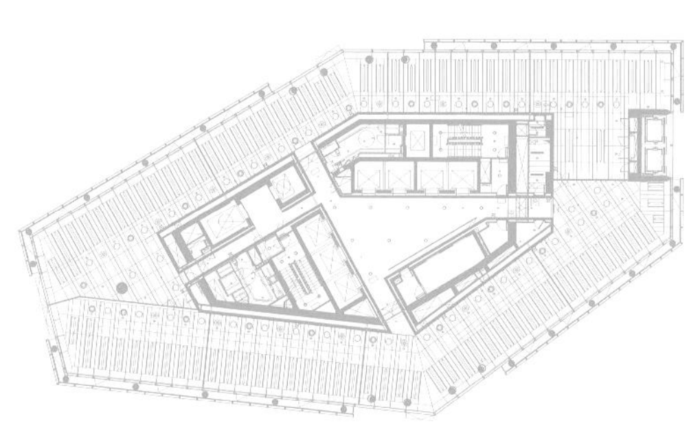

"ARUM"

Corderie dell'Arsenale, Venice, Italy, 2012

Address: not applicable. Area: not applicable
Client: La Biennale di Venezia. Cost: not disclosed

In the old brick-columned space of the Arsenale in Venice, Zaha Hadid's "Arum" stands out, but curiously does not seem like a totally alien presence.

Zaha Hadids „Arum" sticht im Ziegelbau des Arsenale in Venedig deutlich hervor, wirkt jedoch überraschenderweise nicht völlig fremd.

L'Arum de Zaha Hadid se détache dans l'espace de colonnes en briques de l'Arsenal de Venise mais, curieusement, ne semble pas une présence totalement étrangère.

The sculptural pleated metal forms appear to share the weight-bearing burden of the columns, or perhaps to rise up through the ceiling.

Die skulpturale Form aus gefaltetem Metall wirkt ebenso tragend wie die alten Säulen, aber auch, als würde sie durch das Dach streben.

Les formes sculpturales en métal plié semblent partager la charge supportée par les colonnes, ou peut-être s'élever à travers le plafond.

Under the direction of the architect David Chipperfield, the theme of the 2012 Architecture Biennale in Venice (August 29–November 25, 2012), was "Common Ground." One aspect of this theme was the demonstration that architects are often engaged in "historical lineages of collective research," as Zaha Hadid Architects puts it. This reference links Hadid's early work to Russian Suprematism, for example. Zaha Hadid's more recent influences would include the work of the noted German engineer Frei Otto. "From Frei Otto we learned how the richness, organic coherence and fluidity of the forms and spaces we desire could emerge rationally from an intricate balance of forces. We expanded Frei Otto's method to include environmental as well as structural logics, and we moved from material to computational simulations," she states. Lightweight shells in combination with tensile structures are the particular subject of the **"ARUM"** installation. Pleated metal structures were presented with documentation on research and "key reference projects," including work by Felix Candela, Heinz Isler, and Philippe Block, a young researcher who is interested in stone compression shells.

Das Thema der Architekturbiennale 2012 in Venedig unter Leitung von David Chipperfield (29. August–25. November 2012) lautete „Common Ground". Ein Aspekt des Mottos war die Tatsache, dass Architekten oft in einer „kritisch-forschenden Tradition" stehen, wie Zaha Hadid es formuliert. In Hadids Fall ist diese Tradition u. a. der russische Suprematismus. Ein jüngerer Bezugspunkt ist für sie das Werk des bedeutenden deutschen Ingenieurs Frei Otto. „Von Frei Otto haben wir gelernt, dass die Vielschichtigkeit, organische Kohärenz und die fließenden Formen und Räume, die wir erzielen wollen, sich rational aus einem sensiblen Gleichgewicht verschiedener Kräfte ableiten lassen. Wie dachten Frei Ottos Ansatz weiter, integrierten umweltbezogene und konstruktive Prinzipien und verlegten uns von materialhaften Modellen auf digitale Simulation", so Hadid. Bei ihrer Installation **„ARUM"** kombiniert sie Leichtbauschalen mit einer Spannkonstruktion. Präsentiert wurden ihre Strukturen aus gefaltetem Metall mit einer Dokumentation zur Recherche und „Schlüsselreferenzen", darunter Projekte von Felix Candela, Heinz Isler und Philippe Block, einem jungen Wissenschaftler, der an Forschungsprojekten zu Gewölbetragwerken arbeitet.

Sous la direction de l'architecte David Chipperfield, le thème de la Biennale d'architecture de Venise 2012 (29 août–25 novembre 2012) était « Common Ground ». Un de ses aspects était de démontrer que les architectes sont souvent engagés dans « une lignée historique de recherche collective », comme l'affirme Zaha Hadid. Cette référence relie les premiers travaux d'Hadid aux suprématistes russes, par exemple. Parmi ses influences plus récentes, on trouve l'éminent ingénieur allemand Frei Otto. « De Frei Otto, dit-elle, nous avons appris comment la cohérence organique et la fluidité des forces et des espaces auxquelles on aspire peuvent émerger rationnellement d'un équilibre complexe des forces. Nous avons prolongé la méthode de Frei pour y inclure une logique environnementale aussi bien que structurelle, et nous sommes passés de la simulation matérielle à la simulation informatique. » Des coques légères combinées à des structures élastiques sont le sujet propre à l'installation **ARUM**. Des structures en métal plié étaient présentées avec des documents de recherche et des « projets de références », dont des créations de Felix Candela, Heinz Isler et Philippe Block, un jeune chercheur qui s'intéresse aux coques en pierre comprimée.

Seen from below inside (left) or outside (this page), the "Arum" installation provides constant visual surprises vis-à-vis the old structure of the Arsenale.

Ob in Untersicht aus dem Inneren (links) oder von außen betrachtet (diese Seite) – „Arum" bietet stets neue erstaunliche Perspektiven im Zusammenspiel mit dem Arsenale.

Vue de dessous et de l'intérieur (page de gauche) ou de l'extérieur (ici), l'installation Arum crée une surprise visuelle constante par rapport au vieux bâtiment de l'Arsenal.

HANDEL ARCHITECTS

Handel Architects LLP
150 Varick Street, 8th Floor
New York, NY 10013
USA

Tel: +1 212 595 4112
Fax: +1 212 595 9032
E-mail: newyork@handelarchitects.com
Web: www.handelarchitects.com

Born in Israel, **MICHAEL ARAD** was raised there, in the UK, in the United States, and in Mexico. He received a B.A. from Dartmouth College (1994) and an M.Arch from the Georgia Institute of Technology (1999). He became a resident of New York subsequent to his studies and worked with Kohn Pedersen Fox, before joining the Design Department of the New York City Housing Authority, where he was working during the 2003 competition for the National September 11 Memorial. He joined the New York firm of Handel Architects as a Partner in April 2004, where he worked on the realization of the memorial design as a member of the firm. Recent and current work of Handel Architects includes the Flushing Meadows Corona Park Recreation Center (New York, New York, USA, 2009); Nove Residences (San Francisco, California, USA, 2010); Dream Downtown Hotel (New York, New York, USA, 2011); Rosewood Hotel (Abu Dhabi, UAE, expected completion 2013); Shangri-La at the Fort (Manila, Philippines, expected completion 2014); and the Millennium Tower Boston (Boston, Massachusetts, USA, ongoing). Michael Arad won the AIA Presidential Citation (2012) and an AIA Honor Award (2012), both for the National September 11 Memorial (New York, New York, USA, 2006–11, published here).

MICHAEL ARAD kam in Israel zur Welt. Er wuchs in seinem Heimatland, in Großbritannien und Mexiko auf. Seinen B. A. absolvierte er am Dartmouth College (1994), seinen M. Arch. am Georgia Institute of Technology (1999). Nach Beendigung seines Studiums lebte er in New York und war für Kohn Pedersen Fox tätig, bevor er in der Projektierungsabteilung der New Yorker Wohnungsbehörde arbeitete, als die Nationale Gedenkstätte für den 11. September ausgeschrieben wurde. Im April 2004 wurde Arad Partner im New Yorker Büro Handel Architects, wo er die Realisierung des Entwurfs für die Gedenkstätte betreute. Neuere und aktuelle Projekte von Handel Architects sind das Freizeitzentrum im Flushing Meadows Corona Park (New York, 2009), die Nove Residences (San Francisco, Kalifornien, 2010), das Dream Downtown Hotel (New York, 2011), das Rosewood Hotel (Abu Dhabi, VAE, voraussichtliche Fertigstellung 2013), das Hotel Shangri-La at the Fort (Manila, Philippinen, voraussichtliche Fertigstellung 2014), der Millenium Tower Boston (Boston, Massachusetts, in Planung). Das American Institute of Architects verlieh Michael Arad für die Nationale Gedenkstätte für den 11. September (New York, 2006–2011, hier vorgestellt) die Presidential Citation (2012) und einen Honor Award (2012).

MICHAEL ARAD est né en Israël et y a grandi, ainsi qu'au Royaume Uni, aux États-Unis et au Mexique. Il a obtenu son B.A au Dartmouth College (1994) et un M.Arch au Georgia Institute of Technology (1999). Il s'installe à New York après ses études et travaille chez Kohn Pedersen Fox, avant de rejoindre le département de Design de la direction du logement de la ville de New York, où il travaille au moment du concours pour le mémorial du 11-Septembre. En 2004, il rejoint comme associé l'agence new yorkaise Handel Architects, où il travaille à la réalisation du projet de mémorial. Les réalisations récentes ou en cours d'Handel Architects comprennent le Flushing Meadows Corona Park Recreation Center (New York, 2009) ; l'ensemble d'habitations Nove Residences (San Francisco, 2010) ; l'hôtel Dream Downtown (New York, 2011) ; l'hôtel Rosewood (Abou Dhabi, EAU, achèvement prévu en 2013) ; la tour Shangri-La at the Fort (Manille, achèvement prévu en 2014) et la tour Millennium à Boston (en cours). Michael Arad a été récompensé d'une AIA Presidential Citation (2012) et d'un AIA Honor Award (2012), tous deux pour le mémorial du 11-Septembre (New York, 2006–11, présenté ici).

NATIONAL SEPTEMBER 11 MEMORIAL

New York, New York, USA, 2006–11

*Address: 1 Albany Street, New York, NY 10006, USA, www.911memorial.org
Area: 3.2 hectares. Client: National September 11 Memorial & Museum. Cost: $700 million (Memorial and Museum combined). Collaboration: Peter Walker and Partners (Landscape Architects), Davis Brody Bond (Associate Architect)*

Given the scale of destruction witnessed on September 11, 2001, on this site, a void or rather a fountain that seems to pour into the earth is an appropriate symbol.

Angesichts des Ausmaßes der Zerstörung, die diesen Ort am 11. September 2001 heimsuchte, sind Leerräume – oder vielmehr Brunnen, der Wasser in den Boden strömt – ein treffendes Symbol.

Compte tenu de l'étendue des destructions sur ce site, le 11 septembre 2001, un vide, ou plutôt une fontaine semblant se déverser dans le sol, est un symbole pertinent.

The names of the victims of the attack are engraved in the dark bronze panels that ring the two fountains that mark the footprints of the former World Trade Center towers.

Die Namen der Opfer des Terroranschlags wurden in dunkle Bronzepaneele graviert, die entlang der Brunnenkanten – und damit entlang der Konturen des ehemaligen World Trade Centers – verlaufen.

Les noms des victimes de l'attaque sont gravés sur les panneaux en bronze foncé entourant les deux fontaines qui marquent l'empreinte des tours disparues du World Trade Center.

Michael Arad's design for the **NATIONAL SEPTEMBER 11 MEMORIAL** at the World Trade Center site, entitled "Reflecting Absence," was selected by the Lower Manhattan Development Corporation from among more than 5000 entries submitted in an international competition held in 2003. The memorial is located on the site of the former World Trade Center Twin Towers, and is part of the overall 7.5-hectare redevelopment area. A garden area with 400 swamp white oak trees is part of the project. Two reflecting pools, marking the 4000-square-meter footprints of the former towers, are recessed over nine meters into the ground and are lined by waterfalls. As the architects state: "The voids are absence made present and visible." Water tables that are 2.4 meters wide and 61 centimeters high serve as the source of the waterfalls. Both the voids themselves and the water tables are clad in dark gray Virginia granite. The names of the victims are engraved in dark bronze panels, in a carefully chosen order.

Michael Arads Entwurf für die **NATIONALE GEDENKSTÄTTE FÜR DEN 11. SEPTEMBER**, „Reflecting Absence", wurde 2003 von der Lower Manhattan Development Corporation aus über 5000 Entwürfen eines internationalen Wettbewerbs ausgewählt. Die Gedenkstätte befindet sich am ehemaligen Standort der Zwillingstürme des World Trade Centers und ist Teil eines 7,5 ha großen Stadtentwicklungsgebiets, zu dem Grünflächen mit 400 Zweifarbigen Eichen gehören. Zwei große Becken, von deren Rändern Wasser in die Tiefe stürzt, markieren die 4000 m² große Grundfläche der Zwillingstürme und reichen 9 m in den Boden hinab. Die Architekten dazu: „Die Leerräume sind sichtbare und vergegenwärtigte Abwesenheit." Gespeist werden die Wasserfälle aus einem umlaufenden Sockel, der 2,4 m breit und 61 cm hoch ist. Becken und Sockel wurden mit dunklem Granit aus Virginia verblendet. Eingeschrieben in ein dunkles Bronzeband sind die Namen der Opfer, geordnet nach einem speziell konzipierten System.

« Reflecting Absence », le projet de Michael Arad pour le **MÉMORIAL DU 11-SEPTEMBRE** sur le site du World Trade Center, a été retenu parmi plus de 5000 participants du concours international lancé en 2003 par la Lower Manhattan Development Corporation. Le mémorial est situé à l'emplacement des Twin Towers disparues, inclus dans une zone de réaménagement de 7,50 ha. Un jardin planté de 400 chênes bicolores fait partie du projet. Deux miroirs d'eau, marquant l'empreinte des 4000 m² qu'occupaient les tours disparues, sont enfoncés à 9 m dans le sol et bordés de cascades. Selon les architectes, « les vides sont une absence rendue présente et visible ». Des bassins larges de 2,40 m et hauts de 61 cm alimentent les cascades. Les vides et les bassins sont en granit gris de Virginie. Les noms des victimes sont inscrits dans un ordre minutieusement choisi sur des panneaux de bronze foncé.

The scale of the memorial is clearer in these images taken from elevated angles. On the plan to the left, the memorial is seen near the WTC Transportation Hub (Santiago Calatrava) and the National September 11 Museum (Snøhetta).

Von einem erhöhten Standpunkt aus werden die Dimensionen der Gedenkstätte deutlich. Auf dem Lageplan links ist das Mahnmal unweit des WTC Transportation Hub von Santiago Calatrava und des National September 11 Museum von Snøhetta zu erkennen.

L'échelle du mémorial est plus nette sur ces photos prises depuis des points élevés. Sur le plan ci-contre, le mémorial est vu près du WTC Transportation Hub (Santiago Calatrava) et du Musée national du 11-Septembre (Snøhetta).

HERZOG & DE MEURON

Herzog & de Meuron
Rheinschanze 6 / 4056 Basel / Switzerland
Tel: +41 61 385 57 57 / Fax: +41 61 385 57 58
E-mail: info@herzogdemeuron.com / Web: www.herzogdemeuron.com

JACQUES HERZOG and **PIERRE DE MEURON** were both born in Basel, Switzerland, in 1950. They received degrees in architecture from the ETH, Zurich, in 1975, after studying with Aldo Rossi, and founded their partnership in Basel in 1978. The partnership has grown over the years: **CHRISTINE BINSWANGER** joined the practice in 1994, successively followed by **ASCAN MERGENTHALER** in 2004 and **STEFAN MARBACH** in 2006. Herzog & de Meuron won the 2001 Pritzker Prize, and both the RIBA Gold Medal and Praemium Imperiale in 2007. They were chosen to design Tate Modern in London (1994–2000), and, in 2005, they were again commissioned by the Tate to develop a scheme for the extension of the gallery and its surrounding areas: the Tate Modern Project. The first phase of the expansion, the Tanks, opened in 2012 (Southwark, London, UK, 2010–12). Other recent projects include the Forum 2004 Building and Plaza (Barcelona, Spain, 2000–04); the De Young Museum (San Francisco, California, USA, 1999–2005); the Walker Art Center, expansion (Minneapolis, Minnesota, USA, 1999–2005); Allianz Arena (Munich-Fröttmaning, Germany, 2001–05); Plaza de España (Santa Cruz de Tenerife, Canary Islands, Spain, 1998–2008); TEA, Tenerife Espacio de las Artes (Santa Cruz de Tenerife, Canary Islands, Spain, 1999–2008); the CaixaForum (Madrid, Spain, 2001–08); and the National Stadium for the 2008 Olympic Games in Beijing (China, 2002–08). Among their latest works are VitraHaus, a new building to present Vitra's "Home Collection" on the Vitra Campus in Weil am Rhein (Germany, 2006–09); 1111 Lincoln Road, a mixed-use parking facility in Miami Beach (Florida, USA, 2005–10); the new Parrish Art Museum in Water Mill (New York, USA, 2009–12); the Serpentine Gallery Pavilion (with Ai Weiwei; Kensington Gardens, London, UK, 2012, published here); and the New Hall 1 for Messe Basel (Switzerland, 2010–13, also published here). Projects currently under construction include the new Miami Art Museum (Florida, USA, projected completion 2013); and a new building for Roche in Basel, Roche Building 1 (Basel, Switzerland, projected completion 2015).

JACQUES HERZOG und **PIERRE DE MEURON**, beide 1950 in Basel geboren, schlossen ihr Architekturstudium 1975 an der ETH Zürich bei Aldo Rossi ab. Sie arbeiten seit 1978 zusammen. Mit den Jahren kamen weitere Partner hinzu: **CHRISTINE BINSWANGER** 1994, **ASCAN MERGENTHALER** 2004 und **STEFAN MARBACH** 2006. Herzog & de Meuron wurde 2001 der Pritzker-Preis verliehen, 2007 erhielten die Architekten die RIBA Gold Medal sowie den Praemium Imperiale. Sie entwarfen die Tate Modern in London (1994–2000) und wurden 2005 mit der Planung des Tate Modern Project beauftragt (Ausbau des Museums und des umliegenden Geländes). Mit den Tanks (Southwark, London, 2010–12) wurde 2012 der erste Bauabschnitt realisiert. Weitere jüngere Projekte des Büros sind das Forum 2004 mit Plaza (Barcelona, 2000–04), das De Young Museum (San Francisco, 1999–2005), die Erweiterung des Walker Art Center (Minneapolis, 1999–2005), die Allianz Arena (München, 2001–05), die Plaza de España (Santa Cruz de Tenerife, Kanarische Inseln, 1998–2008), das Kunst- und Kulturzentrum Tenerife Espacio de las Artes (Santa Cruz de Tenerife, 1999–2008), das CaixaForum (Madrid, 2001–08) und das Nationalstadion für die Olympischen Spiele 2008 (Peking, 2002–08). Neueste Projekte sind das VitraHaus für die Sammlung des Vitra Design Museums (Weil am Rhein, Deutschland, 2006–09), das Parkhaus 1111 Lincoln Road mit gemischter Nutzung (Miami Beach, 2005–10), das Parrish Art Museum in Water Mill (New York, 2009–12), der Serpentine Gallery Pavilion 2012 (mit Ai Weiwei, London, 2012, hier vorgestellt) und die neue Halle 1 für die Messe Basel (2010–13, ebenfalls hier vorgestellt). Im Bau sind das neue Miami Art Museum (Florida, Fertigstellung voraussichtlich 2013) und ein Neubau für Roche in Basel (voraussichtlich 2015 fertiggestellt).

JACQUES HERZOG et **PIERRE DE MEURON** sont nés tous deux à Bâle en 1950. Diplômés en architecture de l'ETH de Zurich en 1975 après avoir étudié avec Aldo Rossi, ils fondent leur agence à Bâle en 1978. L'agence s'agrandit avec **CHRISTINE BINSWANGER** en 1994, **ASCAN MERGENTHALER** en 2004, puis **STEFAN MARBACH** en 2006. Herzog & de Meuron reçoivent le prix Pritzker en 2001, la médaille d'or du RIBA et le Praemium Imperiale en 2007. Ils sont choisis pour réaliser la Tate Modern à Londres (1994–2000) et, en 2005, sont chargés par celle-ci du projet d'extension du musée et de ses abords : le Tate Modern Project. La première phase de cet agrandissement, les Tanks, est inaugurée en 2012 (Southwark, Londres, 2010–12). Parmi leurs autres projets récents, on compte l'édifice et la place du Forum 2004 (Barcelone, 2000–04) ; le musée De Young (San Francisco, 1999–2005) ; l'extension du Walker Art Center (Minneapolis, 1999–2005) ; le stade Allianz (Munich-Fröttmaning, 2001–05) ; la Plaza de España (Santa Cruz de Tenerife, îles Canaries, 1998–2008) ; le Tenerife Espacio de las Artes (Santa Cruz de Tenerife, îles Canaries, 1999–2008) ; le musée CaixaForum (Madrid, 2001–08) et le Stade national pour les Jeux olympiques de 2008, à Pékin (2002–08). Parmi leur réalisations récentes, on trouve le VitraHaus, un nouveau bâtiment pour la collection « Home » de Vitra, sur le Vitra Campus, à Weil-am-Rhein (Allemagne, 2006–09) ; le 1111 Lincoln Road, un immeuble de parking à Miami Beach (Floride, 2005–10) ; le nouveau musée Parrish Art, à Water Mill (New York, 2009–12) ; le pavillon de la Serpentine Gallery (avec Ai Weiwei ; Kensington Gardens, Londres, 2012, présenté ici) et la nouvelle Halle 1 de la foire de Bâle (Bâle, 2010–13, également présentée ici). Parmi leurs projets en construction, on trouve le Miami Art Museum (Floride, achèvement prévu en 2013) et le Roche Building 1, pour le site de Roche, (Bâle, achèvement prévu en 2015).

MESSE BASEL—NEW HALL

Basel, Switzerland, 2010–13

Address: Messeplatz 1, 4058 Basel, Switzerland, www.mch-group.com
Area: 40 305 m². Client: MCH Swiss Exhibition (Basel) Ltd.
Cost: not disclosed

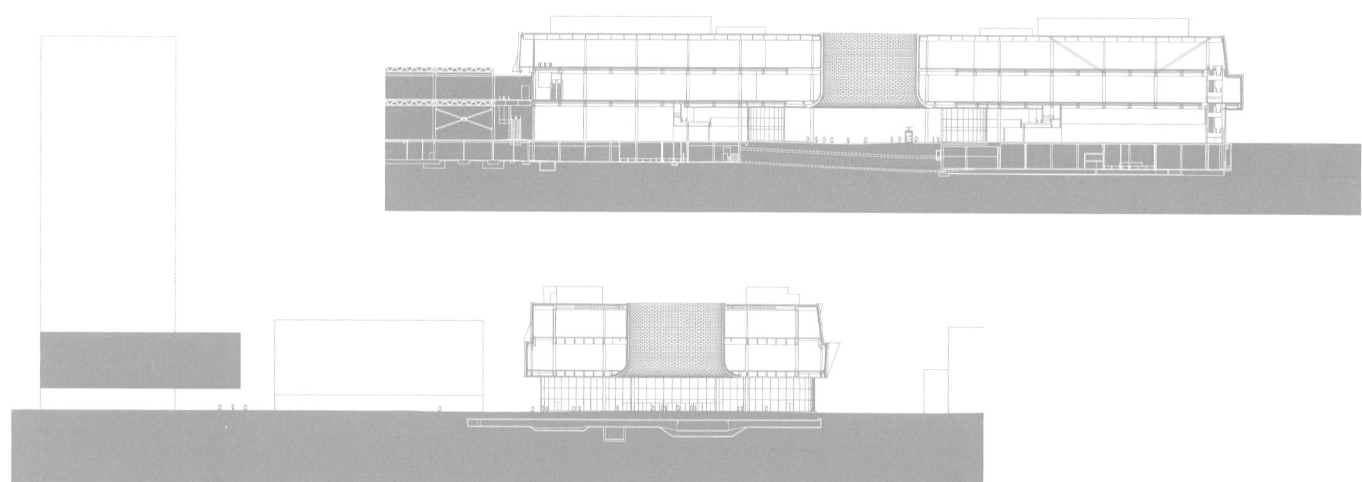

Those who visit the annual Art Basel fair, founded in 1970, are certainly familiar with the facilities located in the Kleinbasel area across the Rhine from the old city. Parts of the former Hall 1 and Hall 3 were deemed to no longer fulfill modern exhibition requirements in terms of ceiling heights, column spacing or load-bearing capacity of the floors. The new structure is a three-story addition to Hall 1 running parallel to the Riehenring. The building contains a multistory exhibition hall, the City Lounge, which is a partially covered city square that steps over the former entrance zone of the Messeplatz, as well as a multifunctional Event Hall for 2500 visitors. A big circular opening in the building provides ample daylight to the areas beneath the largely elevated volume. This fully open space is, in some sense, an echo of the round, enclosed courtyard in Hall 2, which is open only during exhibitions. The entrance at street level, with its large expanses of glass, links the City Lounge to the existing Hall 1, former Hall 3, the new Event Hall, and a number of shops, bars, and restaurants in the foyers. The two exhibition levels above are designed as separate, stacked volumes. The architects state: "The New Hall therefore consists of three individual elements, one on top of the other, each projecting over the street in varying degrees, and allowing them to respond to different urban conditions." A façade made of twisting bands of aluminum unifies the whole. They go on to say: "This is not simply a decorative element but a practical means to regulate the fall of natural light on adjacent properties and to frame specific views from individual spaces, primarily the social areas above the City Lounge, towards the public life of the city."

Wer die 1970 gegründete, jährlich stattfindende Art Basel besucht, kennt die Messeanlagen gegenüber der Altstadt, auf der anderen Seite des Rheins. Teile von Halle 1 und Halle 3 erfüllten im Hinblick auf Deckenhöhe, Gangbreite und statische Belastbarkeit der Böden nicht mehr die Ansprüche, die an moderne Messeflächen gestellt werden. Der dreigeschossige Neubau ergänzt Halle 1 und verläuft parallel zum Riehenring. Das Projekt umfasst eine mehrgeschossige Messehalle und einen teilweise überdachten Platz (die City Lounge), der sich in Stufen über den einstigen Eingangsbereich des Messeplatzes erstreckt, sowie die multifunktionale Event Halle für 2500 Besucher. Durch eine große runde Dachöffnung fällt Licht bis in die unteren Zonen des hoch aufragenden Baus. Dieser offene Teil des Gebäudes zitiert in gewisser Weise den umschlossenen Innenhof von Halle 2, der nur für Messeveranstaltungen geöffnet wird. Der Eingangsbereich mit seinen großflächigen Verglasungen verbindet die City Lounge mit der bestehenden Halle 1, der alten Halle 3, der Event Halle und mit Geschäften, Bars und Restaurants in den Foyers. Die zwei oberen Hallengeschosse sind getrennt und gegeneinander verschoben. Die Architekten: „Die Neue Messe besteht aus drei übereinanderliegenden individuellen Einheiten, die unterschiedlich weit in den Straßenraum hinausragen und auf diese Weise mit dem Stadtraum korrespondieren." Die Fassade aus weißen Aluminiumlamellen gibt dem Projekt ein einheitliches Gepräge. Die Architekten weiter: „Es handelt sich nicht nur um ein dekoratives Element, sondern um ein Mittel zur Regulierung des Einfalls natürlichen Sonnenlichts auf die umgebenden Objekte und zur Rahmung des Blicks auf das städtische Leben, das sich vor allem von den Treffpunkten oberhalb der City Lounge aus darbietet."

Les visiteurs de la foire annuelle Art Basel, créée en 1970, connaissent bien les installations de Kleinbasel, le quartier en face de la vieille ville de l'autre côté du Rhin. Une partie des Halles 1 et 2 ne répondait plus aux besoins des expositions actuelles, en termes de hauteur, d'espacement des poteaux ou de capacité de charge des planchers. La nouvelle structure est une extension sur trois niveaux de la Halle 1, longeant le Riehenring. Le bâtiment contient une halle d'exposition sur plusieurs niveaux, le City Lounge qui est une place partiellement couverte enjambant la zone de l'ancienne entrée de la Messeplatz, et une halle événementielle et multifonction pour 2500 visiteurs. Une grande ouverture circulaire fournit une lumière naturelle à profusion aux espaces en dessous du volume élevé. Cet espace complètement ouvert fait écho à la cour intérieure de la Halle 2, ouverte uniquement pour les expositions. L'entrée au niveau de la rue, largement vitrée, relie le City Lounge à la Halle 1 existante, à l'ancienne Halle 3, à la nouvelle Halle événementielle et à plusieurs boutiques, bars et restaurants dans les foyers. Au-dessus, les deux niveaux d'exposition sont des volumes distincts et empilés. Pour les architectes, « la nouvelle Halle consiste en trois éléments distincts, empilés l'un sur l'autre, chacun s'avançant plus ou moins sur la rue, en réponse aux différentes conditions urbaines ». Une façade de bandes d'aluminium torsadées unifie l'ensemble. « Ce n'est pas un simple élément décoratif, ajoutent-ils, elles contribuent à réguler la lumière naturelle tombant sur les immeubles voisins et à cadrer des vues spécifiques sur la vie de la cité depuis les espaces publics situés au-dessus du City lounge ».

For those who know the Messe Basel area, the new building is situated near the main entrance plaza of the exhibition halls, forming a very open wall between the street and the Messe itself.

Wer die Messe Basel kennt, sieht dass der Neubau unweit des zentralen Messevorplatzes liegt. Das Gebäude bildet eine durchlässige Mauer zwischen Straße und Messegelände.

Pour ceux qui connaissent le quartier de la foire de Bâle, le nouveau bâtiment est situé près de l'entrée principale des halles d'exposition, formant un mur très ouvert entre la rue et la foire proprement dite.

130208

congress

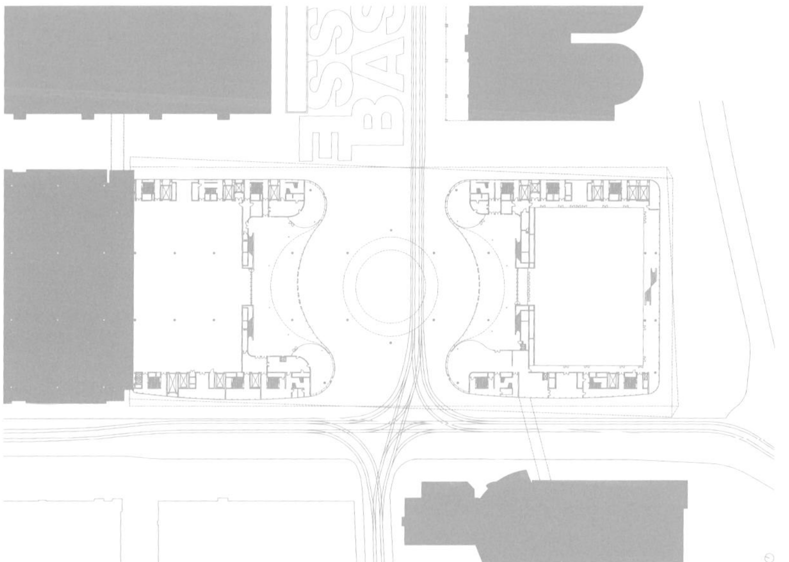

Left, a ground-floor plan of the complex, with the existing Hall 2 to the upper left and Hall 4 to the lower right. Above, detailed views looking through the twisting aluminum band façade.

Links ein Lageplan des Komplexes auf Erdgeschossebene mit der älteren Halle 2 und der neuen Halle 4 rechts unten im Bild. Oben Durchblicke und Detailansichten der gedrehten Aluminiumbänder der Fassade.

Ci-contre, un plan du rez-de-chaussée du complexe, avec la Halle 2 existante en haut à gauche et la Halle 4 en bas à droite. Ci-dessus, des vues de détail à travers la façade en bandes torsadées d'aluminium.

The round central opening is surrounded by equally spectacular interior space. Below, exhibition areas are functional, but it seems clear, nonetheless, that careful attention has been paid to the architecture.

Um die zentrale runde Öffnung gruppieren sich ebenso spektakuläre Innenräume. Die Messeflächen (unten) sind funktional, doch ganz offensichtlich mit hoher Sorgfalt für das architektonische Detail geplant.

L'ouverture centrale ronde est entourée d'un espace intérieur aussi spectaculaire. En bas, les espaces d'exposition sont fonctionnels, mais leur architecture a clairement fait l'objet d'une attention minutieuse.

SERPENTINE GALLERY PAVILION

Kensington Gardens, London, UK, 2012

Address: not applicable. Area: 415 m². Client: Serpentine Gallery
Cost: not disclosed. Design: Herzog & de Meuron and Ai Weiwei

This structure is surely one of the simplest ones designed since the Serpentine started its tradition of summer pavilions in 2000 with Zaha Hadid. It is essentially a 10-meter steel disk rising just over one meter above the level of the lawn, with a cork-clad seating area beneath. The architects explain that after 12 other architects had tried their hand, they would try "instinctively to sidestep the unavoidable problem of creating an object, a concrete shape." They dug down 1.5 meters into the soil of the park to the level of the water table, discovering telephone cables, and the remains of former pavilion foundations or backfills as they descended. The former foundations and footprints form a "jumble of convoluted lines" and were used to inspire the new design, with 11 load-bearing supports corresponding to the previous pavilions, plus a 12th support placed by the designers at their whim. They write of the completed structure: "The roof resembles that of an archeological site. It floats a few feet above the grass of the park, so that everyone visiting can see the water on it, its surface reflecting the infinitely varied, atmospheric skies of London. For special events, the water can be drained off the roof as from a bathtub, from whence it flows back into the waterhole, the deepest point in the pavilion landscape. The dry roof can then be used as a dance floor or simply as a platform suspended above the park." The structure was realized with the generous support of many sponsors, including cork manufacturers Amorim and Usha and Lakshmi N. Mittal; the latter also purchased the structure, which entered their collection, after it closed to the public on October 14, 2012.

Dieser Pavillon ist einer der schlichtesten, seitdem die Serpentine Gallery ihre Sommerpavillontradition 2000 mit Zaha Hadid begonnen hat. Er besteht im Wesentlichen aus einer Stahlscheibe mit 10 m Durchmesser, die kaum mehr als 1 m über die Rasenfläche ragt, darunter eine Sitzlandschaft aus Kork. Nachdem vor ihnen bereits zwölf andere Architekten einen Pavillon entworfen hatten, waren Herzog & de Meuron „instinktiv versucht, das Problem zu umgehen, ein Objekt, eine konkrete Gestalt zu planen". Bei Erdarbeiten, die 1,5 m tief bis auf Grundwasserniveau führten, stießen die Architekten auf Telefonkabel, Fundamentüberreste früherer Pavillons und Aufschüttmaterial. Diese Überreste bildeten ein „Gewirr aus verschlungenen Linien" und inspirierten den neuen Entwurf. Elf Stützelemente markieren die alten Pavillons und werden durch eine zwölfte, ad hoc platzierte Stütze ergänzt. Herzog & de Meuron über den Bau: „Das Dach erinnert an archäologische Ausgrabungsstätten und schwebt etwa 1 m über der Rasenfläche, damit die Besucher den Wasserspiegel sehen können, der die unendlich abwechslungsreichen, atmosphärischen Formationen des Londoner Himmels spiegelt. Für besondere Veranstaltungen kann das Wasser wie aus einer Badewanne abgelassen werden und anschließend zum tiefstgelegenen Punkt der Sitzlandschaft abfließen. Das Dach kann anschließend als erhöhte Tanzfläche oder Podium genutzt werden." Der Pavillon wurde durch Sponsoren wie den Korkhersteller Amorim sowie Usha und Lakshmi N. Mittal ermöglicht. Das Ehepaar erwarb den Pavillon nach der Schließung am 14. Oktober 2012 für seine Sammlung.

Ce bâtiment est certainement un des pavillons d'été de la Serpentine les plus simples depuis le début de cette tradition avec Zaha Hadid en 2000. Il s'agit d'un disque de métal de 10 m de diamètre, suspendu à un mètre de la pelouse, au-dessus d'un espace où l'on peut s'asseoir recouvert de liège. Se prêtant à cet exercice à la suite de 12 autres, les architectes ont voulu essayer « instinctivement d'esquiver l'inévitable problème de créer un objet, une forme concrète ». En creusant le sol du parc sur 1,50 m de profondeur, ils sont tombés sur la nappe phréatique, mais aussi sur des câbles téléphoniques et des restes ou des remblaiements des pavillons précédents. Les anciennes fondations et les traces qui formaient un « fouillis de lignes complexes » ont servi d'inspiration pour le nouveau projet, avec 11 supports de charge correspondant aux pavillons précédents, et un 12e à un emplacement choisi par les concepteurs. De l'ensemble de la structure, ils écrivent que « le toit ressemble à celui d'un site archéologique. Il flotte à quelques dizaines de centimètres au-dessus de l'herbe, pour que les visiteurs puissent voir l'eau au-dessus, sa surface réfléchissant la variété infinie des ciels londoniens. Pour certains événements, l'eau peut être vidée du toit, comme d'une baignoire, d'où elle retourne dans le trou d'eau au point le plus bas du site du pavillon. Le toit peut alors servir de piste de danse ou de plateforme suspendue au-dessus du parc ». Le bâtiment a été réalisé grâce à de nombreux sponsors, dont le fabricant de liège Amorim et Usha et Lakshmi N. Mittal ; ces derniers ont également acheté la structure entrée dans leur collection après sa fermeture au public, le 14 octobre 2012.

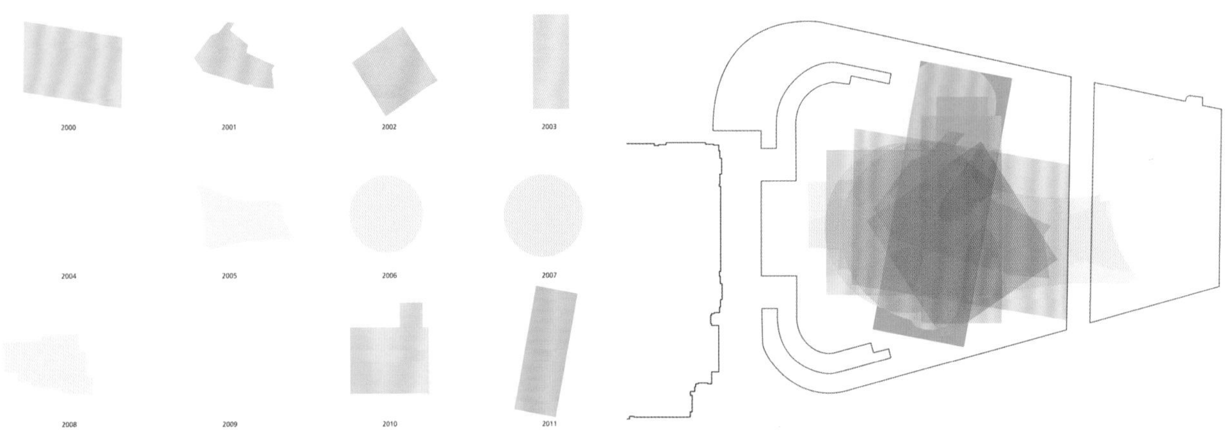

The configuration of the area beneath the pavilion's water-covered disk is based on the remains of earlier Serpentine Summer Pavilions, as the drawing above shows. Right, the completed pavilion.

Die Konfiguration des Bereichs unterhalb der wassergefüllten Scheibe entwickelte sich aus den Spuren früherer Sommerpavillons, wie die Zeichnung oben illustriert. Rechts der realisierte Pavillon.

L'espace sous le miroir d'eau du pavillon tire sa configuration des restes des précédents pavillons d'été de la Serpentine, comme le montrent les dessins ci-dessus. À droite, le pavillon terminé.

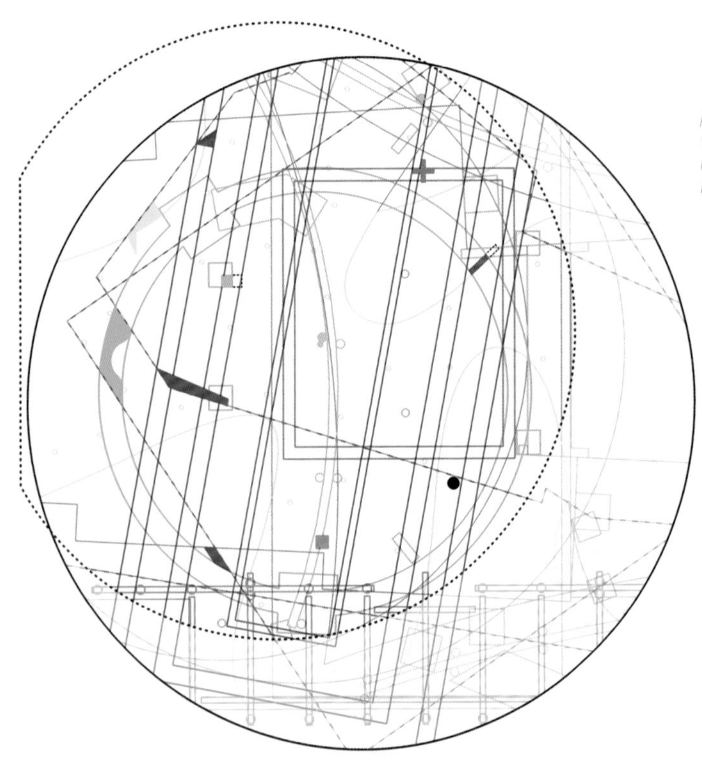

The drawing (left) shows traces of previous pavilion foundations. Below, visitors could enter freely and sit either near the central disk or beneath it.

Die Zeichnung (links) zeigt die Konturen früherer Pavillonfundamente. Besucher hatten ungehinderten Zugang und konnten neben oder unterhalb der Scheibe sitzen (unten).

Le dessin (à gauche) montre les traces de fondation des précédents pavillons. Ci-dessous, les visiteurs entrent librement et s'assoient près du disque central ou en dessous.

The Georgian building of the Serpentine reflected in the pavilion disk. Right, the disk in its grass-surrounded setting.

Der georgianische Bau der Galerie spiegelte sich im Wasser der Pavillonscheibe. Rechts die Scheibe im Kontext der angrenzenden Rasenflächen.

Le bâtiment georgien de la Serpentine se reflète dans le disque du pavillon. Ci-contre, le disque dans son environnement de pelouse.

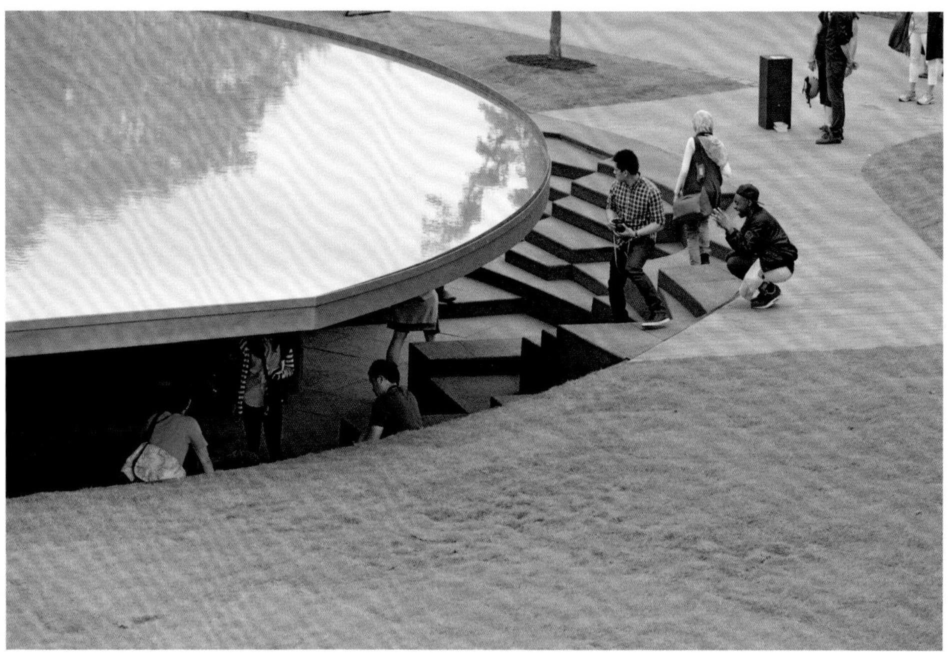

HHF

HHF architects GmbH
Allschwiler Str. 71A / 4055 Basel / Switzerland
Tel: +41 61 756 70 10 / Fax: +41 61 756 70 11
E-mail: info@hhf.ch / Web: www.hhf.ch

HHF architects was founded in 2003 by Tilo Herlach, Simon Hartmann, and Simon Frommenwiler. **TILO HERLACH** was born in 1972 in Zurich, Switzerland. He studied architecture at the ETH Zurich and at the EPFL in Lausanne (1992–98). He subsequently worked with d-company in Bern (2001–03), and with Rolf Furrer Architekten (Basel, 2003). **SIMON HARTMANN** was born in 1974 in Bern, Switzerland, and studied architecture at the EPFL, the Technical University of Berlin, and the ETH (1994–2003). From 1997 to 2003 he worked with Nicola di Battista in Rome, A.B.D.R., Garofalo & Miura, Steuerwald + Scheiwiller Architekten, Basel, and Rolf Furrer Architekten, in Basel. Hartmann has been a teaching assistant at the ETH Studio Basel, working with Jacques Herzog, Pierre de Meuron, Roger Diener, and Marcel Meili since 2002, and head of teaching there since 2005. Since 2009 he has been Professor at the HTA in Fribourg, Switzerland. **SIMON FROMMENWILER** was born in London, UK, in 1972. He attended the ETH in Zurich (1994–2000), and worked subsequently with Bearth & Deplazes, Chur; ARchos Architecture, Basel; and Skidmore, Owings & Merrill in New York. Frommenwiler has been a teaching assistant working with Harry Gugger at the EPFL in Lausanne since 2005. HHF have recently worked on the Jinhua Sculpture Park Baby Dragon (Jinhua, China, 2006); Artfarm, showroom and storage for art (Clinton, New York, USA, 2006–08); Tsai Residence (Ancram, New York, USA, 2006–08); the Kirschgarten High School cafeteria (Basel, Switzerland, 2006–08); Dune House (Ordos, Inner Mongolia, China, 2008–09); Labels 2 (Berlin, Germany, 2008–09); and Confiserie Bachmann (Basel, Switzerland, 2009). In 2011, they completed the Guesthouse (Ancram, New York, USA, in collaboration with Ai Weiwei), and House D (Nuglar, Switzerland), both published here. They are currently working on "Five Houses", a project with buildings in Bali (Indonesia) and in the Hamptons (New York, USA), this again in collaboration with Ai Weiwei.

HHF wurde 2003 von Tilo Herlach, Simon Hartmann und Simon Frommenwiler gegründet. **TILO HERLACH**, 1972 in Zürich geboren, studierte Architektur an der ETH Zürich und der EPFL in Lausanne (1992–98). Anschließend arbeitete er für d-company in Bern (2001–03) und Rolf Furrer Architekten (Basel, 2003). **SIMON HARTMANN** wurde 1974 in Bern geboren und studierte Architektur an der EPFL, der TU Berlin und der ETH Zürich (1994–2003). Von 1997 bis 2003 arbeitete er für Nicola di Battista in Rom, A.B.D.R., Garofalo & Miura, Steuerwald + Scheiwiller Architekten, Basel, und Rolf Furrer Architekten in Basel. Hartmann war ab 2002 Lehrassistent am ETH Studio Basel, wo er mit Jacques Herzog, Pierre de Meuron, Roger Diener und Marcel Meili zusammenarbeitete, seit 2005 leitet er dort die Lehre. Seit 2009 ist er Professor an der HTA Fribourg, Schweiz. **SIMON FROMMENWILER** wurde 1972 in London geboren. Nach seinem Studium an der ETH Zürich (1994–2000) war er für Bearth & Deplazes, Chur, ARchos Architecture, Basel, und Skidmore, Owings & Merrill in New York tätig. Frommenwiler ist seit 2005 Lehrassistent bei Harry Gugger an der EPFL in Lausanne. In den letzten Jahren arbeitete HHF am „Baby Dragon" im Skulpturenpark Jinhua (Jinhua, China, 2006), der Artfarm, Ausstellungsraum und Lager für Kunst (Clinton, New York, 2006–08), der Tsai Residence (Ancram, New York, 2006–08), der Kirschgarten Schulcafeteria (Basel, 2006–08), dem Dune House (Ordos, Innere Mongolei, China, 2008–09), dem Modezentrum Labels 2 (Berlin, 2008–09) und der Confiserie Bachmann (Basel, 2009). 2011 wurden das Gästehaus in Ancram fertiggestellt (New York, mit Ai Weiwei) sowie das Haus D (Nuglar, Schweiz), beide hier vorgestellt. Derzeit arbeitet das Büro an „Five Houses", einem Projekt in Bali (Indonesien) und den Hamptons (New York), wieder in Zusammenarbeit mit Ai Weiwei.

HHF architects a été créé en 2003 par Tilo Herlach, Simon Hartmann et Simon Frommenwiler. Né à Zurich en 1972, **TILO HERLACH** étudie l'architecture à l'ETH de Zurich et à l'EPFL de Lausanne (1992–98). Il travaille ensuite chez d-company à Berne (2001–03) et chez Rolf Furrer Architekten (Bâle, 2003). Né à Berne en 1974, **SIMON HARTMANN** étudie l'architecture à l'EPFL, à l'Université technique de Berlin et à l'ETH (1994–2003). De 1997 à 2003, il travaille chez Nicola di Battista, A.B.D.R. et Garofalo & Miura, à Rome, et chez Steuerwald + Scheiwiller Architekten et Rolf Furrer Architekten, à Bâle. Hartmann est professeur assistant depuis 2002 à l'ETH Studio Basel, avec Jacques Herzog, Pierre de Meuron, Roger Diener et Marcel Meili, et directeur de la formation depuis 2005. Depuis 2009, il est professeur au HTA de Fribourg, en Suisse. **SIMON FROMMENWILER** est né à Londres en 1972. Il étudie à l'ETH de Zurich (1994–2000), puis travaille chez Bearth & Deplazes, Chur, ARchos Architecture, à Bâle, et Skidmore, Owings & Merrill, à New York. Frommenwiler est l'assistant de Harry Gugger à l'EPFL de Lausanne depuis 2005. Parmi les projets récents de HHF, on compte Baby Dragon, pour le parc de sculptures de Jinhua (Chine, 2006) ; Artfarm, une galerie d'art et d'entreposage (Clinton, États-Unis, 2006–08) ; la résidence Tsai (Ancram, New York, 2006–08) ; la cafétéria de l'école Kirschgarten (Bâle, 2006–08) ; la maison Dune (Ordos, Mongolie intérieure, 2008–09) ; Labels 2 (Berlin, 2008–09) et la confiserie Bachmann (Bâle, 2009). En 2011, ils ont achevé la Guesthouse (Ancram, New York, en collaboration avec Ai Weiwei) et la maison D (Nuglar, Suisse), présentées ici. Ils travaillent actuellement sur le projet *Five Houses* à Bali et dans les Hamptons (New York), toujours en collaboration avec Ai Weiwei.

GUESTHOUSE

Ancram, New York, USA, 2010–11

Address: not disclosed. Area: 219 m². Client: not disclosed
Cost: not disclosed. Collaboration: Ai Weiwei,
Mio Tsunemaya, Madeleine Kessler, Jeff Mansfield

The owners of the Tsai Residence, completed by the architects in 2008, asked them to create a guesthouse in collaboration with the Chinese artist Ai Weiwei. The guesthouse required a bedroom, workroom, and an art gallery, that were brought together in a Y-shaped design. Each element of the guesthouse offers a different perspective on the extensive grounds of the Tsai Residence. The timber structure is clad in corrugated Cor-ten steel. With the exception of some white walls, the entire interior of the house is clad in wood panels—floor, walls, and ceiling. The architects state: "The relationship of the Tsai Residence to the guesthouse reflects HHF's philosophy, namely to use what already exists at a site as a source of inspiration." The basement level of the guesthouse contains a garage and measures 99 square meters, meaning that the visible part of the structure is relatively modest in its dimensions.

Die Bauherren der Tsai Residence (2008 von den Architekten fertiggestellt) beauftragten das Büro, in Zusammenarbeit mit Ai Weiwei, mit der Planung eines Gästehauses. Gewünscht waren ein Schlafzimmer, ein Studio und ein Galerieraum: das Programm wurde auf einem Y-förmigen Grundriss realisiert. Von jedem Raum aus bieten sich neue Ausblicke auf das großzügige Anwesen. Die Fassade des Holzbaus wurde mit gewelltem Cor-Ten-Stahl verblendet. Mit Ausnahme weniger weißer Wände wurde der gesamte Innenraum – Böden, Wände, Decken – mit Holz ausgebaut. Die Architekten erklären: „Das Zusammenspiel von Tsai Residence und Gästehaus spiegelt die Philosophie von HHF wider: das jeweils Bestehende an einem Standort als Inspirationsquelle zu nutzen." Im 99 m² großen Untergeschoss des Gästehauses befindet sich eine Garage. Der sichtbare Teil des Baus ist flächenmäßig deshalb recht bescheiden in seinen Dimensionen.

Les propriétaires de la résidence Tsai, achevée par les architectes en 2008, leur ont demandé de créer une annexe en collaboration avec l'artiste chinois Ai Weiwei. Celle-ci comprend une chambre, un bureau et une galerie d'art, réunis par un plan en forme de Y. Chaque élément offre un point de vue différent sur le vaste domaine de la résidence. Le bâtiment en bois est revêtu d'acier Corten ondulé. Excepté quelques murs blancs, l'intérieur de la maison est totalement recouvert de panneaux de bois – sols, murs et plafonds. Selon les architectes, « la relation entre la résidence Tsai et son annexe reflète la philosophie de HHF qui est de s'inspirer de ce qui existe déjà sur le site ». Le sous-sol de l'annexe abrite un garage et mesure 99 m², ce qui fait que la part visible du bâtiment est de taille relativement modeste.

The curving guesthouse sits lightly on its hillside site, with a slight cantilever over the slope. Elevation drawings show its insertion into the ground (right).

Das Gästehaus mit seinen geschwungenen Konturen liegt leicht auf seinem Baugrund und kragt etwas über den Abhang aus. Aufrisse (rechts) illustrieren seine Einbindung in das Grundstück.

La Guesthouse en courbe est délicatement posée sur le site vallonné, avec un léger porte-à-faux au-dessus de la pente. Les élévations montrent son insertion dans le sol (ci-contre).

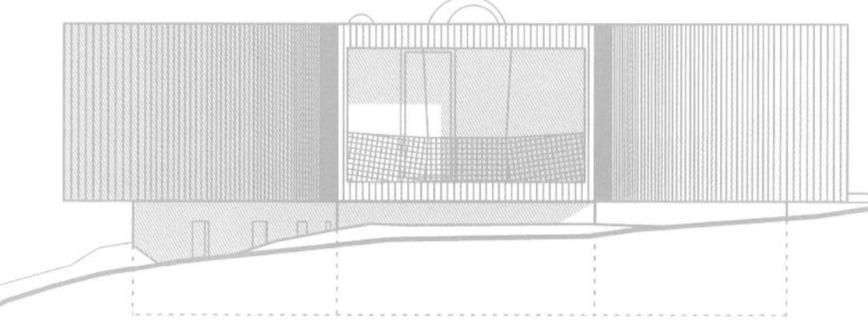

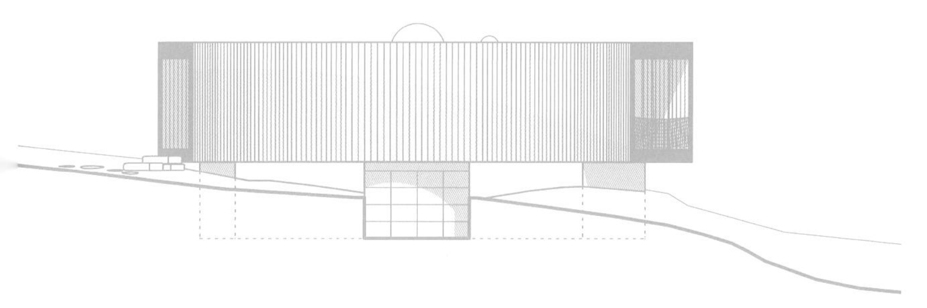

The impression of rather strict lines on the exterior is contrasted with the warm wood of the interiors. Exhibition space (above) and bedroom and living areas are seen here.

Einen Kontrast zu den eher strengen Linien des Außenbaus bilden die warmen Holztöne des Interieurs. Hier die Galerie (oben) sowie Schlaf- und Wohnbereiche.

L'impression stricte des lignes extérieures contraste avec le bois chaud des intérieurs. On peut voir ici l'espace d'exposition (ci-dessus), la chambre à coucher et les espaces de vie.

Above, plans of the garage level (left) and the first floor (right). Below, a bed sits behind an angled wall.

Oben zu sehen: Grundrisse der Garagenebene (links) sowie des Erdgeschosses (rechts). Unten ein Bett hinter einer schrägen Trennwand.

Ci-dessus, les plans du niveau du garage (à gauche) et du rez-de-chaussée (à droite). Ci-dessous, un lit placé derrière un mur oblique.

HOUSE D

Nuglar, Switzerland, 2010–11

Address: not disclosed. Area: 241 m². Client: not disclosed. Cost: not disclosed
Collaboration: Markus Leixner, Anna Smorodinsky, Mio Tsuneyama

The plan of **HOUSE D** is a strict rectangle oriented toward a view of a fruit orchard. Built in Nuglar in the Canton of Solothurn, the house has a kitchen, dining, and living area on the fully glazed main floor. A concrete core neighbors a stairway leading to the upper and lower floors. Proximity to the site is increased dramatically by a 240-square-meter wood deck terrace and a pool. Untreated wood is used for the ceilings and doors in the house, which has three bedrooms, three bathrooms, a gym, and office, aside from the ground-floor living areas. With its many concrete surfaces and strict lines, the house is certainly rigorous and avoids being completely cold because of its close connection to the fields in which it is placed.

Der Grundriss von **HAUS D** ist ein strenges Rechteck, orientiert zum Blick auf den Obstgarten. Das Haus in Nuglar, Kanton Solothurn, verfügt im vollverglasten Erdgeschoss über Küche, Essbereich und Wohnzimmer. Neben dem Hauskern aus Beton führt eine Treppe in Unter- und Obergeschoss. Die Nähe zur Landschaft wird besonders durch die 240 m² große Holzterrasse und ein Schwimmbecken spürbar. Bei Decken und Türen im Haus kam unbehandeltes Holz zum Einsatz. Neben den Wohnbereichen im Erdgeschoss verfügt der Bau über drei Schlafzimmer, drei Bäder, einen Fitnessraum sowie ein Büro. Durch zahlreiche Sichtbetonflächen und schnörkellose Linienführung wirkt das Haus streng, jedoch – dank der engen Einbindung in die umliegenden Felder – nicht kühl.

La **MAISON D** est un rectangle strict, orienté avec une vue sur un verger. Construite à Nuglar, dans le canton de Soleure, en Suisse, elle est dotée, au rez-de-chaussée entièrement vitré, d'un espace cuisine-salle à manger-salon. Un noyau central en béton jouxte un escalier reliant les étages inférieur et supérieur. La proximité avec le site est spectaculairement mise en valeur par une terrasse en bois de 240 m² et une piscine. Du bois non traité est utilisé pour les plafonds et les portes de la maison, qui a trois chambres, trois salles de bain, une salle de sport et un bureau, en sus des aires de séjour du rez-de-chaussée. Avec ses nombreuses surfaces de béton et ses lignes strictes, la maison est certes sévère mais évite la froideur grâce à sa relation étroite avec les champs dans lesquels elle est située.

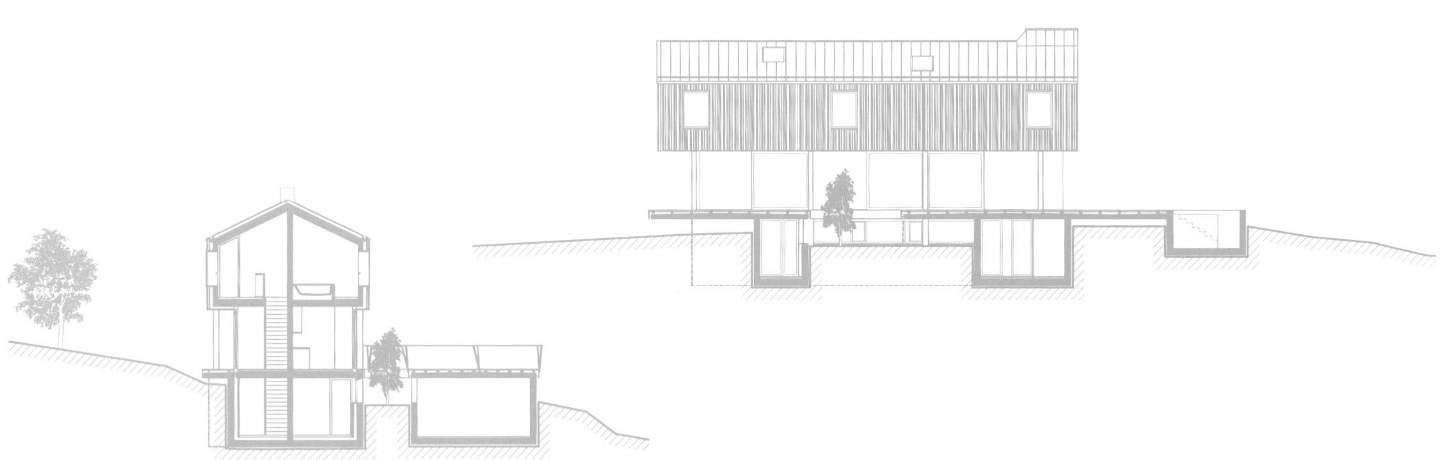

Anchored in a gentle slope, the house seems to have an upper section that is more closed and "traditional" than the fully glazed ground level. Below, a view of the large wooden terrace.

Das Haus, eingebettet in das leicht abschüssige Grundstück, hat ein eher geschlossenes Obergeschoss, das „traditioneller" wirkt als das voll verglaste Erdgeschoss. Unten eine Ansicht der großen Holzterrasse.

Accrochée à une pente douce, la maison semble avoir un étage supérieur plus fermé et « traditionnel » que le rez-de-chaussée entièrement vitré. Ci-dessous, une vue de la grande terrasse en bois.

Wood is used on the upper level ceilings seen to the left, but the concrete gives an impression of a certain coldness.

Die Decken des Obergeschosses sind holzvertäfelt (links), doch Sichtbeton sorgt für eine gewisse Kühle.

Même si l'on a utilisé du bois pour les plafonds de l'étage, ci-contre, le béton laisse une certaine impression de froideur.

To the right, ground-floor spaces with full-height glazing, wooden floors, and white "camouflage"-style curtains.

Rechts Wohnbereiche im Erdgeschoss mit raumhoher Verglasung, Holzböden und weißen Vorhängen im „Camouflage"-Stil.

Page de droite, les espaces entièrement vitrés du rez-de-chaussée, avec des planchers en bois et des rideaux de style « camouflage ».

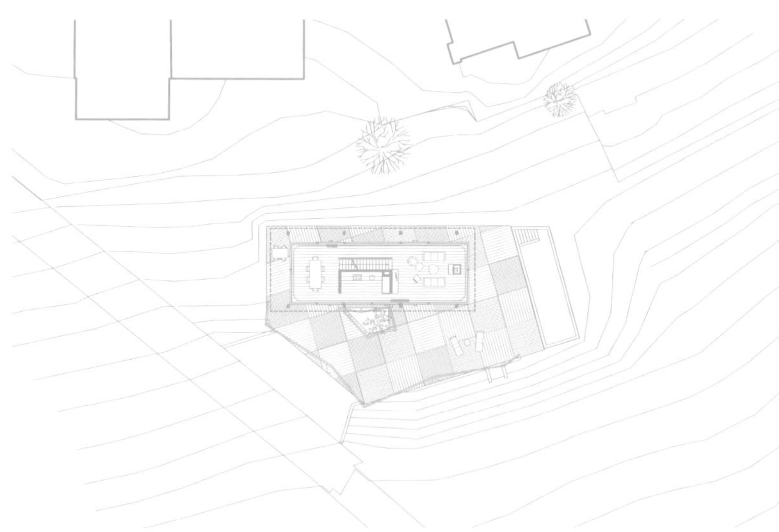

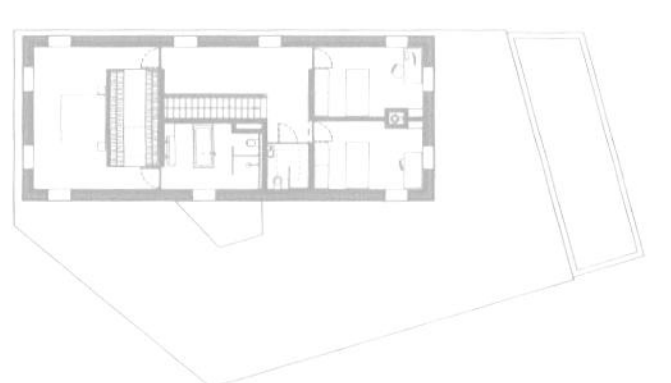

STEVEN HOLL

Steven Holl Architects, P.C.
450 West 31st Street, 11th floor
New York, NY 10001
USA

Tel: +1 212 629 7262
Fax: +1 212 629 7312
E-mail: mail@stevenholl.com
Web: www.stevenholl.com

Born in 1947 in Bremerton, Washington, **STEVEN HOLL** obtained his B.Arch degree from the University of Washington (1970). He studied in Rome and at the Architectural Association in London (1976). He began his career in California and opened his own office in New York in 1976. He won the Alvar Aalto Medal in 1998. His notable buildings include Void Space/Hinged Space, housing (Nexus World, Fukuoka, Japan, 1991); Stretto House (Dallas, Texas, USA, 1992); Chapel of St. Ignatius, Seattle University (Seattle, Washington, USA, 1997); Kiasma Museum of Contemporary Art (Helsinki, Finland, 1998); and an extension to the Cranbrook Institute of Science (Bloomfield Hills, Michigan, USA, 1999). Holl won the competition (2009) for the Glasgow School of Art (Glasgow, UK), and has completed an expansion and renovation of the Nelson-Atkins Museum of Art (Kansas City, Missouri, USA, 1999–2007); Linked Hybrid (Beijing, China, 2005–08); the Knut Hamsun Center (Hamarøy, Norway, 2006–09); HEART: Herning Museum of Contemporary Art (Herning, Denmark, 2007–09); and the Vanke Center (Shenzhen, China, 2008–09). His more recent projects include the Nanjing Museum of Art and Architecture (China, 2008–10); Cité de l'Océan et du Surf (Biarritz, France, 2008–11, with Solange Fabião, published here); Shan-Shui Hangzhou (master plan, Hangzhou, China, 2010–); and the Hangzhou Music Museum (Hangzhou, China, 2010–).

STEVEN HOLL, geboren 1947 in Bremerton, Washington, absolvierte seinen B. Arch. an der University of Washington (1970) und studierte darüber hinaus in Rom und an der Architectural Association in London (1976). Nach Beginn seiner Laufbahn in Kalifornien gründete er 1976 ein Büro in New York. 1998 wurde Holl mit der Alvar-Aalto-Medaille ausgezeichnet. Zu seinen meistbeachteten Projekten zählen die Wohnanlage Void Space/Hinged Space (Nexus World, Fukuoka, Japan, 1991), das Stretto House (Dallas, Texas, 1992), die Chapel of St. Ignatius an der Seattle University (Seattle, Washington, 1997), das Kiasma Museum für zeitgenössische Kunst (Helsinki, 1998) sowie eine Erweiterung des Cranbrook Institute of Science (Bloomfield Hills, Michigan, 1999). Holl gewann den Wettbewerb (2009) für die Glasgow School of Art und realisierte ein Erweiterungs- und Sanierungsprojekt für das Nelson Atkins Museum of Art (Kansas City, Missouri, 1999–2007). Weitere Arbeiten sind das Linked Hybrid (Peking, 2005–09), das Knut-Hamsun-Zentrum (Hamarøy, Norwegen, 2006–09), das Herning Museum für zeitgenössische Kunst (HEART, Herning, Dänemark, 2007–09) und das Vanke Center (Shenzhen, China, 2008–09). Zu seinen jüngeren Projekten zählen das Museum für Kunst und Architektur in Nanjing (China, 2008–10), die Cité de l'Océan et du Surf (Biarritz, Frankreich, 2008–11, mit Solange Fabião, hier vorgestellt), ein Masterplan für Shan-Shui (Hangzhou, China, seit 2010) und das Museum für Musik in Hangzhou (seit 2010).

Né en 1947 à Bremerton, aux États-Unis, **STEVEN HOLL** obtient son B.Arch à l'université de Washington (1970). Il étudie à Rome et à l'Architectural Association à Londres (1976). Il débute sa carrière en Californie et crée son agence à New York en 1976. Il reçoit la médaille Alvar Aalto en 1998. Parmi ses réalisations marquantes, on compte l'ensemble d'habitations Void Space/Hinged Space (Nexus World, Fukuoka, Japon, 1991) ; la maison Stretto (Dallas, 1992) ; la chapelle St. Ignatius de l'université de Seattle (Seattle, 1997) ; le Musée d'art contemporain Kiasma (Helsinki, 1998) et une extension du Cranbrook Institute of Science (Bloomfield Hills, Michigan, 1999). Holl gagne le concours (2009) pour l'École des beaux-arts de Glasgow et achève l'extension et le réaménagement du Musée d'art Nelson-Atkins (Kansas City, Missouri, 1999–2007) ; le complexe résidentiel Linked Hybrid (Pékin, 2005–08) ; le Centre Knut Hamsun (Hamarøy, Norvège, 2006–09) ; le HEART, le Musée d'art contemporain de Herning (Herning, Danemark, 2007–09) et le Centre Vanke (Shenzhen, Chine, 2008–09). Parmi ses projets récents, on compte le Musée d'art et d'architecture de Nankin (Chine, 2008–10) ; la Cité de l'Océan et du Surf (Biarritz, 2008–11, avec Solange Fabião, présenté ici) ; Shan-Shui Hangzhou (plan directeur, Hangzhou, Chine, 2010–) et le Musée de la musique de Hangzhou (Chine, 2010–).

CITÉ DE L'OCÉAN ET DU SURF

Biarritz, France, 2008–11

Address: 1 Avenue de la Plage, 64200 Biarritz, France, +33 559 22 75 40, www.citedelocean.com
Area: 3800 m². Client: SNC Biarritz. Cost: not disclosed
Collaboration: Solange Fabião

This museum explores both surf and sea and their role in leisure-time activities. Steven Holl won the 2005 international competition for the design of this facility in collaboration with Solange Fabião. A concave exterior plaza dubbed "Place de l'Océan" neighbors two glass "boulders" that contain the restaurant and the surfer's kiosk and echo two real boulders on the beach. The building's southwest corner is marked by a surfers' area with a skate pool at the top and an open porch beneath connecting to an auditorium and exhibition spaces inside the museum. The architects explain: "The gardens of the **CITÉ DE L'OCÉAN ET DU SURF** aim at a fusion of architecture and landscape, and connect the project to the ocean horizon. The precise integration of concept and topography gives the building its unique profile." Portuguese cobblestone paving with grass and natural vegetation mark the outside plaza. Here, as he has in other recent projects, Steven Holl places a particular emphasis on the relationship between architecture and landscape.

Das Museum ist dem Meer, der Brandung und dem Surfsport gewidmet. Steven Holls Entwurf, erarbeitet mit Solange Fabião, gewann 2005 einen internationalen Wettbewerb. Gerahmt wird der konkave Museumsplatz, die Place de l'Océan, von zwei Glasbauten, in denen ein Restaurant und ein Kiosk für die Surfer untergebracht sind. Sie wirken wie zwei Felsen und zitieren zwei reale Steinformationen am Strand. An der Südwestseite des Museums liegt ein öffentlicher Platz mit einem Skate-Pool und einer darunter gelegenen Veranda, über die man in das Auditorium und die Ausstellungsräume gelangt. Die Architekten: „Die Außenanlagen der **CITÉ DE L'OCÉAN ET DU SURF** suchen nach einer Symbiose von Architektur und Landschaft und binden das Projekt an den Meereshorizont an. Die präzise Integration von Konzept und Topografie gibt dem Projekt sein unverwechselbares Profil." Der Platz wurde mit portugiesischem Kopfsteinpflaster, Rasen und natürlicher Vegetation gestaltet. Wie schon in anderen Projekten zuvor, geht es Steven Holl auch hier um ein Zusammenspiel von Architektur und Landschaft.

Ce musée explore les rôles du surf et de la mer dans les activités de loisirs. Steven Holl a remporté le concours international de 2005 pour ce complexe, en collaboration avec Solange Fabião. Une place extérieure concave baptisée « place de l'Océan » jouxte deux « rochers » de verre, contenant un restaurant et un kiosque pour les surfeurs, qui font écho à deux rochers réels de la plage. Le coin sud-ouest du bâtiment se distingue par une aire de surf, avec un skate pool au sommet et, en dessous, un porche ouvert donnant accès à un auditorium et à des espaces d'expositions à l'intérieur du musée. Selon les architectes, « les jardins de la **CITÉ DE L'OCÉAN ET DU SURF** visent à fusionner architecture et paysage, et relie le projet à l'horizon de l'océan. La nette intégration du concept et de la topographie donne au bâtiment son profil singulier ». Un pavement portugais avec de l'herbe et de la végétation naturelle marque la place extérieure. Comme dans d'autres de ses projets récents, Steven Holl met ici l'accent sur la relation entre architecture et paysage.

As is frequently the case, parts of Holl's building glow from within at night. A dunelike cobblestone configuration makes the building appear to emerge from a natural setting.

Teile des Baus leuchten bei Nacht, wie so oft bei Holl. Der kopfsteingepflasterte Platz, wie eine Düne geformt, lässt das Gebäude wie aus einer natürlichen Landschaft aufragen.

Comme souvent avec Holl, des parties du bâtiment luisent de l'intérieur, la nuit. Une configuration pavée en forme de dune donne au bâtiment l'impression d'émerger d'un environnement naturel.

Steven Holl has invented a new type of lyrical modern architecture, where sculpture and his favored form of expression—watercolor sketches—never seem far removed from the completed buildings.

Steven Holl definiert eine neue Form lyrischer Architektur: Hier sind die realisierten Bauten nie weit von Skulptur oder Aquarellskizzen entfernt – seinem bevorzugten Medium.

Steven Holl a inventé un nouveau type lyrique d'architecture moderne où les bâtiments achevés ne semblent jamais très éloignés de la sculpture et de son mode d'expression préféré – les esquisses à l'aquarelle.

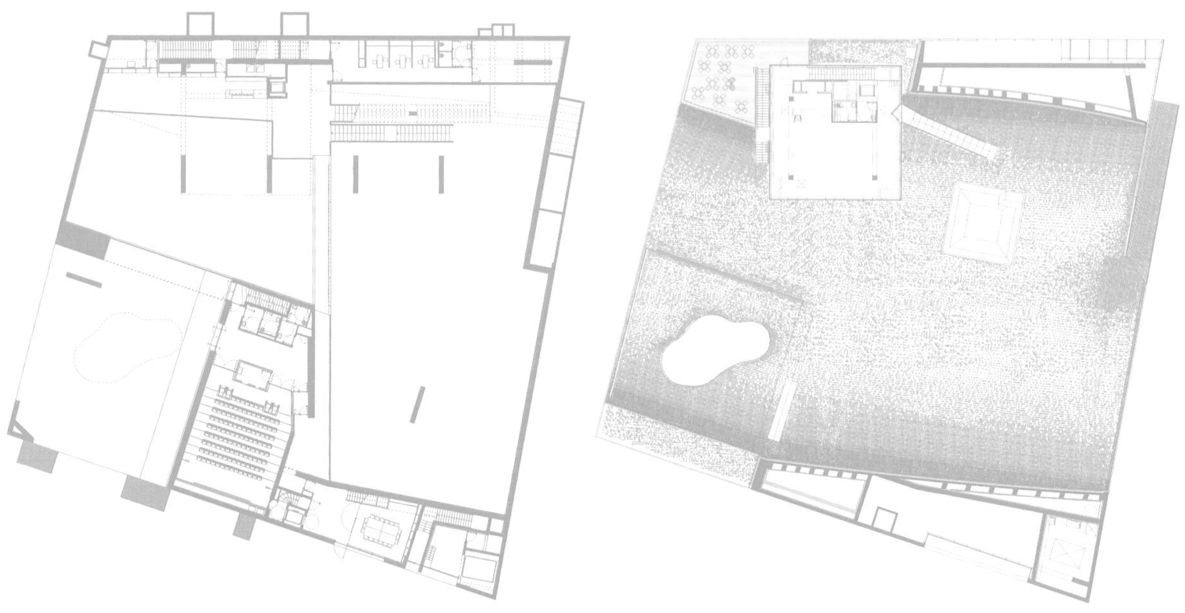

Above, a floor plan (left) and a roof plan (right). Light seems to enter the building from all sides, guided and modulated by the curving surfaces seen in the image below.

Oben ein Etagengrundriss (links) sowie ein Grundriss des Dachs (rechts). Licht fällt von allen Seiten in den Bau ein, geführt und moduliert durch die geschwungenen Oberflächen (unten).

Ci-dessus, un plan de sol (à gauche) et un plan du toit (à droite). Ci-dessous, la lumière, guidée et modulée par les surfaces courbes, semble pénétrer le bâtiment de toute part.

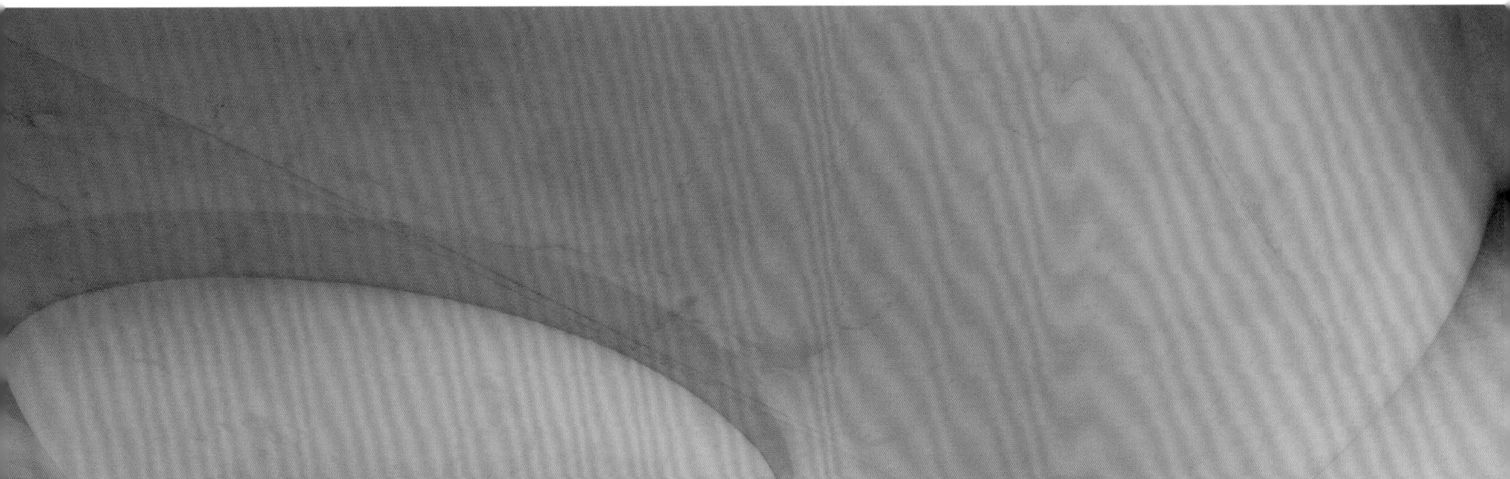

If Holl's designs are lyrical, they are also abstract, fulfilling functional requirements as the elevation drawings below suggest, even as they play on light and space in a poetic manner.

Holls Entwürfe sind nicht nur lyrisch, sondern auch abstrakt und werden zugleich funktionalen Anforderungen gerecht (Aufrisse unten), auch wenn sie Licht und Raum poetisch interpretieren.

Les formes lyriques de Holl sont également abstraites et répondent aux besoins fonctionnels, comme le montrent les élévations ci-dessous, tout en jouant poétiquement avec la lumière et l'espace.

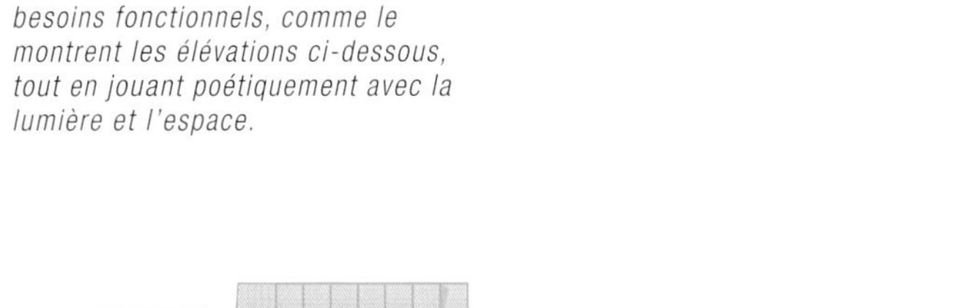

ARATA ISOZAKI

Arata Isozaki & Associates
1-2-7 Shirokane, Minato-ku
Tokyo 108-0072
Japan

Tel: +81 3 3446 2334
Fax: +81 3 6450 2335
E-mail: isozaki@isozaki.co.jp
Web: www.isozaki.co.jp

Born in Oita City on the island of Kyushu, Japan, in 1931, **ARATA ISOZAKI** graduated from the Architectural Faculty of the University of Tokyo in 1954 and established Arata Isozaki & Associates in 1963, having worked in the office of Kenzo Tange. Winner of the 1986 RIBA Gold Medal, his notable buildings include the Museum of Modern Art, Gunma (Gunma, Japan, 1971–74); the Tsukuba Center Building (Tsukuba, Japan, 1978–83); the Museum of Contemporary Art (Los Angeles, California, USA, 1981–86); Art Tower Mito (Mito, Japan, 1986–90); Higashi Shizuoka Convention and Arts Center (Shizuoka, Japan, 1993–98); and Ohio's Center of Science and Industry (COSI, Columbus, Ohio, USA, 1994–99). Recent work includes the Shenzhen Cultural Center (Shenzhen, China, 1997–2008); Central Academy of Fine Art, Museum of Art (Beijing, China, 2003–08); Qatar National Convention Center (Doha, Qatar, 2004–11); the ongoing Milano Fiera (Milan, Italy, 2003–); and Himalayas Center (Shanghai, China, 2007–, published here).

ARATA ISOZAKI, 1931 in Oita auf der Insel Kyushu geboren, schloss sein Studium 1954 an der Fakultät für Architektur der Universität Tokio ab. Anschließend arbeitete er im Büro von Kenzo Tange und gründete 1963 Arata Isozaki & Associates. 1986 wurde er mit der RIBA-Goldmedaille ausgezeichnet. Zu seinen wichtigsten Bauten zählen das Museum für moderne Kunst in Gunma (Gunma, Japan, 1971–74), das Tsukuba Center (Tsukuba, Japan, 1978–83), das Museum of Contemporary Art (Los Angeles, Kalifornien, 1981–86), der Art Tower Mito (Mito, Japan, 1986–90), das Messe- und Kunstzentrum Higashi Shizuoka (Shizuoka, Japan, 1993–98) und das Zentrum für Wissenschaft und Industrie von Ohio (COSI, Columbus, Ohio, 1994–99). Neuere Arbeiten sind u.a. das Kulturzentrum Shenzhen (China, 1997–2008), das Kunstmuseum der Central Academy of Fine Art (CAFA) in Peking (2003–08), das Nationale Kongresszentrum von Katar (Doha, Katar, 2004–11), das laufende Projekt Fiera Milano (Mailand, seit 2003) und das Himalayas Center (Shanghai, China, seit 2007, hier vorgestellt).

Né à Oita, sur l'île de Kyushu, au Japon, en 1931, **ARATA ISOZAKI** obtient son diplôme d'architecte à l'université de Tokyo en 1954. Il fonde Arata Isozaki & Associates en 1963 après avoir travaillé dans l'agence de Kenzo Tange. Il obtient la médaille d'Or RIBA en 1986. Parmi ses réalisations les plus remarquées, on trouve le Musée d'art moderne de Gunma (Japon, 1971–74) ; le Centre civique de Tsukuba (Japon, 1978–83) ; le Musée d'art contemporain de Los Angeles (1981–86) ; la tour de l'Art Mito (Mito, Japon, 1986–90) ; le Centre des congrès et des arts Higashi Shizuoka (Shizuoka, Japon, 1993–98) et le Centre des sciences et de l'industrie COSI (Columbus, Ohio, 1994–99). Ses récents travaux comprennent le Centre culturel de Shenzhen (Chine, 1997–2008) ; le musée de l'École nationale des beaux-arts (Pékin, 2003–08) ; le Centre national des congrès du Qatar (Doha, 2004–11) ; le Milano Fiera, en cours (Milan, 2003–) et le complexe Himalayas (Shanghai, 2007–, présenté ici).

HIMALAYAS CENTER

Shanghai, China, 2007–

Address: 869 Yinghua Road, Pudong, Shanghai, China, +86 21 6075 8555, www.zendaihimalayas.com
Area: 155 000 m². Client: Shanghai Zendai Himalayas Real Estate Company Ltd.
Cost: not disclosed

Located in the newly developed Pudong area of Shanghai, this very large complex plays on numerous ideas seen elsewhere in Isozaki's work, such as the treelike façade of his Qatar National Convention Center.

Der Großkomplex liegt im Neubauviertel Pudong von Shanghai und greift verschiedene Motive auf, die bei Isozaki auch an anderer Stelle auszumachen sind, u. a. das Baummotiv an der Fassade seines Nationalen Kongresszentrums in Katar.

Situé dans le nouveau quartier en expansion de Pudong, à Shanghai, ce très grand complexe joue sur de nombreuses idées présentes dans d'autres projets de Isozaki, comme la façade en forme d'arbre de son Centre national des congrès du Qatar.

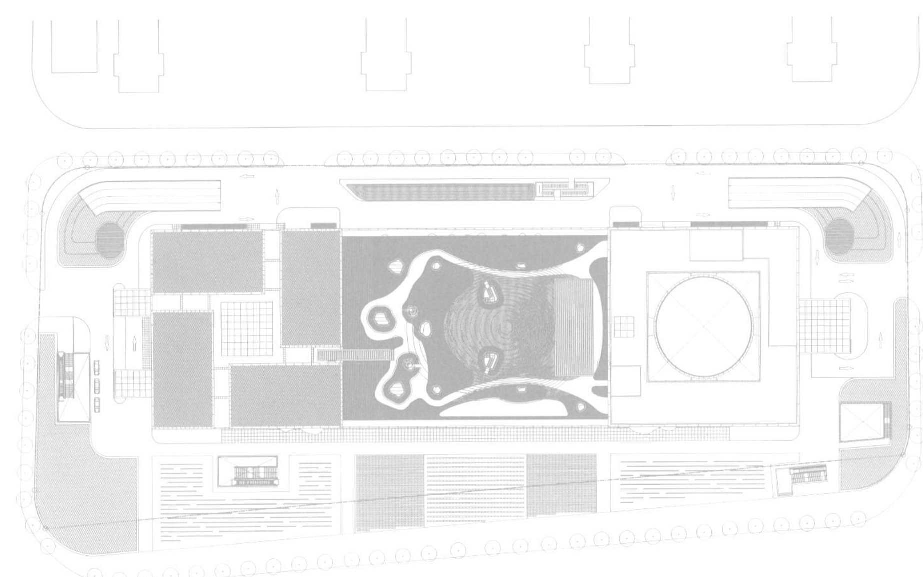

As seen in plan, an open square, a circle inscribed in a square, and the unusual, irregular wall forms seen above are combined by the architect into a rather unexpected whole.

Wie der Lageplan zeigt, organisiert der Architekt ein überraschendes Gesamtkonzept aus einem offenen Quadrat, einem in ein Quadrat eingeschriebenen Kreis und unregelmäßigen Fassadenformen (oben).

Comme on le voit en plan, une place ouverte, un cercle inscrit dans un carré et les formes insolites des murs irréguliers, ci-dessus, se conjuguent en un ensemble assez inattendu.

Located in the Pudong district of Shanghai, this complex has the particularity of having no less than 65 000 square meters of its area below grade. It includes an art center, a five-star hotel, studios for artists, and shopping malls. The hotel is located on the northern end of the site and rises to a height of 100 meters. The artist's studios, occupying 11 500 square meters, are on the southern side in a 67.5-meter-high tower structure. The two towers are connected by the art center, which is the core of the facility. The architect emphasizes the complexity of the structure, which unites very different functions, in a web that is considered both in its horizontal dimension and vertically. At street level, the building includes a number of apparently organic elements that can be likened to the treelike structure of the architect's National Convention Center in Doha, Qatar.

Der Komplex liegt in Pudong, einem Stadtteil von Shanghai. Ganze 65 000 m² des Projekts wurden unterirdisch realisiert. Im Himalayas Center sind ein Museum, ein Fünf-Sterne-Hotel, Künstlerateliers und Einkaufszentren untergebracht. Das Hotel liegt am nördlichen Ende des Grundstücks und misst an der höchsten Stelle 100 m. Die Ateliers haben eine Nutzfläche von 11 500 m² und befinden sich in einem 67,5 m hohen Turm am Südende des Komplexes. Beide Türme sind durch ein Museum verbunden, das den Kern des Projekts bildet. Der Architekt betont die Komplexität des Gebäudes, das dank einer sowohl horizontal als auch vertikal gedachten Netzstruktur höchst verschiedene Funktionen in sich vereint. Auf Straßenniveau präsentiert sich das Gebäude mit einer Reihe organisch wirkender Elemente, die an das Nationale Kongresszentrum von Katar erinnern, das der Architekt in Doha plante.

Ce complexe situé dans le quartier de Pudong à Shanghai, présente la particularité d'avoir au moins 65 000 m² en sous-sol. Il comprend un centre d'art, un hôtel cinq étoiles, des ateliers d'artistes et des galeries marchandes. L'hôtel est situé à la limite nord du site et s'élève à 100 m de hauteur. Les ateliers d'artiste, sur 11 500 m², sont situés au sud, dans une tour de 67,50 m de haut. Les deux tours sont reliées par le centre d'art qui constitue le cœur du complexe. L'architecte met l'accent sur la complexité du bâtiment qui réunit des fonctions très différentes par un réseau à la fois horizontal et vertical. Au niveau de la rue, le bâtiment comporte des éléments d'apparence organique qui rappellent la structure en forme d'arbre du Centre national des congrès de Doha, au Qatar.

As seen from street level (above), the building appears to be composed of very different elements that are nonetheless joined together into a coherent whole.

Auf Straßenebene (oben) präsentiert sich der Komplex als Vielzahl verschiedener Elemente, die sich dennoch zu einem schlüssigen Ganzen fügen.

Vu du niveau de la rue (ci-dessus), le bâtiment semble être composé d'éléments très différents, toutefois réunis en un ensemble cohérent.

In an elevation drawing (below) and the details to the right, different aspects of the design are brought to light—one block has a screen that appears to be inspired in its form by Chinese writing, while cavelike shapes are predominant elsewhere.

Ein Aufriss (unten) und Details (rechts) beleuchten verschiedene Aspekte des Entwurfs – ein Baukörper ist mit einem Fassadenschirm ausgestattet, der an chinesische Schriftzeichen erinnert, während an anderer Stelle höhlenartige Motive dominieren.

Dans une élévation (ci-dessous) et dans les détails ci-contre, différents aspects du projet sont mis en lumière – un des cubes a un claustra dont le dessin s'inspire de l'écriture chinoise tandis qu'ailleurs prédominent des formes de grottes.

The complex is very large, as these images suggest. The architect has created varied interior spaces that echo the external façades. The forms above appear almost organic in their inspiration.

Die Aufnahmen lassen ahnen, wie groß der Komplex tatsächlich ist. Der Architekt gestaltete abwechslungsreiche Räume, die motivisch an die Fassade anknüpfen. Die Formen oben im Bild wirken geradezu organisch.

Le complexe est immense, comme le montrent ces photos. L'architecte a créé différents espaces intérieurs répondant aux façades extérieures. Les formes ci-dessus sont presque d'inspiration organique.

In the image to the right, the play on the contrast between curving, organic, or geological forms with planar elements such as the windows and floor is clear—this contrast is also seen in the plan below.

Rechts im Bild wird das kontrastreiche Zusammenspiel von geschwungenen, organischen oder geologisch inspirierten Formen mit planen Elementen wie Fenstern und Böden deutlich – dieser Kontrast spiegelt sich auch im Grundriss unten.

Dans la photo de droite, le jeu de contraste entre des formes courbes, organiques ou géologiques et des éléments plans, comme les fenêtres ou les sols, est évident – contraste également visible dans le plan ci-dessous.

CARLA JUAÇABA AND BIA LESSA

Carla Juaçaba
Rua Republica do Peru 73/301 / Copacabana
Rio de Janeiro, RJ 22021–040 / Brazil
Tel: +55 21 2547 3488 / Fax: +55 21 8202 2229
E-mail: mail@carlajuacaba.com.br
Web: www.carlajuacaba.com.br

Bia Lessa
Rua Aarão Reis 116 / Santa Teresa Â
Rio de Janeiro, RJ 20240–090 / Brazil
E-mail: bia@bialessa.com
Web: www.bialessa.com

CARLA JUAÇABA was born in 1976 in Rio de Janeiro, Brazil. She studied architecture at Santa Ursula University (Rio de Janeiro). She is currently a Professor at the Pontifícia Universidade Católica (Rio de Janeiro). Carla Juaçaba worked with the architect and scenographer Gisela Magalhãe (1996–2000). She has served as a lecturer at the Latin American Architecture Biennale (BAL, Pamplona, Spain 2009), and as a guest critic at the Staedelschule (Frankfurt, Germany 2010). Her residential projects include the Veranda House (Rio de Janeiro, Brazil, 2007); and the Casa Rio Bonito, Minimal House (Nova Friburgo, Rio de Janeiro, Brazil, 2008). She has also worked on exhibition designs—"Jewelry Brazil" and "Chaumet Jewelry"—both held at the Museu de Arte Moderna, Rio de Janeiro, in 2005. **BIA LESSA** (Beatriz Ferreira Lessa) was born in 1958 in São Paulo, Brazil. Aside from numerous stage and exhibition designs, she was the guest artist of the Brazil Pavilion at Expo 2000 in Hanover, the third most visited pavilion of the expo. Together, they created the Humanidade 2012 Pavilion (Copacabana, Rio de Janeiro, Brazil, 2012, published here).

CARLA JUAÇABA wurde 1976 in Rio de Janeiro, Brasilien, geboren. Hier studierte sie Architektur an der Universität Santa Ursula. Derzeit lehrt sie als Professorin an der Pontifícia Universidade Católica, ebenfalls in Rio de Janeiro. Von 1996 bis 2000 arbeitete Juaçaba mit der Architektin und Szenografin Gisela Magalhãe. Juaçaba hielt Vorträge im Rahmen der Lateinamerikanischen Architekturbiennale (BAL, Pamplona, Spanien, 2009) und war Gastkritikerin an der Frankfurter Städelschule (2010). Zu ihren Wohnbauprojekten zählen die Casa Varanda (Rio de Janeiro, Brasilien, 2007) und die minimalistische Casa Rio Bonito (Nova Friburgo, Rio de Janeiro, 2008). Carla Juaçaba plante außerdem die Ausstellungsarchitekturen für „Jóia Brasil" und „Chaumet", beide 2005 am Museu de Arte Moderna in Rio de Janeiro. **BIA LESSA** (Beatriz Ferreira Lessa) wurde 1958 in São Paulo, Brasilien, geboren. Außer zahlreichen Bühnenbildern gestaltete sie als Gastkünstlerin den Brasilianischen (und drittmeistbesuchten) Pavillon auf der Expo 2000 in Hannover. Gemeinsam entwarfen Carla Juaçaba und Bia Lessa den Pavillon für das Nachhaltigkeitsforum Humanidade 2012 (Copacabana, Rio de Janeiro, 2012, hier vorgestellt).

Née en 1976 à Rio de Janeiro, **CARLA JUAÇABA** étudie l'architecture à l'université Santa Ursula (Rio de Janeiro). Elle enseigne actuellement à l'Université catholique de Rio de Janeiro. Carla Juaçaba a travaillé avec l'architecte et scénographe Gisela Magalhãe (1996–2000). Elle a été maître de conférences à la Biennale latino-américaine de Pampelune (2009) et critique invitée à la Staedelschule (Francfort, 2010). Ses projets résidentiels comprennent la maison Veranda (Rio de Janeiro, 2007) et une maison minimaliste à Rio Bonito (Nova Friburgo, Rio de Janeiro, 2008). Elle a aussi travaillé à des scénographies d'expositions – « Jóia Brasil » et « Jóias de Chaumet » – toutes deux au Musée d'art moderne de Rio de Janeiro, en 2005. **BIA LESSA** (Beatriz Ferreira Lessa) est née en 1958 à São Paulo. Outre ses nombreuses scénographies de théâtre et d'expositions, elle a été l'artiste invitée du pavillon du Brésil (troisième de la manifestation en terme de fréquentation), pour Expo 2000 à Hanovre. Ensemble, elles ont créé le pavillon Humanidade 2012, à Copacabana (Rio de Janeiro, 2012, présenté ici).

O HOMEM
E SUAS CONEXÕES

HUMANIDADE 2012 PAVILION

Copacabana, Rio de Janeiro, Brazil, 2012

Address: not applicable. Area: 6500 m². Client: FIESP / FIRJAN
Cost: not disclosed. Collaboration: Carla Juaçaba / Bia Lessa

Scaffolding is a part of any urban environment, but usually only as a shell surrounding a building under construction—here the scaffolding becomes the building.

Gerüste finden sich in jedem urbanen Kontext, bilden jedoch normalerweise die Hülle um ein entstehendes Gebäude – hier wird das Gerüst selbst zum Bauwerk.

Les échafaudages font partie de tout environnement urbain, quoique habituellement enveloppant un bâtiment en construction – ici, l'échafaudage devient le bâtiment.

Flags of participating nations fly from the highest level of the pavilion, with walkways or inserted container-like forms providing for activities.

Flaggen der teilnehmenden Nationen auf der obersten Ebene des Pavillons. Laufgänge und integrierte container-ähnliche Elemente bieten Raum für Veranstaltungen.

Les drapeaux des nations participantes flottent au sommet du pavillon, au-dessus de passerelles et de volumes en forme de containers destinés aux activités.

In the context of the 2012 United Nations Conference on Sustainable Development (UNCSD), also known as Rio+20, Humanidade 2012 was organized at the initiative of FIESP, the FIRJAN System, the Roberto Marinho Foundation, SESI-Rio, SESI-SP, Senai-Rio and Senai-SP, with sponsorship by the City of Rio de Janeiro and Sebrae, and was designed to highlight the role that Brazil currently plays as a global leader in the debate on sustainable development. The architect Carla Juaçaba and the set designer Bia Lessa were chosen to create a temporary structure at Fort Copacabana to house this event. The building was composed of five structural walls measuring 170 meters in length and 20 meters in height, with 5.40-meter gaps between them, creating "a suspended walkway over Rio's landscape, interrupted when necessary by spaces meant for reflection and thought." Exhibition rooms acted as bracing for the entire structure. Carla Juaçaba states: "We propose a scaffold building, translucent, exposed to all weather conditions: light, heat, rain, sounds of waves and wind, reminding man of his frailty when compared to nature." The concept called for all of the materials used, including scaffolding, enclosures, furniture, and even the garbage generated to be reused after the event. The team attributes the "general concept and direction" to Bia Lessa and the architecture to Carla Juaçaba. Bia Lessa states: "Our main idea with this project was to come up with an exhibition where space and project was one and the same: the space is the exhibition itself… We were given a site in a military base, an unstable terrain. Facing two of Rio's most well-known beaches, Ipanema and Copacabana, and surrounded by exuberant nature, the wind blows harshly, often at 120 kilometers per hour… We were certain about not using materials frequently used for temporary exhibitions (plastic tents, blowups), though we were aware of the provisional character of the project."

Im Rahmen der UN-Konferenz über nachhaltige Entwicklung (UNCSD), auch bekannt unter dem Namen „Rio +20", fand auf Initiative von FIESP, FIRJAN System, SESI-Rio, SESI-SP, Senai-Rio, Senai-SP und der Roberto-Marinho-Stiftung das von der Stadt Rio de Janeiro und Sebrae geförderte Nachhaltigkeitsforum Humanidade 2012 statt. Thema war die Rolle Brasiliens als führender globaler Akteur in der Debatte um nachhaltige Entwicklung. Architektin Carla Juaçaba und Bühnenbildnerin Bia Lessa erhielten den Auftrag, einen temporären Veranstaltungsort in Fort Copacabana zu realisieren. Die Konstruktion bestand aus fünf 170 m langen und 20 m hohen Gerüstwänden. 5,4 m breite Lücken zwischen den Wänden bildeten „schwebende Laufgänge über Rios Landschaft, die Raum zum Verweilen und Nachdenken boten". Die Ausstellungsbereiche dienten bautechnisch zugleich als Konstruktionsverspannung. Carla Juaçaba: „Unser Entwurf besteht aus Gerüsten, ist lichtdurchlässig, der Witterung ausgesetzt: dem Licht, der Hitze, dem Rauschen des Meers und des Windes. Er erinnert daran, wie zerbrechlich der Mensch im Vergleich zur Natur ist." Das Konzept sah vor, sämtliche Materialien, darunter Gerüste, Zäune, Mobiliar und selbst den Müll im Anschluss zu recyceln. Kernkonzept und Ausrichtung verantwortete Bia Lessa, die bauliche Umsetzung lag in den Händen von Carla Juaçaba. Bia Lessa: „Grundidee war die Realisierung einer Ausstellung, bei der Ausstellungsraum und -gegenstand ein und dasselbe sind: Der Ort selbst ist die Ausstellung ... Der uns zugewiesene Standort lag auf einem Militärstützpunkt, ein instabiles Gelände nahe zwei der beliebtesten Strände von Rio, Ipanema und Copacabana, ringsherum üppigste Natur, starke Winde, nicht selten mit bis zu 120 km/h ... Obwohl uns klar war, dass es um ein temporäres Projekt ging, wollten wir keine Plastikzelte oder aufblasbare Elemente verwenden, wie sie bei temporären Ausstellungen häufig zum Einsatz kommen."

Dans le cadre de la Conférence des Nations unies sur le développement durable 2012, dite Rio +20, Humanidade 2012 a été organisé à l'initiative de la FIESP, de FIRJAN System, de la Fondation Roberto Marinho, de SESI-Rio, SESI-SP, Senai-Rio et Senai-SP, avec le soutien de la ville de Rio de Janeiro et du Sebrae. Ce projet avait pour objectif de mettre en lumière le rôle actuel joué par le Brésil, en tant que puissance mondiale, dans le débat sur le développement durable. L'architecte Carla Juaçaba et la scénographe Bia Lessa ont été sélectionnées pour créer un bâtiment temporaire destiné à accueillir cet évènement à Fort Copacabana. Le bâtiment est composé de cinq murs structurels de 170 m de long et 20 m de haut, espacés chacun de 5,40 m, pour créer une « promenade suspendue au-dessus du paysage de Rio, interrompue quand nécessaire par des espaces réservés à la réflexion et à l'analyse ». Les salles d'exposition font office d'entretoise pour l'ensemble du bâtiment. « Nous proposons un bâtiment en échafaudages, explique Carla Juaçaba, translucide et exposé aux éléments : lumière, chaleur, pluie, bruit des vagues et du vent, rappelant à l'homme sa fragilité face à la nature. » Le concept veut que tous les matériaux utilisés, y compris les échafaudages, les clôtures, le mobilier et même les déchets générés soient recyclés après l'évènement. Bia Lessa est chargée de la conception générale et de la direction et Carla Juaçaba de l'architecture. Pour Bia Lessa, « notre idée principale pour ce projet était de parvenir à une exposition dans laquelle l'espace et le projet sont une seule et même chose : l'espace est l'exposition… Nous disposions d'un site sur une base militaire, un terrain instable en face de deux des plus célèbres plages de Rio, Ipanema et Copacabana, entouré d'une nature luxuriante où le vent souffle très fort, souvent à 120 km/h… Nous ne voulions pas utiliser les matériaux habituels des expositions temporaires (tentes en plastique, structures gonflables), tout en étant conscientes du caractère provisoire du projet ».

Seen from a distance (left page) or in an overall drawing, the sheer size of the structure becomes apparent. Inside, the dense web of scaffolding provides a more intimate scale.

Aus der Ferne (linke Seite) oder auf Überblicksplänen wird die enorme Größe der Konstruktion deutlich. Innen entsteht durch ein dichtes Netz aus Gerüstelementen ein kleinteiligerer Maßstab.

De loin (page de gauche) ou dans un dessin d'ensemble, la taille de la structure devient évidente. À l'intérieur, le réseau dense d'échafaudages produit une échelle plus intime.

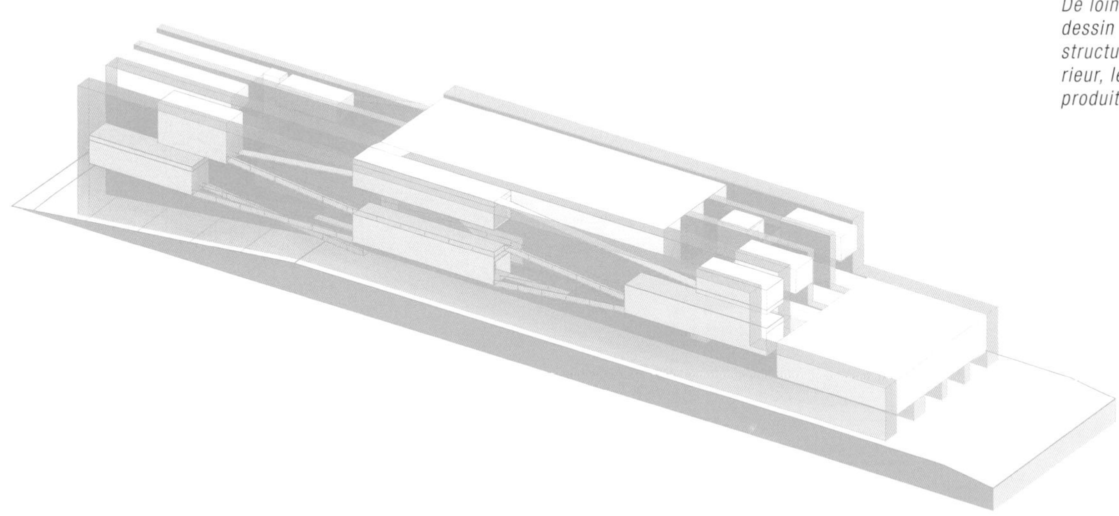

With the involvement of the set designer Bia Lessa, exhibition spaces within the complex take on a decidedly theatrical or artistic character. Below, visitors viewing exhibitions that include paintings.

Durch die Beteiligung der Szenografin Bia Lessa gewinnen die Ausstellungsbereiche im Komplex einen dramatischen, künstlerischen Charakter. Unten Besucher in der Ausstellung, die auch Bilder umfasste.

Avec la participation de la scénographe Bia Lessa, les espaces d'exposition du complexe prennent un caractère résolument théâtral ou artistique. Ci-dessous, des visiteurs d'expositions, entre autres de peintures.

The theatrical element of the installations is again visible in these images, where color and space combine with light and reflections to give an almost vertiginous impression.

Auch hier wird das dramatische Element der Installationen sichtbar: Farbe und Raum, im Zusammenspiel mit Licht und Spiegelungen, sind von fast hypnotischer Wirkung.

L'aspect théâtral des installations est à nouveau visible dans ces photos où la couleur et l'espace se combinent à la lumière et aux reflets pour produire une impression presque vertigineuse.

ANISH KAPOOR AND CECIL BALMOND

Anish Kapoor Studio
London / UK
E-mail: info@kapoorstudio.com
Web: www.anishkapoor.com

Balmond Studio / Unit 9
190a New North Road / London N1 7BJ / UK
Tel: +44 20 70 43 06 51
E-mail: info@balmondstudio.com
Web: www.balmondstudio.com

The artist **ANISH KAPOOR** was born in Bombay, India, in 1954 and has lived and worked in London since the early 1970s. He studied at the Hornsey College of Art (1973–77) and the Chelsea School of Art (1977–78), and he had his first solo exhibition in 1980. He represented Britain at the 1990 Biennale in Venice and won the Turner Prize in 1991. His many exhibitions include architecture-scale works such as *Marsyas* (Tate Modern, London, UK, October 2002–April 2003); *Cloud Gate*, Chicago Millennium Park (Chicago, Illinois, USA, 2004); and *Leviathan*, Monumenta 2011 (Grand Palais, Paris, France, May 11–June 23, 2011). Born in 1943 in Colombo, Sri Lanka, **CECIL BALMOND** was educated at the University of Ceylon (1960). He came to London for postgraduate studies (University of Southampton, 1962–65) and joined Arup in 1968. He is an internationally recognized designer, structural engineer, and author, and was Deputy Chairman of multidisciplinary engineering firm Arup since 2004, where he founded the Advanced Geometry Unit (AGU). Balmond has now set up his own practice: Balmond Studio. He has collaborated with Rem Koolhaas on the Kunsthal (Rotterdam, the Netherlands, 1994); Grand Palais (Lille, France, 1994); Seattle Central Library (Seattle, Washington, USA, 2004); Casa da Música (Porto, Portugal, 2005); the Serpentine Pavilion (London, UK, 2006); and the CCTV Headquarters (Beijing, China, 2005–08). He worked with Álvaro Siza on the Portuguese National Pavilion for Expo '98 in Lisbon (Portugal), and with Shigeru Ban on the design of the new Centre Pompidou-Metz (Metz, France, 2006–10). Anish Kapoor and Cecil Balmond completed the Orbit (London, UK, 2010–12, published here).

Der Künstler **ANISH KAPOOR** wurde 1954 in Mumbai, Indien, geboren. Er lebt und arbeitet seit den frühen 1970er-Jahren in London. Kapoor studierte am Hornsey College of Art (1973–77) und an der Chelsea School of Art (1977–78). Seine erste Einzelausstellung fand 1980 statt, 1990 vertrat er Großbritannien auf der Biennale von Venedig. 1991 erhielt er den Turner-Preis. Zu seinen Arbeiten zählen auch bauliche Installationen wie „Marsyas“ (Tate Modern, London, Oktober 2001–April 2003), „Cloud Gate“ im Chicago Millenium Park (Chicago, Illinois, 2004) und „Leviathan“ auf der Monumenta 2011 (Grand Palais, Paris, 11. Mai–23. Juni, 2011). **CECIL BALMOND** wurde 1943 in Colombo, Sri Lanka, geboren und studierte an der Universität von Ceylon (1960). Für ein Aufbaustudium an der University of Southampton (1962 bis 1965) zog er nach London. Ab 1968 arbeitete er für das multidisziplinär tätige Ingenieurbüro Arup. Cecil Balmond ist weltweit anerkannter Planer, Statiker, Autor und war seit 2004 stellvertretender Geschäftsführer bei Arup, wo er die Abteilung für komplexe Geometrie (Advanced Geometry Unit, AGU) ins Leben rief. Inzwischen hat er mit Balmond Studio sein eigenes Büro gegründet. Mit Rem Koolhaas arbeitete er an folgenden Projekten: Kunsthal (Rotterdam, 1994), Grand Palais (Lille, Frankreich, 1994), Seattle Central Library (Seattle, Washington, 2004), Casa da Música (Porto, Portugal, 2005), Serpentine Pavilion (London, 2006) und CCTV Headquarters (Peking, 2005 bis 2008). Mit Álvaro Siza arbeitete er am Portugiesischen Pavillon für die Expo '98 in Lissabon sowie mit Shigeru Ban am Centre Pompidou Metz (Metz, 2006–10). Orbit (London, 2010–12, hier vorgestellt) ist eine Zusammenarbeit von Anish Kapoor und Cecil Balmond.

L'artiste **ANISH KAPOOR**, né à Bombay en 1954, vit et travaille à Londres depuis le début des années 1970. Il étudie au Hornsey College of Art (1973–77), à la Chelsea School of Art (1977–78) et fait sa première exposition personnelle en 1980. Il représente la Grande-Bretagne à la Biennale de Venise 1990 et gagne le prix Turner en 1991. Ses nombreuses expositions comprennent des œuvres de taille monumentale, comme *Marsyas* (Tate Modern, Londres, octobre 2002–avril 2003) ; *Cloud Gate*, Millennium Park (Chicago, 2004) et *Leviathan*, Monumenta 2011, Grand Palais (Paris, 11 mai–23 juin 2011). Né en 1943 à Colombo, Sri Lanka, **CECIL BALMOND** étudie à l'université de Ceylan (1960). Il poursuit ses études supérieures à Londres (université de Southampton, 1962–65) et rejoint Arup en 1968. Internationalement reconnu comme designer, ingénieur structure et auteur, il devient vice-président du bureau d'études Arup en 2004, où il crée l'Advanced Geometry Unit (AGU). Balmond a maintenant sa propre agence, Balmond Studio. Il a collaboré avec Rem Koolhaas sur le Kunsthal (Rotterdam, 1994) ; Lille Grand Palais (Lille, 1994) ; la Bibliothèque centrale (Seattle, 2004) ; la Casa da Música (Porto, 2005) ; le pavillon de la Serpentine (Londres, 2006) et le siège de CCTV (Pékin, 2005–08). Il collabore avec Álvaro Siza pour le pavillon national portugais d'Expo '98 à Lisbonne et avec Shigeru Ban pour le Centre Pompidou-Metz (2006–10). Anish Kapoor et Cecil Balmond ont réalisé l'Orbit (Londres, 2010–12, présenté ici).

ORBIT

Olympic Park, London, UK, 2010–12

Address: Queen Elizabeth Olympic Park, Stratford, London E20 2ST, UK, www.londonlegacy.co.uk
Area: 600 m². Client: London Legacy Development Corporation
Cost: £22.7 million. Collaboration: Ushida Findlay Architects, Ove Arup & Partners,
Sir Robert McAlpine & Partners, Watsons

Above, three plan drawings emphasize the concept of the structure that is formed as a continuous loop, with a circular platform located 85 meters above the ground.

Drei Grundrisse (oben) unterstreichen den konzeptuellen Aufbau der Konstruktion als unendliche Schleife. In 85 m Höhe schwebt eine runde Plattform.

Ci-dessus, trois plans mettent l'accent sur le concept de la structure en forme de boucle continue et sa plateforme circulaire perchée à 85 m au-dessus du sol.

This unusual form was co-created by Kapoor and Balmond, a team that has previously worked on other large-scale art works. As Cecil Balmond's office describes the project: "Instead of going up linearly, in a straight line, their creation is an 'orbit'—a continuous loop from start to finish that goes around and comes back on itself. By turning, looping, and connecting up every time it passes itself, a unique, highly stable structure is created that compiles space around you, as you move up and down." Prefabricated in four-meter sections, the tower includes 1400 tons of steel. A platform 85 meters off the ground is reached by a spiral stair that wraps around one of the legs of the structure. Each "strand" of the design is made up of eight structural elements "to produce the feeling of a rope instead of a rigid tube." Balmond continues: "Unlike vertical towers that grow by being continually supported one story upon another, the ArcelorMittal Orbit form gathers strength from overlaps and scatter, in a new paradigm for form and its stabilities."

Die ungewöhnlich geformte Konstruktion ist ein Gemeinschaftsprojekt von Anish Kapoor und Cecil Balmond, die zusammen bereits andere monumentale Kunstwerke realisiert haben. Balmonds Büro über das Projekt: „Statt linear aufzuragen, ist das Werk ein ‚Orbit' – eine von Anfang bis Ende durchgehende Schleife, die um sich selbst herumführt. Durch Richtungswechsel, Schleifen und neue Verbindungen bei jedem An-sich-selbst-Vorbeiführen, entsteht eine einmalige, überaus stabile Konstruktion, die den Raum verdichtet, während man sich in ihr auf und ab bewegt." Der Turm besteht aus 4 m langen Einzelteilen und 1400 t Stahl. Die 85 m über dem Boden gelegene Plattform erreicht man über eine Wendeltreppe, die sich um einen der Standfüße der Konstruktion windet. Jeder „Strang" des Turms besteht aus acht Bauelementen, „um die Illusion eines Seils zu erzeugen, statt den Eindruck einer starren Röhre". Balmond weiterhin: „Anders als vertikale Türme, die in die Höhe wachsen, indem ein Stockwerk auf dem nächsten ruht, bezieht der Orbit von ArcelorMittal seine Kraft aus Schnittstellen und Streuung und definiert ein neues Paradigma für Form und Stabilität."

Cette forme insolite est une création de Kapoor et Balmond, qui avaient déjà collaboré sur d'autres projets à grande échelle. « Plutôt que de s'élever en ligne droite, explique le bureau de Balmond, leur création est une "orbite" – une boucle continue du début à la fin qui tourne et revient sur elle-même. En tournant en boucle et en se raccordant à chaque passage, une structure très stable se crée, qui densifie l'espace environnant, quand on monte et descend. » La tour, préfabriquée en tronçons de quatre mètres, totalise 1400 tonnes d'acier. Une plateforme perchée à 85 m du sol est accessible par un escalier qui s'enroule autour d'un des pieds de la structure. Chaque « rang » du projet comporte huit éléments structurels « produisant l'effet d'une corde, plutôt que d'un tube rigide ». « À la différence des tours verticales où chaque étage supporte le suivant, ajoute Balmond, la forme de l'ArcelorMittal Orbit tire sa solidité des chevauchements et de l'éparpillement, offrant ainsi un nouveau paradigme pour une forme et sa stabilité. »

Seen at night, the Orbit, with its striking red color, stands out as a highly unusual structure, not quite anything seen before, a real collaboration between an artist and an engineer at the height of their respective professions.

Nachts zeigt sich der Orbit in seinem markanten Rot als überaus ungewöhnliches Bauwerk, als etwas nie Dagewesenes, als echte Kooperation zwischen einem Künstler und einem Bauingenieur auf dem Höhepunkt ihrer jeweiligen Laufbahn.

Dans la nuit, l'Orbit, d'un rouge frappant, se démarque comme une structure vraiment insolite et inédite, une véritable collaboration entre un artiste et un ingénieur au sommet de leur carrière.

Seen during the day, the Orbit reveals its spiral access stairway. The vocabulary of materials and colors might evoke the forms of industry or amusement parks, but the real subjects are art and engineering.

Auf einer Tagesansicht ist die den Bau erschließende Wendeltreppe zu erkennen. Formensprache, Material und Farbgebung erinnern an industrielle Bauten oder Freizeitparks, doch tatsächlich geht es hier im Kunst und Statik.

De jour, l'Orbit révèle son escalier d'accès en colimaçon. Si le vocabulaire des matériaux et des couleurs peut évoquer des parcs industriels ou d'attractions, son vrai propos concerne l'art et l'ingénierie.

DIÉBÉDO FRANCIS KÉRÉ

Kéré Architecture
Arndtstr. 34
10965 Berlin
Germany

Tel: +49 30 78 95 23 91
Fax: +49 30 78 95 23 98
E-mail: mail@kere-architecture.com
Web: www.kere-architecture.com

DIÉBÉDO FRANCIS KÉRÉ, born in Burkina Faso, studied at the Technische Universität Berlin. He puts an emphasis on education about architecture in his own country. He states: "The community needs to be educated about how to monitor the climatic circumstances and to use local materials. Only people who take part in the building process can maintain and spread the word about these architectural projects." In 2011 Kéré was awarded the UWM Marcus Prize for Architecture, while his first project, a primary school in his native village (Gando, 2001), won a 2004 Aga Khan Award for Architecture because of its exemplarity as well as its concise and elegant architecture. As well as this primary school, his work includes the National Park of Mali (Bamako, Mali, 2009–10); the Earthen Architecture Center (Mopti, Mali, 2010); and the permanent exhibition for the Red Cross Museum (Geneva, Switzerland, 2010–11). Ongoing work includes a women's community center (Gando, Burkina Faso, 2009–); a library (Gando, Burkina Faso, 2010); a training center (in collaboration with DAZ e.V, Dapaong, Togo, 2010–); Zhoushan Harbor Development (Zhoushan, China, 2010–); the Opera Village (Laongo, Burkina Faso, 2010–, published here); and a secondary school in Gando (Burkina Faso, 2011–in construction).

DIÉBÉDO FRANCIS KÉRÉ, geboren in Burkina Faso, studierte an der Technischen Universität Berlin. Sein besonderes Anliegen ist die Vermittlung von Architektur in seinem Geburtsland. Er erklärt: „Es muss gezeigt werden, wie man mit den klimatischen Gegebenheiten umgeht und lokale Materialien nutzt. Nur Menschen, die am Bauprozess teilhaben, können solche Architekturprojekte erhalten und weitervermitteln." 2011 wurde Kéré mit dem UWM Marcus Prize for Architecture ausgezeichnet; für sein erstes Projekt, eine Grundschule in seinem Heimatdorf Gando (2001), erhielt er 2004 den Aga-Khan-Preis für Architektur, der sowohl den Vorbildcharakter als auch die Präzision und Eleganz seiner Architektur würdigte. Neben der Grundschule umfasst sein Werk den Nationalpark von Mali (Bamako, Mali, 2009–10), das Zentrum für Lehmbau (Mopti, Mali, 2010) sowie die Dauerausstellung für das Museum des Roten Kreuzes (Genf, 2010–11). Laufende Projekte sind u. a. ein Frauengemeindezentrum (Gando, Burkina Faso, seit 2009), eine Bibliothek (Gando, 2010), ein Ausbildungszentrum (in Zusammenarbeit mit DAZ e.V., Dapaong, Togo, seit 2010), eine Bauerschließung im Hafen von Zhoushan (China, seit 2010), das Operndorf (Laongo, Burkina Faso, seit 2010, hier vorgestellt) sowie eine Mittelschule in Gando (2011–im Bau).

Né au Burkina Faso, **DIÉBÉDO FRANCIS KÉRÉ** fait ses études à l'Université technique de Berlin. Dans son propre pays, il met l'accent sur l'éducation à l'architecture. Selon lui, « il faut apprendre aux gens à prendre en compte les conditions climatiques et à utiliser les matériaux locaux. Seules les personnes qui participent au processus de construction sont capables de conserver et de faire connaître ces projets architecturaux ». En 2011, Kéré gagne le prix Marcus d'architecture (université du Wisconsin–Milwaukee) et son premier projet, une école primaire dans son village natal (Gando, 2001), remporte le prix Aga Khan d'architecture en 2004 pour son exemplarité, sa concision et son élégance. Il a réalisé également le parc National du Mali (Bamako, Mali, 2009–10), le Centre de l'architecture en terre (Mopti, Mali, 2010) et l'exposition permanente du musée de la Croix-Rouge (Genève, 2010–11). Parmi ses réalisations en cours, on compte une Maison des femmes (Gando, Burkina Faso, 2009–) ; une bibliothèque (Gando, Burkina Faso, 2010) ; un centre de formation (en collaboration avec DAZ e.V, Dapaong, Togo, 2010–) ; la réhabilitation du grand port de Zhoushan (Zhoushan, Chine, 2010–) ; le village-opéra (Laongo, Burkina Faso, 2010–, présenté ici) et une école d'enseignement secondaire à Gando (Burkina Faso, 2011–en construction).

OPERA VILLAGE

Laongo, Burkina Faso, 2010–

Address: Laongo, Burkina Faso, www.operndorf-afrika.com
Area: 8100 m². Client: Festspielhaus Afrika GmbH
Cost: not disclosed

This very unexpected project is the result of a meeting between Christoph Schlingensief and the architect. Christoph Schlingensief was one of Germany's best known directors. He died of cancer in 2010, meaning that this project is in some sense his legacy. Francis Kéré states: "When I was first confronted with the question of an opera house for Africa, I initially thought it was a joke. Such a fantasy could only come from somebody who either doesn't know Africa, or who is so saturated that all he can think up is nonsense." When a flood washed away the potential site for the opera in Ouagadougou in August 2009, it became obvious to the architect and the patron that their project should include housing modules—an "**OPERA VILLAGE**." The result was built on a 14-hectare site in Laongo, a one-hour car drive from the capital of Burkina Faso, overlooking the landscape of the Sahel area. The team plans a festival theater, workshops, a health station, guesthouses, as well as solar panels, a well, and a school for up to 500 children and teenagers with music and film classes. The central element of the as yet incomplete complex will be the Festival Hall. The actual stage was designed and built for a theater in Germany and not used afterwards, and will be transformed for use in the Opera Village. Local materials such as clay, laterite, cement bricks, gumwood, and loam rendering will be used for construction. Concrete is to be used for beams, columns, ring beams, and foundations.

Das ungewöhnliche Projekt entstand nach einer Begegnung zwischen Francis Kéré und dem deutschen Theatermacher Christoph Schlingensief, der 2010 an Krebs starb und das Projekt in gewissem Sinn für sein Erbe hielt. „Als ich zum ersten Mal die Anfrage für eine Oper in Afrika erhielt", so Kéré, „dachte ich, das sei ein Scherz. So etwas kann sich nur jemand ausdenken, der Afrika entweder nicht kennt, oder so gesättigt ist, dass er nur noch dumme Ideen hat." Als das geplante Baugrundstück für die Oper in Ouagadougou im August 2009 überschwemmt wurde, kamen Architekt und Initiator zu dem Schluss, das Projekt um Wohnbaumodule zu erweitern – ein ganzes „**OPERNDORF**" zu bauen. Die Arbeiten begannen schließlich auf einem 14 h großen Gelände in Laongo, eine Autostunde von der Hauptstadt Burkina Fasos entfernt, mit Blick auf die Landschaft der Sahelzone. Geplant sind ein Festspielhaus, Werkstätten, ein Krankenhaus, Gästehäuser, eine Solaranlage, ein Brunnen sowie eine Schule für bis zu 500 Kinder und Jugendliche, die hier auch Musik- und Filmunterricht erhalten. Herzstück des noch nicht abgeschlossenen Projekts ist das Festspielhaus. Die Bühne wurde ursprünglich für ein deutsches Theater gebaut, kam jedoch nie zum Einsatz und wird für das Operndorf angepasst. Gearbeitet wird mit lokalen Baumaterialien wie Lehm, Laterit, Zementbaustein, Gummibaum und Lehmputz. Beton wird für Träger, Stützen, Ringanker und Fundamente verwendet.

Ce projet très inattendu résulte d'une rencontre entre l'architecte et le réalisateur allemand Christoph Schlingensief. « Quand j'ai entendu parler pour la première fois d'un Opéra en Afrique, raconte F. Kéré, j'ai cru qu'il s'agissait d'une blague. Un tel fantasme ne pouvait venir que de quelqu'un qui ne connaissait pas l'Afrique ou qui était si blasé qu'il ne pouvait inventer que des idioties. » Quand une inondation balaye le site potentiel de l'Opéra à Ouagadougou, en août 2009, il devient évident pour l'architecte et le mécène que leur projet doit inclure des modules d'habitation – un « **VILLAGE-OPÉRA** ». Le tout est bâti sur 14 ha, à une heure et demie de route de la capitale du Burkina Faso, dominant le désert du Sahel. L'équipe a en projet un festival de théâtre, des ateliers, une clinique et des installations hôtelières, ainsi que des panneaux solaires, un puits et une école pouvant accueillir 500 enfants et adolescents, avec des classes de cinéma et de musique. L'élément central de ce complexe encore en chantier sera la salle de spectacles. La scène, construite à l'origine pour un théâtre allemand, sera transformée pour y être utilisée. L'on utilisera pour la construction des matériaux locaux tels que l'argile, la latérite, les briques de ciment, le bois de gommier ou l'enduit d'argile. Le béton sera utilisé pour les poutres, colonnes, poutres circulaires et fondations.

Right, a site plan showing the entire complex, including the future opera house. Above and opposite page, the architect has integrated the required functions using a style that is appropriate to the region.

Rechts ein Lageplan des Gesamtkomplexes, einschließlich des geplanten Festspielhauses. Der Architekt setzte die geforderten Funktionen in eine Formensprache um, die der Region entspricht (oben und gegenüber).

Ci-contre, un plan de situation montrant la totalité du complexe, avec le futur Opéra. Ci-dessus et page de gauche, l'architecte a intégré les fonctions requises dans un style approprié à la région.

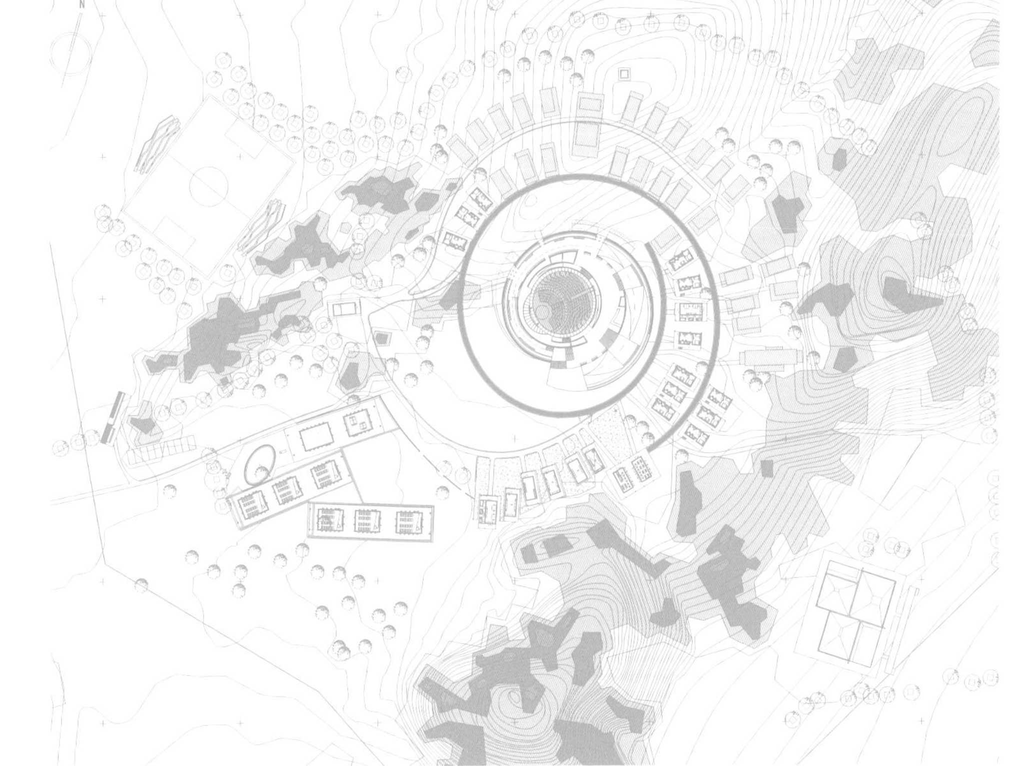

The architecture is simple and elegant, not at all in contradiction with its location even if the operatic function is less apparent here than in the overall scheme.

Die Architektur ist schlicht und elegant und steht keineswegs im Widerspruch zu ihrem Standort, auch wenn der Opernaspekt des Projekts hier weniger erkennbar ist als im Gesamtentwurf.

L'architecture simple et élégante n'est pas du tout contradictoire avec sa localisation, même si sa fonction d'Opéra y est ici moins perceptible que dans le schéma d'ensemble.

Below, a section drawing of the entire Opera Village. Above, simple columns and arched coverings create sheltered outdoor space.

Unten eine Visualisierung des Operndorfs im Querschnitt. Schlichte Stützen und gewölbte Dachsegmente schaffen geschützte Außenbereiche.

Ci-dessous, une coupe de l'ensemble du Village-Opéra. En haut, de simples colonnes et des toitures incurvées créent des espaces extérieurs abrités.

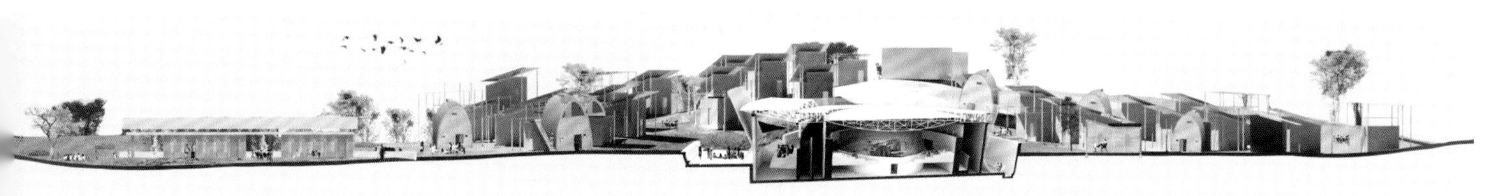

KLAB ARCHITECTURE

KLab Architecture
2 Achaiou Street, Kolonaki
Athens 10675
Greece

Tel: +30 21 03 21 11 39
Fax: +30 21 03 21 11 55
E-mail: info@klab.gr
Web: www.klab.gr

KONSTANTINOS LABRINOPOULOS was born in 1970 in Athens, Greece. He graduated from the School of Architecture, National Technical University of Athens (1994), and continued his studies in the United States. In 1996 he received his Master III degree in Advanced Architectural Design from SCI-Arc, Los Angeles. After working freelance from 1998 to 2001, he co-created klmf architects. In 2007, when the klmf partnership terminated, he founded KLab Architecture (Kinetic Lab of Architecture). The firm opened a second office in London in 2010. In 2012 KLab Architecture won the 2011 best commercial project award for the Placebo Pharmacy (Glyfada, Athens, 2010–11, published here) at the X International Awards organized by the publishing company Salon-Press and the Russian edition of *Domus*. In 2012, they were invited to participate in the Architecture Biennale in Venice, Italy, with their project "Urban Cubes." Other projects include the Guru Bar (Athens, 2008); Cubic Distortion House (Athens, 2009); and Urban Stripes (Athens, 2010), all in Greece.

KONSTANTINOS LABRINOPOULOS wurde 1970 in Athen geboren. Er absolvierte ein Studium an der Fakultät für Architektur der Nationalen Technischen Universität von Athen (1994) und setzte seine Studien in den USA fort. Seinen M. Arch. III im Fach Advanced Architectural Design absolvierte er am SCI-Arc in Los Angeles. Nach freiberuflicher Tätigkeit (1998–2001) gründete Labrinopoulos zusammen mit Kollegen das Büro klmf architects. 2007 rief er KLab Architecture (Kinetic Lab of Architectur) ins Leben. Die Firma eröffnete 2010 ein zweites Büro in London. 2012 erhielt KLab Architecture für die Placebo Pharmacy (Glyfada, Athen, 2010–11, hier vorgestellt) den X International Award 2011 in der Kategorie „Bestes gewerbliches Projekt" (Preis initiiert vom Verlag Salon-Press und der russischen Ausgabe von *Domus*). 2012 nahm KLab Architecture mit dem Projekt „Urban Cubes" an der Architekturbiennale in Venedig teil. Weitere Projekte des Büros sind die Guru Bar (Athen, 2008), das Cubic Distortion House (Athen, 2009) und Urban Stripes (Athen, 2010).

KONSTANTINOS LABRINOPOULOS est né en 1970 à Athènes. Il obtient son diplôme de l'École d'architecture de l'Université technique nationale d'Athènes (1994) et poursuit ses études aux États-Unis. En 1996, il obtient son Master III en design architectural du SCI-Arc, Los Angeles. Après avoir travaillé en free-lance de 1998 à 2001, il participe à la fondation de klmf architects. En 2007, quand la société klmf prend fin, il fonde KLab Architecture (Kinetic Lab of Architecture). L'agence ouvre un deuxième bureau à Londres en 2010. En 2012, KLab Architecture gagne le prix du meilleur projet publicitaire pour la pharmacie Placebo (Glyfada, Athènes, 2010–11, présentée ici) aux X International Awards organisés par la maison d'édition Salon-Press et l'édition russe de *Domus*. En 2012, ils sont invités à participer à la Biennale d'architecture de Venise avec leur projet *Urban Cubes*. Parmi leurs autres réalisations, l'on trouve le Guru Bar (Athènes, 2008), la maison Cubic Distortion (Athènes, 2009) et les Urban Stripes (Athènes, 2010).

PLACEBO PHARMACY

Glyfada, Athens, Greece, 2010–11

Address: Vouliagmenis Avenue 85, Glyfada, Athens, Greece
+30 21 09 63 35 95, www.placebopharmacy.com. Area: 520 m². Client: Morfopoulos, Pharmacist
Cost: €400 000. Collaboration: Xara Marantidou, Enrique Ramirez, Mark Chapman

The octagonal shape of an existing structure was re-formed into a cylinder in order to create a spiral. This idea was inspired by the motion of traffic on Vouliagmenis Avenue, where the building stands. The panels of the façade are perforated using Braille, which alludes to the use of Braille on pharmaceutical packaging while allowing light into the interior. The Pharmacy covers two floors, the ground floor being the primary shop space and the upper mezzanine floor consisting of ancillary office space used as a temporary surgery for visiting health professionals. An interior ramp leading to the upper level echoes the exterior spiral. The pharmacy itself is arranged in a radial pattern with the main cashier's desk as the focal point. The product displays fan out from this focal point giving the cashier the ability to view the whole pharmacy. The drug dispensary, preparation areas, and toilets are also part of the radial pattern.

Ein bestehender achteckiger Bau wurde zu einem Zylinder mit Spiralcharakter umgestaltet. Inspiration für das Konzept war die Verkehrsbewegung auf der Odos Vouliagmeni, an der die Apotheke liegt. Die perforierte Fassadenverblendung erinnert an den Einsatz von Brailleschriftzeichen auf Arzneimittelverpackungen und lässt Licht ins Innere des Baus. Die Apotheke nutzt zwei Etagen: Im Erdgeschoss ist der eigentliche Verkaufsraum untergebracht, während im Mezzaningeschoss zusätzliche Räume liegen, die temporär als Sprechzimmer für Gesundheitsexperten genutzt werden. Eine spiralförmige Rampe im Inneren greift die äußere Form des Gebäudes auf. Der Apothekenraum ist strahlenförmig organisiert: Die Hauptkasse bildet das Zentrum. Von hier strahlen die Regale fächerartig aus. Mitarbeiter an der Kasse können die gesamte Ladenfläche überblicken. Auch Arzneiausgabe, Labor und Toiletten wurden in das strahlenförmige Muster integriert.

La forme octogonale d'une structure existante a été transformée en cylindre pour créer une spirale. L'idée s'inspire de la circulation sur l'avenue Vouliagmenis, où est situé le bâtiment. Les panneaux de la façade sont perforés à la manière de l'alphabet Braille, faisant référence au braille utilisé sur les boîtes de médicaments tout en laissant la lumière pénétrer à l'intérieur. La pharmacie est située sur deux niveaux, le rez-de-chaussée étant l'espace boutique et le premier étage en mezzanine consistant en un espace annexe de consultation temporaire pour les professionnels de la santé. Une rampe intérieure menant au niveau supérieur fait écho à la spirale extérieure. La pharmacie elle-même est disposée en étoile, avec la caisse principale en son centre. Les rayonnages se déploient en éventail à partir de ce centre, permettant au caissier de voir toute la boutique. L'officine, le secteur des préparations et les toilettes font également partie de l'étoile.

As the drawings to the right attest, the architectural concept is quite simple, with wrapped bands forming the main outside form. Lit from within at night, the Pharmacy retains an iconic presence.

Wie die Zeichnungen rechts belegen, ist das architektonische Konzept denkbar einfach: Einander überlagernde Bänder bilden die Außenhaut des Baus. Wenn sie nachts von innen beleuchtet ist, zeigt sich die Apotheke als markante Präsenz.

Les dessins ci-contre montrent le concept architectural assez simple de bandes enroulées créant la forme externe principale. Éclairée de l'intérieur, la pharmacie garde, la nuit, une présence emblématique.

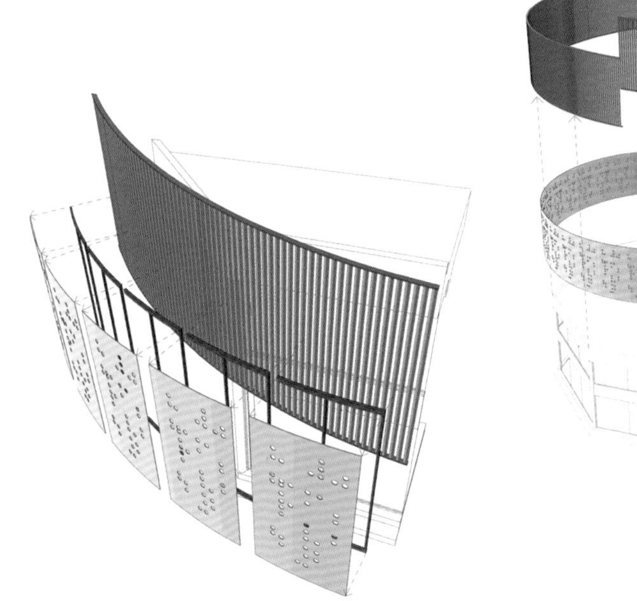

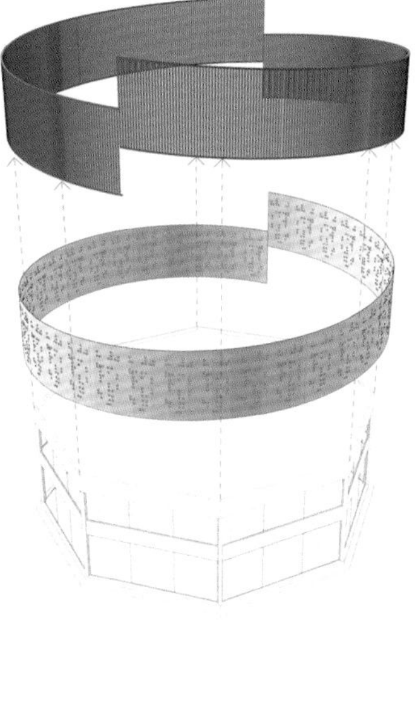

The exterior spiral has inspired the interior ramp and window forms. Below, display cases are integrated into the design as well.

Die Außenspirale inspirierte die Rampe im Innenraum und die Form der Fenster. Regale (unten) wurden ebenfalls in den Entwurf integriert.

La spirale extérieure a inspiré la rampe intérieure et les formes des fenêtres. Ci-dessous, les rayonnages sont également intégrés dans le design.

Right, plans of the two levels of the Pharmacy. Above, the proximity of green plants and ample natural light contribute to the attractive interior space.

Rechts Grundrisse der zwei Apothekenebenen. Unmittelbare Begrünung und reichlich Tageslicht tragen zur angenehmen Raumwirkung bei.

Ci-contre, des plans des deux niveaux de la pharmacie. Ci-dessus, la végétation proche et un éclairage naturel généreux contribuent à l'attrait de l'espace intérieur.

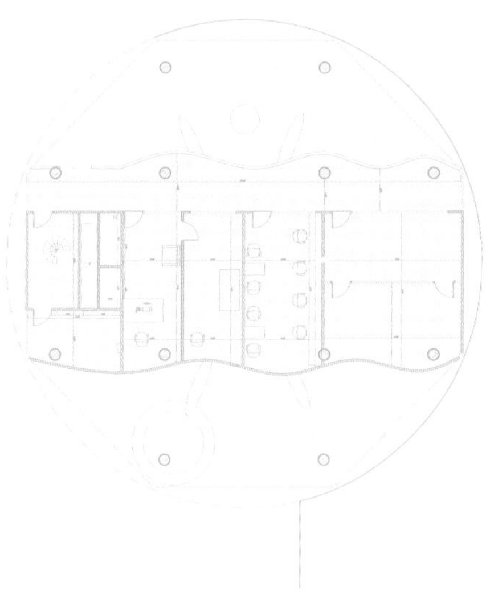

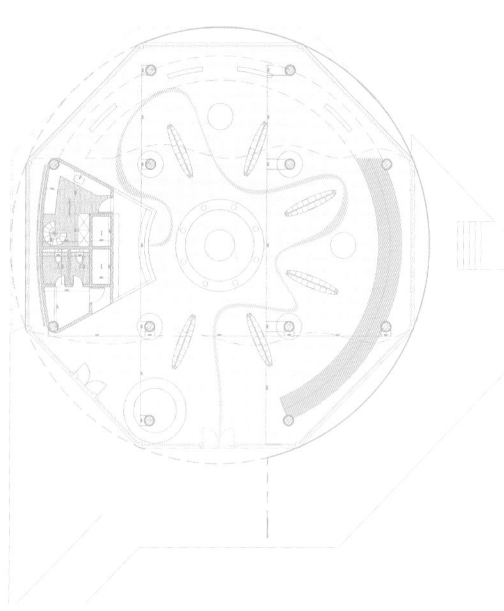

HENNING LARSEN, BATTERÍIÐ, OLAFUR ELIASSON

Henning Larsen Architects
Vesterbrogade 76
1620 Copenhagen V / Denmark
Tel: +45 82 33 30 00 / Fax: +45 82 33 30 99
E-mail: info@henninglarsen.com
Web: www.henninglarsen.com

Batteríið Architects
Tronuhraun 1
220 Hafnarfjordur / Iceland
Tel: +354 545 47 00.
E-mail: batteriid@architect.is
Web: www.arkitekt.is

Studio Olafur Eliasson
Christinenstr. 18/19, Haus 2
10119 Berlin / Germany
E-mail: studio@olafureliasson.net
Web: www.olafureliasson.net

Henning Larsen created his firm in 1959 in Copenhagen. In 2012, he was awarded the Praemium Imperiale for Architecture. **HENNING LARSEN ARCHITECTS** is an international firm with more than 200 employees. Partners in the firm are Henning Larsen, Mette Kynne Frandsen, Louis Becker, Peer Teglgaard Jeppesen, Lars Steffensen, and Jacob Kurek. Their work includes the Ministry of Foreign Affairs in Riyadh (Saudi Arabia, 1982–84); the Nation Center in Nairobi, (Kenya, 1987–92); and the Royal Danish Opera (Copenhagen, Denmark, 2001–05). More recently, they have designed the masterplan for King Abdullah Financial District (Riyadh, Saudi Arabia, 2006–16); Spiegel Headquarters (Hamburg, Germany, 2009–11); and the Siemens Headquarters (Munich, Germany, 2011–15). **BATTERÍIÐ ARCHITECTS** was founded in Iceland in 1988, our portrait shows partner Sigurður Einarsson. Aside from the Harpa, Reykjavik Concert Hall and Conference Center (published here), they participated in the design of the public space around the building together with Landslag, landscape architects (2011). They are currently working on a the Active Living Centre for the University of Manitoba in Canada and a number of other projects. **OLAFUR ELIASSON** was born in 1967 in Copenhagen, Denmark, where he attended the Royal Academy of Arts (1989–95). He represented Denmark in the 2003 Venice Biennale and has had solo exhibitions at MoMA, New York, the Musée d'Art Moderne de la Ville de Paris, and other major museums around the world. Projects in public space include the Serpentine Gallery Pavilion 2007 (London, with Kjetil Thorsen); and *The New York City Waterfalls* (2008). Recent architectural works are *Your rainbow panorama* (Aarhus, Denmark), and the façade of the Harpa Reykjavik Concert Hall and Conference Center (both 2011).

Henning Larsen gründete sein Büro 1959 in Kopenhagen. 2012 erhielt er den Praemium Imperiale für Architektur. **HENNING LARSEN ARCHITECTS** ist eine internationale Firma mit über 200 Mitarbeitern und den Partnern Henning Larsen, Mette Kynne Frandsen, Louis Becker, Peer Teglgaard Jeppesen, Lars Steffensen und Jacob Kurek. Zu ihren Projekten zählen das Außenministerium in Riad (Saudi-Arabien, 1982–84), das Nation Center in Nairobi (Kenia, 1987–92) sowie das Opernhaus in Kopenhagen (2001–05). In jüngerer Zeit entstanden der Masterplan für den King Abdullah Financial District (Riad, Saudi-Arabien, 2006–16), das *Spiegel*-Hochhaus (Hamburg, 2009–11) und die Siemens-Zentrale (München, 2011–15). **BATTERÍIÐ ARCHITECTS** wurde 1988 in Island gegründet. Unser Foto zeigt den Partner Sigurður Einarsson. Neben dem Konzertsaal und Konferenzzentrum Harpa in Reykjavik (2011, hier vorgestellt) war das Büro mit den Landschaftsarchitekten Landslag an der Gestaltung der öffentlichen Flächen um den Komplex (2011) beteiligt. Derzeit arbeitet das Büro am Active Living Centre für die University of Manitoba, Kanada, und verschiedenen anderen Projekten. **OLAFUR ELIASSON** wurde 1967 in Kopenhagen geboren, wo er an der Königlich Dänischen Akademie der Künste studierte (1989–95). Er vertrat Dänemark auf der Biennale 2003 in Venedig und hatte Einzelausstellungen am MoMA (New York), dem Musée d'Art Moderne de la Ville de Paris und weiteren bedeutenden Museen weltweit. Zu seinen Projekten im öffentlichen Raum zählen der Pavillon für die Serpentine Gallery 2007 (London, mit Kjetil Thorsen) und „The New York City Waterfalls" (2008). Jüngere bauliche Projekte sind u. a. „Your rainbow panorama" (Aarhus, Dänemark) sowie die Fassade für Harpa in Reykjavik.

Henning Larsen crée son entreprise en 1959 à Copenhague. En 2012, il reçoit le Praemium Imperiale d'architecture. **HENNING LARSEN ARCHITECTS** est une entreprise internationale de plus de 200 employés. Les associés en sont Henning Larsen, Mette Kynne Frandsen, Louis Becker, Peer Teglgaard Jeppesen, Lars Steffensen et Jacob Kurek. Ils ont réalisé, entre autres, le ministère des Affaires étrangères à Riyad (Arabie Saoudite, 1982–84), le Nation Center à Nairobi (Kenya, 1987–92) et l'Opéra royal danois (Copenhague, 2001–05). Plus récemment, ils ont conçu le plan directeur du quartier financier du roi Abdallah (Riyad, 2006–16), le siège du Spiegel (Hambourg, 2009–11) et de Siemens (Munich, 2011–15). **BATTERÍIÐ ARCHITECTS** est fondé en Islande en 1988. Outre Harpa, le Palais de la musique et des congrès de Reykjavik (présenté ici), l'agence a participé à la conception de l'espace public qui l'entoure avec les architectes paysagistes de Landslag (2011). Elle travaille entre autres projets sur l'Active Living Centre de l'université du Manitoba au Canada. **OLAFUR ELIASSON,** né en 1967 à Copenhague, étudie à l'Académie royale des arts (1989–95). Il représente le Danemark à la Biennale de Venise 2003 et a des expositions personnelles au MoMA, au Musée d'art moderne de la Ville de Paris et dans d'autres grands musées. Parmi ses projets dans l'espace public, l'on trouve le pavillon de la Serpentine Gallery de 2007 (Londres, avec Kjetil Thorsen) et *The New York City Waterfalls* (2008). Ses ouvrages architecturaux récents sont *Your rainbow panorama* (Aarhus, Danemark) et la façade de Harpa, le Palais de la musique et des congrès de Reykjavik (tous deux en 2011).

HARPA

Reykjavik Concert Hall and Conference Center, Reykjavik, Iceland, 2011

Address: Austurbakki 2, 101 Reykjavík, Iceland, +354 528 50 00, www.en.harpa.is
Area: 28 000 m². Client: Austurnhofn TR – East Harbour Project Ltd. Cost: not disclosed

This concert hall forms part of an extensive harbor development project in Reykjavik. Harpa, winner of the European Union Prize for Contemporary Architecture—Mies van der Rohe Award 2013, was completed by Henning Larsen Architects and Batteríið Architects, with façade design and development by Olafur Eliasson and Studio Olafur Eliasson in collaboration with Henning Larsen Architects. The overall objective has been to expand and revitalize the eastern harbor, and create a better connection between it and the city center. The concert hall has a clear view of the sea and mountains surrounding Reykjavik. An arrival and foyer area is at the front of the building; there are four concert halls in the middle, and a backstage area with offices, administration, rehearsal hall, and changing room. The three large halls are placed next to each other with public access on the south side and backstage access from the north. The fourth floor houses a multifunctional hall for more intimate shows and banquets. Eliasson's design of the façades, carried out in close collaboration with Henning Larsen Architects, is based on five-fold symmetry and was inspired by nature and, in particular, characteristic local basalt formations. Made of glass and steel in a 12-sided, space-filling, geometric, modular system called "quasi bricks," which Eliasson developed with Einar Thorsteinn, the building generates a kaleidoscopic play of colors. The southern façade is composed of over 1000 quasi bricks. The principle for the remaining north, east, and west façades and roof derives from sectionalized, two-dimensional variants of the brick. One of the main ideas has "been to 'dematerialize' the building as a static entity and let it respond to surrounding colors—city lights, the ocean, and the glow of the sky. The public spaces in the building respond to and take form from the play of light and shadow through the façade."

Die Konzerthalle gehört zu einem Entwicklungsprojekt für den Hafen von Reykjavik. Harpa, 2013 mit dem Mies-van-der-Rohe-Preis der EU für zeitgenössische Architektur ausgezeichnet, ist eine Kooperation von Henning Larsen Architects und Batteríið Architects mit einer Fassadengestaltung von Olafur Eliasson und Studio Olafur Eliasson mit Henning Larsen Architects. Durch das Projekt sollen der Osthafen erweitert und belebt sowie eine bessere Anbindung an das Stadtzentrum erreicht werden. Der Komplex bietet einen unverstellten Blick auf das Meer und die Berge um Reykjavik. Vorne liegen Foyers, in der Mitte gruppieren sich vier Konzertsäle, dahinter der Backstagebereich sowie Büros, Verwaltung, Probenräume und Umkleiden. Drei große Säle liegen parallel zueinander, mit Publikumszugang von Süden und Bühnenzugang von Norden. Im vierten Stock befindet sich ein Multifunktionssaal für kleinere Aufführungen und Bankette. Eliassons Fassadenentwurf, realisiert in enger Zusammenarbeit mit Henning Larsen Architects, basiert auf fünfzähligen Symmetrien und ist inspiriert von der Natur, speziell von lokalen Basaltformationen. Die Fassade aus Glas und Stahl besteht aus zwölfseitigen, raumfüllenden geometrischen Modulen, „Quasi-Bricks", die Eliasson mit Einar Thorsteinn entwickelte und die ein kaleidoskopisches Farbenspiel erzeugen. Während die Südfassade aus über 1000 „Quasi-Bricks" konstruiert ist, bestehen Nord-, Ost-, Westfassade und Dach aus einer zweidimensionalen Variante der „Bricks". Zentrales Anliegen war es, „den Bau so weit wie möglich als statische Größe zu entmaterialisieren und auf die Farben seiner Umgebung reagieren zu lassen – die Lichter der Stadt, das Meer, das Leuchten des Himmels. Die öffentlichen Bereiche reagieren auf das einfallende Licht- und Schattenspiel und nehmen hierdurch Gestalt an."

Ce Palais de la musique s'inscrit dans un plan d'aménagement de grande envergure du port de Reykjavik. Prix d'architecture contemporaine de l'Union européenne Mies van der Rohe 2013, le Harpa a été conçu par Henning Larsen Architects et Batteríið Architects. Le dessin de la façade et la réalisation sont d'Olafur Eliasson et Studio Olafur Eliasson, en collaboration avec Henning Larsen Architects. L'objectif global était d'étendre et de revitaliser le port est, tout en créant une meilleure liaison entre le port et le centre-ville. Le Palais de la musique a une vue dégagée sur la mer et les montagnes entourant Reykjavik. Le hall d'accueil et le foyer sont à l'avant du bâtiment, les quatre salles de concert au centre, les bureaux, l'administration, la salle de répétition et les loges à l'arrière. Les trois grandes salles sont placées l'une à côté de l'autre, avec l'accès au public au sud, et l'accès aux coulisses au nord. Le quatrième niveau abrite une salle modulable pour des spectacles plus intimistes ou des banquets. Eliasson a dessiné les façades, en étroite collaboration avec Henning Larsen Architects, se référant à la symétrie d'ordre 5 présente dans la nature, et en particulier dans les orgues basaltiques d'Islande. Composé de « quasi-bricks » de verre et d'acier à 12 facettes qu'Eliasson a mises au point avec Einar Thorsteinn, le bâtiment offre un kaléidoscope de couleurs. Plus de 1000 quasi-bricks composent la façade sud. Pour le toit et les façades nord, est et ouest, des variantes à deux dimensions de la brique sectionnée ont été utilisées. L'idée majeure était de « "dématérialiser" le bâtiment en tant qu'entité statique pour qu'il réponde aux couleurs environnantes, comme les lumières de la ville, l'océan et l'éclat du ciel. Les espaces publics à l'intérieur du bâtiment réagissent au jeu d'ombre et de lumière qui traverse la façade ».

Harpa, reflecting the low sun's red light in the picture above, won the 2013 Mies van der Rohe European Architecture Prize. The façade responds well to the frequently changing Icelandic sky (left).

Harpa, oben im Abendlicht, wurde 2013 mit dem Mies-van-der-Rohe-Preis der Europäischen Union ausgezeichnet. Die Fassade reagiert unmittelbar auf die Wechselspiele des isländischen Himmels (links).

Harpa, qui reflète la lumière rouge du soleil couchant ci-dessus, a gagné en 2013 le prix d'architecture de l'Union européenne Mies van der Rohe. La façade répond à merveille aux ciels changeants de l'Islande (à gauche).

In their port-side setting, the angled glass façades are both reflective and partially transparent. Right page, elevation drawings show the entire form of the building, seen in a general view above, right.

Die kantige Glasfassade in ihrem Hafenkontext gibt sich teils reflektierend, teils transparent. Aufrisse (rechts) zeigen den Bau von allen Seiten. Rechts oben eine Gesamtansicht.

Dans leur environnement portuaire, les façades vitrées inclinées sont à la fois réfléchissantes et semi-transparentes. Page de droite, les élévations montrent la forme entière du bâtiment, montré en vue générale, en haut à droite.

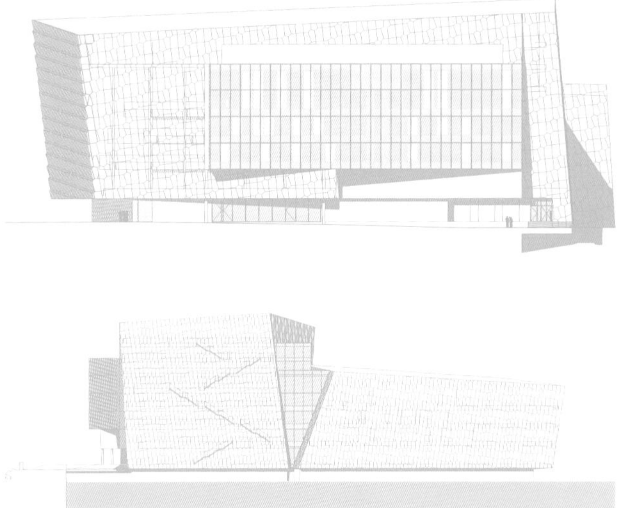

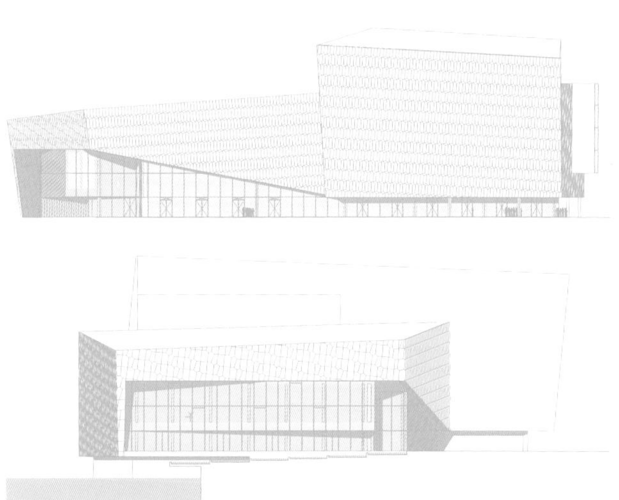

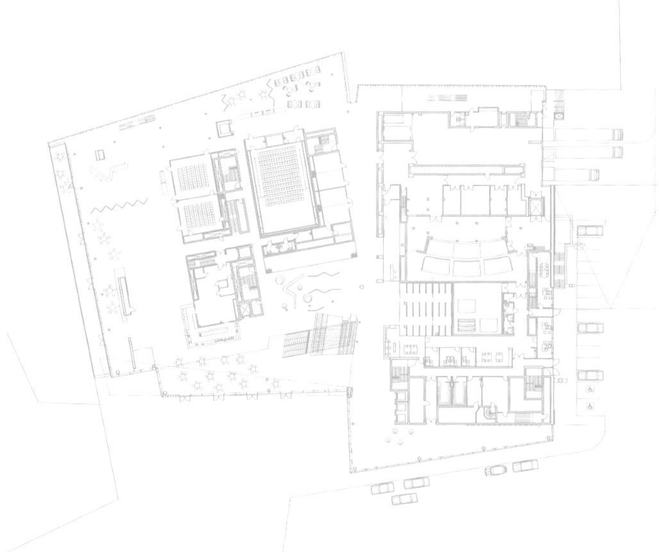

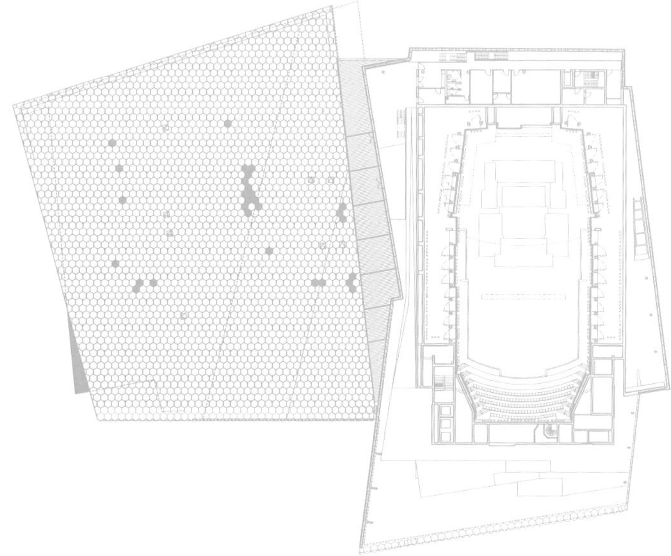

The weblike pattern of the glass façade, together with the use of colored elements, makes for a lively series of patterns inside. Above, plans show that the angles of the façade reflect shifts in the actual building.

Die netzartige Struktur der Glasfassade und der Einsatz einzelner farbiger Elemente sorgen für dynamische Linienspiele im Inneren des Baus. Die Grundrisse (oben) zeigen, dass die Winkel der Fassade Verschiebungen im Gebäude spiegeln.

Associé à des éléments colorés, le motif réticulé de la façade vitrée produit une série de dessins vivants à l'intérieur. Ci-dessus, les plans montrent que les angles de la façade reflètent des décalages dans le bâtiment lui-même.

MAD ARCHITECTS

MAD Architects
7 Banqiao Nanxiang, 3rd Floor West Tower
Beixinqiao
Beijing 1000007
China

Tel: +86 10 6402 6632
Fax: +86 10 6402 3940
E-mail: office@i-mad.com
Web: www.i-mad.com

Founded in 2004 by **MA YANSONG**, MAD first gained attention in 2006 when they won an international competition to design the Absolute Towers near Toronto, completed in 2012 (published here). Born in Beijing, Ma Yansong graduated from the Beijing Institute of Civil Engineering and Architecture before receiving his Master's degree from Yale University. MAD is currently led by Ma Yansong, Dang Qun, and Yosuke Hayano. **DANG QUN**, born in Shanghai, holds an M.Arch from Iowa State University, while **YOSUKE HAYANO** who heads the firm's Tokyo office, trained in architecture at Waseda University (Tokyo, 2000), and at the Architectural Association (London, 2003). Their work includes the Conrad Hotel (Beijing, China, 2008); Fake Hills (Beihai, China, 2008); Hutong Bubble 32 (Beijing, China, 2008–09); Urban Forest (Chongqing, China, 2009); Harbin Culture Island (Harbin, China, 2009); Roma Via Boncompagni (Rome, Italy, 2010); the Ordos Museum (Ordos, Inner Mongolia, 2005–11, published here); Amsterdam Zuidas (Amsterdam, the Netherlands, 2011); Absolute Towers (Mississauga, Canada, 2006–12, also published here); and the China Wood Sculpture Museum (Harbin, China, 2009–12).

MAD wurde 2004 von **MA YANSONG** gegründet und erregte erstmals 2006 Aufmerksamkeit, als sich das Büro bei einer Ausschreibung für die Absolute Towers durchsetzen konnte, die 2012 in der Nähe von Toronto fertiggestellt wurden. Ma Yansong wurde in Peking geboren und absolvierte ein Studium am Institut für Ingenieurwesen und Architektur in Peking, bevor er seinen Masterabschluss an der Yale University absolvierte. Derzeit arbeitet MAD unter Leitung von Ma Yansong, Dang Qun und Yosuke Hayano. **DANG QUN**, geboren in Shanghai, absolvierte seinen M. Arch. an der Iowa State University, während **YOSUKE HAYANO**, die das Büro in Tokio leitet, an der Waseda Universität (Tokio, 2000) und der Architectural Association (London, 2003) studierte. Zu den Projekten von MAD gehören das Conrad Hotel (Peking, 2008), Fake Hills (Beihai, China, 2008), Hutong Bubble 32 (Peking, 2008–09), Urban Forest (Chongqing, China, 2009), Harbin Culture Island (Harbin, China, 2009), Roma Via Boncompagni (Rom, 2010), das Ordos Museum (Ordos, Innere Mongolei, 2005–11, hier vorgestellt), Amsterdam Zuidas (Amsterdam, 2011), die Absolute Towers (Mississauga, Kanada, 2006–12, ebenfalls hier vorgestellt) und das Museum für chinesische Holzbildhauerei (Harbin, 2009–12).

Fondée en 2004 par **MA YANSONG**, MAD s'est fait remarquer pour la première fois en 2006 en gagnant un concours international pour le projet des Absolute Towers, près de Toronto, projet achevé en 2012 (présenté ici). Né à Pékin, Ma Yansong sort diplômé de l'Institut d'ingénierie civile et d'architecture de Pékin avant d'obtenir un master de l'université de Yale. MAD est dirigé actuellement par Ma Yansong, Dang Qun et Yosuke Hayano. **DANG QUN**, né à Shanghai, est titulaire d'un M.Arch de l'université de l'Iowa, tandis que **YOSUKE HAYANO**, qui dirige le bureau de Tokyo, a fait ses études d'architecture à l'université Waseda (Tokyo, 2000) puis à l'Architectural Association (Londres, 2003). Leurs réalisations comprennent l'hôtel Conrad (Pékin, 2008) ; Fake Hills (Beihai, Chine, 2008) ; Hutong Bubble 32 (Pékin, 2008–09) ; Urban Forest (Chongqing, Chine, 2009) ; Harbin Culture Island (Harbin, Chine, 2009) ; Roma Via Boncompagni (Rome, 2010) ; le musée Ordos (Ordos, Mongolie-Intérieure, 2005–11, présenté ici) ; Zuidas (Amsterdam, 2011) ; les Absolute Towers (Mississauga, Canada, 2006–12, présenté ici) et le Musée de la sculpture sur bois (Harbin, Chine, 2009–12).

ORDOS MUSEUM

Ordos, Inner Mongolia, China, 2005–11

Address: the New City District in Ordos City, Inner Mongolia, China, +86 044 7839 0997, www.ordosbwg.com
Area: 41 227 m². Client: City of Ordos. Cost: not disclosed

In 2005, the city of Ordos, near the Gobi Desert, established a master plan for its development. Ordos City is a relatively wealthy coal-mining town with a population of 1.5 million, whose ambitious development plans, including the ambitious Ordos 100 project curated by the artist Ai Weiwei and Herzog & de Meuron, have been largely stalled for economic reasons. In fact, on March 17, 2012, the BBC labeled Ordos "the biggest ghost town in China." MAD was commissioned by the local government to conceive a museum intended as a centerpiece to the new city. Influenced by Buckminster Fuller's geodesic domes, MAD conceived a metallic shell to protect the structure from harsh winters and frequent sand storms. The interior is likened to "an airy monumental cave flushed with natural light through skylights." This entry space marks a void between the galleries and exhibition hall. It is brightly illuminated at the top and crossed by sky bridges. A naturally lit interior garden is shared by the office and research programs of the museum, creating a pleasant work environment. The structure occupies a 27 760-square-meter site and reaches a maximum height of 40 meters. The architects write: "Familiar yet distinct, the Art and City Museum in Ordos appears to have either landed in the desert from another world or to always have existed."

Die am Rand der Wüste Gobi gelegene Stadt Ordos beschloss 2005 einen Masterplan für die Stadtentwicklung. Ordos ist eine relativ wohlhabende Bergbaustadt mit 1,5 Millionen Einwohnern. Ehrgeizige Entwicklungspläne, darunter das von dem Künstler Ai Weiwei mit Herzog & de Meuron kuratierte Projekt „Ordos 100", sind dennoch aus ökonomischen Gründen ins Stocken geraten. Am 17. März 2012 bezeichnete die BBC Ordos als „größte Geisterstadt Chinas". Die Kommunalverwaltung beauftragte MAD mit dem Entwurf eines Museums als Landmarke für die Stadt. Inspiriert von den geodätischen Kuppeln Buckminster Fullers, entwarfen MAD zum Schutz vor den strengen Wintern und häufigen Sandstürmen eine Metallhülle für das Museum. Der Eingangsbereich gleicht „einer gewaltigen, luftigen Höhle, die durchflutet ist von Tageslicht, das durch Oberlichter einfällt". Der lichte Eingangsbereich bildet einen Leerraum zwischen Fluren und zentraler Galerie und wird von sieben Brücken durchkreuzt. Büros und Forschungsabteilung des Museums teilen sich einen als Arbeitsumfeld attraktiven Innengarten mit viel natürlichem Licht. Das Projekt liegt auf einem 27 760 m² großen Grundstück und erreicht eine Maximalhöhe von 40 m. Die Architekten: „Vertraut und doch ungewöhnlich wirkt das Museum für Kunst und Stadtgeschichte entweder wie aus einer anderen Welt mitten in der Wüste gelandet oder als sei es schon immer da gewesen."

En 2005, la ville d'Ordos, près du désert du Gobi, établissait un plan directeur de développement. Ordos est une ville minière relativement cossue d'un million et demi d'habitants. Ses ambitieux projets de développement, dont l'audacieux Ordos 100, sous la tutelle de l'artiste Ai Weiwei et de Herzog & de Meuron, ont calé pour des raisons économiques. Le 17 mars 2012, la BBC étiquetait Ordos « la plus grande ville fantôme de Chine ». Les instances locales ont passé commande à MAD de la conception d'un musée destiné à figurer au centre de la nouvelle ville. S'inspirant des dômes géodésiques de Buckminster Fuller, MAD a conçu une coque métallique pour protéger la structure des hivers rigoureux et des nombreuses tempêtes de sable. L'intérieur peut en être décrit comme « une monumentale grotte baignée de lumière naturelle entrant par des interstices ». Cet espace d'accueil marque un vide entre les galeries et le hall d'exposition. Il est brillamment éclairé en haut et traversé de passerelles aériennes. Un jardin intérieur recevant la lumière naturelle est partagé par les bureaux et le programme de recherche du musée, créant un agréable environnement de travail. La structure, d'une hauteur maximale de 40 m, occupe un site de 27 760 m². Selon les architectes, « tout à la fois familier et singulier, le musée d'Ordos semble avoir atterri dans le désert en provenance d'un autre monde ou avoir toujours été là ».

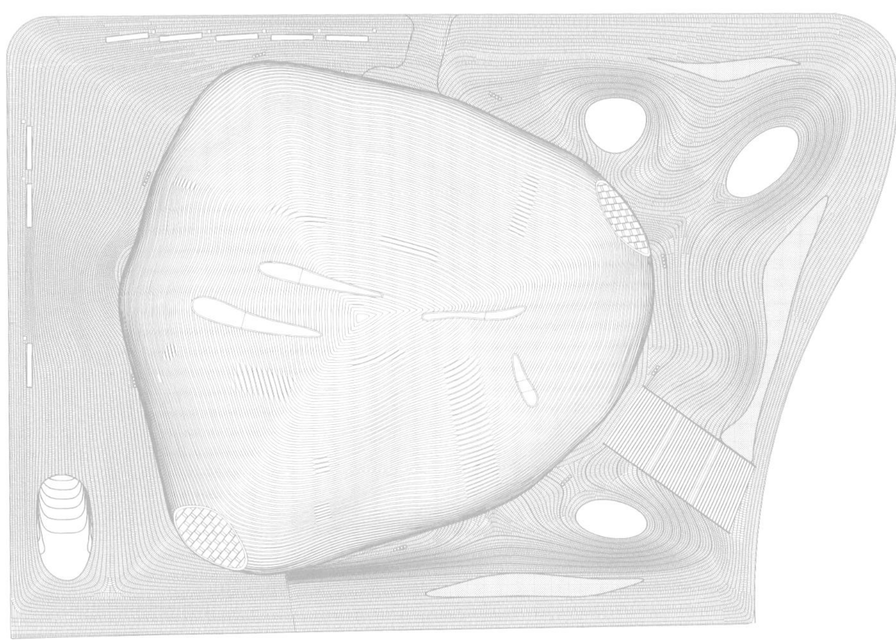

Left, site plan of the museum. Photos show the undulating striated façades of the structure, corresponding to the free curves seen in the site plan.

Links ein Lageplan des Museums. Fotos zeigen die geschwungene Streifenoptik der Fassade, ein visuelles Pendant zur freien Linienführung des Lageplans.

Ci-contre, le plan de situation du musée. Les photos montrent les façades striées ondulantes du bâtiment, correspondant aux courbes déliées du plan de situation.

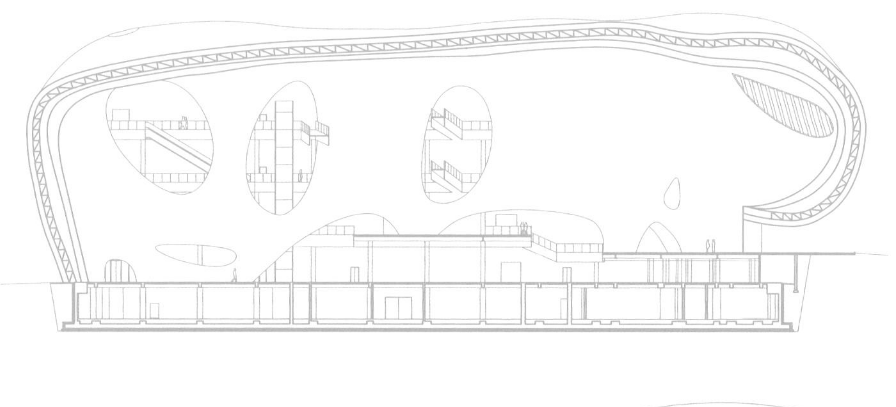

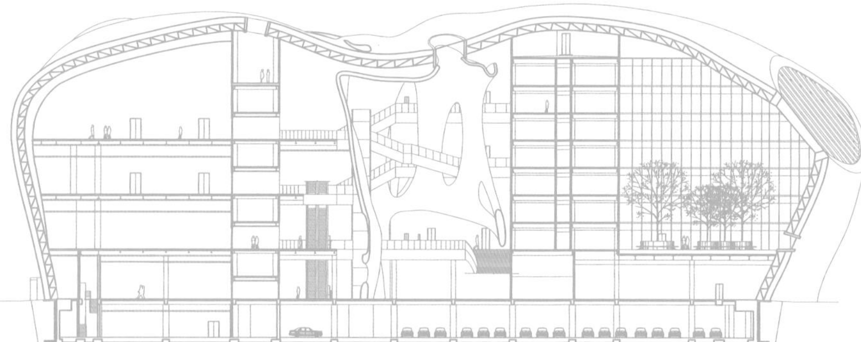

Despite its unusual somewhat geologically inspired forms, the museum clearly deploys usable spaces, as can be seen in the two section drawings on this page. Even the openings are of unexpected shape (right and below).

Trotz seiner eigenwilligen, an geologische Formationen erinnernden Gestalt bietet das Museum nutzbare Räume, wie die zwei Querschnitte auf dieser Seite belegen. Selbst die Fassadenöffnungen (rechts und unten) sind ungewöhnlich geformt.

En dépit de ses formes insolites d'inspiration assez géologique, le musée déploie nettement des espaces utiles, comme on le voit sur les deux coupes de cette page. Même les ouvertures ont des formes inattendues (ci-dessous et page de droite).

The organic and freely curved exterior is echoed by the black and white interior, with its soaring spaces, and somewhat incongruous visitors (above).

Die organischen, frei geschwungenen Formen des Außenbaus wiederholen sich im schwarzweißen Innenraum mit beeindruckend hohen Räumen und eher ungewöhnlichen Besuchern (oben).

L'extérieur organique et librement galbé trouve un écho dans l'intérieur noir et blanc, avec ses volumes élancés et ses visiteurs un peu incongrus (ci-dessus).

Though other projects in Ordos involving well-known architects have been delayed, the museum is quite obviously complete, and stands witness to the rising reputation and talents of its designers.

Während andere Projekte in Ordos, teilweise von bekannten Architekten, Verzögerungen hinnehmen müssen, konnte dieser Museumsbau fertiggestellt werden und zeugt vom wachsenden Renommee und Können seiner Planer.

Bien que d'autres projets d'architectes de renom aient été retardés à Ordos, le musée est à l'évidence terminé et témoigne de la réputation croissante et du talent de ses créateurs.

Very large, open interior space can be seen in the image above. The basic floor plans (seen below) show the central space opening into the more regularly shaped galleries.

Oben im Bild ein monumentaler offener Ausstellungsraum. Die einfachen Grundrisse (unten) zeigen, wie sich der Hauptraum zu eher konventionell konfigurierten Galerieräumen öffnet.

Un très large espace intérieur ouvert est visible dans la photo ci-dessus. Les plans de niveaux (ci-dessous) montrent l'ouverture de l'espace central dans les galeries aux formes plus régulières.

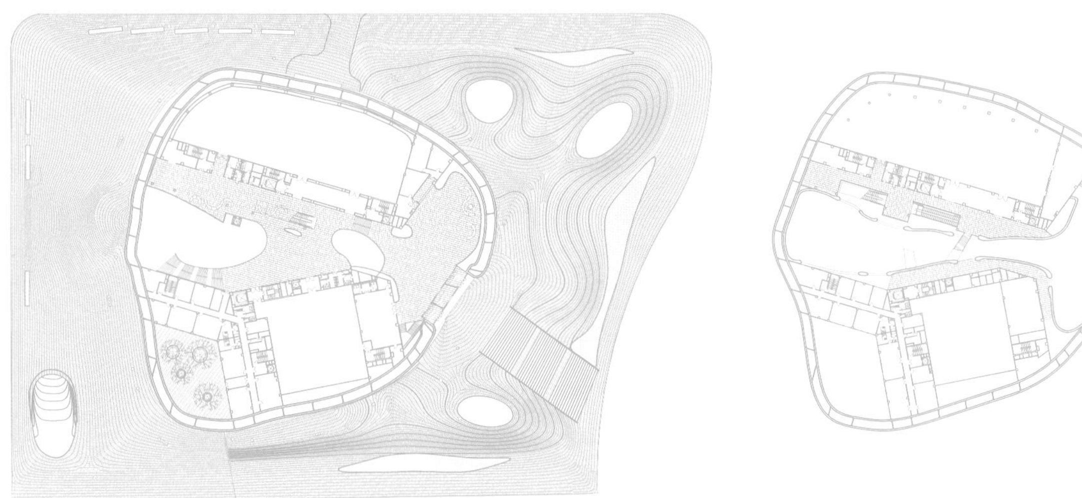

ABSOLUTE TOWERS

Mississauga, Canada, 2006–12

Address: 50–60 Absolute Avenue, Mississauga, ON L4Z 4E8, Canada, +1 416 896 6057, www.absolutecondos.com. Area: 95 000 m². Client: Fernbrook / Cityzen. Cost: not disclosed Collaboration: Burka Architects Inc.

Designing unusual or "iconic" towers is a complex task given the number of architects who have tried and failed. These towers, perhaps because of their responsive duality, give the genre a new idea to work with.

Ungewöhnliche zeichenhafte Hochhäuser zu entwerfen, ist eine komplexe Aufgabe, an der schon viele gescheitert sind. Diese Türme definieren, vielleicht auch dank ihres dialogischen Charakters, neue Ansätze.

Vu l'échec de nombre d'architectes, la conception de tours insolites ou « emblématiques » semble une tâche complexe. Celles-ci, peut-être en raison de leur sensible dualité, donnent de nouvelles pistes au genre.

The surprising, undulating **ABSOLUTE TOWERS** are respectively 56 stories (170 meters) and 50 stories (150 meters) high. According to the architects: "The Absolute Towers parallel the twisting fluidity or natural lines found in life." They explain that Mississauga, near Toronto, has developed rapidly into an independent urbanized area. "Yet," they continue, "the cityscape lacked a unique character. In response, we wanted to add something naturalistic, delicate, and human in contrast to the backdrop of listless, boxy buildings." Each floor plate of the towers is rotated between one and eight degrees, increasing the potential for views from the balconies, but also giving the towers their distinctive undulating forms. The two towers are supported by concrete load-bearing walls. The architects explain: "The bearing walls extend and contract in response to the sectional fluctuation created by the rotation of the floors while the balconies consist of cantilevered concrete slabs. In order to ensure that the elegant edge profiles are as thin as possible, there is a thermal break in the slabs at the exterior glazing such that the insulation need not wrap the entirety of the balconies."

Mit 170 bzw. 150 m sind die **ABSOLUTE TOWER** 56 bzw. 50 Stockwerke hoch. Die Architekten: „Die Absolute Towers greifen fließende Formen und Linien auf, wie sie in der Natur zu finden sind." MAD zufolge hat sich Mississauga bei Toronto in kürzester Zeit zu einem unabhängigen Stadtraum entwickelt. „Dennoch", so MAD weiter, „fehlt es der Stadtlandschaft an Charakter. Wir wollten deshalb die eintönigen Kastenbauten um etwas Naturwüchsiges, Leichtes, Menschliches bereichern." Die Geschossplatten der Türme sind um ein bis acht Grad pro Etage gedreht – sowohl um eine bessere Aussicht von den Balkonen zu ermöglichen, als auch den Gebäuden ihre unverwechselbare Wellenform zu geben. Beide Türme wurden mit tragenden Betonwänden geplant. Die Architekten: „Je nach Gradation der Geschossplatten werden die tragenden Wände breiter oder schmaler, die Balkone sind frei auskragende Betonplatten. Um sicherzustellen, dass die Kantenprofile so dünn wie nur möglich sind, befindet sich in den Platten an der äußeren Verglasung eine thermische Trennung, sodass die Balkone nicht insgesamt gedämmt werden mussten."

Les surprenantes **ABSOLUTE TOWERS** tout en courbes comportent respectivement 56 (170 m) et 50 niveaux (150 m). Selon les architectes, « elles reproduisent l'ondulante fluidité de lignes courbes que l'on trouve dans la nature ». Ils expliquent que Mississauga, près de Toronto, s'est rapidement développée en zone urbanisée indépendante, mais qu'« il manquait un signe fort à son paysage urbain ». Ils ont voulu y « ajouter quelque chose de naturel, de délicat et d'humain, en contraste avec un fond de bâtiments carrés et sans élan ». La torsion d'un à huit degrés appliquée au plancher de chaque étage accroît le potentiel de vue des balcons et donne aux tours cette ondulation si caractéristique. Elles sont soutenues par des murs porteurs de béton qui « se contractent et se dilatent au gré des fluctuations modulaires créées par la torsion des étages. Les balcons sont des dalles de béton en porte-à-faux. Pour garantir la finesse et l'élégance du tout, une barrière thermique sur le revêtement extérieur des plaques évite une isolation complète des balcons ».

To the right, a more distant view confirms the way in which the towers stand out from their relatively bland environment.

Rechts eine Aufnahme aus größerer Distanz, die bestätigt, wie stark die Türme sich von ihrem eher unauffälligem Umfeld abheben.

Page de droite, une vue plus éloignée confirme la façon dont les tours se détachent dans un environnement plutôt terne.

Especially seen from below and in this instance with a wide-angle lens, the deformation of the towers seems quite remarkable. To the right, a basic plan reveals the concept of shifted oval floor plates.

Gerade in der Untersicht, und hier mit einem Weitwinkelobjektiv dokumentiert, ist die „Deformation" der Türme bemerkenswert. Rechts ein einfacher Grundriss, der das Prinzip der gedrehten Geschossplatten illustriert.

Vues de dessous et, ici, avec un objectif grand angle, la déformation des tours est tout à fait remarquable. Un plan basique, ci-contre, révèle le principe de décalage des étages ovales.

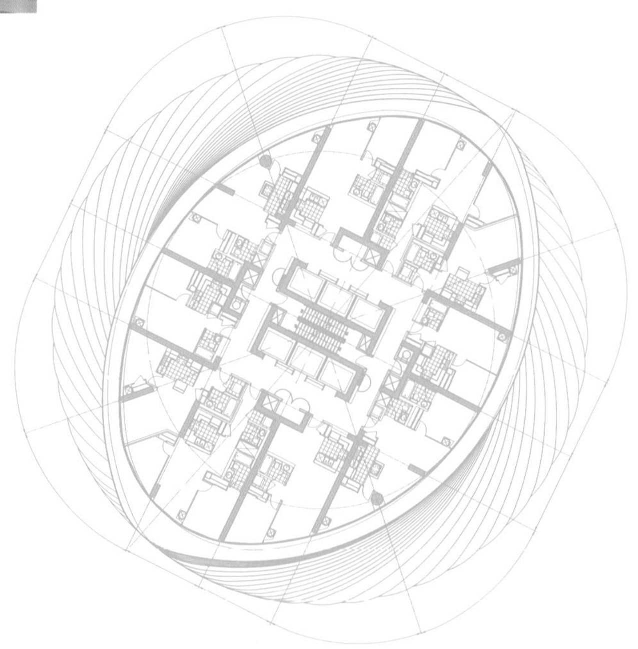

J. MAYER H. ARCHITECTS

J. Mayer H. Architects
Zementhaus
Knesebeckstr. 30
10623 Berlin
Germany

Tel: +49 30 644 90 77 00
Fax: +49 30 644 90 77 11
E-mail: contact@jmayerh.de
Web: www.jmayerh.de

JÜRGEN MAYER H. was born in Stuttgart, Germany, in 1965. He studied at Stuttgart University (Architecture and Town Planning, 1986–92), the Cooper Union (1990–91), and Princeton University (M.Arch, 1992–94). He created his firm J. Mayer H. Architects in Berlin in 1996. Jürgen Mayer H. has taught at Princeton University, University of the Arts Berlin, Harvard University, Kunsthochschule Berlin, Architectural Association (London), Columbia University (New York), and at the University of Toronto. Recent projects include the Town Hall in Ostfildern, Germany; a Student Center at Karlsruhe University (Karlsruhe, Germany, 2006); the Dupli.Casa (near Ludwigsburg, Germany, 2006–08); and the Metropol Parasol, redevelopment of Plaza de la Encarnación (Seville, Spain, 2005–2011). More recently the architect has completed a number of buildings in Georgia—the Sarpi Border Checkpoint (Sarpi, 2010–11, published here); Mestia Police Station (Mestia, 2011–12); and Rest Stops at Gori (Gori, 2011–12; also published here).

JÜRGEN MAYER H. wurde 1965 in Stuttgart geboren. Er studierte an der Universität Stuttgart (Architektur und Stadtplanung, 1986–92), der Cooper Union (1990–91) und der Universität Princeton (M. Arch., 1992–94). 1996 gründete er sein Büro J. Mayer H. Architects in Berlin. Jürgen Mayer H. lehrte u. a. an der Princeton University, der Universität der Künste Berlin, der Harvard University, der Kunsthochschule Berlin-Weißensee, der Architectural Association (London), der Columbia University (New York) und der University of Toronto. Projekte der jüngeren Vergangenheit sind das Stadthaus in Ostfildern, die Mensa der Universität Karlsruhe (2006), die Dupli. Casa (bei Ludwigsburg, 2006–08) sowie die Neugestaltung der Plaza de la Encarnación in Sevilla (Spanien, 2005–11). Aktuelle Projekte sind eine Reihe von Gebäuden in Georgien: der Grenzübergang von Sarpi (2010–11, hier vorgestellt), die Polizeistation von Mestia (2011–12) und die Raststätte Gori (2011–12, ebenfalls hier vorgestellt).

JÜRGEN MAYER H. est né à Stuttgart en 1965. Il fait ses études à l'université de Stuttgart (architecture et urbanisme, 1986–92), à la Cooper Union (1990–91) et à l'université de Princeton (M.Arch, 1992–94). Il fonde son agence J. Mayer H. Architects à Berlin, en 1996. Jürgen Mayer H. a enseigné à Princeton, à l'Université des arts de Berlin, à Harvard, à l'École supérieure des beaux-arts de Berlin-Weissensee, à l'Architectural Association de Londres, à l'université Columbia (New York) et à l'université de Toronto. Ses derniers projets comprennent l'hôtel de ville d'Ostfildern, Allemagne ; un centre d'étudiants à l'université de Karlsruhe (Karlsruhe, Allemagne, 2006) ; la Dupli.Casa (près de Ludwigsburg, Allemagne, 2006–08) et Metropol Parasol, réhabilitation de la Plaza de la Encarnación (Séville, 2005–2011). Plus récemment, l'architecte a réalisé une série de bâtiments en Géorgie – le poste-frontière de Sarpi (Sarpi, 2010–11) et plusieurs aires de repos (Gori, 2011–12) présentés ici –, ainsi que le poste de police de Mestia (Mestia, 2011–12).

georgia

SARPI BORDER CHECKPOINT

Sarpi, Georgia, 2010–11

Address: Sarpi, Georgia. Area: 7351 m². Client: Ministry of Finance of Georgia
Cost: $10.9 million (including equipment)
Collaboration: Beka Pkhakadze, Ucha Tsotseria (Local Architects)

This six-story building reaches a height of 40.4 meters. The concrete and steel structure has a PU coating. Situated at the Georgian border with Turkey, on the shore of the Black Sea, the structure has cantilevered terraces and is used as a viewing platform, with multiple levels overlooking the water and the steep coastline. In addition to the required customs facilities, the checkpoint also includes a cafeteria, staff rooms and a conference room. Indeed surprising in its form, according to the architect, "the building welcomes visitors to Georgia, representing the progressive upsurge of the country."

Der sechsgeschossige Stahlbetonbau erreicht eine Höhe von 40,4 m und ist PU-beschichtet. Das Kontrollgebäude liegt an der georgisch-türkischen Grenze am Ufer des Schwarzen Meers, verfügt über auskragende Terrassen und wird als mehrstufige Aussichtsplattform genutzt, von der aus Besucher das Meer und die steile Küste betrachten können. Außer Räumlichkeiten für die Zollabfertigung sind hier eine Cafeteria, Personalräume und ein Konferenzsaal untergebracht. Der Architekt: „Das Gebäude steht am Eingang zu Georgien und ist ein Zeichen für den gegenwärtigen Aufschwung des Landes."

Ce bâtiment de 40,40 m de haut se compose de 6 étages. La structure de béton et d'acier est recouverte de polyuréthane. Située à la frontière entre la Géorgie et la Turquie, sur les rives de la mer Noire, et dotée de terrasses en porte-à-faux, la structure est utilisée comme plateforme d'observation, avec ses niveaux multiples donnant sur l'eau et son littoral escarpé. En sus des installations nécessaires aux formalités de douane, on y trouve une cafétéria, des salles du personnel et une salle de conférences. Surprenant dans sa forme, « le poste-frontière de Sarpi qui accueille les visiteurs en Géorgie représente, selon l'architecte, le renouveau progressiste du pays ».

With its rippling undulations, this border checkpoint is nothing if not unexpected. Seen at nightfall against the background of the water, it recalls a tall ship, while, above, it might be a strange beached creature on the rocks.

Mit seinen wellenförmigen Einbuchtungen ist der Grenzübergang in jeder Hinsicht überraschend. In einer Ansicht bei Anbruch der Nacht, im Hintergrund das Meer, erinnert er an ein großes Schiff. Oben wirkt er wie ein gestrandetes Fabelwesen.

Avec toutes ses ondulations, ce poste-frontière est pour le moins inattendu. Vu à la tombée de la nuit, avec l'eau en arrière-plan, il fait penser à un grand bateau, alors que, ci-dessus, il ressemble à une étrange créature échouée sur les galets.

The concept and function of border control are more evident in the image above, with the tower giving visitors the clear impression that they are entering a modern country. Interior spaces are open and airy.

Oben im Bild sind Konzept und Funktion des Grenzübergangs deutlich zu erkennen. Der Turm fungiert als Tor in ein modernes Land. Die Innenräume sind hell und offen.

Le concept et la fonction de contrôle aux frontières sont plus évidents sur l'image ci-dessus, avec la tour donnant clairement l'impression aux visiteurs qu'ils entrent dans un pays moderne. Les espaces intérieurs sont ouverts et aérés.

Below, a section drawing. Right, the curved entrance doorway and window clearly echo the form of the building's tower.

Unten ein Querschnitt. Eingang und Fenster nehmen mit ihren geschwungenen Formen deutlich Bezug auf den Turm des Komplexes.

Ci-dessous, une coupe. Ci-contre, la porte d'entrée et la fenêtre en arrondis font écho à la tour du bâtiment.

REST STOPS

Gori, Georgia, 2011–12

Address: Gori, Georgia. Area: 760 m²
Client: PM Motors Ltd. Cost: not disclosed

In 2009, the architects were commissioned by the Public Roads Authority of Georgia to design a series of 20 **REST STOPS** on a new highway running through Georgia and connecting Azerbaijan to Turkey. Two of these Rest Stops have been completed. The architects state: "The new Rest Stops are located on selected scenic viewpoints along the route and serve as activators for their area and neighboring cities, including not only a nearby gas station and supermarket, but also a farmers' market and a cultural space for local arts and crafts." Designed for stations operated by the companies Wissol and Socar, the Rest Stops share a striking concrete design with angled supports and volumes that do not immediately bring to mind the forms of other recent architecture—a feat in itself.

2009 beauftragte das georgische Verkehrsministerium die Architekten mit 20 **RASTSTÄTTEN** für eine neuen Transitautobahn durch Georgien, die Aserbaidschan mit der Türkei verbindet. Zwei dieser Bauten sind inzwischen fertiggestellt. Die Architekten: „Die neuen Raststätten befinden sich an ausgewählten, landschaftlich reizvollen Standorten und bieten außer Tankstellen ein erweitertes Serviceangebot mit Supermärkten, Verkaufsständen lokaler Erzeugnisse und Versammlungs- und Ausstellungsräumen für die Anwohner." Die Raststätten aus Beton wurden für Tankstellen der Unternehmen Wissol und Socar entworfen. Sie eint eine auffälliges Erscheinungsbild mit abgewinkelten Säulen und einer Formensprache, die in der jüngeren Vergangenheit ihresgleichen sucht – für sich genommen schon ein Kunststück.

En 2009, l'administration des Ponts et Chaussées de Géorgie passe commande aux architectes de la conception de 20 **AIRES DE REPOS** sur une nouvelle autoroute qui traverse la Géorgie et relie l'Azerbaïdjan à la Turquie. Deux de ces aires sont terminées. Selon les architectes, « les nouvelles aires de repos sont situées à des endroits pittoresques et dynamisent les villes et les régions voisines, avec la proximité d'une station-service et d'un supermarché, mais aussi d'un marché fermier et d'un espace d'art et artisanat locaux ». Conçues pour des stations-service des compagnies Wissol et Socar, ces aires ont en commun un design frappant de béton, avec des supports et des volumes obliques qui n'ont pas grand-chose à voir avec l'architecture récente – une prouesse en soi.

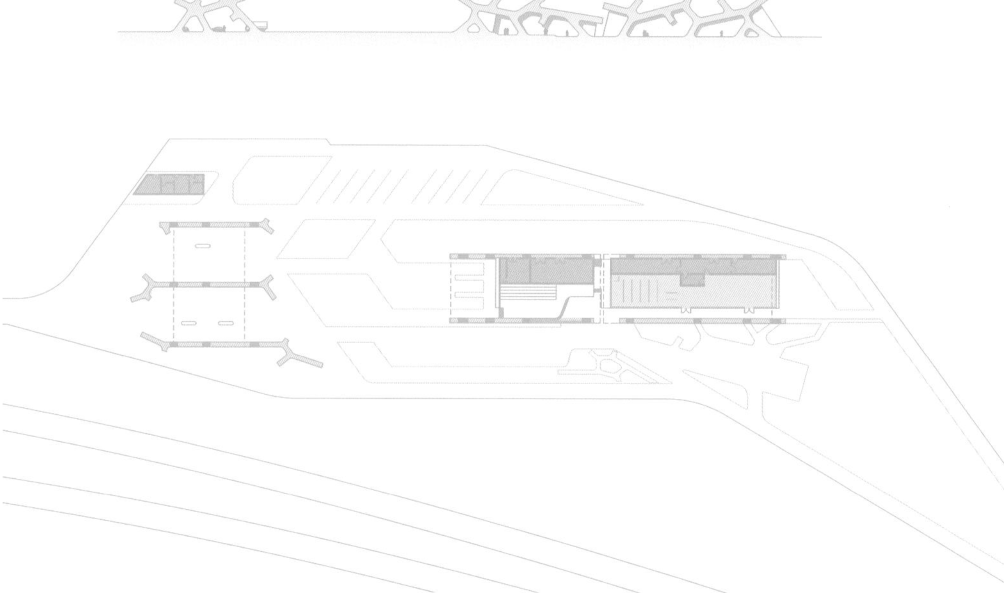

Seen in elevation or in the image on the left page, this rest stop looks something like a defensive structure, but, as the photo below shows, it is quite open.

Auf dem Aufriss und links im Bild wirkt die Raststätte fast wie eine Befestigungsanlage. Die Aufnahme unten jedoch zeigt, dass der Bau tatsächlich ausgesprochen offen ist.

Vue en élévation ou sur l'image page de gauche, cette aire de repos ressemble à un ouvrage défensif, mais, comme le montre la photo ci-dessous, elle est assez ouverte.

Seen from a closer angle, the Rest Stops have both an abstract and a rather defensive aspect. They do not assume the form of a barrier since they run parallel to the road, as seen to the right.

Aus größerer Nähe wirken die Raststätten abstrakt und vergleichsweise defensiv – jedoch nicht wie eine Barriere, denn sie sind parallel zum Straßenverlauf orientiert (rechts im Bild).

Vues sous un angle plus proche, les aires de repos ont un aspect à la fois abstrait et défensif. Comme on le voit ci-contre, elles n'adoptent pas la forme d'une barrière puisqu'elles sont parallèles à la route.

RICHARD MEIER

Richard Meier & Partners Architects LLP
475 10th Avenue
New York, NY 10018 / USA

Tel: +1 212 967 6060 / Fax: +1 212 967 3207
E-mail: mail@richardmeier.com
Web: www.richardmeier.com

RICHARD MEIER was born in Newark, New Jersey, in 1934. He received his architectural training at Cornell University, and worked in the office of Marcel Breuer (1960–63), before establishing his own practice in 1963. In 1984, he became the youngest winner of the Pritzker Prize, and he received the 1988 RIBA Gold Medal. His notable buildings include the Atheneum (New Harmony, Indiana, USA, 1975–79); High Museum of Art (Atlanta, Georgia, USA, 1980–83); Museum of Decorative Arts (Frankfurt, Germany, 1979–84); Canal Plus Headquarters (Paris, France, 1988–91); Barcelona Museum of Contemporary Art (Barcelona, Spain, 1988–95); The Hague City Hall and Library (the Netherlands, 1990–95); and the Getty Center (Los Angeles, California, USA, 1984–97). Recent work includes the US Courthouse and Federal Building (Phoenix, Arizona, USA, 1995–2000); Yale University History of Art and Arts Library (New Haven, Connecticut, USA, 2001); Jubilee Church (Rome, Italy, 1996–2003); Crystal Cathedral International Center for Possibility Thinking (Garden Grove, California, USA, 1998–2003); 66 Restaurant in New York (New York, USA, 2002–03); Ara Pacis Museum (Rome, Italy, 1995–2006); 165 Charles Street (New York, New York, USA, 2003–06); and the Arp Museum (Rolandseck, Germany, 1997–2007). More recently he has completed the ECM City Tower (Pankrác, Prague, Czech Republic, 2001–08); Rickmers Residence (Hamburg, Germany, 2005–08); On Prospect Park (Brooklyn, New York, USA, 2003–09); Italcementi i.lab (Bergamo, Italy, 2008–12); and the OCT Shenzhen Clubhouse (Shenzhen, China, 2010–12, published here).

RICHARD MEIER wurde 1934 in Newark, New Jersey, geboren. Er absolvierte sein Architekturstudium an der Cornell University und arbeitete im Büro von Marcel Breuer (1960–63), bevor er 1963 seine eigene Firma gründete. 1984 war er der bis dato jüngste Empfänger des Pritzker-Preises, 1988 erhielt er die RIBA-Goldmedaille. Zu seinen wichtigsten Projekten gehören das Atheneum (New Harmony, Indiana, 1975–79), das High Museum of Art (Atlanta, Georgia, 1980–83), das Museum für Angewandte Kunst (Frankfurt am Main, 1979–84), der Hauptsitz von Canal Plus (Paris, 1988–91), das Museum für zeitgenössische Kunst MACBA (Barcelona, 1988–95), Rathaus und Bibliothek in Den Haag (1990–95) sowie das Getty Center (Los Angeles, Kalifornien, 1984–97). Jüngere Arbeiten sind u. a. das US Courthouse and Federal Building in Phoenix (Arizona, 1995–2000), die kunsthistorische Bibliothek der Yale University (New Haven, Connecticut, 2001), die Jubiläumskirche (Rom, 1996–2003), das Crystal Cathedral International Center for Possibility Thinking (Garden Grove, Kalifornien, 1998–2003), das Restaurant 66 in New York (2002–03), das Ara-Pacis-Museum (Rom, 1995–2006), 165 Charles Street (New York, 2003–06) und das Arp Museum (Rolandseck, Deutschland, 1997–2007). In der jüngeren Vergangenheit abgeschlossene Projekte sind der ECM City Tower (Pankrác, Prag, Tschechien,2001–08), ein Verwaltungsgebäude für die Reederei Rickmers (Hamburg, 2005–08), On Prospect Park (Brooklyn, New York, 2003–09), Italcementi i.lab (Bergamo, 2008–12) und das OCT Shenzen Clubhouse (Shenzhen, China, 2010–12, hier vorgestellt).

RICHARD MEIER est né à Newark, New Jersey, en 1934. Il fait ses études d'architecture à l'université Cornell et travaille dans le bureau de Marcel Breuer (1960–63) avant d'ouvrir son agence en 1963. En 1984, il devient le plus jeune récipiendaire du prix Pritzker et reçoit la médaille d'or du RIBA en 1988. Ses bâtiments les plus remarquables sont l'Atheneum (New Harmony, États-Unis, 1975–79) ; le High Museum of Art (Atlanta, États-Unis, 1980–83) ; le Musée des arts décoratifs (Francfort, 1979–84) ; le siège de Canal+ (Paris, 1988–91) ; le Musée d'art contemporain de Barcelone (Barcelone, 1988–95) ; l'hôtel de ville et la bibliothèque de La Haye (La Haye, 1990–95) et le Getty Center (Los Angeles, 1984–97). Les plus récents comprennent le Palais de justice et bâtiment fédéral de Phoenix (Phoenix, 1995–2000) ; la bibliothèque d'art et d'histoire de l'art de Yale (New Haven, 2001) ; l'église du Jubilé (Rome, 1996–2003) ; l'International Center for Possibility Thinking de la congrégation Crystal Cathedral (Garden Grove, Californie, 1998–2003) ; le 66 Restaurant (New York, 2002–03) ; le musée de l'Ara Pacis (Rome, 1995–2006) ; 165 Charles Street (New York, 2003–06) et le Arp Museum (Rolandseck, Allemagne, 1997–2007). Plus récemment, il a achevé la tour ECM (Pankrác, Prague, 2001–08) ; la maison Rickmers (Hambourg, 2005–08) ; On Prospect Park (Brooklyn, New York, 2003–09); Italcementi i.lab (Bergame, Italie, 2008–12) et l'OCT Shenzhen Clubhouse (Shenzhen, Chine, 2010–12, présenté ici).

OCT SHENZHEN CLUBHOUSE

Shenzhen, China, 2010–12

Address: OCT Bay, 8 Baishi Road, Shenzhen, China. Area: 11 000 m²
Client: OCT Urban Entertainment Investment Company of Shenzhen. Cost: not disclosed
Collaboration: Dukho Yeon (Associate Partner),
Vivian Lee (Project Manager), Jerome Engelking (Project Architect)

OCT Harbor is located in the central business district of Shenzhen Bay. This area began development in 2005, with Phase One in place by 2011. The Shenzhen Clubhouse is located on an island in the middle of OCT Harbor lake. It offers dining, recreation facilities, a fitness center, and a small exhibition gallery to guests and members. Metal panels and ample natural light, signature elements of Richard Meier's architecture, characterize the interior spaces. The architects explain: "The geometry of the clubhouse follows a precise focal point from which 'layers' of distinct spaces radiate and terminate in a sweeping curve that is seen from the cultural and entertainment center across the water. At the south end of the island, linked to the clubhouse by an outdoor pathway and garden, is the structure that houses the indoor pool and fitness center." The sweeping curve alluded to is resolved in plan in the form of a section of a circle, while the pool and fitness center is a more strictly rectangular volume. The clubhouse is surrounded by gardens that "evoke a strong sense of the Chinese landscape philosophy." The exterior spaces of the complex in general are generous and clearly involve visitors in the drama of the architecture.

OCT Harbor liegt im zentralen Geschäftsbezirk der Bucht von Shenzen. Begonnen wurde mit der Entwicklung dieses Gebiets 2005, der erste Abschnitt konnte 2011 fertiggestellt werden. Das OCT Shenzhen Clubhouse liegt auf einer Insel inmitten des OCT-Harbor-Sees: Clubmitglieder und Gäste können hier essen, das Fitnesscenter nutzen oder eine kleine Galerie besuchen. Die charakteristischen Merkmale von Meiers Architektur, Metallpaneele und viel Tageslicht, finden sich in den Innenräumen. Das Büro hierzu: „Die Geometrie des Gebäudes folgt einem exakt fixierten Brennpunkt, von dem verschiedene ‚Raumschichten' ausstrahlen, die von einer großzügigen Kurvenform begrenzt werden. Diese ist vom Kultur- und Unterhaltungszentrum am anderen Ufer aus gut erkennbar. Am Südende der Insel liegt ein Gebäude mit Indoorpool und Fitnesscenter, das man vom Clubhouse aus über einen Weg durch einen Garten erreicht." Der erwähnte Kurvenschwung erzeugt einen kreissegmentförmigen Grundriss. Der Grundriss des Gebäudes mit Pool und Fitnesscenter ist hingegen weitgehend rechtwinklig gehalten. Das Clubhouse liegt inmitten von Grünanlagen, die „chinesische Landschaftskonzepte" zitieren. Die großzügigen Anlagen beziehen die Besucher in die eindrucksvolle Architektur mit ein.

OCT Harbour est situé dans le quartier d'affaires central de la baie de Shenzhen. Le développement de ce quartier a commencé en 2005, une première phase s'étant achevée en 2011. Le Shenzhen Clubhouse se situe sur une île au milieu du lac d'OCT Harbour. Il propose à ses membres et à ses clients des espaces de divertissement et de restauration, un centre de fitness et une petite galerie d'exposition. Des panneaux de métal et une lumière naturelle prodigue, qui signent l'architecture de Richard Meier, définissent les espaces intérieurs. Les architectes expliquent que « la géométrie du club suit un point de convergence précis à partir duquel rayonnent des "couches" d'espaces distincts qui se terminent en une large courbe que l'on peut voir du centre culturel et de loisirs de l'autre côté de l'eau. À la pointe sud de l'île, reliée au club par une allée extérieure et un jardin, se trouve la structure qui abrite la piscine intérieure et le centre de fitness ». La large courbe mentionnée plus haut se fond en une portion de cercle, tandis que la piscine et le centre de fitness ont un volume plus strictement rectangulaire. Le club est entouré de jardins qui « évoquent fortement les concepts chinois de paysage ». Généreux, les espaces extérieurs du complexe impliquent clairement les visiteurs dans l'histoire que raconte l'architecture.

With this large project, Richard Meier is at the height of his powers, integrating his trademark white geometric forms with tan stone and a lake environment. Right, a site plan showing the lake and the building.

Mit diesem Großprojekt zeigt sich Richard Meier in Bestform, integriert die für ihn typischen weißen geometrischen Formen in einen Kontext aus cremefarbenem Mauerwerk und einem See. Rechts ein Lageplan mit See und Gebäuden.

Avec ce grand projet, Richard Meier est au sommet de son art, intégrant les formes géométriques blanches qui sont sa signature dans la pierre brun clair et le lac environnants. Ci-contre, un plan de situation montrant le lac et le bâtiment.

Below and at the top of the right page, elevation drawings reveal the entire composition, with its often angled forms. Above, thin columns and finely designed surfaces and forms participate in the overall impression of perfection.

Aufrisse zeigen die Gesamtkomposition mit oft winkligen Formen (oben und rechte Seite oben). Schmale Stützen und fein gegliederte Oberflächen und Formen tragen zum makellosen Gesamteindruck bei (oben).

Ci-dessous et en haut de la page de droite, des élévations dévoilent toute la composition, avec ses formes souvent anguleuses. Ci-dessus, les colonnes fuselées et les formes et les surfaces finement dessinées participent à l'impression générale de perfection.

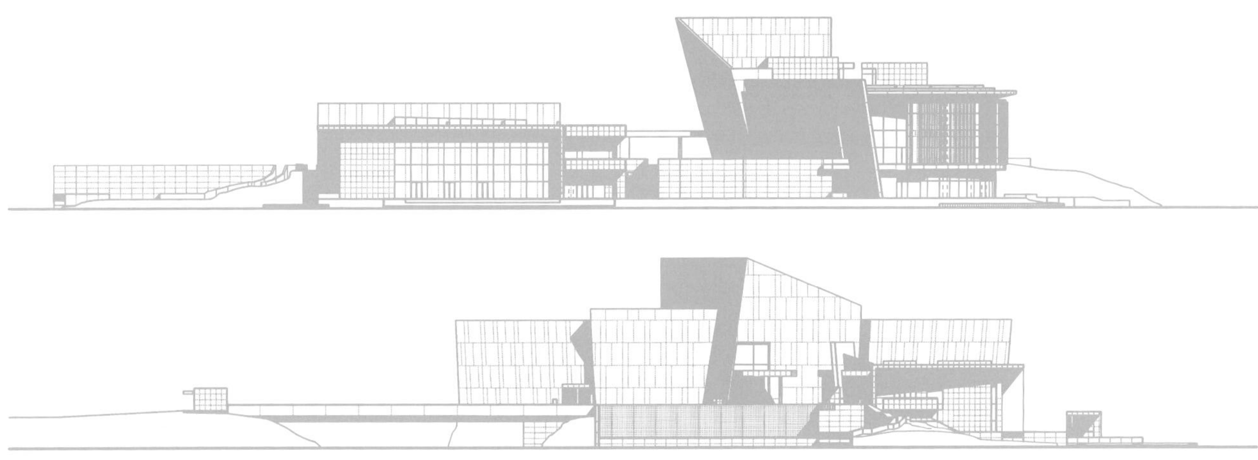

A fountain springs from a plaza with carefully aligned stone pavement. The white forms of the buildings in this area are largely opaque, leaving broad glazing for other zones in the project.

Auf einem Platz mit präziser Pflasterung sorgt ein Brunnen für Wasserspiele. Die weißen Baukörper sind hier weitgehend geschlossen; großflächige Verglasung findet sich in anderen Bereichen.

Des jets d'eau jaillissent d'une place au dallage parfaitement aligné. Les formes blanches des bâtiments sont ici en grande partie opaques, faisant place à de grands vitrages en d'autres endroits.

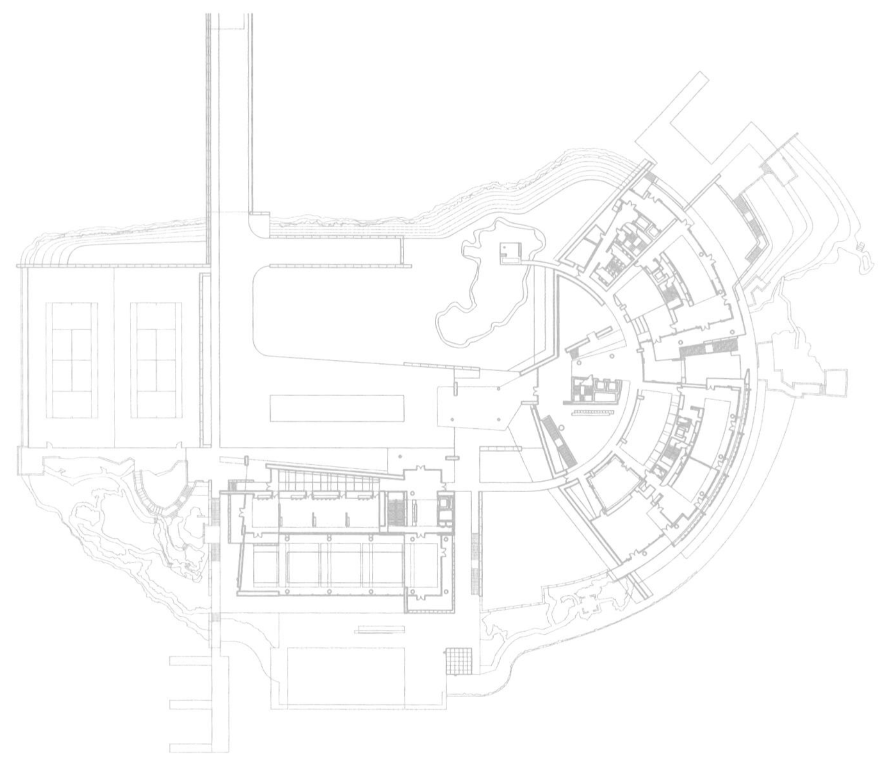

A ground-floor plan shows the large radiating curve that forms the most visible lakeside façade. Below, stairways and overhead glazing make for forms that are readily identifiable as being designed by Richard Meier.

Ein Grundriss des Erdgeschosses zeigt den ausgreifenden Kurvenschwung, der die auffällige Seefassade prägt. Treppen und Oberlichter (unten) haben eine Formensprache, die eindeutig Richard Meier zuzuordnen ist.

Ce plan du rez-de-chaussée montre la large courbe formée par la façade la plus visible côté lac. Les escaliers et vitrages ci-dessous produisent des formes portant clairement la signature de Richard Meier.

The angling and cantilever seen above add a dynamic aspect to the architecture, which is not always present in these proportions in the work of Richard Meier.

Die Verkantungen und Ausleger oben im Bild geben der Architektur eine Dynamik, die in diesem Maß nicht in allen Entwürfen von Richard Meier präsent ist.

Les angles et porte-à-faux ci-dessus ajoutent à l'architecture une dynamique qui n'est pas toujours aussi présente dans l'œuvre de Richard Meier.

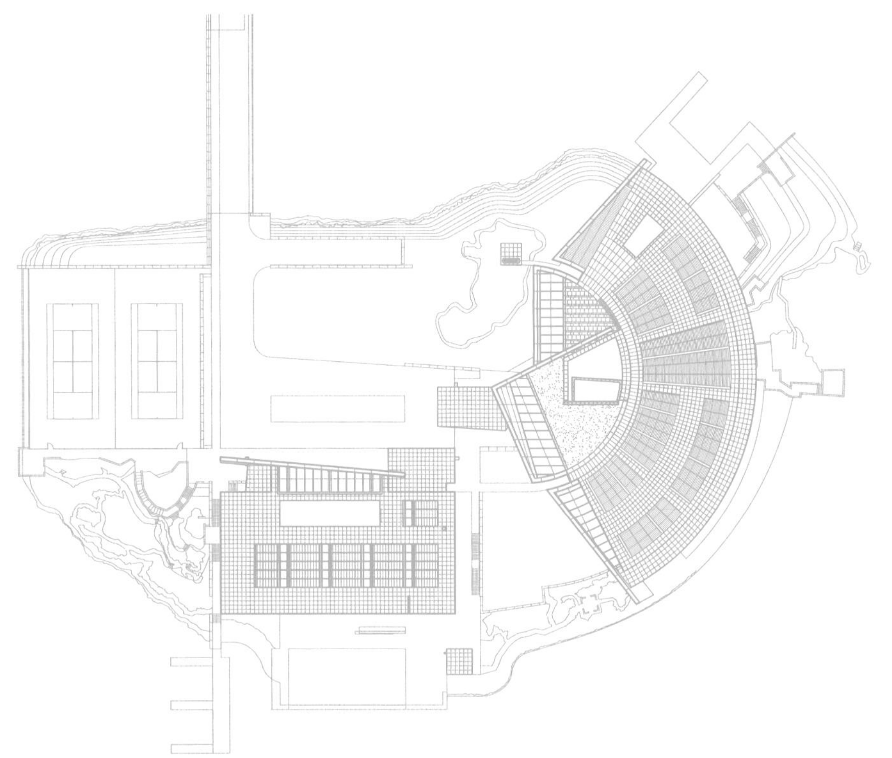

Left, a roof plan of the OCT Clubhouse. On this page, contrasts between white and black but, above all, soaring ceiling heights and ample glazing make for spectacular spaces. Right, an enclosed swimming pool.

Links ein Grundriss des Dachgeschosses des OCT Clubhouse. Schwarzweißkontraste, aber vor allem beeindruckend hohe Decken und großzügige Verglasung (diese Seite), erzeugen spektakuläre Raumwirkungen. Rechts ein Indoorpool.

Ci-contre, un plan du toit du OCT Clubhouse. Sur cette page, le contraste noir/blanc, mais surtout des hauteurs sous plafond impressionnantes et des vitrages en abondance rendent ces espaces spectaculaires. Page de droite, une piscine couverte.

METRO ARQUITETOS

Metro Arquitetos
Rua General Jardim, 645
São Paulo SP 01223-011
Brazil

Tel: +55 11 3255 1221
E-mail: contato@metroo.com.br
Web: www.metroo.com.br

MARTIN CORULLON was born in Argentina in 1973. He received his architecture degree from the Faculdade de Arquitetura e Urbanismo da Universidade de São Paulo (FAUUSP) in 2000, when he founded Metro Arquitetos Associados. Since 1994, Martin Corullon has been a close collaborator of Paulo Mendes da Rocha. In 2008 and 2009, he worked at Foster + Partners, in London. **ANNA FERRARI** was born in São Paulo, Brazil, in 1978. She received her architecture degree from the Faculdade de Arquitetura e Urbanismo (FAU/Mack) Mackenzie (2000). She was a collaborator of the office from the time of its creation and became a Partner in 2005; between 2011 and 2012 she worked at Herzog & de Meuron (Basel), afterwards returning to Metro. **GUSTAVO CEDRONI** was born in São Paulo in 1978. He received his degree at the Fundação Armando Alvares Penteado (FAAP) in 2000. He worked with Pedro Paulo de Melo Saraiva (1999) and Eduardo Colonelli (2000), before joining Metro in 2002. He became a Partner in 2005. Their work includes Votorantim I (São Paulo, São Paulo, 2007); Cais das Artes (Vitória, Espírito Santo, 2008); Nestlé Chocolate Factory (Caçapava, 2011, published here); the LP House (São Paulo, São Paulo, 2010–12); Votorantim II (Alumínio, São Paulo, 2012); New Leme Gallery (based on a design by Paulo Mendes da Rocha, São Paulo, São Paulo, 2012, also published here); and the Itau Movie Theaters in six different cities (2012), all in Brazil.

MARTIN CORULLON wurde 1973 in Argentinien geboren. Sein Architekturstudium schloss er 2000 an der Faculdade de Arquitetura e Urbanismo da Universidade de São Paulo (FAUUSP) ab. Noch im selben Jahr gründete er Metro Arquitetos Associados. Seit 1994 arbeitet Corullon eng mit Paulo Mendes da Rocha zusammen. Von 2008 bis 2009 war Corullon bei Foster + Partners in London tätig. **ANNA FERRARI** wurde 1978 in São Paulo geboren. Sie absolvierte ein Architekturstudium an der Faculdade de Arquitetura e Urbanismo (FAU) der Mackenzie-Universität (2000). Anna Ferrari arbeitet seit Bestehen des Büros mit Metro Arquitetos zusammen und wurde 2005 Partnerin. Zwischen 2011 und 2012 arbeitete sie für Herzog & de Meuron (Basel) und kehrte anschließend zu Metro Arquitetos zurück. **GUSTAVO CEDRONI** wurde 1978 in São Paulo geboren. Sein Studium schloss er 2000 an der Fundação Armando Alvares Penteado (FAAP) ab. Er arbeitete für Pedro Paulo de Melo Saraiva (1999) und Eduardo Colonelli (2000), bevor er sich 2002 Metro anschloss und 2005 Partner wurde. Projekte des Büros sind Votorantim I (São Paulo, 2007), Cais das Artes (Vitória, Espírito Santo, 2008), eine Schokoladenfabrik für Nestlé (Caçapava, 2011, hier vorgestellt), die Casa LP (São Paulo, 2010–12), Votorantim II (Alumínio, São Paulo, 2012), die Galerie Nova Leme (auf der Basis eines Entwurfs von Paulo Mendes da Rocha, São Paulo, 2012, ebenfalls hier vorgestellt) sowie Itaú-Kinos in sechs verschiedenen Städten (2012), alle in Brasilien.

Né en Argentine en 1973, **MARTIN CORULLON** obtient son diplôme d'architecture de la faculté d'architecture et d'urbanisme de l'université de São Paulo (FAUUSP) en 2000, au moment où il fonde Metro Arquitetos Associados. Depuis 1994, Martin Corullon est un proche collaborateur de Paulo Mendes da Rocha. En 2008 et 2009, il travaille chez Foster + Partners, à Londres. Née à São Paulo en 1978, **ANNA FERRARI** obtient son diplôme d'architecture de la faculté d'architecture et d'urbanisme Mackenzie (FAU/Mack) en 2000. D'abord collaboratrice au sein de l'agence depuis sa création, elle en devient associée en 2005 ; entre 2011 et 2012, elle travaille chez Herzog & de Meuron (Bâle), puis retourne chez Metro. **GUSTAVO CEDRONI** est né à São Paulo, en 1978. Il sort diplômé de Fundação Armando Alvares Penteado (FAAP) en 2000. Il travaille avec Pedro Paulo de Melo Saraiva (1999) puis avec Eduardo Colonelli (2000) avant de rejoindre Metro en 2002. Il devient associé de l'agence en 2005. Parmi leurs réalisations, l'on compte Votorantim I (São Paulo, 2007) ; Cais das Artes (Vitória, Espírito Santo, 2008) ; l'usine de chocolat Nestlé (Caçapava, 2011, présentée ici) ; la maison LP (São Paulo, 2010–12) ; Votorantim II (Alumínio, São Paulo, 2012) ; la nouvelle galerie Leme (d'après une idée de Paulo Mendes da Rocha, São Paulo, 2012, également présentée ici) et les cinémas Itau dans six villes du Brésil (2012).

NEW LEME GALLERY

São Paulo, São Paulo, Brazil, 2012

Address: Av. Valdemar Ferreira 130, São Paulo, SP 05501–000, Brazil
+55 11 3093 8184, www.galerialeme.com. Area: 554 m²
Client: Leme Gallery. Cost: not disclosed. Collaboration: Paulo Mendes da Rocha

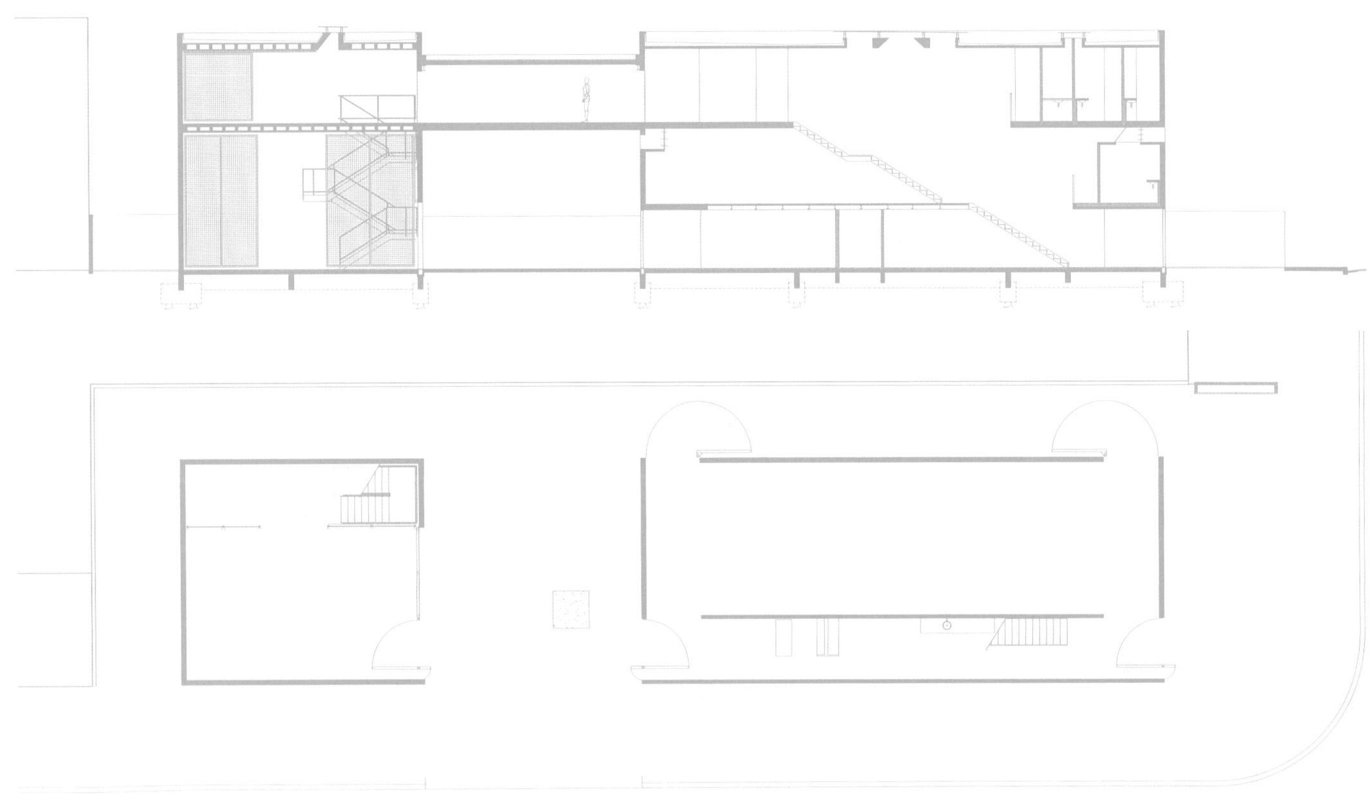

This project is unusual in that it is a homage to, and a collaboration with, the great Brazilian architect Paulo Mendes da Rocha, with whom Metro has frequently worked.

Das Projekt ist ungewöhnlich, weil es eine Zusammenarbeit mit dem großen brasilianischen Architekten Paulo Mendes da Rocha ist, mit dem Metro schon mehrfach gearbeitet hat, und zugleich eine Hommage an ihn.

Ce projet est inhabituel dans le sens qu'il est, en même temps qu'une collaboration, un hommage au grand architecte brésilien Paulo Mendes da Rocha avec lequel Metro a souvent travaillé.

The **NEW LEME GALLERY** was built two blocks away from the original, which was designed by Paulo Mendes da Rocha with Metro. The architects reproduced the original while adding a 9 x 9-meter cube that is connected to the main building by an upper-level footbridge. A new patio was also added, making the transition from the reproduction of the original to the new space clear. This move was negotiated with a large construction company that bought the entire block on which the old gallery was located. For a short period before the old gallery was demolished, visitors were invited to visit and compare the two structures. The New Leme Gallery, like the old one, was built entirely out of reinforced concrete. The exhibition galleries have overhead lighting and areas between six and nine meters high. Administrative areas, with skylights and windows, are above the galleries.

Dieser **NEUBAU FÜR DIE GALERIE LEME** wurde zwei Straßenzüge entfernt von deren ursprünglichem Domizil errichtet, das Paulo Mendes da Rocha mit Metro entworfen hatte. Die Architekten duplizierten das Original und ergänzten es um einen 9 x 9 m großen Kubus, der mit dem Hauptgebäude über eine Brücke verbunden ist. Teil des Projekts ist ein Innenhof, der den Übergang von der Kopie des Originals zur neuen Galerie verdeutlicht. Dank Verhandlungen mit einer großen Baufirma, die einen ganzen Straßenzug gekauft hatte, konnten Besucher für kurze Zeit beide Gebäude vergleichen, bevor die alte Galerie abgerissen wurde. Wie schon ihre Vorgängerin ist auch die neue Galerie in Stahlbetonweise ausgeführt. Die Ausstellungsräume verfügen über Deckenbeleuchtung und Deckenhöhen von 6 bis 10 m. Darüber liegen Büros mit Fenstern und Oberlichtern.

La **NOUVELLE GALERIE LEME** a été construite à deux rues de l'ancienne, conçue par Paulo Mendes da Rocha avec Metro. Les architectes ont reproduit la galerie originale en y ajoutant un cube de 9 x 9 m relié au bâtiment principal par une passerelle piétonne surélevée. Ils y ont adjoint également un patio qui clarifie la transition entre la reproduction du lieu original et le nouvel espace. Ce changement a été négocié avec une grande entreprise de construction qui a acheté la totalité du secteur sur lequel se situait l'ancienne galerie. Avant la destruction de l'ancienne galerie, les visiteurs ont pu, pendant un court laps de temps, comparer les deux structures. La nouvelle galerie Leme, tout comme l'ancienne, est entièrement en béton armé. Les salles d'exposition, entre 6 et 9 m de haut, ont un éclairage au plafond. Les bureaux de l'administration, pourvus de lucarnes et de fenêtres, sont situés au-dessus des salles d'exposition.

The architects return to Mendes da Rocha's trademark powerful concrete surfaces—to the right, only limited glazing brings the exhibition space to life. The architecture seems defensive, but creates privileged spaces for contemporary art.

Die Architekten greifen die für Mendes da Rocha typisch markanten Sichtbetonflächen auf. Der Raum rechts gewinnt auch durch minimale Verglasung an Dynamik. Die Architektur wirkt fast hermetisch geschlossen, schafft jedoch ideale Rahmenbedingungen für zeitgenössische Kunst.

Les architectes reviennent aux solides surfaces de béton, marque de fabrique de Mendes da Rocha. Page de droite, seules des surfaces vitrées limitées animent l'espace d'exposition. Si l'architecture a un côté défensif, elle crée des espaces privilégiés pour l'art contemporain.

NESTLÉ CHOCOLATE FACTORY

Caçapava, Brazil, 2011

Address: Av. Henry Nestlé 1800, Vila Antonio Augusto, Caçapava, SP 12286–140, Brazil, www.nestle.com.br
Area: 1850 m². Client: Nestlé. Cost: not disclosed

The architects have used red glass to considerable effect, signaling the location of the factory and also pointing out their own contribution. The length of the bridge makes it seem to almost hover in space, unsupported.

Die Architekten beeindrucken mit der roten Verglasung; sie signalisiert den Standort der Fabrik und zugleich die Handschrift des Büros. Durch die Länge der Brücke scheint diese fast schwerelos im Raum zu schweben.

Les architectes ont utilisé un vitrage rouge d'un effet puissant, signalant à la fois l'emplacement de l'usine et leur propre contribution. La longueur du pont donne l'impression qu'il flotte sans soutien dans l'espace.

This project was carried out in an existing **NESTLÉ CHOCOLATE FACTORY**, originally built in the 1960s. Given the original layout, visitor circulation posed a problem, and it was decided to install a museum and circuit for these visitors. The architects explain: "The main intention of the design for the Nestlé factory's visiting areas was to create a landmark in the generic landscape of the Dutra highway that connects São Paulo and Rio de Janeiro, revealing the existence of a public and accessible space." The main signal employed is formed by two steel-framed red glass towers connected to foot bridges that wrap around the existing building and give access to the factory. Floors in the towers are made with perforated metal sheets. Ten thematic cores were created in the exhibition area, taking spectators from raw materials to the final packaging. Each of these cores has a specific color and different materials are employed. The architects were also involved in the exhibition design and soundtracks used.

Realisiert wurde das Projekt bei einem bestehenden **FABRIKGEBÄUDE DER FIRMA NESTLÉ** aus den 1960er-Jahren. Die räumliche Organisation der Fabrik war für den gewünschten Besucherverkehr ungeeignet, weshalb man sich entschied, ein Museum und einen Rundgang einzurichten. Die Architekten: „Bei der Gestaltung des Besucherbereichs für Nestlé ging es darum, der charakterlosen Landschaft an der Dutra-Autobahn zwischen São Paulo und Rio de Janeiro eine Landmarke hinzuzufügen. Sie sollte einen öffentlich zugänglichen Ort markieren." Zentrales Signal des Komplexes sind zwei rot verglaste Stahltürme. Diese sind mit Fußgängerbrücken verbunden, die um das bestehende Gebäude führen und den Zugang zur Fabrik bilden. In den Türmen kamen gelochte Bodenbleche zum Einsatz. Der Ausstellungsbereich umfasst zehn Themenbereiche zur Produktion vom Rohmaterial bis zur Verpackung mit jeweils eigenem Farb- und Materialprofil. Die Architekten planten auch die Ausstellungsarchitektur und waren an der Herstellung des Audiomaterials beteiligt.

Ce projet a été mené à bien à l'intérieur d'une **USINE DE CHOCOLAT NESTLÉ** construite dans les années 1960. L'agencement d'origine posait problème quant à la circulation des visiteurs. Il a donc été décidé d'installer un musée et un circuit spécialement pour eux. Selon les architectes, « pour ce qui est des aires de visite de l'usine Nestlé, l'intention principale était de créer, au milieu du paysage générique de la Dutra, l'autoroute qui relie São Paulo et Rio de Janeiro, un point de repère révélant l'existence d'un espace public accessible ». L'on a utilisé comme signal fort deux tours rouges de verre et d'acier reliées par des passerelles qui enveloppent le bâtiment existant et donnent accès à l'usine. Les sols des tours sont faits de plaques de métal perforées. Dix pôles thématiques ont été créés dans l'espace d'exposition pour accompagner le visiteur des matières premières à l'emballage final. Chaque thématique a sa couleur et différents matériaux ont été employés. Les architectes ont également collaboré à la scénarisation et à l'environnement sonore de l'exposition.

Exhibition spaces tell the story of chocolate in a way that blends seamlessly with the striking red architecture of the exterior.

Die Ausstellungsräume präsentieren die Geschichte der Schokolade auf eine Weise, die geradezu selbstverständlich an das markante Rot des Außenbaus anknüpft.

Des espaces d'exposition racontent l'histoire du chocolat d'une façon qui se mélange sans heurt avec le rouge frappant de l'architecture extérieure.

Above, inside the long red passage between the new tower and the older building. A drawing (below) shows the proportions of the different elements.

Oben ein Blick in den langen roten Gang zwischen neuem Turm und älterem Fabrikgebäude. Eine Zeichnung (unten) veranschaulicht die Proportionen der verschiedenen Elemente.

Ci-dessus, l'intérieur du long passage rouge entre la nouvelle tour et l'ancien bâtiment. Le dessin ci-dessous indique les proportions des différents éléments.

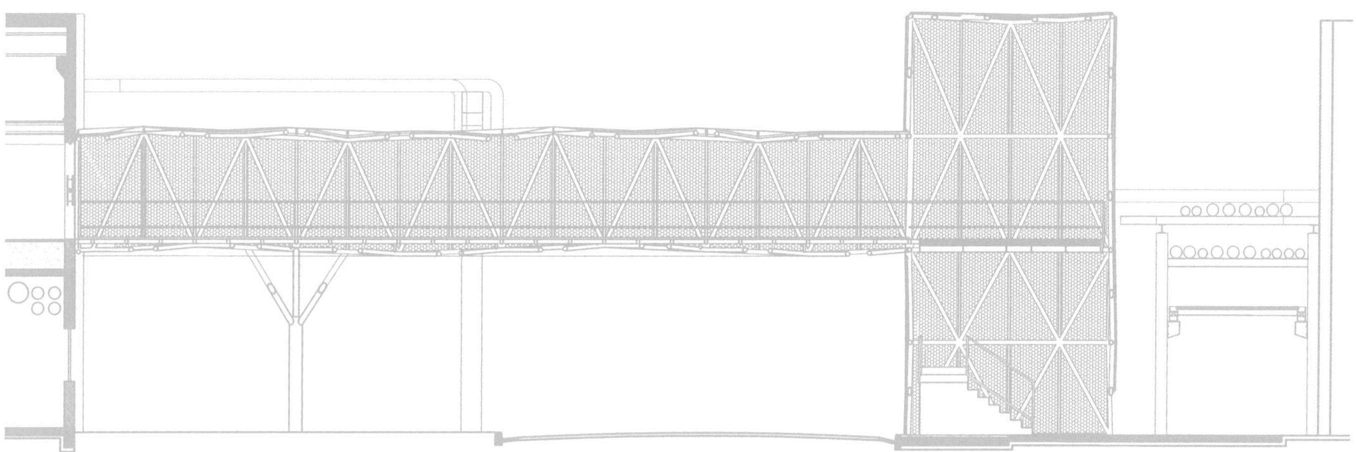

MORPHOSIS

*Morphosis Architects
3440 Wesley Street
Culver City, CA 90232
USA*

*Tel: +1 424 258 6200 / Fax: +1 424 258 6299
E-mail: studio@morphosis.net
Web: www.morphosis.com*

Morphosis Principal **THOM MAYNE**, born in Connecticut in 1944, received his B.Arch in 1968 from the University of Southern California, Los Angeles, and his M.Arch degree from Harvard in 1978. He founded Morphosis in 1972. He has taught at UCLA, Harvard, Yale, and SCI-Arc, of which he was a founding Board Member. Thom Mayne was the winner of the 2005 Pritzker Prize as well as the 2013 AIA Gold Medal. Some of the main buildings by Morphosis are the Kate Mantilini Restaurant (Beverly Hills, California, 1986); Cedars-Sinai Comprehensive Cancer Care Center (Los Angeles, California, 1987–88); Crawford Residence (Montecito, 1988–90); the Blades Residence (Santa Barbara, California, 1993–97); and International Elementary School (Long Beach, California, 1998–99). More recent work includes the NOAA Satellite Operation Facility in Suitland (Maryland, 2001–05); San Francisco Federal Building (San Francisco, California, 2000–07); and 41 Cooper Square (New York, New York, 2006–09). The firm has also completed the Giant Interactive Group Corporate Headquarters (Shanghai, China, 2006–10); Clyde Frazier's Wine and Dine (New York, New York, 2011–12, published here); and the Perot Museum of Nature and Science (Dallas, Texas, 2010–13), all in the USA unless stated otherwise. Ongoing work includes Cornell University's new Computing and Information Science Building (Ithaca, New York, USA, 2014); the Taubman Engineering, Life Sciences, and Architecture (TELSA) Complex (Southfield, Michigan, USA, 2016); the Phare Tower (Paris, France, 2017); and Vialia Vigo (Vigo, Spain, 2017).

THOM MAYNE, Direktor von Morphosis, wurde 1944 in Connecticut geboren. Seine Studien schloss er 1968 mit einem B. Arch. an der University of Southern California, Los Angeles, und 1978 mit einem M. Arch. in Harvard ab. 1972 gründete er Morphosis. Mayne lehrte an der UCLA, in Harvard, in Yale und am SCI-Arc, zu dessen Gründungsmitgliedern er zählt. 2005 wurde Mayne mit dem Pritzker-Preis ausgezeichnet, 2013 mit der AIA-Goldmedaille. Ausgewählte Bauten von Morphosis sind u. a. das Kate Mantilini Restaurant (Beverly Hills, Kalifornien, 1986), die Cedars-Sinai-Krebsklinik (Beverly Hills, Kalifornien, 1987–88), die Crawford Residence (Montecito, 1988–90), die Blades Residence (Santa Barbara, Kalifornien, 1993–97) sowie die International Elementary School (Long Beach, Kalifornien, 1998–99). Jüngere Arbeiten sind u. a. das NOAA-Satellitenzentrum in Suitland (Maryland, 2001–05), das San Francisco Federal Building (San Francisco, Kalifornien, 2000–07) und der 41 Cooper Square (New York, 2006–09). Das Büro plante zudem den Hauptsitz der Giant Interactive Group (Shanghai, China, 2006–10), das Clyde Frazier's Wine and Dine (New York, 2011–12, hier vorgestellt) und das Museum für Naturkunde (Dallas, Texas, 2010–13). Laufende Projekte sind u. a. ein Neubau für die Informatik- und Informationswissenschaften an der Cornell University (Ithaca, New York, 2014), der Taubman Engineering, Life Sciences and Architecture Complex (TELSA, Southfield, Michigan, 2016), das Hochhaus „Le Phare" (Paris, 2017) sowie Vialia Vigo (Vigo, Spanien, 2017).

THOM MAYNE, le directeur de Morphosis, né dans le Connecticut en 1944, obtient son B.Arch en 1968 à l'USC, Los Angeles, et son M.Arch à Harvard en 1978. Il fonde Morphosis en 1972. Il a enseigné à l'UCLA, Harvard, Yale et au SCI-Arc dont il est un membre fondateur. Thom Mayne remporte en 2005 le prix Pritzker ainsi que la médaille d'or 2013 de l'AIA. Les principaux bâtiments dessinés par Morphosis sont le Kate Mantilini Restaurant (Beverly Hills, 1986) ; le Centre de cancérologie de l'hôpital Cedar's Sinai (Los Angeles, 1987–88) ; la maison Crawford (Montecito, 1988–90) ; la maison Blades (Santa Barbara, 1993–97) et l'International Elementary School (Long Beach, Californie, 1998–99). Parmi les projets les plus récents, on trouve le NOAA Satellite Operation Facility de Suitland (Maryland, 2001–05) ; le San Francisco Federal Building (San Francisco, 2000–07) et le 41 Cooper Square (New York, 2006–09). L'agence a également achevé le siège du Giant Interactive Group Corporate (Shanghai, 2006–10) ; le restaurant Clyde Frazier's Wine and Dine (New York, 2011–12, présenté ici) et le Perot Museum of Nature and Science (Dallas, Texas, 2010–13), tous situés aux États-Unis sauf indication contraire. Parmi les projets en cours, on compte le nouveau bâtiment informatique et sciences de l'information de l'université Cornell (Ithaca, New York, 2014) ; le complexe TELSA (Taubman Engineering, Life Sciences, and Architecture) (Southfield, Michigan, 2016) ; la tour Phare (Paris, 2017) et Vialia Vigo (Vigo, Espagne, 2017).

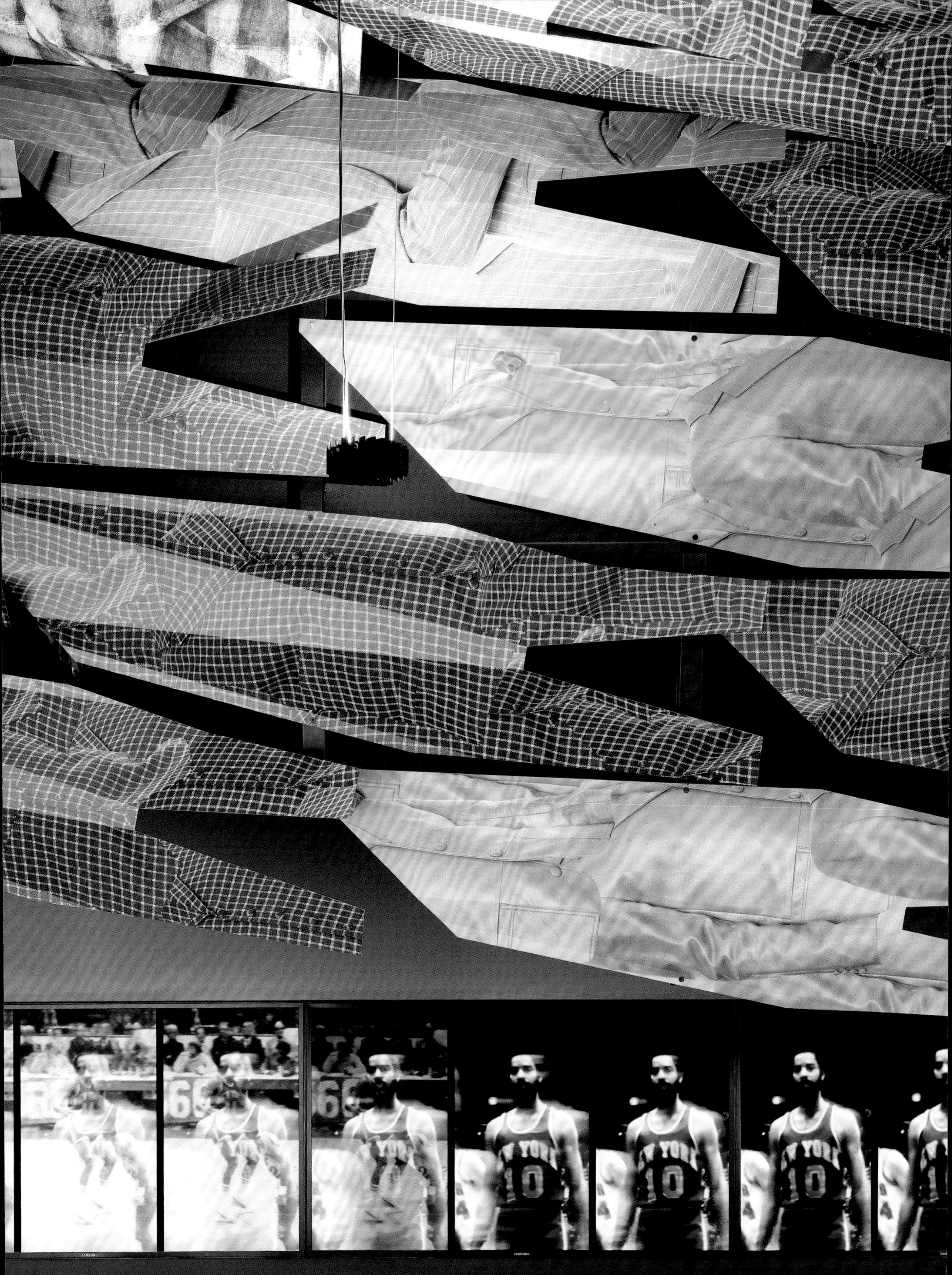
10

CLYDE FRAZIER'S WINE AND DINE

New York, New York, USA, 2011–12

Address: 485 10th Avenue, New York, NY 10003, USA, +1 212 842 1110, www.arkrestaurants.com/clydes.html
Area: 930 m². Client: ARK Restaurants. Cost: not disclosed

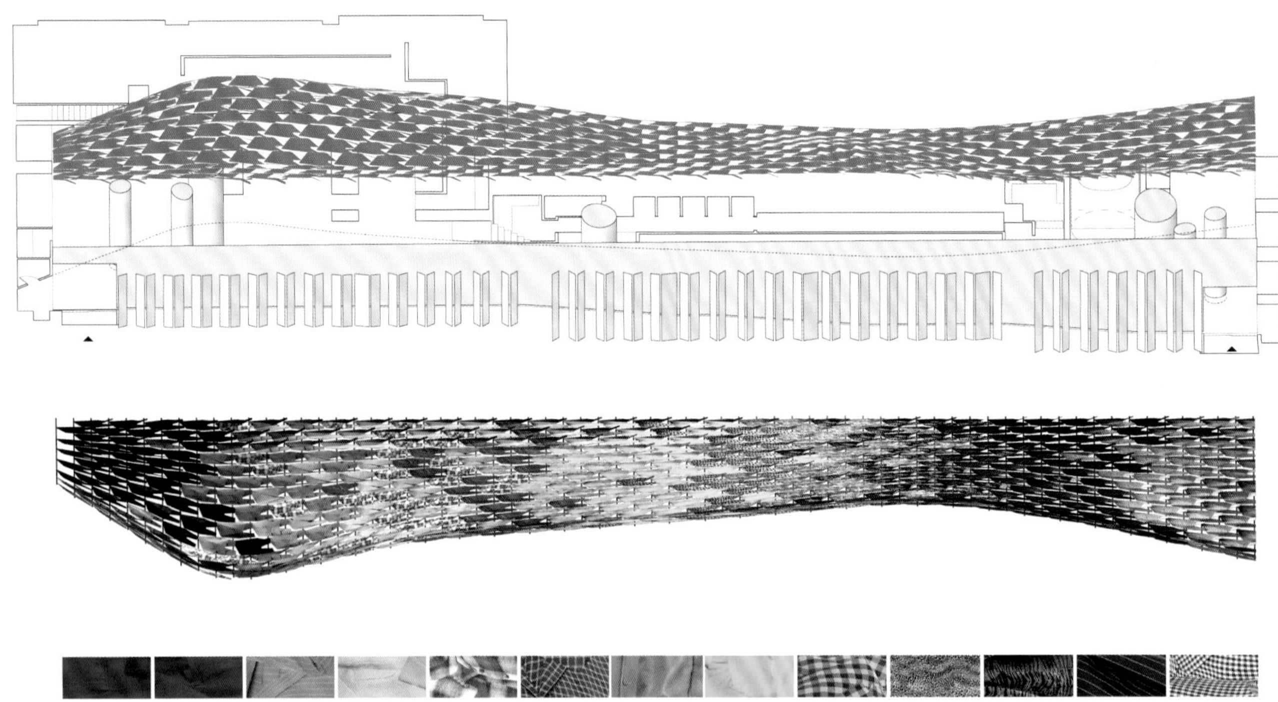

Drawings (above) show the continuous way the architects imagined the interior of the space. As the image to the right shows, the approach is cinematographic, or, in any case, oriented to movement.

Zeichnungen (oben) illustrieren das fließende Kontinuum, als das die Architekten den Raum entwickeln. Die Ansicht rechts illustriert ihren kinematografischen Ansatz, der deutlich als dynamische Bewegung konzipiert ist.

Les dessins ci-dessus montrent comment les architectes ont imaginé l'espace intérieur de façon continue. Page de droite, on voit sur la photo leur approche cinématographique, ou du moins orientée vers le mouvement.

This restaurant is owned by the former basketball star Walt "Clyde" Frazier. The main room of the facility runs over 55 meters between 37th and 38th Streets along 10th Avenue. The restaurant is located on the downtown side, and there is a bar in the middle and a lounge at the uptown end of the interior. Photos of the star's basketball days are used in the décor and his well-known style of dress was also a source of inspiration. Frazier's wardrobe also inspired the 52-meter-long aluminum fin design that hovers over most of the establishment. Polished dark concrete floors and resin countertops for the bar and open kitchen contrast by their sobriety with the more colorful elements of the décor. A space next to the lounge where patrons can take a shot at a basketball hoop is also part of the scheme. Considering that the early reputation of Morphosis was in part made through such eateries as the Kate Mantilini Restaurant in Beverly Hills (1986), it would seem that Thom Mayne and his team still take pleasure from a project that is considerably smaller than most of their other work.

Inhaber des Restaurants ist der ehemalige Basketballstar Walt „Clyde" Frazier. Das Restaurant erstreckt sich über 55 m Länge zwischen der 37th und 38th Street entlang der 10th Avenue. Der Gastraum liegt an der nach Downtown orientierten Seite, im mittleren Abschnitt ist die Bar untergebracht, am entgegengesetzten Ende liegt eine Lounge. Fotos aus der erfolgreichen Vergangenheit des Basketballstars und sein exzentrischer Kleidungsstil inspirierten die Inneneinrichtung – Letzterer vor allem die 52 m lange, lamellenartige Aluminiumkonstruktion, die über einem Großteil des Innenraums schwebt. Die polierten dunklen Betonböden, Harzplatten für die Tresen und eine offene Küche kontrastieren in ihrer Nüchternheit mit dem ansonsten farbintensiven Interieur. In einem Raum neben der Lounge haben Gäste die Möglichkeit, ein paar Körbe zu werfen. Morphosis hat sich nicht zuletzt einen Namen mit Lokalen wie dem Kate Mantilini Restaurant in Beverly Hills (1986) gemacht. Es scheint also, als hätten Thom Mayne und sein Team immer noch Spaß an Projekten wie diesen, die wesentlich kleiner ausfallen als die meisten ihrer Aufträge.

Ce restaurant appartient à l'ancienne star de basketball Walt « Clyde » Frazier. La salle principale court sur 55 m entre la 37e Rue et la 38e Rue, le long de la Dixième Avenue. La partie restaurant est située côté *downtown* et il y a un bar au milieu et un *lounge* à une extrémité côté *uptown*. On a utilisé pour le décor, également inspiré de son fameux style vestimentaire, des photos du temps où la star jouait au basket. La garde-robe de Frazier a aussi influencé le long empennage d'aluminium qui survole presque tout l'établissement sur 52 m. Les sols sombres en béton ciré et les plans de travail en résine pour le bar et la cuisine ouverte contrastent par leur sobriété avec les éléments plus colorés du décor. Un espace proche du *lounge* où les clients peuvent s'essayer à mettre des paniers rajoute encore à l'ensemble. Morphosis s'est en partie taillé sa réputation avec des restaurants comme le Kate Mantilini à Beverly Hills (1986), et il semble que Thom Mayne et son équipe tirent encore du plaisir d'un projet beaucoup plus modeste que la plupart de leurs réalisations.

NEW YORK

Images from the basketball career of Clyde Frazier cover the walls, while the much more abstract ceiling sculpture lends a note of color.

Bilder von der Profilaufbahn des Basketballers Clyde Frazier ziehen sich über die Wände. Die im Vergleich dazu abstraktere Deckenskulptur sorgt für Farbakzente.

Des photos de la carrière de joueur de basket-ball de Clyde Frazier couvrent les murs tandis que le plafond sculptural, beaucoup plus abstrait, ajoute une note de couleur.

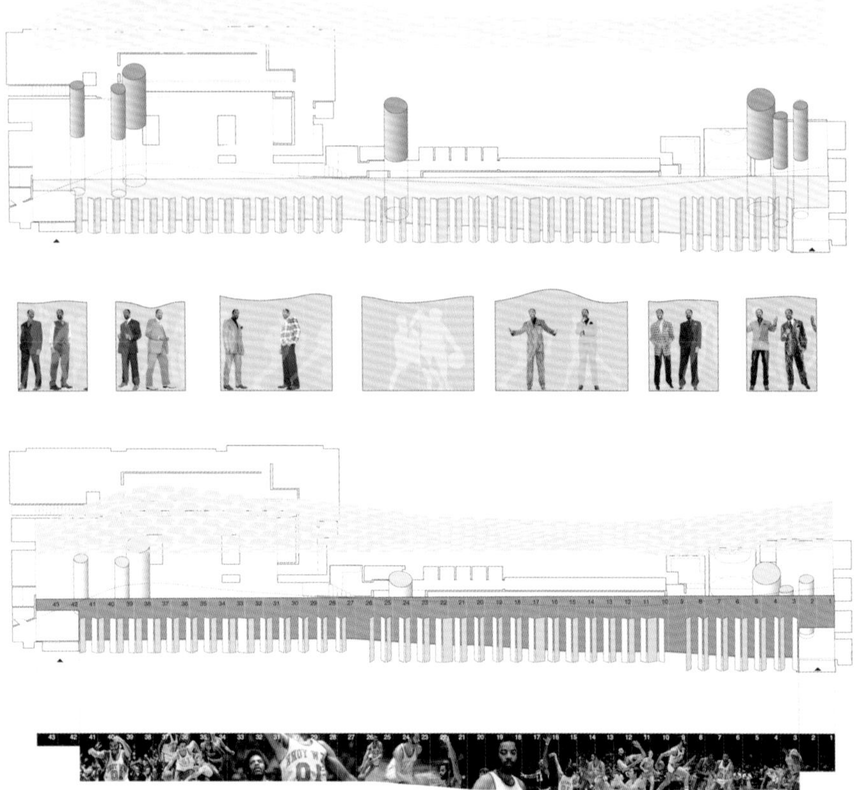

While ceilings are usually relatively "dead" space, in this instance, the upper area is brought to life with the unusual hanging forms of the ceiling design. Left, drawings of the installation, again showing its full length.

Decken sind oft ein relativ „toter" Raum, hier wurde diese Zone jedoch durch ungewöhnliche Hängeobjekte gestaltet und zum Leben erweckt. Links eine Zeichnung der Installation, auch hier in voller Länge zu sehen.

Si les plafonds sont souvent des espaces « morts », ici, leurs formes de design inhabituelles animent l'espace supérieur. Ci-contre, des dessins de l'installation montrant toute sa longueur.

The celebrity of the owner is the starting point for the design, but the end result is an agreeable dining space, as seen in the image above.

Der Prominentenstatus des Inhabers war zwar Ausgangspunkt für den Entwurf, das Resultat jedoch ist ein einladender Gastraum, wie oben zu sehen.

Si la célébrité du propriétaire est le point de départ du design, le résultat final est un espace de restauration agréable, comme on le voit ci-dessus.

TATZU NISHI

Tatzu Nishi
ARATANIURANO
3-1-15-2F, Shirokane
Minato-ku
Tokyo 108-0072
Japan

Tel: +81 3 5422 8320
Fax: +81 3 3444 1224
E-mail: info@arataniurano.com
Web: www.arataniurano.com

TATZU NISHI is an artist who also goes by the names Tazu Rous, Tatzu Oozu, Tatsurou Bashi, and Tazro Niscino. He was born in Nagoya, Japan, in 1960. He studied at the Musashino Art University (Tokyo, 1981–84) and the Kunstakademie Münster (Germany, 1989–97). He currently lives and works in Berlin and Tokyo. His work includes the installations "Hotel Continental" (Aachen, Germany, 2002); "Villa Victoria" (Liverpool, UK, 2002); "Engel" (Basel, Switzerland, 2004); "Café in the Sky—Moon Rider" (Dublin, Ireland, 2005); "Kariforunia," the Museum of Contemporary Art (Los Angeles, USA, 2006); "Chéri in the Sky," Maison Hermès (Tokyo, Japan, 2006); "Sometimes Extraordinary, Sometimes Less Than Common," Aichi Prefectural Museum of Art (Nagoya, Japan, 2009); "Villa Cheminée" (Cordemais, France, 2011); the Merlion Hotel (Singapore, 2012); Hotel Gent (Ghent, Belgium, 2012); and "Discovering Columbus" (New York, New York, USA, 2012, published here).

TAZU NISHI ist Künstler und arbeitet auch unter den Namen Tazu Rous, Tatzu Oozu, Tatsurou Bashi und Tazro Niscino. Er wurde 1960 in Nagoya, Japan, geboren. Nishi studierte an der Musashino Kunsthochschule (Tokio, 1981–84) und der Kunstakademie in Münster (1989–97). Zurzeit lebt und arbeitet er in Berlin und Tokio. Zu seinen Arbeiten zählen die Installationen „Hotel Continental" (Aachen, 2002), „Villa Victoria" (Liverpool, 2002), „Engel" (Basel, 2004), „Café in the Sky – Moon Rider" (Dublin, 2005), „Kariforunia" am Museum of Contemporary Art (Los Angeles, 2006), „Chéri in the Sky" im Maison Hermès (Tokio, 2006), „Sometimes Extraordinary, Sometimes Less Than Common" im Museum für Kunst der Präfektur Aichi (Nagoya, 2009), „Villa Cheminée" (Cordemais, Frankeich, 2011) sowie das Merlion Hotel (Singapur, 2012), das Hotel Gent (Gent, Belgien, 2012) sowie „Discovering Columbus" (New York, 2012, hier vorgestellt).

L'artiste **TATZU NISHI** se fait également appeler Tazu Rous, Tatzu Oozu, Tatsurou Bashi ou Tazro Niscino. Né à Nagoya, au Japon, en 1960, il fait ses études à l'Université d'art de Musashino (Tokyo, 1981–84) et à l'Académie des beaux-arts de Münster (Allemagne, 1989–97). Il vit et travaille entre Berlin et Tokyo. Parmi ses réalisations, on trouve *Hotel Continental* (Aix-la-Chapelle, Allemagne, 2002) ; *Villa Victoria* (Liverpool, 2002) ; *Engel* (Bâle, 2004) ; *Café in the Sky – Moon Rider* (Dublin, 2005) ; *Kariforunia* au Musée d'art contemporain (Los Angeles, 2006) ; *Chéri in the Sky* à la Maison Hermès (Tokyo, 2006) ; *Sometimes Extraordinary, Sometimes Less Than Common* au Musée préfectoral d'art d'Aichi (Nagoya, Japon, 2009) ; *Villa Cheminée* (Cordemais, France, 2011) ; l'hôtel Merlion (Singapour, 2012) ; l'hôtel Gent (Gand, Belgique, 2012) et *Discovering Columbus* (New York, 2012, présenté ici).

ONE WAY
Tatzu Nishi
DISCOVERING
COLUMBUS

"DISCOVERING COLUMBUS"

New York, New York, USA, 2012

Address: not applicable. Area: 12 m² (hallway); 75 m² (living room)
Client: Public Art Fund. Cost: not disclosed
Collaboration: Amiko Takimoto, Gerner Kronick + Valcarcel PC

Those familiar with Manhattan have surely noticed the statue of Christopher Columbus that stands on a 23-meter-high column at Columbus Circle. Tatzu Nishi, faithful to other installations that have involved a similar approach to spaces that normally cannot be acceded to, has actually built a domestic environment around the sculpture. "I am constructing a living room around it—as if to envelop this statue that has for years watched over New York as its immigrants came in—and it will be open to the public. The object, which passersby could previously only see from the sidewalk, will now occupy this room like a familiar sculpture, bringing viewers face to face with it at eye level for the first time in the plaza's over 100-year-long history." Visitors were invited to climb stairs attached to scaffolding, to pass through a long narrow hallway and to enter the "living room." The artist explains: "The interior design is similar to apartments commonly seen in the neighborhood with the exceptions of the presence of an unnaturally large sculpture and the original wallpaper, which is based on my drawings that take American culture and history as their inspiration. The building design and interior only need to serve the minimal function of enabling the contradictory concept of a public sculpture that occupies an indoor 'private' space."

Wer New York kennt, kennt sicher die Statue von Christoph Kolumbus, die auf einer 23 m hohen Säule über dem Columbus Circle steht. Tazu Nishi, der bereits mehrere Installationen schuf, die Räume und Orte thematisieren, die üblicherweise unzugänglich sind, hat einen fiktiven Wohnraum um diese Skulptur herum errichtet. „Ich baue ein Wohnzimmer um die Skulptur herum, um sie gewissermaßen zu verhüllen, nachdem sie jahrelang, während immer neue Einwanderer den Weg in die Stadt finden, über New York gewacht hat, und öffne dieses Wohnzimmer der Öffentlichkeit. Bisher konnten Passanten die Skulptur nur vom Gehweg aus sehen. Jetzt dominiert sie als etwas sehr Vertrautes den Raum, und zum ersten Mal in der über 100-jährigen Geschichte des Columbus Circle können Besucher ihr geradewegs in die Augen sehen." Besucher konnten über eine Treppe das Gerüst hinaufsteigen und über einen schmalen Gang das Zimmer betreten. Der Künstler hierzu: „Abgesehen von der überdimensionalen Skulptur und der originellen Tapete mit von mir gezeichneten Motiven aus der US-amerikanischen Kultur und Geschichte, ist die Inneneinrichtung konventionell. Architektur und Inneneinrichtung erfüllen lediglich die Funktion, den Widerspruch zu illustrieren, der darin liegt, einer Skulptur des öffentlichen Raums in einem ‚privaten' Wohnraum zu begegnen."

Ceux qui connaissent Manhattan auront sûrement remarqué la statue de Christophe Colomb qui s'élève sur une colonne de 23 m de haut à Columbus Circle. Tatzu Nishi, fidèle à d'autres installations impliquant une approche similaire aux espaces habituellement inaccessibles, a construit un environnement domestique autour de la sculpture. « Je construis un salon tout autour, comme pour envelopper cette statue qui a surveillé New York à l'arrivée des immigrants pendant des années, et il sera ouvert au public. Cet objet, que les passants ne pouvaient voir que du trottoir, occupera maintenant cette pièce comme une sculpture familière, mettant les spectateurs au même niveau qu'elle pour la première fois depuis plus de cent ans que la place existe. » Les visiteurs étaient conviés à grimper les escaliers attachés à l'échafaudage, puis à traverser un long couloir étroit pour entrer dans le « salon ». Selon l'artiste, « le design intérieur est semblable aux appartements du voisinage à l'exception de la présence d'une énorme sculpture et du papier peint créé d'après mes dessins, qui s'inspirent de l'histoire et de la culture de l'Amérique. Le design du bâtiment et de l'intérieur ont pour fonction minimale d'exposer au grand jour le concept antinomique d'une sculpture publique occupant un espace intérieur "privé" ».

The artist has perched an intentionally very ordinary domestic space on the top of the column where this sculpture of Columbus is placed. Scale, function, and location are all questioned in an original way.

Der Künstler versetzt ganz bewusst einen konventionellen Wohnraum an die Spitze einer Säule, auf der die Kolumbusstatue steht. So hinterfragt er ironisch Maßstab, Funktion und Standort zugleich.

L'artiste a perché un espace domestique délibérément très banal au sommet de la colonne où est placée cette statue de Christophe Colomb. Il questionne ainsi échelle, fonction et emplacement de façon originale.

JO NOERO

Noero Architects
6 Pepper Street, 9b
Cape Town 8000
South Africa

Tel: +27 21 424 5508
Fax: +27 21 424 7122
E-mail: info@noeroarchitects.com
Web: www.noeroarchitects.com

JO NOERO received his B.Arch degree from the University of Natal (South Africa, 1978) and a Master of Philosophy in Architecture from the University of Newcastle-upon-Tyne (UK, 1980). He had his own firm, Jo Noero Architects, in Johannesburg from 1984 to 1999, before cofounding Noero Wolff Architects in Cape Town (1998–2012). His new firm, Noero Architects, was created in Cape Town in May 2012. Over the span of his career, Jo Noero has completed over 200 buildings that range in scale and complexity from individual houses to large museums and other institutional buildings, such as law courts and schools. Jo Noero was awarded the Gold Medal for Architecture from the Institute of South African Architects in 2010. He was Director of the School of Architecture and Planning, University of Cape Town, South Africa, from 2000 to 2005, and has been a Professor of Architecture in the same institution since 2000. His work includes the Red Location Museum (Port Elizabeth, South Africa, 2006) and Phase Two of the Red Location Precinct (New Brighton, Port Elizabeth, South Africa, 2009–11, published here).

JO NOERO absovierte einen B. Arch. an der University of Natal (Südafrika, 1978) und einen Master in Architekturphilosophie an der Universität im britischen Newcastle-upon-Tyne (1980). Bevor er Noero Wolff Architects in Kapstadt mitbegründete (1998), hatte er von 1984 bis 1999 in Johannesburg ein eigenes Büro (Jo Noero Architects). Seine aktuelle Firma, Noero Architects, praktiziert seit Mai 2012 in Kapstadt. Noero entwarf im Verlauf seiner Karriere bislang über 200 Gebäude, von kleineren Wohnhäusern bis hin zu großen Museen und Institutionen wie Gerichts- und Schulgebäuden. 2010 wurde er vom Institute of South African Architects mit der Goldmedaille für Architektur geehrt. Noero war von 2000 bis 2005 Direktor der Fakultät für Architektur und Stadtplanung an der University of Cape Town, wo er seit 2000 Professor ist. Zu seinen Arbeiten gehören u. a. das Red Location Museum (Port Elizabeth, Südafrika, 2006) und die zweite Phase des Red Location Precinct (New Brighton, Port Elizabeth, South Africa, 2009–11, hier vorgestellt).

JO NOERO obtient son diplôme B.Arch de l'université de Natal (Afrique du Sud, 1978) et une maîtrise en philosophie de l'architecture de l'université de Newcastle-upon-Tyne (GB, 1980). Il possède sa propre agence, Jo Noero Architects, à Johannesburg, de 1984 à 1999, avant de participer à la fondation de Noero Wolff Architects au Cap (1998–2012). Il crée sa nouvelle agence, Noero Architects, au Cap en mai 2012. Au cours de sa carrière, Jo Noero a réalisé plus de 200 bâtiments variant en complexité, allant de maisons individuelles à de grands musées en passant par d'autres bâtiments institutionnels tels que des palais de justice ou des écoles. Jo Noero reçoit la médaille d'or de l'architecture de l'Institute of South African Architects en 2010. Il est directeur de l'École d'architecture et d'urbanisme de l'université du Cap de 2000 à 2005, et il enseigne l'architecture dans cette même institution depuis 2000. Il a réalisé entre autres le musée Red Location (Port Elizabeth, Afrique du Sud, 2006) et la Phase 2 de Red Location Precinct (New Brighton, Port Elizabeth, Afrique du Sud, 2009–11, présenté ici).

RED LOCATION

New Brighton, Port Elizabeth, South Africa, 2009–11

Address: Olof Palme Avenue, New Brighton, Port Elizabeth, South Africa
Area: 950 m² (library), 650 m² (art gallery). Client: Nelson Mandela Bay Municipality
Cost: €2.5 million. Collaboration: Robert McGiven, Stanley Ngarandi, Korine Stegman

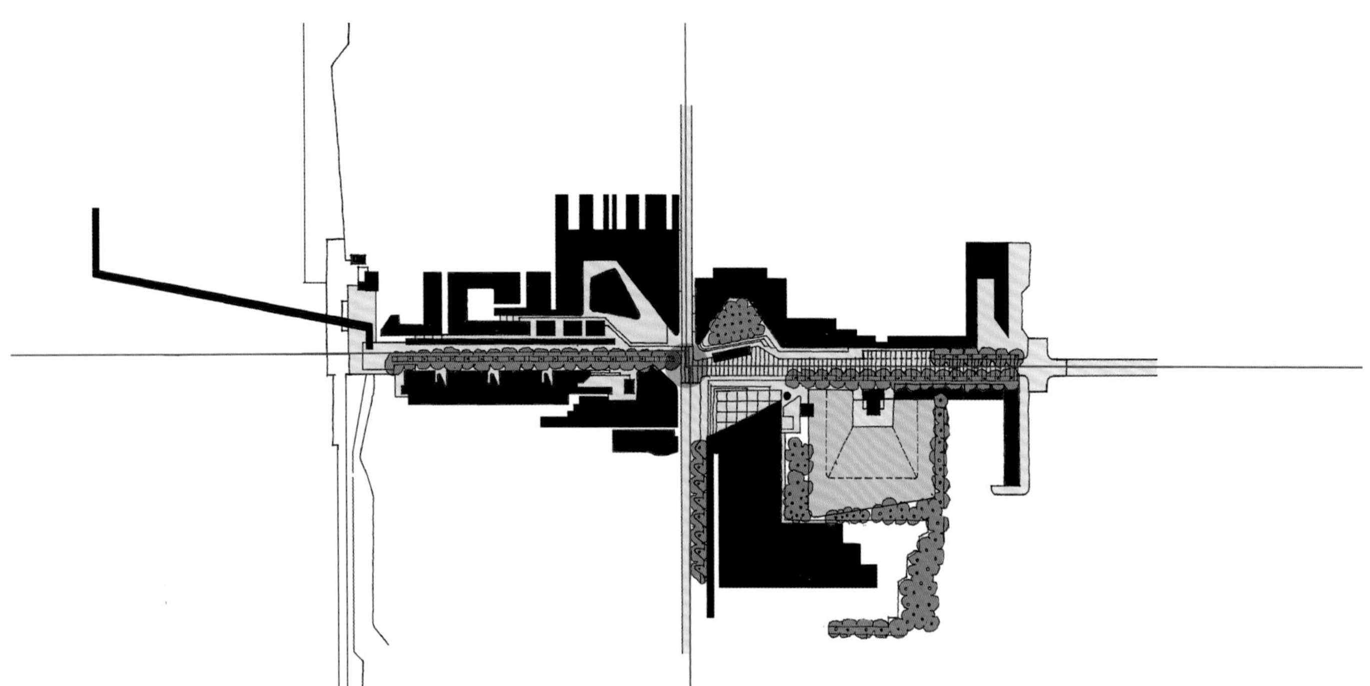

The **RED LOCATION**, which was an area of struggle during the apartheid period, is one of the oldest black townships of Port Elizabeth. Its name is related to the rusted corrugated-iron barrack buildings that date from the turn of the 20th century. The Red Location Museum, by Noero Wolff Architects, won the RIBA Lubetkin Prize in 2006. Phase two of the Red Location Precinct project includes an art gallery, library, and archive. The art gallery will show a collection of Eastern Cape struggle art, which will be shared with the Nelson Mandela Art Gallery. An original 1902 corrugated-iron bungalow is located in the entrance courtyard of the gallery. The library includes a digital library and Internet café computer school. A sawtooth roof admits south light and is modulated to exclude any direct light. The floor of the library is landscaped to create a series of rooms within rooms. The archive is attached to the library and will house the archives of the main city library, as well as the library's collection of struggle literature. The two-story archive library was designed, according to the architect, as "a timber boxlike form that lies parallel to the adjoining road. The idea is that the building will evoke memories and associations with the ark, timber caskets, and treasure chests. The external treatment of the buildings seeks to emphasize these connections."

RED LOCATION ist eines der ältesten Townships in Port Elizabeth und spielte während der Apartheid eine aktive Rolle im Widerstand. Seinen Namen verdankt es den rostroten Wellblechhütten aus der Wendezeit zum 20. Jahrhundert. Das Red Location Museum von Noero Wolff Architects wurde 2006 mit dem RIBA-Lubetkin-Preis ausgezeichnet. Der zweite Bauabschnitt des Red-Location-Precinct-Projekts umfasst eine Galerie, eine Bibliothek und ein Archiv. Die Galerie wird eine mit der Nelson Mandela Art Gallery geteilte Sammlung von Kunst aus der östlichen Kapprovinz zeigen, die den Kampf gegen die Apartheid thematisiert. Auf dem Vorplatz der Galerie steht eine historische Wellblechhütte von 1902. Die Bibliothek verfügt über digitale Medien, ein Internetcafé und eine Computerschule. Ein nach Süden orientiertes Sheddach sorgt für Licht, verhindert jedoch direkte Sonneneinstrahlung. Der Boden der Bibliothek ist so gestaltet, dass Räume in Räumen entstehen. Ein angegliedertes Archiv bietet Platz für die Bestände der zentralen Stadtbibliothek und eine Sammlung von Widerstandsliteratur. Das zweigeschossige Archiv erinnert laut Architekt an eine „parallel zur Straße platzierte Holzbox und weckt Assoziationen an eine Arche, ein Holzkästchen oder eine Schatztruhe. Die äußere Gestaltung der Bauten soll diese Assoziationen gezielt unterstreichen."

RED LOCATION, qui était un quartier de luttes pendant l'apartheid, est l'un des plus vieux townships noirs de Port Elizabeth. Il tire son nom du ton rouille des baraquements en tôle ondulée datant du début du XXe siècle. Le musée Red Location, de Noero Wolff Architects, a gagné le prix du RIBA Lubetkin en 2006. La Phase 2 du projet Red Location Precinct comprend une galerie d'art, une bibliothèque et des archives. La galerie exposera une collection de *struggle art* du Cap-Oriental, partagée avec la galerie Nelson Mendela. Un cabanon en tôle ondulée datant de 1902 est installé dans la cour d'entrée de la galerie. La bibliothèque comprend une bibliothèque numérique, un café internet et une école d'informatique. Une toiture en dents de scie laisse passer une lumière naturelle indirecte venant du sud. Le niveau de la bibliothèque est conçu de façon à créer une série de pièces les unes à l'intérieur des autres. Les archives, reliées à la bibliothèque, abriteront celles de la bibliothèque municipale ainsi que la collection d'ouvrages traitant de la lutte. Les deux étages des archives ont été conçus, selon l'architecte, comme « une boîte en bois parallèle à la route contiguë. Le bâtiment devrait ainsi provoquer les souvenirs en faisant penser à l'arche, aux cercueils de bois et aux coffres au trésor. Le traitement de l'extérieur des bâtiments tend à souligner ces connexions ».

Left, a plan of the entire complex. Below, an aerial image and a ground-level shot show the library and art gallery. Above, the entrance courtyard of the gallery with the original 1902 corrugated-iron bungalow.

Links ein Lageplan des Projekts. Luft- und ebenerdige Aufnahmen der Bibliothek und der Galerie (unten). Oben der Eingangsbereich der Galerie mit der originalen Wellblechhütte von 1902.

Page de gauche, un plan du complexe dans son ensemble. Ci-dessous, une photo aérienne et une prise de vue au sol montrent la bibliothèque et la galerie d'art. La cour d'entrée de la galerie (ci-dessus) avec le cabanon en tôle ondulée d'origine de 1902.

Right, Red Location art gallery floor plan (above) and the plan of the library (below). The two images at the bottom of the page are interior photos of the library.

Rechts ein Grundriss der Galerie von Red Location (oben) und ein Grundriss der Bibliothek (unten). Unten zwei Innenansichten der Bibliothek.

Ci-contre, le plan de la galerie d'art de Red Location (en haut) et le plan de la bibliothèque (en bas). Les deux photos en bas de page montrent l'intérieur de la bibliothèque.

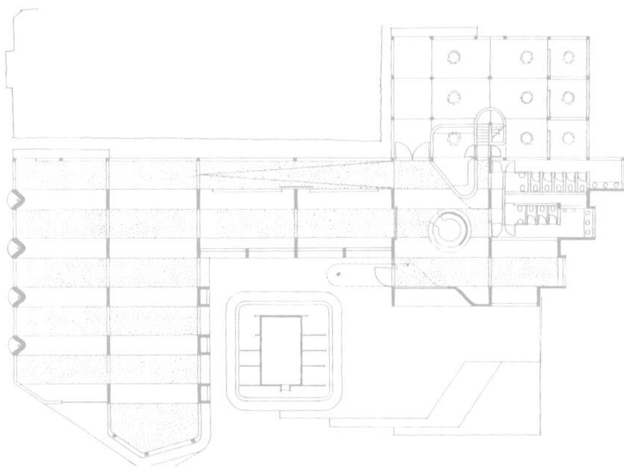

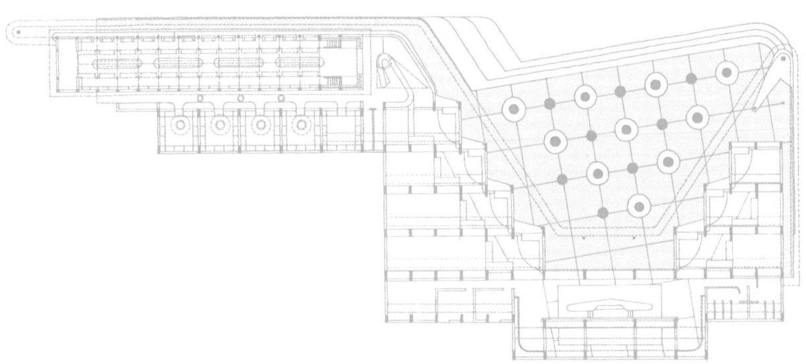

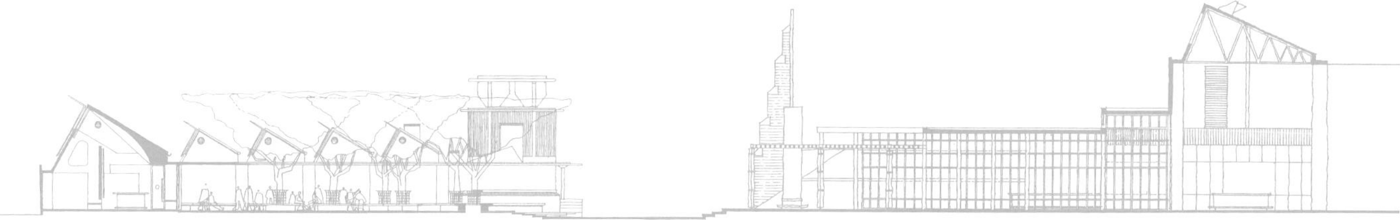

Above, Red Location section through library and museum across the roadway, looking west. Also on this page, two interior views of the library.

Querschnitte durch Bibliothek und Museum mit einer zwischen den Bauten verlaufenden Straße (oben). Außerdem zwei Innenansichten der Bibliothek.

Ci-dessus, un plan de coupe de Red Location représentant la bibliothèque et le musée de l'autre côté de la chaussée, vers l'ouest. Également sur cette page, deux vues intérieures de la bibliothèque.

JEAN NOUVEL

Ateliers Jean Nouvel
10 Cité d'Angoulême
75011 Paris
France

Tel: +33 1 49 23 83 83 / Fax: +33 1 43 14 81 10
E-mail: info@jeannouvel.fr / Web: www.jeannouvel.com

JEAN NOUVEL was born in 1945 in Fumel, France. He studied in Bordeaux and then at the École des Beaux-Arts (Paris, 1964–72). From 1967 to 1970, he was an assistant of the noted architects Claude Parent and Paul Virilio. He created his first office with François Seigneur in Paris in 1970. Jean Nouvel received the RIBA Gold Medal in 2001 and the Pritzker Prize in 2008. His first widely noted project was the Institut du Monde Arabe (Paris, France, 1981–87, with Architecture Studio) and the Fondation Cartier (Paris, France, 1991–94) made him one of the most noted French architects. Major projects since 2000 are the Music and Conference Center (Lucerne, Switzerland, 1998–2000); the Agbar Tower (Barcelona, Spain, 2001–03); an extension of the Reina Sofia Museum (Madrid, Spain, 1999–2005); the Quai Branly Museum (Paris, France, 2001–06); an apartment building in SoHo (New York, New York, USA, 2006); the Guthrie Theater (Minneapolis, Minnesota, USA, 2006); the Danish Radio Concert House (Copenhagen, Denmark, 2003–09); an office tower in Doha (Qatar, 2010); two apartment buildings in Ibiza (Spain, 2006–11); the City Hall in Montpellier (France, 2008–11); Jane's Carousel, Brooklyn Bridge Park (Brooklyn, New York, USA, 2011, published here); and a hotel in Barcelona (Spain, 2011). Current work includes the new Philharmonic Hall in Paris (France, 2012); the Louvre Abu Dhabi (UAE, 2009–13); the Tour de Verre in New York (New York, USA); and the National Museum of Qatar (Doha, Qatar, 2015). Jean Nouvel is the architect-manager of all the projects for the Ile Seguin in Boulogne-Billancourt (Paris, France, 2012–23).

JEAN NOUVEL, geboren 1945 in Fumel, Frankreich, studierte zunächst in Bordeaux und schließlich an der Pariser École des Beaux-Arts (1964–72). Von 1967 bis 1970 war er Assistent bei den renommierten Architekten Claude Parent und Paul Virilio. 1970 gründete er mit François Seigneur sein erstes Büro in Paris. Jean Nouvel wurde 2001 mit der RIBA-Goldmedaille und 2008 mit dem Pritzker-Preis ausgezeichnet. Sein erstes weithin bekannt gewordenes Projekt ist das Institut du Monde Arabe (mit Architecture Studio, Paris, 1981–87). Die Fondation Cartier (Paris, 1991–94) machte ihn zu einem der bekanntesten Architekten Frankreichs. Seine bedeutendsten Projekte seit 2000 sind das Kultur- und Kongresszentrum Luzern (1998–2000), der Agbar-Turm (Barcelona, 2001–03), die Erweiterung des Museums Reina Sofia (Madrid, 1999–2005), das Museum am Quai Branly (Paris, 2001–06), ein Apartmenthaus in SoHo (New York, 2006), das Guthrie-Theater (Minneapolis, 2006), das Konzerthaus für den dänischen Rundfunk (Kopenhagen, 2003–09), ein Bürohochhaus in Doha (Katar, 2010), zwei Apartmenthäuser auf Ibiza (2006–11), das Rathaus in Montpellier (2008–11), Jane's Carousel im Brooklyn Bridge Park (Brooklyn, New York, 2011, hier vorgestellt) und ein Hotel in Barcelona (2011). Laufende Projekte sind u. a. die neue Philharmonie in Paris (2012), der Louvre Abu Dhabi (VAE, 2009–13), der Tour de Verre in New York und das Nationalmuseum von Katar (Doha, Katar, 2015). Jean Nouvel ist leitender Architekt sämtlicher Bauvorhaben auf der Ile Seguin in Boulogne-Billancourt (Paris, 2012–23).

JEAN NOUVEL est né en 1945 à Fumel, en France. Il fait ses études à Bordeaux puis à l'École des beaux-arts de Paris (1964–72). De 1967 à 1970, il est assistant des célèbres architectes Claude Parent et Paul Virilio. Il crée sa première agence avec François Seigneur à Paris en 1970. Jean Nouvel reçoit la médaille d'or du RIBA en 2001 et le prix Pritzker en 2008. Le projet qui le propulse sur la scène internationale est l'Institut du monde arabe (Paris, 1981–87, avec Architecture Studio), et la Fondation Cartier (Paris, 1991–94) fait de lui un des architectes français les plus célèbres. Ses principaux projets depuis 2000 sont le Palais de la culture et des congrès de Lucerne (Suisse, 1998–2000) ; la tour Agbar (Barcelone, 2001–03) ; une extension du musée Reina Sofia (Madrid, 1999–2005) ; le musée du Quai Branly (Paris, 2001–06) ; un immeuble d'habitation de SoHo (New York, 2006) ; le Guthrie Theater (Minneapolis, 2006) ; la salle de concert de la Radio danoise (Copenhague, 2003–09) ; une tour de bureaux à Doha (Qatar, 2010) ; deux immeubles d'habitation à Ibiza (2006–11) ; l'hôtel de ville de Montpellier (2008–11) ; le manège Jane's Carousel au Brooklyn Bridge Park (Brooklyn, 2011, présenté ici) et un hôtel à Barcelone (2011). Parmi ses projets en cours, on trouve la nouvelle Philharmonie de Paris (2012) ; le Louvre d'Abou Dhabi (EAU, 2009–13) ; la Tour de verre à New York et le Musée national du Qatar (Doha, Qatar, 2015). Jean Nouvel est l'architecte-maître d'œuvre de tous les projets de l'île Seguin à Boulogne-Billancourt (Paris, 2012–23).

JANE'S CAROUSEL

Brooklyn Bridge Park, Brooklyn, New York, USA, 2011

Address: Brooklyn Bridge Park, DUMBO, between the Brooklyn and Manhattan Bridges on the East River (entrance at Dock Street or Main Street), Brooklyn, NY 11201, USA, +1 718 222 2502
www.janescarousel.com / www.brooklynbridgepark.org/events/recreation/janes-carousel
Area: 450 m². Client: Jane and David Walentas. Cost: not disclosed. Collaboration: Beyer Blinder Belle Architects, Tim Dumbleton Architect (Associate Architects)

Seen here with the Manhattan Bridge in the background, Jane's Carousel is a most unusual project for Jean Nouvel, a sort of jewel case for a 1922 merry-go-round.

Jane's Carousel, hier mit der Manhattan Bridge im Hintergrund, ist ein für Jean Nouvel sehr ungewöhnliches Projekt, eine Art Schmuckkästchen für ein Karussell von 1922.

Vu ici avec le pont de Manhattan en arrière-plan, le Jane's Carousel, sorte d'écrin pour un manège de 1922, est un projet très inhabituel pour Jean Nouvel.

Built in 1922 in Ohio, **JANE'S CAROUSEL** has been placed in Brooklyn Bridge Park, opposite Manhattan. Jean Nouvel designed a pavilion intended to serve as a protective structure for the carousel. The structure is square (23 x 23 m) and the carousel (diameter 15 m) is placed in its center. The pavilion is 8.2 meters high with a 6.1-meter interior ceiling height. Four cylindrical steel columns set back from the façades and tied together by four steel beams located above the ceiling form the essential structure of the pavilion. Eleven-centimeter-thick acrylic panels form the four façades of the structure—transparent on the east and west sides, and fully operable on the south and north elevations. A glass skylight is located on the roof. The interior of the structure has a polished gray concrete floor. Large recessed screens are lowered at night for a light show featuring shadows of the carousel horses.

JANE'S CAROUSEL, ein 1922 in Ohio gebautes historisches Karussell, steht im Brooklyn Bridge Park mit Blick auf Manhattan. Der von Jean Nouvel entworfene Pavillon wurde als schützende Hülle konzipiert. Im Zentrum des Pavillons (Grundfläche 23 x 23 m) steht das Karussell (Durchmesser 15 m). Der Pavillon ist 8,2 m hoch, die lichte Höhe im Inneren beträgt 6,1 m. Die Konstruktion besteht im Wesentlichen aus vier zurückgesetzten Stahlsäulen, verbunden durch vier Stahlträger in der Decke. Die Fassade des Pavillons besteht aus transparenten, 11 cm starken Acrylpaneelen, die auf Nord- und Südseite vollständig geöffnet werden können. In das Dach des Pavillons ist ein großes Oberlicht integriert, der Fußboden des Innenraums wurde in poliertem grauem Beton realisiert. Nachts werden im Pavillon Wandschirme herabgelassen, auf denen sich durch Hinterleuchtung das Schattenspiel der Karussellpferde abzeichnet.

Construit en 1922 dans l'Ohio, le manège **JANE'S CAROUSEL** a été placé dans le Brooklyn Bridge Park, en face de Manhattan. Jean Nouvel a dessiné un pavillon carré (23 x 23 m) destiné à protéger le manège de 15 m de diamètre placé en son centre. Le pavillon de 8,20 m de haut a une hauteur sous plafond de 6,10 m. Quatre colonnes cylindriques de métal, en retrait des façades et reliées par quatre poutres métalliques situées au-dessus du plafond, forment la structure principale du pavillon. Des panneaux acryliques de 11 cm d'épaisseur forment les quatre façades de la structure – transparents sur les côtés est et ouest, et totalement ouvrables sur les côtés sud et nord. Le toit possède une grande verrière. Le sol intérieur est de béton gris ciré. De grands rideaux se baissent le soir pour permettre des éclairages mettant en valeur les silhouettes des chevaux du manège.

The structure takes the very simple and classical form of a circle inscribed in a square, with four main supporting columns, and folding glass walls.

Der Bau ist formal ausgesprochen schlicht: ein Kreis, eingeschrieben in ein Quadrat. Die Konstruktion ruht auf vier Säulen und hat faltbare Glasfassaden.

La structure prend la forme très simple et classique d'un cercle dans un carré, avec quatre colonnes de soutien et des murs de verre en accordéon.

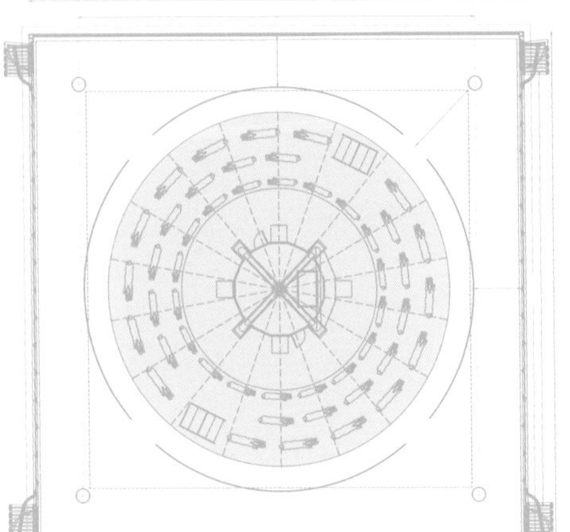

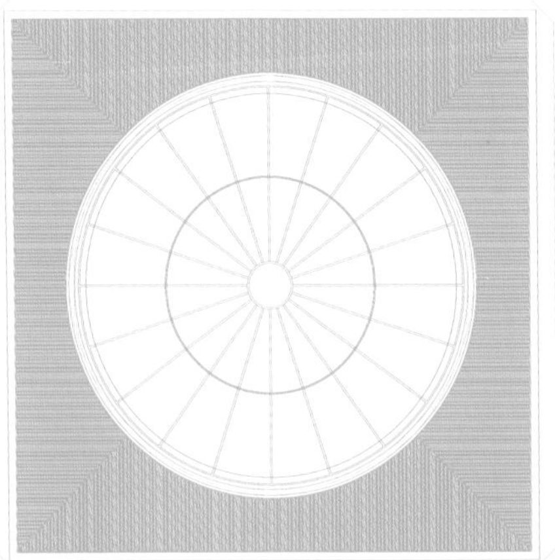

Left, plans of the ground and roof levels. Above, the carousel is lit from within and the walls of the building show its forms.

Grundriss und Deckenebene (links). Auf den Wänden des von innen beleuchteten Baus zeichnet sich das Schattenspiel des Karussells ab (oben).

Ci-contre, des plans du rez-de-chaussée et du toit. Ci-dessus, le manège est éclairé de l'intérieur et ses formes se projettent sur les murs en ombres chinoises.

Right, an elevation drawing of the closed building (below) and a section showing the structural elements of the pavilion and the carousel itself. Below, open walls with the Brooklyn Bridge just behind.

Rechts ein Aufriss mit geschlossener Fassade (unten) und ein Querschnitt des Tragwerks des Pavillons und des Karussells. Unten der Bau mit geöffneter Fassade, im Hintergrund die Brooklyn Bridge.

Ci-contre, une élévation du bâtiment fermé (en bas) et une coupe montrant les éléments structurels du pavillon et du manège. Ci-dessous, les murs ouverts avec, juste à l'arrière-plan, le pont de Brooklyn.

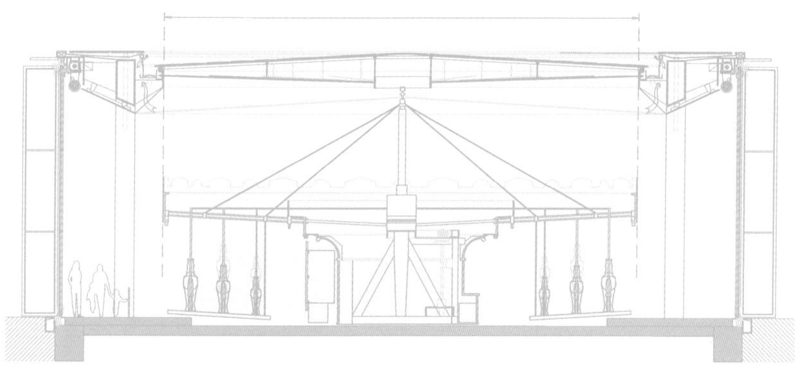

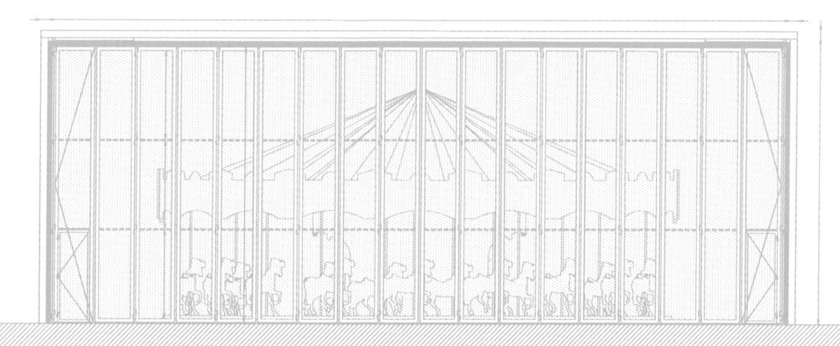

O STUDIO

O Studio Architects
Unit 209, 2/F, Block B, Sea View Estate
2–8 Watson Road
North Point, Hong Kong
China

Tel: +852 2882 2508
Fax: +852 3996 8187
E-mail: office@ostudioarchitects.com
Web: www.ostudioarchitects.com

FAI AU was born in Guangzhou, China, in 1975. He is the founding Principal of O Studio Architects, created in 2009. He received his Master in Design Studies from Harvard GSD, and his B.Arch from the Royal Melbourne Institute of Technology. He worked as a senior designer at OMA in Rotterdam. He was also the founding Director of ADARC Associates Limited from 2005 to 2008. The work of O Studio includes the Fanling Classic Car Museum (Hong Kong, 2007); the Heineken Club (Guangzhou, 2009); Heineken Brewery (Guangzhou, 2009); Luofu Mountain Museum (Huizhou, 2009); Church of Seed (Huizhou, 2010–11, published here); and a short-listed project for the Xiqu Center (West Kowloon Cultural District, Hong Kong, with Foster + Partners, 2012), all in China.

FAI AU wurde 1975 in Guangzhou, China, geboren. Er ist Gründungsdirektor von O Studio Architects (seit 2009). Fai absolvierte seinen Master in Design an der Harvard GSD sowie einen B. Arch. am Royal Melbourne Institute of Technology. Er war als Senior Designer bei OMA in Rotterdam tätig und von 2005 bis 2008 Gründungsdirektor von ADARC Associates Limited. Zu den Projekten von O Studio zählen u. a. das Fanling-Oldtimermuseum (Hongkong, 2007), der Heineken Club (Guangzhou, 2009), die Heineken Brauerei (Guangzhou, 2009), das Luofu-Gebirgsmuseum (Huizhou, 2009), die Church of Seed (Huizhou, 2010–11, hier vorgestellt) und ein Wettbewerbsentwurf für das Xiqu-Zentrum in Kowloon, dem Kunst- und Kulturviertel von Hongkong (mit Foster + Partners, 2012), mit dem das Team in die engere Wahl gekommen ist; alle Projekte in China.

FAI AU est né à Canton, en Chine, en 1975. Il est le principal fondateur de O Studio Architects, créé en 2009. Il obtient un master en Design Studies de la Harvard GSD et un B.Arch de l'Institut royal de technologie de Melbourne. Il travaille ensuite comme concepteur principal à OMA à Rotterdam. Il est aussi directeur fondateur de ADARC Associates Limited, de 2005 à 2008. Les réalisations de O Studio comprennent le Fanling Classic Car Museum (Hong Kong, 2007) ; le club Heineken (Canton, 2009) ; la brasserie Heineken (Canton, 2009) ; le musée Luofu Mountain (Huizhou, 2009) ; l'église de la Graine (Huizhou, 2010–11, présentée ici) et un projet présélectionné pour le centre Xiqu (quartier culturel de West Kowloon, Hong Kong, avec Foster + Partners, 2012), tous en Chine.

CHURCH OF SEED

Huizhou, China, 2010–11

Address: Zhaidao Garden, Guoqian Village, Huizhou, China
Area: 220 m². Client: Mefull (Huizhou) Agricultural Co. Ltd. Cost: $200 000

Built on a 1200-square-meter site, the **CHURCH OF SEED** is located in the Luofu Mountain Scenic Area, one of the seven Taoist mountains in China. It can accommodate 60 worshippers. The enclosing wall adopts the form of a seed, and then splits into three parts. The wall that faces southeast has a cross-shaped opening that allows morning sun into the interior. The wall facing west is solid and blocks the afternoon sun. A stepped roof terrace brings northern light into the interior and allows for ceiling heights that rise from three to 12 meters. The main part of the structure is poured-in-place concrete made with bamboo formwork. Furniture was made by local farmers. The architect states: "This is not a piece of architecture which purely celebrates its sculptural form, but a building which respects the natural environment and local culture."

Die **CHURCH OF SEED** liegt auf einem 1200 m² großen Gelände in der Präfektur Huizhou, in der Landschaft um den Luofu, einem der sieben taoistischen Berge Chinas. Die Kirche bietet Raum für 60 Gottesdienstbesucher. Die Wände des Baus bilden die Form eines Samenkorns und brechen in drei Teile auf. In die Südostwand ist eine kreuzförmige Öffnung eingeschnitten, durch sie fällt morgens Licht in den Innenraum. Die Westwand hat keinerlei Fenster oder Öffnungen und schützt vor der Nachmittagssonne. Eine gestufte Dachterrasse lässt von Norden her Licht in den Bau und definiert stufenförmige Deckenhöhen von 3 bis 12 m. Die Betonarbeiten der Kirche wurden mit Bambusschalung realisiert. Das Mobiliar wurde von Bauern aus der Gegend gefertigt. Die Architekten: „Der Entwurf ist nicht nur eine Hommage an die skulpturale Form, sondern respektiert auch Natur und Kultur der Region."

Bâtie sur un site de 1200 m², l'**ÉGLISE DE LA GRAINE** est située dans la belle région du mont Luofu, un des sept monts taoïstes de Chine. Elle peut accueillir soixante fidèles. Le mur extérieur adopte la forme d'une graine puis se divise en trois. Le mur sud-est possède une ouverture en croix qui laisse entrer la lumière du matin. Un autre mur plein protège du soleil de l'après-midi à l'ouest. Un toit-terrasse en gradins laisse entrer la lumière du nord et tient compte de hauteurs de plafond allant de 3 à 12 m. La partie principale de la structure est faite de béton coulé sur place dans des coffrages de bambou. Le mobilier a été réalisé par des fermiers du pays. « Il ne s'agit pas, dit l'architecte, d'un projet d'architecture qui célèbre simplement sa forme sculpturale, mais d'un bâtiment qui respecte l'environnement et la culture locale. »

Below, the south (left) and north elevations of the building. The photo above shows the north entrance. Left page, a simple path leads up to the church.

Unten ein Süd- (links) und Nordaufriss des Baus. Oben der Nordeingang; auf der Ansicht links der schlichte Weg, der zur Kirche führt.

Ci-dessous, les élévations sud (à gauche) et nord du bâtiment. La photo ci-dessus montre l'entrée nord. Page de gauche, un chemin simple monte à l'église.

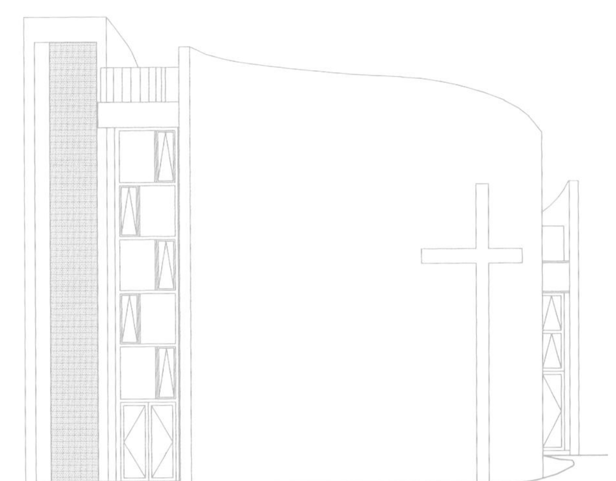

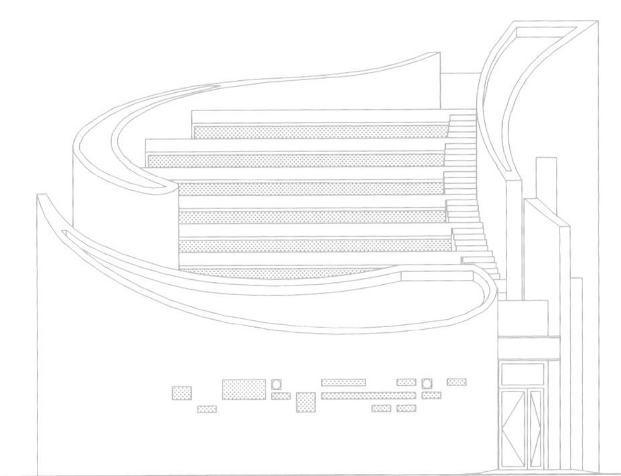

A cross is carved into the striated concrete surface. Left, the church, again seen from the north side. Right page, visitors can walk to the top of the structure and see the view of the natural setting.

Ein Kreuz ist in den gefurchten Sichbeton eingeschnitten. Links eine Nordansicht der Kirche. Besucher können das Dach des Gebäudes begehen und die Landschaft betrachten (rechts).

Une croix est découpée dans la surface de béton strié. Ci-contre, à nouveau la façade nord de l'église. Page de droite, les visiteurs peuvent monter au sommet du bâtiment pour admirer le paysage.

The interior of the church is quite simple, a fact that is emphasized by the wooden furniture chosen. Below, a section drawing of the church showing the ceiling design.

Der Innenraum der Kirche ist schlicht gehalten, was durch die Wahl des Holzmobiliars noch betont wird. Der Querschnitt unten lässt die Beschaffenheit der Decke erkennen.

L'intérieur de l'église est relativement simple, une impression renforcée par le choix du mobilier en bois. En dessous, une coupe de l'église montre le dessin du plafond.

A second view of the church interior, from the position of the altar or lectern. Right, a site plan shows the seedlike form of the building.

Eine zweite Ansicht des Innenraums der Kirche, vom Altar bzw. Lesepult aus. Der Lageplan lässt die Samenform des Gebäudes erkennen.

Une deuxième vue de l'intérieur de l'église, prise de l'autel ou du lutrin. Ci-contre, un plan de situation montre la forme de graine du bâtiment.

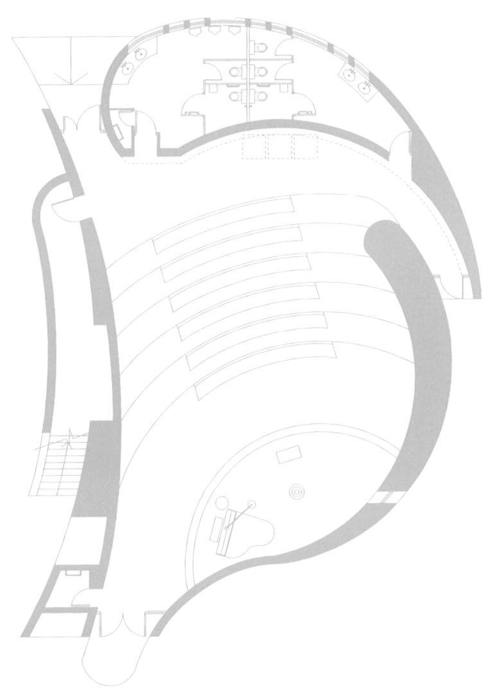

I. M. PEI AND IO ARCHITECTS

I. M. Pei, Architect
88 Pine Street / New York, NY 10005 / USA
Tel: +1 212 872 4010 / Fax: +1 212 872 4222

io Architects LLP
39 East 13th Street / New York, NY 10003 / USA
Tel: +1 212 982 5010
E-mail: info@io-arch.com / Web: www.io-arch.com

Born in 1917 in Canton (now Guangzhou), China, **I. M. PEI** came to the United States in 1935. He received his B.Arch degree from MIT (1940), his M.Arch from Harvard (1942), and a doctorate from Harvard (1946). He formed I. M. Pei & Associates in 1955. He won the AIA Gold Medal (1979), the Pritzker Prize (1983), and the Praemium Imperiale in Japan (1989). His notable buildings include the National Gallery of Art, East Building (Washington, D.C., USA, 1968–78); Bank of China Tower (Hong Kong, China, 1982–89); the Grand Louvre (Paris, France, 1983–93); and the Miho Museum (Shigaraki, Shiga, Japan, 1992–97). His most recent projects include an extension to the German Historical Museum (Berlin, Germany); Mudam, Musée d'Art Moderne Grand-Duc Jean (Luxembourg, Luxembourg); and the Suzhou Art Museum (Suzhou, China), all inaugurated in 2006; and the Museum of Islamic Art (Doha, Qatar, 2008). **HITOSHI MAEHARA**, born in Japan in 1962, received his B.Arch degree from Tama Art University (Tokyo, 1987). He worked with KT Architects (Tokyo, 1989–91), working closely with I. M. Pei on the Miho Museum as a site architect and then on the Luxembourg Musée d'Art Moderne as project architect. He cofounded io Architects in 2007 with his Partners, Simon Hsu and Philip Wu (who left the partnership in 2011). **SIMON HSU** received his M.Arch degree from the Harvard GSD (1995). He worked with Pei Cobb Freed (1995–2007) prior to cofounding io Architects. Hsu collaborated with I. M. Pei on the campus master plan of the Miho Institute of Aesthetics (Shigaraki, Shiga, Japan, 2010–12, published here). In addition, I. M. Pei designed the campus chapel, while io Architects designed the remaining 12 buildings, landscape, and interiors.

I. M. PEI wurde 1917 in Kanton geboren (heute Guangzhou) und lebt seit 1935 in den USA. Er absolvierte einen B. Arch. am MIT (1940) und einen M. Arch. in Harvard (1942), wo er auch promovierte (1946). 1955 gründete er sein Büro I. M. Pei & Associates. Er wurde mit der AIA Gold Medal (1979), dem Pritzker-Preis (1983) und dem japanischen Praemium Imperiale (1989) ausgezeichnet. Zu seinen wichtigsten Projekten gehören u. a. das East Building der National Gallery of Art (Washington D. C., 1968–78), der Tower der Bank of China (Hongkong, 1982–89), der Grand Louvre (Paris, 1983–93) und das Miho Museum (Shigaraki, Präfektur Shiga, Japan, 1992–97). Zu seinen jüngeren Arbeiten zählen ein Erweiterungsbau des Deutschen Historischen Museums (Berlin), das Musée d'Art Moderne Grand-Duc Jean (Mudam, Luxemburg) und das Suzhou Museum (Suzhou, China, alle 2006 eingeweiht) sowie das Museum für islamische Kunst (Doha, Katar, 2008). **HITOSHI MAEHARA** wurde 1962 in Japan geboren und absolvierte seinen B. Arch. an der Kunsthochschule Tama (Tokio, 1987). Er arbeitete zunächst bei KT Architects (Tokio, 1989–91), bevor er als Bauleiter des Miho Museums und anschließend als Projektachitekt für das Luxemburger Musée d'Art Moderne eng mit I. M. Pei kooperierte. 2007 gründete er mit Simon Hsu und Philip Wu, der das Büro 2011 wieder verließ, die Firma io Architects. **SIMON HSU** absolvierte einen M. Arch. an der Harvard GSD (1995) und arbeitete bei Pei Cobb Freed (1995 bis 2007), bevor er io Architects mitgründete. Io Architects entwarf mit I. M. Pei den Masterplan für den Campus des Miho Institute of Aesthetics (Shigaraki, Präfektur Shiga, Japan, 2010–12, hier vorgestellt). I. M. Pei plante außerdem die Kapelle auf dem Campus, während io Architects die übrigen zwölf Gebäude sowie Innenarchitektur und Grünanlagen entwarfen.

Né en 1917 à Canton en Chine, **I. M. PEI** arrive aux États-Unis en 1935. Il obtient son B.Arch au MIT en 1940, son M.Arch puis un doctorat à Harvard en 1942 et 1946. Il fonde I. M. Pei & Associates en 1955. Il gagne la médaille d'or AIA (1979), le prix Pritzker (1983) et le prix japonais Praemium Imperiale (1989). Parmi ses bâtiments les plus célèbres, on trouve la National Gallery of Art, East Building (Washington, 1968–78) ; la tour de la Banque de Chine (Hong Kong, 1982–89) ; le Grand Louvre (Paris, 1983–93) et le musée Miho (Shigaraki, Shiga, Japon, 1992–97). Parmi ses plus récents projets, on compte l'extension du Musée de l'histoire allemande (Berlin) ; le Mudam, Musée d'art moderne Grand-Duc Jean (Luxembourg) et le Musée d'art de Suzhou (Suzhou, Chine), tous inaugurés en 2006, et le Musée d'art islamique (Doha, Qatar, 2008). Né au Japon en 1962, **HITOSHI MAEHARA** obtient son B.Arch à l'Université des beaux-arts Tama (Tokyo, 1987). Il travaille avec KT Architects (Tokyo, 1989–91) avant de collaborer étroitement avec I.M. Pei sur le musée Miho en tant que maître d'œuvre, puis sur le Musée d'art moderne du Luxembourg en tant qu'architecte du projet. Il est cofondateur de io Architects en 2007 avec Simon Hsu et Philip Wu (qui cesse d'être partenaire en 2011). **SIMON HSU** obtient son M.Arch à la Harvard GSD (1995). Il travaille avec Pei Cobb Freed (1995–2007) avant de participer à la fondation de io Architects. Hsu collabore avec I. M. Pei sur le plan directeur du campus de l'École d'esthétique Miho (Shigaraki, Shiga, Japon, 2010–12, présenté ici). I. M. Pei conçoit également la chapelle du campus, alors que io Architects s'occupe des douze bâtiments restants et de l'aménagement des extérieurs et des intérieurs.

MIHO INSTITUTE OF AESTHETICS

Shigaraki, Shiga, Japan, 2010–12

Address: 369 Hata Nishi-gawa, Shigaraki, Kouka-shi, Shiga 529–1813, Japan
Area: 25 319 m². Client: Shinji Shumeikai Miho Institute of Aesthetics Founding Committee
Cost: not disclosed

The **MIHO INSTITUTE OF AESTHETICS**, a private boarding school situated east of Kyoto, in Shigaraki, was inaugurated on April 1, 2012. I. M. Pei designed the central chapel and collaborated on the master plan with io Architects, who provided full architectural design services for the remaining 12 school buildings, from concept design through to construction administration. Additionally, io Architects also rendered the landscape design, interior design, and coordinated the identity branding and signage by Pentagram New York. I. M. Pei had previously designed the Miho Museum in 1997 and the "Joy of Angels" Bell Tower in 1990 for the same client on nearby sites. Located on a cypress-forested eight-hectare site, the facility is intended to serve 240 students from grades 7 through 12. The complex includes 15 700 square meters of teaching facilities, administrative offices, library, gym, and art galleries; 7300 square meters of student residences; a 100-square-meter Japanese pavilion; and Pei's 1800-square-meter chapel. The chapel, with an asymmetrical conical section, has a teardrop plan and measures 19 meters in height at its highest point. It can seat 300 people. The poured-in-place reinforced-concrete structure is clad in bead-blasted stainless-steel panels, each 5 millimeters thick, 18 meters long, and tapering from a width of 1.5 to 0.6 meters. The interior of the chapel is finished in Japanese red cedar plank walls and a flooring of French limestone and white oak. The school buildings are all designed on the basis of a similar architectural vocabulary. The exterior finishes of the school building are beige-colored architectural concrete and custom mosaic tiles. An L-shaped covered walkway on the periphery of the school plaza frames the chapel and links the three distinct school buildings—the Forecourt, the Commons, and the Academic Center. The Forecourt houses a visitor center, security office, and library. The Commons building contains the dining hall on the plaza level and a gym / assembly hall below. The Academic Center accommodates the main entrance and administrative facilities, and also extends to four interlinked classroom buildings via bridges and shared spaces.

Das **MIHO INSTITUTE OF AESTHETICS** – ein privater Internatscampus in Shigaraki, östlich von Kioto – wurde am 1. April 2012 eingeweiht. I. M. Pei entwarf die zentral gelegene Kapelle und entwickelte mit io Architects den Masterplan für den Campus. Die übrigen zwölf Gebäude wurden vom Entwurf bis zur Bauleitung von io Architects betreut, ebenso wie Grünflächenplanung und Innenarchitektur. Io Architects koordinierte außerdem die Umsetzung der von Pentagram New York entwickelten Corporate Identity und des dazugehörigen Leitsystems. Unweit des Internats hatte I. M. Pei für denselben Auftraggeber bereits 1997 das Miho Museum realisiert sowie 1990 den Glockenturm „Joy of Angels". Das Internat liegt auf einem 8 ha großen Gelände mit einem Zypressenwald und bietet Raum für 240 Schüler von der siebten bis zur zwölften Klasse. Außer 15 700 m² Unterrichtsfläche sind hier Verwaltungsräume, eine Bibliothek, eine Sporthalle und Ausstellungsräume untergebracht; zudem Schülerunterkünfte mit 7300 m², ein 100 m² großer japanischer Pavillon und I. M. Peis Kapelle mit 1800 m². Die Kapelle ist ein asymmetrischer angeschnittener Kegel, ihr Grundriss ist tropfenförmig. An seiner höchsten Stelle misst der Bau 19 m und bietet Platz für 300 Personen. Der Bau aus Stahl und Ortbeton wurde mit 5 mm starken und 18 m langen, perlgestrahlten Edelstahlpaneelen verkleidet, die zwischen 0,6 und 1,5 m breit sind. Der Innenraum der Kapelle ist mit japanischer Riesenthuja ausgekleidet, auf dem Boden wurde französischer Kalkstein und Amerikanische Weißeiche verlegt. Die Campusbauten zeichnen sich durch eine einheitliche Formensprache aus, Fassaden wurden mit sandfarbenen Betonpaneelen und speziell gefertigten Mosaikfliesen verblendet. Ein L-förmiger Laubengang entlang des Schulhofs rahmt die Kapelle und verbindet die drei Hauptgebäude: Im „Forecourt" liegen Besucherzentrum, Bibliothek und ein Büro der Sicherheitsfirma. Im „Commons" befindet sich auf Ebene des Schulhofs die Mensa, darunter die auch als Aula genutzte Sporthalle. Im „Academic Center" schließlich sind Verwaltung und Haupteingang untergebracht; dieser Bau erschließt über Brücken und Gemeinschaftsflächen vier weitere Gebäude mit Klassenräumen.

L'**ÉCOLE D'ESTHÉTIQUE MIHO**, un pensionnat privé situé à Shigaraki, à l'est de Kyoto, a été inaugurée le 1er avril 2012. I. M. Pei a conçu la chapelle centrale et collaboré au plan directeur avec io Architects qui a fourni tous les services de création architecturale pour les 12 bâtiments de l'école restants, du concept à l'administration des travaux. io Architects s'est occupé également du design paysager, du design intérieur et a coordonné l'identité de la marque et la signalisation de Pentagram New York. I. M. Pei avait déjà réalisé le musée Miho en 1997 et le campanile « Joy of Angels » en 1990 pour le même client sur des sites voisins. Situées sur un site de 8 ha boisé de cyprès, les installations sont prévues pour 240 étudiants du secondaire. Le complexe englobe sur 15 700 m² les équipements scolaires, les bureaux de l'administration, une bibliothèque, une salle de sport et des galeries d'art, 7300 m² de résidences d'étudiants, un pavillon japonais de 100 m² et la chapelle de 1800 m² de Pei. La chapelle, dotée d'une section en cône asymétrique, possède un plan en larme et mesure 19 m de haut en son point le plus élevé. Elle contient 300 places assises. La structure en béton armé coulé sur place est revêtue de panneaux d'acier inoxydable microbillé de 5 mm d'épaisseur, 18 m de long et qui s'effilent en largeur de 1,50 m à 60 cm. Les murs intérieurs de la chapelle sont revêtus de panneaux de cèdre rouge du Japon et le sol est en pierre de Bourgogne et chêne blanc. Les bâtiments de l'école sont conçus sur la base d'un même vocabulaire architectural. Les finitions extérieures sont de béton architectonique beige et de tuiles de mosaïque faites sur commande. Un passage couvert en forme de L, à la périphérie de la place de l'école, encadre la chapelle et relie les trois bâtiments scolaires distincts – Forecourt, Commons et Academic Center. Le bâtiment Forecourt abrite l'accueil aux visiteurs, le bureau de la sécurité et la bibliothèque. Le bâtiment Commons contient le réfectoire au rez-de-chaussée et une salle de sport/salle de réunion au niveau inférieur. Le bâtiment Academic Center accueille l'entrée principale et l'administration, et se prolonge vers quatre bâtiments de classes reliés entre eux par des ponts et des espaces partagés.

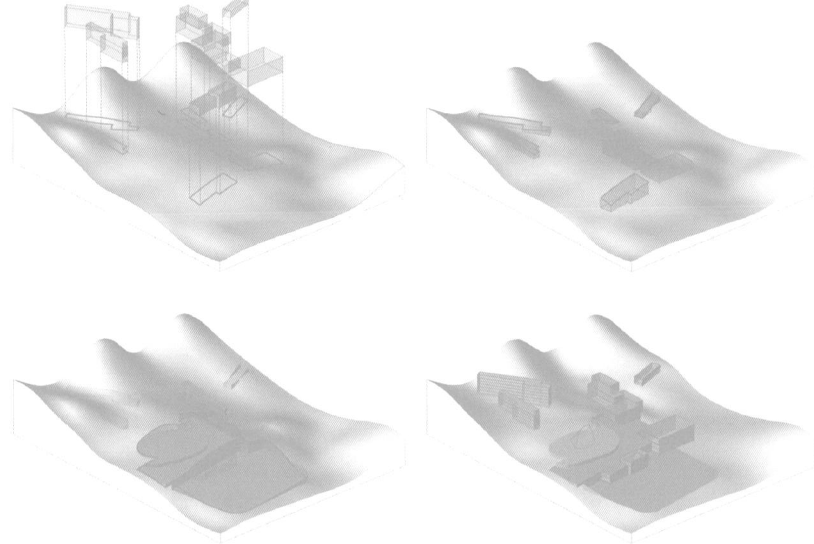

Left, a "siting diagram" shows how the school buildings are inserted into the site, their profile lowered as they go down the slope, finishing in the playing field seen in the aerial image on the opposite page, above. Below, the chapel designed by I. M. Pei.

Eine Grafik veranschaulicht, wie sich die Schulgebäude der Hanglage des Standorts anpassen, der von einem Sportplatz begrenzt wird (Luftbild oben rechts). Unten rechts die von I. M. Pei entworfene Kapelle.

Ci-contre, un « schéma d'implantation » montre l'insertion des bâtiments de l'école dans le site, leur profil s'amenuisant au fur et à mesure de la pente pour finir dans le terrain de sport, comme on le voit dans la vue aérienne (page de droite, en haut). Page de droite, en bas, la chapelle conçue par I. M. Pei.

Inside the school careful attention is paid to materials and lighting. A glazed island planted with bamboo brings the presence of nature and light into a hallway (top).

In der Schule spielen Materialien und Licht eine wesentliche Rolle. Eine mit Bambus bepflanzte Glasinsel holt Natur und Licht in die Flure der Schule (oben).

À l'intérieur de l'école, une attention forte a été portée aux matériaux et à la lumière. Une île vitrée plantée de bambous fait entrer la nature et la lumière dans un couloir (en haut).

Above, classrooms are bright and most have glazed walls facing the natural setting. Below, section drawings show the insertion of the complex into its hilly site.

Viele der hellen Klassenzimmer haben Glasfronten mit Blick in die Natur (oben). Querschnitte veranschaulichen, wie sich der Komplex in den hügeligen Standort einfügt (unten).

Ci-dessus, les salles de classe, souvent dotées de baies vitrées donnant sur la nature, sont lumineuses. Ci-dessous, des dessins de coupe montrent l'insertion du complexe dans un site vallonné.

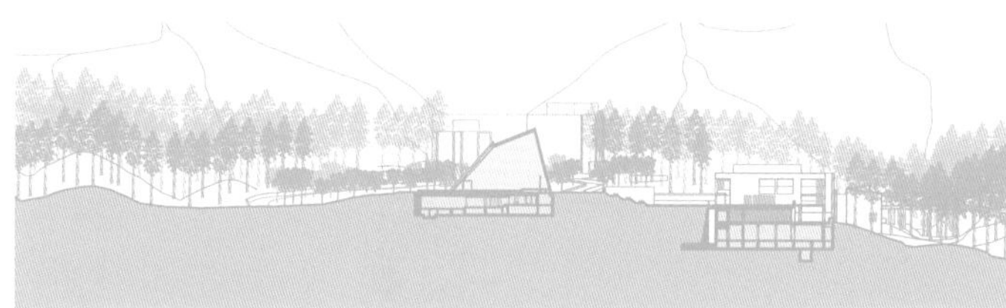

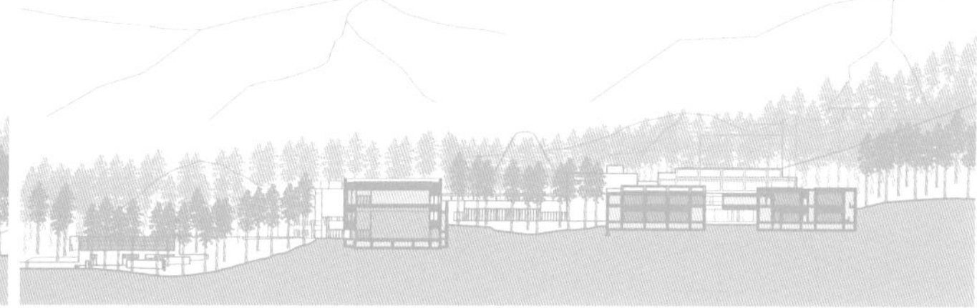

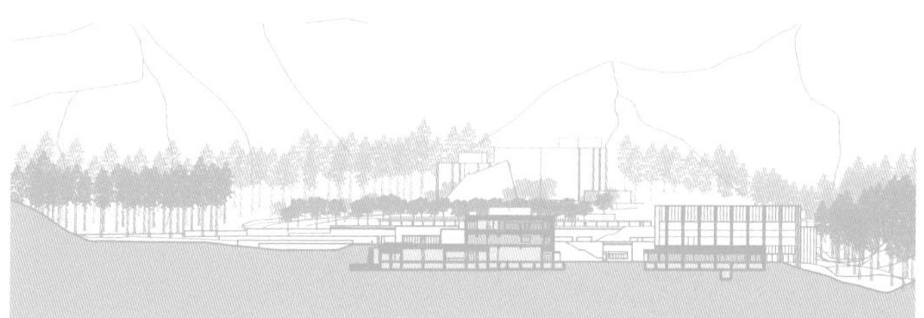

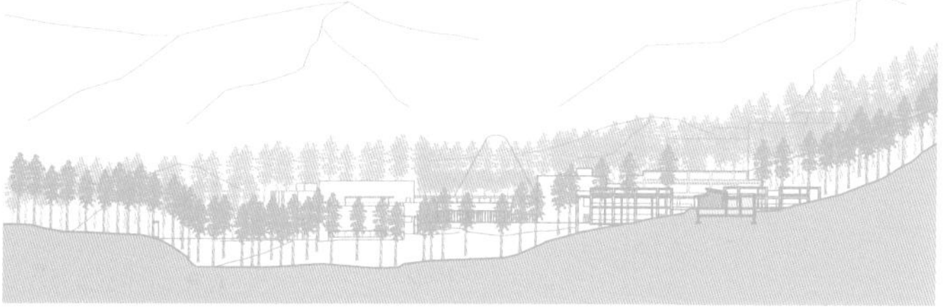

On the right, the interior of the chapel, entirely designed by I. M. Pei with the assistance of io Architects. The very large suspended circular light fixture was also designed by Pei.

Rechts der Innenraum der von I. M. Pei entworfenen Kapelle (unterstützt von io Architects). Der große kreisförmige Leuchter ist ebenfalls ein Entwurf von Pei.

Page de droite, l'intérieur de la chapelle entièrement conçu par I. M. Pei, avec l'aide de io Architects. L'énorme suspension d'éclairage circulaire est également de Pei.

Above, the main entrance to the chapel is fully glazed, revealing the wood-clad interior in this evening view. Right, a plan shows the chapel to the left, and the academic and housing building to the right.

Der Haupteingang zur Kapelle ist vollständig verglast und lässt in dieser Ansicht bei Abend das holzvertäfelte Innere erkennen (oben). Auf dem Lageplan sind links die Kapelle und rechts Schulgebäude und Unterkünfte zu sehen (rechts).

Ci-dessus, sur cette vue de nuit, l'entrée principale entièrement vitrée révèle l'intérieur de bois de la chapelle. Ci-contre, un plan montre la chapelle à gauche et le bâtiment des logements et de l'école à droite.

GUSTAVO PENNA

Gustavo Penna Arquiteto & Associados—GPA&A
Av. Álvares Cabral 414, Centro
Belo Horizonte 30170–000
Minas Gerais
Brazil

Tel: +55 31 3218 2400
Fax: +55 31 3274 2500
E-mail: arquiteto@gustavopenna.com.br
Web: www.gustavopenna.com.br

GUSTAVO PENNA was born in 1950 in Belo Horizonte, Brazil. He graduated with a degree in Architecture from the Escola de Arquitetura da Universidade Federal de Minas Gerais (EA-UFMG, 1973). He has been the Director of Gustavo Penna Arquiteto & Associados since 1973. He has served as a Professor at the EA-UFMG (1977–2009). His work includes a multipurpose space at the Center for Ecological and Cultural Reference, Municipal Park of Belo Horizonte (Belo Horizonte, Minas Gerais, 2006); Japanese Immigration Memorial (Pampulha, Belo Horizonte, 2008); Forluz Headquarters Building (Belo Horizonte, Minas Gerais, 2008); Manacás House (Lima, Minas Gerais, 2009); ZEE Portal, Special Economic Zone (Luanda, Angola, 2009); revitalization of the city center of Araxá (Araxá, Minas Gerais, 2010); All Saints Chapel, Gurita Farm (Martinho Campos, Minas Gerais, 2011, published here); UNIFEI, Campus for the Federal University of Itajubá (Itajubá, Minas Gerais, 2011); and Sete Lagoas High School, Fundação Zerrenner (Sete Lagoas, Minas Gerais, 2012), all in Brazil unless otherwise indicated.

GUSTAVO PENNA wurde 1950 in Belo Horizonte, Brasilien, geboren. Er absolvierte ein Architekturstudium an der Escola de Arquitetura da Universidade Federal de Minas Gerais (EA-UFMG, 1973). Seit 1973 ist er Direktor von Gustavo Penna Arquiteto & Associados. Von 1977 bis 2009 lehrte er als Professor an der EA-UFMG. Zu Pennas Arbeiten gehören das Zentrum für Ökologie und Kultur im Stadtpark von Belo Horizonte (Belo Horizonte, Minas Gerais, 2006), das Denkmal für die japanische Einwanderungsbewegung (Pampulha, Belo Horizonte, 2008), der Forluz-Firmenhauptsitz (Belo Horizonte, Minas Gerais, 2008), die Casa Manacás (Lima, Minas Gerais, 2009), das ZEE Portal in der Sonderwirtschaftszone von Luanda (Angola, 2009), ein Stadterneuerungsprojekt in der Innenstadt von Araxá (Araxá, Minas Gerais, 2010), die Allerheiligenkapelle auf der Gurita Farm (Martinho Campos, Minas Gerais, 2011, hier vorgestellt), der UNIFEI-Campus der Universiät Itajubá (Itajubá, Minas Gerais, 2011) und die Oberschule der Fundação Zerrenner (Sete Lagoas, Minas Gerais, 2012).

Né en 1950 à Belo Horizonte au Brésil, **GUSTAVO PENNA** obtient son diplôme en architecture à l'École d'architecture de l'Université fédérale du Minas Gerais (EA-UFMG, 1973). Il est directeur de Gustavo Penna Arquiteto & Associados depuis 1973. Il enseigne comme professeur à l'EA-UFMG (1977–2009). Ses réalisations comprennent le Centre écologique et culturel du parc municipal de Belo Horizonte (Belo Horizonte, Minas Gerais, 2006) ; le mémorial japonais de l'immigration (Pampulha, Belo Horizonte, 2008) ; le siège de Forluz (Belo Horizonte, Minas Gerais, 2008) ; la Casa Manacás (Lima, Minas Gerais, 2009) ; la ZEE Portal, zone économique spéciale (Luanda, Angola, 2009) ; la revitalisation du centre-ville d'Araxá (Araxá, Minas Gerais, 2010) ; la chapelle de Tous-les-Saints, Fazenda Gurita (Martinho Campos, Minas Gerais, 2011, présentée ici) ; le campus de l'UNIFEI, Université fédérale de Itajubá (Itajubá, Minas Gerais, 2011) et le lycée de Sete Lagoas, Fundação Zerrenner (Sete Lagoas, Minas Gerais, 2012), toutes au Brésil sauf indication contraire.

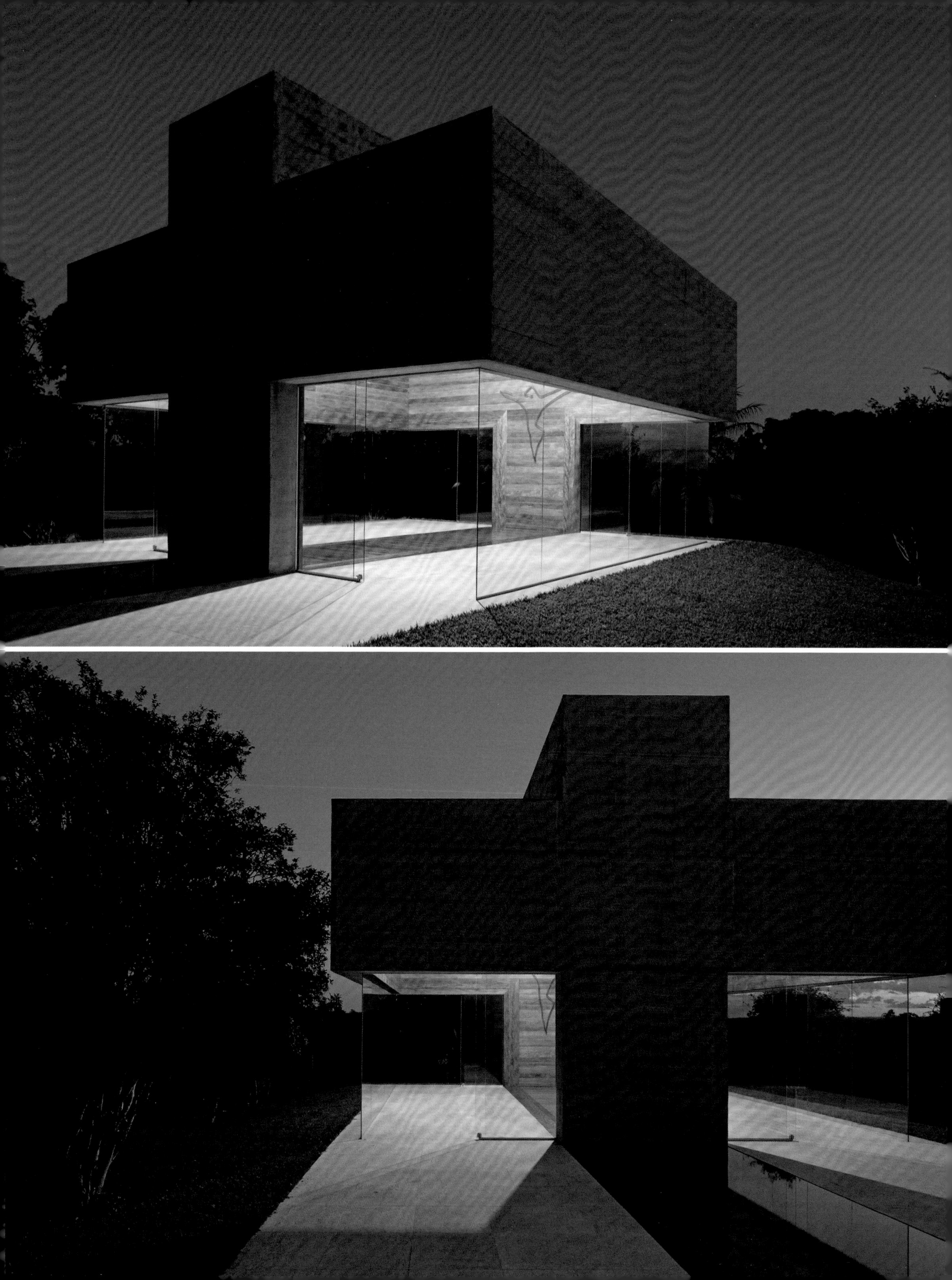

ALL SAINTS CHAPEL

Gurita Farm, Martinho Campos, Minas Gerais, Brazil, 2011

Address: Gurita Farm, Martinho Campos, Minas Gerais, Brazil
Area: 160 m². Client: Eliana Pimentel and Gilmar Dias dos Santos. Cost: not disclosed
Collaboration: Laura Penna, Norberto Bambozzi (Architects)

This powerful chapel assumes the shape of a cross, but unlike the traditional Christian cross it is wider than it is tall. Built on a 2000-square-meter site, the structure is essentially made of concrete and glass with travertine marble and a rare Brazilian wood called *peroba do campo*. Floor-to-ceiling glazing makes the distinction between interior and exterior spaces almost invisible. A stylized crucifix, placed on the interior wood cladding, figures Christ without a cross, which is, indeed, the very substance of the architecture. The rectangular plan of the chapel features a narrow rectangular basin aligned on the center of the building. Gustavo Penna prefers to describe his project in rather poetic terms than to give a more formal series of facts: "First, the baptismal font. A source of pure water—the origin of everything. / Through the two river banks, one reaches the third—religion; the symbol/synthesis, the cross. / Sky and earth—the vertical line. / All men—the horizontal line. / The internal space is created by displacing the sacred form. / The space is the movement. / The wood shelters, embraces, protects. / Nature surrounds, participating in solidarity."

Diese ausdrucksstarke Kapelle ist geformt wie ein Kreuz. Anders jedoch als das traditionelle lateinische Kreuz ist der Querbalken hier länger als der Längsbalken, der Bau damit breiter als hoch. Das Projekt liegt auf einem 2000 m² großen Grundstück und wurde im Wesentlichen aus Beton, Glas, Travertin und dem seltenen brasilianischen Holz *peroba do campo* realisiert. Durch die deckenhohe Verglasung verschwimmen die Grenzen von Innen- und Außenraum. Auf der Holztäfelung im Innenraum zeichnet sich ein stilisiertes Kruzifix ab, das eine Christusfigur andeutet, dabei auf das eigentliche Kreuzsymbol verzichtet, das hier vom Bau selbst gezeichnet wird. Vor der Kapelle befindet sich auf der zentralen Achse des Baus ein schmales Wasserbecken. Statt mit baulichen Daten skizziert Gustavo Penna sein Projekt lieber in poetischen Bildern: „Zunächst das Taufbecken. / Quelle reinen Wassers – Ursprung allen Seins. / Entlang an zwei Flussufern wird ein drittes erreicht – der Glaube, das Kreuz als Symbol und Synthese. / Himmel und Erde: vertikale Linie. / Der Mensch: horizontale Linie. / Der Innenraum: definiert durch die Orientierung des heiligen Symbols. / Der Raum ist Bewegung. / Das Holz bietet Zuflucht, umfängt und schützt. / Ringsum die Natur in Verbundenheit."

Cette chapelle puissante adopte la forme d'une croix mais, contrairement à la croix chrétienne traditionnelle, elle est plus large que haute. Construite sur un site de 2000 m², la structure est faite principalement de béton, verre, travertin et d'un bois rare brésilien, le *peroba do campo*. Des vitrages du sol au plafond rendent presque invisible la séparation entre le dedans et le dehors. Une crucifixion stylisée, placée sur le revêtement intérieur en bois, figure le Christ sans croix, ce qui est la substance même de l'architecture. Le plan rectangulaire de la chapelle présente un étroit bassin rectangulaire aligné sur le centre du bâtiment. Gustavo Penna préfère décrire son projet en termes poétiques plutôt que d'aligner une série de faits plus formels : « D'abord les fonts baptismaux. Une source d'eau pure – l'origine de tout. / Par les deux rives de la rivière, on atteint la troisième – la religion ; le symbole/synthèse, la croix / Ciel et terre – la ligne verticale / L'humanité – la ligne horizontale / L'espace intérieur est créé en déplaçant la forme sacrée. / L'espace est le mouvement. / Le bois abrite, embrasse, protège. / La Nature entoure le tout, participante solidaire. »

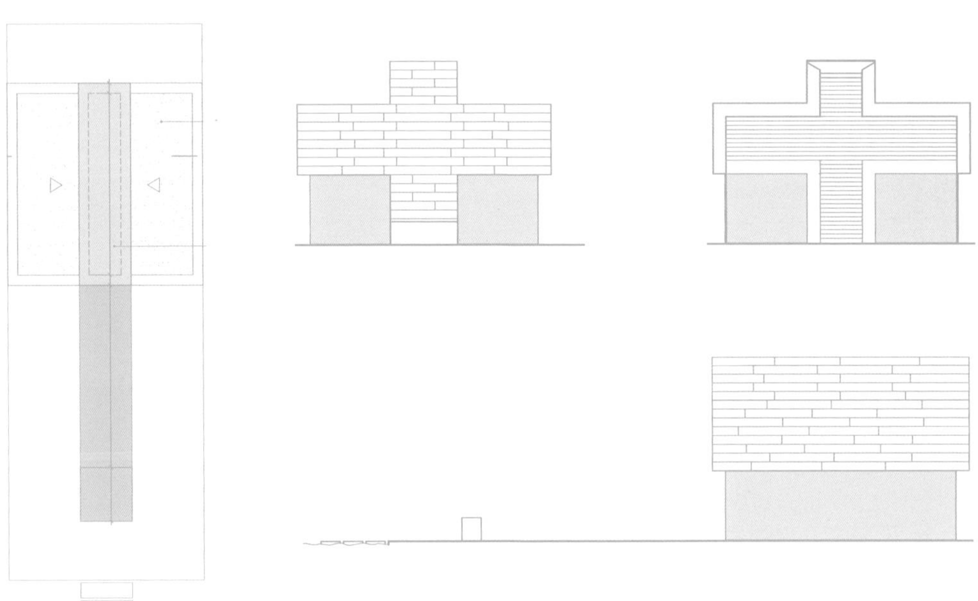

With its powerful concrete exterior form echoed by the tropical wood interior, the chapel is also seen in the floor plan (left, above), as well as in front and side elevations and a section drawing.

Die eindrucksvolle Kapelle aus Beton, deren mit Tropenholz vertäfelter Innenraum die äußere Form aufgreift, hier im Grundriss (links oben), als Frontal- und Seitenaufriss sowie als Querschnitt.

On voit sur le plan (à gauche, ci-dessus), sur des élévations de face et de côté et un plan de coupe, la chapelle avec sa forme extérieure puissante en béton qui renvoie à l'intérieur en bois tropical.

RENZO PIANO

Renzo Piano Building Workshop / 34 Rue des Archives / 75004 Paris, France
Tel: +33 1 42 78 00 82 / Fax: +33 1 42 78 01 98 / E-mail: france@rpbw.com / Web: www.rpbw.com
Renzo Piano Building Workshop / Via P. Paolo Rubens 29 / 16158 Genoa, Italy
Tel: +39 01 06 17 11 / Fax: +39 01 06 17 13 50 / E-mail: italy@rpbw.com / Web: www.rpbw.com

RENZO PIANO was born in 1937 in Genoa, Italy. He studied at the University of Florence and at Milan's Polytechnic Institute (1964). He formed his own practice (Studio Piano) in 1965, associated with Richard Rogers (Piano & Rogers, 1971–78)—completing the Pompidou Center in Paris in 1977—and then worked with Peter Rice (Piano & Rice Associates, 1978–80), before creating the Renzo Piano Building Workshop in 1981 in Genoa and Paris. Piano received the RIBA Gold Medal in 1989. Built work after 2000 includes Maison Hermès (Tokyo, Japan, 1998–2001); Rome Auditorium (Italy, 1994–2002); conversion of the Lingotto Factory Complex (Turin, Italy, 1983–2003); the Padre Pio Pilgrimage Church (San Giovanni Rotondo, Foggia, Italy, 1991–2004); the Woodruff Arts Center Expansion (Atlanta, Georgia, USA, 1999–2005); renovation and expansion of the Morgan Library (New York, New York, USA, 2000–06); and the New York Times Building (New York, New York, USA, 2005–07). More recently completed work includes the Broad Contemporary Art Museum (Phase I of the LACMA expansion, Los Angeles, California, USA, 2003–08); California Academy of Sciences (San Francisco, California, USA, 2008); the Modern Wing of the Art Institute of Chicago (Chicago, Illinois, USA, 2005–09); St. Giles Court mixed-use development (London, UK, 2002–10); the Resnick Pavilion (Phase II of the LACMA expansion, Los Angeles, USA, 2006–10); the Ronchamp Gatehouse and Monastery (France, 2006–11); the London Bridge Tower (London, UK, 2009–12, published here); and the Tjuvholmen Icon Complex (Oslo, Norway, 2009–12, also published here). Ongoing work includes the Stavros Niarchos Foundation Cultural Center (Athens, Greece, 2008–); Valletta City Gate (Valletta, Malta, 2008–); and the Botín Art Center (Santander, Spain, 2010–).

RENZO PIANO wurde 1937 in Genua geboren. Er studierte an der Universität von Florenz und am Polytechnischen Institut von Mailand (1964). 1965 gründete er Studio Piano, später schloss er sich mit Richard Rogers zusammen (Piano & Rogers, 1971–78), mit dem er 1977 das Centre Pompidou in Paris realisierte. Im Anschluss arbeitete er mit Peter Rice (Piano & Rice Associates, 1978–80), bevor er 1981 sein Büro Renzo Piano Building Workshop, mit Sitz in Genua und Paris, gründete. Piano erhielt 1989 die RIBA-Goldmedaille. Zu seinen Arbeiten nach 2000 zählen u. a. die Maison Hermès (Tokio, 1998–2001), das Auditorium Parco della Musica in Rom (1994–2002), ein Umbau der Fiat-Werke in Lingotto (Turin, 1983–2003), die Pilgerkirche Padre Pio (San Giovanni Rotondo, Foggia, 1991–2004), eine Erweiterung des Woodruff Arts Center (Atlanta, Georgia, 1999–2005), die Sanierung und Erweiterung der Morgan Library (New York, 2000–06) sowie das *New York Times* Building (New York, 2005–07). Jüngere Arbeiten sind u. a. das Broad Contemporary Art Museum (1. Bauabschnitt der Erweiterung des LACMA, Los Angeles, Kalifornien, 2003–08), die California Academy of Sciences (San Francisco, Kalifornien, 2008), ein Flügel für moderne Kunst am Art Institute of Chicago (Chicago, Illinois, 2005–09), der St. Giles Court mit Mischnutzung (London, 2002–10), der Resnick Pavilion (2. Bauabschnitt der Erweiterung des LACMA, Los Angeles, 2006–10), Torhaus und Kloster von Ronchamp (Frankreich, 2006–11), der London Bridge Tower (London, 2009–12, hier vorgestellt) und der Icon Complex im Quartier Tjuvholmen (Oslo, 2009–12, ebenfalls hier vorgestellt). Laufende Projekte sind u. a. das Kulturzentrum der Stavros-Niarchos-Stiftung (Athen, seit 2008), das Stadttor von Valletta (Valletta, Malta, seit 2008) und das Botín-Kunstzentrum (Santander, seit 2010).

Né en 1937 à Gênes, en Italie, **RENZO PIANO** fait ses études à l'université de Florence et à l'École polytechnique de Milan (1964). Il s'établit (Studio Piano) en 1965, s'associe avec Richard Rogers (Piano & Rogers, 1971–78) – terminant le Centre Pompidou à Paris in 1977 – puis travaille avec Peter Rice (Piano & Rice Associates, 1978–80) avant de créer Renzo Piano Building Workshop en 1981, à Gênes et Paris. Piano reçoit la médaille d'or du RIBA en 1989. Parmi les réalisations postérieures à 2000, on trouve la Maison Hermès (Tokyo, 1998–2001) ; l'auditorium Parco della Musica (Rome, 1994–2002) ; la reconversion de l'usine Lingotto (Turin, 1983–2003) ; l'église de pèlerinage Padre Pio (San Giovanni Rotondo, Foggia, Italie, 1991–2004) ; l'extension du Woodruff Arts Center (Atlanta, Georgie, 1999–2005) ; la rénovation et l'extension de la bibliothèque Morgan (New York, 2000–06) et la tour du New York Times (New York, 2005–07). Parmi les projets terminés plus récemment, on trouve le Broad Contemporary Art Museum (Phase I de l'extension du LACMA, Los Angeles, 2003–08) ; la California Academy of Sciences (San Francisco, 2008) ; l'aile moderne de l'Art Institute of Chicago (Chicago, 2005–09) ; le projet d'aménagement polyvalent St. Giles Court (Londres, 2002–10) ; le Resnick Pavilion (Phase II de l'extension du LACMA, Los Angeles, 2006–10) ; La Porterie de Notre-Dame-du-Haut et le couvent des Clarisses de Ronchamp (France, 2006–11) ; la London Bridge Tower (Londres, 2009–12, présentée ici) et le complexe Tjuvholmen Icon (Oslo, 2009–12, également présenté ici). Il travaille actuellement aux projets du Centre culturel de la Fondation Stavros Niarchos (Athènes, 2008–) ; de la porte de la ville de La Valette (La Valette, Malte, 2008–) et du Centre d'art Botin (Santander, Espagne, 2010–).

LONDON BRIDGE TOWER

London, UK, 2009–12

Address: 32 London Bridge Street, London SE1, UK, +44 20 74 93 53 11, www.the-shard.com
Area: 12 671 m². Client: Sellar Property Group. Cost: not disclosed
Collaboration: Adamson Associates

Also known as "the Shard," this 72-story, 306-meter-high mixed-use tower stands above London Bridge Station on the South Bank, and is surrounded by lower buildings. The station, redeveloped as part of the overall project, combines rail, bus, and underground lines that handle 200 000 travelers per day. The essentially pyramidal form of the building, generated by eight "shards" that carry 11 000 glass panels, includes offices at the bottom (floors 4 to 28), public areas and a hotel in the middle (floors 31 to 52), and 10 apartments above (on levels 53 to 65). Floors 68 to 72 include a viewing gallery. The concrete core of the structure includes 44 single and double-deck elevators. From its initiation in 2000, this project, which was redesigned to improve its stability and evacuation times after the 9/11 attacks in New York, took more than 10 years to complete, in part because of financial difficulties, which were solved in 2008. This is the first building in London to break the symbolic 1000 foot mark (304.8 meters) and it is nearly twice as tall as Norman Foster's "Gherkin" building, located on the other side of the Thames River.

Der 306 m hohe Turm mit gemischter Nutzung, auch „The Shard" (Splitter oder Scherbe) genannt, hat 72 Stockwerke und ragt an der South Bank über der London Bridge Station auf, umgeben von niedrigerer Nachbarbebauung. Durch die gerade umfassend sanierte London Bridge Station verkehren täglich 200 000 Passagiere per Bus, Bahn und U-Bahn. Die pyramidale Außenhaut des Baus besteht aus acht „Scherben" mit 11 000 Glaspaneelen. Unten liegen Büros (Etagen 4–28), darüber öffentlich zugängliche Bereiche und ein Hotel (Etagen 31–51) sowie oben zehn Apartments (Etagen 53–65). In den Etagen 68 bis 72 ist eine Aussichtsplattform untergebracht. Durch den Betonkern ziehen sich 44 Einzel- und Doppeldeckeraufzüge. Das Projekt wurde 2000 begonnen; nach den Anschlägen vom 11. September wurden Stabilität und Fluchtwege überarbeitet. Bis zum Bauabschluss vergingen über zehn Jahre – auch wegen finanzieller Engpässe, die 2008 gelöst werden konnten. Der Turm übersteigt als erstes Gebäude Londons die Grenze von 1000 Fuß (304,8 m) und ist fast doppelt so hoch wie Norman Fosters „Gherkin"-Turm am anderen Themse-Ufer.

Communément appelée « The Shard », cette tour à usage mixte de 72 étages et 306 m de haut, entourée de bâtiments plus bas, se situe au-dessus de la gare de London Bridge sur la rive sud de la Tamise. La gare, réaménagée dans le cadre du projet global, comprend des lignes de chemin de fer, de bus et de métro qui drainent 200 000 voyageurs par jour. La forme essentiellement pyramidale du bâtiment, créée par huit « éclats » porteurs de 11 000 panneaux de verre, comprend des bureaux (étages 4 à 28), des espaces publics et un hôtel (étages 31 à 52) et 10 appartements au-dessus (étages 53 à 65). Les étages 68 à 72 incluent une galerie panoramique. Au cœur du noyau en béton de la structure, on trouve 44 ascenseurs simples ou à double cabine superposée . Depuis son lancement en 2000, il a fallu plus de dix ans, en partie en raison de difficultés financières résolues en 2008, pour achever ce projet repensé pour améliorer sa stabilité et les délais d'évacuation après les attentats du 11 septembre. Presque deux fois plus haut que le « Gherkin » de Norman Foster, de l'autre côté de la Tamise, c'est le premier bâtiment de Londres à passer la barre symbolique des 1000 pieds (304,80 m).

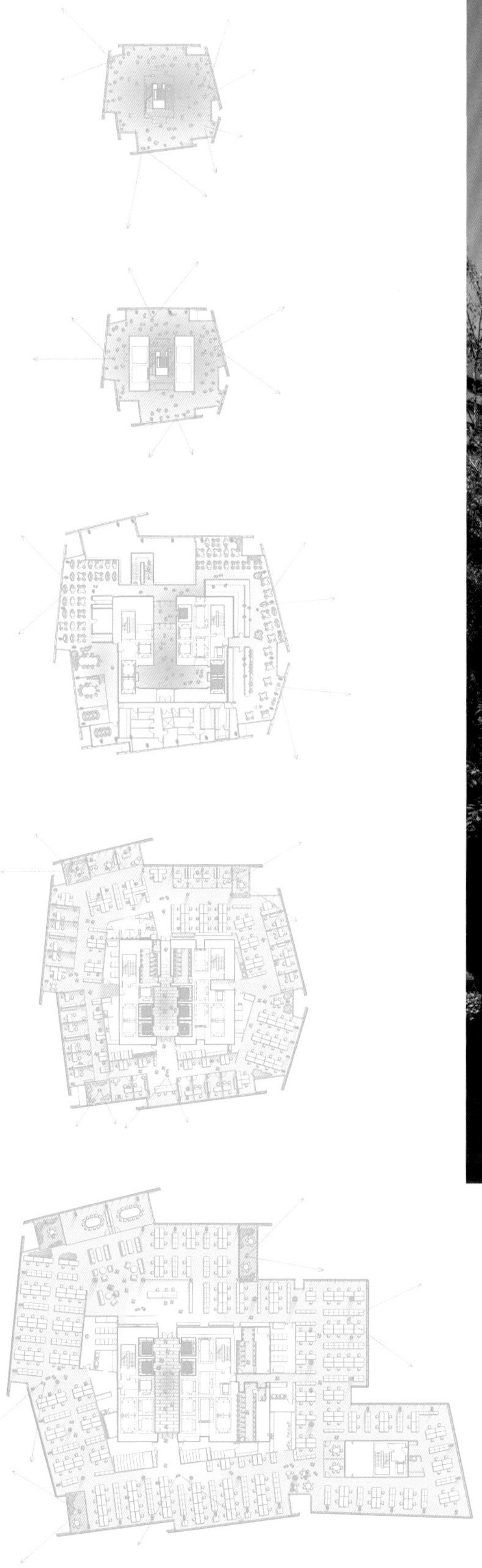

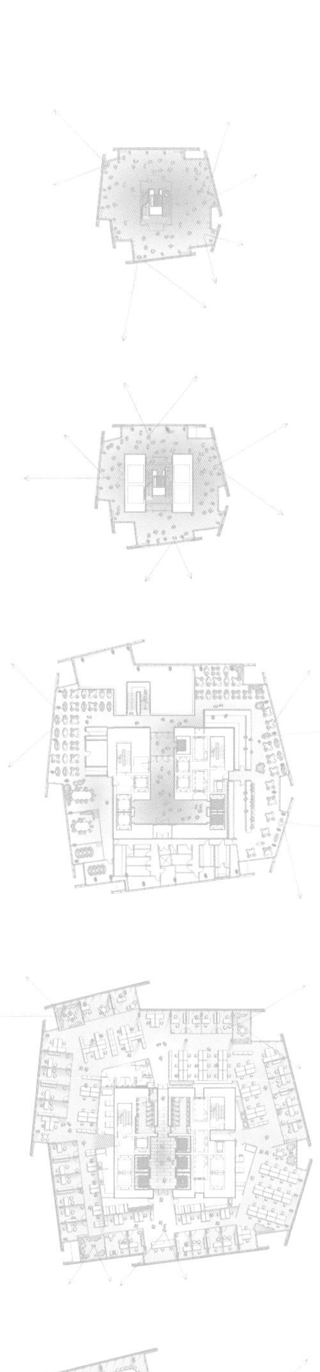

Der Turm fällt auf – ob nun vom Themse-Ufer (linke Seite) oder aus unmittelbarer Nähe gesehen. Die Form des Gebäudes ist durchaus komplex, wie die Grundrisse links erkennen lassen.

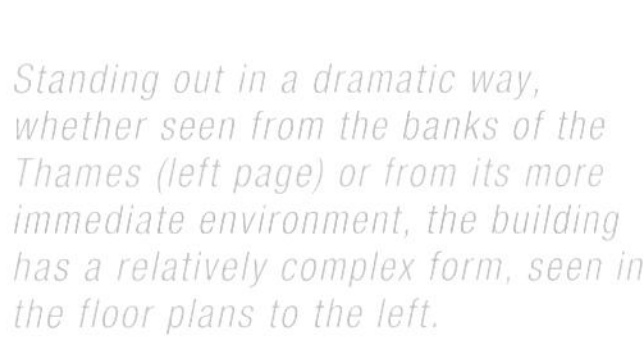

Standing out in a dramatic way, whether seen from the banks of the Thames (left page) or from its more immediate environment, the building has a relatively complex form, seen in the floor plans to the left.

Se démarquant de façon spectaculaire, que ce soit vu des berges de la Tamise (page de gauche) ou dans son environnement immédiat, le bâtiment a une forme relativement complexe, comme le montrent les plans à gauche.

Above, two views of the railway station entrance area at the foot of the tower. Right, a sketch of the building by Renzo Piano, and, opposite page, the Shard standing out against its historic environment.

Zwei Ansichten des Bahnhofseingangs am Fuß des Turms (oben). Rechts der Bau auf einer Skizze Renzo Pianos sowie ganz rechts „The Shard" in seiner historischen Umgebung.

Ci-dessus, deux vues de l'entrée de la gare au pied de la tour. À droite, un croquis du bâtiment par Renzo Piano. Page de droite, le Shard se détachant sur un environnement de bâtiments anciens.

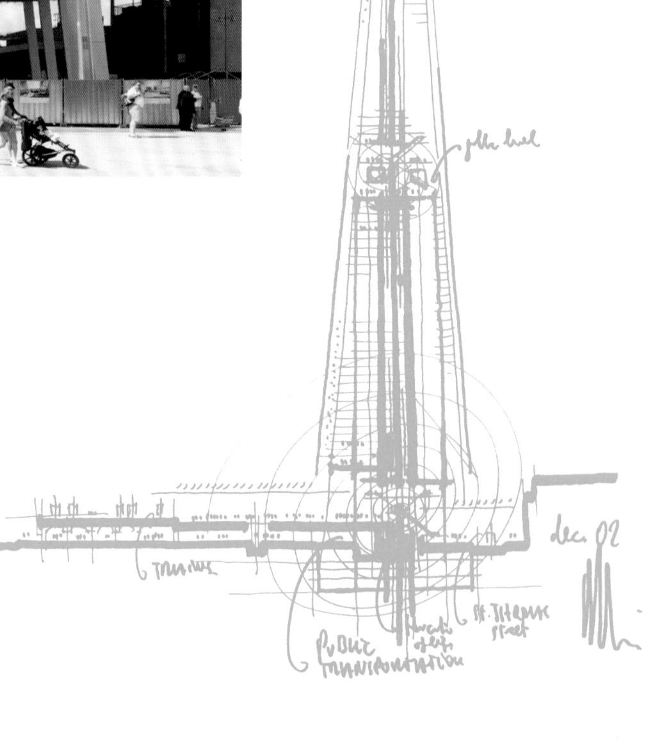

TJUVHOLMEN ICON COMPLEX

Oslo, Norway, 2009–12

Address: Tjuvholmen Byggeplass Kontorrigg, 2.etasje 0250, Oslo, Norway
Area: 15 600 m². Client: Selvaag Gruppen / Aspelin-Ramm Gruppen
Cost: €60 million. Collaboration: Narud Stokke Wiig (Oslo)

Located southwest of the center of Oslo, this project is a continuation of the Aker Brygge development completed in the 1990s. The site of the Tjuvholmen project is one of the most beautiful places in Oslo. The project aims to "transform the formerly closed harbor into a public area connecting the fjord and the center of the city." It includes three buildings located under a single curved glass roof; one for offices and the exhibition of art, and two others for an art museum. The architects explain: "The design strongly identifies the project. Its curved shape, formed by laminated wood beams, crosses the canal between the buildings. The beams are supported by slender steel columns, reinforced with cable rigging, which refer to the maritime character of the site. The roof's geometrical shape is derived from a section of a toroid and it slopes down toward the sea." An 800-meter canal promenade links Aker Brygge to the new complex. A sculpture park is located between the museum and the sea. The exhibition spaces of the art museum on the north side of the canal house a permanent contemporary art collection, with an area continuing at ground level under the office building. The building on the south side of the canal is for temporary exhibitions. The four-story office building has a naturally lit atrium in the center. Weathered timber is used on the opaque façade areas of the complex, with reference to Scandinavian traditions.

Das Projekt südwestlich des Stadtzentrums von Oslo knüpft an die in den 1990er-Jahren realisierte Erschließung von Aker Brygge an. Das Quartier Tjuvholmen, Standort des Projekts, ist eine der schönsten Gegenden der Stadt. Das Projekt soll „das ehemals unzugängliche Hafengelände als öffentlichen Raum nutzbar machen und sowohl mit dem Fjord als auch dem Stadtzentrum verbinden". Der Icon Complex besteht aus drei Baukörpern unter einem geschwungenen Glasdach: Ein Bau beherbergt Büros und Ausstellungsräume, die zwei übrigen ein Museum. Die Architekten: „Das Design gibt dem Projekt sein markantes Profil. Die geschwungene Form ruht auf Schichtholzträgern und überspannt einen Kanal zwischen den Bauten. Die Träger ruhen auf schlanken Stahlstützen, verstärkt durch eine Stahlkabelspannkonstruktion, die motivisch auf den maritimen Standort verweist. Die geometrische Form wurde aus einem Torus-Segment entwickelt und fällt zum Fjord hin ab." Eine 800 m lange Promenade am Kanal verbindet Aker Brygge mit dem neuen Komplex. Zwischen Museum und Fjord liegt ein Skulpturenpark. Die Museumsräume nördlich des Kanals zeigen eine Dauerausstellung zeitgenössischer Kunst. Das Museum setzt sich bis in das Erdgeschoss des Büroriegels fort. Der Bau südlich des Kanals wird für temporäre Ausstellungen genutzt. Das viergeschossige Bürogebäude hat ein zentrales, natürlich beleuchtetes Atrium. Die geschlossenen Bereiche der Fassade wurden in Anlehnung an skandinavische Bautraditionen witterungssicher mit Holz verschalt.

Situé au sud-ouest du centre d'Oslo, ce projet est un prolongement de l'aménagement de la zone Aker Brygge achevé dans les années 1990. Le site du projet Tjuvholmen est l'un des plus beaux d'Oslo. Le projet vise à « transformer le port désaffecté en un espace public reliant le fjord au centre-ville ». Il comprend trois bâtiments situés sous un simple toit courbe de verre ; un pour les bureaux et pour des expositions d'art et les deux autres pour un musée d'art. « Le design, expliquent les architectes, donne une forte identité au projet. Sa forme courbe donnée par des poutres de bois stratifié enjambe le canal entre les bâtiments. De fines colonnes d'acier renforcées de gréements, qui rappellent le contexte maritime du site, soutiennent les colonnes. Le toit, dont la forme géométrique rappelle une section de tore, s'incline vers la mer. » Un canal promenade de 800 m relie Aker Brygge au nouveau complexe. Un parc de sculptures est situé entre le musée et la mer. Sur la rive nord du canal, les espaces d'exposition du musée d'art, avec une partie qui se prolonge sous le bâtiment des bureaux, abritent une collection permanente d'art contemporain. Le bâtiment situé sur la rive sud sert aux expositions temporaires. Le bâtiment de quatre niveaux de bureaux possède en son cœur un atrium éclairé en lumière naturelle. En référence aux traditions scandinaves, on a utilisé du bois vieilli par les intempéries pour les façades opaques du complexe.

Below, a sketch of the building by Renzo Piano. Right page, an aerial view shows the complex at the water's edge. From a lower angle it retains a modest yet confirmed presence thanks to the sloping roof.

Eine Skizze des Gebäudes von Renzo Piano (unten). Eine Luftaufnahme des am Wasser gelegenen Komplexes (rechte Seite). Aus einem niedrigeren Winkel behält das Gebäude dank seiner Dachneigung eine zurückhaltende, aber entschiedene Präsenz.

Ci-dessous, un croquis du bâtiment par Renzo Piano. Page de droite, une vue aérienne montre le complexe au bord de l'eau. Vu d'un angle moins élevé, sa présence plus discrète s'affirme par le toit en pente.

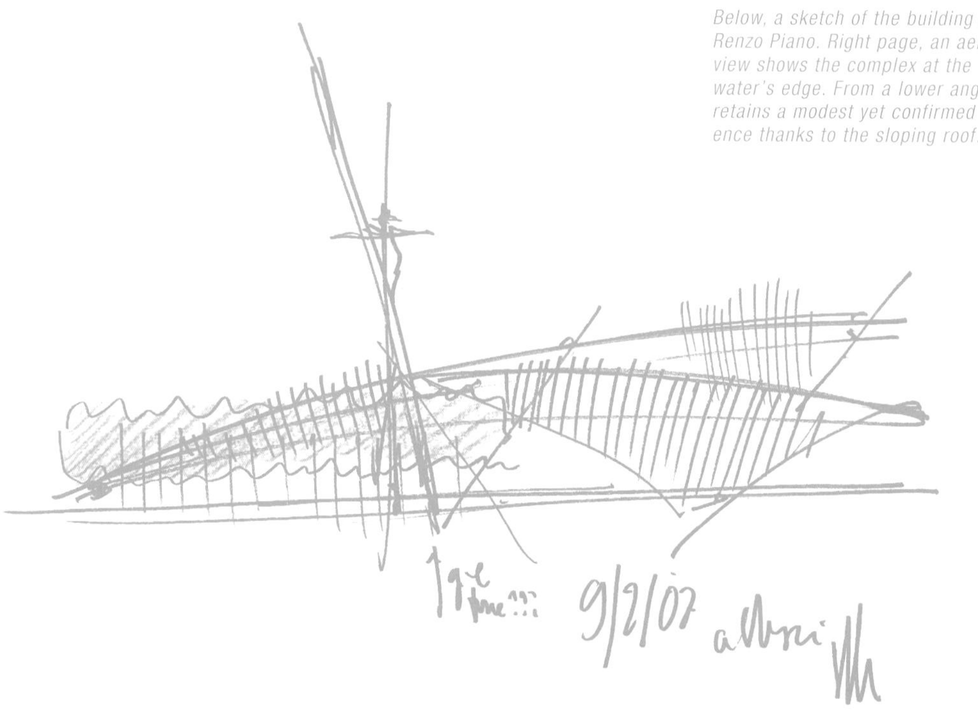

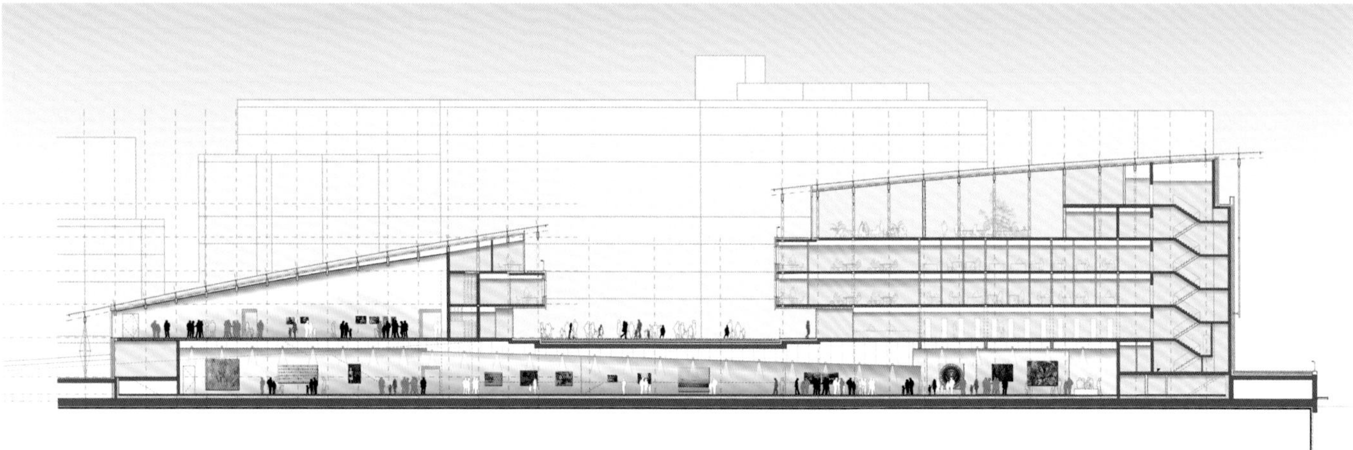

A section drawing shows how the complex is connected at the lowest level, rising in a steady slope away from the water. Below, convivial outdoor spaces are linked by canopies and bridges.

Der Querschnitt lässt das Untergeschoss erkennen, das den Komplex verbindet, der mit zunehmender Entfernung vom Wasser immer höher wird. Die belebten Außenbereiche sind durch Dächer und Brücken miteinander verbunden.

Une coupe montre comment le complexe, solidaire au niveau le plus bas, s'éloigne de l'eau en une inclinaison régulière. Ci-dessous, des espaces exterieurs sont reliés par des auvents et des ponts.

The drawing (right) and photo (above) demonstrate in part how the architect combines a feeling of lightness with architecturally substantial volumes.

Zeichnung (rechts) und Foto (oben) belegen, dass der Architekt Leichtigkeit und teilweise substanzielle Baukörper zu verbinden weiß.

Le dessin (ci-contre) et la photo (ci-dessus) démontrent en partie comment l'architecte associe volumes architecturaux considérables et sensation de légèreté.

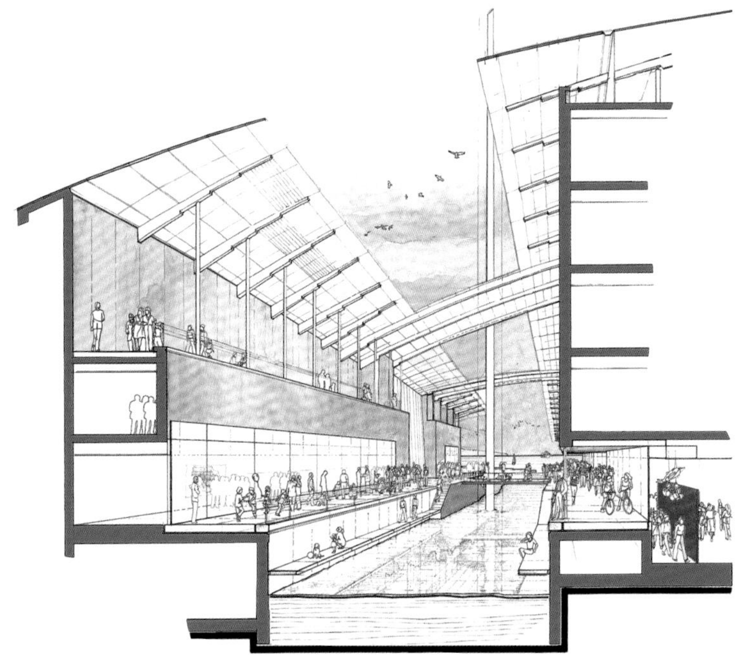

A view from above shows the curving roof with its irregular openings. The buildings are connected over the canal, seen above and also on the right page and in the section drawing below.

Eine Aufsicht zeigt das geneigte Dach mit verschieden großen Öffnungen. Sowohl oben als auch rechts und im Querschnitt unten ist zu erkennen, wie die Gebäude über den Kanal hinweg verbunden sind.

Une vue du dessus montre le toit incurvé et ses ouvertures irrégulières. Les bâtiments sont reliés par-dessus le canal, comme on le voit sur ces images et celle en page de droite, ainsi que sur la coupe ci-dessous.

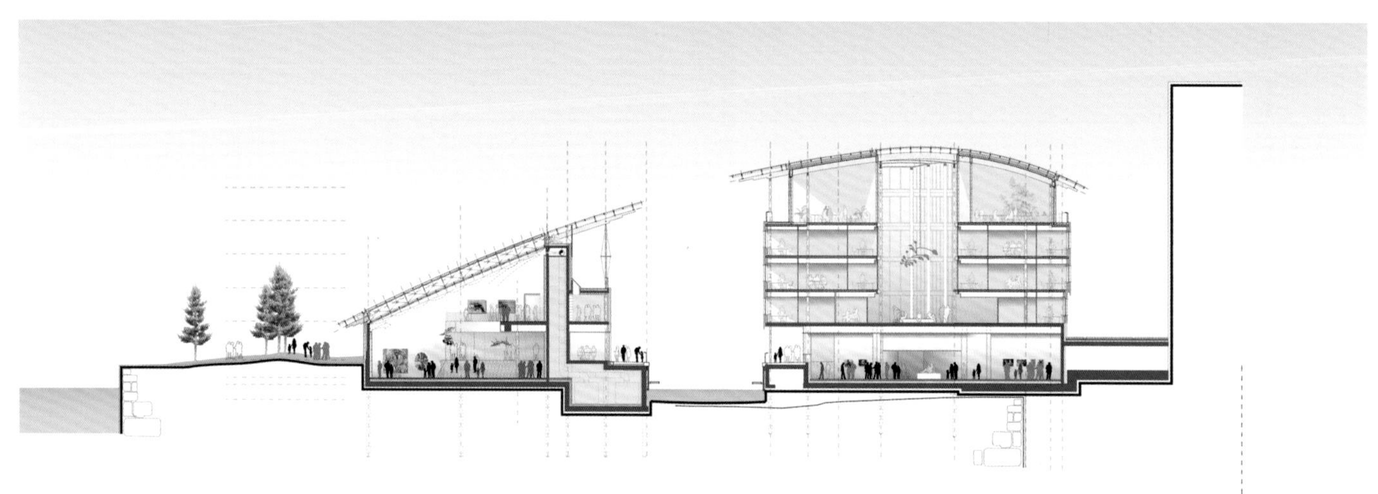

PROJECT ORANGE ARCHITECTS

Project Orange Architects
1st Floor Cosmopolitan House
10A Christina Street
London EC2A 4PA
UK

Tel: +44 20 77 39 30 35
E-mail: mail@projectorange.com
Web: www.projectorange.com

Orange was formed in 1992 as a loose collaboration of young architects. In 1997 a new company called Project Orange was established by Christopher Ash and James Soane. **CHRISTOPHER ASH** completed his architectural training at Cambridge University (UK) in 1991, while **JAMES SOANE** received an M.Arch from Cambridge University and took his Diploma at UCL. He joined Conran & Partners in 1992, becoming a Director in 1999.Their recent work includes the Jerwood Art and Technology building (Oakham, UK, 2009); Fitzwilliam Hotel (Belfast, Northern Ireland, UK, 2009); Whitechapel Gallery Dining Rooms (London, UK, 2009); Cemetery Road (Sheffield, UK, 2010); Riverside Manor House (Oxford, UK, 2011); Monsoon Restaurant (Bangalore, India, 2011); 192 Shoreham Street (Sheffield, UK, 2011–12, published here); and the Summer House (Moscow, Russia, 2012).

Orange wurde 1992 zunächst als loser Architektenzusammenschluss gegründet. 1997 riefen Christopher Ash und James Soane dann als neue Firma Project Orange ins Leben. **CHRISTOPHER ASH** schloss 1991 ein Architekturstudium an der Cambridge University ab, **JAMES SOANE** absolvierte einen M. Arch. an derselben Hochschule und schloss sein Diplom an der UCL ab. 1992 schloss er sich Conran & Partners an und wurde dort 1999 Direktor. Jüngere Projekte von Project Orange sind u. a. das Jerwood Art and Technology Building (Oakham, GB, 2009), das Fitzwilliam Hotel (Belfast, 2009), die Whitechapel Gallery Dining Rooms (London, 2009), Cemetery Road (Sheffield, 2010), Riverside Manor House (Oxford, 2011), Monsoon Restaurant (Bangalore, Indien, 2011), 192 Shoreham Street (Sheffield, 2011–12, hier vorgestellt) und Summer House (Moskau, 2012).

En 1992, de jeunes architectes collaborant librement se regroupent sous le nom d'Orange. En 1997, Christopher Ash et James Soane forment une nouvelle société qu'ils appellent Project Orange. **CHRISTOPHER ASH** achève ses études d'architecte à l'université de Cambridge en 1991. **JAMES SOANE** obtient un M.Arch, également à Cambridge, puis un diplôme à l'UCL. Il rejoint Conran & Partners en 1992 et en devient directeur en 1999. Parmi leurs réalisations récentes, on compte un nouveau bâtiment du Jerwood Art and Technology Building (Oakham, GB, 2009) ; l'hôtel Fitzwilliam (Belfast, 2009) ; les Whitechapel Gallery Dining Rooms (Londres, 2009) ; Cemetery Road (Sheffield, GB, 2010) ; la Riverside Manor House (Oxford, 2011) ; le Monsoon Restaurant (Bangalore, Inde, 2011) ; 192 Shoreham Street (Sheffield, 2011–12, présenté ici) et la Summer House (Moscou, 2012).

192 SHOREHAM STREET

Sheffield, UK, 2011–12

Address: 192 Shoreham Street, Sheffield, South Yorkshire S1, UK
Area: 900 m². Client: Neaversons. Cost: €1.5 million
Collaboration: JP Mooney Ltd. (Project Manager), Project Design Associates (Engineer)

This project involves a Victorian industrial brick building located at the edge of the Cultural Industries Quarter Conservation Area in Sheffield. The architects explain: "The completed development seeks to rehabilitate the once redundant building, to celebrate its industrial heritage, and to allow the building to be once again relevant for use. The brief was to provide mixed use combining a desirable double-height restaurant/bar within the original shell (capitalizing on the raw industrial character of the existing building) with duplex studio office units above. These are accommodated in an upward extension of the existing building in a contrasting but complementary volume, a replacement for the original pitched roof." They further explain that the extension is "parasitical" in nature, but that it allows both the creation of double-height volumes in duplex units, while also giving the entire structure a more modern appearance.

Das Projekt in einem viktorianischen Backsteinbau, einer alten Fabrik, liegt im sog. Cultural Industries Quarter Conservation Area in Sheffield. Die Architekten: „Das realisierte Projekt soll das industrielle Erbe dieses zuletzt leer stehenden Gebäudes unterstreichen und wieder nutzbar machen. Gefragt war ein gemischtes Programm mit attraktiven hohen Räumen für eine Nutzung als Restaurant und Bar im historischen Gebäudeteil (bei Betonung des industriellen Charmes) und Maisonette-Studios und -Büros darüber. Diese sind in einer baulichen Erweiterung untergebracht, die auf den Altbau aufgesetzt wurde. Sie bildet einen ergänzenden Kontrast und ersetzt das alte Satteldach." Die Architekten verstehen den Aufbau zwar als „parasitär", dafür ermöglicht er jedoch doppelte Raumhöhen in den Maisonette-Einheiten und gibt dem Gebäude ein insgesamt moderneres Gesicht.

Il s'agit d'un bâtiment industriel victorien en briques situé en bordure de la zone de protection dite Cultural Industries Quarter, à Sheffield. « Le projet achevé, expliquent les architectes, vise à réhabiliter le bâtiment désaffecté, à honorer son patrimoine industriel et à lui donner une seconde vie. La mission consistait à combiner un restaurant/bar attrayant sur deux étages à l'intérieur de la carcasse d'origine (en tirant parti du caractère industriel brut du bâtiment existant) avec des ateliers/bureaux en duplex au-dessus. Ceux-ci sont installés dans une extension surélevée du bâtiment existant, dans un volume en contraste mais complémentaire, en lieu et place de la toiture en pente d'origine. » Selon eux, l'extension est « parasite » de nature, mais elle permet la création de volumes sur deux niveaux pour les duplex, tout en donnant à toute la structure une apparence plus moderne.

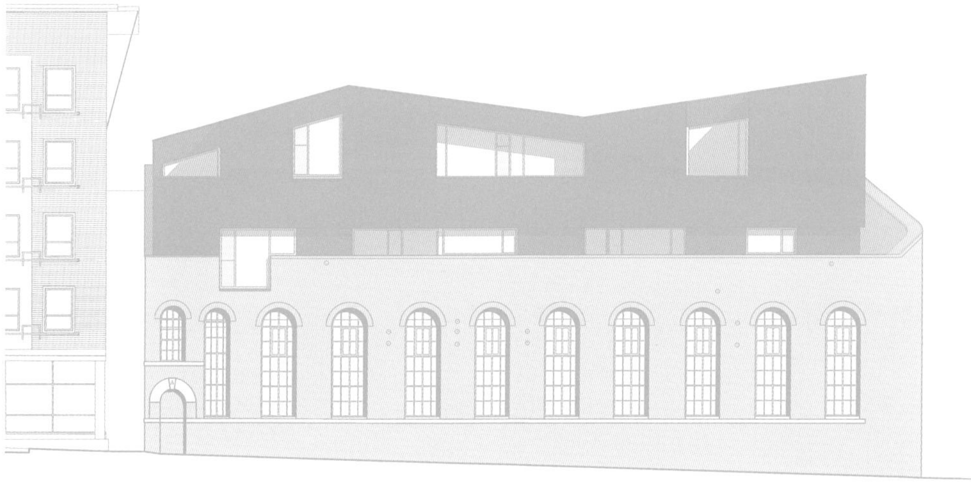

The architects manage to ally the forms of the older industrial brick building with their new black addition. Above, an elevation drawing shows the angled new volume sitting on top of its more regular brick base.

Den Architekten gelingt es, das alte Backsteingebäude mit der schwarzen Ergänzung in Einklang zu bringen. Der Aufriss oben zeigt den winkligen Baukörper auf dem geradlinigeren Backsteingebäude.

Les architectes réussissent à unir les formes du vieux bâtiment industriel en brique à leur extension noire. Ci-dessus, une élévation montre le nouveau volume en obliques reposant sur sa base plus régulière en brique.

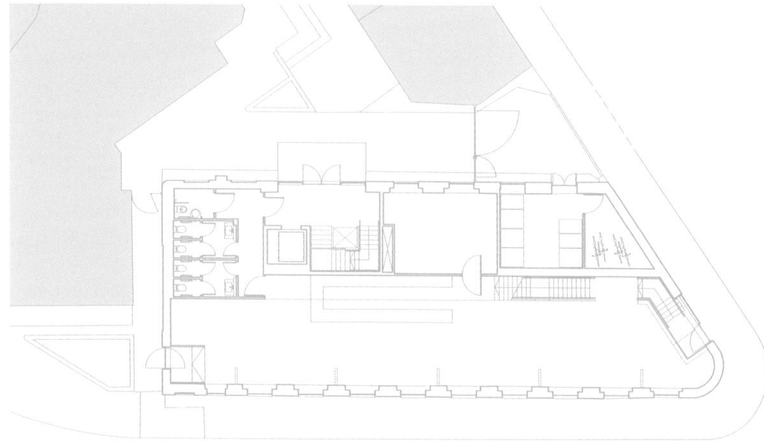

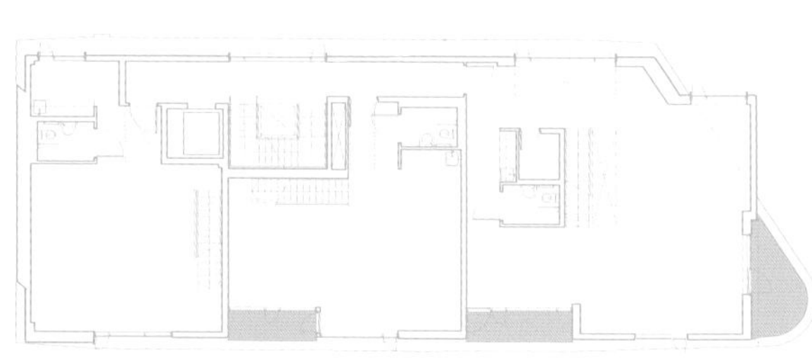

Plans show a greater regularity than might be expected from the exterior forms of the upper volume, and yet the architects also succeed in giving the angled spaces (images below) a logical coherence with the outside shapes.

Die Grundrisse des Neubaus sind regelmäßiger, als es die äußere Form der Aufbauten erwarten lässt. Gleichwohl gelingt es den Architeken, mit der Formensprache der winkligen Innenräume (unten) schlüssig an den Außenbau anzuknüpfen.

Les plans montrent une régularité plus grande que celle escomptée d'après les formes extérieures du volume supérieur. Cependant, les architectes ont réussi à donner aux espaces en obliques (ci-dessous) une logique en cohérence avec les formes extérieures.

Bright, high spaces, where colors such as lime green enliven the otherwise tan and white environment, contribute to the dynamic aspect of the project.

Helle, hohe Räume und kräftige Farben wie Limettengrün geben dem sonst in Hellbraun- und Weißtönen gehaltenen Projekt Dynamik.

Des espaces hauts et lumineux, où des couleurs, comme le vert citron, égaient un environnement plutôt brun clair et blanc, contribuent à l'aspect dynamique du projet.

RUDY RICCIOTTI

Agence Rudy Ricciotti
17 Bd Victor Hugo
83150 Bandol
France

Tel: +33 4 94 29 52 61 / Fax: +33 4 94 32 45 25
E-mail: rudy.ricciotti@wanadoo.fr
Web: www.rudyricciotti.com

Born in 1952 in Algiers, Algeria, **RUDY RICCIOTTI** moved to the south of France as a child. He attended the École Supérieure Technique in Geneva, from which he graduated as an engineer in 1975, and the Architecture School of Marseille, from which he graduated in 1980. He created his office in Bandol, France, in 1980, and won the 2006 Grand Prix National for Architecture, the highest French award in the field. His early work includes a number of private villas in the south of France. His first large-scale project was the stadium in Vitrolles (1994). In 1997 he completed the College 600 Secondary School in Saint-Ouen; and in 1999 a new building for the Luminy Science Faculty in Marseille. Recent work includes the Philharmonic Concert Hall in Potsdam (Germany, 2000); the Tanzmatten Concert and Sports Hall near Strasbourg (France, 2001); the Peace Footbridge in Seoul (South Korea, 2003); the National Choreographic Center (Aix-en-Provence, France, 1999–2005); the "Passerelle des Anges" (Hérault, France, 2009); and the Jean Cocteau Museum (Menton, France, 2009–11, published here). Rudy Ricciotti won competitions for the Department of Islamic Art of the Louvre Museum in Paris (France, 2008–12, also published here); for MuCEM, the European and Mediterranean Civilizations Museum (Marseille, France, 2012); and for the new building of the Venice Film Festival (Venice, Italy, 2005–). He is currently working on Les Arts Gstaad, a new cultural center in a Swiss Alpine village known for its classical music festival founded by Yehudi Menuhin (2012).

RUDY RICCIOTTI wurde 1951 in Algier geboren und zog als Kind mit seiner Familie nach Südfrankreich. 1975 schloss er ein Ingenieurstudium an der École Supérieure Technique in Genf ab und erhielt 1980 in Marseille einen Abschluss in Architektur. Noch im selben Jahr gründete er sein Büro in Bandol, Frankreich. 2006 wurde er mit dem Grand Prix National ausgezeichnet, dem wichtigsten Architekturpreis Frankreichs. Frühe Arbeiten sind eine Reihe von Privatvillen in Südfrankreich. Erstes großes Projekt war das Stadion in Vitrolles (1994). 1997 wurde die Sekundarschule Collège 600 in Saint-Ouen fertiggestellt, 1999 ein Neubau für die naturwissenschaftliche Fakultät in Luminy, Marseille. Neuere Projekte sind die Philharmonie in Potsdam (2000), die Konzert- und Sporthalle Tanzmatten bei Straßburg (2001), die Fußgängerbrücke des Friedens in Seoul (2003), das Nationale Zentrum für Choreografie (Aix-en-Provence, 1999–2005), die „Passerelle des Anges" (Hérault, Frankreich, 2009) und das Jean-Cocteau-Museum (Menton, Frankreich, 2009–11, hier vorgestellt). Rudy Ricciotti gewann die Wettbewerbe für die Abteilung für islamische Kunst im Louvre (Paris, 2008–12, ebenfalls hier vorgestellt), für das Museum für europäische und Mittelmeerkulturen MuCEM (Marseille, 2012) sowie den Neubau der Filmfestspiele in Venedig (seit 2005). Derzeit arbeitet das Büro an Les Arts Gstaad, einem neuen Kulturzentrum im Schweizer Alpendorf, das vor allem für sein von Yehudi Menuhin ins Leben gerufene Musikfestival bekannt ist (2012).

Né en 1952 à Alger, **RUDY RICCIOTTI** grandit ensuite dans le Sud de la France. Il obtient un diplôme d'ingénieur de l'École supérieure technique de Genève en 1975, puis poursuit ses études à l'École d'architecture de Marseille dont il sort diplômé en 1980. Il crée son agence à Bandol en 1980, et gagne en 2006 le grand prix national de l'architecture, la plus haute distinction française dans le domaine. Parmi ses premières réalisations, on trouve plusieurs villas privées dans le Sud de la France. Son premier projet d'envergure est le stade de Vitrolles (1994). En 1997, il achève le Collège 600 à Saint-Ouen, et, en 1999, la reconstruction du grand hall de la faculté des sciences Luminy à Marseille. Ses projets récents comprennent la salle de concert philharmonique de Potsdam (Allemagne, 2000) ; la salle de spectacles et la salle festive Les Tanzmatten près de Strasbourg (2001) ; la passerelle de la Paix à Séoul (Corée-du-Sud, 2003) ; le Centre national chorégraphique d'Aix en Provence (1999–2005) ; la passerelle des Anges (Hérault, 2009) et le musée Jean Cocteau (Menton, 2009–11, présenté ici). Rudy Ricciotti a gagné des concours pour le département des Arts de l'islam du Louvre (Paris, 2008–12, également présenté ici) ; pour le MuCEM, Musée des civilisations de l'Europe et de la Méditerranée (Marseille, 2012) et pour le nouveau Palais du cinéma de la Mostra de Venise (Venise, 2005–). Il travaille actuellement sur Les Arts Gstaad, le nouveau centre culturel d'un village des Alpes suisses connu pour son festival de musique classique créé par Yehudi Menuhin (2012).

JEAN COCTEAU MUSEUM

Menton, France, 2009–11

Address: 2 Quai de Monléon, 06500 Menton, France, +33 489 81 52 50, www.museecocteaumenton.fr
Area: 1656 m². Client: City of Menton. Cost: €11.78 million
Collaboration: Marco Arioldi (Assistant Architect)

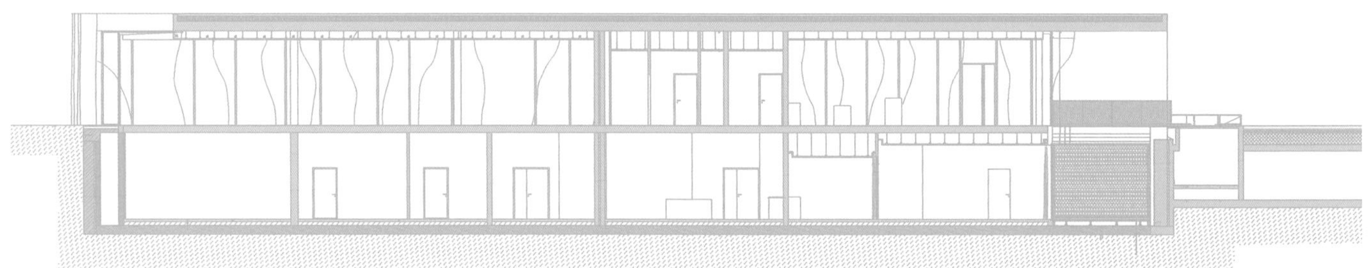

A section drawing (above) shows the two rectilinear floor plates. The structure itself is simple and straightforward.

Der Querschnitt (oben) zeigt die beiden geradlinigen Geschossplatten. Die Konstruktion selbst ist schlicht und schnörkellos.

Une coupe (ci-dessus) montre les deux planchers rectilignes. La structure elle-même est simple et sobre.

Rudy Ricciotti was the winner of a 2007 international competition to design a museum intended to display works by Jean Cocteau donated by Severin Wunderman to the city of Menton in the south of France. The architect had to deal with underground parking and water purification facilities that already existed on the site, as well as a busy urban setting and exposure to sea spray. A further complication was added by a neighboring 19th-century market building that had to be left fully intact. The architect quotes Jean Cocteau, who said: "There is nothing more vulgar than a work which sets out to prove something; acting without proof requires a leap of faith." The sculptural white concrete design engages not only the exterior walls, but also the roof. "The museum's roof will paint an allegorical picture," says Ricciotti, "its lines visible by day as well as at night." The architect goes on to say: "For this museum, we needed to create an atmosphere conveying the full force of the diametrical oppositions between light and dark, this play of shadows thus provoking 'the emotion inspiring us to see, believe, think, and dream,' in the words of Henri Alekan, director of photography of *La Belle et la Bête*, who added, 'I will record what I see on the roll of film as if I were writing in ink.' Alekan honors the poetic vision of Cocteau, who often juxtaposed light and dark in his films, with surfaces and depths set against each other, fully conscious of the psychological role of light and shadow for feeling and knowledge." Black and white, light and dark are thus the architect's palette as well.

Rudy Ricciotti gewann 2007 mit seinem Entwurf für das Jean-Cocteau-Museum einen internationalen Wettbewerb. Die Cocteau-Sammlung wurde der südfranzösischen Stadt Menton von Severin Wunderman gestiftet. In seine Planung musste der Architekt eine Tiefgarage und Wasseraufbereitungsanlagen einbeziehen, die sich bereits auf dem Gelände befanden. Eine Herausforderung waren das geschäftige urbane Umfeld, die Salzwassergischt und eine Markthalle aus dem 19. Jahrhundert, die sich in unmittelbarer Nachbarschaft befindet und erhalten bleiben sollte. Der Architekt zitiert Cocteau: „Nichts ist vulgärer als ein Werk, das sich beweisen will; ohne Beweis zu handeln, erfordert den Schritt ins Ungewisse." Skulptural erscheinen nicht nur die weißen Außenwände des Museums, sondern auch seine Dachlandschaft. Der Architekt: „Das Museumsdach soll ein (Sinn-)Bild zeichnen, das Tag und Nacht zu erkennen ist." Ricciotti weiter: „Wir wollten eine Atmosphäre schaffen, die den Gegensatz von Licht und Dunkel markant vermittelt, ein Schattenspiel, das ‚emotional berührt, uns inspiriert zu sehen, zu glauben, zu denken und zu träumen', wie Henri Alekan, Kameramann bei ‚Die Schöne und das Biest' formuliert. Alekan ergänzt: ‚Was ich sehe, banne ich auf Film als schriebe ich mit Tinte.' Alekan würdigt Cocteaus poetische Vision, der in seinen Filmen Licht und Dunkel oft als Oberflächen und Abgründe kontrastiert – wohl wissend, dass Licht und Schatten emotional wie intellektuell eine zentrale psychologische Rolle spielen." Folgerichtig arbeitet der Architekt hier mit Schwarz und Weiß, Licht und Dunkel.

En 2007, Rudy Ricciotti gagne un concours international pour la conception d'un musée destiné à exposer les œuvres de Jean Cocteau données par Severin Wunderman à la ville de Menton. L'architecte a dû composer avec un parking souterrain et une station d'épuration préexistants, ainsi qu'un tissu urbain chargé et une exposition soumise aux embruns maritimes. Complication supplémentaire, un marché couvert voisin, du XIXe siècle, devait rester intact. Les architectes citent Jean Cocteau : « Tout ce qui se prouve est vulgaire, agir sans preuve exige un acte de foi. » Le design sculptural de béton blanc engage les murs extérieurs comme la toiture. « Sa toiture, dit Ricciotti, est un tableau allégorique au graphisme lisible de jour et de nuit. Penser ce musée, ajoute l'architecte, c'était imaginer un principe architectural capable de porter le contraste entre lumière et obscurité et le sublimer par un jeu d'ombres provoquant "l'émotion qui donne à voir, à penser, à réfléchir et à rêver", comme le disait Henri Alekan, directeur de la photographie sur le film *La Belle et la Bête*, ajoutant "Je vais écrire en pellicule comme avec de l'encre". Alekan traduit l'expression poétique de Cocteau qui, dans ses films, joue avec le clair/obscur, conscient du rôle psychologique de la lumière et des ombres pour l'émotion et la connaissance. » Ainsi, le noir et le blanc, l'ombre et la lumière sont aussi la palette de l'architecte.

The flat surfaces of the building are broken up or rather penetrated by irregular cracks that bring light into the interiors.

Die glatte Außenhaut des Gebäudes wird von unregelmäßigen Öffnungen zerschnitten, durch die Licht ins Innere des Baus fällt.

Les surfaces planes du bâtiment sont fêlées ou plutôt percées de fissures irrégulières qui laissent entrer la lumière à l'intérieur.

Seen from below, the openings in the façades of the building take on a sculptural and surprisingly light form.

Von unten betrachtet erscheinen die Fassadenöffnungen skulptural und erstaunlich leicht.

Vues du dessous, les ouvertures dans les façades du bâtiment prennent une forme sculpturale et étonnamment légère.

Right page, a plan of the lower level of the museum and a view of light-filled gallery space, with the irregular shadows engendered by the façade design.

Rechts ein Grundriss der unteren Ebene des Museums und ein Blick in einen lichtdurchfluteten Ausstellungsraum mit einem Licht- und Schattenspiel, das durch die Fassadenöffnungen entsteht.

Page de droite, un plan du niveau inférieur du musée et une vue d'une galerie inondée de lumière, avec ses ombres irrégulières créées par le dessin de la façade.

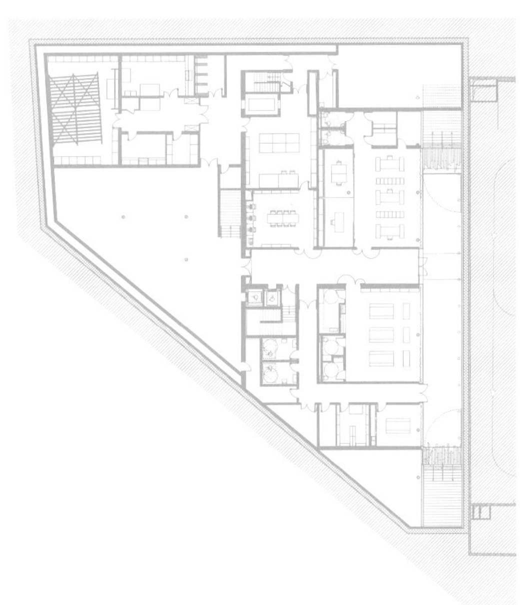

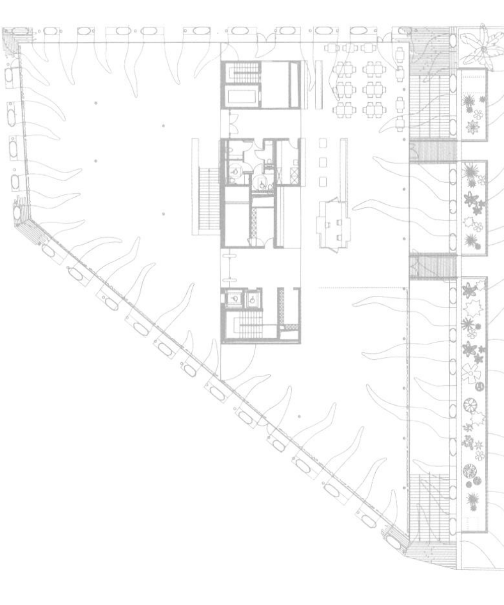

DEPARTMENT OF ISLAMIC ART

Louvre Museum, Paris, France, 2008–12

Address: Cours Visconti, Musée du Louvre (metro Palais-Royal), 75001 Paris, France +33 140 20 53 17, www.louvre.fr. Area: 2800 m² (galleries). Client: Musée du Louvre. Cost: €98.5 million. Architects: Rudy Ricciotti, Mario Bellini

Right page, the Cour Visconti in the Louvre, on the Seine River side of the palace, with the restored façades of the old building surrounding the undulating roof of the Department of Islamic Art.

Rechts der zur Seine gelegene Cour Visconti des Louvre mit den restaurierten Fassaden des historischen Palasts, die das geschwungene Dach der Abteilung für islamische Kunst rahmen.

Page de droite, en bord de Seine, la cour Visconti du Louvre, avec les façades restaurées du bâtiment historique entourant la toiture ondulante du département des Arts de l'islam.

Above, the interior gallery areas of the ground floor where visitors enter the department. The woven aspect of the roof is visible in this image.

Oben die ebenerdigen Ausstellungsräume, auf deren Niveau auch der Eingang liegt. Hier ist die gewebeartige Dachstruktur gut zu erkennen.

Ci-dessus, la galerie intérieure du rez-de-chaussée par laquelle les visiteurs entrent dans le département. On découvre sur cette photo l'aspect tissé du toit.

Located in the hitherto empty Cour Visconti of the Louvre not far from the Seine River, this space offers two levels of entirely new galleries for the rich collections of Islamic art of the Louvre. Rather than simply glassing over the courtyard or building a new structure inside the Napoleon III façades, the architects chose to place an undulating cover over the new galleries—a cover which does not touch the old façades at all but, instead, stands back from them by a margin of 2.5 to 4 meters. Made up of 2350 metallic triangles, the roof weighs approximately 135 tons, but it appears to float on the glass walls that stand on each side. The lower-level exhibition spaces, which are below grade, offer some glimpses of light but are largely darkened for the display of such delicate objects as oriental rugs. This project was carried out in collaboration between Rudy Ricciotti and the architect and designer Mario Bellini. Bellini was born in 1935 and graduated in 1959 from the Politecnico di Milano. He lives and works in Milan. His activities range from architecture and urban design to furniture and industrial design. As Bellini states: "The new space is not a building in the traditional sense of the word, nor is it a mere 'cover' for the courtyard. It's more like an enormous veil that undulates as if suspended in the wind, almost touching the ground of the courtyard at one point, but without totally encumbering it or contaminating the historic façades." Bellini also designed the exhibition installation with Renaud Pierard.

Das Projekt wurde im bisher ungenutzten Cour Visconti des Louvre realisiert, unweit der Seine. Auf zwei Ebenen entstanden hier neue Ausstellungsräume für die umfangreiche Sammlung islamischer Kunst. Statt eines Glasdachs über dem Innenhof oder eines Neubaus zwischen den historischen Fassaden aus der Zeit Napoleons III. planten die Architekten ein wellenförmiges Dach über der Galerie, das nicht bis an die Fassaden heranreicht, sondern einen Abstand von 2,5 bis 4 m wahrt. Das Dach aus 2350 Metalldreiecken wiegt rund 135 t, scheint aber auf den darunterliegenden Glaswänden zu schweben. Die unter Bodenniveau liegenden Ausstellungsbereiche sind nur verhalten beleuchtet, um empfindliche Exponate, darunter orientalische Teppiche, effektvoll zu akzentuieren. Rudy Ricciotti realisierte das Projekt mit Architekt und Designer Mario Bellini. Bellini wurde 1935 geboren und graduierte 1959 am Politecnico di Milano. Er lebt und und arbeitet in Mailand, in den Bereichen Architektur, Stadtplanung, Möbel- und Industriedesign. Bellini: „Hier handelt es sich nicht um ein Gebäude im üblichen Wortsinn oder eine schlichte Hofüberdachung. Eher ähnelt die Intervention einem großen Schleier, der im Wind weht, an einer Stelle fast den Boden des Hofs berührt, ohne ihn jedoch zu verbauen oder die Wirkung der historischen Fassaden zu schmälern." Gemeinsam mit Renaud Pierard entwarf Bellini auch die Ausstellungsräume.

Situé dans la cour Visconti du Louvre, vide jusqu'alors et non loin de la Seine, cet espace offre deux niveaux de nouvelles galeries pour les magnifiques collections d'art de l'islam du Louvre. Plutôt que de recouvrir la cour d'une simple verrière ou de construire une nouvelle structure à l'intérieur des façades Napoléon III, les architectes ont choisi de couvrir les nouvelles galeries d'une verrière ondulante – verrière qui, au lieu d'être collée aux façades historiques, s'en écarte d'une distance allant de 2,50 à 4 m. Faite de 2350 triangles métalliques, la toiture qui pèse environ 135 tonnes semble malgré tout flotter sur les murs de verre posés de chaque côté. Les espaces d'exposition du niveau inférieur, en sous-sol, ne reçoivent que peu de lumière pour présenter des objets aussi délicats que des tapis d'Orient. Ce projet est le fruit d'une collaboration entre Rudy Ricciotti et l'architecte et designer Mario Bellini. Né en 1935, sorti diplômé de l'École polytechnique de Milan en 1959, Bellini vit et travaille à Milan. Ses activités s'étendent de l'architecture au design urbain, en passant par le design industriel ou de mobilier. « Le nouvel espace, déclare Bellini, n'est pas un bâtiment dans le sens traditionnel du terme, non plus qu'une simple "couverture" de la cour. Il s'agit plutôt d'un immense voile qui ondule, comme suspendu dans le vent, touchant presque le sol de la cour à une extrémité, sans encombrer totalement ni altérer les façades historiques. » Bellini a également conçu la muséographie aux côtés de Renaud Piérard.

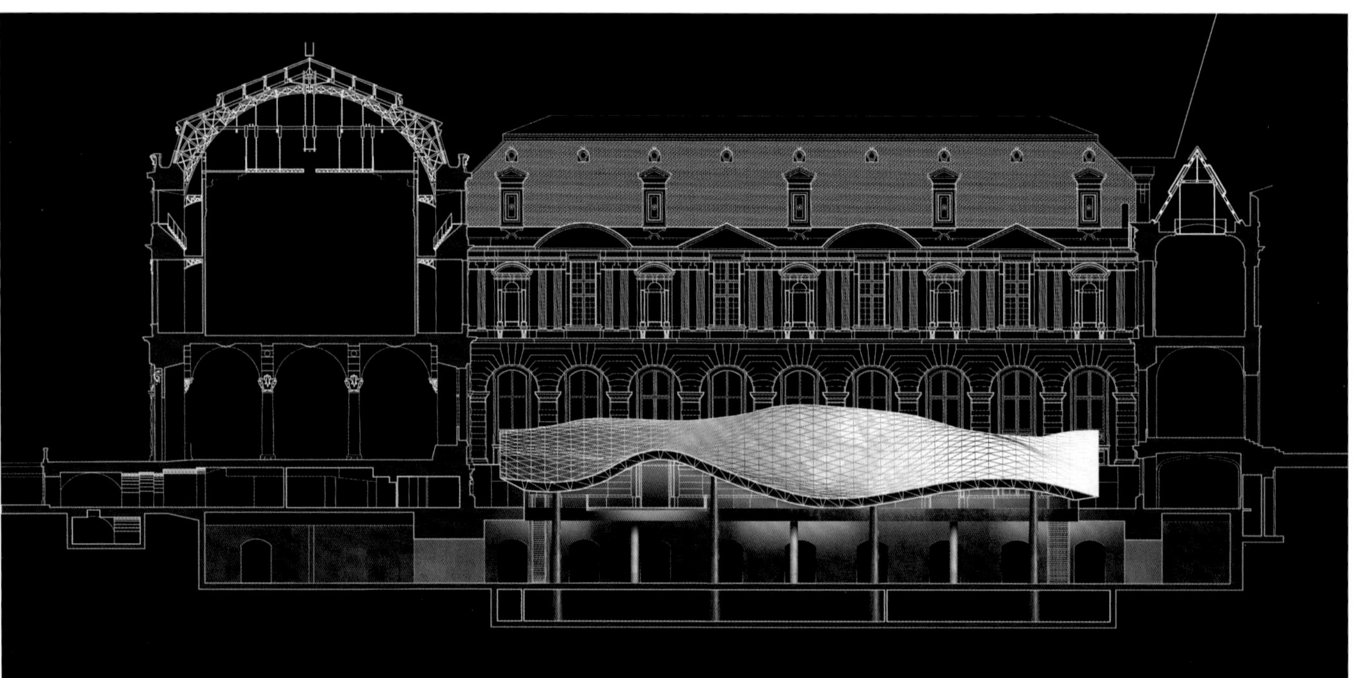

Above, a section drawing shows the golden form of the roof. To the right, the new structure is clearly delineated and separated from the older architecture. Bottom right, the larger and darker underground exhibition gallery.

Der Querschnitt lässt das goldene Dach erkennen (oben). Der Neubau hebt sich deutlich vom historischen Altbau ab (rechts). Unten rechts der abgedunkelte, größere Ausstellungsbereich im Untergeschoss.

Ci-dessus, une coupe montre la forme dorée de la toiture. Page de droite, la nouvelle structure est clairement définie et séparée de l'architecture historique. En bas, les galeries d'exposition, plus grandes et plus sombres.

"Beyond Infinity I"

SERGE SALAT

Serge Salat Architect
16, Rue de la Glacière
Paris 75013
France

Tel: +33 1 45 35 72 58
E-mail: serge.salat@free.fr
Web: www.serge-salat.com

To say that **SERGE SALAT** is the most highly educated and academically qualified participant in this book would be an understatement. Born in 1956, he graduated from the École Polytechnique as an engineer (Paris, 1976–79), from the equally prestigious Institut d'Études Politiques (Paris, 1979–82), and from the École Nationale d'Administration (Paris, 1984). He obtained a Ph.D. in Economics (Université Paris IX Dauphine, 1979–82); a Ph.D. in Architecture (École d'Architecture de Paris La Villette, 1989); and a Ph.D. in History and Civilizations (EHESS, Paris, 2010). He is a Professor at Paris-Est Marne-la-Vallée, at the École Nationale Supérieure des Mines de Paris, and at the École Nationale Supérieure des Ponts et Chaussées. In 2008, he founded the Urban Morphology Laboratory in Paris. The Lab "explores the theories of complexity and applies them to urban development, to building a science of urban energetics, to climate change mitigation and adaptation." He was a Project Director at Aéroports de Paris (Chief Architect and Engineer), while other main projects were Phnom Penh Airport (Cambodia), Ekaterinburg (Russia), Catania (Italy), and Abu Dhabi (UAE). He has also been Project Director of Ecocities urban planning in China and is a member of the board of IARO (International Air Rail Association). In particular, he designed the first structural titanium roof with a length of 500 meters and a 60-meter span. Published here, instead, are two art-architecture installations.

SERGE SALAT ist zweifellos der am vielseitigsten gebildete und qualifizierte Architekt in diesem Band. Geboren wurde er 1956. An der École Polytechnique schloss er zunächst ein Ingenieursstudium ab (Paris, 1976–79), danach folgten Studien am ebenso renommierten Institut d'Études Politiques (Paris, 1979–82) und der École Nationale d'Administration (Paris, 1984). Salat promovierte in Wirtschaftswissenschaften (Université Paris IX Dauphine, 1979–82), Architektur (École d'Architecture de Paris La Villette, 1989) und Geschichte und Kultur (EHESS, Paris, 2010). Er ist Professor an der Université Paris-Est Marne-la-Vallée, der École Nationale Supérieure des Mines de Paris und der École Nationale Supérieure des Ponts et Chaussées. 2008 gründete er das Urban Morphology Laboratory in Paris. Das Labor nutzt „Komplexitätstheorien für Stadtentwicklungsprojekte, für die Entwicklung einer Wissenschaft urbaner Energetik sowie zur Eindämmung und Lenkung des Klimawandels". Salat war Projektleiter beim Flughafenbetreiber Aéroports de Paris (Chefarchitekt und -ingenieur), wo er Großprojekte betreute, darunter die Flughäfen von Phnom Penh (Kambodscha), Jekaterinburg (Russland), Catania (Italien) und Abu Dhabi (VAE). Salat war zudem Projektdirektor von Eco Cities in China und ist Vorstandsmitglied von IARO (International Air Rail Association). Als Erster entwarf er eine Dachkonstruktion aus Titan, mit 500 m Länge und 60 m Breite. Hier vorgestellt sind zwei Installationen an der Schnittstelle von Kunst und Architektur.

Ce serait peu dire que **SERGE SALAT** est la personne au parcours académique le plus brillant de ce livre. Né en 1956, il sort diplômé de l'École polytechnique (Paris, 1976–79), puis du tout aussi prestigieux Institut d'études politiques (Paris, 1979–82) et enfin de l'École nationale d'administration en 1984. Il obtient un doctorat en sciences économiques de l'université Paris-Dauphine (1979–82), un doctorat en architecture de l'École d'architecture de Paris-La Villette en 1989 et un doctorat en histoire et civilisations de l'EHESS en 2010. Il enseigne à Paris-Est Marne-la-Vallée, à l'École nationale supérieure des Mines de Paris et à l'École nationale supérieure des ponts et chaussées. En 2008, il fonde Urban Morphology Laboratory à Paris. Le Lab « explore les théories de la complexité et les applique au développement urbain, à l'édification d'une science des énergies urbaines, de la réduction du dérèglement climatique et de l'adaptation à ce dérèglement ». Il a été directeur de projets chargé de l'architecture et de l'ingénierie pour les Aéroports de Paris. Dans ce cadre, il a dirigé la conception de grands aéroports comme ceux de Phnom Penh (Cambodge), Ekaterinburg (Russie), Catane (Italie) et Abou Dhabi (EAU). Il a été également directeur de projet pour la planification urbaine de écovilles en Chine et siège au conseil d'administration de l'IARO (International Air Rail Association). Il a conçu la première toiture en titane de 500 m de long et 60 m de large. Mais ce sont deux installations d'art-architecture qui sont présentées ici.

"BEYOND INFINITY I"

Shanghai, Beijing, Guangzhou, China, 2007

Address: not applicable. Area: 240 m²
Client: Buick China. Cost: €300 000

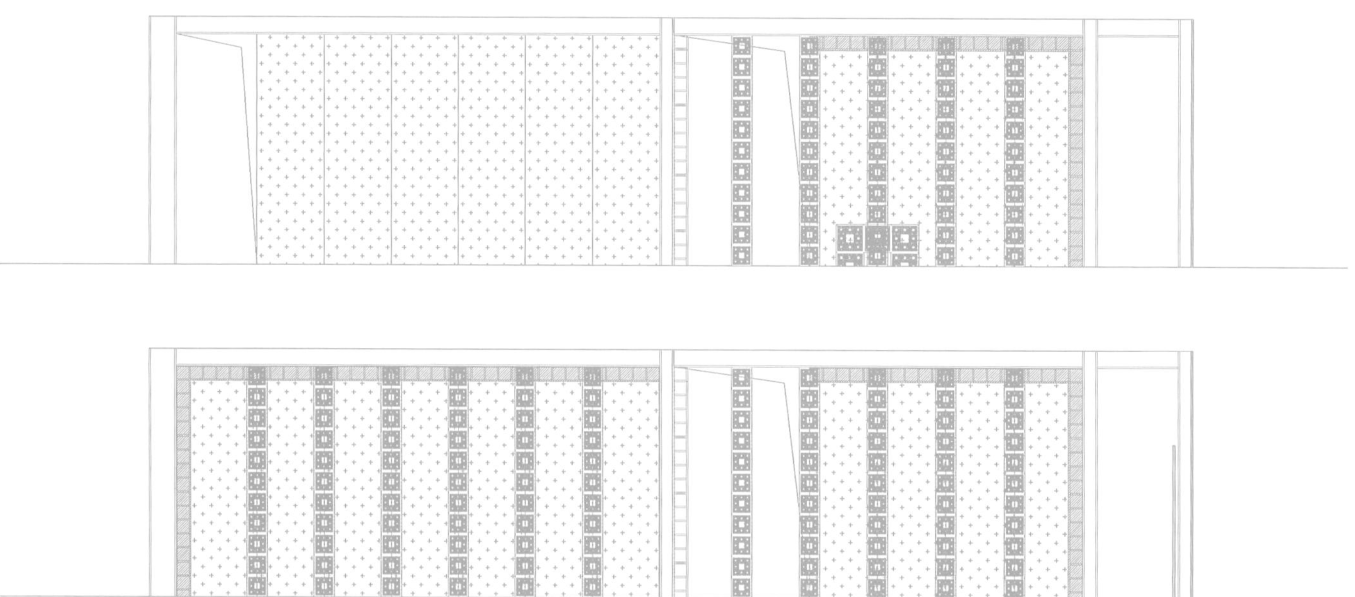

This art and architecture installation was made up of three linked rooms. According to Serge Salat: "It explores at the same time the Japanese concepts of architectural space and the space of closed and open Chinese courtyards." The goal of the architect is to "make the spectator get out of normal space to enter a highly paradoxical space, floating, dreamlike, with deeper and deeper layers of dreams." Architectural shapes such as columns, walls, and cubes are used so that the visitor will not be completely disoriented. Positive and negative spaces are employed, as are "manipulations of scale." The fractal patterning of all surfaces, an emphasis on the "heavenly colors" gold, red, and blue, the use of ultraviolet light, and the slow rhythmic fluctuation of the lighting are other techniques employed. Salat states: "They may look very abstract, my works are reminiscences and amplifications of personal experiences in space, experiences where you feel the encounter of time and some feeling of eternity. More generally, philosophy and literature played an important role in their creation: Leibniz in the 17th century describes in the *Theodicy* a dream very close to my installations, with a pyramid of virtual worlds extending to infinity and a brighter one, the real, chosen by God. I have been fascinated by Borges' *Fictions* and in particular *The Aleph.*"

Die Kunst- und Architekturinstallation besteht aus einer dreiteiligen Raumsequenz. Serge Salat: „Die Installation bezieht sich sowohl auf japanische Vorstellungen von architektonischem Raum als auch auf die Bauweise geschlossener und offener chinesischer Hofanlagen." Der Architekt lädt die Betrachter ein, „aus ihrem vertrauten Umfeld in einen faszinierend paradoxen, fließenden, traumartigen Raum mit immer tieferen Schichten von Träumen einzutreten". Architektonische Elemente wie Säulen, Wände und Kuben helfen den Besuchern, nicht völlig die Orientierung zu verlieren. Salat arbeitet mit positivem und negativem Raum ebenso wie mit „manipulierten Maßstäben". Weitere Stilmittel sind fraktale Muster auf den Oberflächen, ein bervorzugter Einsatz der „Farben des Himmels" wie Gold, Rot und Blau sowie ultraviolettes Licht und rhythmisch wechselnde Lichtmodulationen. Serge Salat: „Meine Arbeiten wirken mitunter sehr abstrakt. Sie gehen zurück auf persönliche Raumerlebnisse, Erlebnisse, die eine Begegnung mit der Zeit zulassen, eine Ahnung von Ewigkeit geben. Philosophie und Literatur sind hierbei eine wichtige Inspirationsquelle. Im 17. Jahrhundert beschrieb Leibniz in seiner *Theodizee* einen Traum, dem meine Installationen nahe kommen: Eine Pyramide virtueller Welten scheint sich ins Unendliche und damit in eine hellere, wirklichere, von Gott auserwählte Welt fortzusetzen. Auch Borges' *Fiktionen* faszinieren mich, vor allem *Das Aleph.*"

Cette installation d'art-architecture est composée de trois pièces reliées entre elles. Selon Serge Salat : « Elle explore tout à la fois les concepts japonais de l'espace architectural et de l'espace des cours chinoises ouvertes ou fermées. » L'architecte vise « à faire sortir le spectateur de l'espace normal pour qu'il entre dans un espace hautement paradoxal, flottant, onirique, fait de couches de rêves de plus en plus profondes ». Il utilise des formes architecturales telles que des colonnes, des murs ou des cubes pour que le visiteur ne soit pas totalement désorienté. Il emploie également des espaces positifs et négatifs, tout comme des « manipulations d'échelle ». Il emploie aussi d'autres techniques comme les motifs fractals sur toutes les surfaces, l'accent mis sur les « couleurs célestes » or, rouge et bleue, l'utilisation de la lumière ultraviolette ou la fluctuation rythmiquement lente de l'éclairage. « Mes œuvres, affirme Salat, peuvent paraître très abstraites, ce sont des réminiscences et des amplifications d'expériences personnelles dans l'espace, expériences où l'on rencontre le temps et un certain sentiment d'éternité. Plus généralement, la philosophie et la littérature ont joué un rôle important dans leur création : au XVIIe siècle, Leibniz décrit dans ses *Essais de Théodicée* un rêve très proche de mes installations, avec une pyramide de mondes virtuels s'étendant à l'infini, et un monde meilleur, le monde réel, choisi par Dieu. J'ai été fasciné par les *Fictions* de Borges, en particulier par *L'Aleph.* »

The section drawings on the left page show the rather extreme simplicity of the design, which is used to obtain very complex light and spatial effects, as seen in the image above.

Der Querschnitt links lässt die schlichte Strenge des Entwurfs erkennen, der dennoch höchst komplexe Licht- und Raumeffekte erzielt, wie oben im Bild zu sehen.

Page de gauche, la coupe montre l'extrême simplicité du design utilisé pour obtenir des effets de lumière et d'espace très complexes, comme on le voit sur la photo ci-dessus.

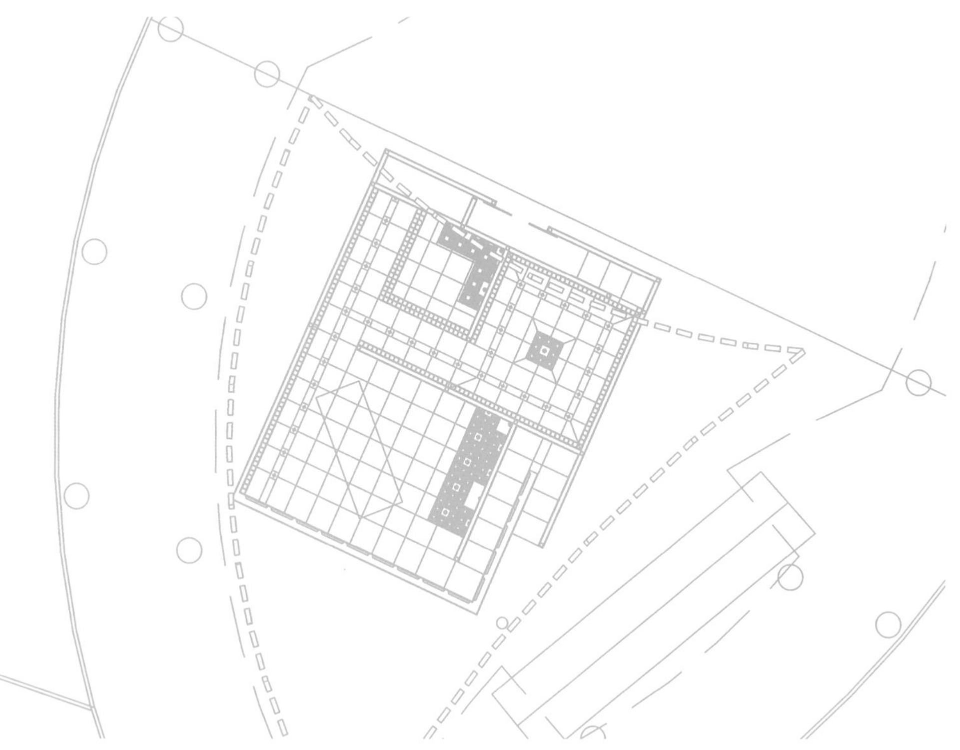

Left, a plan of the installation. With changing light patterns and reflections, the installation gives an impression of infinite space, definitely related to architecture, but not defined as "normal" space.

Links ein Grundriss der Installation. Wechselnde Lichtsequenzen und Spiegeleffekte vermitteln den Eindruck von Unendlichkeit. Auch wenn es sich hier um Architektur handelt, ein gewöhnlicher Raum ist dies keineswegs.

Ci-contre, un plan de l'installation. Avec ses motifs changeants de lumières et de reflets, l'installation offre une impression d'espace infini, vraiment en lien avec l'architecture mais non défini comme espace « normal ».

It is not clear for the visitor where the glowing forms begin and end, and where their reflections take over; they are in a sense lost in space defined by Serge Salat.

Für den Besucher ist nicht auszumachen, wo die leuchtenden Formen anfangen oder aufhören und in Spiegelungen übergehen – sie verlieren sich in diesem Raumkonstrukt von Serge Salat.

Le visiteur ne sait pas où commencent et où finissent les formes lumineuses, ni où leurs reflets prennent le pas. Elles sont perdues dans un espace défini par Serge Salat.

"BEYOND INFINITY II"

Shanghai, Beijing, and 10 other cities in China, 2011

Address: not applicable. Area: 144 m²
Client: Buick China. Cost: €500 000

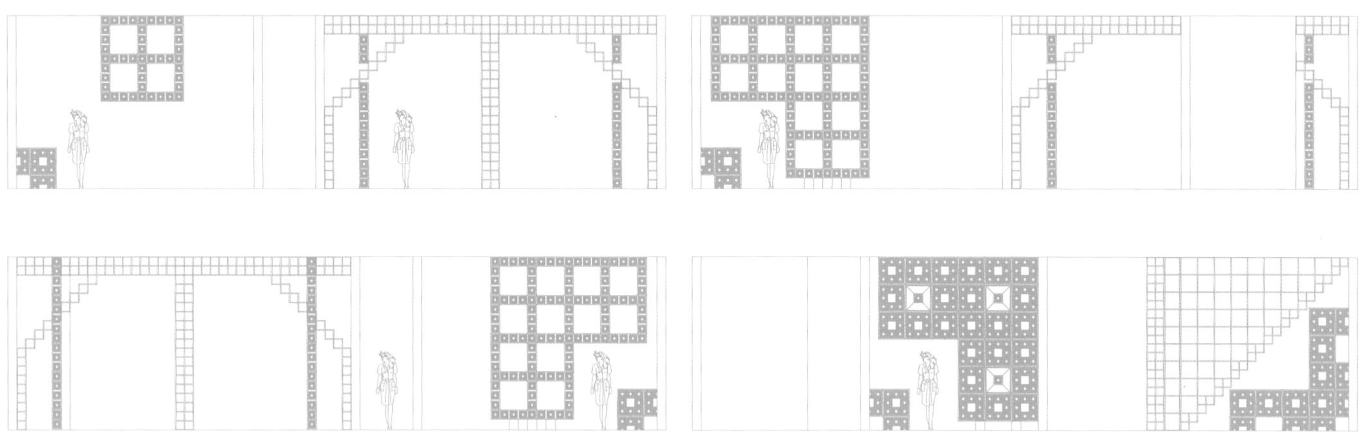

Serge Salat describes this work as "a highly complex, architectural 4D infinite maze. The composition is cinematographic and the experience is theatrical." Staircases are "cubic abstract reinterpretations of the Jantar Mantar cosmological observatories of Jaipur." A "traditional basilica plan structured by a Greek cross" is employed. A 1.8-meter "fractal cube" that is blue on the outside and gold in its interior occupies the center of the pavilion. Salat's description of the effects sought verges on the unreal. Visitors, he says, "pass under the steps of the inverted stairs and they face a fractal hyper cross, whose apparent magnitude measures 5.4 meters, and that extends its six arms toward them, one of which seems to sink into the void. Visitors are levitating in the median plane of this giant structure whose replicas to infinity sink into the abyss." In more general terms, Serge Salat explains that the installation is based on a fractal overall pattern, which is a 3D generalization of the Yi Ching trigrams. "In a certain sense," he states, "the installation is a giant immersive 4D mandala… A strong challenge for me is to recreate inside ultra modernity the spiritual meaning of space and time, which was so strong in ancient culture."

Serge Salat beschreibt seine Arbeit als „hochkomplexes, architektonisches, unendliches 4D-Labyrinth. Die Komposition ist kinematografisch, das Raumerlebnis dramatisch". Die Treppen sind eine „abstrahierte, kubische Neuinterpretation der historischen Jantar-Mantar-Sternwarten in Jaipur". Die Installation basiert auf einem „traditionell als griechisches Kreuz konstruierten Basilikengrundriss". Im Zentrum des Pavillons wurde ein außen blauer, innen goldener „fraktaler Kubus" mit einer Seitenlänge von 1,8 m platziert. Die von Serge Salat beschriebenen Effekte muten unwirklich an: Besucher „laufen unter den Stufen einer kopfstehenden Treppe hindurch auf ein monumentales, 5,4 m großes fraktales Kreuz zu, das sechs Arme nach den Besuchern ausstreckt. Einer der Arme scheint sich im Nichts aufzulösen. Die Besucher schweben in einer Zwischenebene der raumgreifenden Konstruktion, deren ins Unendliche gespiegelte Repliken unter ihnen in einen Abgrund stürzen." Die Installation basiert auf einem fraktalen Muster, einer 3D-Ableitung der Trigramme des I Ging. „In gewisser Hinsicht", so Salat, „ist die Installation ein raumgreifendes, immersives 4D-Mandala … Ich sehe es als Herausforderung an, in einer ultramodernen Welt die spirituelle Bedeutung von Zeit und Raum wiederzubeleben, die die Kulturen des Altertums so stark prägte."

Serge Salat décrit cette œuvre comme « un labyrinthe infini, complexe et architectural, en 4D. La composition en est cinématographique et l'expérience théâtrale ». Les escaliers sont « des réinterprétations cubiques abstraites de l'observatoire astronomique Jantar Mantar à Jaipur ». C'est un « plan de basilique traditionnel structuré par une croix grecque » qui est employé ici. Un « cube fractal » de 1,80 m, bleu à l'extérieur et doré à l'intérieur, occupe le centre du pavillon. La description par Salat des effets recherchés frise l'irréel. « Les visiteurs, dit-il, passent sous les marches de l'escalier inversé et se retrouvent face à une immense croix fractale dont l'envergure apparente est de 5,40 m et qui étend ses six bras vers eux, bras dont l'un semble plonger dans le vide. Les visiteurs sont en lévitation dans le plan médian de cette structure gigantesque dont les répliques à l'infini sombrent dans l'abîme. » En termes plus généraux, Serge Salat explique que l'installation est basée sur un motif global fractal qui est une généralisation en 3D des trigrammes du Yi King. « En un sens, poursuit-il, l'installation est un mandala géant immersif en 4D… Le principal défi pour moi est de recréer, à l'intérieur de l'ultra-modernité, le sens spirituel de l'espace et du temps si prégnant dans les cultures anciennes. »

Above, section drawings of the installation. Right, images evoke complex space where it is very difficult to differentiate "reality" from virtual depth and height.

Oben ein Querschnitt der Installation. Bilder evozieren einen komplexen Raum, in dem „Realität" kaum von virtueller Tiefe und Höhe zu unterscheiden ist (rechts).

En haut, des dessins de coupe de l'installation. Page de droite, des images évoquent un espace complexe où il est très difficile de différencier la « réalité » de hauteurs et de profondeurs virtuelles.

Serge Salat evokes the idea of a "4D mandala" to explain his motivations in creating this work. In the image below, a form like a Greek cross emerges.

Die Motivation für diese Arbeit war, so Serge Salat, ein „4D-Mandala" zu realisieren. Auf der Aufnahme unten zeichnet sich ein griechisches Kreuz ab.

Serge Salat évoque l'idée d'un « mandala en 4D » pour expliquer les motivations de son œuvre. Dans l'image ci-dessous émerge une forme de croix grecque.

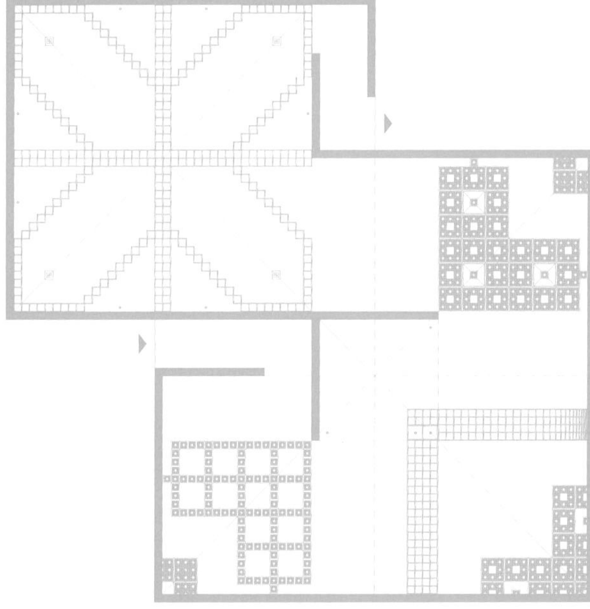

Left, a general plan of the installation. Above, a kind of virtual palace of light, where the usual orientation of directions is very difficult to define.

Links ein Grundriss der Installation. Oben ein virtueller Lichtpalast, in dem es höchst schwierig ist, sich zu orientieren.

Ci-contre, un plan général de l'installation. Ci-dessus, un palais virtuel de lumière où il est très difficile de retrouver l'orientation habituelle des directions.

SANAA / KAZUYO SEJIMA + RYUE NISHIZAWA

SANAA / Kazuyo Sejima + Ryue Nishizawa
1–5–27 Tatsumi, Koto-ku
Tokyo 135–0053
Japan

Tel: +81 3 5534 1780 / Fax: +81 3 5534 1757
E-mail: sanaa@sanaa.co.jp
Web: www.sanaa.co.jp

Born in Ibaraki Prefecture, Japan, in 1956, **KAZUYO SEJIMA** received her M.Arch from the Japan Women's University in 1981 and went to work in the office of Toyo Ito the same year. She established Kazuyo Sejima & Associates in Tokyo in 1987. **RYUE NISHIZAWA** was born in Tokyo in 1966, and graduated from the National University in Yokohama in 1990. They began working together in 1990, and created the new firm Kazuyo Sejima + Ryue Nishizawa / SANAA in 1995. In 2010 SANAA was awarded the Pritzker Prize. The built work of Kazuyo Sejima includes the Saishunkan Seiyaku Women's Dormitory (Kumamoto, 1990–91); Gifu Kitagata Apartment (Gifu, 2000); House in a Plum Grove (Tokyo, 2003); and Inujima Art House Project (1st phase: Okayama, 2010; 2nd phase: 2013), all in Japan. The work of SANAA includes the 21st Century Museum of Contemporary Art (Kanazawa, Ishikawa, Japan, 2002–04); the Glass Pavilion of the Toledo Museum of Art (Ohio, USA, 2003–06); Zollverein School of Management and Design (Essen, Germany, 2006); a Theater and Cultural Center in Almere (the Netherlands, 2004–07); a building for the New Museum of Contemporary Art in New York (New York, USA, 2005–07); the Rolex Learning Center of the EPFL in Lausanne (Switzerland, 2007–09); the Serpentine Pavilion (London, UK, 2009); and the new Louvre-Lens (Lens, France, 2009–12, published here).

Die 1956 in der Präfektur Ibaraki geborene **KAZUYO SEJIMA** absolvierte 1981 ihren M. Arch. an der Japanischen Frauenuniversität und begann noch im selben Jahr für Toyo Ito zu arbeiten. 1987 gründete sie in Tokio ihr Büro Kazuyo Sejima and Associates. **RYUE NISHIZAWA** wurde 1966 in Tokio geboren und schloss sein Studium 1990 an der Nationaluniversität in Yokohama ab. Noch im gleichen Jahr begann er, mit Sejima zusammenzuarbeiten. Gemeinsam gründeten sie 1995 ihr Büro Kazuyo Sejima + Ryue Nishizawa/SANAA. 2010 erhielt SANAA den Pritzker-Preis. Zu den Projekten von Kazuyo Sejima zählen das Frauenwohnheim Saishunkan Seiyaku (Kumamoto, 1990–91), das Gifu Kitagata Apartment (Gifu, 2000), das House in a Plum Grove (Tokio, 2003) und das Inujima Kunsthaus (Okayama, 1. Bauabschnitt 2010; 2. Bauabschnitt 2013), alle in Japan. Zu den Arbeiten von SANAA zählen das Museum für Kunst des 21. Jahrhunderts (Kanazawa, Ishikawa, 2002–04), der Glaspavillon des Toledo Museum of Art (Ohio, 2003–06), die Zollverein School of Management and Design (Essen, 2006), ein Theater- und Kulturzentrum in Almere (Niederlande, 2004–07), ein Neubau für das New Museum of Contemporary Art in New York (2005–07), das Rolex Learning Center an der EPFL in Lausanne (Schweiz, 2007–09), ein Pavillon für die Serpentine Gallery (London, 2009) und ein Neubau für den Louvre in Lens (2009–12, hier vorgestellt).

Né en 1956 dans la préfecture d'Ibaraki au Japon, **KAZUYO SEJIMA** obtient son M.Arch de l'Université pour les femmes du Japon en 1981 et commence à travailler la même année dans l'agence de Toyo Ito. Elle fonde Kazuyo Sejima & Associates à Tokyo en 1987. Né à Tokyo en 1966, **RYUE NISHIZAWA** sort diplômé de l'Université nationale de Yokohama en 1990. Ils travaillent ensemble à partir de 1990 et créent la nouvelle agence Kazuyo Sejima + Ryue Nishizawa / SANAA en 1995. En 2010, SANAA reçoit le prix Pritzker. Parmi les réalisations de Kazuyo Sejima, on trouve le dortoir pour femmes de la firme Saishunkan Seiyaku (Kumamoto, 1990–91) ; l'immeuble d'habitation Gifu Kitagata (Gifu, 2000) ; la House in a Plum Grove (Tokyo, 2003) et le centre d'art contemporain d'Inujima (phase 1 : Okayama, 2010 ; phase 2 : 2013), toutes au Japon. Les projets de SANAA comprennent le Musée d'art contemporain du XXIe siècle de Kanazawa (Ishikawa, Japon, 2002–04) ; le Glass Pavilion du Toledo Museum of Art (Ohio, 2003–06) ; l'École de gestion et de design Zollverein (Essen, Allemagne, 2006) ; un théâtre et un centre culturel à Almere (Pays-Bas, 2004–07) ; un bâtiment pour le New Museum of Contemporary Art de New York (New York, 2005–07) ; le Rolex Learning Center de l'EPFL de Lausanne (2007–09) ; le pavillon de la Serpentine Gallery (Londres, 2009) et le nouveau Louvre-Lens (Lens, 2009–12, présenté ici).

LOUVRE-LENS

Lens, France, 2009–12

Address: Rue Paul Bert, Lens 62300, France, +33 3 21 18 62 10, www.louvrelens.fr
Area: 28 000 m². Client: Région Nord-Pas-de-Calais, Musée du Louvre
Cost: €150 million. Collaboration: Imrey Culbert, Adrien Gardère, Catherine Mosbach

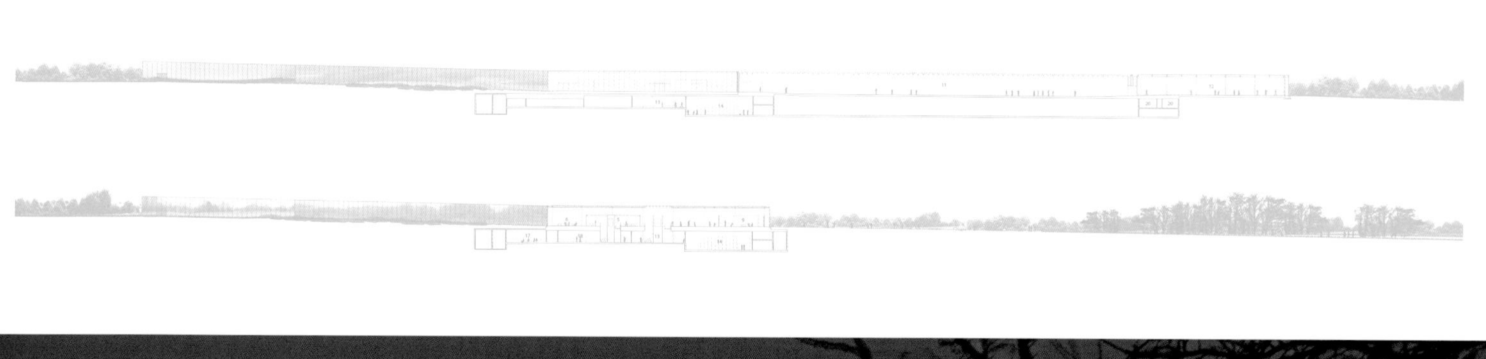

This ambitious project occupies a 20-hectare site. The entrance foyer is a glass hall measuring 68 by 58 meters, or 4000 square meters. Permanent exhibition space (3000 m²) and temporary exhibition space (1800 m², 1000 m²) is complemented by a 950-square-meter auditorium, a multimedia library and resource center, educational workshops, a gift and bookstore, restaurant, and cafeteria. Approximately 700 000 visitors are expected in the first year of operation with about 550 000 per year thereafter. Twenty years after the opening of the Grand Louvre with its Pyramid and new spaces by I. M. Pei, the Louvre is once again turning to contemporary architects for its new spaces—the Department of Islamic Art by Ricciotti and Bellini in Paris (page 392), and the Japanese firm SANAA for the new **LOUVRE-LENS**. SANAA's open, bright project is an assemblage of slightly skewed rectangular forms and high, broadly glazed spaces that bring to mind their 21st Century Museum of Contemporary Art (Kanazawa, Ishikawa, 2002–04). On semipermanent display will be 600 to 800 works from the Louvre in Paris. Displays are designed by Adrien Gardère. The building is set in a broad green space, created by the noted French garden designer Catherine Mosbach. The architecture and museum design also saw the participation of Tim Culbert and Celia Imrey (Imrey Culbert); in fact the intellectual property rights for the project are shared by SANAA, Imrey Culbert, and Catherine Mosbach.

Das Areal des ambitionierten Projekts ist 20 ha groß. Das Glasfoyer misst 68 x 58 m (4000 m²). Außer den Räumen für die Dauerausstellung (3000 m²) und temporäre Ausstellungen (1800 m², 1000 m²) gibt es hier ein 950 m² großes Auditorium, eine Multimediabibliothek, museumspädagogische Werkstätten, einen Museumsshop, ein Restaurant und eine Cafeteria. Für das erste Betriebsjahr werden 700 000 Besucher erwartet, im Folgejahr 550 000. 20 Jahre nach Eröffnung des Grand Louvre mit seiner Pyramide und den neuen Ausstellungsräumen von I. M. Pei setzte der Louvre bei seiner neuen islamischen Kunstabteilung von Ricciotti und Bellini in Paris (Seite 392) und dem Neubau **LOUVRE-LENS** von SANAA erneut auf zeitgenössische Architektur. SANAA's Entwurf zeichnet sich durch Offenheit und Helligkeit aus, verbindet leicht versetzte rechtwinklige Grundrisse mit hohen, großzügig verglasten Räumen und erinnert damit an ihr Museum für Kunst des 21. Jahrhunderts (Kanazawa, Ishikawa, 2002–04). Im Rahmen einer langfristigen Ausstellung sollen hier 600 bis 800 Werke aus dem Louvre gezeigt werden. Die Ausstellungsarchitektur wurde von Adrien Gardère entworfen. Der Neubau liegt inmitten großzügiger Grünanlagen, gestaltet von der französischen Gartenarchitektin Catherine Mosbach. Beteiligt an Architektur und Museumsplanung waren außerdem Tim Culbert und Celia Imrey (Imrey Culbert). Der Gesamtentwurf ist damit eine Gemeinschaftsleistung von SANAA, Imrey Culbert und Catherine Mosbach.

Cet ambitieux projet occupe un site de 20 ha. Le hall d'accueil de 68 m x 58 m, soit 4000 m², est entièrement vitré. Aux espaces d'expositions permanentes (3000 m²) et d'expositions temporaires (1800 m², 1000 m²) s'ajoutent un auditorium de 950 m², une bibliothèque multimédias/centre de ressources, des ateliers éducatifs, une librairie-boutique, un restaurant et une cafétéria. Environ 700 000 visiteurs sont attendus la première année, puis environ 550 000 par an. Vingt ans après l'ouverture du Grand Louvre d'I. M. Pei, avec sa pyramide et ses nouveaux espaces, le Louvre se tourne à nouveau vers des architectes contemporains, Ricciotti et Bellini, pour le département des Arts de l'islam à Paris (page 392), et l'agence japonaise SANAA pour le nouveau **LOUVRE-LENS**. Le projet de SANAA, tout en ouverture et en lumière, est un assemblage de formes rectangulaires légèrement obliques et de hauts espaces largement vitrés qui rappellent leur Musée d'art contemporain du XXIe siècle (Kanzawa, Ishikawa, 2002–04). Entre 600 et 800 œuvres du Louvre de Paris seront exposées de façon semi-permanente. La muséographie est d'Adrien Gardère. Le bâtiment est situé dans un immense espace vert dessiné par la célèbre paysagiste française Catherine Mosbach. Tim Culbert et Celia Imrey (Imrey Culbert) ont également participé à l'architecture et à la muséographie ; en fait, SANAA, Imrey Culbert et Catherine Mosbach se partagent les droits de propriété intellectuelle du projet.

The building is completely flat and relatively low, emerging in this image from the garden designed by Catherine Mosbach.

Der Bau ist gerade und relativ niedrig und liegt inmitten von Grünanlagen, einem Entwurf von Catherine Mosbach.

Le bâtiment, totalement plat et relativement bas, émerge sur cette photo prise du jardin dessiné par Catherine Mosbach.

Seen from a greater distance, the building appears as an almost evanescent form—a concept that is very much in the architects' line of thinking.

Aus der Ferne erscheint das Gebäude nahezu ephemer – ein Eindruck, der die Philosophie der Architekten spiegelt.

Vu d'une plus grande distance, le bâtiment apparaît comme une forme presque évanescente – un concept tout à fait dans la ligne de pensée des architectes.

Below, an overall site plan. Above, volumes are not so much clearly defined as they are formed by glass walls and thin columns that allow free communication between spaces and views as well.

Unten ein Lageplan. Oben: Der Baukörper ist nicht klar umrissen, sondern wird von Glaswänden und schlanken Säulen definiert, die Kommunikation und Blickachsen zwischen den Bereichen erlauben.

Ci-dessous, un plan d'ensemble du site. Ci-dessus, formés de murs de verre et de fines colonnes permettant une libre communication entre espaces et vues, les volumes ne sont pas clairement définis.

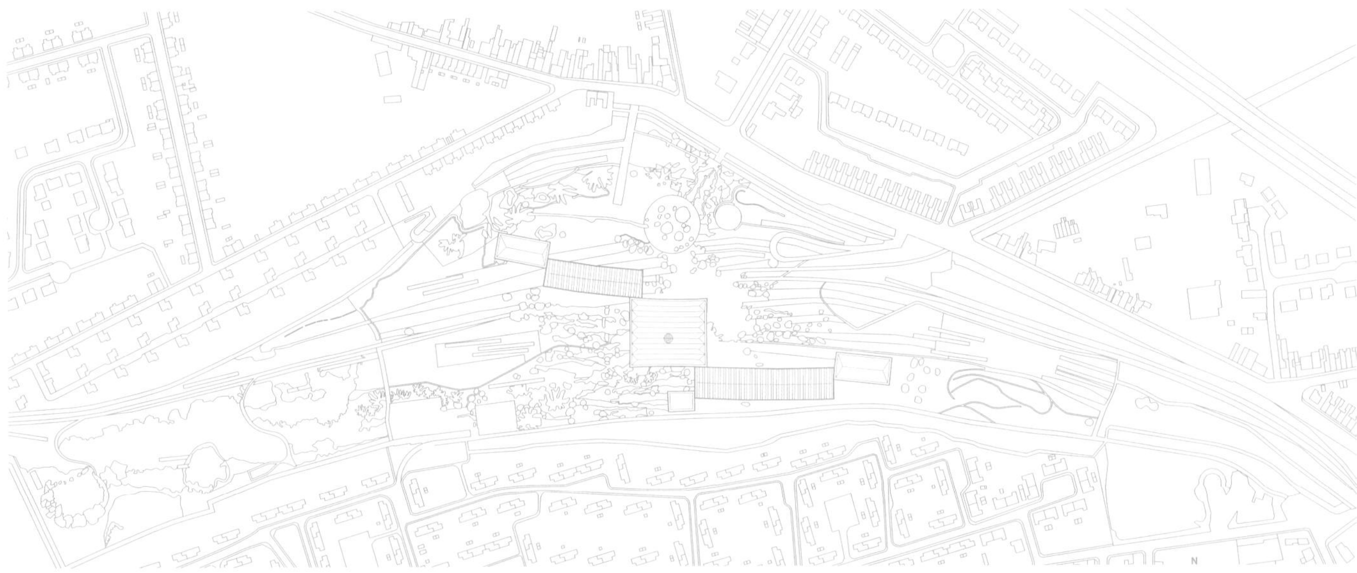

Exhibition galleries are deployed in the vast white spaces designed by the architects. Exhibition design is simple, in keeping with the architectural concept.

Die von den Architekten entworfenen, weitläufigen weißen Räume werden als Galerien genutzt. Die Präsentation ist schlicht und im Einklang mit dem architektonischen Gesamtkonzept.

Des galeries d'exposition se déploient dans les vastes espaces blancs conçus par les architectes. La muséographie est sobre, en accord avec le concept architectural.

SO – IL

Solid Objectives—Idenburg Liu
68 Jay Street #501
Brooklyn, NY 11201
USA

Tel: +1 718 624 6666
Fax: +1 718 624 6616
E-mail: office@so-il.org
Web: www.so-il.org

FLORIAN IDENBURG was born in 1975 in Heemstede, the Netherlands. He received an M.Sc. degree in Architectural Engineering from the Technical University of Delft (1999), and worked with SANAA in Tokyo from 2000 to 2007. **JING LIU** was born in 1980 in Nanjing, China. She received her M.Arch II degree from Tulane University in 2004 and worked from 2004 to 2007 with KPF in New York. Recent work includes Upto35, student housing (Athens, Greece, competition winner 2009); The Hague Dance and Music Center (the Netherlands, competition 2010); the "Pole Dance" installation (PS1, Long Island City, New York, 2010); a park pavilion (Amsterdam, the Netherlands, project 2010–11); a wedding chapel (Nanjing, China, 2008–12); Kukje Art Gallery (Seoul, South Korea, 2009–12, published here); and a housing block (Athens, Greece, project 2010–12). They have also completed an installation for the Frieze Art Fair (New York, 2012, also published here).

FLORIAN IDENBURG wurde 1975 im niederländischen Heemstede geboren. Er absolvierte seinen M. Sc. im Fach Bauingenieurwesen an der TU Delft (1999) und arbeitete von 2000 bis 2007 für SANAA in Tokio. **JING LIU** wurde 1980 in Nanjing, China, geboren. Sie absolvierte 2004 ihren M. Arch. II an der Tulane University und arbeitete von 2004 bis 2007 für KPF in New York. Jüngere Arbeiten des Büros sind u. a. das Studentenwohnheim Upto35 (Athen, 1. Preis, Wettbewerb 2009), das Zentrum für Tanz und Musik in Den Haag (Wettbewerb 2010), die Installation „Pole Dance" (PS1, Long Island City, New York, 2010), ein Parkpavillon (Amsterdam, Projekt 2010 bis 2011), eine Hochzeitskapelle (Nanjing, China, 2008–12), die Kukje Gallery (Seoul, Südkorea, 2009–12, hier vorgestellt) und ein Wohnblock (Athen, Projekt 2010–12). Idenburg und Liu entwarfen außerdem eine Messeinstallation für die Frieze Art Fair (New York, 2012, ebenfalls hier vorgestellt).

FLORIAN IDENBURG est né en 1975 à Heemstede, aux Pays-Bas. Il obtient un M.Sc. en ingénierie architectonique à l'Université de technologie de Delft en 1999 et travaille chez SANAA à Tokyo de 2000 à 2007. **JING LIU** est née en 1980 à Nankin. Elle obtient son M.Arch II à l'université Tulane en 2004 et travaille chez KPF à New York entre 2004 et 2007. Leurs projets récents comprennent la résidence universitaire Upto35 (Athènes, gagnant du concours 2009) ; le Centre de la danse et de la musique de La Haye (concours 2010) ; l'installation *Pole Dance* (PS1, Long Island, New York, 2010) ; un pavillon de parc (Amsterdam, projet 2010–11) ; une chapelle des mariages (Nankin, 2008–12) ; la galerie d'art Kukje (Séoul, 2009–12, présentée ici) et un ensemble immobilier (Athènes, projet 2010–12). Ils ont également achevé une installation pour la Frieze Art Fair (New York, 2012, également présentée ici).

KUKJE ART GALLERY

Seoul, South Korea, 2009–12

Address: Jongro-gu, Samcheong-ro 54, Jongno-gu, Seoul 110–200, South Korea, +82 2735 8449, www.kukje.org
Area: 1500 m². Client: Kukje Art Gallery. Cost: not disclosed

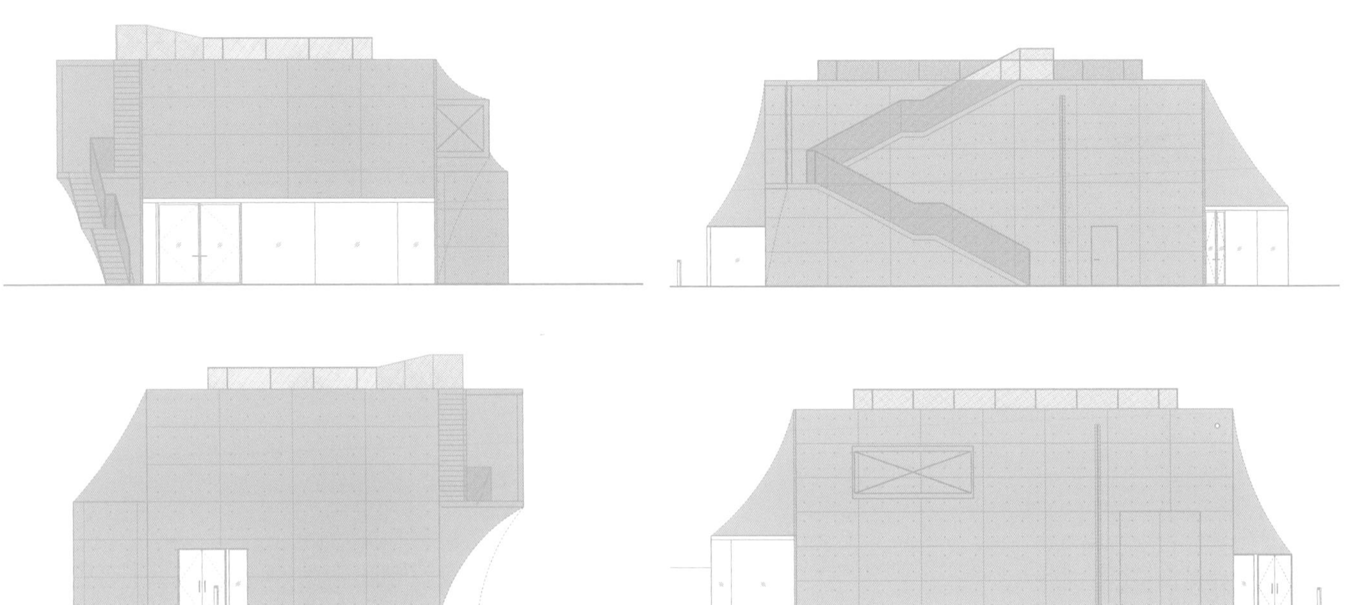

Above, elevation drawings show the curved, tilting forms of the building, with extrusions such as the one at the right seemingly flowing out of the main volume.

Die Aufrisse lassen die geschwungenen, schrägen Konturen des Gebäudes erkennen, ebenso wie Ausbuchtungen, die aus dem Baukörper herauszuwachsen scheinen (oben).

Ci-dessus, des élévations montrent les formes penchées et incurvées du bâtiment, avec des protubérances telle celle en page de droite qui semble jaillir du volume principal.

The architects have developed a master plan for the "art campus" imagined by the gallery in the historic Sogyeok-dong area of northern Seoul. Part of this master plan is the single-story gallery published here. The ground floor will be used for large installations, performances, and other events, while the two sublevel floors house a conference room, a lecture space, and storage areas. A perimeter skylight admits natural light. Rather than a simple white cube, the building is wrapped in a stainless-steel mesh. Referring to this mesh as a "permanent nebula," the architects write that it "produces a layer of diffusion in front of the actual building mass, through a combination of multidirectional reflection, openness, and the moiré pattern generated through interplay of its shadows. An additional quality of the material is that it can stretch, thus avoiding creasing. It is strong yet pliable, and can easily wrap around crude geometries."

Die Architekten entwarfen einen Masterplan für den „Kunstcampus" der Galerie im historischen Stadtteil Sogyeok-dong im Norden von Seoul, zu dem auch die Galerie selbst gehört. Dort werden im Erdgeschoss größere Ausstellungen präsentiert, in den zwei Untergeschossen sind Konferenz-, Vortrags- und Lagerräume untergebracht. Ein umlaufendes Dachfenster lässt Licht ins Innere. Statt einen schlichten weißen Kubus zu planen, hüllten die Architekten das Gebäude in ein Netz aus rostfreiem Stahl, einen „immerwährenden Nebel". Dieser bildet „vor dem eigentlichen Baukörper eine diffuse Schicht, die durch multidirektionale Reflexionen, Transparenz und das Moirémuster entsteht, das durch das erzeugte Schattenspiel zustande kommt. Eine weitere Materialeigenschaft ist seine Biegsamkeit, die Faltungen verhindert. Das Netz ist stabil und elastisch und lässt sich selbst um unregelmäßige Formen hüllen."

Les architectes ont conçu un plan directeur pour ce « campus de l'art » imaginé par la galerie dans le quartier historique de Sogyeok-dong du nord de Séoul. La galerie à un étage, présentée ici, fait partie de ce plan. Le rez-de-chaussée sert pour des installations de grande taille, des performances et d'autres événements, et les deux sous-niveaux abritent une salle de conférences, un espace de lecture et des réserves. Une ouverture périphérique laisse entrer la lumière naturelle. Loin d'être un simple cube blanc, le bâtiment est enveloppé dans un filet en acier inoxydable. Parlant de ce filet comme d'une « nébuleuse permanente », les architectes écrivent qu'il « produit une nappe de diffusion devant la masse du bâtiment, grâce au mélange des reflets multidirectionnels, de l'ouverture et du motif moiré créé par le jeu de ses ombres. Ce matériau possède une autre qualité qui est d'être extensible, évitant ainsi les faux plis. Il est solide mais souple et peut aisément s'enrouler autour de géométries brutes ».

Though it appears to be relatively opaque from certain angles, as it does in the photos above, the building's mesh exterior means that it is actually more permeable than it may seem.

Obwohl das Gebäude aus bestimmten Blickwickeln relativ geschlossen wirkt, erlaubt das Netz eine auf den ersten Blick nicht zu erwartende Durchlässigkeit (oben).

Même s'il apparaît relativement opaque sous certains angles, comme sur les photos ci-dessus, l'extérieur en mailles du bâtiment le rend plus perméable qu'il ne semble.

A window in the image above gives a glimpse of the art on display. Right, a section shows the main building and the two "sublevels" including a lecture space and storage area.

Einblick in die Galerieräume durch ein Fenster (oben). Der Querschnitt zeigt das Hauptgebäude mit den beiden Untergeschossen, in denen Vortrags- und Lagerräume liegen.

Dans l'image ci-dessus, une fenêtre laisse voir les œuvres exposées. Ci-contre, une coupe montre le bâtiment principal et les deux « sous-niveaux » comprenant un espace de lecture et des réserves.

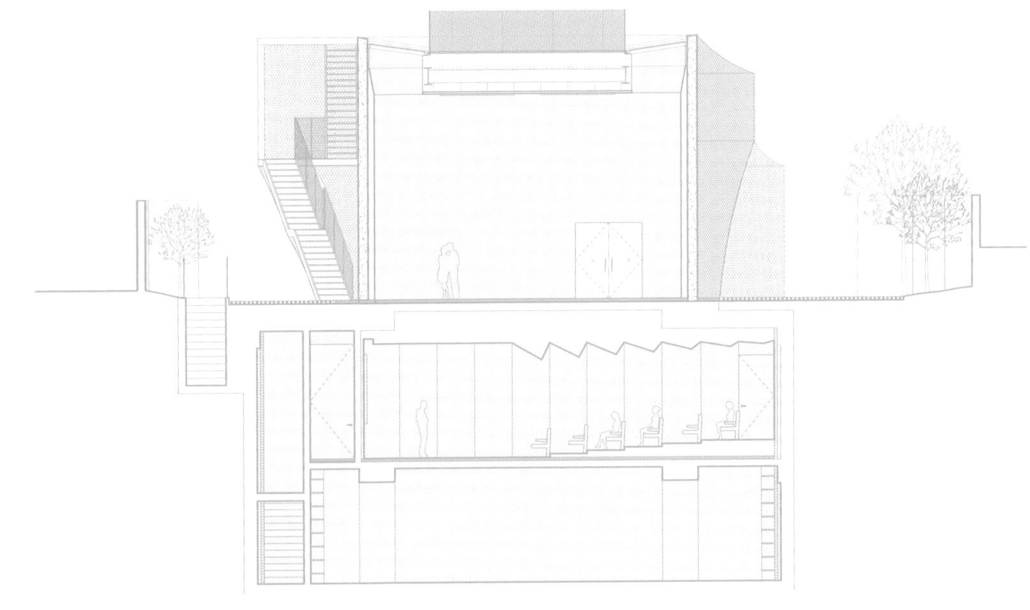

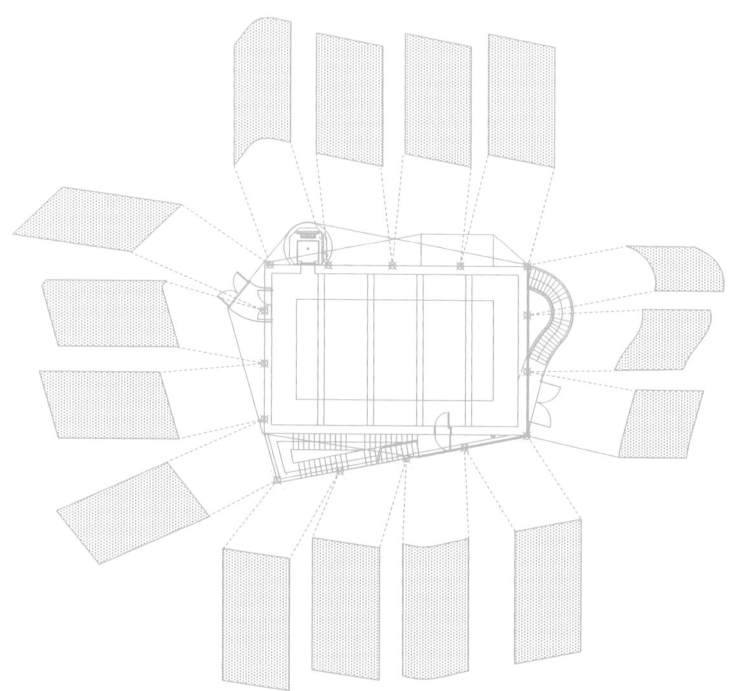

Left, an exploded drawing of the plan and, below, images that contrast the curving exterior glazing with the more traditional buildings nearby.

Eine Explosionszeichnung (links) und Aufnahmen der geschwungenen Außenverglasung – ein Kontrast zur eher traditionellen nachbarschaftlichen Bebauung (unten).

Ci-contre, un dessin éclaté du plan et, ci-dessous, des photos qui mettent en contraste le vitrage extérieur incurvé et les bâtiments voisins plus traditionnels.

Below, a plan of the underground spaces, and, right, an image of the main exhibition gallery with its double-height space.

Ein Grundriss der Räume im Untergeschoss (unten) und ein Blick in den zentralen Ausstellungsraum mit doppelter Raumhöhe (rechts).

Ci-dessous, un plan des espaces en sous-sol et, ci-contre, une photo de la grande galerie d'exposition avec sa double hauteur.

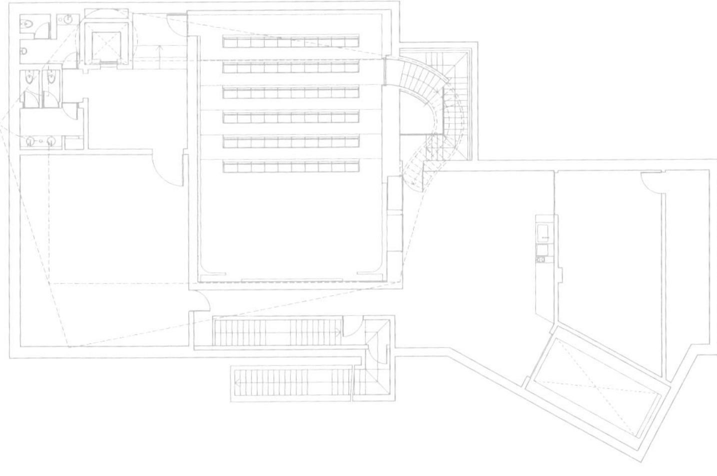

FRIEZE ART FAIR

New York, New York, USA, 2012

Address: not applicable. Area: 20 900 m². Client: Frieze Art Fair
Cost: not disclosed

The architects worked in this instance with an essentially prefabricated structure no less than 457 meters in length. Erected on Randall's Island, which is located between Manhattan, the Bronx, and Queens, the tent housed the prestigious **FRIEZE ART FAIR**, which is dedicated to contemporary art. The solution of SO – IL to alleviate the problem of the standardization of the tent system was to insert new pie-shaped wedges between six tent sections, offering amenities and bending "the otherwise straight tent into a meandering, supple shape," according to the architects. They continue: "The winding form animates it on the unusual waterfront site, as well as establishing the temporary structure as an icon along the water." SO – IL also extended the tent roof fabric with stripes at the end of the gable section of each tent. As they say, "this gesture serves to dissolve the tent into the ground," and "the playful entrances introduce visitors to the experience within."

Bei diesem Projekt arbeiteten die Architekten mit einem vorhandenen Zeltsystem von beeindruckender Länge (457 m). Standort der **FRIEZE ART FAIR**, einer renommierten Messe für zeitgenössische Kunst, war Randall's Island, eine Insel zwischen Manhattan, der Bronx und Queens. Um die Wirkung des standardisierten Systems aufzubrechen, entschied sich SO – IL, die Zeltkonstruktion durch keilförmige Einschübe in sechs Zonen zu gliedern. In den Keilen waren Serviceeinrichtungen untergebracht, außerdem gaben sie laut den Architekten „der sonst geradlinigen Zeltkonstruktion eine mäandernde, weichere Form". „Die Wellenform gibt dem Zelt an seinem ungewöhnlichen Standort am Wasser Dynamik und ein markantes Gesicht." Zusätzlich verlängerten SO – IL die Stirnseiten der Konstruktion mit Stoffbahnen. Den Architekten zufolge „setzt sich die Zeltkonstruktion durch diese Geste fließend in den Boden fort", während die so definierten „spielerischen Eingangszonen die Gäste auf das Besuchserlebnis einstimmten".

Les architectes ont travaillé ici sur une structure essentiellement préfabriquée d'au moins 457 m de long. Érigée sur l'île de Randall, située entre Manhattan, le Bronx et Queens, l'installation de tentes a abrité la prestigieuse **FRIEZE ART FAIR** dédiée à l'art contemporain. Pour soulager le problème de la standardisation du système de la tente, SO – IL a imaginé d'intercaler de nouveaux coins en forme de triangle entre six sections de tente, offrant des équipements et infléchissant « la tente rigide en une forme souple et sinueuse ». Selon les architectes : « La forme ondulante anime la structure sur un site en front de mer inhabituel et en fait un emblème au bord de l'eau. » SO – IL a également prolongé le toit de tente avec des bandes au bout du pignon de chaque tente. « Ce geste, disent-ils, sert à fondre la structure dans le sol. Et les entrées facétieuses familiarisent les visiteurs avec l'expérience qui les attend à l'intérieur. »

The long snaking form of the temporary structure is visible in the aerial view to the left and in the site plan on this page. Below, the extended tent fabric strips tie the structure to the site.

Die längliche geschwungene Form der temporären Konstruktion in einer Luftaufnahme (links) und als Lageplan auf dieser Seite. Stoffbahnen binden die Konstruktion an den Boden an (unten).

Le long serpent de la structure éphémère est visible sur la photo aérienne en page de gauche et sur le plan de situation ci-contre. Ci-dessous, les bandes de toile de tente relient la structure au site.

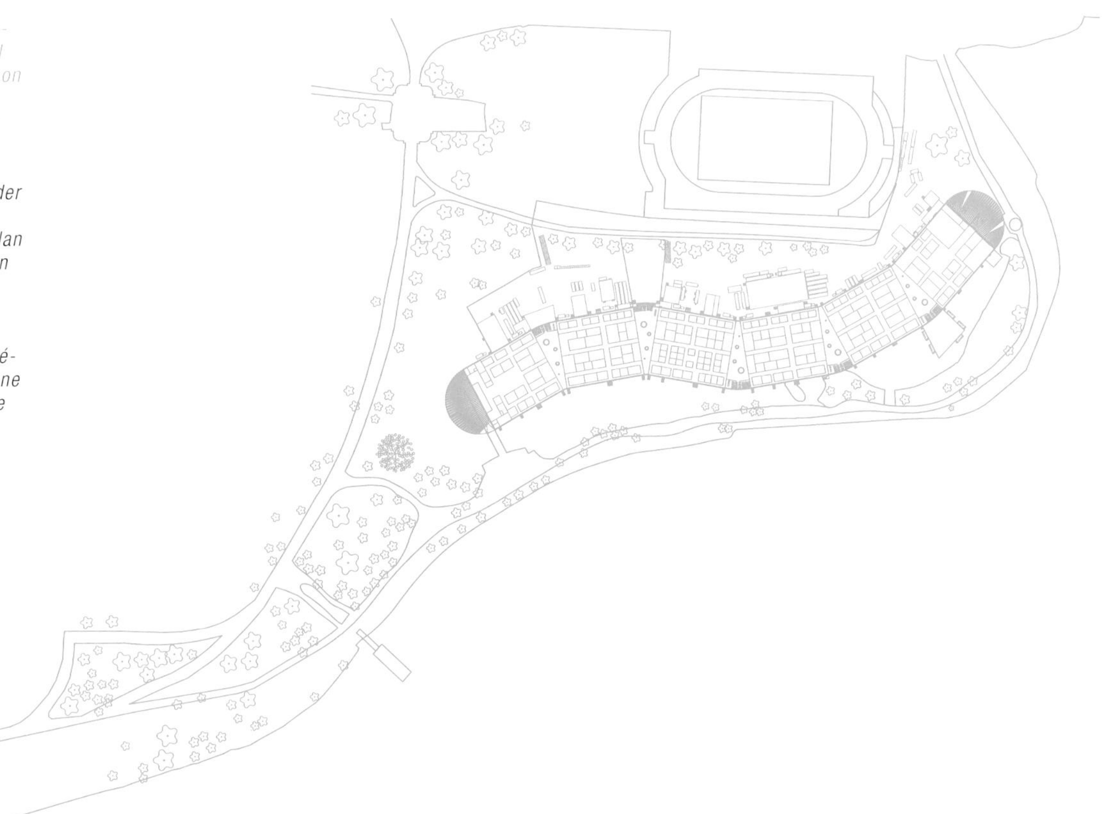

Seen at night with light emerging, the Frieze tents certainly gave an impression of a specially designed structure, but were made with fairly standard elements. Below, interior views.

Beleuchtet und bei Nacht wirkte das Zelt der Frieze wie ein speziell konzipierter Bau, bestand jedoch aus Standardelementen. Unten Innenansichten.

Vues de nuit avec la lumière qui en émerge, les tentes de Frieze, même composées d'éléments relativement standards, donnent l'impression d'une structure sophistiquée. Ci-dessous, des vues d'intérieur.

The "stripes" at the end of the tents offered a partially covered space, both indoors and outdoors at the same time.

Die „Streifen" an den Stirnseiten des Zelts ließen teilgeschützte Bereiche entstehen, in denen Innen- und Außenraum fließend ineinander übergingen.

Les « bandes » à l'extrémité des tentes offrent un espace partiellement couvert, à la fois intérieur et extérieur.

TABANLIOĞLU ARCHITECTS

Tabanlıoğlu Architects
Mesrutiyet Cad. No: 67
Istanbul 34430
Turkey

Tel: +90 21 2251 2111
Fax: +90 21 2251 2332
E-mail: info@tabanlioglu.com
Web: www.tabanlioglu.com

Tabanlıoğlu Architects was created by Murat Tabanlıoğlu in collaboration with Hayati Tabanlıoğlu in 1990. Melkan Gürsel Tabanlıoğlu joined the group in 1995 as a Partner. Based in Istanbul, Turkey, the office consists of more than 120 employees, operating mainly in Turkey, the Middle East, and CIS (Commonwealth of Independent States) countries. **MURAT TABANLIOĞLU** studied architecture at Vienna Technical University and graduated in 1992. **MELKAN GÜRSEL TABANLIOĞLU** studied architecture at Istanbul Technical University. After graduating in 1993, she attended the Polytechnic University of Metropolitan Catalonia for her M.Arch degree. Their recent work includes the Istanbul Modern (Istanbul, Turkey, 2004); DMC Ankara (Ankara, Turkey, 2007); Levent Loft (Istanbul, Turkey, 2007); Loft Gardens (Istanbul, Turkey, 2009); Astana Arena (Astana, Kazakhstan, 2009); Tripoli Congress Center (Tripoli, Libya, 2010); Istanbul Sapphire (Istanbul, Turkey, 2011); Sipopo Congress Center (Malabo, Equatorial Guinea, 2011, published here); Astana Media Center (Astana, Kazakhstan, 2012); and the Bodrum International Airport (Bodrum, Turkey, 2012).

Tabanlıoğlu Architects wurde 1990 von Murat Tabanlıoğlu und Hayati Tabanlıoğlu gegründet. Melkan Gürsel Tabanlıoğlu schloss sich dem Team 1995 als Partnerin an. Das Büro in Istanbul beschäftigt derzeit über 120 Mitarbeiter, die vorwiegend an Projekten in der Türkei, im Nahen Osten und den GUS-Staaten (Gemeinschaft Unabhängiger Staaten) arbeiten. **MURAT TABANLIOĞLU** schloss sein Architekturstudium 1992 an der Technischen Universität Wien ab. **MELKAN GÜRSEL TABANLIOĞLU** studierte Architektur an der TU Istanbul. Nach ihrem Abschluss 1993 absolvierte sie einen M. Arch. an der Universitat Politècnica de Catalunya. Jüngere Arbeiten sind u. a. das Istanbul Modern (Istanbul, 2004), DMC Ankara (Ankara, 2007), Levent Loft (Istanbul, 2007), Loft Gardens (Istanbul, 2009), die Astana Arena (Astana, Kasachstan, 2009), das Kongresszentrum in Tripolis (Tripolis, Libyen, 2010), Istanbul Sapphire (Istanbul, 2011), das Sipopo-Kongresszentrum (Malabo, Äquatorial-Guinea, 2011, hier veröffentlicht), das Astana Media Center (Astana, Kasachstan, 2012) und der internationale Flughafen in Bodrum (Türkei, 2012).

Tabanlıoğlu Architects est créé par Murat Tabanlıoğlu en collaboration avec Hayati Tabanlıoğlu en 1990. Melkan Gürsel Tabanlıoğlu rejoint l'agence en 1995 en tant qu'associé. Basée à Istanbul, l'agence emploie plus de 120 personnes travaillant principalement en Turquie, au Moyen-Orient et dans la CEI (Communauté des États indépendants). **MURAT TABANLIOĞLU** sort diplômé de l'Université technologique de Vienne en 1992. **MELKAN GÜRSEL TABANLIOĞLU** étudie l'architecture à l'Université technologique d'Istanbul. Après avoir obtenu son diplôme en 1993, elle étudie l'architecture à l'Université polytechnique de Catalogne. Parmi leurs réalisations récentes, on trouve le Musée d'art moderne d'Istanbul (Istanbul, 2004) ; le DMC Ankara (Ankara, 2007) ; le Levent Loft (Istanbul, 2007) ; les Loft Gardens (Istanbul, 2009) ; l'Astana Arena (Astana, Kazakhstan, 2009) ; le Palais des congrès de Tripoli (Tripoli, Libye, 2010) ; l'Istanbul Sapphire (Istanbul, 2011) ; le Palais des congrès de Sipopo (Malabo, Guinée équatoriale, 2011, présenté ici) ; le Centre de médias Astana (Astana, Kazakhstan, 2012) et l'aéroport international de Bodrum (Bodrum, Turquie, 2012).

SIPOPO CONGRESS CENTER

Malabo, Equatorial Guinea, 2011

Address: Malabo, Equatorial Guinea. Area: 13 708 m²
Client: Oficina Nacional de Planification Y Seguimiento de Proyectos de Guinea Ecuatorial "GE-Proyectos"
Cost: not disclosed

This rectangular two-story building is in good part surrounded by semi-transparent metal mesh screens that stand out from the façade, acting as a shield against the sun while assuring the security of the structure. Metal panels are placed at different levels and angles, but the façades are largely glazed. The glass wall system allows for maximum viewing area with no horizontal or vertical mullions to obstruct the vision toward the ocean. Set near the shores of the Gulf of Guinea on the outskirts of the capital of Equatorial Guinea, and close to wooded areas, the building stands on a thin podium and is linked via a glass bridge to an existing conference hall which is clad in travertine marble. The main conference hall is a rectangular space on the first floor with a circular seating arrangement. A restaurant, overlooking the bay, is also located on the first floor, flanked by the foyer on two intersecting sides. The three dimensional walls of each space are designed with reference to local sources, such as the bark of pine trees depicted in timber and mirrored in the restaurant, or the geometric motifs related to African tradition on the walls of the lobby.

Das geradlinige zweigeschossige Gebäude ist zu weiten Teilen mit semitransparenten, netzartigen Metallblenden versehen, die der Fassade vorgehängt sind. Sie dienen als Sonnen- und zugleich als Fassadenschutz. Abstand und Winkel der Blenden variieren; die Fassade ist dabei fast vollständig verglast. Das System aus besonders großflächigen Scheiben erlaubt einen Blick aufs Meer, der frei von Fensterkreuzen bleibt. Das Gebäude liegt an der Küste des Golfs von Guinea, in Waldnähe am Stadtrand der Hauptstadt Äquatorial-Guineas. Es ruht auf einem niedrigen Sockel und ist über eine Glasbrücke mit einer älteren, travertinverkleideten Kongresshalle verbunden. Der zentrale Konferenzsaal, ein rechteckiger Raum mit kreisförmiger Sitzordnung, liegt im Erdgeschoss, ebenso wie ein Restaurant mit Blick auf die Bucht, das an zwei Seiten vom Foyer umfangen wird. Die reliefartig strukturierten Wände nehmen Bezug auf regionale Motive: im Restaurant auf die Rinde von Pinienbäumen, die im verwendeten Bauholz nachempfunden wurde, sowie im Foyer auf traditionelle geometrische Muster.

Ce bâtiment rectangulaire de deux niveaux est en grande partie entouré d'écrans métalliques semi-transparents à mailles qui se détachent de la façade, servant de protection contre le soleil tout en assurant la sécurité de la structure. Des panneaux de métal sont placés à différents angles et niveaux, mais les façades sont largement vitrées. Les murs de verre sont sans meneaux horizontaux ni verticaux afin de ne pas obstruer la vue sur l'océan. Situé près des rives du golfe de Guinée, en périphérie de la capitale de la Guinée équatoriale et à proximité de zones boisées, le bâtiment sur son fin podium est relié par un pont de verre à une salle de conférence préexistante habillée de travertin. La salle de conférence principale est un espace rectangulaire au rez-de-chaussée avec un placement circulaire. Sur ce même niveau, on trouve également un restaurant avec vue sur le golfe flanqué du hall d'entrée au croisement de deux côtés. Le design des murs en trois dimensions de chaque espace vient puiser aux sources locales, comme par exemple l'imitation de l'écorce de pin pour le bois utilisé dans le restaurant ou les motifs géométriques de tradition africaine sur les murs du hall.

Set up off the ground, the building appears to hover on its site. Its basic forms are quite simple, rendered more complex by the external treatment.

Der aufgeständerte Bau scheint über dem Boden zu schweben. Seine Grundform ist schlicht und gewinnt erst durch die Fassadengestaltung an Komplexität.

Détaché du sol, le bâtiment semble flotter sur le site. Ses formes relativement simples sont rendues plus complexes par le traitement extérieur.

The angled metal mesh screens employed by the architects provide protection from the sun but also animate the façades. Below, an elevation drawing of the complex.

Die von den Architekten entworfenen, netzartig strukturierten Metallblenden bieten Sonnenschutz und beleben die Fassade. Unten ein Aufriss des Komplexes.

Les écrans obliques de mailles en métal employés par les architectes offrent une protection contre le soleil tout en égayant les façades. Ci-dessous, une élévation du complexe.

At night, the building assumes its natural transparency, glowing from within. Below, a bridge links the building to an older structure.

Dank seiner Transparenz leuchtet das Gebäude nachts von innen. Eine Brücke verbindet es mit einem älteren Bau.

La nuit, le bâtiment illuminé de l'intérieur assume sa transparence naturelle. Dessous, un pont relie le bâtiment à une structure plus ancienne.

Under certain angles, the metal mesh screens appear to form the entire façade of the building. To the right, a site plan.

Je nach Blickwinkel scheinen die Metallblenden die gesamte Fassade des Gebäudes auszumachen. Rechts ein Lageplan.

Sous certains angles, la totalité de la façade semble être constituée d'écrans à mailles de métal. Ci-contre, un plan de masse.

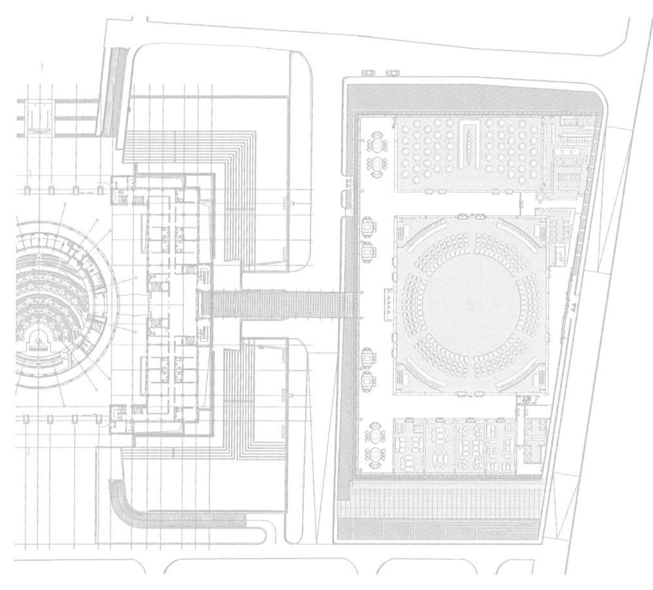

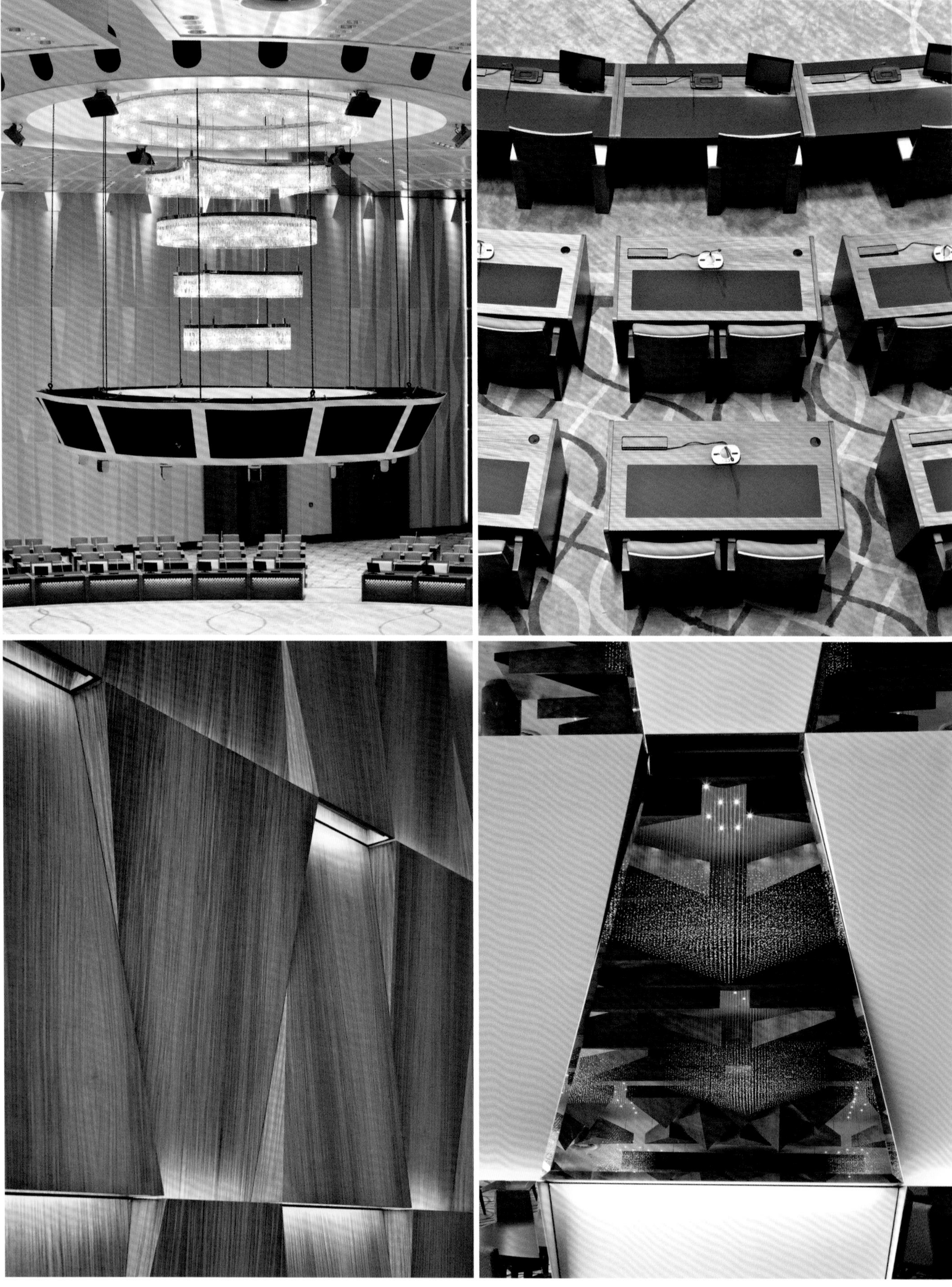

The interior spaces offer a considerable variety of surfaces and colors, as might be expected from the exterior.

Innen besticht das Projekt durch eine Vielfalt an Oberflächen und Farben, wie der Außenbau erwarten lässt.

Les espaces intérieurs offrent une variété considérable de surfaces et de couleurs, comme peut le laisser espérer l'extérieur.

UNSTUDIO

UNStudio
Stadhouderskade 113
1073 AX Amsterdam
The Netherlands

Tel: +31 20 570 20 40 / Fax: +31 20 570 20 41
E-mail: info@unstudio.com
Web: www.unstudio.com

BEN VAN BERKEL was born in Utrecht, the Netherlands, in 1957 and studied at the Rietveld Academy in Amsterdam and at the Architectural Association (AA) in London, receiving the AA Diploma with honors in 1987. After working briefly in the office of Santiago Calatrava in 1988, he set up his practice in Amsterdam with **CAROLINE BOS**, under the name United Network Studio (UNStudio). Their work includes the Karbouw and ACOM (1990–92) office buildings, and the REMU Electricity Station (1989–93), all in Amersfoort; and the Erasmus Bridge in Rotterdam (1990–96). Other works include the Möbius House (Naarden, 1993–98); Het Valkhof Museum (Nijmegen, 1995–99); and NMR Laboratory (Utrecht, 1997–2000), all in the Netherlands; VilLA NM (Upstate New York, USA, 2000–06); and the Mercedes-Benz Museum (Stuttgart, Germany, 2001–06). More recent work includes a music theater (Graz, Austria, 1998–2008); Star Place (Kaohsiung, Taiwan, 2006–08); Burnham Pavilion (Chicago, Illinois, USA, 2009); Haus am Weinberg (Stuttgart, Germany, 2008–11); the Center for Virtual Engineering (ZVE), Fraunhofer Institute (Stuttgart, Germany, 2006–12, published here); I'Park City (Suwon, South Korea, 2008–12); King David the Builder International Airport in Kutaisi (Georgia, 2011–12); and Arnhem Station (the Netherlands, 1996–2014). Ongoing work includes Raffles City (Hangzhou, China, 2008–14); Singapore University of Technology and Design (Singapore, 2010–14); and the Dance Palace in St. Petersburg (Russia, 2009–).

BEN VAN BERKEL wurde 1957 im niederländischen Utrecht geboren und studierte an der Rietveld-Akademie in Amsterdam und der Architectural Association (AA) in London, wo er 1987 sein Diplom mit Auszeichnung absolvierte. Nach einem kurzen Arbeitseinsatz 1988 bei Santiago Calatrava gründete er mit **CAROLINE BOS** das Büro United Network Studio (UNStudio) in Amsterdam. Neben Bürogebäuden für Karbouw und ACOM (1990–92) baute das Team auch das Kraftwerk REMU (1989 bis 1993), beide in Amersfoort, und die Erasmusbrücke in Rotterdam (1990–96). Weitere Projekte sind u. a. das Haus Möbius (Naarden, 1993–98), das Museum Het Valkhof (Nijmegen, 1995–99) und das Labor NMR (Utrecht, 2000), alle in den Niederlanden, sowie die VilLA NM (bei New York, 2000–06) und das Mercedes-Benz-Museum (Stuttgart, 2001–06). Jüngere Arbeiten sind u. a. ein Musiktheater in Graz (1998–2008), der Star Place (Kaohsiung, Taiwan, 2006–08), der Burnham-Pavillon (Chicago, Illinois, 2009), das Haus am Weinberg (Stuttgart, 2008–11), das Zentrum für Virtuelles Engineering (ZVE) der Fraunhofer IAO (Stuttgart, 2006–12, hier vorgestellt), I'Park City (Suwon, Südkorea, 2008–12), der internationale Flughafen King David the Builder Kutaisi (Georgien, 2011–12) und der Bahnhof Arnhem (1996–2014). Laufende Projekte sind u. a. Raffles City (Hangzhou, 2008–14), die Hochschule für Technik und Design in Singapur (2010–14) und der Tanzpalast in St. Petersburg (seit 2009).

Né à Utrecht aux Pays-Bas en 1957, **BEN VAN BERKEL** fait ses études à la Gerrit Rietveld Academie et à l'Architectural Association de Londres dont il sort diplômé avec les honneurs en 1987. Après avoir travaillé brièvement chez Santiago Calatrava en 1988, il ouvre son agence à Amsterdam avec **CAROLINE BOS**, sous le nom United Network Studio (UNStudio). L'agence a réalisé entre autres les immeubles de bureaux Karbouw et ACOM (1990–92) et la sous-station électrique REMU (1989–93), tous à Amersfoort, ainsi que le pont Erasmus à Rotterdam (1990–96). Parmi les autres projets, l'on peut mentionner la maison Möbius (Naarden, 1993–98) ; le musée Het Valkhof (Nijmegen, 1995–99) et le laboratoire NMR (Utrecht, 1997–2000), tous aux Pays-Bas ; VilLA NM (nord de l'État de New York, 2000–06) et le musée Mercedes-Benz (Stuttgart, 2001–06). Les réalisations plus récentes comprennent la Maison de la musique et du théâtre musical de Graz (Graz, Autriche, 1998–2008) ; le grand magasin Star Place (Kaohsiung, Taïwan, 2006–08) ; le Burnham Pavilion (Chicago, 2009) ; la Haus am Weinberg (Stuttgart, 2008–11) ; le Zentrum für Virtuelles Engineering (ZVE), Fraunhofer IAO (Stuttgart, 2006–12, présenté ici) ; le I'Park City (Suwon, Corée-du-Sud, 2008–12) ; l'aéroport international de Kutaisi (Géorgie, 2011–12) et la gare d'Arnhem (Pays-Bas, 1996–2014). L'agence travaille actuellement sur les projets de Raffles City (Hangzhou, Chine, 2008–14), de l'Université de technologie et du design de Singapour (Singapour, 2010–14) et du Palais de la danse de Saint-Pétersbourg (Russie, 2009–).

CENTER FOR VIRTUAL ENGINEERING (ZVE)

Fraunhofer Institute, Stuttgart, Germany, 2006–12

Address: Nobelstr. 11, 70569 Stuttgart, Germany, +49 711 970-2124, www.iao.fraunhofer.de
Area: 3220 m². Client: Fraunhofer – Gesellschaft zur Förderung der angewandten Forschung e.V.
Cost: not disclosed. Collaboration: Asplan Architekten BDA, Harm Wassink,
Florian Heinzelmann, Marc Herschel

The flowing lines of the building are emphasized by bands of windows whose height varies along the length of the façade.

Die fließenden Linien des Gebäudes werden durch Fensterbänder akzentuiert, deren Höhe über die gesamte Breite der Fassade variiert.

Les lignes fluides du bâtiment sont renforcées par des bandeaux de fenêtres dont la hauteur varie le long de la façade.

Fond as always of computer-generated forms, UNStudio innovates in both section and plan, as can be seen by the shapes of the building revealed in this image and the plan to the right.

Mit der Vorliebe für computergeneriertes Design entwickelt UNStudio innovative Konturen und Grundrisse, wie die Gebäudeform und der Grundriss rechts erkennen lassen

Toujours fervent des formes générées par ordinateur, UNStudio innove en coupe comme en plan, comme le prouve la configuration de ce bâtiment sur la photo ci-dessus et sur le plan ci-contre.

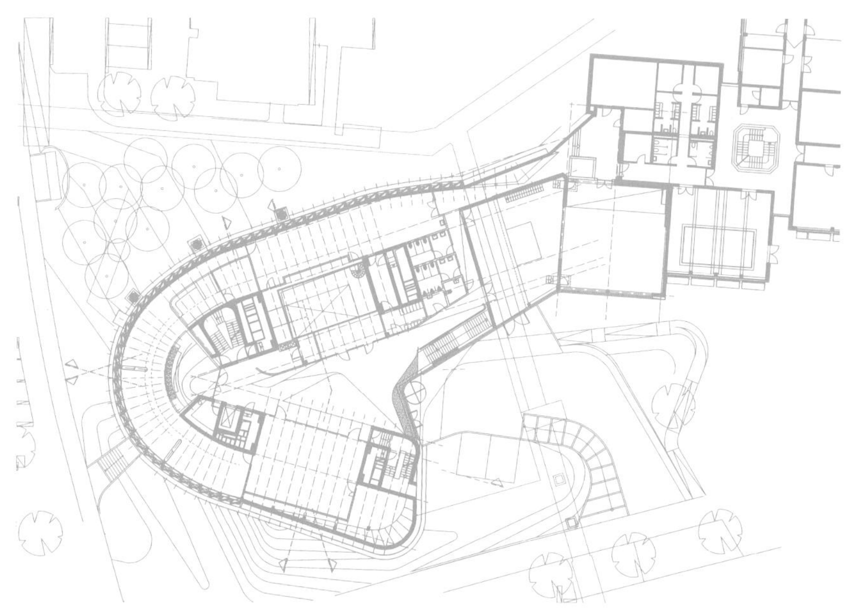

The Fraunhofer Institute is a German research organization that groups 60 institutes that focus on applied science. This building is located on the research campus of the institute in Stuttgart Vaihingen. UNStudio worked in collaboration with Asplan from Kaiserslautern on the architectural services for the center. UNStudio was responsible for the design development, the required 3D-planning, and implementation during all planning processes. Asplan was responsible for the development of the construction documents and the site supervision. Laboratory and research functions are combined with public exhibition areas and a routing of the visitors into an open and communicative building. Working areas merge into each other in order to promote interdisciplinary collaboration. The different programmatic elements are distinguished by a selection of colors. A rounded shape allowed the architects to optimize the building's aluminum envelope, with a contour that is seven percent smaller than that of a rectangular form of the same area. Operable windows are used, and daylight is brought into the structure to the greatest extent possible. Recyclable and low-maintenance materials were used for the skeleton, and interior and façade construction. The structure obtained Gold certification from the DGNB (German Sustainable Building Council). The building is 20.7 meters high and has four floors above grade and one below. The substructure and superstructure are made of concrete.

Die Fraunhofer-Gesellschaft ist eine Forschungseinrichtung, die über 60 Institute für angewandte Wissenschaften umfasst. Der Neubau steht auf dem Forschungscampus eines der Institute in Stuttgart Vaihingen. Bei der Realisierung arbeitete UNStudio mit dem Büro Asplan aus Kaiserslautern zusammen. UNStudio verantwortete Entwurf, 3D-Planung sowie die Umsetzung der Gesamtplanung. Asplan übernahm die Entwicklung der Baupläne und die Bauleitung. Labor- und Forschungsbereiche sowie öffentliche Ausstellungsflächen werden durch ein Leitsystem zu einem offenen und kommunikativen Gebäudekonzept verbunden. Arbeitsräume gehen ineinander über und sollen die interdisziplinäre Zusammenarbeit fördern. Die verschiedenen Elemente des Programms sind farbig gekennzeichnet. Die runde Gebäudeform ermöglichte es den Architekten, die Aluminiumhülle zu optimieren, sodass sie 7 % kleiner ausfällt als bei einem rechteckigen Gebäude mit vergleichbarer Grundfläche. Fenster lassen sich öffnen; der Tageslichteinfall wurde maximiert. Skelett, Innenausbau und Fassadenkonstruktion wurden in recyclingfähigen und wartungsarmen Materialien ausgeführt. Das Projekt erhielt ein Goldzertifikat der Deutschen Gesellschaft für nachhaltiges Bauen (DGNB). Der Bau ist 20,7 m hoch, verfügt über vier Obergeschosse und ein Untergeschoss. Auf- und Unterbau wurden als Betonkonstruktion realisiert.

Le Fraunhofer IAO est un organisme allemand spécialisé dans la recherche en sciences appliquées qui regroupe 60 instituts. Ce bâtiment est situé sur le campus de l'institut à Stuttgart Vaihingen. UNStudio a collaboré avec Asplan de Kaiserslautern pour les services architecturaux. UNStudio était responsable de la conception, de la modélisation 3D et de la mise en œuvre durant le processus de planification. Asplan était responsable du développement des plans de construction et de la supervision du site. Les fonctions de laboratoire et de recherches sont combinées avec des espaces publics d'expositions et l'acheminement des visiteurs à l'intérieur d'un bâtiment ouvert et convivial. Les espaces de travail se fondent les uns dans les autres aux fins d'encourager une collaboration interdisciplinaire. Les différents éléments programmatiques se distinguent par leur couleur. Les architectes ont choisi une forme arrondie pour optimiser l'enveloppe d'aluminium du bâtiment, avec un contour 7 % plus petit que pour une forme rectangulaire sur la même zone. Ils laissent le plus de lumière naturelle possible entrer dans la structure, entre autres par des fenêtres ouvrantes. Des matériaux recyclables et à entretien réduit ont été utilisés pour l'ossature, les façades et l'intérieur. La structure a obtenu la certification Gold du DGNB (Conseil allemand pour la construction durable). Haut de 20,70 m, le bâtiment possède quatre étages au-dessus du niveau du sol, et un en dessous. L'infrastructure, comme la superstructure, sont en béton.

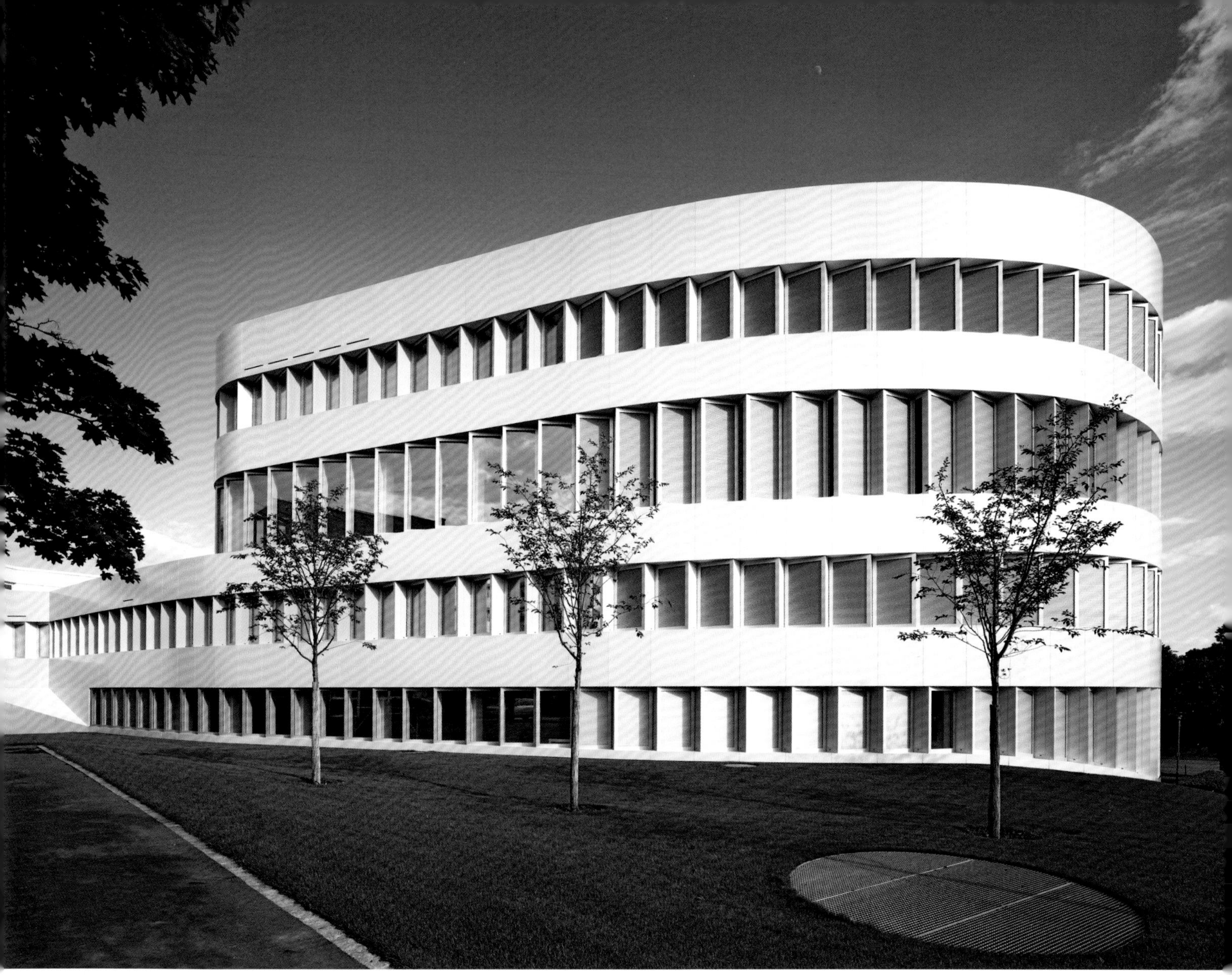

Though much of its formal vocabulary is defined by computer-generated curves, the building provides well-designed and functional interior spaces, as suggested by the section drawing below.

Das Formenvokabular besticht vor allem durch computergenerierte Kurven, zugleich bietet der Bau funktionale und schlüssig geplante Innenräume, wie der Querschnitt unten zeigt.

Même avec un vocabulaire formel surtout défini par des courbes générées par ordinateur, le bâtiment offre des espaces intérieurs bien conçus et fonctionnels, comme suggéré par la coupe ci-dessous.

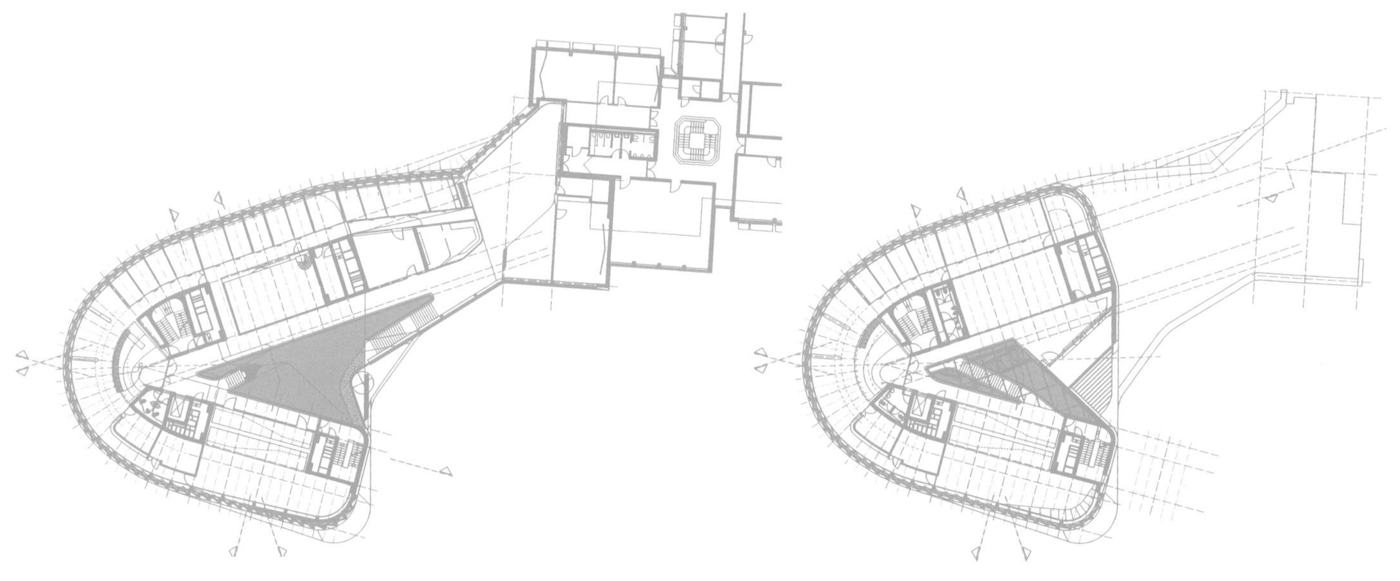

Plans and images begin to reveal the rather considerable complexity of the project, with the high atrium seen below, allowing natural light into the lowest level.

Grundriss und Aufnahmen illustrieren die Komplexität des Projekts mit seinem hohen Atrium, das Licht bis in die unterste Ebene lässt (unten).

Plans et images révèlent la complexité assez considérable du projet, avec le haut atrium ci-dessous qui laisse entrer la lumière au niveau le plus bas.

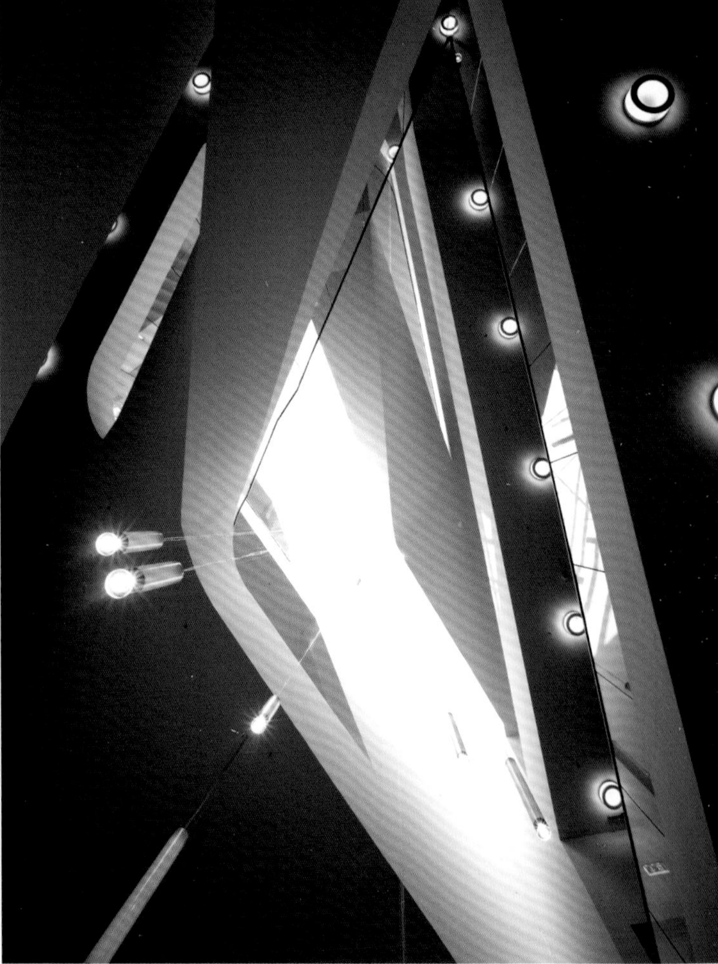

Bridges and open passageways allow free movement through the interior. A drawing of the building shows the circulation patterns (right).

Brücken und offene Flure erschließen das Gebäude fließend. Ein Diagramm illustriert den Rundlauf (rechts).

Des ponts et des passages ouverts permettent une libre circulation à l'intérieur. Un dessin du bâtiment montre les schémas de circulation (ci-contre).

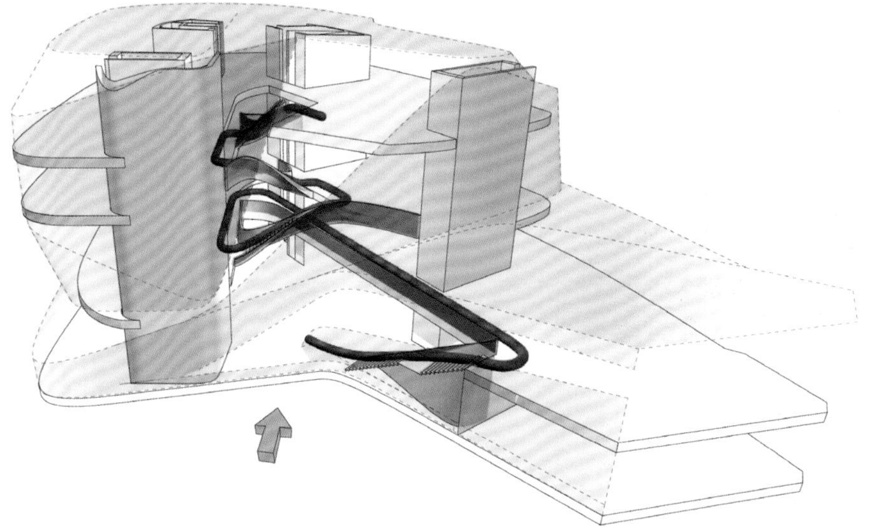

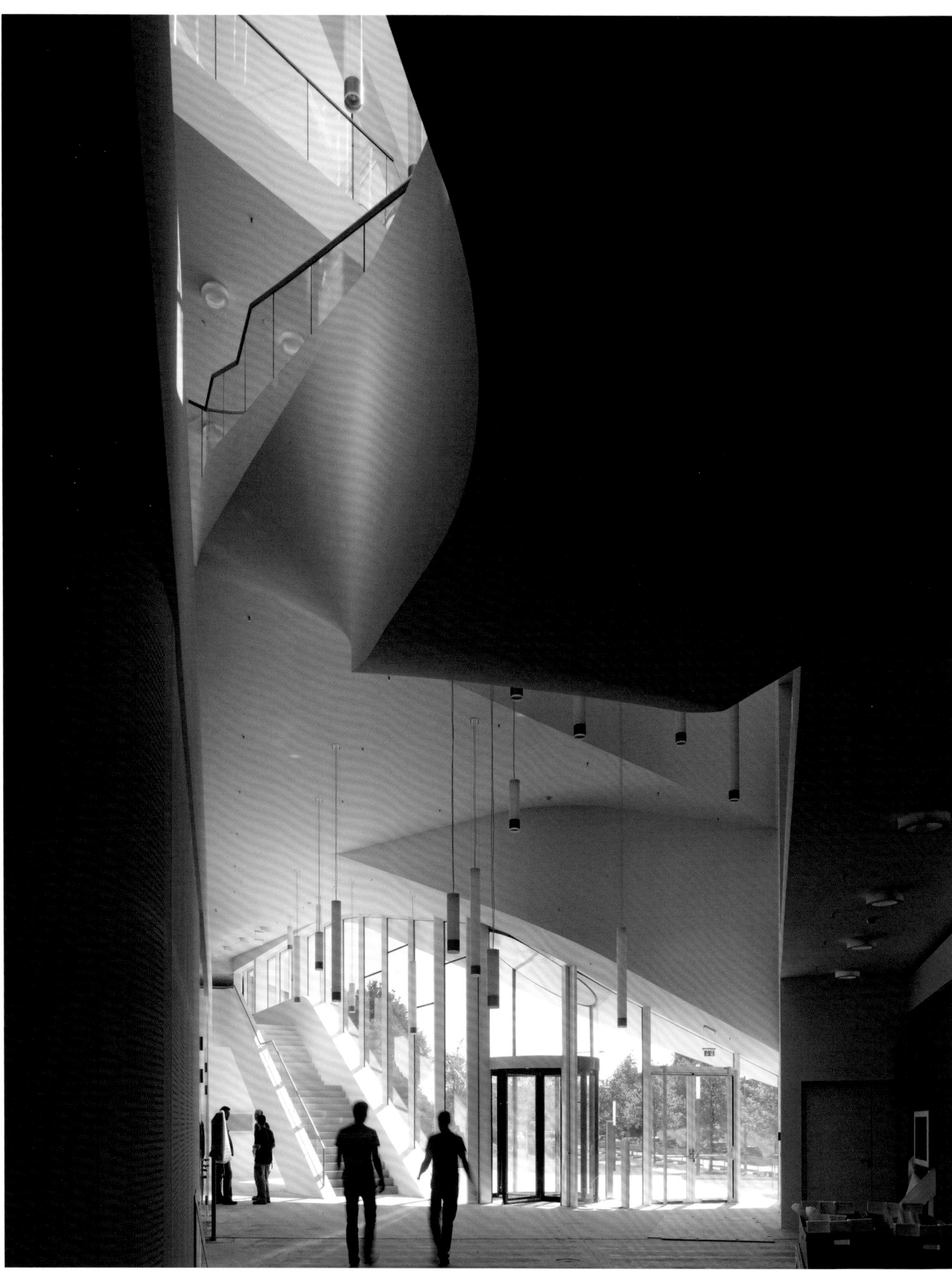

Interior views and plans demonstrate the almost organic layering and juxtaposition of forms and passages. Surfaces and stairs seem to flow into each other in a natural way.

Innenansichten und Grundrisse lassen eine organische Schichtung und Verbindung von Formen und Verkehrsflächen erkennen. Oberflächen und Treppen scheinen ineinanderzufließen.

Des vues et des plans de l'intérieur démontrent la juxtaposition presque organique des formes et des passages. Les surfaces et les escaliers semblent se fondre les uns dans les autres de façon naturelle.

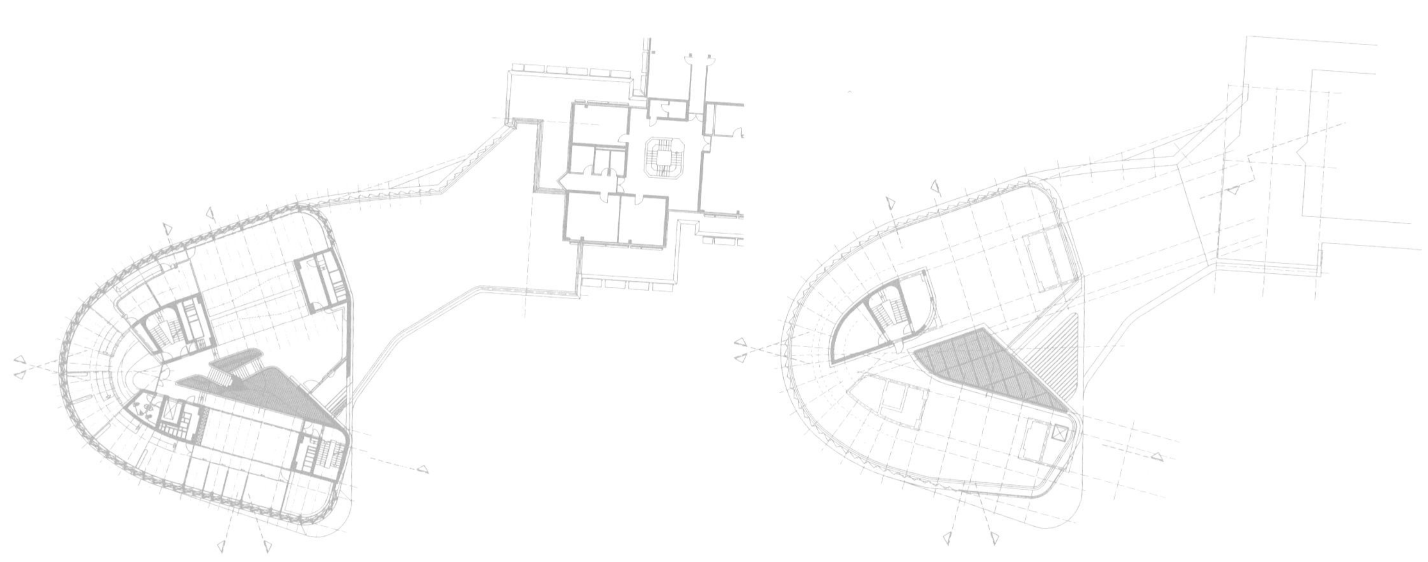

Nanshan Marriage Registration Center

URBANUS

URBANUS Architecture & Design, Inc.
Building E6, 2nd Floor, OCT Loft
Huaqiaocheng Dongbu Industrial Zone
Nanshan District
Shenzhen 518053
China

Tel: +86 755 8609 6345 / Fax: +86 755 860 6336
E-mail: office@urbanus.com.cn / Web: www.urbanus.com.cn

Urbanus was founded in 1999 by Liu Xiaodu, Meng Yan, and Wang Hui. Prior to cofounding Urbanus, **MENG YAN** was a project architect and designer at Kohn Pedersen Fox Associates P.C., Meltzer Mandl Architects in New York, Brown & Bills Architects in Dayton, and Yongmao Architects and Engineers in Beijing. **LIU XIAODU** was previously a project architect and project designer at Design Group Inc. (Columbus, Ohio) and Stang & Newdow Inc. in Atlanta, Georgia. He received his B.Arch degree from Tsinghua University (1985), and M.Arch from Miami University (Oxford, Ohio, 1997). **WANG HUI** previously worked with Gruzen Samton Architects, Gensler, and Gary Edward Handel + Associates, and, like his two Partners, he was educated at Tsinghua University and Miami University. Their recent works include Shenzhen International Yacht Club (Shenzhen, 2006); Public Art Plaza (Shenzhen, 2006); Dafen Art Museum (Shenzhen, 2006); Shanghai Multimedia Valley Office Park (Shanghai, 2007); Digital Beijing (with Pei Zhu; Beijing, 2007); the Nanyou Shopping Park (Shenzhen, 2007); the Tangshan Urban Planning Museum (Tangshan, 2008–11); Nanshan Marriage Registration Center (Shenzhen, 2009–11, published here); OCT Loft Renovation (Shenzhen, 2012); Library of South University of Science and Technology (Shenzhen, 2012); Longcheng Industry Park Core Area Urban Design (Shenzhen, 2012); and Wenjing Plaza (Shenzhen, 2012), all in China.

Urbanus wurde 1999 von Liu Xiaodu, Meng Yan und Wang Hui gegründet. Zuvor arbeitete **MENG YAN** als Projektarchitekt und -planer bei Kohn Pedersen Fox Associates P. C., Meltzer Mandl Architects (New York), Brown & Bills Architects (Dayton) und Yongmao Architects and Engineers (Peking). **LIU XIAODU** war zuvor als Projektarchitekt und -planer für die Design Group Inc. (Columbus, Ohio) sowie Stang & Newdow Inc. (Atlanta, Georgia) tätig. Er absolvierte einen B. Arch. an der Tsinghua-Universität (1985) und einen M. Arch. an der Miami University (Oxford, Ohio, 1997). **WANG HUI** arbeitete zunächst für Gruzen Samton Architects, Gensler und Gary Edward Handel + Associates. Ebenso wie seine Partner studierte er an der Tsinghua-Universität und der Miami University. Jüngere Arbeiten des Büros sind u. a. der Shenzhen International Yacht Club (Shenzhen, 2006), die Public Art Plaza (Shenzhen, 2006), das Dafen Art Museum (Shenzhen, 2006), der Shanghai Multimedia Valley Office Park (Shanghai, 2007), Digital Beijing (mit Pei Zhu; Peking, 2007), der Nanyou Shopping Park (Shenzhen, 2007), das Museum für Stadtplanung in Tangshan (2008–11), das Standesamt im Stadtteil Nanshan (Shenzhen, 2009–11, hier veröffentlicht), das Umbauprojekt OCT-Loft (Shenzhen, 2012), die Bibliothek der South University of Science and Technology (Shenzhen, 2012), Longcheng Industry Park Core Area Urban Design (Shenzhen, 2012) und Wenjing Plaza (Shenzhen, 2012), alle in China.

Urbanus est créé en 1999 par Liu Xiaodu, Meng Yan et Wang Hui. Avant de participer à la fondation de Urbanus, **MENG YAN** a été architecte et concepteur de projets chez Kohn Pedersen Fox Associates P.C., Meltzer Mandl Architects à New York, Brown & Bills Architects à Dayton et Yongmao Architects and Engineers à Pékin. **LIU XIAODU** a été architecte et concepteur de projets chez Design Group Inc. (Columbus, Ohio) et Stang & Newdow Inc. à Atlanta. Il obtient son B.Arch à l'université Tsinghua en Chine (1985) et son M.Arch à l'université Miami (Oxford, Ohio, 1997). **WANG HUI** a d'abord travaillé chez Gruzen Samton Architects, Gensler, et Gary Edward Handel + Associates, et, comme ses deux associés, il a fait ses études à l'université Tsinghua et à l'université Miami. Parmi leurs réalisations récentes, l'on peut mentionner le Shenzhen International Yacht Club (Shenzhen, 2006) ; Public Art Plaza (Shenzhen, 2006) ; le Dafen Art Museum (Shenzhen, 2006) ; le Shanghai Multimedia Valley Office Park (Shanghai, 2007) ; Digital Beijing (avec Pei Zhu ; Pékin, 2007) ; le Nanyou Shopping Park (Shenzhen, 2007) ; le Tangshan Urban Planning Museum (Tangshan, 2008–11) ; le centre de déclaration des mariages de Nanshan (Shenzhen, 2009–11, présenté ici) ; la rénovation d'OCT Loft (Shenzhen, 2012) ; la bibliothèque de l'Université du sud de science et technologie (Shenzhen, 2012) ; Longcheng Industry Park Core Area Urban Design (Shenzhen, 2012) et Wenjing Plaza (Shenzhen, 2012), toutes en Chine.

NANSHAN MARRIAGE REGISTRATION CENTER

Shenzhen, China, 2009–11

Address: the intersection of Changxing Road and Nantou Street, Nanshan District, Shenzhen, China
Area: 977 m². Client: Public Works Bureau of Nanshan
Cost: $1.578 million. Collaboration: Guoqun Studio (Interior Design)

The architects have sought with this project to do nothing less than create a "new architectural typology for marriage registration in China," which is typically a bureaucratic process. Located in the northeastern corner of Lijing Park in the Nanshan District, the structure is about 100 meters long and 25 meters wide. The main building is at the north side of the site, close to the street corner. A small pavilion at the south side is connected with the main building by two bridges that appear to float on a reflecting pool. A continuous spiral path links areas for photos, registration, and meeting with relatives. Relatively small areas are provided for to allow for some privacy. The double-skin structure has an outer layer of floral aluminum mesh and an inner glass wall. Both interior spaces and the exterior façade are white, "in order to show the spiritual atmosphere of marriage registration."

Den Architekten schwebte für dieses Projekt eine „neue Architekturtypologie für die Eheschließung in chinesischen Standesämtern" vor, die üblicherweise als bürokratischer Akt gilt. Der Komplex befindet sich im äußersten Nordosten des Lijing-Parks im Stadtteil Nanshan und ist rund 100 m lang und 25 m breit. Das Hauptgebäude liegt nach Norden in der Nähe einer Straße. Zur Südseite ist ein kleiner Pavillon über zwei Brücken, die über einem reflektierenden Teich zu schweben scheinen, mit dem Hauptgebäude verbunden. Ein spiralförmiger Rundgang verbindet Bereiche, in denen sich die Besucher fotografieren lassen können, getraut werden und mit Verwandten zusammenkommen. Nur wenige Bereiche im Gebäude bieten Privatsphäre. Die Doppelfassade hat eine Außenhaut aus floral inspirierten Aluminiumlamellen und eine Innenhaut aus Glas. Räumlichkeiten und äußere Fassade sind in Weiß gehalten „ein Symbol für den spirituellen Aspekt der Eheschließung".

Pour ce projet, les architectes ont cherché à créer « une nouvelle typologie architecturale pour la déclaration des mariages en Chine » qui est une démarche typiquement bureaucratique. Située à l'angle nord-est du parc Lijing dans le district de Nanshan, la structure fait environ 100 m de long sur 25 m de large. Le bâtiment principal se trouve au nord du site, près de la rue. Au sud, un petit pavillon est relié au bâtiment principal par deux ponts qui semblent flotter sur un miroir d'eau. Un chemin tout en spirale relie les espaces dédiés aux photos, à la déclaration et aux réunions avec la famille. D'autres espaces relativement petits offrant une certaine intimité sont également disponibles. La structure double peau possède un revêtement extérieur de mailles d'aluminium aux motifs floraux et un mur de verre intérieur. Les espaces intérieurs, comme les façades extérieures, sont blancs « pour montrer l'atmosphère de spiritualité de la déclaration de mariage ».

The basic concept of this building—a truncated cylinder surrounded by water and approached by angled paths—brings to mind Tadao Ando's UNESCO Meditation Space (Paris, 1995), albeit using different materials and on a larger scale.

Die Grundidee für den von Wasser umgebenen Zylinderbau, den man über schräge Brücken und Pfade erreicht, erinnert an Tadao Andos UNESCO Meditation Space (Paris, 1995), hier jedoch in größerem Maßstab und mit anderen Materialien.

Le concept de base de ce bâtiment – un cylindre tronqué entouré d'eau et que rejoignent des voies d'accès en oblique – rappelle l'Espace de méditation de l'UNESCO de Tadao Ando (Paris, 1995), bien qu'utilisant des matériaux différents et à une plus grande échelle.

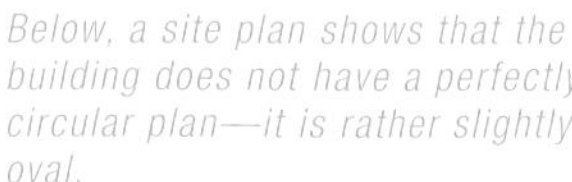

Below, a site plan shows that the building does not have a perfectly circular plan—it is rather slightly oval.

Der Lageplan lässt erkennen, dass der Grundriss nicht exakt kreisförmig, sondern leicht oval ist (unten).

Ci-dessous, un plan de situation montre que la surface du bâtiment n'est pas parfaitement circulaire, mais plutôt légèrement ovale.

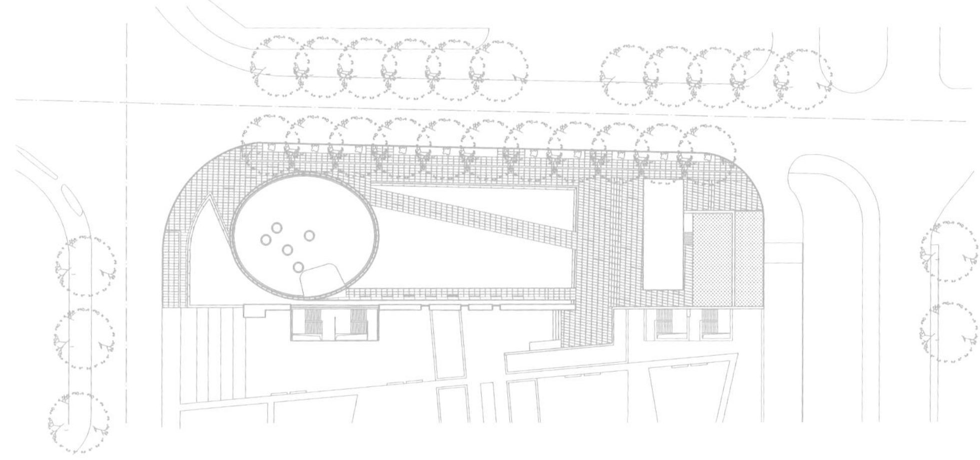

Generous interior space with natural lighting is seen below—section drawings show the interior forms.

Unten großzügige Räume mit viel Tageslicht. Querschnitte zeigen die Gliederung des Innenraums.

Ci-dessous, un espace intérieur généreux, éclairé en lumière naturelle, dont on voit la forme dans les coupes ci-contre.

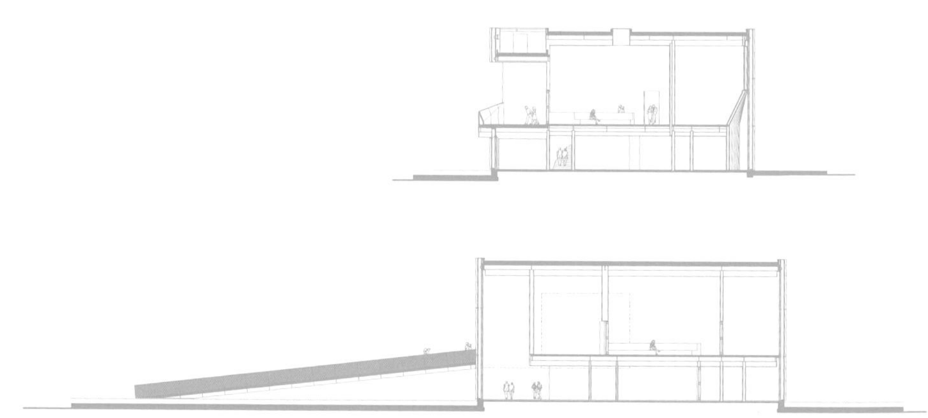

Children on the entrance path are reflected in the pond. The combination of geometric forms assumes a poetic appearance when seen under certain angles.

Kinder laufen auf einem Steg über den Teich und spiegeln sich im Wasser. Aus gewissen Blickwinkeln wirkt die Komposition geometrischer Formen sehr stimmungsvoll.

Sur la voie d'accès, des enfants qui se reflètent dans la nappe d'eau. Sous certains angles, le mélange des formes géométriques adopte une apparence poétique.

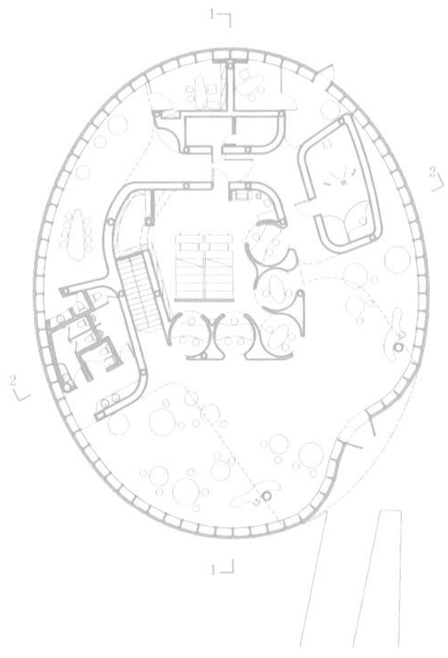

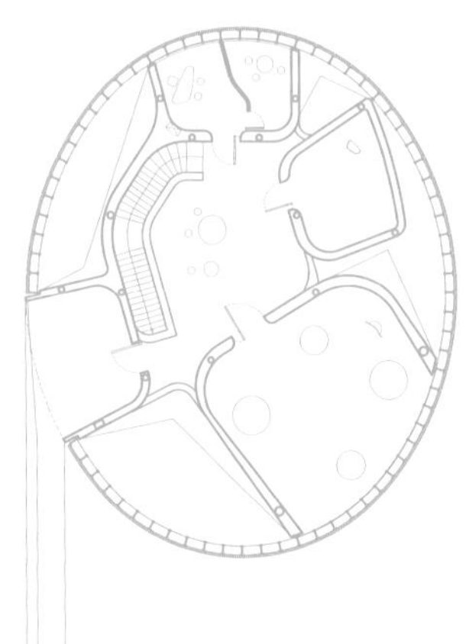

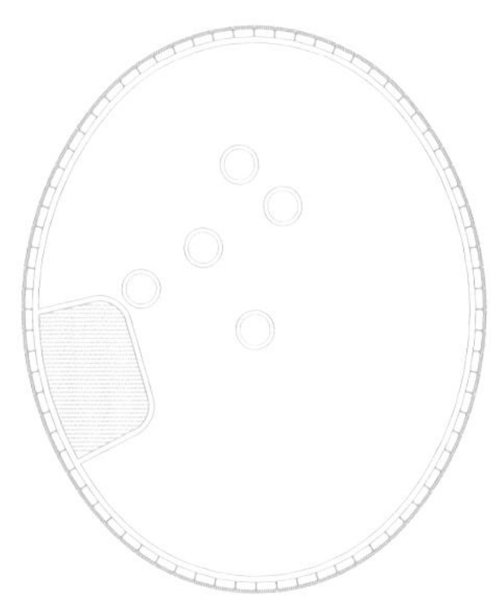

Above, floor plans show the use of the oval spaces of the interior. Left, newlyweds photographed against a wooden background near the high windows of the center.

Grundrisse illustrieren die Nutzung der ovalen Räume (oben). Frisch Vermählte lassen sich vor vertäfeltem Hintergrund neben den hohen Fenstern fotografieren (links).

Ci-dessus, les plans de niveaux montrent l'utilisation des espaces ovales de l'intérieur. Ci-contre, des jeunes mariés photographiés sur un arrière-plan en bois à proximité des hautes fenêtres.

Curving walls and bright colors animate the interior, which also changes with passing clouds and exterior light conditions.

Geschwungene Wände und kräftige Farben beleben das Innere des Gebäudes, dessen Eindruck je nach Bewölkung und Lichtverhältnissen variiert.

Des murs incurvés et des couleurs vives égaient un intérieur qui change au rythme du passage des nuages et de la lumière extérieure.

WILLIAMS AND TSIEN

Tod Williams Billie Tsien Architects
222 Central Park South
New York, NY 10019
USA

Tel: +1 212 582 2385 / Fax: +1 212 245 1984
E-mail: mail@twbta.com
Web: www.twbta.com

TOD WILLIAMS was born in Detroit, Michigan, in 1943. He received his B.A. (1965) and Master of Fine Arts (1967) degrees from Princeton University. After six years as an Associate Architect in the office of Richard Meier in New York, he began his own practice in New York in 1974. **BILLIE TSIEN** was born in Ithaca, New York, in 1949. She received her B.A. at Yale, and her M.Arch from UCLA (1977). She was a painter and graphic designer (1971–75), cofounding Tod Williams Billie Tsien Architects in 1986. Their built work includes the New College, University of Virginia (Charlottesville, Virginia, 1992); the Neurosciences Institute (La Jolla, California, 1995); the renovation and extension of the Phoenix Art Museum (Arizona,1996; Phase II, 2006); the Cranbrook Natatorium (Bloomfield, Michigan, 1999); and the American Folk Art Museum (New York, New York, 2001). Recent and future work includes the Asia Society Hong Kong Center (Hong Kong, China, 2011); the Barnes Foundation (Philadelphia, Pennsylvania, 2010–12, published here); the Reva and David Logan Center for Creative and Performing Arts, University of Chicago (Chicago, Ilinois, 2012); Orchard Student Residences, Haverford College (Haverford, Pennsylvania, 2012); Tata Consultancy Services Campus (Mumbai, India, Phase I, 2013); Lakeside Center at Prospect Park (Brooklyn, New York, 2014); and the Andlinger Center for Energy and the Environment, Princeton University (Princeton, New Jersey, 2015), all in the USA unless stated otherwise.

TOD WILLIAMS wurde 1943 in Detroit, Michigan, geboren. Er absolvierte einen B. A. (1965) und einen Master of Fine Arts (1967) an der Princeton University. Nach sechs Jahren als Associated Architect im New Yorker Büro von Richard Meier arbeitete er ab 1974 selbstständig. **BILLIE TSIEN** wurde 1949 in Ithaca, New York, geboren. Sie absolvierte einen B. A. in Yale und einen M. Arch. an der UCLA (1977). Sie war als Malerin und Grafikdesignerin tätig (1971–75) und gründete mit Williams 1986 das Büro Tod Williams Billie Tsien Architects. Zu ihren Arbeiten gehören das New College der University of Virginia (Charlottesville, Virginia, 1992), das Neurosciences Institute (La Jolla, Kalifornien, 1995), die Renovierung und Erweiterung des Phoenix Art Museum (Arizona, 1996; 2. Abschnitt 2006), die Cranbrook Schwimmhalle (Bloomfield, Michigan, 1999) und das American Folk Art Museum (New York, 2001). Jüngere und anstehende Projekte sind das Asia Society Hong Kong Center (Hongkong, 2011), die Barnes Foundation (Philadelphia, Pennsylvania, 2010–12, hier vorgestellt), das Reva and David Logan Center for Creative and Performing Arts, University of Chicago (Chicago, Ilinois, 2012), das Orchard-Studentenwohnheim, Haverford College (Haverford, Pennsylvania, 2012), der Tata Consultancy Services Campus (Mumbai, Indien, 1. Bauabschnitt, 2013), das Lakeside Center im Prospect Park (Brooklyn, New York, 2014), das Andlinger Center for Energy and the Environment, Princeton University (Princeton, New Jersey, 2015).

Né à Détroit, Michigan, en 1943, **TOD WILLIAMS** obtient son B.A. (1965) et son master des beaux-arts (1967) à l'université de Princeton. Après six ans comme architecte associé dans l'agence de Richard Meier à New York, il ouvre sa propre agence à New York en 1974. Née à Ithaca, New York, en 1949, **BILLIE TSIEN** obtient son B.A. à Yale et son M.Arch à l'UCLA (1977). Elle est d'abord peintre et graphiste (1971–75) avant de participer à la fondation de Tod Williams Billie Tsien Architects en 1986. Parmi leurs réalisations, l'on peut mentionner le New College, université de Virginie (Charlottesville, Virginie, 1992) ; le Neurosciences Institute (La Jolla, Californie, 1995) ; la rénovation et l'extension du Phoenix Art Museum (Arizona, 1996, Phase II, 2006) ; le Cranbrook Natatorium (Bloomfield, Michigan, 1999) et l'American Folk Art Museum (New York, 2001). Parmi leurs projets récents ou futurs, on trouve l'Asia Society Hong Kong Center (Hong Kong, 2011) ; la Fondation Barnes (Philadelphie, 2010–12, présentée ici) ; le Reva and David Logan Center for Creative and Performing Arts de Chicago (Chicago, 2012) ; la résidence pour étudiants Orchard, Haverford College (Haverford, Pennsylvanie, 2012) ; Tata Consultancy Services Campus (Bombay, Phase I, 2013) ; le Lakeside Center à Prospect Park (Brooklyn, New York, 2014) et l'Andlinger Center for Energy and the Environment, de l'université de Princeton (Princeton, New Jersey, 2015), tous aux États-Unis sauf indication contraire.

THE BARNES FOUNDAT
WOOD
ONE WAY

THE BARNES FOUNDATION

Philadelphia, Pennsylvania, USA, 2010–12

Address: 2025 Benjamin Franklin Parkway, Philadelphia, PA 19130, USA,
+1 215 278 7000, www.barnesfoundation.org
Area: 8640 m². Client: The Barnes Foundation. Cost: $150 million

THE BARNES FOUNDATION, long known for its idiosyncratic galleries in Merion, Pennsylvania, and for one of the most significant collections of Post-Impressionist and early modern paintings in the United States, opened its new building on Benjamin Franklin Parkway in Center City, Philadelphia, to the public on May 19, 2012. The architects conceived the new structure as "a gallery in a garden and a garden in a gallery." The two-story building is clad in Negev limestone and has an additional level below grade. The gallery houses the collection, adjoining a generous courtyard space that also leads to an L-shaped support building. The 1115-square-meter gallery seeks to replicate the scale, proportion, and configuration of the original Merion rooms. The galleries also include a classroom on each floor and an internal garden. A light box runs the length of the building and cantilevers over a terrace, bringing daylight into the courtyard space below. At night, the light box becomes "an iconic beacon for the Barnes Foundation." The building achieved LEED Platinum certification from the United States Green Building Council.

DIE BARNES FOUNDATION ist bekannt für ihre ungewöhnlichen Ausstellungsräume in Merion, Pennsylvania, und eine der bedeutendsten Sammlungen postimpressionistischer und moderner Malerei in den USA. Der Neubau der Stiftung auf dem Benjamin Franklin Parkway im Zentrum von Philadelphia ist seit dem 19. Mai 2012 für die Öffentlichkeit zugänglich. Die Architekten konzipierten das Gebäude als „Galerie in einem Garten und Garten in einer Galerie". Das zweigeschossige Gebäude ist mit Kalkstein aus der Negev-Wüste verkleidet und verfügt zudem über ein Untergeschoss. Die Galerie beherbergt die Sammlung und über einen großzügigen Hof gelangt man in ein L-förmiges Nebengebäude. Das 1115 m² große neue Museum knüpft an die Proportionen und Gliederung der älteren Ausstellungsräume in Merion an, verfügt über Unterrichtsräume auf jeder Etage und einen Innengarten. Ein Leuchtkasten liegt auf dem Gebäude, kragt über die Terrasse aus und lässt Licht in den darunter liegenden Hof fallen. Nach Einbruch der Dunkelheit wird er zum „Leuchtturm der Barnes Foundation". Das Gebäude erhielt ein LEED-Platinzertifikat vom United States Green Building Council.

LA FONDATION BARNES, connue depuis longtemps pour ses singulières galeries à Merion, en Pennsylvanie, et pour posséder l'une des plus importantes collections de toiles postimpressionnistes et des premiers modernes des États-Unis, a ouvert un nouveau bâtiment au public, sur Benjamin Franklin Parkway en plein centre de Philadelphie, le 19 mai 2012. Les architectes ont conçu la structure comme « une galerie dans un jardin et un jardin dans une galerie ». Le bâtiment de deux niveaux est revêtu de pierre de Jérusalem et possède un niveau en sous-sol. La galerie qui abrite la collection est contigüe à une grande cour menant à un autre bâtiment en forme de L. Les 1115 m² de la galerie cherchent à reproduire l'échelle, les proportions et la configuration des salles de Merion. Les galeries comprennent également une salle de cours à chaque étage et un jardin intérieur. Un caisson lumineux court sur toute la longueur du bâtiment et finit en surplomb d'une terrasse, laissant entrer la lumière naturelle dans l'espace de la cour au-dessous. La nuit, le caisson devient « un signal lumineux emblématique de la Fondation Barnes ». Le bâtiment a obtenu la certification LEED Platinum du United States Green Building Council.

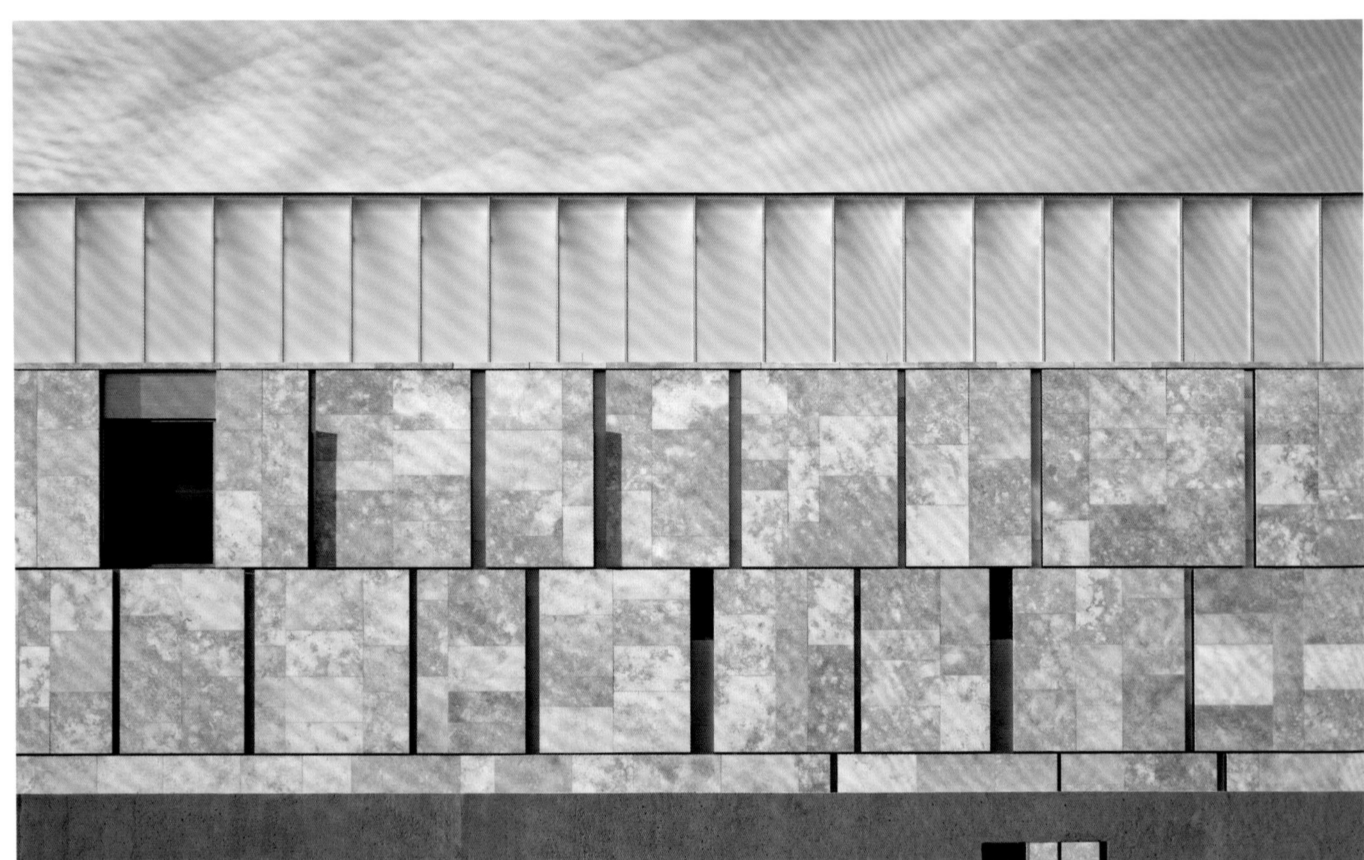

The walls of the building are marked by slightly irregular vertical openings. Above, seen at night, the upper volume of the building glows from within. Right, a floor plan.

Die Fassaden sind von vertikalen, unterschiedlich großen Öffnungen durchzogen. Der Aufbau des Gebäudes leuchtet bei Nacht von innen (oben). Unten ein Etagengrundriss.

Les murs du bâtiment sont marqués par des ouvertures verticales légèrement irrégulières. Ci-dessus, de nuit, son volume supérieur est illuminé de l'intérieur. Ci-contre, un plan de sol.

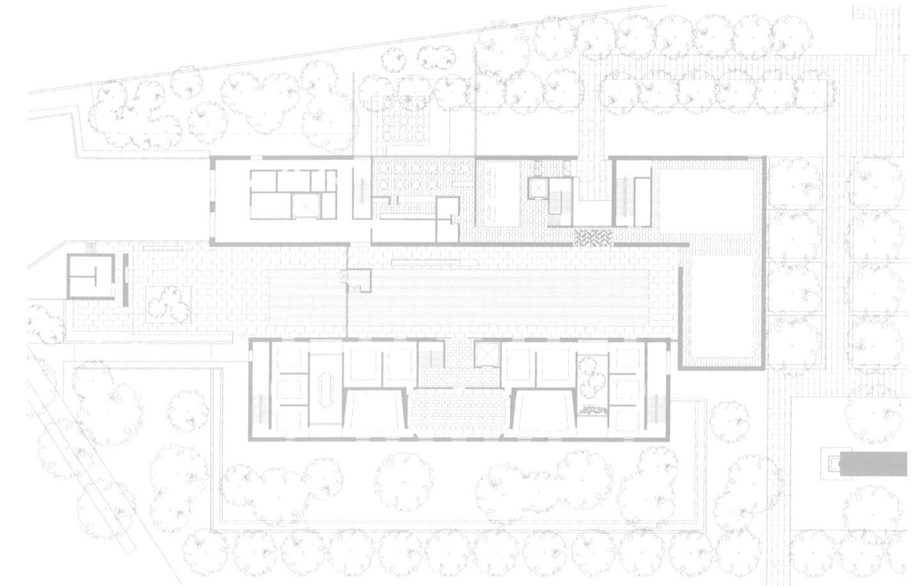

Hangings such as the one above, also seen through an exterior window, reproduce those in the celebrated Barnes Foundation building in Merion, Pennsylvania. Below, a lower-level plan.

Die Hängung – oben rechts und durch das Fenster links zu erkennen – orientiert sich an der Barnes Foundation in Merion, Pennsylvania. Unten der Grundriss einer Untergeschossebene.

Des accrochages comme celui ci-dessus, vu également de l'extérieur, reproduisent ceux du bâtiment de la célèbre Fondation Barnes à Merion, en Pennsylvanie. Ci-dessous, le plan d'un étage inférieur.

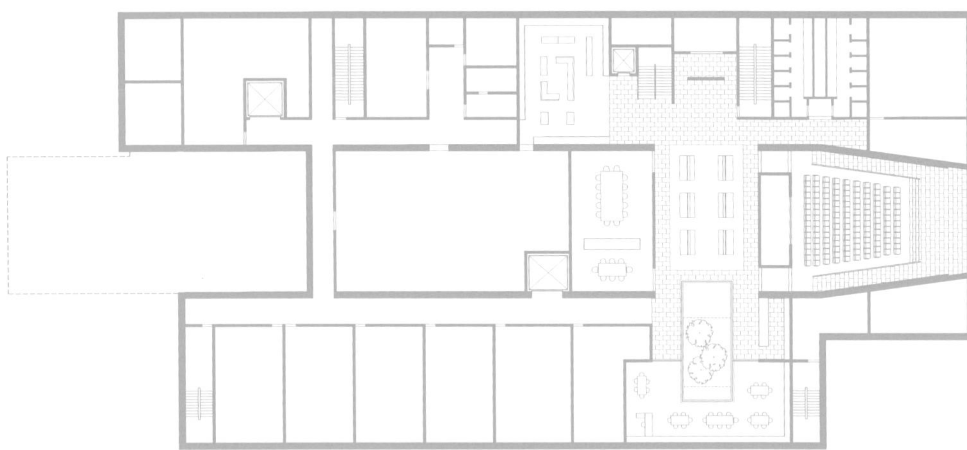

Right, above, an east-west section, and, underneath, the north-south section. Image below, an inner courtyard with a small reflecting pond.

Ein Ost-West-, darunter ein Nord-Südquerschnitt (rechts oben). Darunter ein Innenhof mit einem kleinen Spiegelbecken.

En haut ci-contre, une coupe est-ouest et, en bas, la coupe nord-sud. Ci-dessous, la photo d'une cour intérieure avec un petit miroir d'eau.

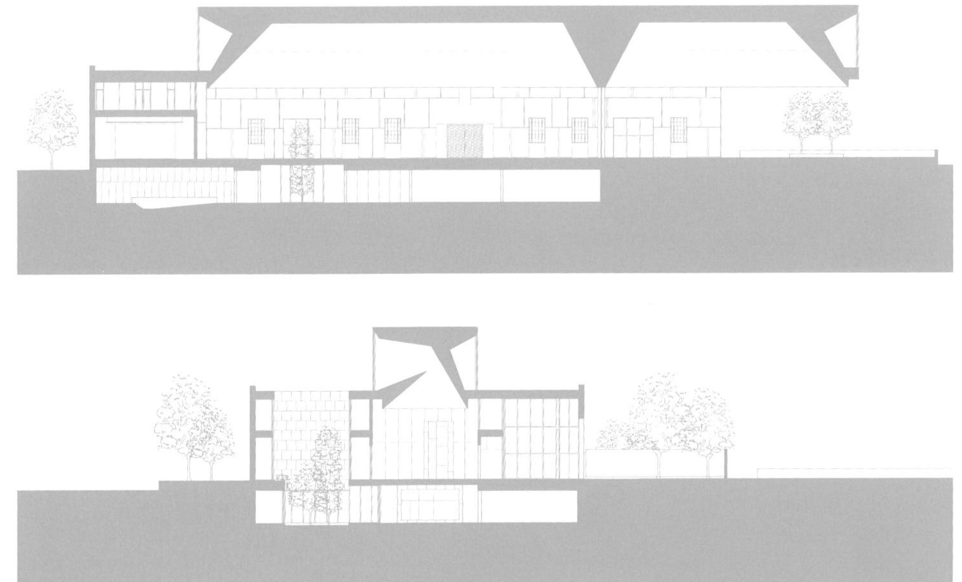

Presented as they were in the Barnes Foundation in Merion, works by Matisse, such as his mural The Dance *(1932–33), are amongst the major attractions of the collection. Above, a generous open area between the entrance and the collections. Below, the level two plan.*

Zu den bedeutendsten Werken der Sammlung zählen Arbeiten wie „Der Tanz“ (1932–33) von Henri Matisse, die wie zuvor in der Barnes Foundation in Merion präsentiert werden. Oben eine großzügige Halle zwischen Eingang und Ausstellungsräumen. Unten ein Grundriss der ersten Etage.

Présentées comme elles l'étaient à la Fondation Barnes de Merion, des œuvres de Matisse, tel son tableau La Danse *(1932–33), font partie des attractions majeures de la collection. Ci-dessus, un vaste espace ouvert entre l'entrée et les collections. Ci-dessous, le plan du niveau deux.*

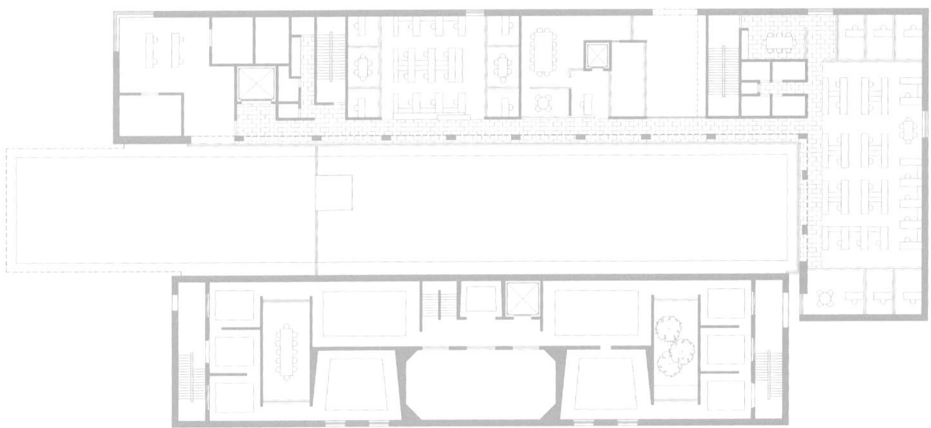

ZHANG LEI

AZL Architects
15th Floor–1517 Feiyimin Mansion
West Beijing Road
Nanjing 210093
China

Tel: +86 25 5186 1369 / Fax: +86 25 5186 1367
E-mail: atelierzhanglei@163.com
Web: www.azlarchitects.com

ZHANG LEI was born in 1964 in Jiangsu province (China), whose major city is Nanjing. From 1981 to 1985, he studied architecture at the Nanjing Institute of Technology, and then went on to complete postgraduate studies at the ETH in Zurich (1992–93). He created his own office, Atelier Zhanglei, in 2000. He has been a Professor of Architectural Design at Nanjing University since 2000, and has also taught at the ETH and the University of Hong Kong. His major projects include the student dormitory at Nantong Foreign Language School (Nantong, 1998–99); the pottery studio at Nanjing Normal University (2001); the Taoyuan 02 Graduate Student Dormitory, Nanjing University (Nanjing, 2001–03); the office building for the Xinhua Construction Company (Xinhua, 2002–03); the office and lab building for the Model Animal Genetic Research Center (Nanjing, 2002–03); the staff residence of Dongguan Institute of Technology (Dongguan, 2002–04); the Jianye Sport Mansion (Nanjing, 2004–05); the Cross Show Room (Qingpu, Shanghai, 2005); and the Concrete Slit House (Nanjing, 2005–07). More recent work includes the N-Park, Jiangsu Software Park (Nanjing, 2006–07); the N4A Museum (Liyang, 2006–07); the Zhengdong District Urban Planning Exhibition Hall (Zhengzhou 2009–11); No. 4 House, CIPEA (Nanjing, 2008–12, published here); and Xixi Artists' Clubhouse (Hangzhou, 2008–12, also published here), all in China.

ZHANG LEI wurde 1964 in der chinesischen Provinz Jiangsu (deren Hauptstadt Nanjing ist) geboren. Von 1981 bis 1985 studierte er am Institut für Technologie in Nanjing und schloss ein Postgraduiertenstudium an der ETH Zürich ab (1992–93). Sein Büro Atelier Zhanglei gründete er 2000. Seit 2000 ist er zudem Professor für Architektur an der Universität von Nanjing und lehrt an der ETH und der Universität Hongkong. Zu seinen wichtigsten Projekten zählen das Studentenwohnheim der Nantong Fremdsprachenschule (Nantong, 1998–99), das Töpferei-Atelier der Nanjing Normal University (2001), das Taoyuan 02 Studentenwohnheim an der Universität von Nanjing (2001–03), Büros für das Bauunternehmen Xinhua (Xinhua, 2002–03), das Büro- und Laborgebäude des Forschungszentrums für Tiergenetik (Nanjing, 2002 bis 2003), die Mitarbeiterunterkünfte des Dongguan-Instituts für Technologie (Dongguan, 2002–04), das Sporthaus Jianye (Nanjing, 2004–05), der Cross Show Room (Qingpu, Shanghai, 2005) und das Concrete Slit House (Nanjing, 2005–07). Jüngere Arbeiten sind der N-Park im Jiangsu Software Park (Nanjing, 2006–07), das N4A Museum (Liyang, 2006–07), eine Ausstellungshalle für ein Stadtplanungsprojekt (Zhengzhou, 2009–11), das No. 4 House von CIPEA (Nanjing, 2008–12, hier vorgestellt) und das Künstlerclubhaus Xixi (Hangzhou, 2008–12, ebenfalls hier vorgestellt), alle in China.

ZHANG LEI est né en 1964 dans la province de Jiangsu (Chine) dont la ville la plus importante est Nankin. Entre 1981 et 1985, il étudie l'architecture à l'Institut de technologie de Nankin, puis poursuit ses études supérieures à l'ETH de Zurich (1992–93). Il monte son agence, Atelier Zhanglei, en 2000. Professeur de design architectural à l'université de Nankin depuis 2000, il a également enseigné à l'ETH et à l'université de Hong Kong. Parmi ses projets majeurs, on compte la résidence universitaire de l'École de langues étrangères de Nantong (Nantong, 1998–99) ; l'atelier de poterie de l'université normale de Nankin (2001) ; la résidence universitaire Taoyuan 02 de l'université de Nankin (Nankin, 2001–03) ; l'immeuble de bureaux de l'entreprise de construction de Xinhua (Xinhua, 2002–03) ; le bâtiment des bureaux et du laboratoire du Centre de recherche sur la génétique animale (Nankin, 2002–03) ; la résidence du personnel de l'Institut de technologie de Dongguan (Dongguan, 2002–04) ; la Maison du sport Jianye (Nankin, 2004–05) ; le Cross Show Room (Qingpu, Shanghai, 2005) et la Maison fendue en béton (Nankin, 2005–07). Parmi ses projets plus récents, l'on peut noter le N-Park, Jiangsu Software Park (Nankin, 2006–07) ; le musée N4A (Liyang, 2006–07) ; la salle d'exposition de la planification du district de Zhengdong (Zhengzhou 2009–11) ; la No. 4 House de la CIPEA (Nankin, 2008–12, présentée ici) et le Xixi Artists' Clubhouse (Hangzhou, 2008–12, également présenté ici), tous en Chine.

XIXI ARTISTS' CLUBHOUSE

Hangzhou, China, 2008–12

Address: Xixi Wetland, Hangzhou, China. Area: 4000 m²
Client: not disclosed. Cost: not disclosed
Collaboration: Architectural Design Institute of Zhejiang Industrial University

The complex forms a small community with varying forms and angles, but an overall aesthetic is imposed by the architect.

Die Einzelbauten des Komplexes mit ihren variierenden Formen und Winkeln bilden eine dörfliche Struktur, die der Architekt durch eine schlüssige Ästhetik zusammenhält.

Le complexe forme une petite communauté avec des formes et des angles variés, mais une esthétique générale est imposée par l'architecte.

Located near the wetlands west of central Hangzhou, the **XIXI ARTISTS' CLUBHOUSE** was designed like a village with five clusters. Each cluster is composed of three Y-shaped volumes in two sizes, capped with six- and three-meter-square frameless windows, offering panoramas of the surrounding landscape. Twisting fiberglass installations redefine the internal spaces, bringing walls, floors, and ceilings together. The larger six-meter structure is made of concrete, while the smaller sections employ translucent white PC panels to diffuse direct sunlight. The architect states: "The confrontation between the oblique and the linear, the translucent panels with the concrete, and the external shape with the interior installations create a heightened sense of space."

Das wie ein Dorf angelegte **KÜNSTLERCLUBHAUS XIXI** liegt in der Nähe einer Moorlandschaft im Westen von Zentral-Hangzhou. Die fünf baulichen Cluster bestehen aus je drei Y-förmigen Baukörpern in zwei Größen und sind an der Stirnseite mit rahmenlosen quadratischen Fenstern (Seitenlänge 6 bzw. 3 m) ausgestattet, die einen Ausblick auf die umliegende Landschaft bieten. Gekrümmte Fiberglaseinbauten geben dem Innenraum ein besonderes Profil und verbinden Wände, Böden und Decken. Die Wände der größeren Baukörper (6 m) wurden aus Beton gefertigt, bei den kleineren Gebäuden kamen lichtstreuende Paneele aus Polycarbonat zum Einsatz. Die Architekten: „Das Zusammenspiel von geschwungenen und geraden Linien, lichtdurchlässigen Paneelen und Beton, von äußerer Form und Inneneinbauten verstärkt das Raumerlebnis."

Situé à proximité des zones humides de l'ouest de Hangzhou, le **XIXI ARTISTS' CLUB** est conçu comme un village en cinq grappes. Chaque grappe est composée de trois volumes en forme de Y dont les branches de taille différente se terminent par des fenêtres sans cadre de 6 ou 3 m² offrant une vue panoramique sur le paysage environnant. Des installations en fibre de verre en zigzag redéfinissent les espaces intérieurs, rassemblant murs, sols et plafonds. La structure la plus grande, de 6 m, est faite en béton, alors que l'on a employé pour les sections plus petites des panneaux en PVC blanc translucides pour diffuser la lumière naturelle directe. Selon les architectes : « La confrontation entre l'oblique et le linéaire, les panneaux translucides et le béton, et la forme extérieure et les installations intérieures crée un sens plus aigu de l'espace. »

Contrasting with the light coloring of exterior volumes, the interior view with a use of a dark palette of materials.

Im Kontrast zur hellen Farbgebung der Gebäude kommen im Inneren dunklere Materialien zum Einsatz.

En contraste avec les couleurs claires des volumes extérieurs, l'intérieur déploie une palette de matériaux sombres.

Above, an overall view of the complex in its verdant setting. Below, first- and second-floor plans of one of the buildings.

Oben eine Gesamtansicht des Komplexes in seiner grünen Umgebung. Grundrisse von Erdgeschoss und erster Etage eines der Gebäude (unten).

Ci-dessus, une vue d'ensemble du complexe dans son environnement verdoyant. Ci-dessous, les plans des premier et deuxième niveaux d'un des bâtiments.

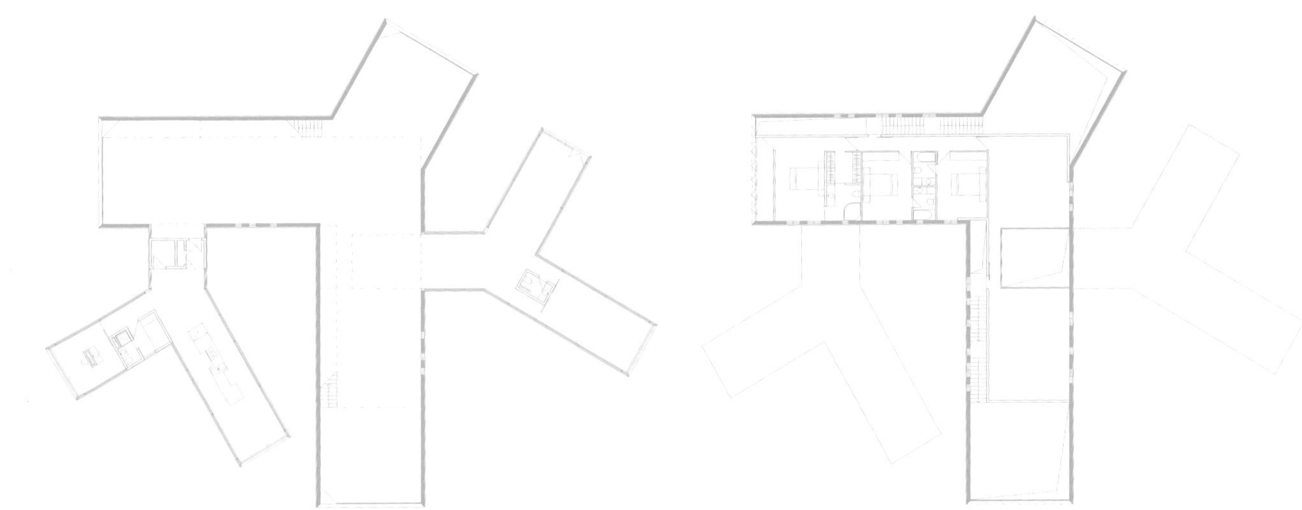

CIPEA NO. 4 HOUSE

Nanjing, China, 2008–12

Address: Foshouhu Lake, Nanjing, China. Area: 500 m²
Client: not disclosed. Cost: not disclosed
Collaboration: Architectural Design & Planning Institute, Nanjing University

Located in Laoshan Forest to the west of central Nanjing, the China International Practical Exhibition of Architecture (CIPEA) was initiated in 2003. The goal was to bring 24 well-known international architects together onto one site. CIPEA is divided into four public buildings and 20 small houses, and, in accordance with the brief, the small houses incorporate no fewer than five bedrooms, public spaces, and hospitality accommodations amounting to 500 square meters. The No. 4 "Blockhouse" is situated on a dramatic valley site. Four cubic floors are stacked vertically, allowing for minimal site excavation and land use. Each floor features living and dining spaces overlooking the forest and a stream. The architects state: "The concept of the Blockhouse corresponds to the attitude of many Chinese: a minimal opening to the surrounding landscape is the only perforation of the richness inside the house. The horizontal break of each floor—in combination with larger unique curved apertures on each floor—frame vistas in the spirit of Chinese landscape scrolls. Prescribed views have a long tradition in Chinese art history and traditional Chinese gardens, designed to make the viewer reconsider and contemplate the landscape."

Die Architekturausstellung „China International Practical Exhibition of Architecture“ (CIPEA) wurde 2003 initiiert und wird im Waldgebiet Laoshan westlich von Zentral-Nanjing realisiert. Für das Projekt sollten 24 international bekannte Architekten gewonnen werden. Das Gelände umfasst vier öffentliche Bauten und 20 kleinere Wohnhäuser. Laut Ausschreibung müssen die kleineren Wohnbauten auf 500 m² fünf Schlafzimmer sowie Gemeinschaftsbereiche und Raum für Gäste bieten. House No. 4 liegt in einer eindrucksvollen Tallandschaft. Durch die vier vertikal übereinander geschichteten, quaderförmige Bauebenen konnten Erdarbeiten und Grundfläche minimiert werden. Auf jeder Etage liegen Wohn- und Essbereiche mit Blick auf die Wald- und Flusslandschaft. Die Architekten: „Das Blockhauskonzept entspricht der Vorstellung vieler Chinesen, dass kleinere Öffnungen des Baus in die Landschaft den Reichtum des Hauses bewahren. Die horizontalen Durchbrüche in der Fassade mit ihren unterschiedlich geformten, kurvenförmigen Öffnungen rahmen das Landschaftspanorama wie auf einer chinesischen Bildrolle. Klar definierte Ausblicke haben eine lange Tradition in der chinesischen Kunst sowie der chinesischen Gartenbaukunst und sollen den Betrachter anregen, die Landschaft neu zu sehen und sich in ihr zu versenken.“

Située dans la forêt de Laoshan à l'ouest du centre de Nankin, l'Exposition internationale pratique d'architecture de Chine (CIPEA) est lancée en 2003. Elle a pour but de rassembler sur un seul site 24 architectes internationaux de renom. La CIPEA est divisée en quatre bâtiments publics et vingt petites maisons et, selon le cahier des charges, les maisons de 500 m² doivent contenir au moins cinq chambres, des espaces publics et des salons d'accueil. La « maison blockhaus » N° 4 est située dans une vallée spectaculaire. Quatre niveaux cubiques sont empilés verticalement pour éviter au maximum de creuser le site et utiliser le moins de terrain possible. Chaque étage offre des espaces de vie ou de restauration avec vue sur la forêt et un ruisseau. Selon les architectes : « Le concept de blockhaus correspond à la conception de nombreux Chinois : une ouverture minimum sur le paysage environnant préserve la richesse à l'intérieur de la maison. La rupture horizontale de chaque étage – en association avec de vastes ouvertures courbes – encadre des vues qui sont dans l'esprit des paysages des manuscrits chinois. Les vues prescrites sont de longue tradition dans l'histoire de l'art chinoise et dans les jardins chinois traditionnels conçus pour que le spectateur reconsidère le paysage et le contemple. »

In its relatively unspoiled setting the CIPEA No. 4 House stands out as a man-made object, but is not incongruous because of its subtle design.

In der weitgehend unberührten Naturlandschaft fällt das CIPEA No. 4 House durchaus als künstliches Element auf. Aufgrund seiner einfühlsamen Architektur wirkt es jedoch nicht fehl am Platz.

Dans un environnement relativement préservé, la No. 4 House de la CIPEA se détache comme un objet artificiel, sans être incongru grâce à son design délicat.

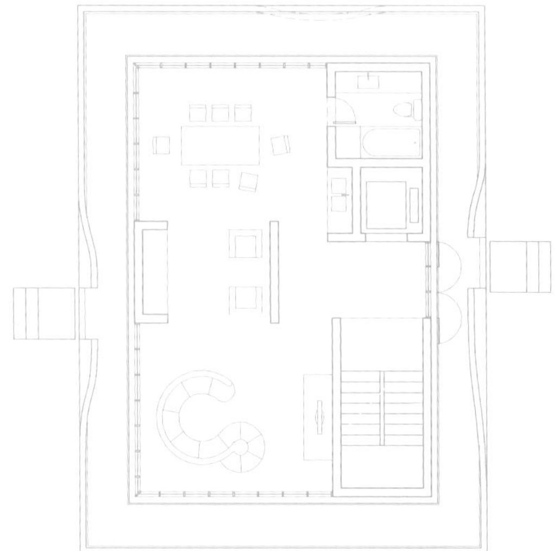

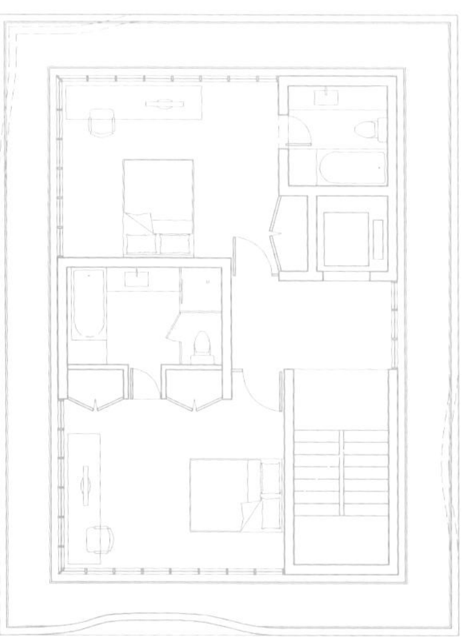

On this page, floor plans for levels one and two of the rectangular building. Below, a view through neighboring trees, and, right, the full elevation of the structure, with its irregular, almost "geological" openings.

Grundrisse von erster und zweiter Ebene des geradlinigen Gebäudes (links). Unten ein Blick durch Bäume und ein Gesamtansicht des Baus mit seinen unregelmäßigen, „geologisch" anmutenden Öffnungen (rechts).

Sur cette page, les plans de sol des premier et deuxième niveaux du bâtiment rectangulaire. Ci-dessous, une vue à travers des arbres proches et, page de droite, l'élévation de la structure, avec ses ouvertures irrégulières, presque « géologiques ».

The irregular openings frame views of the countryside and provide shelter for the small outdoor terraces.

Die ungleichmäßigen Aussparungen rahmen den Blick auf die Landschaft. Die schmalen Balkone sind geschützt

Les ouvertures irrégulières offrent des vues de la campagne et abritent de petites terrasses extérieures.

Right, plans of levels three and four. Below, an image of a living room with designs by the architect combining white surfaces and laminated wood.

Rechts Grundrisse der dritten und der vierten Ebene. Unten der Blick in einen Wohnraum, in dem die Architekten weiße Oberflächen mit Schichtholz kombinieren.

Ci-contre, des plans des troisième et quatrième niveaux. Ci-dessous, l'image d'un salon avec un décor conçu par l'architecte qui mêle surfaces blanches et bois laminé.

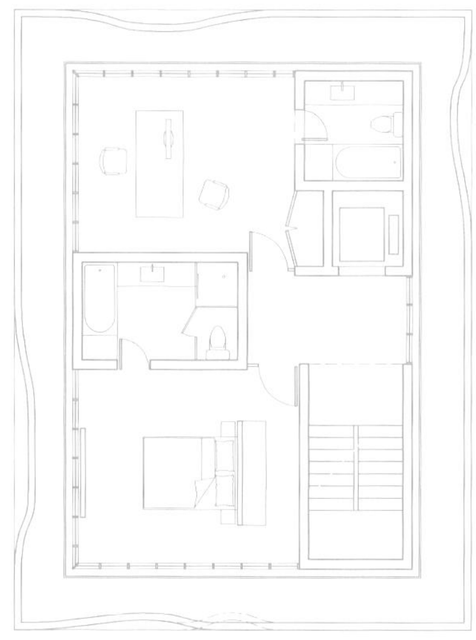

INDEX OF ARCHITECTS, BUILDINGS, AND PLACES

INDEX OF ARCHITECTS, BUILDINGS, AND PLACES

CREDITS

PHOTO CREDITS — 2 © Iwan Baan / **7** © Filip Dujardin / **8** © Go Sugimoto / **11** © Didier Boy de la Tour / **12** © Sanchez y Montoro / **13** © Higashide Photo Studio / **15** © Iwan Baan / **16** © Sergio Pirrone / **19** © Christian Richters / **21** © Michel Denancé / **22** © Gehry Partners, LLP / **25** © Leonardo Finotti / **26** © J. Mayer H. Architects / **28** © Kéré Architecture / **30** © Amit Geron / **31** © Iwan Baan / **33** © Roland Halbe / **37** © Cecil Balmond / **38** © Scott Frances/OTTO / **39** © Iwan Baan / **40** © Leonardo Finotti / **43** © Paul Warchol / **44** © Iwan Baan / **45** © Tom Arban / **47** © Duccio Malagamba / **48** © Christian Richters / **50** © Ed Reeve / **51-55** © Edmund Sumner/VIEW / **56** © ALA Architects / **57, 60 bottom left** © Hufton + Crow / **58-59, 60 top and bottom right, 61** © Tuomas Uusheimo / **62** © Chiaki Arai Urban & Architecture Design / **63-71** © Sergio Pirrone / **72** © ELEMENTAL / **73-77** © Cristóbal Palma / **78, 80-81** © Atelier Bow-Wow / **79, 82-85** © Solomon R. Guggenheim Foundation / **86** © Shigeru Ban Architects / **87-91** © Sanchez y Montoro / **92** © Benthem Crouwel Architects / **93-97** © Iwan Baan / **98** © Courtesy of Cadaval & Solà-Morales / **99** © Santiago Garces / **100-103** © Iwan Baan / **104, 106-109** © Sandra Pereznieto / **105** © Diego Berruecos / **110** © Preston Scott Cohen, Inc. / **111-119** © Amit Geron / **120** © Coop Himmelb(l)au / **122-123, 125-133** © Duccio Malagamba / **121, 124** © Markus Pillhofer / **134** © Studio Odile Decq / **135-141** © Roland Halbe / **142** © Delugan Meissl Associated Architects / **143-151** © Iwan Baan / **152-153, 155-156, 158-159** © Evan Joseph Images / **154, 157** © Gage/Clemenceau Architects / **160-171** © Roland Halbe / **172** © Gehry Partners, LLP / **173-177** © Roland Halbe / **178** © Gijs Van Vaerenbergh / **179-185** © Filip Dujardin / **186** © Courtesy of Zaha Hadid Architects / **187, 193** © Iwan Baan / **188-192, 194** © Roland Halbe / **195-197** © Sergio Pirrone / **198** © Karen Smul / **199** © Port Authority of New York and New Jersey / **200-203** © Joe Woolhead / **204** © Herzog & de Meuron / **205-215** © Iwan Baan / **216** © Matthias Willi / **217-221** © Iwan Baan / **222-225** © Tom Bisig / **226** © Steven Holl Architects / **227-231** © Iwan Baan / **232, 235 right** © Arata Isozaki & Associates / **233-234, 235 left, 236-241** © Sergio Pirrone / **242** © Carla Juaçaba and Bia Lessa / **243-249** © Leonardo Finotti / **250 left** © Jillian Edelstein / **250 right, 251, 254-255** © Cecil Balmond / **252-253** © Clive Little / **256, 260 bottom** © Kéré Architecture / **257-259, 260 top and middle, 261** © Iwan Baan / **262** © KLab architecture / **263-267** © Panos Kokkinias / **268** © Henning Larsen Architects, Batteríið Architects, Studio Olafur Eliasson / **269-275** © Nic Lehoux / **276** © MAD architects / **277-291** © Iwan Baan / **292** © Paul Green / **293-296 top, 297-301** © Jesko Malkolm Johnsson-Zahn / **296 bottom** © Beka Pkhakadze / **302** © Richard Meier & Partners Architects / **303-311** © Roland Halbe / **312** © Metro Arquitetos / **313-321** © Leonardo Finotti / **322** © Morphosis Architects / **323-329** © Roland Halbe / **330** © Courtesy of Tatzu Nishi and Public Art Found / **331-332** © Tom Powel Imaging / **333** © GION / **334** © Jo Noero / **335-339** © Iwan Baan / **340** © Ateliers Jean Nouvel, photo by Gaston Bergeret / **341-345** © Roland Halbe / **346** © O Studio Architects / **347-353** © Iwan Baan / **354 left** © I. M. Pei, Architect / **354 middle and right** © io Architects LLP / **355-358, 359 bottom, 360-363** © Higashide Photo Studio / **359 top** © Fujita Photo Studio / **364** © Jomar Bragança e Ana Valadares / **365-367** © Leonardo Finotti / **368** © Renzo Piano Building Workshop / **369, 373** © Dennis Gilbert/VIEW / **270** © Hufton + Crow/VIEW / **371-372** © Michel Denancé / **374-379** © Nic Lehoux / **380** © Marco Micceri / **381-385** © Jack Hobhouse / **386, 391-395 top** © Agence Rudy Ricciotti / **387-390** © Oliver Amsellem / **395 bottom** © Lisa Ricciotti / **396** © Serge Salat Architect / **397-407** © Didier Boy de la Tour / **408** © SANAA/Kazuyo Sejima + Ryue Nishizawa / **409-413** © Hisao Suzuki / **414-415** © Iwan Baan / **416** © SO – IL / **417-427** © Iwan Baan / **428** © Tabanlıoğlu Architects / **429-437** © Emre Dörter / **438** © UNStudio / **439-447** © Christian Richters / **448-455** © URBANUS / **456** © Tod Williams Billie Tsien Architects, photo by Dorothy Alexander / **457-463** © Michael Moran/OTTO / **464-475** © AZL Architects

CREDITS FOR PLANS / DRAWINGS / CAD DOCUMENTS — 53, 55 © Adjaye Associates / **61** © ALA Architects / **65-68, 70** © Chiaki Arai Urban & Architecture Design / **80, 82, 84** © Atelier Bow-Wow / **90** © Schigeru Ban Architects / **102-103, 105, 109** © Courtesy of Cadaval & Solà-Morales / **114, 118** © Preston Scott Cohen, Inc. / **122, 127-128, 131-133** © Coop Himmelb(l)au / **136, 139, 141** © Studio Odile Decq / **149-150** © Delugan Meissl Associated Architects / **155, 157** © Gage/Clemenceau Architects / **163-164, 167-168, 170** © Ensamble Studio / **183-184** © Gijs Van Vaerenbergh / **188-189, 192-193** © Courtesy of Zaha Hadid Architects / **200, 203** © Handel Architects / **206, 210** © Herzog & de Meuron / **212, 214** © Herzog & de Meuron and Ai Weiwei / **219, 221, 223-224** © HHF architects GmbH / **230-231** © Steven Holl Architects / **235, 237, 241** © Arata Isozaki & Associates / **247** © Carla Juaçaba Office / **252** © Anish Kapoor / **259, 261** © Kéré Architecture / **265, 267** © KLab architecture / **273, 275** © Henning Larsen Architects / **281-282, 287, 290** © MAD architects / **297, 299** © J. Mayer H. Architects / **305-308, 310** © Richard Meier & Partners Architects / **314, 321** © Metro Arquitetos / **324, 328** © Morphosis Architects / **336, 338-339** © Jo Noero / **344-345** © Beyer Blinder Belle / **349, 352-353** © O Studio Architects / **358, 361-362** © io Architects LLP / **366** © Gustavo Penna Arquiteto & Associados / **371-372, 374, 376-378** © Renzo Piano Building Workshop / **383-384** © Project Orange Architects / **388, 391-392, 394** © Agence Rudy Ricciotti / **398, 400, 402, 407** © Serge Salat / **411, 414** © SANAA/Kazuyo Sejima + Ryue Nishizawa / **418, 421-423, 425** © SO – IL / **431, 435** © Tabanlıoğlu Architects / **441, 443-445, 447** © UNStudio / **451-452, 454** © URBANUS / **459-461, 463** © Tod Williams Billie Tsien Architects / **469, 472, 475** © AZL Architects